Psychology of Women
Selected Readings

Also by Juanita H. Williams

Psychology of Women: Behavior in a Biosocial Context

Psychology of Women

Selected Readings

Edited by

Juanita H. Williams

Professor of Psychology
Director of Women's Studies Program
University of South Florida, Tampa

W · W · Norton & Company · New York

Published simultaneously in Canada by George J. McLeod Limited, Toronto. Printed in the United States of America.

First Edition

Library of Congress Cataloging in Publication Data
Main entry under title:

Psychology of women.

Includes bibliographies. Selected Readings
1. Women—Psychology—Addresses, essays, lectures.
I. Williams, Juanita Hingst, 1922–
HQ1206.P77 1979 301.41′2 79-1337
ISBN 0-393-09068-X

1 2 3 4 5 6 7 8 9 0

Contents

Preface ix

1 Myths, Stereotypes, and the Psychology of Women 1

The Psychology of Woman
G. T. W. Patrick 3
Functionalism, Darwinism, and the Psychology of Women
Stephanie A. Shields 12

2 Psychoanalysis and the Woman Question 35

Femininity
Sigmund Freud 40
On Freud's View of Female Psychology
Margaret Mead 53
The Problem of Feminine Masochism
Karen Horney 62
Once More the Inner Space
Erik Erikson 71

3 Biology and Behavior 85

Brain, Body, and Behavior
Ruth H. Bleier 87

The Premenstrual Syndrome
Mary Brown Parlee 99
The Symbolic Significance of Menstruation and the Menopause
Vieda Skultans 115

4 Sex Differences 129

The Eye of the Beholder: Parents' Views on Sex of Newborns
Jeffrey Z. Rubin, Frank J. Provenzano, and Zella Luria 134
Early Sex Differences in the Human: Studies of Socioemotional Development
Michael Lewis 142
Psychology
Reesa M. Vaughter 149
Androgyny Reconsidered
Kathleen E. Grady 172

5 Growing Up Female 179

How Nursery Schools Teach Girls to Shut Up
Lisa A. Serbin and K. Daniel O'Leary 183
Implications and Applications of Recent Research on Feminine Development
Grace K. Baruch and Rosalind C. Barnett 188
Social Values, Femininity, and the Development of Female Competence
Julia A. Sherman 200
Growing Up Black
Joyce A. Ladner 212

6 Sexuality 225

Women's Liberation and Human Sexual Relations
Patricia Spencer Faunce and Susan Phipps-Yonas 228
Social Dimensions of the Menstrual Taboo and the Effects on Female Sexuality
Etta Bender Breit and Marilyn Myerson Ferrandino 241
The Realities of Lesbianism
Del Martin and Phyllis Lyon 255

7 Birth Control 263

Contraceptives for Males
William J. Bremner and David M. de Kretser 266
The Psychosocial Factors of the Abortion Experience: A Critical Review
Lisa Roseman Shusterman 275
!Kung Hunter-Gatherers: Feminism, Diet, and Birth Control
Gina Bari Kolata 298
Sex Preferences, Sex Control, and the Status of Women
Nancy E. Williamson 303

8 Pregnancy, Childbirth, and Breast-feeding 317

Childbirth in Crosscultural Perspective
Niles Newton and Michael Newton 321
Breast Feeding
Niles Newton 342
Maternal Attachment: Importance of the First Post-Partum Days
Marshall H. Klaus, Richard Jerauld, Nancy C. Kreger, Willie McAlpine, Meredith Steffa, and John H. Kennell 351

9 Lifestyles: Tradition and Change 359

Anger and Tenderness
Adrienne Rich 363
Big-Time Careers for the Little Woman: A Dual-Role Dilemma
Susan A. Darley 377
The Role of Models in Women's Professional Development
Elizabeth Douvan 388
The Male Sex Role: Definitions, Problems, and Sources of Change
Joseph H. Pleck 401

10 Psyche and Society: Variations from the Norm 409

The Nature of Female Criminality
Dale Harrentsian 413

Sex Differences and Psychiatric Disorders
Bruce P. Dohrenwend and Barbara Snell Dohrenwend 429
Cinderella's Stepsisters: A Feminist Perspective on Anorexia Nervosa and Bulimia
Marlene Boskind-Lodahl 436
The Consciousness-Raising Group as a Model for Therapy with Women
Annette M. Brodsky 449

11 Middle Age and Aging 457

The Double Standard of Aging
Susan Sontag 462
Women in the Middle Years: Conceptions and Misconceptions
Rosalind Barnett and Grace Baruch 479
A Cross-Cultural Investigation of Behavioral Changes at Menopause
Joyce Griffen 488
Women in Widowhood
Carol J. Barrett 496

Preface

For this book of readings I have relied upon my experiences in six years of teaching the psychology of women and other women's studies courses to select important, interesting papers by outstanding scholars with a wide range of approaches to the field. Tested in both undergraduate and graduate courses, these pieces are valuable for courses in the psychology of women, sociology of women, women's studies, and sex roles. They can also provide significant supplementary material for traditional courses in psychology and sociology. The purpose of this book is to bring together for all such courses a selection of the most recent scholarship, set in historical perspective.

This book of readings may be used either alone or as a supplement to *Psychology of Women: Behavior in a Biosocial Context.* Its organization is parallel and the readings are keyed to the major topics in the textbook. Either way, it makes available to the student and the instructor important theoretical, empirical, and review articles in critical areas of the subject.

Each of the eleven parts of the book is preceded by an introduction which integrates the papers and identifies the issues relevant to the topic. Part 1 presents some "scientific" ideas about woman and her behavior as interpreted by the young science of psychology, as well as contemporary commentaries on both scientific and social mythology as they pertain to the psychology of women. The second part presents some major psychoanalytic views and counterviews which show how thinking about women was influenced by the status and roles of women and men, and by the social values attached to them.

Beginning with Part 3, the book consists of recent research organized by a life cycle approach to the study of women. Papers on various aspects of the biological substratum of behavior and its sociocultural significance are followed in Part 4 by others on sex differences and the concept of androgyny. Implications of the experience of growing up female are examined in Part 5, including a description of black urban girlhood.

The authors of the papers on female sexuality in Part 6 bring controversial viewpoints to the topic. Included here is an original analysis on the menstrual taboo and sexuality, written especially for this volume. The topic of birth control in Part 7 is represented by papers on the effects of abortion and life style changes, as well as on new developments in male contraception and sex control and what they mean for women. The reproductive events of pregnancy, childbirth, and breast-feeding are examined from an experiential perspective in Part 8. Here, too, is a provocative study of the effects for mother and baby of their contact in the post-partum period.

The papers in Part 9 contrast a traditional and a contemporary life style, and elucidate the problems and rewards of each. An important paper on the male sex role analyzes the pressures for the adaptation of men to the growth of women as they assume stronger and more varied roles in the society.

Atypical behavior of women, its incidence, causes, and social significance, are subjects of the papers in Part 10. The feminist perspective is especially noted as an organizing principle in these analyses.

The last group of papers in Part 11 deals with the experiences for women of growing older in our society, including some examples from other cultures and a research on widowhood.

The field of psychology of women is unique in psychology because it cuts across so many of the subdisciplines: developmental, abnormal, social, personality, learning, comparative, physiological. In addition, its study must include theory and research from other disciplines. Its subject matter is the behavior of women, and one cannot begin to understand that without taking into consideration data from history, biology, anthropology, economics, and philosophy, to mention just a few. This book attempts to show how the psychology of women can integrate material from many sources of inquiry. Such integration is sorely needed as knowledge burgeons and as areas of individual expertise become narrower and narrower. An interdisciplinary and integrative field such as the psychology of women has the potential for facilitating community, for lowering the walls which separate disciplines and scholars from each other. Thus by its very being it introduces values which have been woman-identified into the agentic world of science.

Our enterprise, the understanding of women, became viable and infused with energy because of the women's movement and the surging interest in feminist philosophy. This has had the effect not only of generating new research, but of causing the re-evaluation and re-interpretation of old concepts in psychology and other disciplines. The papers in this book, as they move from past to present, demonstrate the new awareness of scholars as they look at theories of personality, psychotherapy, sexuality, and sex roles. They exemplify, too, corrections of old biases, introduction of new and revised theories, and reports of new research, all of which help us more adequately to understand the phenomena of behavior.

For help in evaluating the selections and in reviewing the manuscript,

I want to give appreciative recognition to Mary Brown Parlee of Barnard College, Katherine Schneider of the University of Arkansas, and Reesa Vaughter of Fordham University. My editor at Norton, Don Fusting, was especially helpful with the introductions, and I am very grateful for his objective and knowledgeable assistance. Many students read all or part of the papers, and their reactions and comments, too, helped guide the final selection.

J.H.W.

May, 1978

Psychology of Women
Selected Readings

PART 1

Myths, Stereotypes, and the Psychology of Women

Beliefs about woman's "nature" and her special qualities which distinguish her from man have always been part of the human record. To the ancient Egyptian she was "a deep water whose twisting men know not,"[1] and in later times she was variously described as a childlike nonentity, a dangerous plaything, the devil's gateway, a ministering angel, and a symbol of the fecund and bounteous earth.

It has been typical for man to be regarded as the archetype of a human being and for woman to be seen as a special case. Thus she was often described in terms of her differences from him, usually with emphasis on her basic inferiority or on her sexual and reproductive qualities.

Since science seeks to abjure myth in its search for objective facts and explanatory truths, one would expect the mystique of female behavior to be banished forever in the twentieth century. But in attempts to understand human behavior, the social sciences have often pursued explanations which rest on old untried assumptions whose core consists of basic beliefs about human "nature."

This section includes both archival and contemporary commentaries on the nature of woman, her role in society, and the various ways that these have been explained in the past. "The Psychology of Woman," written by G. T. W. Patrick in 1895, was an examination of woman's physical and psychological characteristics, in order to determine their bearing, if any, on the movement for woman's political, educational, and economic equality. Sex differences in viability, brain size, intellectual functioning, and character were interpreted by Patrick as unsupportive of the doctrine of woman's

[1] Bullough, V. *The Subordinate Sex.* Urbana, Ill.: The University of Illinois Press, 1973, p. 39.

inferiority. Woman was biologically less vulnerable to stress and disease. Though her brain was smaller than man's, her brain-to-body ratio was equal to his. She excelled in quickness of perception, memory, and language development, but was deficient in logical powers and in the ability to think analytically and critically. Morally she was man's superior, being more altruistic and self-sacrificing than he, but a fallen woman easily surpassed man in her capacity for cruelty and depravity.

Such data led Patrick to his central thesis, which was that woman was a case of arrested development. Physically and mentally she was closer to the primitive archetype of the race. For example, the division of labor which marked progress in the civilized world was not found in the work of women; their work was undiversified and their tools primitive. Though richly endowed with the essentials of humanity, woman did not share man's variability, by which he adapted so readily to his environment. These observations, thought Patrick, formed the scientific basis for granting woman a "reverent exemption" from those worldly duties requiring the "restless and active" nature of her consort, man.

Stephanie A. Shields, in a contemporary paper on "Functionalism, Darwinism, and the Psychology of Women," examines the influence on the young science of psychology of Darwin's theory of evolution. She shows how beliefs about women's special qualities, such as those expressed in Patrick's paper, became incorporated into the scientific enterprise as psychologists tried to explain women's roles by looking for their origins in woman's special nature, and in the ways in which she was different from man. Differences in male and female brains were held to account for differences in mental capacities and in cultural achievement. In addition, the belief that women were more alike than men were explained the greater representation of men among the eminent as well as among the mentally handicapped. Finally, the concept of the maternal instinct, already popular, received strong support from the extension to behavior of evolutionary biology: woman was related to the other primates, not only in her reproductive functions, but in her nurturing behavior as well. The tenacity of such ideas, Shields says, is witness to the service that science gave to social values, a justification for the sociocultural status quo.

Beliefs and ideas about the relation of woman to her body, to nature, and to man, and about her place in the scheme of life, have profoundly influenced the ways that she has been treated and the accommodations that have been made for her. The articles in this section demonstrate the continuity and coherence of ideas about women through history, linking today's myths to their origins in the past.

The Psychology of Woman

G. T. W. Patrick

Every thoughtful observer of both the popular and the scientific movements of the day must have noticed the frequent lack of harmony or co-operation between them. Such lack of co-operation, if not of harmony, is well illustrated in the woman question. Two vigorous movements are now in progress. The first is a popular movement, whose end, apparently being very rapidly realized, is the advancement of woman to a position of complete political, legal, educational, and social parity with man—a position which means much more than mere equality of rights for woman; it means for her a changed sphere of activity, with new duties and new burdens, and may in the end involve radical changes in the state and in the family. The second is a scientific movement in anthropology, conducted by laborious and painstaking research, whose end is to ascertain the constitutional differences, both physical and psychical, between man and woman. It may be that these two movements will be found to support each other; but, if so, it is to be feared that it will be by happy chance rather than by intelligent co-operation.

It is the purpose of this article to bring together some of the results of these anthropological studies relating especially to the psychology of woman, in order that we may see what bearing, if any, they may have upon the above-mentioned popular movement. The most devoted patron of woman's political and educational advancement would hardly deny that the success and permanence of the reform will depend in the end upon the fact that there shall be no inherent contradiction between her new duties and her natural physical and mental constitution. It should be borne in mind,

"The Psychology of Woman" by G. T. W. Patrick. *Popular Science Monthly,* 47 (1895), 209–225.

however, that the mere fact of woman's present intellectual or physical weakness, should such be shown, would not be a justifiable ground for denying to her full political and educational privileges. It might be quite the reverse, if it should appear that such weakness were itself the result of the subordinate position which she has been compelled to hold. It would, however, be a justifiable ground for advising woman to assume her new duties gradually, in order that disaster to her cause might not follow the overtaxing of her strength.

In outlining some of the psychological peculiarities of woman as revealed by modern anthropological researches, I shall endeavor to confine myself to those points upon which investigators generally agree, simply omitting those still in dispute, or mentioning them only as questioned.

All facts are best studied in the light of an idea. It may be conducive to clearness, therefore, to mention first the leading theories now in the field concerning woman's peculiarities. It has often been asserted since Aristotle that woman is a stunted or inferior man and represents arrested development. Again, it has been said that woman is a grown-up child, that she belongs to the child type, and must ever to some extent retain the child relation. Again, more recently, it has been maintained that although woman belongs to the child type, yet the child type is in truth the race type and represents greater perfection than is represented by man, whose natural characteristic is senility. Finally, it has been said that throughout the whole animal world, where artificial circumstances have not modified natural relations, the female stands for physical superiority in size and vitality, and more truly represents the essential qualities of the species. Without prejudice for or against any of these theories, let us see what evidence there may be for each. . . .

Some interesting differences are now clearly made out between man and woman in respect to birth, death, and disease. Statistics show that about one hundred and five boys are born to every one hundred girls in Europe and America. The proportion in other countries and among uncivilized races is said to be nearly the same. The greater mortality of males, however, begins with birth and continues throughout childhood and adolescence and the greater proportion of adult years. If, therefore, a count be made of boys and girls or men and women at any age after the first year, the females are found to be in a considerable excess, and this notwithstanding the decimation of women by diseases incidental to the child-bearing stage of their lives. These results, formerly attributed to accidental causes, are now known to be due to the greater natural mortality of males, and this is found to be in harmony with another series of sexual differences, namely, the greater power of woman to resist nearly all diseases. Hospital statistics show that women are less liable to many forms of disease, such as rheumatism, haemorrhages, cancer, and brain diseases; and that while they are more liable to others, such as diphtheria, phthisis, scarlet fever, and whooping-cough, even in these the percentage of fatal cases is so much less that the absolute number of deaths falls considerably below that of men. Sudden deaths from internal causes are much less frequent among women. They endure surgical operations better than men, and recover more easily from the effects of wounds. They also grow old less rapidly and live longer. Among centenarians there are twice as many women as men. Women retain longer the use of their legs and of their hands. Their hair becomes gray later, and they suffer less from senile irritability and from loss of sight, hearing, and memory. In brief, contrary to popular opinion, woman is more hardy than man, and possesses a larger reserve of vitality. In this connection the absence of physical abnormalities in woman should be noted. A mass of evidence from anthropological studies in Italy and England shows that degeneration marks, monstrosities, and almost all kinds of variations from the normal type are much less common in woman than in man. Here, too, we may note that statistics of the diseases to which men, women, and children are severally most subject, show a somewhat marked similarity between the diseases of woman and of children. . . .

The long-disputed questions about woman's brain are now approaching solution in a few leading points. In the first place, woman's brain is of less absolute weight than man's, the proportion among modern civilized races being about nine to ten. This fact in itself has little significance, as man is heavier and taller than woman. If we consider the weight of the brain relatively to the height of the body, it still appears that woman's brain is smaller; but if, as is more just, we consider the weight of the brain relatively to the weight of the body, it appears that there is nearly perfect equality, the difference, if any, being in favor of woman. These results are still of little value, for, as fairly pointed out by Havelock Ellis, other corrections must be made, such as this, that woman has relatively more fat and less muscle than man, the latter, of course, making greater demands upon the brain. On the whole it appears that there is no considerable difference, such as there is being in woman's favor. Of more significance in its bearing upon woman's mental capacity is the relative size of the different parts of the brain. Here it is shown that the lower centers as compared with the hemispheres are larger in the female brain. In the cerebrum itself the frontal region is not, as has been supposed, smaller in woman, but rather larger relatively. The same is true of the occipital lobe. But the parietal lobe is somewhat smaller. It is now believed, however, that a preponderance of the frontal region does not imply intellectual superiority, as was formerly supposed, but that the parietal region is really the more important. As a balance, perhaps, to these female deficiencies, we may note that the circulation of the blood seems to be somewhat greater in woman's brain. In respect to her whole physical structure woman is less modified than man and shows less tendency to variation. Women are more alike than men. . . .

We come now to the well-worn theme of the purely mental differences between the sexes, and here I shall make a brief summary of the more important and well-recognized differences, citing experiments and statistics where they are possible. In perception, woman is in general decidedly quicker than man. She reads a paragraph or book more quickly, and, knowledge of the subject being equal, she grasps more of it. In perception of objects she grasps more quickly a number of wholes or groups, and has a rapid unreasoned perception of relations which has the appearance of intuition. Her perception of details, however, is less accurate than man's, and her rapid reference of things to their proper classes extends only to matters of common human experience. In apperception the subjective factor is larger in woman, and she sees things more from the standpoint of her own experience, wishes, and prejudices. Even more than in man, where feeling is strong, objective perception is blind. Hence women make poorer critics than men, and more rarely are they impartial judges. For the formation of concepts, especially the more abstract ones, woman's mind is less adapted than man's. She thinks more in terms of the concrete and individual. Hence number forms and the associations of colors with sounds are, as is found, more common among women. Differences in habits of thought between the sexes may be well illustrated by a simple experiment in association. If fifty men and fifty women be required to write as rapidly as possible one hundred words without time for thought, in the women's lists more than in the men's will be found words relating to the concrete rather than the abstract, the whole rather than the part, the particular rather than the general, and associations in space rather than in time. As Lotze keenly remarks, women excel in arranging things in the order of space, men in the order of time. Men try to bring things under a general rule, without so much regard to the fitness or symmetry of the result. Women care less for general rules, and are inclined to look only to the immediate end in view, aiming to make each thing complete in itself and harmonious with its surroundings.

In respect to memory, as far as any general statements can be made, woman is superior. In memory tests college girls surpass boys. In Gilbert's tests on New Haven school children, however, the boys were superior in the exact reproduction of an interval of time. In reasoning of the quick associative kind women are more apt than men, but in slow logical reasoning, whether deductive or inductive, they are markedly deficient. They lack logical feeling, and are less disturbed by inconsistency. Analysis is relatively distasteful to them, and they less readily comprehend the relation of the part to the whole. They are thus less adapted to the plodding, analytical work of science, discovery, or invention. Their interest lies rather with the finished product. Of the 483,517 patents issued by the U.S. Patent Office prior to October, 1892, 3,458 were granted to women. In general, woman's thought is less methodical and less deep. The arts, sciences, and philosophy owe their progress more to man than to woman. Whether one studies the history of logic, mathematics, or philosophic thought, of the special sciences or scientific discovery and invention, of poetry or general literature, of musical composition or technique, of painting, sculpture, or architecture, one is engaged more with the names of men than of women. Even in those spheres for which woman by her peculiar physical or mental qualities is particularly adapted, such as vocal music, the stage, and the writing of novels, it is doubtful whether a list of the greatest artists would include more women than men. Even in the arts of cooking and dressmaking, when men undertake them they often excel. Woman, owing to her greater patience, her intuition, and her retentive memory, as well as her constant association with the young, is especially qualified for teaching and has equal or greater success in this work than man. Yet all educational reforms, from the kindergarten to the university, have originated with the latter.

What woman loses in profundity she gains in quickness. She excels in tact, and extricates herself from a difficulty with astonishing adroitness. In language she is more apt than man. Girls learn to speak earlier than boys, and old women are more talkative than old men. Among the uneducated the wife can express herself more intelligently than the husband. Experience in coeducational institutions shows that women are more faithful and punctilious than men, and at least equally apt. In colleges where a record of standing is kept the women gain probably a somewhat higher average. In the years immediately following graduation the men make much greater intellectual progress. Women reach their mental maturity at an earlier age, and develop relatively less after maturity. In many kinds of routine work, especially that requiring patience, women are superior, but they are less able to endure protracted overwork.

We have seen that woman is less modified physically than man and varies less from the average. The same is true mentally. Women are more alike than men and more normal, as it were. The geniuses have been men for the most part, and so have the cranks. Woman's thought pursues old rather than new lines. Her tendency is toward reproduction, while man's is toward production. Woman loves the old, the tried, and the customary. She is conservative, and acts as society's balance-wheel. Man represents variation. He reforms, explores, thinks out a new way.

One of the most marked differences between man and woman is the greater excitability of the nerve centers in the latter. Woman possesses in a higher degree than man the fundamental property of all nervous tissue, irritability, or response to any stimulus. The vasomotor system is particularly excitable, and this fact is in immediate connection with her emotional life. That woman is more emotional than man is only another way of stating the same fact. Various expressions and bodily changes which are really the ground of emotions, such, for instance, as laughing, crying, blushing, quickening of the heart-beat, are more common in woman, and in general her face is more mobile and witnesses more to her mental states. Various forms of abnormal mental conditions, closely connected with the emotions, such as hysteria, are more frequent among women. Women are more easily influenced by suggestion than men, and a larger percentage of them may be hypnotized. Trance mediums are usually women. The word witch has been narrowed almost wholly to the female, and this may be explained by the fact that various forms of mental disturbance connected with superstitious notions are more frequently manifested in women. Sympathy, pity, and charity are stronger in woman, and she is more prominent in works that spring from these sentiments, such as philanthropy and humane and charitable movements. Woman is more generous than man. Her maternal instincts lead her to lend her sympathy to the weak and helpless. She cares for the sick and protects the friendless, and, seeing present rather than remote consequences, she feeds the pauper and pardons the criminal.

In morals a few distinctions between the sexes are well determined. Male criminals outnumber female criminals about six to one. Woman's sympathy and love, her physical weakness and timid nature, her domestic and quiet habits, ill adapt her to the criminal life. Morally bad women too usually find other more attractive fields open to them. Some forms of crime, indeed, such as murder by poisoning, domestic theft, and infanticide, are much more common among women. When women do become criminals their crimes are often marked by greater heinousness, cruelty, and depravity. It is said by Lombroso and his school that in respect to cruelty in general woman surpasses man, particularly in her conduct to her own sex. Woman's appetites are not so strong and her passions are less intense. She is freer from intemperance and related forms of vice. The most marked moral superiority of woman appears in her altruism; her greatest moral defect is her untruthfulness. In her altruistic life of love and self-sacrifice woman shows herself the leader in the supreme virtue of Christian civilization. As far as she leads in this, so far does she fall behind in veracity. She has not the same conception of abstract truth as man, but thinks more of the good to be attained. Deception and ruse in woman, far more than in man, have become a habit of thought and speech. A series of conditions, social, intellectual, and physiological, have forced this habit upon her as a means of self-defense.

Woman's religious nature is stronger than man's. She possesses in a marked degree the qualities of reverence, dependence, devotion, trust, and fidelity. Fear and timidity are feminine qualities, while faith is so natural to woman that she is disposed to credulity rather than to skepticisim.

Let us pause a second time to see what theory, if any, our results establish. Here, again, from her mental differences the doctrine of woman's inferiority receives no support—inferior, no doubt, in philosophy, science, and invention, and in her conception of abstract truth and justice, but superior in intuition, in charity, in temperance, in fidelity, in balance. But here again, as in her physical peculiarities, woman approaches the child type. This is seen in the preponderance of the emotional life over the discriminative, and of the impulsive over the voluntary. So also the quick perception and the retentive memory remind us of the child more than do the stern logical processes of the man. Woman's mental associations, selecting the concrete, the individual, the whole rather than the part, relations in space rather than in time, are also those of the child. Woman's receptivity, her faith and trust, her naïve freedom from skepticism, her fear and timidity, her feeling of dependence, her religious instincts, are all child traits. Children, like women, have slower reaction-time and lesser motor ability, are more easily hypnotized, have more number forms and color associations, have less power of inhibition, express their emotions more in their faces, and more readily give way to tears and smiles. Modern child study has shown that children are more cruel than adults and have little power to discriminate between truth and falsehood. They also are sympathetic and changeable, and act with reference to present rather than remote ends. Woman in respect to her altruism, pity, and charity has less resemblance to the child, but these traits are so intimately connected with her duties of motherhood as to have little bearing upon the theory of her naturally infantile constitution.

The hypothesis that woman approximates to the primitive rather than to the child type, that she represents arrested development, may be said to receive a certain amount of confirmation from her mental traits. Indifference to physical and psychical pain, freedom from color blindness, the preponderance of memory and intuition over reason, lack of mechanical inventiveness, conservatism and adherence to custom, precocity, changeableness, cruelty, tact, deceitfulness, emotional expression, religious feeling, are all traits conspicuous among primitive races, and, as we have seen, are more noticeable in women than in men. That women are less modified mentally and are more alike than men also argues for arrested development. It is well known that in insane asylums the female patients are more destructive, noisy, abusive, and vicious than the male patients, although their insanity is less serious and more curable. This fact, together with the other, that when women become bad they become more hopelessly bad, has led some too hastily to conclude that women, like children, are natural savages. The fact that woman has less logical and philosophical ability and has taken so little part in the development of the sciences, arts, and inventions, which are considered to represent human progress, is adduced as further confirmation of this theory. But in many of her mental traits woman departs further than man from the savage type. In her moral qualities she represents higher evolution. This is notably true in respect to her altruism, charity, sympathy, and pity. Woman's greater humanity, philanthropy, conscientiousness, fidelity, self-sacrifice, modesty, and patience, as well as her lesser disposition to crime, are qualities which separate her further than man from the savage. The same may be said of certain other subtle and scarcely definable feminine qualities, such, for instance, as grace and refinement. Woman's development along these lines certainly has not been arrested, and although it may be argued that these qualities are the logical outcome partly of her physical weakness and partly of her maternal duties, still it would be difficult to show that evolution in this direction represents less progress than in the more intellectual direction in which man has developed. It must be admitted, however, that woman's purely intellectual development has been retarded, and this may have a practical significance considering that on these qualities the struggle for existence now so largely turns. . . .

Certain other facts . . . point, it is said, to woman's arrested development. The division of labor which marks the progress of civilization has reached no such extent in the work of woman as in that of man. In fact, it may be said that there is in woman's work hardly any division of labor, except in so far as, in recent years, she has entered upon pursuits formerly followed only by men. As we have seen that women are more alike physically and mentally than men, so their work is more alike. In domestic life, which still includes the mass of representative women, each one either does her own housework, or has it done by female servants whose labor is equally unspecialized. No man now in civilized communities makes his own clothes, yet this is not uncommon among women, and in primitive communities they may even spin and weave the material. Not only is their work and manner of work more primitive, but also their tools. In the German cities on market day, for instance, may be seen numbers of men and women bringing their produce from the country, the men using carts or wagons propelled by themselves or their horses, but the women bearing their burdens in baskets upon their backs in quite the primitive fashion.

Before attempting any summary of our results I must call attention to some recent biological researches which may throw new light on the natural relation of the sexes. It has been shown by Geddes and Thomson, Fouillée and others, that in many of the lower and simpler orders of animals the female is larger than the male. This is true, with exceptions, throughout the animal world as high as the amphibians, and is in close logical connection with certain other important differences between the sexes. These, observed also best among the lower orders, are as follows: The male is active, restless, agile. The female is passive and quiescent. She has lower temperature, greater longevity, and a larger fund of vitality; her birth is the accompaniment of conditions of better nourishment. The male is katabolic, representing the expenditure of energy, individualism, variation, and progress. The female is anabolic, representing economy and the building up, conserving, and reproductive functions. She is nearer to and more representative of the race. These, it is said, are natural sexual differences seen at the very threshold of life in the contrast between the male and female cells, and so far as these same differences appear in man and woman they can not and need not be accounted for by any theories of natural or sexual selection nor by artificial social conditions. Those peculiarities of modern woman which are contrary to the natural constitution of the female, such as her smaller size and her alleged retarded development, are rather the qualities in need of explanation. It has been suggested that the greater size and strength of the male among the higher vertebrates may be explained as the indirect result, in part, of his combats with rivals, and, in part, of his greater activity in protecting and supporting himself and his mate when the maternal duties of the latter incapacitate her for these actions, and furthermore that the retarded development of woman is due to artificial and unnatural restrictions arising from a sort of bondage which the above conditions have made possible. Again, if it should be shown that woman conspicuously resembles the infant in body and mind, very unwarranted inferences might be drawn from this. It is true that the infant of the human species has certain curious points of resemblance to the lower animals, notably the ape, but it is equally true that the infant ape has certain marked resemblances to the human species which the adult ape does not have. By analogy we may infer that the human infant has closer resemblance to the more highly developed being of the future than the human adult has, and if woman is more like the child than man is, then she is more representative of the future being. The matter, in fact, reduces itself probably to this: that woman, like the child, represents the race type, while man represents those variable qualities by which mankind adapts itself to its surroundings. Every woman is, as it were, a composite picture of the race, never much worse nor much better than all. Man is, as it were, Nature's experiment, modified to reflect, if possible, the varying conditions of his environment. If superiority consists in adaptation to present environment, then man is superior; if it consists in the possession of those underlying qualities which are essential to the race—past, present, and future—then woman is superior.

The facts examined in this article, then, lend a certain amount of confirmation to all of the four theories mentioned at the beginning, except so far as woman's inferiority may have been implied in them. Woman's more intimate connection with the life history of the race, her childlike, representative, and typical nature, her embodiment of the everlasting essentials of humanity, her at present arrested or retarded development—all these are indicated by modern anthropological studies. These results are indicated, not proved. They must be verified, supplemented, and no doubt, in some instances, corrected by future studies along these lines.

From these studies there would be no want of lessons for political and social reformers, if they would learn them. From woman's rich endowment with all that is essentially human, the most devoted enthusiast for woman's rights and equality might gain new inspiration. From her retarded development the educational and political reformer might learn that woman's cause may suffer irretrievable damage if she is plunged too suddenly into duties demanding the same strain and nervous expenditure that is safely borne by man, and if it is attempted to correct in a century the evil of ages. From woman's childlike nature the thoughtful "spectator of all time and all existence" might learn yet a deeper and more significant lesson. May it not be that woman, representative of the past and future of humanity, whose qualities are concentration, passivity, clamness, and reserve of force, and upon whom, more than upon man, rest the burdens and responsibilities of the generations, is too sacred to be jostled roughly in the struggle for existence, and that she deserves from man a reverent exemption from some of the duties for which his restless and active nature adapts him?

Functionalism, Darwinism, and the Psychology of Women

A Study in Social Myth

Stephanie A. Shields

The psychology of women is acquiring the character of an academic entity as witnessed by the proliferation of research on sex differences, the appearance of textbooks devoted to the psychology of women, and the formation of a separate APA division, Psychology of Women. Nevertheless, there is almost universal ignorance of the psychology of women as it existed prior to its incorporation into psychoanalytic theory. If the maxim "A nation without a history is like a man without a memory" can be applied, then it would behoove the amnesiacs interested in female psychology to investigate its pre-Freudian past.

This article focuses on one period of that past (from the latter half of the 19th century to the first third of the 20th) in order to clarify the important issues of the time and trace their development to the position they occupy in current psychological theory. Even a limited overview leads the reader to appreciate Helen Thompson Woolley's (1910) early appraisal of the quality of the research on sex differences:

> There is perhaps no field aspiring to be scientific where flagrant personal bias, logic martyred in the cause of supporting a prejudice, unfounded assertions, and even sentimental rot and drivel, have run riot to such an extent as here. (p. 340)

The Functionalist Milieu

Although the nature of woman had been an academic and social concern of philosopher psychologists throughout the ages, formal psychology (its inception usually dated 1879) was relatively slow to take up the topic of female psychology. The "woman question" was a social one, and social problems did not fall within the sharply defined limits of Wundt's "new" psychology. The business of psychology was the description of the "generalized adult mind," and it is not at all clear whether "adult" was meant to include both sexes. When the students of German psychology did venture outside of the laboratory, however, there is no evidence that they were sympathetic to those defending the equality of male and female ability (cf. Wundt, 1901).

It was the functionalist movement in the United States that fostered academic psychology's study of sex differences and, by extension, a prototypic psychology of women. The incorporation of evolutionary theory into the practice of psychology made the study of the female legitimate, if not imperative. It would be incorrect to assume that the psychology of women existed as a separate specialty within the discipline. The female was discussed only in relation to the male, and the function of the female was thought to be distinctly different from and complementary to the function of the male. The leitmotiv of evolutionary theory as it came to be applied to the social sciences was the evolutionary supremacy of the Caucasian male. The notion of the supplementary, subordinate role of the female was ancillary to the development of that theme.

The influence of evolutionary theory on the psychology of women can be traced along two major conceptual lines: (a) by emphasizing the biological foundations of temperament, evolutionary theory led to serious academic discussion of maternal instinct (as one facet of the general topic of instinct); and (b) by providing a theoretical justification of the study of individual differences, evolutionary theory opened the door to the study of sex differences in sensory, motor, and intellectual abilities. As a whole, the concept of evolution with its concomitant emphasis on biological determinism provided ample "scientific" reason for cataloging the "innate" differences in male and female nature.

This article examines three topics that were of special significance to the psychology of women during the functionalist era: (a) structural differences in the brains of males and females and the implications of these differences for intelligence and temperament, (b) the hypothesis of greater male variability and its relation to social and educational issues, and (c) maternal instinct and its meaning for a psychology of female "nature." As the functionalist paradigm gave way to behaviorism and psychoanalytic theory, the definition and "meaning" of each of these issues changed to fit the times. When issues faded in importance, it was not because they were resolved but because they ceased to serve as viable scientific "myths" in the changing social and scientific milieu. As the times change, so must the myths change.

The Female Brain

The topic of female intelligence came to 19th-century psychology via phrenology and the neuroanatomists. Philosophers of the time (e.g., Hegel, Kant, Schopenhauer) had demonstrated, to their satisfaction, the justice of woman's subordinate social position, and it was left to the men of science to discover the particular physiological determinants of female inadequacy. In earlier periods, woman's inferiority had been defined as a general "state" intimately related to the absence of qualities that would have rendered her a male and to the presence of reproductive equipment that destined her to be female. For centuries the mode of Eve's creation and her greater guilt for the fall from grace had been credited as the cause of woman's imperfect nature, but this was not an adequate explanation in a scientific age. Thus, science sought explanations for female inferiority that were more in keeping with contemporary scientific philosophy.

Although it had long been believed that the brain was the chief organ of the mind, the comparison of male and female mental powers traditionally included only allusions to vague "imperfections" of the female brain. More precise definition of the sites of these imperfections awaited the advancement of the concept of cortical localization of function. Then, as finer distinctions of functional areas were noted, there was a parallel recognition of the differences between those sites as they appeared in each sex.

At the beginning of the 19th century, the slowly increasing interest in the cerebral gyri rapidly gathered momentum with the popularization of phrenology. Introduced by Franz Joseph Gall, "cranioscopy," as he preferred to call it, postulated that the seat of various mental and moral faculties was located in specific areas of the brain's surface such that a surfeit or deficiency could be detected by an external examination of the cranium. Phrenology provided the first objective method for determining the neurological foundation of sex differences in intelligence and temperament that had long been promulgated. Once investigation of brain structure had begun, it was fully anticipated that visible sex differences would be found: Did not the difference between the sexes pervade every other aspect of physique and physiological function? Because physical differences were so obvious in every other organ of the body, it was unthinkable that the brain could have escaped the stamp of sex.

Gall was convinced that he could, from gross anatomical observation, discriminate between male and female brains, claiming that "if there had been presented to him in water, the fresh brains of two adult animals of any species, one male and the other female, he could have distinguished the two sexes" (Walker, 1850, p. 317). Gall's student and colleague, Johann Spurzheim, elaborated on this basic distinction by noting that the frontal lobes were less developed in females, "the organs of the perceptive faculties being commonly larger than those of the reflective powers." Gall also observed sex differences in the nervous tissue itself, "confirming" Malebranche's belief that the female "cerebral fibre" is softer than that of the male, and that it is also "slender and long rather than thick" (Walker, 1850, p. 318). Spurzheim also listed the cerebral "organs" whose appearance differed commonly in males and females: females tended to have the areas devoted to philoprogenetiveness and other "tender" traits most prominent, while in males, areas of aggressiveness and constructiveness dominated. Even though cranioscopy did not survive as a valid system of describing cortical function, the practice of comparing the appearance of all or part of the brain for anatomical evidence of quality of function remained one of the most popular means of providing proof of female mental inferiority. Most comparisons used adult human brains, but with the rise of evolutionary theory, increasing emphasis was placed on the value of developmental and cross-species comparisons. The argument for female mental inferiority took two forms: some argued that quality of intellect was proportional to absolute or relative brain size; others, more in the tradition of cortical localization, contended that the presence of certain mental qualities was dependent upon the development of corresponding brain centers.

The measurement of cranial capacity had long been in vogue as one method of determining intellectual ability. That women had smaller heads than men was taken by some as clear proof of a real disparity between male and female intelligence. The consistently smaller brain size of the female was cited as another anatomical indicator of its functional inferiority. More brain necessarily meant better brain; the exception only proved this rule. Alexander Bain (1875) was among those who believed that the smaller absolute brain size of females accounted for a lesser mental ability. George Romanes (1887) enumerated the "secondary sex characteristics" of mental abilities attributable to brain size. The smaller brain of women was directly responsible for their mental inferiority, which "displays itself most conspicuously in a comparative absence of originality, and this more especially in the higher levels of intellectual work" (p. 655). He, like many, allowed that women were to some degree compensated for intellectual inferiority by a superiority of instinct and perceptual ability. These advantages carried with them the germ of female failure, however, by making women more subject to emotionality.

Proof of the male's absolute brain-size superiority was not enough to secure his position of intellectual superiority, since greater height and weight tended to offset the brain-size advantage. Reams of paper were, therefore, dedicated to the search for the most "appropriate" relative measures, but results were equivocal: if the ratio of brain weight to body weight is considered, it is found that women possess a proportionately larger brain than men; if the ratio of brain surface to body surface is computed, it is found to favor men. That some of the ratios "favored" males while others "favored" females led some canny souls to conclude that there was no legitimate solution to the problem. That they had ever hoped for a solution seems remarkable; estimates of brain size from cranial capacity involve a large margin of error because brains differing as much as 15% have been found in heads of the same size (Elliott, 1969, p. 316).

Hughlings Jackson has been credited as the first to regard the frontal cortex as the repository of the highest mental capacities, but the notion must have held popular credence as early as the 1850s because that period saw sporadic references to the comparative development of the frontal lobes in men and women. Once the function of the frontal lobes had been established, many researchers reported finding that the male possessed noticeably larger and more well-developed frontal lobes than females. The neuroanatomist Hischke came to the conclusion in 1854 that woman is *homo parietalis* while man is *homo frontalis* (Ellis, 1934). Likewise, Rudinger in 1877 found the frontal lobes of man in every way more extensive than those of women, and reported that these sex differences were evident even in the unborn fetus (Mobius, 1901).

At the turn of the century, the parietal lobes (rather than the frontal lobes) came to be regarded by some as the seat of intellect, and the necessary sex difference in parietal development was duly corroborated by the neuroanatomists. The change in cerebral hierarchy involved a bit of revisionism:

> the frontal region is not, as has been supposed smaller in woman, but rather larger relatively. . . . But the parietal lobe is somewhat smaller, [furthermore,] a preponderance of the frontal region does not imply intellectual superiority . . . the parietal region is really the more important. (Patrick, 1895, p. 212)

Once beliefs regarding the relative importance of the frontal and parietal lobes had shifted, it became critical to reestablish congruence between neuroanatomical findings and accepted sex differences. Among those finding parietal predominance in men were Paul Broca,[1] Theodore Meynert, and the German Rudinger (see Ellis, 1934, p. 217).

Other neuroanatomical "deficiencies" of the female were found in (a) the area of the corpus callosum, (b) the complexity of the gyri and sulci, (c) the conformation of gyri and sulci, and (d) the rate of development of the cortex of the fetus (Woolley, 1910, p. 335). Franklin Mall (1909) objected to the use of faulty research methods that gave spurious differences the appearance of being real. Among the most serious errors he noted was the practice of making observations with a knowledge of the sex of the brain under consideration.

The debate concerning the importance of brain size and anatomy as indicators of intelligence diminished somewhat with the development of mental tests; nevertheless, the brain-size difference was a phenomenon that many felt obligated to interpret. Max Meyer (1921) attempted to settle the matter by examining the various measures of relative difference that had been employed. After finding these methods far too equivocal, he concluded, in the best behavioristic terms, that sex differences in intelligence were simply "accidents of habits acquired."

Characteristics of the female brain were thought not simply to render women less intelligent but also to allow more "primitive" parts of human nature to be expressed in her personality. Instinct was thought to dominate woman, as did her emotions, and the resulting "affectability" was considered woman's greatest weakness, the reason for her inevitable failure. Affectability was typically defined as a general state, the manifestation of instinctive and emotional predispositions that in men were kept in check by a superior intellect.[2]

One of the most virulent critics of woman was the German physiologist Paul Mobius (1901), who argued that her mental incapacity was a necessary condition for the survival of the race. Instinct rendered her easily led and easily pleased, so much the better for her to give her all to bearing and rearing children. The dependence of woman also extracted a high price from man:

> All progress is due to man. Therefore the woman is like a dead weight on him, she prevents much restlessness and meddlesome inquisitiveness, but she also restrains him from noble actions, for she is unable to distinguish good from evil. (p. 629)

Mobius observed that woman was essentially unable to think independently, had strong inclinations to be mean and untrustworthy, and spent a good deal of her time in an emotionally unbalanced state. From this he was forced to conclude that: "If woman was not physically and mentally weak, if she was not as a rule rendered harmless by circumstances, she would be extremely dangerous" (Mobius, 1901, p. 630). Diatribes of this nature were relatively common German importations; woman's severest critics in this country seldom achieved a similar level of acerbity. Mobius and his ilk (e.g., Weininger, 1906) were highly publicized and widely read in the United States, and not a little of their vituperation crept into serious scientific discussions of woman's nature. For example, Porteus and Babcock (1926) resurrected the brain-size issue, discounting the importance of size to intelligence and instead associating it with the "maturing of other powers." Males, because of their larger brains would be more highly endowed with these "other powers," and so more competent and achieving. Proposals such as these, which were less obviously biased than those of Mobius, Weininger, and others, fit more easily into the current social value system and so were more easily assimilated as "good science" (cf. Allen, 1927, p. 294).

The Variability Hypothesis

The first systematic treatment of individual differences in intelligence appeared in 1575. Juan Huarte attributed sex differences in intelligence to the different humoral qualities that characterized each sex, a notion that had been popular in Western thought since ancient Greece. Heat and dryness were characteristic of the male principle, while moisture and coolness were female attributes. Because dryness of spirit was necessary for intelligence, males naturally possessed greater "wit." The maintenance of dryness and heat was the function of the testicles, and Huarte (1959) noted that if a man were castrated the effects were the same "as if he had received some notable dammage in his very braine" (p. 279). Because the principles necessary for cleverness were only possessed by males, it behooved parents to conduct their life-style, diet, and sexual intercourse in such a manner as to insure the conception of a male. The humoral theory of sex differences was widely accepted through the 17th century, but with the advent of more sophisticated notions of anatomy and physiology, it was replaced by other, more specific, theories of female mental defect: the lesser size and hypothesized simpleness of the female brain, affectability as the source of inferiority, and complementarity of abilities in male and female. It was the developing evolutionary theory that provided an overall explanation for why these sex differences existed and why they were necessary for the survival of the race.

The theory of evolution as proposed by Darwin had little to say regarding the intellectual capacity of either sex. It was in Francis Galton's (Charles Darwin's cousin) anthropometric laboratory that the investigation of intellectual differences took an empirical form (Galton, 1907). The major conclusion to come from Galton's research was that women tend in all their capacities to be inferior to men. He looked to common experience for confirmarion, reasoning that:

> If the sensitivity of women were superior to that of men, the self interest of merchants would lead to their being always employed; but as the reverse is the case, the opposite supposition is likely to be the true one. (pp. 20–21)

This form of logic—women have not excelled, therefore they cannot excel—was often used to support arguments denigrating female intellectual ability. The fact of the comparative rarity of female social achievement was also used as "evidence" in what was later to become a widely debated issue concerning the range of female ability.

Prior to the formulation of evolutionary theory, there had been little concern with whether deviation from the average or "normal" occurred more frequently in either sex. One of the first serious discussions of the topic appeared in the early 19th century when the anatomist Meckel concluded on pathological grounds that the human female showed greater variability than the human male. He reasoned that because man is the superior animal and variability a sign of inferiority, this conclusion was justified (in Ellis, 1903, p. 237). The matter was left at that until 1871. At that time Darwin took up the question of variability in *The Descent of Man* while attempting to explain how it could be that in many species males had developed greatly modified secondary sexual characteristics while females of the same species had not. He determined that this was originally caused by the males' greater activity and "stronger passions" that were in turn more likely (he believed) to be transmitted to male offspring. Because the females would prefer to mate with the strong and passionate, sexual selection would insure the survival of those traits. A tendency toward greater variation per se was not thought to be responsible for the appearance of unusual characteristics, but "development of such characters would be much aided, if the males were more liable to vary than the females" (Darwin, 1922, p. 344). To support this hypothesis of greater male variability, he cited recent data obtained by anatomists and biologists that seemed to confirm the relatively more frequent occurrence of physical anomaly among males.

Because variation from the norm was already accepted as the mechanism of evolutionary progress (survival and transmission of adaptive variations) and because it seemed that the male was the more variable sex, it soon was universally concluded that the male is the progressive element in the species. Variation for its own sake took on a positive value because greatness, whether of an individual or a society, could not be achieved without variation. Once deviation from the norm became legitimized by evolutionary theory, the hypothesis of greater male variability became a convenient explanation for a number of observed sex differences, among them the greater frequency with which men achieved "eminence." By the 1890s it was popularly believed that greater male variability was a principle that held true, not only for physical traits but for mental abilities as well:

> That men should have greater cerebral variability and therefore more originality, while women have greater stability and therefore more "common sense," are facts both consistent with the general theory of sex and verifiable in common experience. (Geddes & Thomson, 1890, p. 271)

Havelock Ellis (1894), an influential sexologist and social philosopher, brought the variability hypothesis to the attention of psychologists in the first edition of *Man and Woman.* After examining anatomical and pathological data that indicated a greater male *variational tendency* (Ellis felt this term was less ambiguous than *variability*), he examined the evidence germane to a discussion of range of intellectual ability. After noting that there were more men than women in homes for the mentally deficient, which indicated a higher incidence of retardation among males, and that there were more men than women on the roles of the eminent, which indicated a higher incidence of genius among males, he concluded that greater male variability probably held for all qualities of character and ability. Ellis (1903) particularly emphasized the wide social and educational significance of the phenomenon, claiming that greater male variability was "a fact which has affected the whole of our human civilization" (p. 238), particularly through the production of men of genius. Ellis (1934) was also adamant that the female's tendency toward the average did not necessarily imply inferiority of talent; rather, it simply limited her expertise to "the sphere of concrete practical life" (p. 436).

The variability hypothesis was almost immediately challenged as a "pseudo-scientific superstition" by the statistician Karl Pearson (1897). Though not a feminist, Pearson firmly believed that the "woman question" deserved impartial, scientific study. He challenged the idea of greater male variability primarily because he thought it contrary to the fact and theory of evolution and natural selection. According to evolutionary theory (Pearson, 1897), "the more intense the struggle the less is the variability, the more nearly are individuals forced to approach the type fittest to their surroundings, if they are to survive" (p. 258). In a "civilized" community one would expect that because men have a "harder battle for life," any difference in variation should favor women. He took Ellis to task by arguing it was (a) meaningless to consider secondary sex characteristics (as Ellis had done) and, likewise, (b) foolish to contrast the sexes on the basis of abnormalities (as Ellis had done). By redefining the problem and the means for its solution, he was able to dismiss the entire corpus of data that had been amassed: "the whole trend of investigations concerning the relative variability of men and women up to the present seems to be erroneous" (Pearson, 1897, p. 261). Confining his measurements to "normal variations in organs or characteristics not of a secondary sexual character," he assembled anthropometric data on various races, from Neolithic skeletons to modern French peasants. He also challenged the adequacy of statistical comparison of only the extremes of the distribution, preferring to base his contrasts on the dispersion of measures around the mean. Finding a slight tendency toward greater female variability, he concluded that the variability hypothesis as stated remained a "quite unproven principle."

Ellis countered Pearson in a lengthy article, one more vicious than that ordinarily due an intellectual affront.[3] Pearson's greatest sins (according to Ellis) were his failure to define "variability" and his measurement of characteristics that were highly subject to environmental influence. Ellis, of course, overlooked his own failure to define variability and his inclusion of environmentally altered evidence.

In the United States the variability hypothesis naturally found expression in the new testing movement, its proponents borrowing liberally from the theory of Ellis and the statistical technique of Pearson. The favor that was typically afforded the hypothesis did not stem from intellectual commitment to the scientific validity of the proposal as much as it did from personal commitment to the social desirability of its acceptance. The variability hypothesis was most often thought of in terms of its several corollaries: (A) genius (seldom, and then poorly, defined) is a peculiarly male trait; (b) men of genius naturally gravitate to positions of power and prestige (i.e., achieve eminence) by virtue of their talent; (c) an equally high ability level should not be expected of females; and (d) the education of women should, therefore, be consonant with their special talents and special place in society as wives and mothers.

Woman's Education

The "appropriate" education for women had been at issue since the Renaissance, and the implications of the variability hypothesis favored those who had been arguing for a separate female education. Late in the 18th century, Mary Wollstonecraft Godwin (1759–1797) questioned the "natural" roles of each sex, contending that for both the ultimate goal was the same: "the first object of laudable ambition is to obtain a character as a human being, regardless of the distinction of sex" (Wollstonecraft, 1955, p. 5). Without education, she felt, women could not contribute to social progress as mature individuals, and this would be a tragic loss to the community. Though not the first to recognize the social restrictions arbitrarily placed on women, she was the first to hold those restrictions as directly responsible for the purported "defective nature" of women. She emphasized that women had never truly been given an equal chance to prove or disprove their merits. Seventy years later, John Stuart Mill (1955) also took up the cause of women's education, seeing it as one positive action to be taken in the direction of correcting the unjust social subordination of women. He felt that what appeared as woman's intellectual inferiority was actually no more than the effort to maintain the passive-dependent role relationship with man, her means of support:

> When we put together three things—first, the natural attraction between the sexes; secondly, the wife's entire dependence on the husband . . . and lastly, that the principal object of human pursuit, consideration, and all objects of social ambition, can in general be sought or obtained by her only through him, it would be a miracle if the object of being attractive to men had not become the polar star of feminine education and formation of character. (pp. 232–233)[4]

Although Mill objected to fostering passivity and dependency in girls, other educators felt that this was precisely their duty. One of the more influential of the 19th century, Hannah More, rejected outright the proposal that women should share the same type of education as men, because "the chief end to be proposed in cultivating the understanding of women" was "to qualify them for the practical purposes of life" (see Smith, 1970, p. 101). To set one's sights on other than harmonious domesticity was to defy the natural order. Her readers were advised to be excellent women rather than indifferent men; to follow the "plain path which Providence has obviously marked out to the sex . . . rather than . . . stray awkwardly, unbecomingly, and unsuccessfully, in a forbidden road" (Smith, 1970, pp. 100–101). Her values were consonant with those held by most of the middle class, and so her *Strictures on the Modern System of Female Education* (more, 1800) enjoyed widespread popularity for some time.

By the latter part of the century, the question had turned from whether girls should be educated like boys to how much they should be educated like boys. With the shift in emphasis came the question of coeducation. One of the strongest objections to coeducation in adolescence was the threat it posed to the "normalization" of the menstrual period. G. Stanley Hall (1906) waxed poetic on the issue:

> At a time when her whole future life depends upon normalizing the lunar month, is there not something not only unnatural and unhygienic, but a little monstrous, in daily school associations with boys, where she must suppress and conceal her instincts and feelings, at those times when her own promptings suggest withdrawal or stepping a little aside to let Lord Nature do his magnificent work of efflorescence. (p. 590)

Edward Clarke (see Sinclair, 1965, p. 123) had earlier elucidated the physiological reason for the restraint of girls from exertion in their studies: by forcing their brains to do work at puberty, they would use up blood later needed for menstruation.

Hall proposed an educational system for girls that would not only take into consideration their delicate physical nature but would also be tailored to prepare them for their special role in society. He feared that women's competition with men "in the world" would cause them to neglect their instinctive maternal urges and so bring about "race suicide." Because the glory of the female lay in motherhood, Hall believed that all educational and social institutions should be structured with that end in mind. Domestic arts would therefore be emphasized in special schools for adolescent girls, and disciplines such as philosophy, chemistry, and mathematics would be treated only superficially. If a girl had a notion to stay in the "male" system, she should be able to, but, Hall warned, such a woman selfishly interested in self-fulfillment would also be less likely to bear children and so be confined to an "agamic" life, thus failing to reproduce those very qualities that made her strong (Hall, 1918).

Throughout Hall's panegyric upon the beauties of female domestic education, there runs an undercurrent of the *real* threat that he perceived in coeducation, and that was the "feminization" of the American male. David Starr Jordan (1902) shared this objection but felt that coeducation would nevertheless make young men more "civilized" and young women less frivolous, tempering their natural pubescent inclinations. He was no champion of female ability though, stressing that women "on the whole, lack originality" (p. 100). The educated woman, he said, "is likely to master technic rather than art; method, rather than substance. She may know a good deal, but she can do nothing" (p. 101). In spite of this, he did assert that their training is just as serious and important as that of men. His position strongly favored the notion that the smaller range of female ability was the cause of lackluster female academic performance.

The issue of coeducation was not easily settled, and even as late as 1935, one finds debates over its relative merits (*Encyclopedia of the Social Sciences,* 1935, pp. 614–617).

The Biological Bases of Sex Differences

The variability hypothesis was compatible not only with prevailing attitudes concerning the appropriate form of female education but also with a highly popular theory of the biological complementarity of the sexes. The main tenet of Geddes and Thomson's (1890) theory was that males are primarily "catabolic," females "anabolic." From this difference in metabolism, all other sex differences in physical, intellectual, and emotional makeup were derived. The male was more agile, creative, and variable; the female was truer to the species type and therefore, in all respects, less variable. The conservatism of the female insured the continuity of the species. The authors stressed the metabolic antecedents of female conservatism and male differentiation rather than variational tendency per se, and also put emphasis on the complementarity of the two natures:

> The feminine passivity is expressed in greater patience, more open-mindedness, greater appreciation of subtle details, and consequently what we call more rapid intuition. The masculine activity lends a greater power of maximum effort, of scientific insight, or cerebral experiment with impressions, and is associated with an unobservant or impatient disregard of minute details, but with a more stronger grasp of generalities. (p. 271)

The presentation of evolutionary theory anchored in yin–yang concepts of function represents the most positive evaluation of the female sex offered by 19th-century science. Whatever woman's shortcomings, they were necessary to complete her nature, which itself was necessary to complete man's: "Man thinks more, woman feels more. He discovers more, but remembers less; she is more receptive, and less forgetful" (Geddes & Thomson, 1890, p. 271).

Variability and the Testing Movement

Helen Thompson (later Woolley) put Geddes and Thomson's and other theories of sex differences in ability to what she felt was a crucial experimental test (see Thompson, 1903). Twenty-five men and 25 women participated in nearly 20 hours of individual testing of their intellectual, motor, and sensory abilities. Of more importance than her experimental results (whether men or women can tap a telegraph key more times per minute has lost its significance to psychology) was her discussion of the implications of the resulting negligible differences for current theories of sex differences. She was especially critical of the mass of inconsistencies inherent in contemporary biological theories:

> Women are said to represent concentration, patience, and stability in emotional life. One might logically conclude that prolonged concentration of attention and unbiased generalization would be their intellectual characteristics, but these are the very characteristics assigned to men. (p. 173)

In the face of such contradictions, she was forced to conclude that "if the author's views as to the mental differences of sex had been different, they might as easily have derived a very different set of characteristics" (pp. 173–174). Thompson singled out the variability hypothesis for special criticism, objecting not only to the use of physical variation as evidence for intellectual variation but also to the tendency to minimize environmental influences. She held that training was responsible for sex differences in variation, and to those who countered that it is really a fundamental difference of instincts and characteristics that determines the differences in training, she replied that if this were true, "it would not be necessary to spend so much time and effort in making boys and girls follow the lines of conduct proper to their sex" (p. 181).

Thompson's recommendation to look at environmental factors went unheeded, as more and more evidence of woman's incapability of attaining eminence was amassed. In the surveys of eminent persons that were popular at the turn of the century, more credence was given to nature (à la Hall) than nurture (à la Thompson) for the near absence of eminent women (Cattell, 1903; Ellis, 1904). Cattell (1903) found a ready-made explanation in the variability hypothesis: "Women depart less from the normal than man," ergo "the distribution of women is represented by a narrower bell-shaped curve" (p. 375). Cora Castle's (1913) survey of eminent women was no less critical of woman's failure to achieve at the top levels of power and prestige.

One of the most influential individuals to take up the cause of the variability hypothesis was Edward Thorndike. Much of the early work in the testing movement was done at Columbia University, which provided the perfect milieu for Thorndike's forays into the variability problem as applied to mental testing and educational philosophy. Thorndike based his case for the acceptance of the variability hypothesis on the reevaluation of the results of two studies (Thompson, 1903; Wissler, 1901) that had not themselves been directed toward the issue. Thorndike insisted that greater male variability only became meaningful when one examined the distribution of ability at the highest levels of giftedness. Measurement of more general sex differences could only "prove that the sexes are closely alike and that sex can account for only a very small fraction of human mental differences in the abilities listed" (Thorndike, 1910, p. 185). Since the range of female ability was narrower, he reasoned, the talents of women should be channeled into fields in which they would be most needed and most successful because "this one fundamental difference in variability is more important than all the differences between the average male and female capacities" (Thorndike, 1906):

> Not only the probability and the desirability of marriage and the training of children as an essential feature of woman's career, but also the restriction of women to the mediocre grades of ability and achievement should be reckoned with by our educational systems. The education of women for . . . professions . . . where a very few gifted individuals are what society requires, is far less needed than for such professions as nursing, teaching, medicine, or architecture, where the average level is the essential. (p. 213)

He felt perfectly justified in this recommendation because of "the patent fact that in the great achievements of the world in science, as, invention, and management, women have been far excelled by men" (Thorndike, 1910, p. 35). In Thorndike's view, environmental factors scarcely mattered.

Others, like Joseph Jastrow (1915), seemed to recognize the tremendous influence that societal pressures had upon achievement. He noted that even when women had been admitted to employment from which they had previously been excluded, new prejudices arose; "allowances and considerations for sex intrude, favorably or unfavorably; the avenues of preferment, though ostensibly open are really barred by invisible barriers of social prejudice" (pp. 567–568). This was little more than lip service because he was even more committed to the importance of variational tendency and its predominance over any possible extenuating factors: the effects of the variability of the male and the biological conservatism of the female "radiates to every distinctive aspect of their contrasted natures and expressions" (p. 568).

A small but persistent minority challenged the validity of the variability hypothesis, and it is not surprising that this minority was composed mainly of women. Although the "woman question" was, to some degree, at issue, the larger dispute was between those who stressed "nature" as the major determinant of ability (and therefore success) and those who rejected nature and its corollary, instead emphasizing the importance of environmental factors. Helen Thompson Woolley, while remaining firmly committed to the investigation of the differential effects of social factors on each sex, did not directly involve herself in the variability controversy. Leta Stetter Hollingworth, first a student and then a colleague of Thorndike's at Teachers College of Columbia University, actively investigated the validity of the hypothesis and presented sound objections to it. She argued that there was no real basis for assuming that the distribution of "mental traits" in the population conforms without exception to the Gaussian distribution. The assumption of normality was extremely important to the validity of the variability hypothesis, because only in a normal distribution would a difference in variability indicate a difference in range. It was the greater range of male ability that was used to "prove" the ultimate superiority of male ability. Greater range of male ability was usually verified by citing lists of eminent persons (dominated by men) and the numbers and sex of those in institutions for the feebleminded (also dominated by men). Hollingworth (1914) saw no reason to resort to biological theory for an explanation of the phenomenon when a more parsimonious one was available in social fact. Statistics reporting a larger number of males among the feebleminded could be explained by the fact that the supporting data had been gathered in institutions, where men were more likely to be admitted than women of an equal degree of retardation. The better ability of feebleminded women to survive outside the institutional setting was simply a function of female social role:

> Women have been and are a dependent and non-competitive class, and when defective can more easily survive outside of institutions, since they do not have to compete *mentally* with normal individuals, as men do, to maintain themselves in the social *milieu.* (Hollingworth, 1914, p. 515)

Women would therefore be more likely to be institutionalized at an older age than men, after they had become too old to be "useful" or self-supporting. A survey of age and sex ratios in New York institutions supported her hypothesis: the ratio of females to males increased with the age of the inmates (Hollingworth, 1913). As for the rarity of eminence among women,

Hollingworth (1914) argued that because the social role of women was defined in terms of housekeeping and child-rearing functions, "a field where eminence is not possible," and because of concomitant constraints placed on the education and employment of women by law, custom, and the demands of the role, one could not possibly validly compare the achievements of women with those of men who "have followed the greatest possible range of occupations, and have at the same time procreated unhindered" (p. 528). She repeatedly emphasized (Hollingworth, 1914, 1916) that the true potential of woman could only be known when she began to receive social acceptance of her right to choose career, maternity, or both.

Hollingworth's argument that unrecognized differences in social training had misdirected the search for *inherent* sex differences had earlier been voiced by Mary Calkins (1896). Just as Hollingworth directed her response particularly at Thorndike's formulation of the variability hypothesis, Calkins objected to Jastrow's (1896) intimations that one finds "greater uniformity amongst women than amongst men" (p. 431).

Hollingworth's work was instrumental in bringing the variability issue to a crisis point, not only because she presented persuasive empirical data to support her contentions but also because this was simply the first major opposition that the variability hypothesis had encountered. Real resolution of this crisis had to await the development of more sophisticated testing and statistical techniques. With the United States' involvement in World War I, most testing efforts were redirected to wartime uses. This redirection effectively terminated the variability debate, and although it resumed during the postwar years, the renewed controversy never attained the force of conviction that had characterized the earlier period. "Variational tendency" became a statistical issue, and the pedagogic implications that had earlier colored the debate were either minimized or disguised in more egalitarian terms.

After its revival in the mid-1920s, investigation of the variability hypothesis was often undertaken as part of larger intelligence testing projects. Evidence in its favor began to look more convincing than it ever had. The use of larger samples, standardized tests, and newer methods of computing variation gave an appearance of increased accuracy, but conclusions were still based on insubstantial evidence of questionable character. Most discussions of the topic concluded that there were not enough valid data to resolve the issue and that even if that data were available, variation within each sex is so much greater than the difference in variation between sexes that the "meaning" of the variability hypothesis was trivial (Shields, Note 1).

Maternal Instinct

The concept of maternal instinct was firmly entrenched in American psychology before American psychology itself existed as an entity. The first book to appear in the United States with "psychology" in its title outlined the psychological sex differences arising from the physical differences between men and women. Differences in structure were assumed to imply differences in function, and therefore differences in abilities, temperament, and intelligence. In each sex a different set of physical systems was thought to predominate: "In man the arterial and cerebral systems prevail, and with them irritability; in woman the venous and ganglion systems and with them plasticity and sensibility" (Rausch, 1841, p. 81). The systems dominant in woman caused her greatest attributes to lie in the moral sphere in the form of love, patience, and chastity. In the intellectual sphere, she was not equally blessed, "and this is not accidental, not because no opportunity has offered itself to their productive genius . . . but because it is their highest happiness to be mothers" (Rausch, 1841, p. 83).[5]

Although there was popular acceptance of a maternal instinct in this country, the primary impetus for its incorporation into psychology came by way of British discussion of social evolution. While the variability hypothesis gained attention because of an argument, the concept of maternal instinct evolved without conflict. There was consistent agreement as to its existence, if not its precise nature or form. Typical of the evolutionary point of view was the notion that woman's emotional nature (including her tendency to nurturance) was a direct consequence of her reproductive physiology. As Herbert Spencer (1891) explained it, the female's energies were directed toward preparation for pregnancy and lactation, reducing the energy available for the development of other qualities. This resulted in a "rather earlier cessation of individual evolution" in the female. Woman was, in essence, a stunted man. Her lower stage of development was evident not only in her interior mental and emotional powers but also in the resulting expression of the parental instinct. Whereas the objectivity of the male caused his concern to be extended "to all the relatively weak who are dependent upon him" (p. 375), the female's propensity to "dwell on the concrete and proximate rather than on the abstract and remote" made her incapable of the generalized protective attitude assumed by the male. Instead, she was primarily responsive to "infantile helplessness."

Alexander Sutherland (1898) also described a parental instinct whose major characteristic (concern for the weak) was "the basis of all other sympathy," which is itself "the ultimate basis of all moral feeling" (p. 156). Like his contemporaries (e.g., McDougall, 1913, 1923; Shand, 1920; Spencer, 1891), Sutherland revered maternal sentiment but thought the expression of parental instinct in the male, that is, a protective attitude, was a much more significant factor in social evolution, an attitude of benevolent paternalism more in keeping with Victorian social ethic than biological reality. The expression of the parental instinct in men, Sutherland thought, must necessarily lead to deference toward women out of "sympathetic regard for women's weakness." He noted that male protectiveness had indeed wrought a change in the relations between the sexes, evident in a trend away from sexual motivations and toward a general improvement in moral tone, witness the "large number of men who lead perfectly chaste lives for ten or twenty years after puberty before they marry," which demonstrated that the "sensuous side of man's nature is slowly passing under the control of sympathetic sentiments" (p. 288).[6]

Whatever facet of the activity that was emphasized, there was common agreement that the maternal (or parental) instinct was truly an instinct. A. F. Shand (1920) argued that the maternal instinct is actually composed of an ordered "system" of instincts and characterized by a number of emotions. Despite its complexity, "maternal love" was considered to be a hereditary trait "in respect not only of its instincts, but also of the bond connecting its primary emotions, and of the end which the whole system pursues, namely, the preservation of the offspring" (p. 42). The sociologist L. T. Hobhouse (1916) agreed that maternal instinct was a "true" instinct, "not only in the drive but in some of the detail." He doubted the existence of a corresponding paternal instinct, however, since he had observed that few men have a natural aptitude with babies.

The unquestioning acceptance of the maternal instinct concept was just as prevalent in this country as it was in Britain. William James (1950) listed parental love among the instincts of humans and emphasized the strength with which it was expressed in women. He was particularly impressed with the mother-infant relationship and quoted at length from a German psychologist concerning the changes wrought in a woman at the birth of her child: "She has, in one word, transferred her entire egoism to the child, and lives only in it" (p. 439). Even among those who employed a much narrower definition of instinct than James, maternal behavior was thought to be mediated by inherent neural connections. R. P. Halleck (1895) argued that comparatively few instincts are fully developed in humans, because reason intervenes and modifies their expression to fit the circumstances. Maternal instinct qualified as a clear exception, and its expression seemed as primitive and unrefined as that of infants' reflexive behavior.

Others (e.g., Jastrow, 1915; Thorndike, 1914a, 1914b) treated instinct more as a quality of character than of biology. Edward Thorndike (1911) considered the instincts peculiar to each sex to be the primary source of sex differences: "it appears that if the primary sex characters—the instincts directly related to courtship, love, child-bearing, and nursing—are left out of account, the average man differs from the average woman far less than many men differ from one another" (p. 30). Thorndike taught that the tendency to display maternal concern was universal among women, although social pressures could "complicate or deform" it. He conceded that males share in an instinctive "good will toward children," but other instincts, such as the "hunting instinct," predominated (Thorndike, 1914b). He was so sure of the innate instinctual differences between men and women that it was his contention (Thorndike, 1914b) that even "if we should keep the environment of boys and girls absolutely similar these instincts would produce sure and important differences between the mental and moral activities of boys and girls" (p. 203). The expression of instincts therefore was thought to have far-reaching effects on seemingly unrelated areas of ability and conduct. For example, woman's "nursing instinct," which was most often exhibited in "unreasoning tendencies to pet, coddle, and 'do for' others," was also "the chief source of woman's superiorities in the moral life" (Thorndike, 1914a, p. 203). Another of the female's instinctive tendencies was described as "submission to mastery":

> Women in general are thus by original nature submissive to men in general. Submissive behavior is apparently not annoying when assumed as the instinctive response to its natural stimulus. Indeed, it is perhaps a common satisfier. (Thorndike, 1914b, p. 34)

The existence of such an "instinct" would, of course, validate the social norm of female subservience and dependence. An assertive woman would be acting contrary to instinct and therefore contrary to *nature*. There is a striking similarity between Thorndike's description of female nature and that of the Freudians with their mutual emphasis on woman's passivity, dependency, and masochism. For Thorndike, however, the *cause* of such a female attitude was thought to be something quite different from mutilation fears and penis envy.

The most vocal proponent of instinct, first in England and later in this country, was William McDougall (1923). Unlike Shand, he regarded "parental sentiment" as a primary instinct and did not hesitate to be highly critical of those who disagreed with him. When his position was maligned by the behaviorists, his counterattack was especially strong:

> And, when we notice how in so many ways the behavior of the human mother most closely resembles that of the animal-mother, can we doubt that . . . if the animal-mother is moved by the impulse of a maternal instinct, so also is the woman? To repudiate this view as baseless would seem to me the height of blindness and folly, yet it is the folly of a number of psychologists who pride themselves on being strictly "scientific." (p. 136)

In McDougall's system of instincts, each of the primary instincts in humans was accompanied by a particular emotional quality. The parental instinct had as its primary emotional quality the "tender emotion" vaguely defined as love, tenderness, and tender feeling. Another of the primary instincts was that of "pairing," its primary emotional quality that of sexual emotion or excitement, "sometimes called love—an unfortunate and confusing usage" (p. 234). Highly critical of what he called the "Freudian dogma that all love is sexual," McDougall proposed that it was the interaction of the parental and pairing instincts that was the basis of heterosexual "love." "Female coyness," which initiated the courtship ritual, was simply the reproductively oriented manifestation of the instincts of self-display and self-abasement. The appearance of a suitable male would elicit coyness from the female, and at that point the male's parental instinct would come into play:

> A certain physical weakness and delicacy (probably moral also) about the normal young woman or girl constitute in her a resemblance to a child. This resemblance . . . throws the man habitually into the protective attitude, evokes the impulse and emotion of the parental instinct. He feels that he wants to protect and shield and help her in every way. (p. 425)

Once the "sexual impulse" had added its energy to the relationship, the young man was surely trapped, and the survival of the species was insured. McDougall, while firmly committed to the importance of instinct all the way up the evolutionary ladder, never lost his sense of Victorian delicacy: while pairing simply meant reproduction in lower animals, in humans it was accorded a tone of gallantry and concern.

The fate of instinct at the hands of the radical behaviorists is a well-known tale. Perhaps the most adamant, as well as notorious, critic of the instinct concept was J. B. Watson (1926). Like those before him who had relied upon observation to prove the existence of maternal instinct, he used observation to confirm its nonexistence:

> We have observed the nursing, handling, bathing, etc. of the first baby of a good many mothers. Certainly there are no new ready-made activities appearing except nursing. The mother is usually as awkward about that as she can well be. The instinctive factors are practically nil. (p. 54)

Watson attributed the appearance of instinctive behavior to the mother's effort to conform to societal expectations of her successful role performance. He, like the 19th-century British associationist Alexander Bain, speculated that not a little of the mother's pleasure in nursing and caring for the infant was due to the sexually stimulating effect of those activities.[7]

Even the most dedicated behaviorists hedged a bit when it came to discarding the idea of instinct altogether. Although the teleology and redundancy of the concept of instinct were sharply criticized, some belief in "instinctive activity" was typically retained (cf. Dunlap, 1919–1920). W. B. Pillsbury (1926), for example, believed that the parental instinct was a "secondary" instinct. Physical attraction to the infant guided the mother's first positive movements toward the infant, but trial and error guided her subsequent care. Instinct was thought of as that quality which set the entire pattern of maternal behavior in motion.

In time instinct was translated into *drive* and *motivation,* refined concepts more in keeping with behavioristic theory. Concomitantly, interest in the maternal instinct of human females gave way to the study of mothering behavior in rodents. The concept of maternal instinct did find a place in psychoanalytic theory, but its definition bore little resemblance to that previously popular. Not only did maternal instinct lose the connotation of protectiveness and gentility that an earlier generation of psychologists had ascribed to it, but it was regarded as basically sexual, masochistic, and even destructive in nature (cf. Rheingold, 1964).

The Ascendancy of Psychoanalytic Theory

The functionalists, because of their emphasis on "nature," were predictably indifferent to the study of social sex roles and cultural concepts of masculine and feminine. The behaviorists, despite their emphasis on "nurture," were slow to recognize those same social forces. During the early 1930s, there was little meaningful ongoing research in female psychology: the point of view taken by the functionalists was no longer a viable one, and the behaviorists with their emphasis on nonsocial topics (i.e., learning and motivation) had no time for serious consideration of sex differences. While the functionalists had defined laws of behavior that mirrored the society of the times, behaviorists concentrated their efforts on defining universal laws that operated in any time, place, or organism. Individual differences in nature were expected during the functionalist era because they were the sine qua non of a Darwinian view of the world and of science. The same individual differences were anathema to early learning-centered psychology because, no longer necessary or expedient, they were a threat to the formulation of universal laws of behavior.

In the hiatus created by the capitulation of functionalism to behaviorism, the study of sex differences and female nature fell within the domain of psychoanalytic theory—the theory purported to have all the answers. Freudian theory (or some form of it) had for some years already served as the basis for a psychology of female physiological function (cf. Benedek & Rubenstein, 1939). The application of principles popular in psychiatry and medicine (and their inescapable identification with pathology) to academic psychology was easily accomplished. Psychoanalytic theory provided psychology with the first comprehensive theoretical explanation of sex differences. Its novelty in that respect aided its assimilation.

Psychology proper, as well as the general public, had been well-prepared for a biological, and frankly sexual, theory of male and female nature. Havelock Ellis, although himself ambivalent and even hostile toward Freudian teachings, had done much through his writing to encourage openness in the discussion of sexuality. He brought a number of hitherto unmentionable issues to open discussion, couching them in the commonly accepted notion of the complementarity of the sexes, thus insuring their popular acceptance. Emphasis on masculinity and femininity as real dimensions of personality appeared in the mid-1930s in the form of the Terman Masculinity-Femininity Scale (Terman & Miles, 1968). Although Lewis Terman himself avoided discussion of whether masculinity and femininity were products of nature or nurture, social determinants of masculinity and femininity were commonly deemphasized in favor of the notion that they were a type of psychological secondary sexual characteristic. Acceptance of social sex role soon came to be perceived as an indicator of one's mental health.

The traps inherent in a purely psychoanalytic concept of female nature were seldom recognized. John Dewey's (1957) observation, made in 1922, merits attention, not only for its accuracy but because its substance can be found in present-day refutations of the adequacy of psychaoanlytic theory as an explanation of woman's behavior and "nature":

> The treatment of sex by psycho-analysts is most instructive, for it flagrantly exhibits both the consequences of artificial simplification and the transformation of social results into psychic causes. Writers, usually male, hold forth on the psychology of women, as if they were dealing with a Platonic universal entity, although they habitually treat men as individuals, varying with structure and environment. They treat phenomena which are peculiarly symptoms of civilization of the West at the present time as if they were the necessary effects of fixed nature impulses of human nature. (pp. 143–144)

The identification of the psychology of women with psychoanalytic theory was nearly complete by the mid-1930s and was so successful that many psychologists today, even those most deeply involved in the current movement for a psychology of women, are not aware that there was a psychology of women long before there was a Sigmund Freud. This article has dealt only with a brief period in that history, and then only with the most significant topics of that period. Lesser issues were often just as hotly debated, for example, whether there is an innate difference in the style of handwriting of men and women (cf. Allen, 1927; Downey, 1910).

And what has happened to the issues of brain size, variability, and maternal instinct since the 1930s? Where they are politically and socially useful, they have an uncanny knack of reappearing, albeit in an altered form.

For example, the search for central nervous system differences between males and females has continued. Perhaps the most popular form this search has taken is the theory of prenatal hormonal "organization" of the hypothalamus into exclusively male or female patterns of function (Harris & Levine, 1965). The proponents of this theory maintain an Aristotelian view of woman as an incomplete man:

> In the development of the embryo, nature's first choice or primal impulse is to differentiate a female. . . . The principle of differentiation is always that to obtain a male, something must be added. Subtract that something, and the result will be a female. (Money, 1970, p. 428)

The concept of maternal instinct, on the other hand, has recently been taken up and refashioned by a segment of the woman's movement. Pregnancy and childbirth are acclaimed as important expressions of womanliness whose satisfactions cannot be truly appreciated by males. The idea that women are burdened with "unreasoning tendencies to pet, coddle, and 'do for' others" has been disposed of by others and replaced by the semiserious proposal that if any "instinctive" component of parental concern exists, it is a peculiarly male attribute (Stannard, 1970). The variability hypothesis is all but absent from contemporary psychological work, but if it ever again promises a viable justification for existing social values, it will be back as strongly as ever. Conditions which would favor its revival include the renaissance of rugged individualism or the "need" to suppress some segment of society, for example, women's aspirations to positions of power. In the first case the hypothesis would serve to reaffirm that there are those "born to lead," and in the latter that there are those "destined to follow."

Of more importance than the issues themselves or their fate in contemporary psychology is the recognition of the role that they have played historically in the psychology of women: the role of social myth. Graves (1968, p. v) included among the functions of mythologizing that of justification of existing social systems. This function was clearly operative throughout the evolutionist-functionalist treatment of the psychology of women: the "discovery" of sex differences in brain structure to correspond to "appropriate" sex differences in brain function; the biological justification (via the variability hypothesis) for the enforcement of woman's subordinate social status; the Victorian weakness and gentility associated with maternity; and pervading each of these themes, the assumption of an innate emotional, sexless, unimaginative female character that played the perfect foil to the Darwinian male. That science played handmaiden to social values cannot be denied. Whether a parallel situation exists in today's study of sex differences is open to question.

NOTES

1. Ellis (1934) claimed that Broca's opinion changed over time. Broca

> became inclined to think that it [the hypothesized male superiority of intellect] was merely a matter of education—of muscular . . . not merely mental, education—and he thought that if left to their spontaneous impulses men and women would tend to resemble each other, as happens in the savage condition. (p. 222)

2. Burt and Moore (1912, p. 385), inspired by contemporary theories of cortical localization of function, proposed a nuerological theory of female affectability. On the basis of the popular belief that the thalamus was "the centre for the natural expression of the emotions" while "control of movements and the association of ideas" was localized in the cortex and the common assumption that the male was more inclined to be intellectual and rational and the female more passionate and emotional, they concluded that in the adult male the cortex would tend to be "more completely organized," while in the adult female "the thalamus tends to appear more completely organized." They came to the general conclusion that "the mental life of man is predominantly cortical; that of woman predominantly thalamic."
3. One of Ellis's biographers (Calder-Marshall, 1959, pp. 97–98) has suggested that Ellis was "wildly jealous" of Karl Pearson's influence on Olive Schreiner, the controversial South African writer. Schreiner first met Pearson in 1885, over a year after she had met Ellis, and according to Calder-Marshall "was vastly attracted to him [Pearson] in what she considered to be a selfless Hintonian sense. . . . She regarded him as a brilliant young man, dying of tuberculosis, whose few remaining years it was her selfless duty to solace" (Pearson died in 1936). Calder-Marshall summed up the triangle in few, but insinuating, phrases:

   > Exactly what was happening between Karl Pearson and Olive Schreiner during these months [August 1885–December 1886] is a matter more for any future biographer of Olive Schreiner . . . it is enough to know that Olive did her best to remain loyal to both her friends without telling too many lies, and that while Olive remained the most important person in Havelock's life, the most important person in Olive's was Karl Pearson from the time she first met him to a considerable time after she left England. (p. 98)

   Ellis's rivalry with Pearson could explain his bitter and supercilious treatment of Pearson's venture into "variational tendency," since Ellis was not one to easily accept an assault on his ego. For his part Pearson "despised the Hinton group, including Ellis. He thought they were flabby-minded, unhealthy and immoral" (p. 97). But these opinions, while possibly influencing him to write on variation originally, did not intrude upon a fair-minded scientific discussion of the matter.
4. One of the severest critics of Mill's defense of women was Sigmund Freud. He felt Mill's propositions were in direct contradiction to woman's "true" nature:

   > It is really a stillborn thought to send women into the struggle for existence exactly as men. . . . I believe that all reforming action in law and education would break down in front of the fact that, long before the age at which a man can earn a position in society, Nature has determined woman's destiny through beauty, charm, and sweetness. Law and custom have much to give women that has been withheld from them, but the position of women will surely be what it is: in youth an adored darling and in mature years a loved wife. (quoted in Reeves, 1971, pp. 163–164)

5. This sentiment was echoed by Bruno Bettelheim (1965) over 100 years later: "as much as women want to be good scientists or engineers, they want first and foremost to be womanly companions of men and to be mothers" (p. 15).
6. Similar observations were made concerning women. Sutherland (1898) noted that because social morality had developed to such a high level, women "now largely enter upon marriage our of purely sympathetic attractions, in which sex counts for something, but with all its grosser aspects gone." He happily reported another's finding that "sexual desire enters not at all into the minds of a very large proportion of women when contemplating matrimony" (p. 288).
7. Bain's (1875) position was similar except that he believed that there *was* an innate tendency to nurture that initiated the entire cycle of positive affect-positive action. The instinct was thought to be a natural "sentiment," which was fostered by the long period of gestation and the "special energies" required of the mother to sustain the infant. The positive affect arising from activity connected with the infant then brought about increased nurturance and increased pleasure. At least part of this pleasure was thought to be physical in nature.

REFERENCES

ALLEN, C. N. Studies in sex differences. *Psychological Bulletin,* 1927, *24,* 294–304.

BAIN, A. *Mental science.* New York: Appleton, 1875.

BENEDEK, T., & RUBENSTEIN, B. B. The correlations between ovarian activity and psychodynamic processes. II. The menstrual phase. *Psychosomatic Medicine,* 1939, *1,* 461–485.

BETTELHEIM, B. The commitment required of a woman entering a scientific profession in present-day American society. In J. A. Mattfield & C. G. Van Aken (Eds.), *Women and the scientific professions.* Cambridge, Mass.: M.I.T. Press, 1965.

BURT, C., & MOORE, R. C. The mental differences between the sexes. *Journal of Experimental Pedagogy,* 1912, *1,* 355–388.

CALDER-MARSHALL, A. *The sage of sex.* New York: Putnam, 1959.

CALKINS, M. W. Community of ideas of men and women. *Psychological Review,* 1896, *3,* 426–430.

CASTLE, C. A. A statistical study of eminent women. *Columbia Contributions to Philosophy and Psychology,* 1913, *22*(27).

CATTELL, J. MCK. A statistical study of eminent men. *Popular Science Monthly,* 1903, *62,* 359–377.

DARWIN, C. *The descent of man* (2nd ed.). London: John Murray, 1922. (Originally published, 1871; 2nd edition originally published, 1874.)

DEWEY, J. *Human nature and conduct.* New York: Random House, 1957.

DOWNEY, J. E. Judgment on the sex of handwriting. *Psychological Review,* 1910, *17,* 205–216.

DUNLAP, J. Are there any instincts? *Journal of Abnormal and Social Psychology,* 1919–1920, *14,* 307–311.

ELLIOTT, H. C. *Textbook of neuroanatomy* (2nd ed.). Philadelphia: Lippincott, 1969.

ELLIS, H. *Man and woman: A study of human secondary sexual characters.* London: Walter Scott; New York: Scribner's, 1894.

ELLIS, H. Variation in man and woman. *Popular Science Monthly,* 1903, *62,* 237–253.

ELLIS, H. *A study of British genius.* London: Hurst & Blackett, 1904.

ELLIS, H. *Man and woman, a study of secondary and tertiary sexual characteristics* (8th rev. ed.). London: Heinemann, 1934.

Encyclopedia of the Social Sciences. New York: Macmillan, 1935.

GALTON, F. *Inquiries into the human faculty and its development.* London: Dent, 1907.

GEDDES, P., & THOMSON, J. A. *The evolution of sex.* New York: Scribner & Welford, 1890.

GRAVES, R. Introduction. In *New Larousse encyclopedia of mythology* (Rev. ed.). London: Paul Hamlyn, 1968.

HALL, G. S. The question of coeducation. *Munsey's Magazine,* 1906, *34,* 588–592.

HALL, G. S. *Youth, its education, regimen and hygiene.* New York: Appleton, 1918.

HALLECK, R. *Psychology and psychic culture.* New York: American Book, 1895.

HARRIS, G. W., & LEVINE, S. Sexual differentiation of the brain and its experimental control. *Journal of Physiology,* 1965, *181,* 379–400.

HOBHOUSE, L. *Morals in evolution.* New York: Holt, 1916.

HOLLINGWORTH, L. S. The frequency of amentia as related to sex. *Medical Record,* 1913, *84,* 753–756.

HOLLINGWORTH, L. S. Variability as related to sex differences in achievement. *American Journal of Sociology,* 1914, *19,* 510–530.

HOLLINGWORTH, L. S. Social devices for impelling women to bear and rear children. *American Journal of Sociology,* 1916, *22,* 19–29.

HUARTE, J. *The examination of mens wits* (trans. from Spanish to Italian by M. Camilli; trans. from Italian to English by R. Carew). Gainesville, Fla.: Scholars' Facsimiles and Reprints, 1959.

JAMES, W. *The principles of psychology.* New York: Dover, 1950.

JASTROW, J. Note on Calkins' "Community of ideas of men and women." *Psychological Review,* 1896, *3,* 430–431.

JASTROW, J. *Character and temperament.* New York: Appleton, 1915.

JORDAN, D. S. The higher education of women. *Popular Science Monthly,* 1902, *62,* 97–107.

MALL, F. P. On several anatomical characters of the human brain, said to vary according to race and sex, with especial reference to the weight of the frontal lobe. *American Journal of Anatomy,* 1909, *9,* 1–32.

MC DOUGALL, W. *An introduction to social psychology* (7th ed.). London: Methuen, 1913.

MC DOUGALL, MEYER, M. *Psychology of the other-one.* Columbia: Missouri Book, 1921.

MILL, J. S. *The subjection of women.* London: Dent, 1955.

MOBIUS, P. J. The physiological mental weakness of woman (A. McCorn, Trans.). *Alienist and Neurologist,* 1901, *22,* 624–642.

MONEY, J. Sexual dimorphism and homosexual gender identity. *Psychological Bulletin,* 1970, *74,* 425–440.

MORE, H. *Strictures on the modern system of female education. With a view of the principles and conduct prevalent among women of rank and fortune.* Philadelphia, Pa.: Printed by Budd and Bertram for Thomas Dobson, 1800.

PATRICK, G. T. W. The psychology of woman. *Popular Science Monthly,* 1895, *47,* 209–225.

PEARSON, K. Variation in man and woman. In *The chances of death* (Vol. 1). London: Edward Arnold, 1897.

PILLSBURY, W. B. *Education as the psychologist sees it.* New York: Macmillan, 1926.

PORTEUS, S., & BABCOCK, M. E. *Temperament and race.* Boston: Gorham Press, 1926.
RAUSCH, F. A. *Psychology; Or, a view of the human soul including anthropology* (2nd rev. ed.). New York: Dodd, 1841.
REEVES, N. *Womankind.* Chicago: Aldine-Atherton, 1971.
RHEINGOLD, J. *The fear of being a woman.* New York: Grune & Stratton, 1964.
ROMANES, G. J. Mental differences between men and women. *Nineteenth Century,* 1887, *21,* 654–672.
SHAND, A. F. *The foundations of character.* London: Macmillan, 1920.
SINCLAIR, A. *The better half: The emancipation of the American woman.* New York: Harper & Row, 1965.
SMITH, P. *Daughters of the promised land.* Boston: Little, Brown, 1970.
SPENCER, H. *The study of sociology.* New York: Appleton, 1891.
STANNARD, U. Adam's rib, or the woman within. *Trans-Action,* 1970, *8,* 24–35.
SUTHERLAND, A. *The origin and growth of the moral instinct* (Vol. 1). London: Longmans, Green, 1898.
TERMAN, L., & MILES, C. C. *Sex and personality.* New York: Russell and Russell, 1968.
THOMPSON, H. B. *The mental traits of sex.* Chicago: University of Chicago Press, 1903.
THORNDIKE, E. L. Sex in education. *The Bookman,* 1906, *23,* 211–214.
THORNDIKE, E. L. *Educational psychology* (2nd ed.). New York: Teachers College, Columbia University, 1910.
THORNDIKE, E. L. *Individuality.* Boston: Houghton Mifflin, 1911.
THORNDIKE, E. L. *Educational psychology* (Vol. 3). New York: Teachers College, Columbia University, 1914. (a)
THORNDIKE, E. L. *Educational psychology briefer course.* New York: Teachers College, Columbia University, 1914. (b)
WALKER, A. *Woman physiologically considered.* New York: J. & H. G. Langley, 1850.
WATSON, J. B. Studies on the growth of the emotions. In *Psychologies of 1925.* Worcester, Mass.: Clark University Press, 1926.
WEININGER, O. *Sex and character* (trans.). London: Heinemann, 1906.
WISSLER, C. The correlation of mental and physical tests. *Psychological Review Monograph Supplements,* 1899–1901, *3*(6, Whole No. 16).
WOLLSTONECRAFT, M. *A vindication of the rights of woman.* New York: Dutton, 1955.
WOOLLEY, H. T. Psychological literature: A review of the recent literature on the psychology of sex. *Psychological Bulletin,* 1910, *7,* 335–342.
WUNDT, W. *Ethics.* Vol. 3: *The principles of morality, and the departments of the moral life* (M. F. Washburn, Trans.). London: Sonnenschein, 1901.

PART 2

Psychoanalysis and the Woman Question

Psychoanalysis is a complex theory of human behavior. Beginning with the turn-of-the-century work of Sigmund Freud and his colleagues, it evolved into the Western world's most influential theory of the development of personality and behavior, both normal and disturbed. It rests upon the concept of unconscious motivation, that much of our behavior is motivated by psychic forces of which we are unaware. These forces, or drives, originate in the developmental events of early childhood, which, according to the theory, are fraught with conflicts. If not successfully resolved and integrated into the personality, these conflicts can disrupt normal development, resulting in neuroses and other maladaptive outcomes. An example is the well-known *Oedipal conflict,* whose resolution requires the child to abandon the unrealistic desire for exclusive possession of the opposite sex parent, to identify with the same sex parent, and, later, to transfer the old desire to an appropriate mate.

Psychoanalysis is also a treatment procedure by means of which people are supposed to come to an understanding of their inner conflicts and thereby be relieved of their neurotic symptoms. Techniques such as dream interpretation and the free expression of thoughts in a relaxed state were developed by Freud and his followers in order to elicit material buried in the unconscious. The theory provides a framework for the understanding of such material, thus giving the patient and the therapist insight into the nature of the long-ago-repressed conflicts.

The psychology of women was not a central concern of Freud's theory. In fact, he commented more than once that the topic was an enigma, that the mental life of women was less accessible than that of men and that it was impossible to know what women were really like. Nevertheless, he wrote three papers on the psychology of women, and his ideas were enormously influential in directing the thinking of his colleagues and followers, many of whom elaborated and expanded what he had to say.

Psychoanalytic ideas about women have been bitterly attacked by feminists because of their phallocentric bias, that is, their implicit assumption that the male is the model human being. Given the anatomical differences between the sexes, if the male is the model then the female can only emerge as an inferior and mutilated counterpart. Envy of the penis, arising very early in the girl's development, could be resolved by identification with the mother and acceptance of the feminine role, including one day a baby of her own as a reward for her renunciation of the old envious fantasy. The female body was thus defined as less impressive and valuable, inducing a feeling of having been deprived which could only be resolved through her reproductive function. Feminists have responded that female behavior is not innately determined by biology, but rather by female social roles in patriarchal society, by the uses to which her body has destined her in a world controlled by men.

The papers in this section include an example of Freud's thinking about the psychology of women and a recent critique of Freud's paper by anthropologist Margaret Mead; a 1935 paper by psychoanalyst Karen Horney in which she takes issue with Freud and invokes a cultural explanation for women's "nature"; and a recent discussion by psychoanalyst Erik Erikson of the ways in which the psychic experiences of women have their counterparts in men's experiences. They all present ideas which variously influence the ways that women are understood and treated, both in and out of therapy. Freud's paper represents the classic psychoanalytic position. Mead's and Horney's show how assumptions arising from a given social order can be mistaken for universal truths. Erikson's contribution attempts to find in the life experiences of women and men a kind of compensatory balance. As theory and as critical evaluation of theory, they show how intimate indeed is the connection between beliefs based on observations limited by time and place, and that way of knowing which we call science.

"Femininity" was the third of Freud's three papers on the psychology of women. Appearing in 1933 as one of a series of lectures on psychoanalysis, it is an inquiry into "how a woman develops out of a child." By this time he had already published his theory of penis envy as the key concept in female psychosexual development. The present paper is more concerned with female sexuality, from the bisexuality of the early years when the clitoris is used in masturbatory activity as a penis equivalent to the discovery of the vagina and the transfer of the locus of erotic experience from the clitoris to the vagina: "With the change to femininity the clitoris should wholly or in part hand over its sensitivity, and at the same time its importance, to the vagina." The female thus abandons, in the normal course, her "masculine" clitoral sexuality in favor of the "feminine" sexuality of the passive-receptive vagina.

Freud also discussed in this paper another major developmental task girls must achieve: the abandonment of the mother as love-object in favor of the father. This turning away from the mother, often accompanied by hostility, even hate, grows out of the girl's castration complex, her discovery that she has no penis, for which she blames her mother. Her subsequent attachment to her father she can later transfer to a mate by whom she can have the long-awaited child.

These dual necessities of normal female development—the need to change both the erotogenic zone and the love-object—were accomplished at great psychic cost to the female, Freud thought. They resulted in an early, compared to man, termination of psychic development, so that she seemed more rigid and less open to the possibility of further growth and development. Other character traits of hers, such as jealousy and shame, also had their genesis in these early trials. The universal depreciation of women could be understood as a psychic consequence of the discovery of her castration: "as a result of the discovery of women's lack of a penis they are debased in value for girls as they are for boys and later perhaps for men."

Margaret Mead's response, "On Freud's View of Female Psychology," looked at Freudian theory not only within its own culturally limited context but also from an extrapolation of its tenets to a crosscultural application. Finding the notions of penis envy and the normality of vaginal orgasms naive and culture bound, Mead saw that Freud's attitudes about women are nevertheless an expression of contemporary beliefs which are present feminists' targets. But in other societies where people wear fewer clothes and are less inhibited, bodies and their functions, such as menstruation, pregnancy, lactation, and penile erection, are openly observed by all, and womb-envy is, if anything, more common than penis envy. The boy, who can never bear a child, knows that he must achieve his identity in other ways, and the girl accepts her female body and its functions as positive.

Mead traces, in her essay, the history of the division of labor along sex lines, showing its historical necessity and the effects on such role segregation of social and technological revolutions. Regarding the present "commotion" about sex roles and male and female relations, she cautions against over-compensatory statements and extreme reactions. Because of the great importance of the issues, it becomes important to examine, given the inadequacy of Freud's theory of penis envy, whether and to what extent anatomy and destiny are in fact correlated. The fact that women's bodies are made to bear children may not be crucial for the appearance of certain traits usually regarded as feminine. On the other hand some qualities which women more than men seem to have may have evolved because of their adaptive value over the millennia. A valuable part of Mead's message is that we must not confuse ideology with science. While the former may support women's struggles, it is the latter which holds out, for all of us, the hope of freedom.

While psychoanalytic views about women have been widely disseminated and criticized, it is ironic that dissenting and refuting statements which began to appear with Freud's own time have attracted much less attention. Current feminist criticism of Freud, for example, often completely ignores the fact that Freud had critics who took sharp exception to his theories of female personality and sexuality.

In "The Problem of Feminine Masochism" Karen Horney directly attacked the Freudian position that masochism was biologically inherent in the female condition, that it was thus normal for women to exhibit masochistic trends in their approach to life and in their relations with others. In this detailed and carefully reasoned paper Horney pointed out that such ideas were based on studies of small samples of neurotic women, and that there were no substantive data to support generalizations of such personality characteristics to normal women. In addition to calling attention to this important methodological error, Horney compellingly argued for the power of cultural conditioning as a causal factor for the appearance of masochism in women. Inhibiting self-assertion, presenting oneself as weak and helpless and in need of special consideration, and permitting oneself to be exploited are all observable in masochistic women. But such phenomena could be expected, Horney said, in societies which restricted opportunities for women, held them to be inferior, made sure that they were economically dependent, and confined them to a life space consisting of emotional bonds and to the duties of caring for others. Furthermore, in such societies ideologies about woman's "true nature"—that she was weak, emotional, dependent, and so on—would arise, and her value as an erotic partner would then become dependent upon her conformity to the beliefs about her. The marvel is, Horney observed, that any woman could escape becoming masochistic under such conditions. Yet many did escape. Thus it is clear, Horney argued, that biological factors have been greatly overestimated as determinants of female personality.

The final paper in this section is a commentary by Erik Erikson on an earlier paper, "Womanhood and the Inner Space" published in 1968. In that paper Erikson set forth the idea that woman's "inner space," the somatic design of her body, was a determinant of her destiny, a biological psychological, and ethical commitment to take care of the human infant. Her productive inner space is an inescapable criterion of sexual differentiation, since mammalian ecology is built around the fact that the human fetus grows in the womb and the human infant must be suckled (or, at any rate, raised within a maternal world). Further, according to Erikson the disposition of this commitment was the core problem of female identity. Such a theory shared with earlier psychoanalytic thought the aura of biological determinism which has been examined and found wanting by Horney and later feminist scholars as well.

Erikson's purpose in writing "Once More the Inner Space" was to clarify misinterpretations of the earlier paper. In it, he describes what emphasis can be placed on the cultural determinants of female behavior. Here he wishes to bring the discussion into balance by describing correspondences between the experiences of women and men in any era. Thus if woman envies man his real or imagined superiority and power, so too does he envy her the ability to bring forth life and to live certain powerful roles of her own. If woman has assented to an exploitation of her masochistic potential, so too has man accepted slavery, injury, and death as the price for his conquests.

Erikson made an interesting analogy between birth control and arms control, the one going to the heart of womanhood, the other to the core of man's identity. As children more often become planned for and wanted, a world order becomes possible wherein women have control over the uses of their bodies and each child chosen to be born has the opportunity to develop fully. And as arms and war, "the age-old stance of militancy," become less salient to man's identity he will be freer to move into roles which relate to the potentials of life rather than to those which feature exploitation and death. Chosen children can grow into adults who have learned to humanize their own inventions, and women, as equal planners of the world's affairs, will bring their attention to the whole earth as an inner space—"no matter how far out any of the outer spaces may reach."

As theory, the early psychoanalytic view of female personality represented here by Freud's paper is easy to criticize. Its importance lies in its explanation of behavior within a social order, and in its widespread acceptance and application by professionals whose task it was to provide understanding and advice to women and men on the subject of the psychology and sexuality of women. Alternative views and critical reappraisals are now in the ascendancy, and set the stage for new theoretical developments based on empirical research conducted in a different sociocultural climate. In no other literature can we see the relation between scientific inquiry and social values so clearly revealed.

Femininity

Sigmund Freud

To-day's lecture should have no place in an introduction; but it may serve to give you an example of a detailed piece of analytic work, and I can say two things to recommend it. It brings forward nothing but observed facts, almost without any speculative additions, and it deals with a subject which has a claim on your interest second almost to no other. Throughout history people have knocked their heads against the riddle of the nature of femininity—

> Häupter in Hieroglyphenmützen,
> Häupter in Turban und schwarzem Barett,
> Perückenhäupter und tausend andre
> Arme, schwitzende Menschenhäupter. . . .[1]

Nor will *you* have escaped worrying over this problem—those of you who are men; to those of you who are women this will not apply—you are yourselves the problem. When you meet a human being, the first distinction you make is 'male or female?' and you are accustomed to make the distinction with unhesitating certainty. Anatomical science shares your certainty at one point and not much further. The male sexual product, the spermatozoon, and its vehicle are male; the ovum and the organism that harbours it are female. In both sexes organs have been formed which serve exclusively for the sexual functions; they were probably developed from the same [innate] disposition into two different forms. Besides this, in both sexes the other

"Femininity" in *The Standard Edition of the Complete Psychological Works of Sigmund Freud* (Vol. 22), translated and edited by James Strachey. Reprinted by permission of Sigmund Freud Copyrights Ltd., The Institute for Psycho-Analysis, The Hogarth Press Ltd., and by W. W. Norton & Company, Inc.

organs, the bodily shapes and tissues, show the influence of the individual's sex, but this is inconstant and its amount variable; these are what are known as the secondary sexual characters. Science next tells you something that runs counter to your expectations and is probably calculated to confuse your feelings. It draws your attention to the fact that portions of the male sexual apparatus also appear in women's bodies, though in an atrophied state, and vice versa in the alternative case. It regards their occurrence as indications of *bisexuality,*[2] as though an individual is not a man or a woman but always both—merely a certain amount more the one than the other. You will then be asked to make yourselves familiar with the idea that the proportion in which masculine and feminine are mixed in an individual is subject to quite considerable fluctuations. Since, however, apart from the very rarest cases, only one kind of sexual product—ova or semen—is nevertheless present in one person, you are bound to have doubts as to the decisive significance of those elements and must conclude that what constitutes masculinity or femininity is an unknown characteristic which anatomy cannot lay hold of.

Can psychology do so perhaps? We are accustomed to employ 'masculine' and 'feminine' as mental qualities as well, and have in the same way transferred the notion of bisexuality to mental life. Thus we speak of a person, whether male or female, as behaving in a masculine way in one connection and in a feminine way in another. But you will soon perceive that this is only giving way to anatomy or to convention. You cannot give the concepts of 'masculine' and 'feminine' *any* new connotation. The distinction is not a psychological one; when you say 'masculine', you usually mean 'active', and when you say 'feminine', you usually mean 'passive'. Now it is true that a relation of the kind exists. The male sex-cell is actively mobile and searches out the female one, and the latter, the ovum, is immobile and waits passively. This behaviour of the elementary sexual organisms is indeed a model for the conduct of sexual individuals during intercourse. The male pursues the female for the purpose of sexual union, seizes hold of her and penetrates into her. But by this you have precisely reduced the characteristic of masculinity to the factor of aggressiveness so far as psychology is concerned. You may well doubt whether you have gained any real advantage from this when you reflect that in some classes of animals the females are the stronger and more aggressive and the male is active only in the single act of sexual union. This is so, for instance, with the spiders. Even the functions of rearing and caring for the young, which strike us as feminine *par excellence,* are not invariably attached to the female sex in animals. In quite high species we find that the sexes share the task of caring for the young between them or even that the male alone devotes himself to it. Even in the sphere of human sexual life you soon see how inadequate it is to make masculine behaviour coincide with activity and feminine with passivity. A mother is active in every sense towards her child; the act of lactation itself may equally be described as the mother suckling the baby or as her being sucked by it. The further you go from the narrow sexual sphere the more obvious will the 'error of superimposition'[3] become. Women can display great activity in various directions, men are not able to live in company with their own kind unless they develop a large amount of passive adaptability. If you now tell me that these facts go to prove precisely that both men and women are bisexual in the psychological sense, I shall conclude that you have decided in your own minds to make 'active' coincide with 'masculine' and 'passive' with 'feminine'. But I advise you against it. It seems to me to serve no useful purpose and adds nothing to our knowledge.[4]

One might consider characterizing femininity psychologically as giving preference to passive aims. This is not, of course, the same thing as passivity; to achieve a passive aim may call for a large amount of activity. It is perhaps the case that in a woman, on the basis of her share in the sexual function, a preference for passive behaviour and passive aims is carried over into her life to a greater or lesser extent, in proportion to the limits, restricted or far-reaching, within which her sexual life thus serves as a model. But we must beware in this of underestimating the influence of social customs, which similarly force women into passive situations. All this is still far from being cleared up. There is one particularly constant relation between femininity and instinctual life which we do not want to overlook. The suppression of women's aggressiveness which is prescribed for them constitutionally and imposed on them socially favours the development of powerful masochistic impulses, which succeed, as we know, in binding erotically the destructive trends which have been diverted inwards. Thus masochism, as people say, is truly feminine. But if, as happens so often, you meet with masochism in men, what is left to you but to say that these men exhibit very plain feminine traits?

And now you are already prepared to hear that psychology too is unable to solve the riddle of femininity. The explanation must no doubt come from elsewhere, and cannot come till we have learnt how in general the differentiation of living organisms into two sexes came about. We know nothing about it, yet the existence of two sexes is a most striking characteristic of organic life which distinguishes it sharply from inanimate nature. However, we find enough to study in those human individuals who, through the possession of female genitals, are characterized as manifestly or predominantly feminine. In conformity with its peculiar nature, psycho-analysis does not try to describe what a woman is—that would be a task it could scarcely perform—but sets about enquiring how she comes into being, how a woman develops out of a child with a bisexual disposition. In recent times we have begun to learn a little about this, thanks to the circumstance that several of our excellent women colleagues in analysis have begun to work at the question. The discussion of this has gained special attractiveness from the distinction between the sexes. For the ladies, whenever some comparison seemed to turn out unfavourable to their sex, were able to utter a suspicion that we, the male analysts, had been unable to overcome certain deeply-rooted prejudices against what was feminine, and that this was being paid for in the partiality of our researches. We, on the other hand, standing on the ground of bisexuality, had no difficulty in avoiding impoliteness. We had only to say: 'This doesn't apply to *you*. You're the exception; on this point you're more masculine than feminine.'

We approach the investigation of the sexual development of women with two expectations. The first is that here once more the constitution will not adapt itself to its function without a struggle. The second is that the decisive turning-points will already have been prepared for or completed before puberty. Both expectations are promptly confirmed. Furthermore, a comparison with what happens with boys tells us that the development of a little girl into a normal woman is more difficult and more complicated, since it includes two extra tasks, to which there is nothing corresponding in the development of a man. Let us follow the parallel lines from their beginning. Undoubtedly the material is different to start with in boys and girls: it did not need psycho-analysis to establish that. The difference in the structure of the genitals is accompanied by other bodily differences which are too well known to call for mention. Differences emerge too in the instinctual disposition which give a glimpse of the later nature of women. A little girl is as a rule less aggressive, defiant and self-sufficient; she seems to have a greater need for being shown affection and on that account to be more dependent and pliant. . . . One gets an impression, too, that little girls are more intelligent and livelier than boys of the same age; they go out more to meet the external world and at the same time form stronger object-cathexes. I cannot say whether this lead in development has been confirmed by exact observations, but in any case there is no question that girls cannot be described as intellectually backward. These sexual differences are not, however, of great consequence: they can be outweighed by individual variations. For our immediate purposes they can be disregarded.

Both sexes seem to pass through the early phases of libidinal development in the same manner. It might have been expected that in girls there would already have been some lag in aggressiveness in the sadistic-anal phase, but such is not the case. Analysis of children's play has shown our women analysts that the aggressive impulses of little girls leave nothing to be desired in the way of abundance and violence. With their entry into the phallic phase the differences between the sexes are completely eclipsed by their agreements. We are now obliged to recognize that the little girl is a little man. In boys, as we know, this phase is marked by the fact that they have learnt how to derive pleasurable sensations from their small penis and connect its excited state with their ideas of sexual intercourse. Little girls do the same thing with their still smaller clitoris. It seems that with them all their masturbatory acts are carried out on this penis-equivalent, and that the truly feminine vagina is still undiscovered by both sexes. It is true that there are a few isolated reports of early vaginal sensations as well, but it could not be easy to distinguish these from sensations in the anus or vestibulum; in any case they cannot play a great part. We are entitled to keep to our view that in the phallic phase of girls the clitoris is the leading erotogenic zone. But it is not, of course, going to remain so. With the change to femininity the clitoris should wholly or in part hand over its sensitivity, and at the same time its importance, to the vagina. This would be one of the two tasks which a woman has to perform in the course of her development, whereas the more fortunate man has only to continue at the time of his sexual maturity the activity that he has previously carried out at the period of the early efflorescence of his sexuality.

We shall return to the part played by the clitoris; let us now turn to the second task with which a girl's development is burdened. A boy's mother is the first object of his love, and she remains so too during the formation of his Oedipus complex and, in essence, all through his life. For a girl too her first object must be her mother (and the figures of wet-nurses and foster-mothers that merge into her). The first object-cathexes occur in attachment to the satisfaction of the major and simple vital needs,[5] and the circumstances of the care of children are the same for both sexes. But in the Oedipus situation the girl's father has become her love-object, and we expect that in the normal course of development she will find her way from this paternal object to her final choice of an object. In the course of time, therefore, a girl has to change her erotogenic zone and her object—both of which a boy retains. The question then arises of how this happens: in particular, how does a girl pass from her mother to an attachment to her father? or, in other words, how does she pass from her masculine phase to the feminine one to which she is biologically destined?

It would be a solution of ideal simplicity if we could suppost that from a particular age onwards the elementary influence of the mutual attraction between the sexes makes itself felt and impels the small woman towards men, while the same law allows the boy to continue with his mother. We might suppose in addition that in this the children are following the pointer given them by the sexual preference of their parents. But we are not going to find things so easy; we scarcely know whether we are to believe seriously in the power of which poets talk so much and with such enthusiasm but which cannot be further dissected analytically. We have found an answer of quite another sort by means of laborious investigations, the material for which at least was easy to arrive at. For you must know that the number of women who remain till a late age tenderly dependent on a paternal object, or indeed on their real father, is very great. We have established some surprising facts about these women with an intense attachment of long duration to their father. We knew, of course, that there had been a preliminary stage of attachment to the mother, but we did not know that it could be so rich in content and so long-lasting, and could leave behind so many opportunities for fixations and dispositions. During this time the girl's father is only a troublesome rival; in some cases the attachment to her mother lasts beyond the fourth year of life. Almost everything that we find later in her relation to her father was already present in this earlier attachment and has been transferred subsequently on to her father. In short, we get an impression that we cannot understand women unless we appreciate this phase of their pre-Oedipus attachment to their mother.

We shall be glad, then, to know the nature of the girl's libidinal relations to her mother. The answer is that they are of very many different kinds. Since they persist through all three phases of infantile sexuality, they also take on the characteristics of the different phases and express themselves by oral, sadistic-anal and phallic wishes. These wishes represent active as well as passive impulses; if we relate them to the differentiation of the sexes which is to appear later—though we should avoid doing so as far as possible—we may call them masculine and feminine. Besides this, they are completely ambivalent, both affectionate and of a hostile and aggressive nature. The latter often only come to light after being changed into anxiety ideas. It is not always easy to point to a formulation of these early sexual wishes; what is most clearly expressed is a wish to get the mother with child and the corresponding wish to bear her a child—both belonging to the phallic period and sufficiently surprising, but established beyond doubt by analytic observation. . . . You will recall an interesting episode in the history of analytic research which caused me many distressing hours. In the period in which the main interest was directed to discovering infantile sexual traumas, almost all my women patients told me that they had been seduced by their father. I was driven to recognize in the end that these reports were untrue and so came to understand that hysterical symptoms are derived from phantasies and not from real occurrences. It was only later that I was able to recognize in this phantasy of being seduced by the father the expression of the typical Oedipus complex in women. And now we find the phantasy of seduction once more in the pre-Oedipus prehistory of girls; but the seducer is regularly the mother. Here, however, the phantasy touches the ground of reality, for it was really the mother who by her activities over the child's bodily hygiene inevitably stimulated, and perhaps even roused for the first time, pleasurable sensations in her genitals.[6]

I have no doubt you are ready to suspect that this portrayal of the abundance and strength of a little girl's sexual relations with her mother is very much overdrawn. After all, one has opportunities of seeing little girls and notices nothing of the sort. But the objection is not to the point. Enough can be seen in the children if one knows how to look. And besides, you should consider how little of its sexual wishes a child can bring to preconscious expression or communicate at all. Accordingly we are only within our rights if we study the residues and consequences of this emotional world in retrospect, in people in whom these processes of development had attained a specially clear and even excessive degree of expansion. Pathology has always done us the service of making discernible by isolation and exaggeration conditions which would remain concealed in a normal state. And since our investigations have been carried out on people who were by no means seriously abnormal, I think we should regard their outcome as deserving belief.

We will now turn our interest on to the single question of what it is that brings this powerful attachment of the girl to her mother to an end. This, as we know, is its usual fate; it is destined to make room for an attachment to her father. Here we come upon a fact which is a pointer to our further advance. This step in development does not involve only a simple change of object. The turning away from the mother is accompanied by hostility; the attachment to the mother ends in hate. A hate of that kind may become very striking and last all through life; it may be carefully overcompensated later on; as a rule one part of it is overcome while another part persists. Events of later years naturally influence this greatly. We will restrict ourselves, however, to studying it at the time at which the girl turns to her father and to enquiring into the motives for it. We are then given a long list of accusations and grievances against the mother which are supposed to justify the child's hostile feelings; they are of varying validity which we shall not fail to examine. A number of them are obvious rationalizations and the true sources of enmity remain to be found. I hope you will be interested if on this occasion I take you through all the details of a psycho-analytic investigation. . . .

An abundant source of a child's hostility to its mother is provided by its multifarious sexual wishes, which alter according to the phase of the libido and which cannot for the most part be satisfied. The strongest of these frustrations occur at the phallic period, if the mother forbids pleasurable activity with the genitals—often with severe threats and every sign of displeasure—activity to which, after all, she herself had introduced the child. One would think these were reasons enough to account for a girl's turning away from her mother. One would judge, if so, that the estrangement follows inevitably from the nature of children's sexuality, from the immoderate character of their demand for love and the impossibility of fulfilling their sexual wishes. It might be thought indeed that this first love-relation of the child's is doomed to dissolution for the very reason that it is the first, for these early object-cathexes are regularly ambivalent to a high degree. A powerful tendency to aggressiveness is always present beside a powerful love, and the more passionately a child loves its object the more sensitive does it become to disappointments and frustrations from that object; and in the end the love must succumb to the accumulated hostility. Or the idea that there is an original ambivalence such as this in erotic cathexes may be rejected, and it may be pointed out that it is the special nature of the mother-child relation that leads, with equal inevitability, to the destruction of the child's love; for even the mildest upbringing cannot avoid using compulsion and introducing restrictions, and any such intervention in the child's liberty must provoke as a reaction an inclination to rebelliousness and aggressiveness. A discussion of these possibilities might, I think, be most interesting; but an objection suddenly emerges which forces our interest in another direction. All these factors—the slights, the disappointments in love, the jealousy, the seduction followed by prohibition—are, after all, also in operation in the relation of a *boy* to his mother and are yet unable to alienate him from the maternal object. Unless we can find something that is specific for girls and is not present or not in the same way present in boys, we shall not have explained the termination of the attachment of girls to their mother.

I believe we have found this specific factor, and indeed where we expected to find it, even though in a surprising form. Where we expected to find it, I say, for it lies in the castration complex. After all, the anatomical distinction [between the sexes] must express itself in psychical consequences. It was, however, a surprise to learn from analyses that girls hold their mother responsible for their lack of a penis and do not forgive her for their being thus put at a disadvantage.

As you hear, then, we ascribe a castration complex to women as well. And for good reasons, though its content cannot be the same as with boys. In the latter the castration complex arises after they have learnt from the sight of the female genitals that the organ which they value so highly need not necessarily accompany the body. At this the boy recalls to mind the threats he brought on himself by his doings with that organ, he begins to give credence to them and falls under the influence of fear of castration, which will be the most powerful motive force in his subsequent development. The castration complex of girls is also started by the sight of the genitals of the other sex. They at once notice the difference and, it must be admitted, its significance too. They feel seriously wronged, often declare that they want to 'have something like it too', and fall a victim to 'envy for the penis', which will leave ineradicable traces on their development and the formation of their character and which will not be surmounted in even the most favourable cases without a severe expenditure of psychical energy. The girl's recognition of the fact of her being without a penis does not by any means imply that she submits to the fact easily. On the contrary, she continues to hold on for a long time to the wish to get something like it herself and she believes in that possibility for improbably long years; and analysis can show that, at a period when knowledge of reality has long since rejected the fulfilment of the wish as unattainable, it persists in the unconscious and retains a considerable cathexis of energy. The wish to get the longed-for penis eventually in a spite of everything may contribute to the motives that drive a mature woman to analysis, and what she may reasonably expect from analysis—a capacity, for instance, to carry on an intellectual profession—may often be recognized as a sublimated modification of this repressed wish.

One cannot very well doubt the importance of envy for the penis. You may take it as an instance of male injustice if I assert that envy and jealousy play an even greater part in the mental life of women than of men. It is not that I think these characteristics are absent in men or that I think they have no other roots in women than envy for the penis; but I am inclined to attribute their greater amount in women to this latter influence. . . .

The discovery that she is castrated is a turning-point in a girl's growth. Three possible lines of development start from it: one leads to sexual inhibition or to neurosis, the second to change of character in the sense of a masculinity complex, the third, finally, to normal femininity. We have learnt a fair amount, though not everything, about all three.

The essential content of the first is as follows: the little girl has hitherto lived in a masculine way, has been able to get pleasure by the excitation of her clitoris and has brought this activity into relation with her sexual wishes directed towards her mother, which are often active ones; now, owing to the influence of her penis-envy, she loses her enjoyment in her phallic sexuality. Her self-love is mortified by the comparison with the boy's far superior equipment and in consequence she renounces her masturbatory satisfaction from her clitoris, repudiates her love for her mother and at the same time not infrequently represses a good part of her sexual trends in general. No doubt her turning away from her mother does not occur all at once, for to begin with the girl regards her castration as an individual misfortune, and only gradually extends it to other females and finally to her mother as well. Her love was directed to her *phallic* mother; with the discovery that her mother is castrated it becomes possible to drop her as an object, so that the motives for hostility, which have long been accumulating, gain the upper hand. This means, therefore, that as a result of the discovery of women's lack of a penis they are debased in value for girls just as they are for boys and later perhaps for men. . . .

Along with the abandonment of clitoridal masturbation a certain amount of activity is renounced. Passivity now has the upper hand, and the girl's turning to her father is accomplished principally with the help of passive instinctual impulses. You can see that a wave of development like this, which clears the phallic activity out of the way, smooths the ground for femininity. If too much is not lost in the course of it through repression, this femininity may turn out to be normal. The wish with which the girl turns to her father is no doubt originally the wish for the penis which her mother has refused her and which she now expects from her father. The feminine situation is only established, however, if the wish for a penis is replaced by one for a baby, if, that is, a baby takes the place of a penis in accordance with an ancient symbolic equivalence. It has not escaped us that the girl has wished for a baby earlier, in the undisturbed phallic phase: that, of course, was the meaning of her playing with dolls. But that play was not in fact an expression of her femininity; it served as an identification with her mother with the intention of substituting activity for passivity. *She* was playing the part of her mother and the doll was herself: now she could do with the baby everything that her mother used to do with her. Not until the emergence of the wish for a penis does the doll-baby become a baby from the girl's father, and thereafter the aim of the most powerful feminine wish. Her happiness is great if later on this wish for a baby finds fulfilment in reality, and quite especially so if the baby is a little boy who brings the longed-for penis with him. Often enough in her combined picture of 'a baby from her father' the emphasis is laid on the baby and her father left unstressed. In this way the ancient masculine wish for the possession of a penis is still faintly visible through the femininity now achieved. But perhaps we ought rather to recognize this wish for a penis as being *par excellence* a feminine one.

With the transference of the wish for a penis-baby on to her father, the girl has entered the situation of the Oedipus complex. Her hostility to her mother, which did not need to be freshly created, is now greatly intensified, for she becomes the girl's rival, who receives from her father everything that she desires from him. For a long time the girl's Oedipus complex concealed her pre-Oedipus attachment to her mother from our view, though it is nevertheless so important and leaves such lasting fixations behind it. For girls the Oedipus situation is the outcome of a long and difficult development; it is a kind of preliminary solution, a position of rest which is not soon abandoned, especially as the beginning of the latency period is not far distant. And we are now struck by a difference between the two sexes, which is probably momentous, in regard to the relation of the Oedipus complex to the castration complex. In a boy the Oedipus complex, in which he desires his mother and would like to get rid of his father as being a rival, develops naturally from the phase of his phallic sexuality. The threat of castration compels him, however, to give up that attitude. Under the impression of the danger of losing his penis, the Oedipus complex is abandoned, repressed and, in the most normal cases, entirely destroyed [see p. 92], and a severe super-ego is set up as its heir. What happens with a girl is almost the opposite. The castration complex prepares for the Oedipus complex instead of destroying it; the girl is driven out of her attachment to her mother through the influence of her envy for the penis and she enters the Oedipus situation as though into a haven of refuge. In the absence of fear of castration the chief motive is lacking which leads boys to surmount the Oedipus complex. Girls remain in it for an indeterminate length of time; they demolish it late and, even so, incompletely. In these circumstances the formation of the super-ego must suffer; it cannot attain the strength and independence which give it its cultural significance, and feminists are not pleased when we point out to them the effects of this factor upon the average feminine character.

To go back a little. We mentioned as the second possible reaction to the discovery of female castration the development of a powerful masculinity complex. By this we mean that the girl refuses, as it were, to recognize the unwelcome fact and, defiantly rebellious, even exaggerates her previous masculinity, clings to her clitoridal activity and takes refuge in an identification with her phallic mother or her father. What can it be that decides in favour of this outcome? We can only suppose that it is a constitutional factor, a greater amount of activity, such as is ordinarily characteristic of a male. However that may be, the essence of this process is that at this point in development the wave of passivity is avoided which opens the way to the turn towards femininity. The extreme achievement of such a masculinity complex would appear to be the influencing of the choice of an object in the sense of manifest homosexuality. Analytic experience teaches us, to be sure, that female homosexuality is seldom or never a direct continuation of infantile masculinity. Even for a girl of this kind it seems necessary that she should take her father as an object for some time and enter the Oedipus situation. But afterwards, as a result of her inevitable disappointments from her father, she is driven to regress into her early masculinity complex. The significance of these disappointments must not be exaggerated; a girl who is destined to become feminine is not spared them, though they do not have the same effect. The predominance of the constitutional factor seems indisputable; but the two phases in the development of female homosexuality are well mirrored in the practices of homosexuals, who play the parts of mother and baby with each other as often and as clearly as those of husband and wife. . . .

It is not my intention to pursue the further behaviour of femininity through puberty to the period of maturity. Our knowledge, moreover, would be insufficient for the purpose. But I will bring a few features together in what follows. Taking its prehistory as a starting-point, I will only emphasize here that the development of femininity remains exposed to disturbance by the residual phenomena of the early masculine period. Regressions to the fixations of the pre-Oedipus phases very frequently occur; in the course of some women's lives there is a repeated alternation between periods in which masculinity or femininity gains the upper hand. Some portion of what we men call 'the enigma of women' may perhaps be derived from this expression of bisexuality in women's lives. But another question seems to have become ripe for judgement in the course of these researches. We have called the motive force of sexual life 'the libido'. Sexual life is dominated by the polarity of masculine–feminine; thus the notion suggests itself of considering the relation of the libido to this antithesis. It would not be surprising if it were to turn out that each sexuality had its own special libido appropriated to it, so that one sort of libido would pursue the aims of a masculine sexual life and another sort those of a feminine one. But nothing of the kind is true. There is only one libido, which serves both the masculine and the feminine sexual functions. To it itself we cannot assign any sex; if, following the conventional equation of activity and masculinity, we are inclined to describe it as masculine, we must not forget that it also covers trends with a passive aim. . . .

The sexual frigidity of women, the frequency of which appears to confirm this disregard, is a phenomenon that is still insufficiently understood.

Sometimes it is psychogenic and in that case accessible to influence; but in other cases it suggests the hypothesis of its being constitutionally determined and even of there being a contributory anatomical factor.

I have promised to tell you of a few more psychical peculiarities of mature femininity, as we come across them in analytic observation. We do not lay claim to more than an average validity for these assertions; nor is it always easy to distinguish what should be ascribed to the influence of the sexual function and what to social breeding. Thus, we attribute a larger amount of narcissism to femininity, which also affects women's choice of object, so that to be loved is a stronger need for them than to love. The effect of penis-envy has a share, further, in the physical vanity of women, since they are bound to value their charms more highly as a late compensation for their original sexual inferiority. Shame, which is considered to be a feminine characteristic *par excellence* but is far more a matter of convention than might be supposed, has as its purpose, we believe, concealment of genital deficiency. We are not forgetting that at a later time shame takes on other functions. It seems that women have made few contributions to the discoveries and inventions in the history of civilization; there is, however, one technique which they may have invented—that of plaiting and weaving. If that is so, we should be tempted to guess the unconscious motive for the achievement. Nature herself would seem to have given the model which this achievement imitates by causing the growth at maturity of the pubic hair that conceals the genitals. The step that remained to be taken lay in making the threads adhere to one another, while on the body they stick into the skin and are only matted together. If you reject this idea as fantastic and regard my belief in the influence of lack of a penis on the configuration of femininity as an *idée fixe,* I am of course defenceless.

The determinants of women's choice of an object are often made unrecognizable by social conditions. Where the choice is able to show itself freely, it is often made in accordance with the narcissistic ideal of the man whom the girl had wished to become. If the girl has remained in her attachment to her father—that is, in the Oedipus complex—her choice is made according to the paternal type. Since, when she turned from her mother to her father, the hostility of her ambivalent relation remained with her mother, a choice of this kind should guarantee a happy marriage. But very often the outcome is of a kind that presents a general threat to such a settlement of the conflict due to ambivalence. The hostility that has been left behind follows in the train of the positive attachment and spreads over on to the new object. The woman's husband, who to begin with inherited from her father, becomes after a time her mother's heir as well. So it may easily happen that the second half of a woman's life may be filled by the struggle against her husband, just as the shorter first half was filled by her rebellion against her mother. When this reaction has been lived through, a second marriage may easily turn out very much more satisfying.[7] Another alteration in a woman's nature, for which lovers are unprepared, may occur in a marriage after the first child is born. . . . The difference in a mother's reaction to the birth of a son or a daughter shows that the old factor of lack of a penis has even now not lost its strength. A mother is only brought unlimited satisfaction by her relation to a son; this is altogether the most perfect, the most free from ambivalence of all human relationships.[8] A mother can transfer to her son the ambition which she has been obliged to suppress in herself, and she can expect from him the satisfaction of all that has been left over in her of her masculinity complex. Even a marriage is not made secure until the wife has succeeded in making her husband her child as well and in acting as a mother to him. . . .

The fact that women must be regarded as having little sense of justice is no doubt related to the predominance of envy in their mental life; for the demand for justice is a modification of envy and lays down the condition subject to which one can put envy aside. We also regard women as weaker in their social interests and as having less capacity for sublimating their instincts than men. The former is no doubt derived from the dissocial quality which unquestionably characterizes all sexual relations. Lovers find sufficiency in each other, and families too resist inclusion in more comprehensive associations.[9] The aptitude for sublimation is subject to the greatest individual variations. On the other hand I cannot help mentioning an impression that we are constantly receiving during analytic practice. A man of about thirty strikes us as a youthful, somewhat unformed individual, whom we expect to make powerful use of the possibilities for development opened up to him by analysis. A woman of the same age, however, often frightens us by her psychical rigidity and unchangeability. Her libido has taken up final positions and seems incapable of exchanging them for others. There are no paths open to further development; it is as though the whole process had already run its course and remains thenceforward insusceptible to influence—as though, indeed, the difficult development to femininity had exhausted the possibilities of the person concerned. As therapists we lament this state of things, even if we succeed in putting an end to our patient's ailment by doing away with her neurotic conflict.

That is all I had to say to you about femininity. It is certainly incomplete and fragmentary and does not always sound friendly. But do not forget that I have only been describing women in so far as their nature is determined by their sexual function. It is true that that influence extends very far; but we do not overlook the fact that an individual woman may be a human being in other respects as well. If you want to know more about femininity, enquire from your own experiences of life, or turn to the poets, or wait until science can give you deeper and more coherent information.

NOTES

1. Heads in hieroglyphic bonnets,
   Heads in turbans and black birettas,
   Heads in wigs and thousand other
   Wretched, sweating heads of humans. . . .
   (Heine, *Nordsee* [Second Cycle, VII, 'Fragen'].)
2. Bisexuality was discussed by Freud in the first edition of his *Three Essays on the Theory of Sexuality* (1905*d*), *Standard Ed.*, 7, 141–4. The passage includes a long footnote to which he made additions in later issues of the work.
3. I.e. mistaking two different things for a single one. The term was explained in *Introductory Lectures*, XX, *Standard Ed.*, vol. 16, 304.
4. The difficulty of finding a psychological meaning for 'masculine' and 'feminine' was discussed in a long footnote added in 1915 to the *Three Essays* (1905*d*), *Standard Ed.*, vol. 7,

219–20 and again at the beginning of a still longer footnote at the end of Chapter IV of *Civilization and its Discontents* (1930*a*), ibid., vol. 21, 105–6.

5. Cf. *Introductory Lectures,* XXI, *Standard Ed.,* vol. 16, 328–9.
6. In his early discussions of the aetiology of hysteria Freud often mentioned seduction by adults as among its commonest causes (see, for instance, the second paper on the neuro-psychoses of defence (1896*b*), *Standard Ed.,* vol. 3, 164 and 'The Aetiology of Hysteria' (1896*c*), ibid., 208). But nowhere in these early publications did he specifically inculpate the girl's father. Indeed, in some additional footnotes written in 1924 for the *Gesammelte Schriften* reprint of *Studies on Hysteria,* he admitted to having on two occasions suppressed the fact of the father's responsibility (see *Standard Ed.,* vol. 2, 134 *n,* and 170 *n.*). He made this quite clear, however, in the letter to Fliess of September 21, 1897 (Freud, 1950*a,* Letter 69), in which he first expressed his scepticism about these stories told by his patients. His first published admission of his mistake was given several years later in a hint in the second of the *Three Essays* (1905*d*), *Standard Ed.,* vol. 7, 190, but a much fuller account of the position followed in his contribution on the aetiology of the neuroses to a volume by Löwenfeld (1906*a*), ibid., vol. 7, 274–5. Later on he gave two accounts of the effects that this discovery of his mistake had on his own mind—in his 'History of the Psycho-Analytic Movement' (1914*d*), ibid., vol. 14, 17–18 and in his *Autobiographical Study* (1925*d*), ibid., vol. 20, 33–5. The further discovery which is described in the present paragraph of the text had already been indicated in the paper on 'Female Sexuality' (1931*b*), ibid., vol. 21, 238.
7. This had already been remarked upon earlier, in 'The Taboo of Virginity' (1918*a*), *Standard Ed.,* vol. 11, 206.
8. This point seems to have been made by Freud first in a footnote to Chapter VI of *Group Psychology* (1921*c*), *Standard Ed.,* vol. 18, 101 *n.* He repeated it in the *Introductory Lectures,* XIII, ibid., vol. 15, 206 and in *Civilization and its Discontents* (1930*a*), ibid., vol. 21, 113.
9. Cf. some remarks on this in Chapter XII (D) of *Group Psychology* (1921*c*), *Standard Ed.,* vol. 18, 140.

On Freud's View of Female Psychology

Margaret Mead

When I accepted the invitation to write this comment, I began composing it in my head before I reread the last of Freud's famous essays on women, an essay I had not read for perhaps thirty years. I thought I knew what he had said, and I was bored and impatient with the current attacks of some militant women writers against the inevitably limited but highly percipient insights of Freud into the importance of early periods of development and the way perception of one's own body and the bodies of the opposite sex influences character formation. I expected that I would emphasize first that pregenital phases of development are indeed important, that the Oedipus complex is a reality in all societies, since in all societies boys and girls go through a period in which their investment in their budding sexuality is both threatening to their elders and inappropriate for their stage of physical and mental maturity. The resolution of this socially inappropriate surge of sexual feeling (which is treated in psychoanalytically-based shorthand as the boy's desire to kill his father and possess his mother) can also be characterized as the point at which small boys decide to give it all up, during the latency period, and submit to the authority of the dominant elders. This world-wide phenomenon (in which small boys turn away from women, enjoy being unkempt and dirty, and show intense hostility to girls) has only a pallid complementary reflection in the lives of little girls. But here, too, we do find a period in which an active response to the opposite sex is apparently latent, if perhaps only in response to the inhibition of a stronger relationship to the father, and the recurrent unresponsiveness and hostility of boys of the same age.

I then expected to examine the special etiological series which Freud postulates: infantile sexual sensitivity in the male's penis and the girl's clitoris, followed by the shocking discovery, based on comparison between male and female children, that a boy has a penis and a girl has none, resulting in the girl's anger and the boy's fear that his penis might be lost. This series of postulated stages continues with the enhancement of the boy's fear of castration, followed by his submission and development of a superego, and the girl's reconciliation of her disappointment by blaming her mother, and transference of her early mother attachment to love for her father and her disappointment and chagrin to a desire to have a baby by her father, with the equation baby = penis. According to Freud, the girl ultimately recognizes that this also is impossible; this recognition is accompanied by her angry rejection of her clitoris and her transfer of genital sensitivity to the vagina, with a consequent capacity for a vaginal orgasm.

I expected to point out that Freud was writing when very little work had been done on children. He also worked in a specific social situation, in which women with enough initiative to come to psychoanalysis had also had to display an enormous amount of initiative to get an education reserved for men. Furthermore, his patients had been reared in a society where women's reproductive capacities were shrouded and denied recognition, and the display of male activities had reached great heights—in architecture, invention, commerce, science, and the arts—so that the male world was one of achievement and the women's world was one in which her specific type of creativity was denigrated.

I then intended to carry the discussion out of its nineteenth-century European setting into the rest of the world, and particularly into the primitive world, where I have studied the growth and development of boys and girls, the ways in which they are treated, and the ways their attitudes toward themselves and the opposite sex are expressed in myth and ritual. I expected to point out the importance of womb envy—particularly well-illustrated in Pacific island cultures, where women's reproductive role is neither hidden nor denigrated. Indeed, women's reproductivity represents an achievement that is very conspicious in comparison with the rather small exploits of men in making canoes, relatively minor building, and hunting small harmless animals. In the parts of New Guinea I have studied, it is men who envy women their feminine capacities. It is men who spend their ceremonial lives pretending that it was they who had borne the children, that they can "make men." Boys are taught to bleed their penises in imitation of girls' menstruation, which was seen as a salutary bleeding, getting rid of "bad blood." Men hide their complicated noisemaking instruments—flutes, bull roarers, water drums—from the women, for these instruments impersonate the mythical monster the *tamberan,* which is the patron of the men's cult. Interestingly enough also, this monster *tamberan* is then reassigned to women as the men speak of childbirth as the "women's *tamberan,*" reassigning to the women the powers which have been ceremonially denied. It is also this area of the world that men tell how their noisemaking impersonators of their mythical man-making powers were invented by a woman and stolen from her by men. I discussed these activities in *Male and Female* in 1949. In 1954 Bruno Bettelheim published a book called *Symbolic Wounds,* originally triggered by observations of disturbed teenagers in his special school, and, without acknowledgment, using material I had used, wrote a whole chapter speculating on why men said they had stolen their supernatural imitative feminine powers from women!

I expected also to add a few further remarks about present hypotheses concerning the origin of the kinds of precocious sexuality discovered by psychoanalysis, and to suggest that this may be a residue of a period, millions of years ago, in which early hominid creatures matured without latency. In this period, the readiness of the young male to take on his senescent elders could appear, not inappropriately, as it does now, but appropriately at the age of six, and young females may have had offspring at five or six. At present, the existence of the Oedipal phase is treated by psychoanalysis as a function of our particular kind of monogamous nuclear family, although its appearance in today's children is far from making any kind of biological or evolutionary sense. I also intended to add something about the possible origin of our present patterns of sexual behavior in a shrinking of the reproductive period, with the menopause appearing at one end of the reproductive period and latency at the other. The advantage given to a group of early prehuman beings if the lives of some of the knowledgeable old females could be preserved is patent, while the immediate functional value of a period of latency, although of immense value in the process of learning, would not be so immediately apparent in the competition among small groups of hominids.

This is what I meant to say, responding as I was to the fifty years of psychoanalytic understanding to which I have been exposed on the one hand, and to my own intensive studies of primitive people on the other. With this outline in mind, I turned to the last of Freud's three papers, and I experienced a deep shock. It is only too true that the militant feminists have a case against Freud, but not the case they thought they had: that it is only his ideas about penis envy and the normality of vaginal orgasms that have permeated and contaminated our society. Rather, Freud's ideas on women, far from expressing the early culturally limited phases of the development of one of our most important sciences, are actually an expression, and an extraordinarily naïve one, of the still contemporary attitudes about women against which the militants are battling.

Summed up, in brief, Freud asserts that girls have a hard time developing—and in fact never quite reach the heights of moral character that boys do—because they observe that they have no penises. In order that their sexual affection can be transferred to their fathers (and so to males in general) they have to suppress their previous pleasure in their clitoris, and learn to hate their mothers and accept a possible baby from their fathers as compensation for not having a penis. And this he gives as the whole story. The entire argument ignores what we have come to feel is the basis of psychoanalytic understanding: the importance of a child's experience of his or her body in *all* its manifestations.

In Freud's treatment of the subject, nowhere is any attention given to the reproductive capacities as opposed to the pleasure-giving aspects of distinctive anatomical sex differences. An active sperm and a passive ovum are mentioned once, as a sort of loose analogy, but the vagina is seen not as the entry to the womb, but simply as the appropriate displacement from the clitoris. Nor does the male fare any better. As there is no discussion of the girl's discovery of the inside of her body facilitated by her experience of pregnancy and birth in women, so also there is no discussion of the boy's bewildered and vulnerable response to the growth, retraction, and final, painful emergence of his testicles. As babies are seen merely as substitutes for the penis, the entire creative miracle of their production is overlooked, even to the actual paternal contribution.

Karen Horney pointed out years ago that what Freud, an analyst, thought little girls thought was merely what little boys thought little girls thought. Freud's entire explanation of the differential development of super-ego, object love, and search for achievement lay simply in the high valuation of the penis—by both sexes—and the denigration of a baby, because a girl's wish for a child was treated as only a wish for a substitute penis.

With regrets for this particular socially conditioned naïveté, we may turn again to what a sophisticated cross-cultural application of Freud's great and real discoveries about pregenital behavior suggest in regard to the importance of children's early experience of anatomical sex differences. We then can explore children's behavior where middle-class Euro-American culture no longer sets the stage. In a primitive society human bodies are relatively unclothed; menstruation and defloration, pregnancy, delivery, and lactation are openly recognized. Both boys and girls learn about the males' capacities for erection, penetration, and ejaculation, and the females' capacity to produce children inside their bodies. There is no more reason for a girl to envy a boy than for a boy to envy a girl, for the contrasting and differentiated functions of each are fully apparent to children of each sex. True, in some societies the achievements of males are valued far more greatly than those of females (societies, for example, in which men herd large animals or hunt large game), but in other societies (especially those associated with horticulture) the fertility of women is highly valued. The superiority of a penis may be emphasized and reinforced by the salience of male activity over female, or, as happens in the womb-envying cultures, the little boy's desire to have a baby may be built up into compensatory ceremonial behavior among men. The fact that little boys do desire to have babies and also do experience profound disturbances in which their unpredictable testicles are identified as feminine, has now been well documented by clinical studies on little boys in our own society. So we find that a little girl—who is not, as Freud suggested, a small man without a penis, but a small female who has a womb—learns she will someday be a woman who can bear children, and that a little boy learns that he is a creature with a penis and without a womb. He, who can never bear a child, must seek achievement in other ways. In such societies, as girls accept their femininity, they accept it as positive, and as boys accept the fact that they cannot have children, they learn to place a very high valuation on achievement.

However, in all cultures, without any known exception, male activity is seen as achievement; whatever women do—gathering seeds, planting, weeding, basket-making, pot-making—is valued less than when the same activity, in some other culture, is performed by men. When men cook, cooking is viewed as an important activity; when women cook it is just a household chore. And correspondingly, if an activity once performed by women becomes more important in a society, it may be taken over by men.

For example, midwifery, once a profession in which the female practitioners were both constricted and feared, has been taken over by male obstetricians.

Freud speaks of how easy it is for a boy to continue his love for his first love object, his mother, and how hard it is for a girl, who must turn against her mother. But the mother, the boy's first love object, pushes him away, out of her arms, off her lap, into activity that will demonstrate he is a male. The girl can remain near her mother, be held more warmly by both parents, cherished as she waits while her brother must go out and act, and in acting, challenge his father's superior position, and finally demonstrate to some waiting woman that he will be a fit father for her children. The more active girl may find all this discouraging: the more passive boy may find this an unbearably difficult task. But as long as both boys and girls are reared by women, the treatment of each sex has to be different, if later sex identity is to be attained.

As long as women were given the principal responsibility for the care of small children, and this responsibility included breast feeding and the need to have many children if a few were to survive, and as long as the great majority of males had to devote themselves to lifelong maintenance of households in which children were reared, an educational system which reared all females to be wives and mothers and almost all males to be husbands and fathers characterized every human society. And we find concomitants of this situation throughout history. Work that required long distances and long periods away from home—hunting, warfare, and exploration—belonged to men. Activities congruent with staying near the hearth and close to breast-feeding children belonged to women.

The first great change in the social assignment of the entire population to rearing the next generation came with the invention of agriculture, which freed some men from subsistence food-getting, and freed a few women of rank and wealth from the care and feeding of their children (but did not free even a queen from childbearing) and substituted wet nurses. Although there were periods in history when men were withdrawn from parenthood into a monastic life, and women were allowed a complementary celibacy, it was not until the Industrial Revolution that work for mere individual survival, independent of supporting households, became important. Then the lifelong support which society had always provided for child-producing, child-rearing women was withdrawn, and the working woman, often with children, was left completely on her own to fulfill the previous male task of working outside the home to support the children.

In Freud's time, a small number of women were already responding to this situation by demanding to be treated as persons independently of their roles as wives and mothers, to have a chance to have education, a chance to go to medical school, a chance to work in the world of men. The tremendous effort that it takes to break the hold of tradition when it is expressed in terms of such basic differences as sex (and of physique where different roles have been assigned to different racial groups) appeared to Freud and to many of the early analysts as associated with a tremendous drive to be masculine, and this was indeed the most obvious path to take. If a little girl was not allowed to do what her brother was allowed and encouraged to do, then obviously, all early childhood experiences of sex difference that valued his anatomical endowment would seem to devalue hers. All admonitions toward passivity (to be quiet, to be modest, to be chaste) take on invidious connotations, just as the adoption of celibacy has so often in religious history been seen as making males more feminine.

Thus the century and a half of feminism through which we have just gone has witnessed a continuing interpretation of psycho-sexual development as females suffering from the discovery that they were not born males and free.

At the same time that females were making what came to be called in psychoanalytically influenced circles a "masculine protest," periodically there appeared social movements that emphasized the importance of maternity and the need for an extension of the maternal functions into society. While the early social revolutionaries in Europe were offering women freedom from the degrading position of being treated as property by males, there were other social reformers who were glorifying childbearing, and working to abolish child labor, protect the health of working mothers, and to provide contraception to give women control other their own bodies. Just as the emphasis upon the need to share a man's world focused upon a repudiation of women's primary sex characters and the role that accompanied them, so the emphasis upon women's primary sex characters underlay the emphasis on women's maternal aspects. The extreme extension of the first position presents women as handicapped by childbearing and envious of men, women who would like to reduce procreation to as brief as possible a moment in life—as it is for men—with the logical extension being artificial insemination and test-tube babies. The extreme extension of the second position, in which women are seen as handicapped because they cannot exercise their maternal functions to the full, is the emphasis on every woman's right to have a child, the right to elective abortion in which no husband or future father shares in the decision—women are pictured as capable of rearing their children alone, or with the help of other women only.

For a brief time in the period following World War II, there was an emphasis upon the father's involvement in the care of an infant, and the right of a man to be included in the delivery of his child and the enjoyment of its early infancy. These demands have lingered on, with prenatal classes for fathers as well as mothers, presence of fathers at delivery, and the demands of fathers to keep illegitimate infants whom the mothers wish to give away for adoption. In Sweden, there is an organized attempt to include men in the domestic responsibilities of the home, and to rear boys and girls with an expectation of choice between and competence in both the previously masculine roles of breadwinning outside the home and the previously feminine roles of child care and homemaking.

So over the last century we have seen a series of perturbations in the relationships between the sexes, and the interpretations placed by psychiatry and medicine in general on the compatibility or incompatibility of achievement in masculine-defined roles and women's biological functions.

One set of social changes, set in motion by a series of inventions, which began with the invention of agriculture and culminated in the Industrial Revolution, has changed the role of men in society, permitting more and more men to devote themselves to diversified activities other than the primary activities of subsistence and defense. Changes in women's roles only pallidly reflected these changes, which placed greater and greater burdens on women, who could now be turned adrift from male support and protection, but were provided little real relief from the contradiction between a sociologically defined role that placed primary importance on childbearing and childrearing, and an increasing opportunity and desire by some women to be able to live as human beings, as persons, rather than subject their entire lives to caring for the next generation.

Meanwhile, another revolution (as far-reaching in effect as the successive agricultural, industrial, and electronic revolutions, which have transformed the economic life of society) was getting under way: the medical revolution. The practice of obstetrics was taken out of the hands of women, first professionalized as midwifery, and childbirth converted from a natural part of life to a quasi-surgical procedure in a hospital in which women were reduced to the passivity that men had hopefully attributed to them through the centuries. Artificial feeding was invented to replace the mother's breast, and the age-old mystery of the interior of women's bodies was now open to inspection by properly qualified male practitioners. The spread of public health measures is completing the transformation of society; the infant death rate has been markedly reduced with no comparable reduction in the infant birth rate, and the world is now faced with a population explosion that in both the industrialized and the unindustrialized countries threatens the prosperity and wellbeing of almost every society. The perception of this situation has produced the new climate within which societies are seeking to reduce the childbearing role of women, and simultaneously demanding that women take a part in producing activities outside the home.

The stage has thus been set for a new attempt, on the part of both men and women, to redefine their relationships to each other and to the entire social process, to redefine the role of marriage as an institution, and to examine again whether there are any biologically given ways in which anatomy is destiny, as Freud originally put it. The seriousness of this worldwide situation is reflected in the tremendous commotion going on everywhere, in renewed interest in exploring female sexuality, the female body, and in various compensatory and extreme statements, of the tit-for-tat order, like the recent one in *The New York Times* (November 14, 1972) that because "women can achieve five to six sexual climaxes to a man's one; if continuously stimulated they can reach over fifty" this means that "obviously women were not designed for monogamous or polygamous marriage." The very extremity of the present discussion signals the magnitude of the changes in store for us, and reemphasizes the importance of examining whether there are any respects in which, in spite of the inadequacy of any theory of penis envy, Freud's insistence that anatomy is destiny may not, in some deeper sense, be true.

Although it is possible to demonstrate that the social definition of male and female roles throughout prehistory and history have reflected practical conditions—such as the need to breast feed and carry infants, and the need for men to work all their lives to provide for the next generation—there are many unanswered questions. We do not know whether a failure to bear a child, whatever the origin of that failure, may in some way damage a woman's capacity to realize herself as a person, hasten aging, or expose her to other risks more psychologically incapacitating than the hazards and wear and tear of many pregnancies. We do not know whether an abortion, however brief the period after conception, may not be, at least for many women, and for women of many different religious beliefs, a grievous and damaging experience. We do not know whether a bottle-fed mother can transmit to her bottle-fed baby the kind of tactile reassurance and security that infants appear to need, if they in turn, whether they be male or female, are to develop their full potentialities.

We do not know whether there may not be a value, both for women and for men, in the way that a woman's body reflects, in striking and dramatic fashion, the repetitive cycles of reproduction, and gives all of life, including aging, a different dimension from the lives of men, whose bodies register no such periodic and climactic events. We live in a period when much of human behavior has been seen as a nuisance to be eliminated—mechanically, biochemically, chemically. Menstrual cramps, defloration, pregnancy, delivery, and the menopause are all to be subjected to manipulations which limit or suppress entirely their individual and cultural significance. And we are almost completely ignorant of what the consequences of such interventions in very ancient biologically given sex differences may be. These are areas in which Freud's dictum—anatomy is destiny—must be kept very much in mind. We might easily choose a course that in its emphasis on artificial intervention in natural processes transforms human beings into beings who are incapable of the primary love and loyalty for kith and kin and country. Yet these loves and loyalties may be absolutely necessary, if we are to invoke enough devotion to the collective good to cope with the environmental crises that have resulted from Man's imposing his will, irrespective of consequences, on the natural world.

We do not know whether the fact that women's bodies are prepared to bear children may not also be a crucial determinant of certain aspects of behavior traditionally regarded as feminine. Feminine intuition may only be the result of having been the girl child of a mother who was alert to her child's slightest need; but girls continue to be born from their mother's bodies, in a nine-month-long gestation, so that alertness to tiny cues may continue to be transmitted from mother to daughter, and inhibited in sons, even if both boys and girls come to be reared equally by both parents from birth.

It may be that the fact that women's bodies are prepared for a so much lengthier participation in the creation of a human being may make females—even those who bear no children—more prone to take their own bodies as the theater of action. There may be a difference, although it would be a very slight one on the very edge of genius, between the highest creative faculties of men and women, even though women can learn what men have discovered and men can learn what women have discovered. For example, men may have an edge in physics and women in psychology.

Freud opened up a whole new way of understanding ourselves, our development through history, our behavior today. It is a pity that he understood women so little, but those who have followed in his footsteps and studied children, as well as those of us who have studied human development in other societies, are nonetheless indebted to him. The path he outlined, although in his discussion of the psychology of women he was completely culture-bound, still suggests that the rhythms of human development, patterned during a million years, are ignored at our peril, and understood, give us wisdom.

BIBLIOGRAPHY

BELL, ANITA I. "The Significance of Scrotal Sac and Testicles for the Prepuberty Male." *Psychoanalytic Quarterly,* 34, No. 2 (1965), 182–206.

BETTELHEIM, B. *Symbolic Wounds: Puberty Rites and the Envious Male,* rev. ed. New York: Macmillan, 1962.

ERIKSON, ERIK H. *Childhood and Society,* rev. ed. New York: Norton, 1963.

FREUD, SIGMUND. "Some Psychological Consequences of the Anatomical Distinctions Between the Sexes." In *Collected Papers,* James Strachey, translator and ed. (The International Psycho-Analytic Library, ed. Ernest Jones, No. 37.) London: Hogarth Press, 1953, 186–197.

———. "Female Sexuality." In *The Complete Edition of the Psychological Works of Sigmund Freud,* vol. 21: *The Future of an Illusion, Civilization and Its Discontents and Other Works,* James Strachey, translator and ed. London: Hogarth Press, 1961, 225–243.

———. "Lecture 33: Femininity." In *The Complete Edition of the Psychological Works of Sigmund Freud,* Vol. 22: *New Introductory Lectures on Psycho-Analysis and Other Works,* James Strachey, translator and editor. London: Hogarth Press, 1964, 112–135.

HOGBIN, IAN. *The Island of Menstruating Men.* Scranton: Chandler Publications, 1970.

HORNEY, KAREN. "The Flight from Womanhood. The Masculinity Complex in Women, As Viewed by Men and by Women," *International Journal of Psycho-Analysis,* 7 (1926), 324–339.

JACOBSON, EDITH. "Development of the Wish for a Child in Boys," *Psycho-Analytic Study of the Child,* 5 (1950), 139–152.

KINSEY, A. C., and others. *Sexual Behavior in the Human Male.* Philadelphia: Saunders, 1948.

———. *Sexual Behavior in the Human Female.* Philadelphia: Saunders, 1953.

MASTERS, W. H., and V. E. JOHNSON. *Human Sexual Response.* Boston: Little, Brown, 1966.

———. *Human Sexual Inadequacy.* Boston: Little, Brown, 1970.

MEAD, MARGARET. *Sex and Temperament in Three Primitive Societies.* New York: Morrow, 1963. Reprinted with new preface, Apollo editions, New York: Morrow, 1967.

———. *Male and Female.* New York: Morrow, 1949. Reprinted Apollo Editions, New York: Morrow, 1967.

———. "*Totem and Taboo* Reconsidered with Respect," *Bulletin of the Menninger Clinic,* 27, No. 4 (July 1963), 185–199.

SHERFEY, MARY JANE. "The Rib Belonged to Eve: I. Formidable Jargon," *The New York Times,* November 13, 1972, p. 370.

———. "The Rib Belonged to Eve: II. Ancient Man Knew His Place," *The New York Times,* November 14, 1972, p. 47.

The Problem of Feminine Masochism

Karen Horney

Interest in the problem of feminine masochism extends far beyond the merely medical and psychological spheres, for to students of the Western culture at least, it touches on the very roots for evaluating woman in her cultural definition. The facts appear to be that in our cultural areas, masochistic phenomena are more frequent in women than in men. Two ways of approaching an explanation of this observation have appeared. By one, there is an attempt to discover if masochistic trends are inherent in, or akin to, the very essence of female nature. By the other, one undertakes to evaluate the weight of social conditionings in the genesis of any sex-limited peculiarities in the distribution of masochistic trends.

In psychoanalytic literature . . . the problem has been tackled only from the viewpoint of regarding feminine masochism as one psychic consequence of anatomical sex differences. Psychoanalysis thus has lent its scientific tools to support the theory of a given kinship between masochism and female biology. The possibility of social conditioning has as yet not been considered from the psychoanalytical side.

The task of this paper is to contribute to the efforts of determining the weight of biological and cultural factors in this problem; to review carefully the validity of the psychoanalytical data given in this direction; and to raise the question of whether psychoanalytical knowledge can be utilized for an investigation of a possible connection with social conditionings.

One may summarize the psychoanalytic views thus far presented somewhat as follows:

"The Problem of Feminine Masochism" by Karen Horney. *The Psychoanalytic Review,* Vol. 22 (1935), through the courtesy of the Editors and the Publisher, National Psychological Association for Psychoanalysis, New York, N.Y.

The specific satisfactions sought and found in female sex life and motherhood are of a masochistic nature. The content of the early sexual wishes and fantasies concerning the father is the desire to be mutilated, that is, castrated by him. Menstruation has the hidden connotation of a masochistic experience. What the woman secretly desires in intercourse is rape and violence, or in the mental sphere, humiliation. The process of childbirth gives her an unconscious masochistic satisfaction, as is also the case with the maternal relation to the child. Furthermore, as far as men indulge in masochistic fantasies or performances, these represent an expression of their desire to play the female role. . . .

It is assumed at least implicitly that masochistic character trends of all kinds also are much more frequent in women than in men. This conclusion is inevitable when one holds the basic psychoanalytic theory that general behavior in life is modeled on the sexual behavior pattern, which in women is deemed masochistic. It then follows that if most or all women are masochistic in their attitude toward sex and reproduction, they would indubitably reveal masochistic trends in their nonsexual attitude toward life more frequently than would men. . . .

The foregoing observations are sufficient to build a working hypothesis to the effect that wishes for masculinity of some origin or other, play a role in female sex life, and this hypothesis may be used in seeking explanations for certain neurotic phenomena in women. It must be realized, however, that this is an hypothesis, not a fact; and that it is not even indisputably useful as an hypothesis. When it is claimed, moreover, that the desire for masculinity is not only a dynamic factor of primary order in neurotic females, but in every human female, independent of individual or cultural conditions, one cannot but remark that there are no data to substantiate this claim. Unfortunately little or nothing is known of psychically healthy women, or of women under different cultural conditions, due to limitations of historical and ethnological knowledge.

Therefore, as there are no data about frequency, conditioning, and weight of the observed reactions of the little girl to the discovery of the penis, the assumption that this is a turning point in female development is stimulating, but can scarcely be used in a chain of proof. Why, indeed, should the girl turn masochistic when she realizes the lack of a penis? . . .

Let us ask again: What are the data? As far as I can see, only the fact that there may exist in small children early sadistic fantasies. This is partly elicited by direct psychoanalytic observation of neurotic children (M. Klein), and partly by reconstruction out of analysis of neurotic adults. There is no evidence for the ubiquity of these early sadistic fantasies, and I wonder, for instance, whether little American Indian girls, or little Trobriand girls have them. However, even taking for granted that this occurrence was in fact ubiquitous, there still remain three further assumptions necessary for completion of the picture:

(1) That these sadistic fantasies are generated by the active-sadistic libido cathexis of the clitoris.

(2) That the girl renounces her clitoris-masturbation in consequence of the narcissistic injury of having no penis.

(3) That the hitherto active-sadistic libido turns automatically inward and becomes masochistic.

All three assumptions seem highly speculative. It is known that people can become frightened of their hostile aggressions and subsequently prefer the suffering role, but how a libido-cathexis of an organ can be sadistic and then turn inward, seems mysterious. . . .

As the evidence has not yet been presented, one looks around for analogous reactions that might lend plausibility to the assumption. A correspondent example would have to fulfill the same preconditions given in the case of the little girl: a sudden interruption of customary sexual outlets by the occurrence of some painful event. Consider, for example, the case of a man who has led a hitherto satisfactory sex life, and is then jailed and placed under such close supervision that all sexual outlets are barred. Will such a man become masochistic? That is, will he become sexually incited by witnessing beatings, by imagining beatings, or receiving actual beatings and maltreatment? Will he indulge in fantasies of persecution and inflicted suffering? No doubt such masochistic reactions may occur. But no doubt also this represents only one of several possible reactions, and such masochistic reactions will occur only in a man who *previously* had masochistic tendencies. Other examples lead to the same conclusion. A woman deserted by her husband, and without any immediate sexual outlet or the anticipation of one, may react masochistically; but the more poised she is, the better able she will be to renounce sexuality temporarily and find some satisfaction in friends, children, work, or pleasure. Again, a woman in such a situation will react masochistically only if she already had an established pattern of masochistic trends. . . .

Masochistic phenomena in women can be detected as a result of directed and sharpened observation, where they might otherwise have passed unnoticed, as in social rencontres with women (entirely outside the field of psychoanalytic practice), in feminine character portrayals in literature, or in examination of women of somewhat foreign mores, such as the Russian peasant woman who does not feel she is loved by her husband unless he beats her. In the face of this evidence, the psychoanalyst concludes that he is here confronted with an ubiquitous phenomenon, functioning on a psychobiological basis with the regularity of a law of nature.

The onesidedness or positive errors in the results obtained by a partial examination of the picture are due to a neglect of cultural or social factors—an exclusion from the picture of women living under civilizations with different customs. The Russian peasant woman of the Tsaristic and patriarchal regime was invariably cited in discussions aimed at proving how deeply masochism is ingrained in female nature. Yet this peasant woman has emerged into the self-assertive Soviet woman of today who would doubtless be astonished if beatings were administered as a token of affection. The change has occurred in the patterns of culture rather than in the particular women. . . .

For sociological and ethnological approaches, data concerning the following questions would be pertinent:

1—What is the frequency of occurrence of masochistic attitudes towards female functions under various social and cultural conditions?

II—What is the frequency of general masochistic attitudes or manifestations in women, as compared with men, under various social and cultural conditions?

If both these inquiries gave color to the view that under all social conditions there is a masochistic conception of the female role, and if equally there is a decided preponderance of general masochistic phenomena among women as compared with men, then, and only then, would one be justified in seeking further psychologic reasons for this phenomenon. If, however, such an ubiquitous feminine masochism did not appear, one would wish of the sociological-ethnological research the answer to the further questions:

(1) What are the special social conditions under which masochism connected with female functions is frequent?

(2) What are the special social conditions under which general masochistic attitudes are more frequent in women than in men?

The task of psychoanalysis in such an investigation would be to supply the anthropologist with psychological data. With the exception of perversions and masturbatory fantasies, masochistic tendencies and gratifications are unconscious. The anthropologist cannot explore these. What he needs are criteria by which he can identify and observe the manifestations that in high probability indicate the existence of masochistic drives.

To give these data is comparatively simple as in question (1), concerning masochistic manifestations in female functions. On the basis of psychoanalytic experience it is reasonably safe to assume masochistic tendencies:

(1) When there is a great frequency of functional menstrual disorders, such as dysmenorrhea and menorrhagia.

(2) When there is great frequency of psychogenic disturbance in pregnancy and childbirth, such as fear of childbirth, fuss about it, pains, or elaborate means to avoid pain.

(3) When there is a frequency of such attitudes toward sexual relations as to imply that it is debasing for, or an exploitation of, women.

These indications are not to be taken as absolute, but rather with the following two restricting considerations:

(a) It seems to have become habitual in psychoanalytic thinking to assume that pain, suffering, or fear of suffering are prompted by masochistic drives, or result in masochistic gratification. It is therefore necessary to point out that such assumptions require evidence. Alexander, for instance, assumes that people climbing mountains with heavy knapsacks are masochistic, particularly if there is a car or railway by which they might get to the top of a mountain more easily. This may be true, but more frequently the reasons for carrying heavy knapsacks are very realistic ones.

(b) Suffering, or even self-inflicted pain, in more primitive tribes, may be an expression of magical thinking meant to ward off danger, and may have nothing to do with individual masochism. Therefore, one can only interpret such data in connection with a basic knowledge of the entire structure of the tribal history concerned.

The task of psychoanalysis in regard to question (2), data concerning indications for general masochistic attitudes is much more difficult, because understanding of the whole phenomenon is still limited. In fact, it has not advanced much beyond Freud's statement that it has something to do with sexuality and with morality. There are, however, these open questions: Is it a primarily sexual phenomenon that extends also into the moral sphere, or a moral phenomenon extending also into the sexual sphere? Are the moral and the erogenic masochism two separate processes, or only two sets of manifestations arising from a common underlying process? Or is masochism perhaps a collective term for very complex phenomena?

One feels justified in using the same term for widely discrepant manifestations because all of them have some trends in common: tendencies to arrange in fantasies, dreams, or in the real world, situations that imply suffering; or to feel suffering in situations that would not have this concomitant for the average person. The suffering may concern the physical or the mental sphere. There is some gratification or relief of tension connected with it, and that is why it is striven for. The gratification or relief of tension may be conscious or unconscious, sexual or nonsexual. The nonsexual functions may be very different: reassurances against fears, atonements for committed sins, permission to commit new ones, strategy in reference to goals otherwise unattainable, indirect forms of hostility.

The realization of this wide range of masochistic phenomena is more bewildering and challenging than encouraging, and these general statements certainly cannot be of much help to the anthropologist. More concrete data are at his disposal, however, if all scientific worries about conditions and functions are swept aside, and only those surface attitudes that have been observable in patients with distinct and widespread masochistic tendencies within the psychoanalytic situation are made the basis of his investigations. For this purpose, therefore, it may suffice to enumerate these attitudes without tracing them back in detail to their individual conditions. Needless to say, they are not all present in every patient belonging to this category; yet the whole syndrome is so typical (as every analyst will recognize), that if some of these trends are apparent at the beginning of a treatment, one can safely predict the entire picture, though of course the details vary. The details concern sequence of appearance, distribution of weight among the single trends, and particularly form and intensity of defenses built up for protection against these tendencies.

Let us consider what observable data there are in patients with widespread masochistic trends. As I see it, the main lines of the surface structure in such personalities are somewhat as follows:

There are several ways in which one can find reassurance against deep fears. Renunciation is one way; inhibition, another; denying the fear and becoming optimistic, a third one; and so on. Being loved is the particular means of reassurance used by a masochistic person. As he has a rather free-floating anxiety, he needs constant signs of attention and affection, and as he never believes in these signs except momentarily, he has an excessive need for attention and affection. He is therefore, generally speaking, very emotional in his relations with people; easily attached because he expects them to give him the necessary reassurance; easily disappointed because he never gets, and never can get, what he expects. The expectation or illusion of the "great love" often plays an important role. Sexuality being one of the most common ways of getting affection, he also tends to overvalue it and clings to the illusion that it holds the solution of all life's problems. How far this is conscious, or how easily he has actual sexual relations, depends on his inhibitions on this score. Where he has had sexual relations, or attempts at such, his history shows a frequency of "unhappy loves"; he has been deserted, disappointed, humiliated, badly treated. In nonsexual relations, the same tendency appears in all gradations from being or feeling incompetent, self-sacrificing, and submissive, to playing the martyr role and feeling or actually being humiliated, abused, and exploited. While he otherwise feels it as a given fact that he *is* incompetent or that life *is* brutal, one can see in the psychoanalytic situation that it is not facts, but an obstinate tendency, which makes him insist upon seeing or arranging it this way. This tendency, moreover, is revealed in the psychoanalytic situation as an unconscious arrangement motivating him to provoke attacks, to feel ruined, damaged, ill-treated, humiliated, without any real cause.

Because other people's affection and sympathy are of vital importance to him, he easily becomes extremely dependent, and this hyperdependency also shows clearly in relations with the analyst.

The next observable reason he never believes in any form of affection he may actually receive (instead of clinging to it as representing the coveted reassurance) lies in his greatly diminished self-esteem; he feels inferior, absolutely unlovable and unworthy of love. On the other hand, just this lack of self-confidence makes him feel that appealing to pity by having and displaying inferiority feelings, weakness, and suffering is the only means by which he can win the affection he needs. One sees that the deterioration of his self-esteem lies rooted in his paralysis of what may be termed "adequate aggressiveness." By this I mean the capacities for work, including the following attributes: taking initiative; making efforts; carrying things through to completion; attaining success; insisting upon one's rights; defending oneself when attacked; forming and expressing autonomous views; recognizing one's goals and being able to plan one's life according to them.[1] In masochistic persons one usually finds widespread inhibitions on this score, which in their entirety account for the feeling of insecurity, or even helplessness, in the life struggle, and explain the subsequent dependency on other people, and a predisposition to look to them for support or help.

Psychoanalysis reveals the tendency to recoil from competition of any kind as the next observable reason for their incapacity to be self-assertive. Their inhibitions thus result from efforts to check themselves in order to avoid the risk of competition.

The hostile feelings inevitably generated on the basis of such self-defeating tendencies, also cannot be expressed freely because they are conceived as jeopardizing the reassurance attendant on being loved, which is the mainspring of protection against anxieties. Weakness and suffering, therefore, already serving many functions, now also act as a vehicle for the indirect expression of hostility.

The use of this syndrome of observable attitudes for anthropologic investigation is subject to one source of possible major error; namely, masochistic attitudes are not always apparent as such because they are frequently concealed by defenses, often appearing clearly only after the latter have been removed. As an analysis of these defenses clearly is beyond the sphere of such an investigation, the defenses must be taken at face value, with the result that these instances of masochistic attitudes must escape observation.

Reviewing then, the observable masochistic attitudes, regardless of their deeper motivation, I suggest that the anthropologist seek data concerning questions like these: under what social or cultural conditions do we find more frequently in women than in men

(1) the manifesting of inhibitions in the direct expression of demands and aggressions;

(2) a regarding of oneself as weak, helpless, or inferior and implicitly or explicitly demanding considerations and advantages on this basis;

(3) a becoming emotionally dependent on the other sex;

(4) a showing of tendencies to be self-sacrificing, to be submissive, to feel used or to be exploited, to put responsibilities on the other sex;

(5) a using of weakness and helplessness as a means of wooing and subduing the other sex.[2]

Besides these formulations, which are direct generalizations of the psychoanalytic experience with masochistic women, I may also present certain generalizations as to the causative factors that predispose to the appearance of masochism in women. I should expect these phenomena to appear in any culture-complex that included one or more of the following factors:

(1) Blocking of outlets for expansiveness and sexuality.

(2) Restriction in the number of children, inasmuch as having and rearing children supplies the woman with various gratifying outlets (tenderness, achievement, self-esteem), and this becomes all the more important when having and rearing children is the measuring rod of social evaluation.

(3) Estimation of women as beings who are, on the whole, inferior to men (insofar as it leads to a deterioration of female self-confidence).

(4) Economic dependence of women on men or on family, inasmuch as it fosters an emotional adaptation in the way of emotional dependence.

(5) Restriction of women to spheres of life that are built chiefly upon emotional bonds, such as family life, religion, or charity work.

(6) Surplus of marriageable women, particularly when marriage offers the principal opportunity for sexual gratification, children, security, and social recognition.[3] This condition is relevant inasmuch as it favors [as do also (3) and (4)] emotional dependence on men, and generally speaking, a development that is not autonomous but fashioned and molded by existing male ideologies. It is pertinent also insofar as it creates among women a particularly strong competition from which recoil is an important factor in precipitating masochistic phenomena.

All the factors enumerated overlap; for example, strong sexual competition among women will be more potent if other outlets for competitive strivings (as for professional eminence) are concurrently blocked. It would seem that no one factor is ever solely responsible for the deviating development, but rather a concatenation of factors.

In particular one must consider the fact that when some or all of the suggested elements are present in the culture-complex, there may appear certain fixed ideologies concerning the "nature" of woman; such as doctrines that woman is innately weak, emotional, enjoys dependence, is limited in capacities for independent work and autonomous thinking. One is tempted to include in this category the psychoanalytic belief that woman is masochistic by nature. It is fairly obvious that these ideologies function not only to reconcile women to their subordinate role by presenting it as an unalterable one, but also to plant the belief that it represents a fulfillment they crave, or an ideal for which it is commendable and desirable to strive. The influence that these ideologies exert on women is materially strengthened by the fact that women presenting the specified traits are more frequently chosen by men. This implies that women's erotic possibilities depend on their conformity to the image of that which constitutes their "true nature." It therefore seems no exaggeration to say that in such social organizations, masochistic attitudes (or rather, milder expressions of masochism) are favored in women while they are discouraged in men. Qualities like emotional dependence on the other sex (clinging vine), absorption in "love," inhibition of expansive, autonomous development, etc., are regarded as quite desirable in women but are treated with opprobrium and ridicule when found in men.

One sees that these cultural factors exert a powerful influence on women; so much so, in fact, that in our culture it is hard to see how any woman can escape becoming masochistic to some degree, from the effects of the culture alone, without any appeal to contributory factors in the anatomical-physiological characteristics of woman, and their psychic effects.

Certain writers, however, . . . have generalized from psychoanalytical experience with neurotic women, and have held that the culture complexes to which I have referred are themselves the very effect of these anatomical-physiological characteristics. It is useless to argue this overgeneralization until the type of anthropological investigation suggested has been made. Let us look, however, at the factors in the somatic organization of women, which actually contribute to their acceptance of a masochistic role. The anatomical-physiological factors in women that may prepare the soil for the growth of masochistic phenomena, seem to me to be the following:

(a) Greater average physical strength in men than in women. According to ethnologists this is an acquired sex difference. Nevertheless it exists nowadays. Though weakness is not identical with masochism, the realization of an inferior physical strength may fertilize an emotional conception of a masochistic female role.

(b) The possibility of rape similarly may give rise in women to the fantasy of being attacked, subdued, and injured.

(c) Menstruation, defloration, and childbirth, insofar as they are bloody or even painful processes, may readily serve as outlets for masochistic strivings.

(d) The biologic differences in intercourse also serve for masochistic formulation. Sadism and masochism have fundamentally nothing whatsoever to do with intercourse, but the female role in intercourse (being penetrated) *lends* itself more readily to a personal misinterpretation (when needed) of masochistic performance; and the male role, to one of sadistic activity.

These biological functions have in themselves no masochistic connotation for women, and do not lead to masochistic reactions; but if masochistic needs of other origin[4] are present, they may easily be involved in masochistic fantasies, which in turn causes them to furnish masochistic gratifications. Beyond admitting the possibility of a certain preparedness in women for a masochistic conception of their role, every additional assertion as to the relation of their constitution to masochism is hypothetical; and such facts as the disappearance of all masochistic tendencies after a successful psychoanalysis, and the observations of nonmasochistic women (which, after all, exist), warn us not to overrate even this element of preparedness.

In summary: The problem of feminine masochism cannot be related to factors inherent in the anatomical-physiological-psychic characteristics of woman alone, but must be considered as importantly conditioned by the culture-complex or social organization in which the particular masochistic woman has developed. The precise weight of these two groups of factors cannot be assessed until we have the results of anthropological investigations using valid psychoanalytical criteria in several culture areas significantly different from ours. It is clear, however, that the importance of anatomical-psychological-psychic factors has been greatly overestimated by some writers on this subject.

NOTES

1. In the field of psychoanalytic literature Schultz-Hencke, "Schicksal und Neurose," has particularly emphasized the pathogenic importance of these inhibitions.
2. It may strike the psychoanalytic reader that in the enumeration of factors, I have not restricted myself to those that are influential in childhood only. One has to consider, however, that (1) the child is bound to feel the influence of those factors indirectly through the medium of the family, and particularly through the influence they have exerted on the women in her surroundings; and (2) though masochistic attitudes (like other neurotic attitudes) generate primarily in childhood, the conditions of later life determine for the average case (that is, cases in which childhood conditions have not been so severe that they alone definitely shape the characteristics).
3. It must be borne in mind, however, that social regulations, such as marriage arrangement by families, would greatly reduce the effectiveness of this factor. This consideration also throws a light on Freud's assumption that women generally are more jealous than men. The statement probably is correct so far as the present German and Austrian cultures are concerned. To deduce this, however, from more purely individual anatomical-physiological sources (penis envy) is not convincing. While it may be so in individual cases, the generalization—independent of consideration of the social conditions—is subject to the same fundamental objection as previously mentioned.
4. What I have in mind as the sources of masochistic attitudes, I shall present in a later communication.

Once More the Inner Space

Erik Erikson

"Womanhood and the Inner Space" originated in a symposium on The Woman in America of the American Academy of Arts and Sciences in 1963. There, divergent aspects of the main theme were discussed by representative scholars from a number of fields and advocates of a variety of viewpoints. I emphasize this here again, because in these matters context is all—as one quickly learns from the fate of such efforts in times when their subject matter becomes "political." Then, single passages are separated from the rest and isolated phrases assume a slogan-like life of their own. They are not merely quoted "out of context," but forcibly put into a new one. This, at any rate, was impressed on me when on revisiting the Harvard area I heard my essay cited among writings deemed inimical to womanhood.

So I am now asked whether the woman's movement has affected my thinking about women, I cannot bypass these developments. In fact, I must take account of them in some detail not only as a personal experience but also as a phenomenon characteristic of some stages in liberation movements. For if we recognize in such intellectual militancy a necessarily ruthless replowing of the ground of consciousness, we must also note that it

Based on my response to a request from a former student, Jean Strouse, who was editing an anthology of psychoanalytic essays on women, from Freud's early writings on. For each item, she commissioned a contemporary critique. Since I was the last of the reprinted essayists in the volume, and extant, Jean Strouse thoughtfully asked me to write my own critique of the essay "Womanhood and the Inner Space,"[1] and she provided me with some questions which, she felt, the essay raised.

is apt again to plow under insights into unconscious motivation that seem indispensable to the flowering of any modern liberation. But before I come to that, let me confess that I also have been affected by the more recent and still growing impression that many young women do, indeed, seem to embody a new womanhood—at once competent and thoughtful, outspoken and loving. Here, as elsewhere, new and more universal identities are evolving. I must truthfully say, however, that this has confirmed rather than "affected" what, through a long life in a number of countries, I have learned to feel womanhood can be or would become wherever it will free itself from the mere obligatory and fashionable aspects of the dominant roles, with all their built-in neuroticisms, *and* from mere reactive rebelliousness.

But if it should be now insisted that I enlarge on what I mean by womanhood, I would not know how to answer. The special polarity of the erotic encounter and of lifelong love is so close to the secret of life that only poets would attempt to find words for it. I am son and brother, husband and father to women: each a radiant and unique being, they are part of my existence and essence as I am part of theirs. Our joint experience at its best is an interplay of divergence appreciated and affinity confirmed. And this is true for women in other spheres, where intellectual interplay transcends all differences. At any rate, I could not write about women as a definable category of otherness—except in a clearly comparative subcontext such as the one to which I gave at first the admittedly slogan-like title, "The Inner and the Outer Space." As a matter of fact, wherever in human life a category of others turns into a bunch of "them," there is already something very wrong. And I have come to understand that many young women have been able to face the suddenly highlighted awareness of their having been implicitly treated as "them" in such a variety of confining (even if sometimes flattering) roles throughout history, only by vindictively lumping men together as "them," and by mistrusting totally what might prove treacherous. But vindication is not yet liberation.

In the symposium on womanhood for which the article was written, my job clearly was to start with a psychosexual theme. I had to explain where and why my own observations could not be fitted into those classicial psychoanalytic formulations of womanhood which emphasized exclusively the organ that was *not* there. And I had to focus on what was very much there on the inside—visible and touchable only in its vestibular access, but certainly "known" early to all children except the most underprivileged urban elite.

But alas, in the minds of many feminists, I merely seem to have been granting—and with some condescension—a reasonable equivalent to maleness; and, worse, I still seemed to believe in anatomy as well as in the unconscious. And let us face it right now: it is the idea of being unconsciously possessed by one's body, rather than owning it by choice and using it with deliberation, which cuases much of the most pervasive anger. Here I had to learn that in women's liberation, as in other liberations spearheaded by the educated middle class, a corollary to the attempt to raise consciousness is the determination to repress the awareness of unconscious motivation, especially where it demands an adjustment to what suddenly appear to be the physical stigmata of sex, age, or race. Thus, in this post-Freudian era we face not only some of the standard repressions unearthed by Freud but the re-repression of much that has so far been, shall we say, widely half understood and that, more fully understood in a new key, could help importantly in true liberation. To be sure, some of the theoretical paradigms of early psychoanalytic interpretation are badly dated. But to continue a once truly revolutionary enlightenment, to redate systematically what belongs to the passage of time and to sift out what is lasting—that can mean to accept historical responsibility.

So, we turn to my paper and its (partial) fate. Let us see how some sentences, when used for political rhetoric, lost their theoretical half tones and, instead, took on one (inflammable) color. For example, I am asked:

> One of the chief points which feminist writers take issue with, in your formulations about womanhood, has to do with the old controversy about nature vs. nurture. You write that, "The basic modalities of woman's commitment and involvement naturally also reflect the ground plan of her body; and that anatomy, history and personality are our combined destinty." Anatomy, feminists would argue, is only destiny insofar as it determines cultural conditioning . . . "Erikson's whole theory," claims Kate Millet, "is built in psychoanalysis' persistent error of mistaking learned behavior for biology." What is your answer to this charge?

My answer is that if even staunch feminists concede that anatomy, to some extent, "determines cultural conditioning," then we really have no basic argument. We could start here as well as anywhere; the question is, only, Where do we think we are going? To clarify *my* direction, I need only ask readers (if in an uncomfortably professorial manner) to take another look at what I am quoted as saying and to mark the little words "also" in the first part of my sentence and "and" in the second. "Also" means that the modalities of a woman's existence reflect the ground plan of her body among other things—as do men's modalities reflect that of the male body. "And" says that history and personality and anatomy are our joint destiny. And if we should go all out and italicize "combined," too, then an all-round relativity is implied: each of the three aspects of human fate—anatomy, history, and personality—must always be studied in its relation to the other two, for each codetermines the others. Such "systematic going around in circles" (as I have called it, so as not to overdo the word "relativity") takes some thought which is indispensable to the study of human facts.

Incidentally, I did not start this destiny business, and Freud did not, either. Napoleon was the "man of destiny" to whom, naturally, history was all. Freud the doctor wanted to make things more concrete (and, no doubt, shake the great usurper's throne a bit) by reminding him of the power of motivations (even some imperial ones) based on anatomy. And I, an heir of ego psychology, asked rather modestly whether we ourselves are not also part of our destiny. I find myself in a body that exists in a particular social place and historical period, and I must attempt to make the most and the best of that, while helping others to make the most and the best of themselves—and of me. A freer choice nobody can claim or grant to anybody, even if it would seem (and I will quote one such suggestion later) that it is implicitly guaranteed by the American Constitution.

In my article, I describe a play procedure which was employed in the context of a long-range study of a large group of California boys and girls. For most of the first two decades of their lives, they were seen twice a year in the Guidance Study of the Institute for Child Development of the University of California, to be measured, interviewed, and tested. On the occasion of their visits during their eleventh, twelfth, and thirteenth years, I asked one child at a time to come into my study, to arrange with given toys on a given table "an exciting scene from an imaginary moving picture," and then to tell the "plot." The story was recorded and the scene photographed. An open-ended observational procedure, then, but not what the critics halfmockingly refer to as an "experiment" meant to find "evidence" for a "theory."

How the *clinical* observation of free play has become an important tool in the recognition of a disturbed or anxious child's central problems is summarized in *Childhood and Society*. What I learned in Berkeley was that children outside of a clinical context, too, would willingly, and some eagerly, invent a toy scene, projecting on the play construction (unconsciously, one must assume) themes which often proved to be significantly related to life themes revealed as central and dominant in a wide variety of other data systematically collected over the years by observers of various theoretical persuasions. The wider implications of such play phenomena I have discussed more recently in my Godkin Lectures, which will appear under the title (suggested by a line from William Blake) *The Child's Toys and the Old Man's Reasons*. Thanks to the wealth of data in the Berkeley Guidance Study's "follow-up," I have, in fact, been able to review a few of those play constructions (now nearly thirty years old) and show their relevance in the light of these subjects' further course of life.

At the time of the original procedure, I was fascinated by what I soon perceived as the "language" of *spatial representation* facilitated by the use of blocks: How the constructions-in-progress moved forward to the outer edge of the table or back to the wall to which it was attached; how they rose to shaky heights or remained close to the table surface; how they were spread over the available space or constricted to a portion of that space. Now, the spatial aspect of the matter probably makes more immediate sense to persons who are visually inclined and who have learned to "read" what children "say" as they move in space and play with things and forms. At any rate, it soon became apparent that these girls and boys tended to use space differently, and that certain configurations as well as themes occurred strikingly often in the constructions of one sex and rarely in those of the other.

Let me restate the main trends here, in order to emphasize that to build with blocks and to arrange toys are modes of spatial action. Where the boys represented outdoor scenes without using any of the blocks, they emphasized the free motion of animals, cars, and people in the open spaces. If they built streets and crossroads, they channeled traffic, which, in turn, might lead to collisions or be stopped by the traffic policeman. Where the boys built structures, they were apt to build relatively high ones, to erect towers, and to add protruding ornaments in the form of cones and cylinders. On occasion, they accentuated such height by playing out the danger of collapse. And their structures enclosed fewer people and animals than did those of the girls.

In comparison and contrast, the girls, when arranging configurations of furniture without building any surrounding walls, emphasized the interior of houses. Where walls were built, the configuration was one of simple and low enclosure. And, indeed, these contained many more people and animals. When the girls added a more elaborate structure, it was apt to be an ornate doorway leading into the enclosure; and there were scenes in which animals and (male) people entered or intruded into the predominantly peaceful interior.

Interestingly enough, some critical writers are teased into playing with the material even as they read about it. Elizabeth Janeway, in referring to my "famous experiment," summarized it thus: "Boys . . . use their toys and blocks to construct outdoor scenes of action where wild animals threaten and automobiles collide. Little girls prefer interiors where their dolls serve each other tea, or play the piano."[2] None of these California children mentioned tea; nor did I. The significance of such reinterpretations seems to lie not only in the attraction of play but also in the readers' inclination to embellish role stereotypes in the play content over the more mysterious spatial configurations on which my analysis of the use of outer and of inner space rests.

If I, then, abstract the configurations more often done by the boys as dominated by height and downfall and by strong motion and its channelization or arrest and those done by the girls as dominated by static interiors which were open or simply enclosed, peaceful or intruded upon, it is obvious that in the actual play constructions there was a rich interplay between form and content, between the spatial position and the narrative themes assigned to the dolls and toys. In the end, however, it would have taken a special effort to overlook the fact that the sex differences in the use of play space did correspond to the morphology of genital differentiation, or, as I put it: "In the male, an external organ, erectable and intrusive in character, serving the channelization of mobile sperm cells: in the female, internal organs, with vestibular access, leading to expectant ova."

But the matter certainly does not rest with this seeming reduction to some basic elements. It begins here. If I concluded that these differences may suggest a "difference in the experience of the ground plan of the human body," which, in turn, "influences the experience of existence in space," I proceeded, in the rest of the article, to apply this assumption to corresponding configurations observed under other conditions, such as in clinical experience, in the observation of animal behavior, and in anthropological accounts. A configurational exploration, then, but no "theory" as yet. But all these wider demonstrations are usually omitted in references to the essay, although they explain the "inner space" as a configuration denoting a series of concentric "surroundings," from the womb of origin and the maternal body and presence to social organization and styles of dwellings, and from the quality of domestic or communal life to the "feel" of the universe.

To some readers, it seems to follow immediately that, on the basis of my "proof," I declare men to *be this* and women to *be that:* as one publication (approvingly) had it, men, to me, are "penetrators" and women, "enclosers"; men are oriented outward, women inward. Likewise, where I claim that "male and female principles in body construction . . . remain relevant throughout life for the elaboration of sex roles in cultural spacetimes,"

Janeway (in all her well-known clarity, warmth, and responsibility) concludes that "according to this formula, men are active, women intuitive; men are interested in things and ideas, women in people and feelings." Worse, "there is a limit to learning . . . in Erkison's view, and that limit is involved with the ground plan of the body and is inescapable."

Well, I have been forced to re-read the paper and to clarify it again for myself. Let me add that I feel the need to change very little except a few imprudent words and phrases as well as some ambivalently poetic ones. It was imprudent to say, "the emphasis here is in predisposition and predilection, rather than on exclusive ability, for both sexes (if otherwise matched in maturation and intelligence) learn readily to *imitate* the spatial mode of the other sex." I should have said, instead, "to make use of, to share, and at times to imitate, the configurations most typical of the other sex." Play configurations can mean many things, and a variety of bodily and spatial experiences are shared, in principle, by both sexes. Both sexes, for example, grow up and stand upright, or may be living in high-rise apartments, and therefore have a variety of "reasons" to build tower-like structures, not to speak of the mere pleasure of putting block upon block. Likewise, both have a bodily interior and live in houses, and thus may wish to build enclosures. It is quite probable, therefore, that the play space will at different ages be used variously for the expression of common and of different experiences, even as single children will demonstrate quite individual meanings. This, to me, makes it all the more convincing that our pubertal children demonstrated more clearly how differences in the experience of sexual maturation may appear in the play space. But no matter how the interior and the exterior space are experinced, used, and represented at different ages, the sexual and procreative orientation becomes and remains—that much I must claim—a significant aspect of existence in space.

Now back to the department of clarification by italics. When Kate Millet makes the (horrible) suggestion that I "define" the female as a 'creature with a woundlike aperture," she refers to a sentence which claims that "children of both sexes sooner or later 'know' the penis to be missing in one sex, leaving in its place a woundlike aperture" (*Identity: Youth and Crisis,* p. 267). The mere underscoring of the word "children" would emphasize that I am referring to infantile observations made at a stage of development when the inviolacy of the body is a matter of anxious concern leading to the well-known phobic "theories" which (as I insist throughout) are counteracted in the growing child's eventual awareness of a "protective innerbodily space safely set in the center of female form and carriage."

That, in another passage, I did fail to italicize two even shorter words seems to have invited an even weirder misunderstanding. On page 278 of the same book, I speak as a clinician and note a particular *quality* in the transitory as well as the chronic depressions of women: "In female experience an 'inner space' is at the center of despair even as it is the very center of potential fulfillment. Emptiness is the female form of perdition." Such hurt—and I now italicize—"*can* be re-experienced in each menstruation; *it* is a crying to heaven in the mourning over a child; and it becomes a permanent scar in the menopause." Millet read "it" to mean mourning over each menstrual loss, wherefore she undertook to count how many periods women average in a lifetime and how often, therefore, Erikson thinks, they are crying to heaven over a child not conceived. To older people like myself, the loss of a child by death was once a more expectable experience in family life, whereas in past generations all living children represented a triumph of survival.

Come to think of it, there must be some historical relativity in much that is written about such matters—and in much that is misunderstood, Janeway clarified for me one such issue mentioned in the paper, namely, the special historical dilemma of American women.

> To be told in Erik Erikson's words one is "never not a woman" comes as rather a shock. This is especially true for American women becase of the way in which the American ethos has honored the idea of liberty and individual choice. We can find, in fact, an excellent description of the psychological effect of these traditional American attitudes in Professor Erikson's own clasical study, *Childhood and Society*. "The process of American identity formation," he writes, "seems to support an individual's ego identity as long as he can preserve a certain element of deliberate tentativeness of autonomous choice. The individual must be able to convince himself that the next step is up to him." Very well; but then what about the limiting restrictions of being "never-not-a-woman" . . . it is more than restricting, because it involves women in the kind of conflict with their surroundings that no decisions and no action open to them can be trusted to resolve.[3]

This challenging quotation makes plain the fact that I should not have written about American identity formation without specifying its meaning for American women—a theme I have approached in my recent Jefferson Lectures (*Dimensions of a New Identity,* 1974). But it makes equally clear that such traditional oversight cannot now be corrected by focusing on the fate of women exclusively, instead of studying the *correspondences* in male and female experience in different historical periods.

To make this systematic will be a gigantic job, since correspondences, in any instance under discussion, can counterpoint sameness as well as difference, mutual complementation as well as irreversible antagonism, compensatory rewards as well as irretrievable sacrifices.

I can touch here on only a few of these correspondences. For example, if the reiteration (by a man) of such a verity as "never-not-a-woman" appears to be shocking, one must consider that a man is never-not-a-man, either. If to this some may respond with conviction the corresponding fact "but that is what he wants to be!" it should be remembered that a boy, under certain conditions, is not even permitted to *think* that he might ever *want* to be not-a-man or not-quite-a-man with all the proud trimmings of manhood in his culture. In America, this has meant to want to be or to make like being a *self-made man,* made in America, an ideal most invigorating and unifying under historical conditions which permitted and demanded a new national identity made out of a multiplicity of immigrant identifications, on a wide continent of expanding opportunities. That eventually a stance developed which maintained, at all cost, the semblance of self-chosen roles, sometimes to the point of caricature—all this only parallels other national stereotypes; and one could, no doubt, relate the unfreedom of women in this as in any culture to the kind of freedom enjoyed by some men and barely lived up to by most. But in America, the emphasis on *choice* in all social roles has become an ideological faith which Janeway seems to feel is violated by any suggestion "that woman's role differs from man's because women are born differently." Her crescendo of complaint can make a man feel quite guilty (somewhat like a mean older brother) for ever having brought up the subject; for such a suggestion, Janeway says, "destroys any value that can be derived from the notion of roles . . . it knocks to the ground the idea of the role as a means of learning, of getting things done, and of communicating by means of behavior . . . it seems a sad waste to throw away such a valuable concept simply to put women back in their place."[4]

If here the self-made role is at stake, together with its time honored method of convincing oneself that the next step is always up to the individual's choice, then, indeed, it must be said that American women have not only enjoyed equal political and economic rights but have also been forced to assume (and learn to flourish as best they could in) roles which were meant, above all, to *complement* the male ideal of self-madeness and mobility in a "Man's world" which thus by and large did dictate "woman's place."

Janeway, as you can see, alternately calls a role a "notion," an "idea," and a "concept." And, indeed, it seems important to differentiate between the role concepts which emerge in a given country (such as Talcott Parsons' in this country) and the role ideology dominant in it. No true role *concept* would ignore the fact that functioning roles, if ever so flamboyant, are tied to certain conditions: a role can only provide leeway within the limits of what bodily constitution can sustain, social structure can make workable, and personality formation can integrate. A role *ideology,* however, would induce persons to convince themselves and each other at all cost that their role choices can surmount all or some of these limitations. Women in America, having for so long lived in and with the ideology of the self-made man without partaking of it except vicariously, may plausibly feel that in this very country of liberty and equality they have in some ways further to go than women in some other democracies, and this not only in the mere acquisition of the right and chance to participate equally in the game of economics and politics. For the very nature of that game, as is obvious in its procedural and verbal habits, excluded all but exceptionally adaptable and insistent women from being "one of the boys." And one may well ask whether women *should* play the game, even if they could, without changing its nature. Even where political and economic liberty provides the belated right to join men in self-made stances cultivated in American history, it will soon become obvious to liberated women that the American male must now learn to adjust to a limitation of *his* aspirations and dreams, namely, where they have led not only to the overexpansion of goals but also to the corruption of means, to the mechanization of motives, and to a restriction of personality potentials.

Equal opportunity for women, then, can only mean the right and the chance to give new meaning and a new kind of competence to (so far) "male" occupations. Only thus can women really influence future work conditions and marriage arrangements, life styles, and forms of communal collaboration. At the end, only a renewal of social creativity can liberate both men and women from reciprocal roles which, in fact, have exploited both.

In my essay, I concentrated on those aspects of the "inner space" which mark its central importance—relatively neglected in psychoanalytic literature—for the woman's positive identity, and more or less unconsciously envied by men. If one then inquires about the fate of those *negative self-images* which the girl inevitably absorbs as she grows up under conditions in which, as Jean Strouse emphasizes, she cannot fail to make the "observation that the qualities associated with having a penis (action, adventure, change, fighting, building, aggressing) are valued more highly than those associated with having a vagina," we must learn to think of them, too, in *correspondences.* This means we must evaluate the negative as well as positive elements in the identity formation of both sexes, and this not only in their importance for the "inner *economy*" of the individual person, as clinical thinking all too easily suggests, but rather as part of the emotional *ecology* shared by persons of both sexes. Where one sex harbors negative images of the other, the resulting mutual defensiveness leads not only to acknowledged antagonisms but also to attempted resolutions in (more or less conscious) *social deals.* Incidentally, I have learned to like this word "deals" because it suggests a reciprocal bartering and bargaining, an apportioning and allocating of rights and duties, and this with varying outcomes, such as square deals, double and fast deals—and, of course, dirty ones. To speak of such deals helps me to relate (or to think we may learn to relate) the inner defenses studied by psychoanalysis and the "political" machinations common in daily life. So let us play with a few correspondences between male and female existence, to see what happens to the negative identities in each.

Readers by now will be fully informed, probably to the point of ennui, of all the proliferations of penis envy. It may provide just relief to remember that males must suffer a corresponding discomfort, namely, the fear of losing or damaging a vulnerable and exposed organ of such magic prowess—and competitiveness. For there are, of course, real and imagined differences in male equipment, too, and a resulting *inter-male* penis envy. But if there is an element of what we call "overcompensation" in men's search for arenas of majestic accomplishment, men are making up not only for a fear of being immobilized and found to be wanting in stature and status but probably also for a deep envy of the maternal capacity to produce what in all its newborn weakness is and remains, after all, the most miraculous human product in the universe: and it breathes!

Boys, of course, have mothers, too, and have internalized mother love with their (or some) milk. But only the girl has it literally in her to become a mother herself. Whether she learned to like or dislike her particular mother and what she stood for, she must transfom her own early dependency into her own style of adult dependability. In whatever context she later chooses to be thus depended on, however, there are always deals permitting her to remain in some respects dependent—and to make others overly so. The boy's and man's developmental job is apt to be quite different and yet reciprocal: namely, to doubly compensate for the pull to infantile dependence and to establish male autonomy while also finding ways of becoming clandestinely dependent on women (and men) in the adult scene. At any rate, to the boy and man, womanhood combines the highest as well as the lowest connotations, so that part of his own negative identity—the "effeminate" traits he must suppress in himself as he becomes a man—is in stark conflict with the maternal ideals he received from and continues to seek in motherly persons. Such conflicts, incidentally, creative men and women are able to resolve on a grand scale because they learn to feel and to depict the otherness usually suppressed; and although they suffer some well-publicized agony on the way, they are sure of universal applause. For ordinary men and women love to witness, at least in the printed page or on stage and screen, the playing out of some bisexual freedom (and even the resulting tragedy) denied to them. Modern life may come to permit a much freer inter-identification of the sexes in everyday life: we will return to this point.

If the little girl, then, feels inferior because of the boy's negative attitude to the woman in himself, she also knows that she is going to be assigned superior roles by a compensatory—if variably ambivalent—valuation given her traditionally in the role of mother and sister, value giver and teacher, lady of the house, mistress, and playmate—all potentially confining roles and yet each endowed with a specific power which forces the man, in turn, to live up to his part. No wonder that, faced with some pained awareness of all this, some individuals of both sexes prefer trying out homosexual or otherwise interchangeable roles. However, without rare gifts or insights, they do not escape transparently analogous role complications.

Does all this express a clinician's habitual pessimism? The point is that these age-old conflicts call not only for liberty in socio-economic matters but also for emotional liberation—whatever comes first. And a specifically psychoanalytic re-evaluation of sexual differences must ask not only what defensive deals individuals make with their own manifold identifications but also what deals men and women have made or are making with each other, in order to complement each other's defenses, and to come to some workable division of roles.

But one must also always allow for the ideal in a given period. Indeed, a strong *ego-ideal* provided by parents, elders, and leaders with consistent values is a prime psychological necessity, and this especially as a counterforce against the (developmentally) more infantile and (collectively) more atavistic *super-ego* which mortgages all choices in life and in history. It is, therefore, especially important to watch, in the sudden shift of awareness brought about by an attempted liberation, the comparative fate of new ideals and of old super-ego pressures. The latter, after all, are always the inner mainstay that helped to secure and to maintain the traditional status quo. Often, it can permit a liberation only at the price of turning old guiltiness into a new and consuming righteousness, and an erstwhile negative self-image into blind accusations against others, now newly appointed enemies. As youth in much of the world captured a great vision of peace (which *has* made a difference), it also vented a moralistic fury on the whole adult generation, and in the name of peace created new and hateful confrontations across the generational border. We are now aware of the moral exhaustion which can follow such moralistic realignment of images. In the women's movement, one can discern a corresponding moralistic projection of erstwhile negative self-images upon men as representing evil oppressors and exploiters. This may be necessary; but it must not replace that cold *self*-appraisal in historical terms which no true revolutionary movement can do without; and in our time such historical self-appraisal must include some "psycho-historical" insight.

Do I mean that women should recognize their masochism in that inner collusion which I have postulated? When it comes to masochism, I again invoke the formula that "only a total configurational approach—somatic, historical, individual—can help us to see single traits in context rather than in isolated and senseless comparison." True, woman is prepared by physical constitution and by tradition to bear some unique discomfort and pain and some special sensitivity associated with her procreative endowment; but this becomes a masochistic love of suffering only when she "exploits pain perversely or vindictively, which means that she steps out of rather than deeper into her female function." So I do not ascribe to a simple female masochism (or, indeed, to a male sadism) the historical fact that woman through the ages has assented to an *accentuation* of the inner space as an over-all confinement and to an *exploitation* of masochistic potentials in roles in which she was "immobilized, infantilized, and prostituted, deriving from it at best what in pathology we call 'secondary gains' of devious dominance."

But so, we must now continue, have men accepted and inflicted on their own kind hardship and slavery, injury and death, for the sake of the defense and conquest of those outer spaces which they needed for their victories. The corresponding exploitation of *their* masochistic as well as sadistic potentials has been hidden only by the imagery of heroism, of duty, and of work. So I should extend to men, also, my suggestion that only a new biocultural history (created by women and men articulately self-observing and communicative) could clarify the evolution of the masochistic potential in our man-made world, and of our overadjustment to it.

The inner psychological division necessary to maintain such a world of accentuated inner and outer spaces as I outlined in my paper harbors, then, negative and positive identity elements in both men and women. It would take more than one essay to specify how all this *develops,* either ontogenetically or historically. But it is clear that where in girls a certain "inner-directedness," and, indeed, a certain self-contained strength and peace, was cultivated, they were also forced to abandon (and sometimes later to overdo) much of the early locomotor vigor and the social and intellectual initiative and intrusiveness which, potentially, girls share with boys; while most boys, in pursuing the male role beyond what came naturally, had to dissimulate and to disavow what receptivity and intuitiveness they shared with girls. How each sex overdeveloped what was given; how each compensated for what it had to deny; how, thus, each managed to get special approbation for a divided self-image; and to what extent "oppressor" and "oppressed" (beyond and behind the overt scene of blatant political and economic exploitation) colluded with each other in both flattering and enslaving each other and themselves—*that* is what I mean by the deals which men and women must learn to study and discuss.

I am asked what effect the relative accessibility of abortion and birth control may have on the identity of women. These two words always strike me as being dangerously negative for an issue which makes mankind face the responsibility for its own life-giving power: "birth control" seems to associate the matter (choose one) with price, pest, or arms control, and "abortion" with the elimination of waste. "Planned parenthood" is better; it emphasizes initiative and thoughtfulness, and assumes that the wish for parenthood exists. And, indeed, among many young adults planned parenthood is becoming a voluntary joint experience of great meaning. For it attempts to give a few children their due, while it applies the energies saved from parental overcommitment to wider communal responsibilities. I have always called the dominant task of adulthood *generativity* rather than procreativity or productivity, because I did want to allow for a variety of activities other than parenthood or the making of goods or money—activities which are, well, "generative" because they contribute to the life of the generations. Here, indeed, is a field of new leadership for young adults privileged enough to have choices and to recognize them.

The ideological leadership of young adulthood also seems all important at this time just because it emphasizes the adventure of new ideals and plays down the grim moralism of old. True, we can see now—now that we can avoid it technologically—how motherhood was used to enslave women by the combined forces of instinctual drive, social tradition, and inner collusion. But, again, the mere attempt to right a wrong by turning it upside down, and to claim that there is no instinctual need for parenthood and that parenthood is *nothing but* social convention and coercion, will not liberate anybody's choices. A choice is free when it can be made with a minimum of denial and of guilt and with a maximum of insight and conviction.

In view of all this, questions regarding birth control, when addressed to *me,* can only mean: If what we have subsumed in the image "inner space" is, indeed, so significant, both as the inner bodily ground of female procreation and as a dominant configuration in self-images and social roles, how can modern woman be aware of this *and* choose to be or not to be a mother if and when it suits her? And we are facing the age-old question all over again, of whether a person or a generation can simply choose to disregard as inconvenient or unnecessary any part of the instinctuality essential to our bodily existence. In other words, on our way to liberate genitality but to restrict procreation, are we about to repress yet another "basic drive"? Or *is* it "yet another"?

Mankind, it is true, has learned to transform sexuality into a source of vital personal expression and into an art of intimate communication. Love has learned to borrow from necessity, and self-fulfillment from a natural mandate. All this—and sublimation—has helped to civilize mankind and has provided much of the fuel for its creativity. But it has also made us frightfully self-indulgent—and I mean indulgent of the single self, licensed by an ideology of individualism.

This is the time, then, to face a simple fact just because it was never more unpopular: not even psychoanalysis, while investigating the power of the libido, has sufficiently accounted for the procreative core of genital activity. In my article, I point to modern investigations of the human sexual response which seem to reveal a vigorous involvement of the inner procreative organs in the erotic excitement due to every kind of sexual act. And, as I have insisted, even the great aim of psychosexual maturation (and of psychoanalytic cure), namely, the "primacy" of genital sexuality, does not, in itself, assure adult maturity, unless genitality, in turn, becomes an intrinsic part of erotic intimacy, and such intimacy, in turn, part of joint generative commitments. In reminding you of this, I realize why both pro- and anti-psychoanalytic liberationists may look at my contributions with mistrust: for how can one be really liberated in one's genitality *and* remain committed to generative tasks?

A theory of the life cycle rather suggests the opposite question: How can one really maintain genital liberation and not come to terms with the deep urges of generativity? In fact, we face here the question (and psychiatry will soon be up against it) whether the need for procreation can be simply ignored or repressed either for the sake of convenience or for that of the most stringent economic considerations, either in the name of "free" sexuality, or in that of fashionable role playing—even as genitality was once unsuccessfully repressed for the sake of, say, Victorian status seeking. I have already given, or implied, my answer: birth control calls for new and combined insights both psychological and political. The hybris of planned progeny calls for a new creedal context: a world order with the provision of an equal opportunity to develop fully for each child chosen to be born, and backed up by the generative commitment of all adults.

Much is being written now by and about the new woman. My impression is that what is published is all too often written by writers, of writers, for writers. I point this out because writers have a shared investment in a specific type of generativity. Fair enough; but one would wish that in matters so close to the core of human life, more writers would include in their awareness the less verbal, or, at any rate, less intellectual masses of women—whether workers or mothers or both—and ask what makes up the sense of existence in their days and nights, their years and stages of life—including their old age. To liberate *them* means to create new and convincing functions and duties as well as rights beyond the mere know-how of birth control.

But to return once more to the men. Considering the brazen way in which, in the essay under discussion, I juxtaposed the inner and the outer space, it will not be too shocking if I now claim that, indeed, *birth control* and *arms control* are two corresponding technological developments which are stirring up both the male and the female self-images in order to combine them in a more all-human identity. As birth control goes to the core of womanhood, the implications of arms control go the core of the male identity, as it has emerged through evolution and history.

Atavistically speaking, armament originates in the extension of the man's strong right arm as the carrier of weapons and tools employed and perfected in all those righteous wars which the human pseudo-species have waged against each other, wars such as no self-respecting species wages against itself in nature. Warfare, to be sure, has become a self-perpetuating institution, which justifies itself on grounds of technical perfection as well as on political grounds as the logical outcome of former wars and of the treaties that ended them forever incompletely. But warfare, as we surely have come to realize, also serves the periodical reaffirmation of uniformed masculinity with its simultaneous function of making an impression on one another, on womankind, and on the enemy. This, too, has served ideals, inventions, and deeds which mankind considers part of its proudest history. In these days, however, we are becoming aware of war's thoughtless exploitation and the extermination of defenseless populations anywhere and the periodical and mandatory sacrifice of a generation of fittest sons which our heroic history has entailed. Today, we suddenly hear Homer in a new key;

and we view with less admiration the sight of full-grown men deploying the age-old stance of armed militancy plus righteousness, from far jungles and coasts to the Wall Streets and Washingtons. But such new awareness, instead of exhausting itself in perpetual protest, must also lead to an assessment of the warrior's evolution from the man-to-man fighting spirit to the impersonal exercise of mechanical warfare and the cold engineering of annihilation. It now seems that arms control comes first, and that the economic and motivational investment in super-weaponry must first be contained in an over-all attitude of mutual deterence which will also deter the deterrer.

This, no doubt, will make, and is already making, specific demands on the male psyche, and must cause grave bewilderment in young men, whose adolescent mores still reflect the anticipation of periodic combat with some people of some other kind. Today, even when there is no war, the availability of small, manageable weapons at home makes it possible for some peculiarly crazed young people to appoint any group and any person to be that "other kind" that must be exterminated. If birth control, then, frees women for a choice of (alternating or simultaneous) roles other than motherhood or spinsterhood, arms control, if understood in all its emotional implications, would permit men to become freer for roles not originally defined by a hunter's or a conqueror's imagery. Parenthetically, the widespread concern with inwardness on the part of many young men may well be pointing to a withdrawal of commitment from a variety of overextended fighting fronts and a new search for anchor in that inner space which we all share.

Which brings me to my conclusion—and I do mean also the conclusion of my previous paper. For (should I apologize?) I still believe what I said there in somewhat creedal terms about the Ultimate residing in the Immediate. But I must apply this now, of course, to both sexes. To put a fuller existence above uncontrolled parenthood, and planned peace above unrestricted war, would call not only for new inventions but also for the redirection of much of human instinctuality. A more conscious and concerted sublimation of generativity from generation to generation cannot rely on the mere avoidance, prohibition, or inhibition of either careless procreation or thoughtless violence. Mankind needs a guiding vision. And fate usually makes it only too clear what the next vision *must* be: today, it must be a world order which would permit all children chosen to be born to develop to an adulthood that may learn to humanize its inventions—experientially as well as technologically. I cannot see how such an adulthood could evolve except through an equal involvement of women and of their special modes of experience in the over-all planning and governing so far monopolized by men.

NOTES

1. Erik H. Erikson, "Womanhood and the Inner Space," in *Identity: Youth and Crisis* (New York: Norton, 1968).
2. Elizabeth Janeway, *Man's World Woman's Place* (New York: Morrow, 1971), p. 8.
3. Ibid., p. 93.
4. Ibid.

PART 3

Biology and Behavior

Conception begins the process of sexual differentiation which culminates in a firmly established gender identity, the knowledge of oneself as a member of one sex and not the other. The development of gender identity is normally contingent upon the body, its form and its functions. For woman, the form and functions of her body have always caused her to be viewed as special, have determined her particular place, her roles, the kinds of explanations made for her, and her fate in the society. Explanatory concepts, such as penis envy and inner space, have been derived from the anatomy of the female body, and attributes of personality, such as emotional, sensitive, and nurturant, have been identified directly with female reproductive functions.

Questions about the relationship between soma and psyche have become political since women have defined themselves as members of a class subject to demeaning and restrictive discrimination on the basis of their sex. Women share a common biology, and such biological events as menstruation and pregnancy are important to them. But what are the influences of biology on behavior? Do biological events such as the menstrual cycle, pregnancy, and the menopause and their associated hormonal changes affect women in such remarkable ways that their social destinies must inevitably be different from those of men? Or are the mystique and the meanings assigned to woman's body potent rationalizations for maintaining old oppressions?

The papers presented here look at some of the research in this area and offer some perspectives for evaluating it. Ruth Bleier is especially interested in the brain and its regulatory effect on the endocrine system, including the ovaries and its hormones. She also examines the evidence for sexual differentiation of the brain, and for the effects of androgen on mating and aggressive behavior. Most valuable is her discussion of the methodological problems in such research and her warning of the assumptions which guide the inquiries and the interpretations of the data. Unlike research in the physical sciences, in which theories and interpretations do not effect the phenomena under investigation, research in the behavioral sciences, Bleier points out, may not only rest on biased concepts and assumptions but may give rise to interpretations which support those very biases. The literature on "masculine" aggression and "feminine" passivity is cited to show how evidence can be distorted to fit social and psychiatric myths.

Menstruation and its attendant phenomena have always been invested with great significance and with special meanings for both women and men. Perhaps more than any other of the biological events of woman's body, the menstrual cycle has been held to have important affects on woman's behavior, affects which would diminish her functional abilities, restrict her activities, and disrupt her emotional equilibrium. Especially during the premenstruum, females are expected to manifest a variety of symptoms which are incapacitating to some degree. Mary Parlee reviewed the research in "The Premenstrual Syndrome" and found grounds for criticizing the scientific status of such a hypothesized syndrome. While a great many women do report behavioral and other changes in the few days before the onset of the menses, such symptoms are not consistent for groups of women or even for one woman from month to month. Since the research has not yet demonstrated a definable syndrome, we can conclude that generalizations and policies about women based on the menstrual cycle are not warranted.

More important than the biological events themselves are the meanings with which they are invested in a given culture. In "The Symbolic Significance of Menstruation and the Menopause," Vieda Skultans presents an example of research on such meanings among middle-aged women in a village in Wales. In structured interviews women related their life histories, their medical histories, attitudes toward their husbands, and their beliefs and reactions concerning menstruation and menopause. Skultans found that the women fell into two categories: those who saw the menses as cleansing, and wanted to bleed as much as possible for as long as possible, and those who believed that the loss of blood was damaging to their health and wanted to cease menstruating as early as possible. Skultans also provides a fascinating analysis of the language the women used to talk about menstruation and menopause, and its relation to their sociosexual roles. Menopause, especially, may be understood as a *rite de passage,* whereby the woman passes from a reproductive to a nonreproductive role.

Conclusions about the affects of woman's biology on her behavior are not possible at the present time, although contemporary research and theory substantially support the more important contributions of environment and experience. As Bleier has said, a basic scientific principle is involved: "The effect of one variable [biology] cannot be measured when other variables are uncontrolled and even undefined. To what degree biology determines behavior can never be known until clearly existing cultural determinants are controlled."

Brain, Body, and Behavior

Ruth H. Bleier

In a sense, the brain serves as the link among all the topics in this book; it is, after all, the organ of our consciousness. With it we perceive the external world, store our perceptions in the form of memory, which we call experience and learning, and then use this body of experience to determine our unique responses to our perceptions of the external world. The brain thus becomes the single most potent force in our development, our self-conception, our self-expression; and it is also the instrument for the construction and transmission of the body of ideas and practices that constitute our culture.

The basic structure and organization as well as mechanisms of functioning are the same for brains of all vertebrate species, though certain areas subserving particular functions are more highly developed in certain species: touch in raccoons, vision-flight coordination in birds, and so forth.

The part of the brain that, in its organizational development and volume, distinguishes human beings from other species is the cortex, the outer surface layers. In all animals, the cortex receives and transforms into conscious perceptions the various modalities of stimuli from the external world—visual, auditory, tactile, olfactory, gustatory. In an animal with a smooth-surfaced brain, such as the rabbit, almost the entire cortex is involved in receiving such stimuli; thus, most of the cortex constitutes *primary receiving areas.* The intricately and deeply folded pattern of the human cortex provides a larger volume and area of cortex relative to the rest of the brain than that of other animals, and the primary receiving areas constitute considerably less than half of the total cortex. The rest of the cortex is involved in a further processing of the primary information it receives—storing perceptions and experiences (memory and learning) and associating them with other previous and ongoing perceptions and experiences. All of these together determine one's intellectual, emotional, and motor responses to a stimulus.

These *association areas* provide the substrate for the infinite variety of responses of humans (and, to a lesser degree, other primates) to a particular stimulus as contrasted with the relatively stereotypic nature of responses of animals with a less complex cortex. This presents an important paradox. Humanity in general manifests a variety of responses to a given stimulus. But as individuals, with the cortical capacity for creative, novel, variegated responses, we become bound and imprisoned by stereotypic responses to certain sets of stimuli (our culture) even while our creativity is responsible for the very existence of a culture. Personal liberation and creativity require freeing oneself from stereotyped responses, which are in any case unworthy of our cerebral cortex.

The Hypothalamus and Cycles

The hypothalamus, a part of the brain that particularly concerns us here, does not participate in higher intellectual functions. It is, however, concerned with functions essential to the survival of the individual and the species: feeding and drinking behavior, body-temperature regulation, blood pressure and heart rate, mating behavior and reproduction. There is another important difference between the hypothalamus and the rest of the brain: It functions in part like an endocrine gland. Its nerve cells (neurons) are influenced not only by impulses from other nerve cells like the rest of the brain but also directly by hormones in the body—ovarian, testicular, thyroid, adrenal, and pituitary. This fact is of significance in the influence of the hypothalamus on certain behavioral and physiological sex differences. In addition, neurons of the hypothalamus manufacture hormones that regulate the hormonal output of the "master" endocrine gland, the pituitary.

The hypothalamus thus regulates the various functions of the pituitary gland, which is attached to the hypothalamus and, through it, the ovaries as well as other endocrine glands. The pituitary secretes two hormones that regulate cyclic activity of the ovaries: follicle stimulating hormone (FSH) and luteinizing hormone (LH). The hypothalamus secretes an FSH-releasing factor (FSH-RF) and an LH-releasing factor (LH-RF). At a particular point near the beginning of a normal human female's 28-day menstrual cycle, the hypothalamus begins to increase its production of FSH-RF, causing the pituitary to release increasing amounts of FSH, which in turn results in the growth and maturation of one ovarian egg and its envelope, the follicle. The follicle produces the hormone estrogen, which has two important effects on the hypothalamus. As the blood level of estrogen rises, it *suppresses* hypothalamic production of FSH-RF (negative feedback) and *stimulates* hypothalamic production of LH-RF (positive feedback). The surge of LH-RF on approximately the fourteenth day of the cycle causes the mature egg to erupt from its follicle (ovulation). The follicle then begins to produce the hormone progesterone, which *suppresses* hypothalamic production of LH-RF and of FSH-RF. The interplay of these opposing effects at different phases of the 28-day period results in menstrual cyclicity in females.

The purpose and effect of the "pill," a combination of estrogen and progesterone, is precisely to disrupt this delicately balanced mechanism in order to prevent ovulation. What the long-term effects may be of such hormonal manipulation of neuronal function are unknown. This and other unknown as well as known hazards require greater caution than is now generally exercised in the prescribing and taking of contraceptive pills.

The Hypothalamus and Sexual Differentiation

In contrast to females, in males there is a fairly constant level of pituitary production of LH having a continual effect on the testicular cells that produce the male androgenic hormone testosterone, although there is evidence in several species to suggest cyclic fluctuations of sex hormone levels in males also (Kihlstrom 1971). Studies have shown that cyclicity of sex hormone production is regulated by the hypothalamus. Studies in rats have suggested to some investigators that the differentiation of hypothalamic mechanisms regulating cyclicity appears to be determined by the presence or absence of androgens in the fetus or newborn. They have concluded that in the absence of androgens, a cycling type of hypothalamus develops; if androgen is present, a noncycling type results (Levine 1971). Thus, if a male rat is castrated at birth, his pattern of pituitary release of FSH-LH at maturity is cyclic. Ovarian transplants into such a male undergo cyclic ovulation (Harris 1964). If a newborn female rat is given a single injection of testosterone in the newborn period, she will not have cyclic ovaluation at maturity (Harris and Levine 1965). Control studies have been done to eliminate both the pituitary and the gonads (ovaries and testes) as the organs responsible for regulation of cyclicity. It is clear, however, as Johnson (1972) emphasizes, that this scheme of androgen-dependent sexual differentiation of the brain is oversimplified and that much critical data have yet to be acquired before an adequate theory can be developed. Furthermore, recent work indicates that results in rodents may not apply to primates since all attempts thus far to demonstrate such an organizing or developmental effect of androgens on the primate hypothalamus have been unsuccessful (Karsch et al. 1973).

The Hypothalamus and Mating Behavior

Experiments have also been interpreted as demonstrating that the presence or absence of androgenic effect on the hypothalamus of the newborn or fetal rat (and monkey) determines the predominant pattern of mating behavior at maturity. (For a review of this complex field of research, hormonal effects on brain development and behavior, see Davidson and Levine 1972.)

The female rat comes into heat or estrus at the phase of her five-day cycle when estrogen and progesterone are in a particular balance. At this time her stereotyped behavior pattern is to assume the lordotic posture (elevation of the rump) in the presence of mature males. The male, being acyclic, is stimulated by the presence of the estrous female (her odor and her presentation) to his sterotyped mating behavior which is to mount and attempt intromission. Neither will perform these behaviors in the absence of their own or administered sex hormones. Both sexes will, however, normally also exhibit some sexual activity which is characteristic of that of the opposite sex; i.e., females sometimes mount and males are sometimes mounted. Early experiments produced some expected results. They showed that a male rat, castrated *in adulthood* and given estrogen, will not exhibit lordosis. The sexual behavior of a male rat castrated *at birth* and given estrogen as an adult is, however, indistinguishable from that of a normal female; indistinguishable not only to the human observer but to other male rats who respond to him as to an estrous female (Levine 1971). If a newborn uncastrated female rat is given an injection of testosterone, her female pattern of sexual behavior ("receptivity") as an adult is abolished, even following injections of estrogen and progesterone. Her behavior following injections of androgens as an adult resembles that of a male with increased mounting and attempts at intromission (Harris and Levine 1965).

Results of other studies, however, exploring unanticipated (i.e., heterotypical or unstereotyped) hormonal effects, confound this simple scheme. Beach (1942) found that the lordosis response was enhanced in females castrated and given *testosterone* prepuberally. Other workers have demonstrated that estrogen given to newborn female rats abolishes the lordosis response in the mature animal (Levine and Mullins 1964) and increases her mounting activity with estrous females (Sodersten 1972).

The literature on animal studies is vast and has been recently reviewed by Money and Ehrhardt (1971, 1972), who summarize their conclusions concerning animal data thus:

> Experimental animal studies of the influence of prenatally or neonatally administered sex hormones on the subsequent manifestations of sexual behavior implicate an organizing action of sex hormones and related substances on the brain, probably the region of the hypothalamus. The rule would appear to be that female-male bipotentiality applies initially prior to the influence of any sex hormone in the course of brain development. Bipotentiality would appear to persist when the early hormonal environment is feminine, so that either the feminine or the masculine component of mating behavior can be elicited in adulthood, dependent, among other things, on whether the eliciting hormone is estrogen or androgen. Bipotentiality is resolved in favor of unipolar masculinity of mating behavior if the early hormonal influence at the critical differentiating period is androgenic. The feminine component is then inhibited. Once this is accomplished, the feminine component will, in many, though perhaps not in all species, be elicited only under special conditions, for example, direct brain stimulation, or not at all. In the course of normal differentiation, the initial completeness of feminine potential varies across species. Thus it is more complete in the rat than the hamster. In man it is probably not

very complete, and is perhaps individually variable, as well. (Money and Ehrhardt 1971).

Implications of Animal Studies for Human Behavior

What might be the implications of these studies for humans and their patterns of sexual activity and sex identity? A number of problems make any generalizations about animal and especially human behavior based on hormone studies risky at this time: First, this field of research is new and many critical experiments have not been done. Second, the action of a given hormone may vary with the species of animal used, the dosage, and the timing of administration or withdrawal. Third, ovaries produce *androgens* in addition to estrogens and testes produce *estrobens* in addition to androgens, and the adrenal cortex of both sexes produces both hormones during fetal and postnatal life. In addition, fetuses of both sexes are exposed throughout pregnancy to estrogens and high levels of progesterone from the maternal ovaries and placenta. Thus, what physiological levels of any of these compounds may be present at various stages of development are quite unknown. Fourth, there is a *family* of androgens and a *family* of estrogens being produced. All the forms are closely related structurally or chemically both within and between the two families and are easily transformed metabolically one into the other in both sexes. To what degree this is constantly occurring is also unknown. Fifth, a recent significant finding in all species thus far studied, including primates, is that the brain *itself* converts androgens to estrogens (Ryan et al. 1972). For other reasons also, such as the fact that estrogen rather than androgen is localized in the nucleus of the cell, this finding raises the possibility that estrogen is the metabolic form in which these compounds act at their target sites, such as the brain.

There are obvious and clear-cut physical differences between the sexes that are related to different levels of estrogens and androgens. It is nonetheless interesting to speculate about the possibility that there are in the course of development relative and shifting rather than absolute blood levels of both types of hormones and that physical development and some aspects of sexual behavior may be to some degree influenced not only by genetic and cultural factors, but also be relative levels of hormones in the developing individual.

The examination of human behavior is further complicated by the absence of known stereotyped patterns of sexual activity which can be used as a measure of female- or male-type, such as lordosis and mounting frequency in animals.

Sexual expression and sex identity for humans occur within an individual and cultural as well as a biologically defined context. In the adult of both sexes, either estrogen or androgen may increase libido. But people are not dependent on sex hormones as are animals since, following removal of the ovaries or testes, most men and women continue the same pattern of sexual activity as that prior to removal. Furthermore, it is clear that women are not tied to their cycle phase as are other mammalian species.

Of overriding importance is the presence of an adequate stimulus. A multitude of cultural, experiential, and perceptual factors will determine at any moment whether a woman wishes to and does indeed engage in sexual activity. Similarly such factors will determine the object of sexual interest—which person and which sex. It goes without saying that all our social and legal institutions, mores, and ideologies approve and support only monogamous heterosexual relationships. And this cultural conditioning to one's sex role and sex identity begins within months after birth.

It is also probable that most deviations from the expected norm are themselves the result of a complex of cultural and experiental factors that are unique for each individual. Observations of animals in which cultural influences play an insignificant role make one wonder how humans might behave were cultural restraints removed. Is it possible that bisexuality is a biologic norm and heterosexuality an anatomic convenience that is, to be sure, enhanced as the dominant pattern by certain stimuli—odors or colors in certain species and by cultural conditioning in humans?

The power of one's immediate cultural environment or social interactions is demonstrated by studies of hermaphrodites (Money 1970). These indicate that psychosexual differentiation and sex identity are independent of genetic and hormonal sex (and also, therefore, of appearance of external genitalia). Gender identity is, rather, congruent with sex assignment; i.e., the person sees her/himself as belonging to the sex of assignment (usually by parents) and rearing.

Relationship between Biology and Behavior: Conceptual and Methodological Problems

It is clearly for women to begin to examine every field of knowledge for its set of assumptions and premises since every field has been developed and dominated by men. Problems and issues are thus often defined from a particular perspective with a particular set of biases or blindnesses.

The question, for example, of the relationship between biology and behavior is a most difficult one because too little is known and too much emotion is invested. There are, of course, measurable biological and measurable psychological and behavioral differences (viewed statistically) between men and women. The serious logical fallacy often made, however, is to assume that there is a necessary *causal* relationship between these differences; for example between androgen and "aggressiveness." For this assumption there is no convincing evidence whatsoever in humans, and to use animal data as evidence that particular psychological or behavioral sex differences in humans are caused by particular *biological* sex differences is to ignore a fact that in other contexts is recognized to be of supreme importance: that humans are *qualitatively* different from all other animals. They are different precisely because of their brain and their culture which is the unique product of that brain. Individual social behavior is, in turn, formed by and expressed within the context of that individual's culture and is, in fact, nonexistent without it.

As described earlier, while neuronal structures and mechanisms in the hypothalamus and the rest of the brain of rats, cats, and so on, are retained in primates, the critical development in the latter, especially in humans, is in the growth and organization of the cerebral cortex. Cortical mechanisms, specifically as they are manifested in their most dramatic products—learning and culture—come to be dominant as determinants of human behavior, as contrasted with the biologically based stereotyped behavior of most other animals.

One cannot, for example, talk about "maternal instinct" as a biological fact or product as long as every baby girl is given a baby doll before she can walk or talk, as long as every little girl has to read books about what *girls* do and what *boys* do, as long as little girls see their mothers and other women being only mothers. In short, one cannot begin to assess the existence of such an "instinct" until society ceases to prescribe the maternal or the familial as the sole valid, useful, acceptable, and normal role for women.

Or take the matter of intelligence. Any aspect of human behavior, whether a pathological complex such as schizophrenia or tuberculosis, or a normal variant such as intelligence, manual dexterity, athletic ability, or mathematical skill, is determined by the interaction between that individual's biological state (prenatally and throughout postnatal life) and her environment, including her unique history of accumulated experiences. Of overriding importance as determinants of specific behavioral reactions of individuals are, however, the latter—her culture or tradition, her socialization, her experiences. That this is true is implicit in the fact that it is precisely culture or the accumulated effect of individual and social experience that sets human behavior apart from that of every other species.

There is no evidence whatsover that women are not as intelligent or as creative as men, given the fact that they are (although in tiny numbers) in fields for which they have both been allowed to be educated only during the last fifty to a hundred years. Women have not only made it but have been outstanding in every field once considered exclusively male—mathematics, physics (including Nobel laureates), business, banking, economics, mechanical and electrical and electronic engineering, philosophy, and so on. That is, there are women who excel in abstract thinking, mathematical thinking, hard-headed business; women who are aggressive, independent, and creative. As with blacks and the periodic controversy over their intelligence as compared with whites, so long as there are women or blacks who can and do accomplish all the things that men or whites do, then it is clear that these characteristics are not outside the biological capabilities of the group. Therefore, one must look to the effects of culture or characteristics that are peculiarly human and peculiarly cultural. Intelligence, aggressiveness, and the like, are, after all, developed and manifested only within a social and cultural context.

Psychological tests showing sex differences in children in certain concepts, e.g., those involving spatial perception, should be used not as reflections of *innate* characteristics but as indices of the *plasticity* of the human mind as it is affected and molded by social attitudes and practices.

A basic scientific principle is involved here. The effect of one variable cannot be measured when other variables are uncontrolled and even undefined. To what degree biology determines behavior can never be known until clearly existing cultural determinants are controlled.

Another serious methodological error obstructs some scientific approaches to truth. Concepts and terms that embody certain social biases, stereotypes, and assumptions are used to interpret data observed, for example, by experimental psychologists or by psychiatrists. These interpretations and conclusions are then used as evidence to support and "prove" those very stereotypes and assumptions.

Biases, incorrect assumptions, faulty interpretations, erroneous conclusions are not unknown in any field or science, even one so seemingly objective as anatomy. These may even approach fad proportions; but sooner or later the truth will emerge and generally, little except time has been lost and little damage done. This is because in the biological or physical sciences, the behavior or structure or function of the object of study is not changed one whit by all the scientific nonsense that might be said about them. Einstein's theory, whether right or wrong, would have no effect whatsoever upon the movement of celestial bodies. In the behavioral sciences, however, theories and pronouncements by "experts" have potentially a very real effect upon the phenomena observed. Here the objects studied—people—are conscious and aware, and theories interpreting their character and behavior affect that behavior often in destructive and self-fulfilling ways.

Women are "shown" (either directly or by extrapolation from animal studies) to be passive or instinctively maternal or incapable of abstract thought or lacking in libido. These characteristics then constitute the stamp of approval for feminine normality. The pressure is there, subtle or blatant, unremitting and nearly inescapable except for those who dare to be viewed as deviant: Either behave in the way (pseudo)science has described as normal and healthy for your sex; or be suspect and, consequently, guilty, insecure, and unable to acknowledge your own needs, goals, or abilities.

Thus, having a female body invites a set of assumptions—about one's mind, intelligence, capabilities, skills, motives, intentions, emotions, and goals—and worst of all, a set of behavior patterns: The woman graduate student is asked, "What's a good-looking girl like you doing in physics?" The woman student wanting to go into botany and ecological research is told she ought to be a journalist instead. Nursing is recommended to the woman premed since it is "less arduous" and she'll get married anyhow. Untold numbers of women are daily being channeled from fields of their choice to those that men traditionally have reserved for them.

Aggressiveness as Conceptual Problem

One example of such a biased concept is *aggressiveness,* a word charged with value—a different value for men and for women—and applied anthropomorphically to the interpretation of animal behavior. In our culture aggressiveness in men is desirable; it is rewarded and encouraged in business, sports, and war, and is considered a male characteristic. Aggressiveness in women is, however, a social liability; it is considered unattractive, undesirable, embarrassing, and downright unfeminine. Passivity is thus a feminine characteristic. What is perhaps even more insidious is an implication that aggressiveness includes such characteristics as independence of mind, decisiveness, imagination—all, therefore, masculine qualities.

The observation is made that male rats in a cage fight; females do not. When given an electric shock, the male rats fight more; the females do not.

Aha! Now we have more proof that males *are* naturally aggressive. What about the equally obvious (or ridiculous?) conclusion that females must be more intelligent since fighting each other is clearly an inappropriate response to being shocked by some human being?

Starting, presumably, with the assumption that "aggressiveness" is an androgen-linked male characteristic, early studies demonstrated that male rats castrated at birth were less "aggressive" (i.e., fought less) as adults (Conner and Levine 1969) and that female mice given androgen at birth were more "aggressive" following androgen injections as adults (Edwards 1969). The fact seems to be little known that a subsequent study (Edwards and Herndon 1970) showed that newborn female mice given *estrogen* at birth also fought more as adults.

Strangely enough, the same freedom and ease with which the generalization is made linking aggressiveness with masculinity are not exercised in interpreting data that have possible implications for feminine characteristics that do not fit the stereotype. In open-field tests, female rats exhibit greater exploratory activity and less defecation. I have yet to see the conclusion that females, then, are more curious, inquisitive, adventuresome, and since they defecate less, less anxious.

Nor, of course, should such conclusions be drawn any more than those concerning aggressiveness. One of the problems is conceptual. *Aggressiveness* is clearly a behavioral complex, not a sex-linked gene. The behavioral response of *fighting* or *attack* is not synonymous with *aggressiveness.* Fighting behavior can and will be elicited in any species or sex given the appropriate stimulus. A female rabbit may be ferocious in defense of her young. Female hamsters, *which are larger than males,* fight more. Odors, especially those of the estrous female, will elicit fighting in male rats. The fact that androgen may prove to be an important element in activating the olfactory (smelling) mechanisms of male rats in response to an estrous female (resulting in their fighting each other) will have obvious implications for species survival mechanisms rather than for a universal masculine characteristic of aggressiveness.

Female Sexuality

The other side of "masculine aggressiveness" is, of course, "feminine passivity and receptivity" and the associated social and psychiatric myths that have become established concerning women's sexuality. It is interesting that the concept of feminine sexual passivity should have arisen at all with so little evidence. Among animals, it is the male who is passive until an estrous female displays her presence by odor, color, posture, and so on. Serious studies of human behavior indicate what women have long known or suspected—that their libido starts as young as, and lasts longer than, that of men. Furthermore, women are capable of (and probably usually prefer) several orgasms, particularly if they have escaped the legislated nonsense of the compulsory vaginal orgasm (Sherfey 1966).

Sherfey (1966) develops a convincing hypothesis about the suppression of female sexuality. "In every culture studied, the crucial transition from the nomadic, hunting, and food-gathering economy to a settled, agricultural existence was the beginning of family life, modern civilization, and civilized man. . . . With the domestication of animals and the agricultural revolution, for the first time in all time, the survival of species lay in the extended family with its private property, kinship lineages, inheritance laws, social ordinances, and, most significantly, many surviving children. . . . Many factors have been advanced to explain the rise of the patriarchal, usually polygynous, system and its concomitant ruthless subjugation of female sexuality (which necessarily subjugated her entire emotional and intellectual life). However, if the conclusions reached here are true, it is conceivable that the *forceful* suppression of women's inordinate sexual demands was a prerequisite to the dawn of every modern civilization and almost every living culture."

The suggestion is made by Sherfey that women for physiological reasons are and always have been sexually insatiable, unlike men. With the accumulation of private property, she implies, it was necessary for men, who became the producers in settled agricultural economies, to ensure that their wealth be passed on only to their own sons. For this reason, the man had to suppress the ebullient sexuality of the bearer of his children lest she present him with the sons of other men. The protection of lineages for the inheritance of private property was considered by Engels (1970) also to be a crucial factor in the origin of the family (i.e., institutionalized monogamy) and state.

Recent studies (at this writing, still in press; see Kolata 1974) of the !Kung people provide important evidence that the transition from a food gathering–hunting economy to a settled agricultural mode was critical to the change in women's status from one of equality. Nomadic hunters and gatherers for the past 11,000 years in the Kalahari Desert, the !Kung have begun in the last decade to settle in agrarian villages near the Bantus; less than 5 percent are still nomads.

Formerly the women provided at least half the food consumed, and child care and food preparation were shared by men and women. Since settling into agrarian villages, the men clear the fields and tend the cattle while the women perform domestic chores. The channeling of skills is further accentuated by the fact that the men, since they tend the cattle of the Bantus, learn their language; consequently, the men are the ones who conduct business with the Bantus. Along with the loss of economic status by women, presumed biological effects of dietary changes are reinforcing their domestication through a marked increase in their fertility and consequent frequency of pregnancy.

While it may indeed be the case that the accumulation of private property and the establishment (by men) of institutions and suppressive mores to protect their property were, as Sherfey states, "a prerequisite to the dawn of every modern civilization," it is important to acknowledge that they are only modern civilizations as we know them to be, capitalist and imperialist, based upon the oppression by one class of all other classes. The implication is clear from the analyses of both Engels and Sherfey that sexual oppression, with men ruling women, may well have been the original form of class oppression and a model and training ground for all subsequent forms.

That "civilization" may indeed have evolved in that way hardly precludes all other possible forms nor justifies the continuation of ideologies and institutions that limit potential and destroy the lives of one group in the interests of another.

Society, aided by some psychiatric theories and practice, has established passivity and receptivity as the norm for feminine sexual and other behavior. If she deviates sexually, she is called promiscuous or a nymphomaniac; if she deviates socially, she is called aggressive and castrating. A norm is set which is social, *not* biological; and the woman who deviates is stigmatized. Stereotypes are thus constructed which serve the purpose of maintaining the status quo in our homes and professions.

The myths of female passivity have served well to keep the little woman back at the ranch and busy at the range and, until recently, quietly guilty about the restiveness she feels under a variety of restraints imposed upon her being. The findings of Masters and Johnson (1966) ought to explode the myths about female sexuality; the assertive self-determination of women themselves will explode the remaining myths of biological inferiority.

REFERENCES

BEACH, F. S. "Male and Female Mating Behavior in Prepuberally Castrated Female Rats Treated with Androgen." *Endocrinology* 31 (1942): 672–78.

CONNER, R. L., AND LEVINE, S. "Hormonal Influences on Aggressive Behavior." In *Aggressive Behaviour,* edited by S. Garattini and E. B. Sigg. Amsterdam: Excerpta Med., 1969. Pp. 150–63.

DAVIDSON, J. M., AND LEVINE, S. "Endocrine Regulation of Behavior." *Annual Review of Physiology* 34 (1972): 375–408.

EDWARDS, D. A. "Early Androgen Stimulation and Aggressive Behavior in Male and Female Mice." *Physiology and Behavior* 4 (1969): 333–38.

EDWARDS, D. A., AND HERNDON, J. "Neonatal Estrogen Stimulation and Aggressive Behavior in Female Mice." *Physiology and Behavior* 5 (1970): 993–95.

ENGELS, F. *The Origin of the Family, Private Property and the State* (1891). New York: International Publishers, 1970.

HARRIS, G. W. "Sex Hormones, Brain Development and Brain Function." *Endocrinology* 75 (1964): 627–48.

HARRIS, G. W., AND LEVINE, S. "Sexual Differentiation of the Brain and Its Experimental Control." *Journal of Physiology* 181 (1965): 379–400.

JOHNSON, D. C. "Sexual Differentiation of Gonadotropic Patterns." *American Zoologist* 12 (1972): 193–205.

KARSCH, F. J.; DIERSCHKE, D. J.; AND KNOBIL, E. "Sexual Differentiation of Pituitary Function: Apparent Difference between Primates and Rodents." *Science* 179 (1973): 484–86.

KIHLSTROM, J. E. "A Male Sexual Cycle." In *Current Problems in Fertility,* edited by A. Ingleman-Sundberg and N. O. Lunell. New York: Plenum Press, 1971. Pp. 50–54.

KOLATA, G. B. "!Kung Hunter-Gatherers: Feminism, Diet, and Birth Control." *Science* 185 (1974): 932–34.

LEVINE, S. "Sexual Differentiation: The Development of Maleness and Femaleness." *California Medicine* 114 (1971): 12–17.

LEVINE, S., AND MULLINS, R. "Estrogen Administered Neonatally Affects Adult Sexual Behavior in Male and Female Rats." *Science* 144 (1964): 185–87.

MASTERS, W. H., AND JOHNSON, V. E. *Human Sexual Response.* Boston: Little, Brown, 1966.

MONEY, J. "Sexual Dimorphism and Homosexual Gender Identity. *Psychological Bulletin* 74 (1970): 425–40.

MONEY, J., AND EHRHARDT, A. A. "Fetal Hormones and the Brain: Effect on Sexual Dimorphism of Behavior—A Review." *Archives of Sexual Behavior* 1 (1971): 241–62.

MONEY, J., AND EHRHARDT, A. A. *Man and Woman, Boy and Girl.* Baltimore, Md.: Johns Hopkins Press, 1972.

RYAN, K. J.; NAFTOLIN, F.; REDDY, V.; FLORES, F.; AND PETRO, Z. "Estrogen Formation in the Brain." *American Journal of Obstetrics and Gynecology* 114 (1972): 454–60.

SHERFEY, M. J. *The Nature and Evolution of Female Sexuality.* New York: Random House, 1966.

SODERSTEN, P. "Mounting Behavior in the Female Rat during the Estrous Cycle, after Ovariectomy, and after Estrogen or Testosterone Administration." *Hormones and Behavior* 3 (1972): 307–20.

The Premenstrual Syndrome

Mary Brown Parlee

Psychological studies of the premenstrual syndrome are discussed in four methodological categories: (a) *studies reporting a positive correlation between specific behavioral acts and phase of the menstrual cycle;* (b) *those using retrospective questionnaires concerning symptom and mood changes;* (c) *studies involving day-to-day (self-) ratings of various behaviors, symptoms, and moods; and* (d) *thematic analyses of verbal material gathered in an unstructured situation throughout the cycle. The scientific status of the hypothesis of a premenstrual syndrome is considered, together with more general topics—in particular the question of control groups, the choice of a base line for describing changes in behavior, and the difficulties involved in physiological explanations of psychological phenomena. Brief consideration is given to publication practices of psychological journals as they affect the kind of scientific information available on behavioral changes associated with the menstrual cycle.*

Considerable biological evidence is now available to support Seward's (1934) observation that "Rhythm is a universal characteristic of natural phenomena [p. 153]." In human beings, circadian rhythms have been reported to exist in a variety of processes including cell division, adrenal cortical activity, and glucose tolerance, as well as in sleeping and waking, pain tolerance, and susceptibility to asthmatic attacks (Luce, 1970). Cyclic changes with periods of greater than 24 hours are also well established (Richter, 1968). One rhythm that has been studied in detail is the menstrual cycle of the human female.

Southam and Gonzaga (1965) extensively reviewed studies of physiological changes occurring throughout the menstrual cycle. While a full specification of the neuroendocrine mechanisms controlling menstruation depends upon the development of appropriate techniques (e.g., Neill, Johansson, Datta, & Knobil, 1967), these mechanisms are understood in rough outline and will no doubt eventually provide explanations for the various bodily changes observed. Of more interest to the psychologist, however, are the numerous reports of behavioral changes associated with the menstrual cycle. Such studies would seem to be important for at least two

"The Premenstrual Syndrome" by Mary Brown Parlee. *Psychological Bulletin,* 83, 6 (1973), 454–465.

reasons, the first being that psychological changes accompanying the menstrual cycle are phenomenologically significant to many women and are thus an appropriate topic for psychological research. The second reason, however, lies not in their contribution to the body of scientific knowledge, but in the fact that they raise methodological and theoretical issues which have implications for the study of other psychological phenomena as well. The purpose of the present article is to consider the literature on those psychological changes associated with the menstrual cycle which have been called the premenstrual syndrome(s) (Dalton, 1964; Moos, 1968) or premenstrual tension (Frank, 1931; Rees, 1953a). Another major topic in the study of behavioral changes accompanying the menstrual cycle—fluctuations in sexual behavior—will not be included here; this literature has been reviewed by Kane, Lipton, and Ewing (1969).

The Premenstrual Syndrome: Four Types of Studies

Correlational Data

The syndrome first described by Frank (1931) as a premenstrual feeling of "indescribable tension," irritability, and "a desire to find relief by foolish and ill-considered actions [p. 1054]" has been studied in a variety of ways, one of which is simply to look for correlations between the phase of the menstrual cycle and statistical data on the occurrence of specific, well-defined behaviors. Correlations have been reported, for example, between the premenstrual or menstrual phase of the cycle and commission of violent crimes (Cooke, 1945; Dalton, 1961; Morton, Additon, Addison, Hunt, & Sullivan, 1953; Ribeiro, 1962), death from accident or suicide (MacKinnon & MacKinnon, 1956; Mandell & Mandell, 1967), accidents (Dalton, 1960b), admission to a hospital with acute psychiatric illness (Dalton, 1959; Janowsky, Gorney, Castelnuovo-Tedesco, & Stone, 1969), taking a child to a medical clinic (Dalton, 1966), and loss of control of aircraft (Whitehead, 1934). Such data were summarized by Dalton (1964) who has been a major contributor in this area of research.

In statistical studies, the behavioral act—when considered as one term of the correlation—is readily identifiable; if either occurs (and often becomes part of a public record) or it does not. It is usually the case that the other term of the correlation—the phase of the menstrual cycle—is also objectively determined by the investigators either by questioning the women shortly after the behavioral event (Dalton) or by basal body temperature (Altman, Knowles, & Bull, 1941; Ivey & Bardwick, 1968), vaginal smears (Benedek & Rubenstein, 1939a, 1939b), or data from autopsies (MacKinnon & MacKinnon, 1956; Ribeiro, 1962). Some frequently cited correlational studies, however, are methodologically less than sound. Morton et al. (1953), for example, reported that 62% of violent crimes committed by women took place during the premenstrual week, 19% during midcycle, and 17% during menstruation, but they did not define the length in days of these latter two phases. Nor did they say precisely how they determined the phase of the cycle at the time of the crime. "Review of the inmates' records . . . [Morton et al., 1953, p. 1191]" suggested that onset of menstruation may be part of a prisoner's record, but in a table presenting the data themselves (p. 1189), 8 of the 58 women are listed in a "cannot remember" category which does not support the notion that a record was kept for all prisoners.

In spite of possible weaknesses in method, however, the Morton et al. (1953) study does not have as many flaws as some others of this correlational type. Cooke (1945), for example, whose study is cited by Morton et al., Greene and Dalton (1953), MacKinnon and MacKinnon (1956), and Coppen and Kessel (1963) in support of a relationship between menstrual cycle phase and commission of violent crime, included exactly one sentence on the topic. It reads:

> That this ["the hypersensitization of the nervous system which occurs during the premenstrual phase of the cycle"] is a very potent factor in the psychology of women is evidenced by the report of a Parisian prefect of police: that 84 per cent of all the crimes of violence committed by women are perpetrated during the premenstrual and early menstrual phases of the cycle [Cooke, 1945, p. 459].

Although several relatively recent papers refer to an association between the menstrual cycle and crashes by women airplane pilots (Dalton, 1960b; Moos, 1968, 1969b; Pierson & Lockhart, 1963), the only reference offered is to Whitehead (1934) or to Dalton (1964) who cited only Whitehead. Whitehead's article consisted of reports of three airplane crashes over a period of eight months in which the women pilots were said to be menstruating at the time of the crash.

While methodologically sound in terms of specifying both the behavioral event and the phase of the menstrual cycle, even Dalton's much-cited work does not always establish the correlations between menstrual cycle and behavior as clearly as might be desirable. As Sherman (1971) and Sommer (1972) pointed out, Dalton (1960a) reported a decrease in 27% of her schoolgirl subjects' test performance during the premenstrual phase of the cycle but did not provide a statistical test of the significance of this decrease, and references to her work fail to note that a premenstrual increase in 17% of the schoolgirls' performance was also found, while 56% of the girls showed no change.

Reynolds (1966) has documented the persistence of at least one "myth" in psychology (that there are sex differences in color discrimination) and suggests that such myths tend to be perpetuated when authors cite studies from other reviews or repeat the original author's conclusions without checking the data as they appeared in the original report. Given the variable quality of the basic data in correlational studies of the menstrual cycle, it would seem necessary for contemporary authors to be familiar with the methodological adequacy of the original studies before citing them as factual evidence—a caution which does not, of course, apply alone to studies of the premenstrual syndrome.

Putting aside questions of method, however, and assuming that many of the correlations between phase of the cycle and behavior are true as reported, how should the studies be interpreted and to whom can the results be generalized? Most of the investigators in this area do not explicitly point to a causal relationship between hormonal changes and the occurrence of various behaviors, but they do use phrases which tend strongly to imply that the hormones are the cause of the behaviors. Rarely is it suggested that it is the behavioral events that affect the menstrual cycle, although gynecology tests state that psychological stress may delay menstruation (Lloyd, 1962, p. 473) or precipitate its onset (Benson, 1964, p. 573); Balint (1937) offered an elaborate psychodynamic interpretation of how this might occur.[1] It is also important to note in interpreting correlational studies that data from particular groups cannot provide a basis for a generalization about all women or about any woman selected at random unless it is assumed that women are equally likely to be or become a member of the groups in which the data were collected. From knowing, for example, that crimes are likely to *have been committed* during certain phases of the cycle, it is not possible to assume the truth of the inverse—that women in these phases of the cycle are more likely to commit crimes; this latter is true only for women who will at some time commit crimes. It is possible that studies of different populations of women might reveal correlations between the premenstrual and menstrual phases of the cycle and more positively valued acts such as, for example, bursts of creative energy. Without further correlational studies of more diverse populations, and in the absence of additional information as to which subgroup a woman belongs (e.g., potential criminal, potential artist), it is difficult to predict anything about an individual's behavior from the fact that she is in the premenstrual or menstrual phase of the cycle.

Retrospective Questionnaires

A second type of data which is available to support the hypothesis of a premenstrual syndrome is based upon questionnaires asking women to report (their memory of) their experience of various "symptoms" and moods at different phases of the cycle. The symptoms and moods listed on the questionnaires are usually negative ones, and the subjects are questioned primarily about their experiences just before and during menstruation. Moos (1968, 1969b) has described the development of a comprehensive questionnaire of this sort; Coppen and Kessel (1963) and Sutherland and Stewart (1965) provided earlier examples. None of these questionnaires can be considered well-developed psychometric instruments, since no reliability data or external validity data (with the exception of Coppen & Kessel) are offered to support their usefulness. The Moos Menstrual Distress Questionnaire, which is relatively recent and frequently used (Moos, Kopell, Melges, Yalom, Lunde, Clayton, & Hamburg, 1969; Silbergeld, Brast, & Nobel, 1971), suffers from additional methodological inadequacies. In his articles describing the development of the questionnaire, Moos failed to report the fact that of the 839 subjects in the normative sample, 420 were taking oral contraceptives, 81 were pregnant, and 40 did not answer the questions about their use of oral contraceptives. These data are presented elsewhere (Moos, 1969a) along with the fact that significant differences in responses on the questionnaire were found between those women who were taking the pill and those who were not. In light of the suggestion that clinical studies and retrospective questionnaires have been the primary source of evidence that there are behavioral changes associated with the menstrual cycle (Moos et al., 1969, p. 37), the methodological soundness of individual questionnaires must be carefully considered in evaluating the relevance of such data to the hypothesis of a premenstrual syndrome.

Daily Self-Reports or Observations

Another approach to the study of the premenstrual syndrome also involves women's self-ratings of various symptoms and moods, but is different from the simple questionnaire in that the ratings are made regularly throughout the cycle and do not depend upon a retrospective account. McCance, Luff, and Widdowson (1937) collected self-reports from 167 women (over 4–6 menstrual cycles) of their experience of 10 carefully defined symptoms and moods. The data, consisting of records kept over 780 cycles, showed discrepancies between the daily-record technique and the results of a preliminary questionnaire on menstrual cycle symptoms given before the study was made, discrepancies "so frequent that they throw considerable doubt upon the value of any work on this subject based upon history or a questionnaire [pp. 579–580]." McCance et al. reported that the majority of individual records showed no evidence of rhythm during the period of the study. When records were combined, however, cyclic changes were observed, related to the menstrual cycle, in fatigue, abdominal and—to a lesser extent—back pain, headache, breast changes, sexual feelings and intercourse, tendency to cry, irritability, and effort required for intellectual work. Rees (1953a) also collected day-to-day records of reports of symptoms from 30 women (over a period of "some months") and found overall patterns of premenstrual increases in tension, irritability, depression, emotional lability, anxiety, swelling of extremities and breasts, fatigue, and headaches. In a similar study with more subjects, Rees (1953b) noted that 56% of the women did not report any significant "premenstrual tension symptoms"; the method section is not sufficiently detailed, however, to determine precisely what data were collected to support this conclusion. The Nowlis (1965) Mood Adjective Check List has been used to study daily changes in self-ratings over the course of the menstrual cycle, with inconsistent results (Moos et al., 1969); Silbergeld et al., 1971).

Altman et al. (1941) followed 10 subjects over a total of 55 menstrual cycles, recording variations in physiological events associated with ovulation (basal body temperature, "bioelectric ovulatory potentials," skin temperature) and psychological changes (sleep, physical and mental activity, mood, worry, tension, irritability, and fatigue). The psychological changes were assessed by the experimenter during daily interviews which apparently were conducted after the physiological measures had been taken (see pp. 200–201). Their psychological data showed the presence at ovulation of elation and activity, and the presence during the premenstrual phase of depression, tension, and activity. Individual women showed considerable variability in patterns of behavior. Abramson and Torghele (1961) reported changes in daily recordings of weight, temperature, and "psychosomatic symptomatology" (ratings of abdominal pain, irritability, bloating, depression, etc.). As was the case in Rees' reports, information which might have been gained in a longitudinal study is lost since the authors did not report the ratings for individual symptoms at different points throughout the cycle; instead, they presented bar graphs of the total number of times individual signs and symptoms were reported. The most frequently indicated symptom was headache, which was mentioned 90 times (the study involved 34 subjects who reported in all approximately 3,000 times on the presence or absence of headache). In the absence of a fuller presentation of the data and of control groups of nonmenstruating individuals, it is unclear whether such "psychosomatic symptomatology" can be taken as evidence of a premenstrual syndrome. Dalton's (1964) use of control groups, unusual in studies of this kind, raises an interesting question about the interpretation of any fluctuations in day-to-day records of activities; she reported that punishment records in prisons and schools failed to show 28-day cycles for males but did show them for female prisoners and school-girls, both those who were menstruating *and those who had not yet begun to menstruate* (pp. 81–82).

Thematic Analysis of Unstructured Verbal Material

A final approach to the study of the premenstrual syndrome is one which also records data on a day-to-day basis, but this technique, first put in quantitative form by Gottschalk, Kaplan, Gleser, and Winget (1962), differs from those above in that the subjects are not rated or asked to rate themselves on specific symptoms, but rather are requested to talk into a tape recorder for five minutes "about any life experience they cared to [p. 301]." Gottschalk and his co-workers developed a standardized method of scoring which allowed them to analyze the verbal material gathered in this way in terms of the levels of "hostility directed inwards," "hostility directed outwards," and "anxiety" manifested by the subject. Studying five women over a period of 30–60 days, they found that "four of the 5 women showed statistically significant rhythmical changes in the magnitude of at least one of the affects . . . during the sexual cycle [test and significance level not specified]. The changes in these affects were not similar among the women [Gottschalk et al., 1962, pp. 307–308]." It should be noted that they did not say that these rhythmic changes are linked to the phase of the menstrual cycle.

Using the Gottschalk technique with a larger sample of subjects (26 women, data collected four times over the course of two cycles), Ivey and Bardwick (1968) confirmed the Gottschalk et al. (1962) report of transient "decreases in levels of anxiety and hostility [p. 307]," finding that the ovulatory anxiety level was significantly lower than that during the premenstrual phase. Paige (1971) also gathered unstructured verbal material from an even larger sample at four different times throughout the cycle, and used Gottschalk's scoring procedure to assess anxiety, hostility, and negative affect (the latter being the sum of the anxiety and hostility scales). In the 38 subjects not taking oral contraceptives, she found that all three scores varied significantly throughout the cycle. These cyclic variations were not present in the group of 52 subjects who were taking oral contraceptives containing both estrogens and progestin.

While not relying upon a standardized scoring technique such as

Gottschalk, Benedek and Rubenstein's (1939a, 1939b) classic study also involved day-by-day analysis of women's speech in a relatively unstructured setting. In their case, the data consisted of "verbal material" (not verbatim records) collected over the course of psychoanalysis of women diagnosed as neurotic. Studying nine patients over a total of 75 cycles, Benedek found that she could predict, solely on the basis of a patient's reports of dreams, the day on which ovulation occurred, a prediction which was corroborated independently by Rubenstein's analysis of vaginal smears. Benedek (1963) noted the difficulty she experienced in formalizing what it was in the records which allowed her to make such precise predictions; the fact that her data are described in terms which are inseparable from her theoretical orientation makes it difficult to specify operationally the procedures by which she was able to infer the phase of the menstrual cycle from the women's reports of their dreams.

Scientific Status of the Premenstrual Syndrome

The four kinds of studies discussed above—correlations between behavioral acts and phase of the menstrual cycle, retrospective questionnaires, daily self-ratings or observations, and thematic analyses of verbal material—represent the sorts of evidence that are cited in support of the hypothesis of the existence of a premenstrual syndrome. Given the variety of types of supporting data, it is not surprising that the terms "premenstrual syndrome" and its associated "symptoms" seem to have been used somewhat broadly. Premenstrual syndrome, for example, has been taken to include the "recurrence of [any] symptoms always at the same time in each menstrual cycle [Dalton, 1954, p. 339]" or even "any combination of emotional or *physical* features which occur cyclically in a female before menstruation [Sutherland & Stewart, 1965, p. 1182; italics added]." Moos (1969b) found from a review of the literature that over 150 different symptoms have been associated with the menstrual cycle, including such various ones as elation, depression, back pain, sexual desire, and a great many other more or less specific behaviors and inferred psychological states. Sutherland and Stewart suggested that "the only common denominator to all the symptoms described is that, when they occur, they do so at regular [28-day?] intervals[p. 1183]." Given the broad and not always consistent use of "premenstrual syndrome" and its constituent "symptoms," estimates of the prevalence of "menstrual symptoms" or of the premenstrual syndrome are useless for most purposes (Ferguson & Vermillion, 1957; see Moos, 1968, p. 854, for other references).

In spite of the lack of agreement on the precise nature of the premenstrual syndrome or even its relationship to the phases of the menstrual cycle, a wide variety of physiological factors have been proposed in the past to account for it. Among them are "female sex hormones" (Frank, 1931), estrogen-progesterone imbalance (Morten et al., 1953), altered suprarenal cortex activity (MacKinnon & MacKinnon, 1956), water retention caused by high estrogen-progesterone ratio (Greene & Dalton, 1953); see Southam and Gonzaga (1965) for others. This physiologic explanatory bias dictated some of the early attempts to "cure" the syndrome: Sterilization by X-ray was reported to have been successful for some of Frank's (1931) patients; Greene (1954) reported, however, that "not only does hysterectomy fail to cure the premenstrual syndrome, but it may actually initiate it, a fact which we have so far failed to explain [p. 338]." Less drastic measures such as diuretics (Eichner & Waltner, 1955) and hormone therapy (Rees, 1953a) were also reported.

Recently, several investigators have suggested that monoamine oxidase activity might be the means through which estrogens and progesterone affect neural firing and behavior (Grant & Pryse-Davies, 1968; Klaiber, Broverman, Vogel, Kobayashi, & Moriarty, 1972; Paige, 1971). As in the case of earlier proposals, evidence supporting a hypothetical mechanism involving monoamine oxidase is indirect, and a number of currently untested assumptions about physiological processes are required.[2] On the basis of available data, such an hypothesis seems premature since physiological knowledge is not yet sufficiently detailed to put serious limits on the kinds of physiological processes which might mediate hormone-behavior relationships, and more importantly, psychological studies have not yet clarified the nature and extent of the behavioral changes which are to be explained by the proposed mechanism.

There is clearly a need for a more precise definition of the premenstrual syndrome and for a specification, in terms of the methods used to identify them, of the symptoms of which it is thought to be composed. This definition should be accompanied by a conceptual scheme for relating to each other the data collected by different methods. Is a premenstrual increase in irritability (e.g., found in daily self-ratings) causally related to a premenstrual increase in commission of violent crimes? Is the anxiety found through thematic analysis related to the increased likelihood of a mother's taking her child to a clinic? Questions such as these illustrate the need for an explicit statement of the hypothetical psychological mechanisms relating one kind of data to another. Before such theories can be elaborated and tested, however, it must be shown that data collected by different methods are in fact correlated, since one would expect that any psychological state that is included in a description of the premenstrual syndrome would be measurable by more than one method. There is some evidence that this is not always the case. The premenstrual syndrome as assessed by the Moos (1968, 1969b) Menstrual Distress Questionnaire, for example, includes symptom scales labeled Autonomic Reactions and Concentration (which includes as one item "lowered motor coordination"), but in his own work with Kopell, Lunde, Clayton, and Moos (1969), Moos reported failure to find fluctuations throughout the menstrual cycle in galvanic skin potential and in reaction time. Pierson and Lockhart (1963) and Zimmerman and Parlee (1973) also reported failure to find changes in reaction time and in galvanic skin potential. McCance et al. (1937) found cyclic variations in subjects' self-ratings of "effort required for intellectual work," but Sommer (1972) could not demonstrate changes in intellectual performance when subjects were tested repeatedly over the course of the menstrual cycle. Using three different measures within a single study—the Moos Menstrual Distress Questionnaire (retrospective questionnaire), the Nowlis Mood Adjective Check List (daily self-report), and the Gottschalk technique of thematic analysis—Silbergeld et al. (1971) concluded that "the three methods of behavioral assessment produced scores which were, at best, only weakly correlated [p. 411]."

Coppen and Kessel (1963) have attempted to make the generalized use of premenstrual syndrome more precise by distinguishing between dysmenorrhea—pain specifically associated with and occurring during menstruation—and the premenstrual syndrome which they define in a more limited way as irritability, depression, nervousness or tension, and anxiety. While it is not clear that all of the symptoms which have previously been studied in conjunction with the menstrual cycle can be placed reliably into one of these two categories (e.g., how would "headache" be classified?), the distinction does have some empirical justification. On the basis of a retrospective questionnaire administered to 500 women, Coppen and Kessel reported that the premenstrual syndrome as they defined it is correlated with neuroticism (Maudsley Personality Inventory), while dysmenorrhea is negatively correlated with age and with parity, and is uncorrelated with neuroticism. Although the authors offered no speculation concerning the causes of either dysmenorrhea or the premenstrual syndrome, their discussion implied that dysmenorrhea has a more direct physiological basis (it occurs during menstruation and is not "a psychosomatic condition or one that calls for psychological treatment, [p. 720]") while "the subjects with premenstrual symptoms had abnormal personality traits [p. 718]." Lennane and Lennane (1973) have also noted that, contrary to a considerable body of medical opinion, evidence strongly suggests that dysmenorrhea is primarily of physiological rather than psychogenic origin.

Thompson (1950), Shainess (1961), Paige (1971), and others have suggested, on the other hand, that a woman's psychological response to the physiological changes associated with her menstrual cycle may also be shaped or modified by cultural practices which attach values to menstruation and to femininity. In this view, what Coppen and Kessel (1963) call the premenstrual syndrome would be the result of complex psychological processes arising from an interaction between physiological changes and environmental factors specifically related to femininity and sexuality. As such, it would be associated with other aspects of the personality to the extent that these also are related to sexuality, and considerable individual differences might be expected.

Whether a distinction between dysmenorrhea and a more limited and precise definition of the premenstrual syndrome will prove useful for psychological theory construction remains to be seen, but in its present form it represents one attempt to deal with at least some of the various aned complex factors which must be considered in dealing with phenomena involving both physiological and psychological processes. Statements which simply assume a direct causal relationship between physiological processes and complex psychological experiences and behaviors are abundant in the literature,[3] but they are inadequate as contributions to psychology since they neither specify in at least outline form the nature of the hypothetical mechanism supposed to link physiological and psychological events nor make explicit the underlying beliefs about the conceptually difficult relationship between mind and body (Borst, 1970; Fodor, 1968).

General Issues

Many of the studies of the premenstrual syndrome discussed above involve certain assumptions which, when made explicit, raise some interesting general questions about the description and explanation of behavior. One of these assumptions is that the syndrome (however it may be defined in a particular study) can best be described as a premenstrual or menstrual "increase" in certain symptoms, moods, or behaviors. With some exceptions, the data seem equally consistent with an hypothesis of a midcycle syndrome of lowered incidence of crime (Dalton, 1961) and epileptic seizures (Hamburg, 1966), increased self-esteem and elation (Ivey & Bardwick, 1968), and increased sexual desire and sexual activity (Benedek & Rubenstein, 1939a, 1939b; McCance et al., 1937). What is the base line compared with which *changes* in behavior are described as an increase or decrease? If control groups of males are used in studies of cyclic behavior, the question of what to use as a base line for description of behaviors also arises. To take a hypothetical example, if female performance on a digit-symbol substitution task should be found to fluctuate with the menstrual cycle, it would seem incomplete and therefore misleading to say only that females' performance is worse at certain times in the cycle than at others, since it may at all times be better than the average performance of males on this task. One can say, of course, that male performance is by definition irrelevant to the study of behavioral changes associated with the menstrual cycle, but it is not irrelevant—though it is not often investigated—to studies of rhythmic changes in human behavior, which may be a more useful concept in a general psychological theory.

The question of control groups, then, points to a second assumption which seems to underlie studies of the premenstrual syndrome—that is, the assumption that the menstrual cycle is relevant to the interpretation of a great many cyclic changes in behavior in human females. In view of the evidence of the pervasiveness of cyclic phenomena in human beings (Luce, 1970), control groups would appear to be essential for proper interpretation of data on adult female subjects. Hersey (1931), for example, has reported finding cycles of emotionality in males (determined on the basis of daily observations of behavior and self-reports. These cycles varied from three and one-half to nine weeks in length, but were constant, within ± one week, and predictable for a given individual. Lieber and Sherin (1972) have reported finding lunar cycles in the occurrence of violent crimes—whether committed by males or females. As noted above, Dalton (1964) described 28-day cycles in the behavior of prepubertal schoolgirls, cycles comparable to those found in menstruating females of various ages (though not found in men and boys). Whatever the cause of such rhythmic behaviors in nonmenstruating individuals, their existence points to the necessity of control groups for interpretation of cyclic phenomena as well as for determining a base line for describing any changes which may be found only in one sex.

A final issue which is raised by the literature on the premenstrual syndrome has to do with some of the conventions governing the publication of psychological research. One of these is the generally accepted practice of not publishing "negative" results. In the menstrual cycle literature, for example, numerous investigators have tested reaction time at various phases of the menstrual cycle and have found no changes (the data were included as part of a report of a larger study in which some other change was found; e.g., Kopell et al., 1969). There is, on the other hand, at least one report of positive findings (Voitsechovsky, 1909) which presumably could be cited in support of a claim that reaction time varies throughout the menstrual cycle. Given the conventions governing the availability of "facts" in psychology, it is difficult to document a claim of "no change" or "no difference." The issue of negative results is, of course, a complex one, involving questions about the sensitivity of the tests used, random sampling errors and the like. Nevertheless, in a problem area where there may be a general expectation of finding a "result," there would seem to be a danger that the literature will be encumbered with more Type II errors than is desirable simply because a result frequently sought may occur by chance at least a few times and make its way into print.

Also related to publication practices is another difficulty illustrated by the menstrual cycle literature, one which arises when investigators have data on which a large number of correlations can be computed. What should be the editorial policy regarding publication of such data when only a few of the correlations are significant? In studies of the menstrual cycle, this generally occurs when correlations are computed between each item on a lengthy questionnaire and individual items on other questionnaires or tests. Kopell et al. (1969), for example, found 12 of at least 72 correlations (the exact number cannot be determined from their report) to be statistically significant, Levitt and Lubin (1967) found 14 of 75, and Silbergeld et al. (1971) found 13 of 129 variables to vary significantly during the cycle. In interpreting such data, it seems that either the authors do not attempt to make even ad hoc sense out of the data in terms of a coherent psychological theory (Silbergeld et al., 1971), or else they draw a conclusion which seems more elaborate than is justified by the data. Kopell et al., for example, found that time estimation varied significantly during the menstrual cycle; time estimation and two-flash threshold were found to be positively correlated on three out of four tests; and self-ratings of "concentration" and "social affection" were negatively correlated with time estimation at each of the four phases of the cycle tested. From these data they posed the "intriguing question" of whether the "subjective changes experienced during the premenstrual period" are "an expression of a distortion of the basic time sense which, in turn, might be part of a very mild, transient, confusional state [p. 186]."

In light of these various methodological and theoretical considerations, then, it seems fair to conclude:

1. Psychological studies of the premenstrual syndrome have not as yet established the existence of a class of behaviors and moods, *measurable in more than one way,* which can be shown in a longitudinal study to fluctuate throughout the course of the menstrual cycle, or even a class of such behaviors which is regularly correlated with any particular phase of the cycle for groups of women. This is not to say that such a set of behaviors does not exist—many women spontaneously attest that they do—but that as a scientific hypothesis the existence of a premenstrual syndrome has little other than face validity.

2. Psychological studies of the premenstrual syndrome are difficult to interpret without control groups to establish a base line for describing changes in behavior in one sex and to determine the presence or absence of cyclic changes in the behaviors of nonmenstruating individuals. The use of control groups—automatic in most psychological studies—might yield new data on rhythmic behaviors of hitherto unsuspected generality and, if so, would broaden the interpretation of those previously studied only in adult females.

3. Given the paucity of data showing actual changes in nonverbal behavior throughout the menstrual cycle, careful consideration should be given to the nature of the data in a particular study: Do they show what the subject *says* about menstruation or what she does—nonverbally—throughout the cycle? In view of the prevalence of culturally transmitted beliefs and attitudes about menstruation, this distinction is important in considering the relative influence of social and physiological factors both in interpreting the data and in formulating new hypotheses.

4. Given the variety of methods and the variable quality of data on the premenstrual syndrome, investigators proposing a physiological mechanism to explain hormone-behavior relationships should make clear both what behaviors they propose to account for and also the nature of the empirical and conceptual assumptions upon which their psychophysiological hypotheses rest.

NOTES

1. The suggestion that behavior can indeed influence levels of reproductive hormones is supported by the recent finding that testosterone levels in primates are affected by manipulations of the social setting (Rose, Gordon, & Bernstein, 1972). McClintock's (1971) study demonstrated in another context the effects of social factors on the timing of menstruation in human beings: Menstrual cycles of females living together in a college dormitory were found to become more closely synchronized over the course of an academic year. While it is clear that many of the correlational data mentioned above cannot be interpreted in this way, a consideration of possible psychological effects on the menstrual cycle as well as the reverse would be useful in assessing the extent and limitations of the statistical evidence cited in support of a hormone-"related" (with connotations of "caused") premenstrual syndrome of "neurotic and antisocial reactions [Janowsky et al., 1969, p. 189]."
2. The argument is that estrogens and progesterones affect levels of monoamine oxidase which in turn affect catecholamine-mediated neural activity in the brain; this central nervous system activity is, according to the hypothesis, related to psychological states of depression and irritability. Supporting evidence is indirect: (*a*) endometrial monoamine oxidase fluctuates throughout the human menstrual cycle (Cohen, Belensky, & Chaym, 1965; Southgate, Grant, Pollard, Pryse-Davies, & Sandler, 1968), (*b*) drugs which inhibit monoamine oxidase activity—and possibly affect other physiologically significant substances as well—transiently relieve psychological depression (Crane, 1970), (*c*) oral contraceptives affect both endometrial monoamine oxidase levels and psychological depression (method for assessing "depression" not stated; Grant & Pryse-Davies, 1968). Several assumptions are obviously required if these data and others like them are to be interpreted as supporting the hypothesis that naturally occurring fluctuations in estrogen and progesterone levels during the menstrual cycle are responsible—by means of a mechanism involving monoamine oxidase—for clearly established cycles in depression and irritability. Some of these assumptions are (*a*) that the pharmacologic doses of estrogen and progesterone present in oral contraceptives have similar psychological effects on the physiologic levels of these hormones; (*b*) that peripheral, systemic measures of monoamine oxidase activity (blood plasma, endometrial monoamine oxidase) reflect central levels; (*c*) that monoamine oxidase

regulates the functional levels of catecholamines in the brain; and (*d*) that central nervous system activity involving catecholamines as transmitter substances is directly related to psychological states of depression and irritability. Relevant to these assumptions, respectively, are the following considerations: (*a*) behavioral effects of drug substances are not always a monotonic function of dosage; (*b*) one of the basic functions of the blood-brain barrier is to maintain constant levels of some substances in the brain in the presence of fluctuating systemic levels; (*c*) even if there were direct evidence that monoamine oxidase influences absolute levels of brain catecholamines, it would still be necessary to establish that monoamine oxidase affects direct measures of neural transmission in the same way; and (*d*) no evidence is available showing the existence of a one-to-one relationship between brain activity of a specified kind and psychological states. As an example of the relationship between the sort of physiological knowledge now available and the psychophysiological assumptions required by the monoamine oxidase-catecholamine hypothesis, compare Assumptions *b* and *c* above with the Southgate et al. (1968) report in which they were able to show a correlation between two methods for assessing human endometrial monoamine oxidase activity. In this article they noted that "at present there is insufficient information to decide whether the observed changes are localized to the endometrium or are part of a more generalized cyclical variation in MAO [monoamine oxidase] activity [p. 724]" and that "in recent years it has become increasingly obvious that there are not one but a series of MAOs, each differing in its action towards substrates and inhibitors [p. 725]."

While none of the assumptions required by the monoamine oxidase hypothesis is itself inherently implausible, considerable physiological and psychophysiological research would be needed to establish each of them, research which is not cited by supporters of the monoamine oxidase-catecholamine hypothesis. In view of the considerations bearing on the correctness of each assumption, furthermore, any hypothesis which depends upon the validity of all of them must be regarded as far from established.

3. "The personality changes associated with the menstrual cycle occur in spite of individual personality differences and may even be extreme; they are consequences of endocrine and related physical changes . . . [Bardwick, 1971, p. 27]." "We felt assured that the phases of ovarian function were reflected in psychic processes [Benedek, 1963, p. 315]." "There was a tendency for the levels of tension measured—specifically, anxiety and hostility inward—to decrease transiently around the time of ovulation. The presumed cause is some hormonal change . . . [Gottschalk et al., 1962, p. 308]." "The menstrual cycle imposes on the human female a rhythmic variability encompassing all aspects of her being, from the biochemical to the psychosocial [Silbergeld et al., 1971, p. 411]." "The theory that the pathological emotional findings are hormonally influenced is widely accepted [Janowsky, Gorney, & Kelley, 1966, p. 243]." Janowsky et al., regard these hormonal influences as having considerable scope, listing the following as

> some [sic] of the cyclically recurring phenomena of the premenstrual and menstrual phases . . . depression, irritability, sleep disturbances, lethargy, alcoholic excesses, nymphomania, feelings of unreality, sleep disturbances, epilepsy, vertigo, syncope, paresthesias, nausea, vomiting, constipation, bloating, edema, colicky pain, enuresis, urinary retention, increased capillary fragility, glaucoma, migraine headaches, relapses of meningiomas, schizophrenic reactions and relapses, increased susceptibility to infection, suicide attempts, admission to surgical and medical wards, crime rates, work morbidity, manic reactions, and dermatological diseases [p. 242].

REFERENCES

ABRAMSON, M., & TORGHELE, J. R. Weight, temperature changes, and psychosomatic symptomatology in relation to the menstrual cycle. *American Journal of Obstetrics and Gynecology,* 1961, 81, 223–232.

ALTMAN, M., KNOWLES, E., & BULL, H. D. A psychosomatic study of the sex cycle in women. *Psychosomatic Medicine,* 1941, 3, 199–224.

BALINT, M. A contribution to the psychology of menstruation. *Psychoanalytic Quarterly,* 1937, 6, 346–352.

BARDWICK, J. M. *Psychology of women: A study of biocultural conflicts.* New York: Harper & Row, 1971.

BENEDEK, T. An investigation of the sexual cycle in women: Methodologic considerations. *Archives of General Psychiatry,* 1963, 8, 311–322.

BENEDEK, T., & RUBENSTEIN, B. B. The correlations between ovarian activity and psychodynamic processes: I. The ovulative phase. *Psychosomatic Medicine,* 1939, 1, 245–70. (a)

BENEDEK, T., & RUBENSTEIN, B. B. The correlations between ovarian activity and psychodynamic processes: II. The menstrual phase. *Psychosomatic Medicine,* 1939, 1, 461–485. (b)

BENSON, R. C. *Handbook of obstetrics and gynecology.* Los Angeles: Lange Medical Publications, 1964.

BORST, C. V. (Ed.) *The mind/brain identity theory.* New York: Macmillan, 1970.

COHEN, S., BELENSKY, L., & CHAYM, J. The study of monoamine oxidase activity by histochemical procedures. *Biochemical Pharmacology,* 1965, 14, 223–228.

COOKE, W. R. The differential psychology of the American woman. *American Journal of Obstetrics and Gynecology,* 1945, 49, 457–472.

COPPEN, W. R., & KESSEL, N. Menstruation and personality. *British Journal of Psychiatry,* 1963, 109, 711–721.

CRANE, G. E. Use of monoamine oxidase inhibiting antidepressants. In W. G. Clark & J. del Giudice (Eds.), *Principles of psychopharmacology: A textbook for physicians, medical students, and behavioral scientists.* New York: Academic Press, 1970.

DALTON, K. Discussion on the premenstrual syndrome. *Proceedings of the Royal Society of Medicine,* 1954, 48, 339–346.

DALTON, K. Menstruation and acute psychiatric illness. *British Medical Journal,* 1959, 1, 148–149.

DALTON, K. Effect of menstruation on schoolgirls' weekly work. *British Medical Journal,* 1960, 1, 326–328. (a)

DALTON, K. Menstruation and accidents. *British Medical Journal,* 1960, 2, 1425–1426. (b)

DALTON, K. Menstruation and crime. *British Medical Journal,* 1961, 2, 1752–1753.

DALTON, K. *The premenstrual syndrome.* Springfield, Ill.: Charles C Thomas, 1964.

DALTON, K. The influence of mother's menstruation on her child. *Proceedings of the Royal Society of Medicine,* 1966, 59, 1014.

EICHNER, E., & WALTNER, C. Premenstrual tension. *Medical Times,* 1955, 83, 771–779.

FERGUSON, J. H., & VERMILLION, M. B. Premenstrual tension: Two surveys of its prevalence and a description of the syndrome. *Obstetrics and Gynecology,* 1957, 9, 615–619.

FODOR, J. A. Functional explanation in psychology. In M. Brodbeck (Ed.), *Readings in the philosophy of the social sciences.* New York: Macmillan, 1968.

FRANK, R. T. The hormonal causes of premenstrual tension. *Archives of Neurology and Psychiatry,* 1931, 26, 1053–1057.

GOTTSCHALK, L. A., KAPLAN, S. M., GLESER, G. C., & WINGET, C. M. Variations in magnitude of emotions: A method applied to anxiety and hostility during phases of the menstrual cycle. *Psychosomatic Medicine,* 1962, 24, 300–311.

GRANT, C., & PRYSE-DAVIES, J. Effects of oral contraceptives on depressive mood changes and on endometrial monoamine oxidase and phosphates. *British Medical Journal,* 1968, 1, 777–780.

GREENE, R. Discussion on the premenstrual syndrome. *Proceedings of the Royal Society of Medicine,* 1954, 48, 337–338.

GREENE, R., & DALTON, K. The premenstrual syndrome. *British Medical Journal,* 1953, 1, 1007–1013.

HAMBURG, D. A. Effects of progesterone on behavior. *Research Publications. Association for Research in Nervous and Mental Diseases,* 1966, 43, 251–265.

HERSEY, R. B. Emotional cycles in man. *Journal of Mental Science,* 1931, 77, 151–169.

IVEY, M., & BARDWICK, J. M. Patterns of affective fluctuation in the menstrual cycle. *Psychosomatic Medicine,* 1968, 30, 336–345.

JANOWSKY, D. S., GORNEY, R., CASTELNUOVO-TEDESCO, P., & STONE, C. B. Premenstrual-menstrual increase in psychiatric hospital admission rates. *American Journal of Obstetrics and Gynecology,* 1969, 103, 189–191.

JANOWSKY, D., GORNEY, R., & KELLEY, B. "The curse"—Vicissitudes and variations of the female fertility cycle: Part I. Psychiatric aspects. *Psychosomatics,* 1966, 7, 242–247.

KANE, F. J., LIPTON, M. A. & EWING, J. A. Hormonal influences in female sexual response. *Archives of General Psychiatry,* 1969, 20, 202–209.

KLAIBER, E. L., BROVERMAN, D. M., VOGEL, W., KOBAYASHI, Y., & MORIARTY, D. Effects of estrogen therapy on plasma MAO activity and EEG driving responses of depressed women. *American Journal of Psychiatry,* 1972, 128, 1492–1498.

KOPELL, B. S., LUNDE, D. T., CLAYTON, R. B., & MOOS, R. H. Variations in some measures of arousal during the menstrual cycle. *Journal of Nervous and Mental Diseases,* 1969, 148, 180–187.

LENNANE, M. B., & LENNANE, R. J. Alleged psychogenic disorders in women—a possible manifestation of sexual prejudice. *New England Journal of Medicine,* 1973, 288, 288–292.

LEVITT, E. E., & LUBIN, B. Some personality factors associated with menstrual complaints and menstrual attitude. *Journal of Psychosomatic Research,* 1967, 11, 267–270.

LIEBER, A., & SHERIN, C. The case of the full moon. *Human Behavior,* 1972, 1, 29.

LLODY, C. W. The ovaries. In R. H. Williams (Ed.), *Textbook of endocrinology.* (3rd ed.) Philadelphia: W. B. Saunders, 1962.

LUCE, G. G. *Biological rhythms in psychiatry and medicine.* (USPHS Pub. No. 2088) Washington, D.C.: U.S. Department of Health, Education and Welfare, 1970.

MACKINNON, P. C. B., & MACKINNON, I. L. Hazards of the menstrual cycle. *British Medical Journal,* 1956, 1, 555.

MANDELL, A., & MANDELL, M. Suicide and the menstrual cycle. *Journal of the American Medical Association,* 1967, 200, 792–793.

MCCANCE, R. A., LUFF, M. C., & WIDDOWSON, E. E. Physical and emotional periodicity in women. *Journal of Hygiene,* 1937, 37, 571–605.

MCCLINTOCK, M. K. Menstrual synchrony and suppression. *Nature,* 1971, 229, 244–245.

MOOS, R. H. The development of a menstrual distress questionnaire. *Psychosomatic Medicine,* 1968, 30, 853–867.

MOOS, R. H. Assessment of psychological concomitants of oral contraceptives. In H. A. Salhanick et al. (Eds.), *Metabolic effects of gonadal hormones and contraceptive steroids.* New York: Plenum Press, 1969. (a)

MOOS, R. H. Typology of menstrual cycle symptoms. *American Journal of Obstetrics and Gynecology,* 1969, 103, 390–402. (b)

MOOS, R. H., KOPELL, B. S., MELGES, F. T., YALOM, I. D., LUNDE, D. T., CLAYTON, R. B., & HAMBURG, D. A. Fluctuations in symptoms and moods during the menstrual cycle. *Journal of Psychosomatic Research,* 1969, 13, 37–44.

MORTON, J. H., ADDITON, H., ADDISON, R. G., HUNT, L., & SULLIVAN, J. J. A clinical study of premenstrual tension. *American Journal of Obstetrics and Gynecology,* 1953, 65, 1182–1191.

NEILL, J. D., JOHANSSON, E. D. B., DATTS, J. K., & KNOBIL, E. Relationship between the plasma levels of leutinizing hormone and progesterone during the normal menstrual cycle. *Journal of Clinical Endocrinology,* 1967, 27, 1167–1173.

NOWLIS, V. Research with the Mood Adjective Check List. In S. S. Tomkins & C. E. Izard (Eds.), *Affect, cognition, and personality.* New York: Springer, 1965.

PAIGE, K. E. Effects of oral contraceptives on affective fluctuations associated with the menstrual cycle. *Psychosomatic Medicine,* 1971, 33, 515–537.

PIERSON, W. R., & LOCKHART, A. Effect of menstruation on simple reaction and movement time. *British Medical Journal,* 1963, 1, 796–797.

REES, L. The premenstrual tension syndrome and its treatment. *British Medical Journal,* 1953, 1, 1014–1016. (a)

REES, L. Psychosomatic aspects of the premenstrual tension syndrome. *Journal of Mental Science,* 1953, 99, 62–73. (b)

REYNOLDS, L. T. A note on the perpetuation of a "scientific fiction." *Sociometry,* 1966, 29, 85–88.

RIBEIRO, A. L. Menstruation and crime. *British Medical Journal,* 1962, 1, 640.

RICHTER, C. P. Periodic phenomena in man and animals: Their relation to neuroendocrine mechanisms (a monthly or near monthly cycle). In R. P. Michael (Ed.), *Endocrinology and human behavior.* London: Oxford University Press, 1968.

ROSE, R. M., GORDON, T. P., & BERNSTEIN, I. S. Plasma testosterone levels in the male rhesus: Influences of sexual and social stimuli. *Science,* 1972, 178, 643–645.

SEWARD, G. H. The female sex rhythm. *Psychological Bulletin,* 1934, 31, 153–192.

SHAINESS, N. A re-evaluation of some aspects of femininity through a study of menstruation: A preliminary report. *Comparative Psychiatry,* 1961, 2, 20–26.

SHERMAN, J. A. *On the psychology of women: A survey of empirical studies.* Springfield, Ill.: Charles C Thomas, 1971.

SILBERGELD, S., BRAST, N., & NOBEL, E. P. The menstrual cycle: A double-blind study of symptoms, mood and behavior, and biochemical variables using Enovid and placebo. *Psychosomatic Medicine,* 1971, 33, 411–428.

SOMMER, B. Menstrual cycle changes and intellectual performance. *Psychosomatic Medicine,* 1972, 34, 263–269.

SOUTHAM, A. L., & GONZAGA, F. P. Systemic changes during the menstrual cycle. *American Journal of Obstetrics and Gynecology,* 1965, 91, 142–165.

SOUTHGATE, J., GRANT, E. C. G., POLLARD, W., PRYSE-DAVIES, J., & SANDLER, M. Cyclical variations in endometrial monoamine oxidase: Correlation of histochemical and quantitative biochemical assays. *Biochemical Pharmacology,* 1968, 17, 721–726.

SUTHERLAND, H., & STEWART, I. A critical analysis of the premenstrual syndrome. *Lancet,* 1965, 1, 1180–1193.

THOMPSON, C. Some effects of the derogatory attitude toward female sexuality. *Psychiatry,* 1950, 13, 349–354.

VOITSECHOVSKY, N. V. [The influence of menstruation upon the nervous and psychic apparatus of women.] Thesis from the Imperial Military Academy, St. Petersburg, Russia, 1909, No. 6. Cited by G. H. Seward, The female sex rhythm. *Psychological Bulletin,* 1934, 31, 153–192.

WHITEHEAD, R. E. Women pilots. *Journal of Aviation Medicine,* 1934, 5, 47–49.

ZIMMERMAN, E., & PARLEE, M. B. Behavioral changes associated with the menstrual cycle: An experimental investigation. *Journal of Applied Social Psychology,* 1973, in press.

The Symbolic Significance of Menstruation and the Menopause

Vieda Skultans

This article reports some provisional results of a social medicine study which I am currently conducting in south Wales.

Menstruation and the menopause were chosen as subjects of research for several reasons which suggested their anthropological interest. Firstly, it was noted that more than any other period of time in a woman's life, the menopause has gained popular attention as a topic of concern, apprehension and speculation. Furthermore, it has been selected by popular termininology as a period of transition *par excellence.* The corresponding processes of biological change at puberty, for example, have no such popular designation, nor do they command the same degree of attention. It was, therefore, realised that there existed the necessity to isolate and examine certain concepts relating to structural features of the female cycle. An altogether different approach, and one not involving a consideration of the menopause within the female life-history, is one which would compare the differential emphasis put upon male and female sexual histories. Even though it be admitted that the male reproductive system has no by-products as spectacular as those of menstruation, there is still, to the best of my knowledge, no comparable collection of beliefs and theories surrounding the male sexual life cycle. Yet perhaps a case exists for a comparative study of theories about changes in male and female sexual activities. More specifically, a comparative study of attitudes to 'losses' is called for, which would relate such ideas to salient features of the male and female life-cycle.

Such considerations as these have led to the formulation of the main

"The Symbolic Significance of Menstruation and Menopause" by Vieda Skultans in *Man* (new series 1970), 641–651. Reprinted by permission of the Royal Anthropological Institute of Great Britain and Ireland.

theme of this article. Namely, that at menstruation women are using a biological given, that is the loss of menstrual blood, in order not only to express their femininity, but also to reaffirm their acceptance of the female social role. The movement here is away from the biological to the social. This reaffirmation is expressed through attitudes towards and beliefs about menstruation. Furthermore, this analysis of a particular set of ideas about menstruation in terms of the reaffirmation of a particular kind of social role for women, leads very easily to a consideration of the menopause or 'change' as a *'rite de passage'*, a passage from one kind of role to another. I shall return to a discussion of this topic later, after first considering the significance of menstrual loss *per se*.

This introduction should show that my analysis makes claims different from the one made by Mary Douglas (unpublished article). She says: 'People's ideas about menstruation are part and parcel of their general ideas about how the relations between the sexes should be governed. If they take a very relaxed attitude to premarital sex and to family size they are not likely to think of menstruation as dangerous. The private instruction of European mothers might come somewhere near the scale one might draw of tribal reactions which vary from joyful congratulation, through solemn teaching to intense preoccupation with danger.' I would agree with the statement that ideas about menstruation reflect ideas about how the relations between the sexes should be conducted, or the norms governing inter-sexual behaviour, but would go on to qualify this statement differently. I have not found much evidence which would tend to support a relationship between the degree of danger attributed to menstruation and attitudes towards family size or towards premarital intercourse. The connexion which I shall try to establish, however, will be one between the dangers of menstruation on the one hand and the reaffirmation of one's social roles as sexual partner, mother and housewife.

This connexion between the polluting qualities of menstrual blood, the subsequent need for purging and the fulfilment of the duties regarded as traditional for married women, was suggested not only by the results of research directed specifically towards the topic of menstruation and the menopause, but also by previous research on spiritualism which I had been carrying out in Swansea. In the first place it was noted that membership of Spiritualist meetings was largely female. Secondly, that most of the women were at least middle-aged. Furthermore, a high proportion of the messages received from 'Spirit' could be most obviously interpreted as referring to menopausal troubles, especially to the feelings of uncertainty and lack of direction which are a frequent accompaniment of the physical symptoms of the 'change'. Moreover, it was painstakingly explained to me by Spiritualists that what they termed the menopause, or at least menopausal symptoms, could occur at any time in a woman's life from the age of twenty-three onwards; and that it is not necessarily associated with an impaired capacity for child-bearing, nor with the disappearance of this capacity nor with the cessation of menstrual bleeding. Such assertions made me realise that my own conception of the menopause had hitherto been a far too literal one, at least by the standards of Spiritualist women, if by no others. It became apparent that the concept of the 'menopause' was a cultural rather than a biological one and that the concept was being used to express a cultural or social rather than a biological truth. This judgement was confirmed by subsequent research. However, in keeping with the general orientations of the research, which viewed Spiritualism as an expression of dissatisfaction with the female sexual role and a substitute for it, the presentation of menstrual symptoms such as back-ache, flooding and tiredness were treated as revealing ' deep-seated rejection of woman's basic roles'. In fact, it was found that subsequent evidence did not support this theory. It was found that many Spiritualist women had problematical relationships with men and it was, therefore, originally thought that Spiritualism was a further retreat from men. Now, however, I would regard Spiritualism, for those women I studied at least, as an attempt to understand and accommodate oneself to an, at times, uncomfortable role.

Another topic which figured very largely in my thinking about the planned study on menstruation and the menopause was that of 'hysterectomies'. I was told by a general practitioner in south Wales that there exists a large body of medical literature which claims that in a substantial percentage of cases the hysterectomy was not justified on strictly medical grounds but was performed at the woman's insistence, whose reasons were psychosocial rather than medical. This suggestion gains plausibility if it is borne in mind that in the case of hysterectomies, assessment of the need for operation relies more heavily upon the verbal presentation of symptoms which could counterweigh medical examination. Estimates of the percentage of unnecessary hysterectomies, that is cases recording no pathological condition, have varied from 30·8 per cent. (Miller 1946) to 12·5 per cent. (Doyle 1952). Since 1844 when the first hysterectomy was performed, enthusiasm for the operation has increased continuously. Miller says: 'Indeed, extirpation purely as a measure of preventive medicine is by no means unheard of'. Doctors are frequently confronted with such bald statements as: 'I want to have it all out', or, 'I want to get rid of the lot' (personal communication from the general practitioner). Such choice of expressions would indicate the wish to put a definitive end to one's sexual life and even one's female identity, rather than the simple rejection of one particular organ. The extreme attitudes of the unnecessarily hysterectomised will, therefore, provide a theoretical model around which the residual category of women who attach no special value to menstruation can be grouped.

Research was carried out in a mining village in south Wales with the very generous co-operation of a local general practitioner. The village in question established its character as a mining community in the 1870's at the same time as the mining communities of the Rhondda were set up. Its population of 1,700 is contained in uniformly neat terraced houses. At the centre of the village, occupying the same patch of fenced-in land as does the athletic club, lies the health centre.

Fieldwork began in January 1970. Working from an already-compiled age/sex register, the names of all the women born between 1919 and 1921 were extracted. These were judged to be the three years producing the highest proportion of women now presenting menopausal symptoms. A total of thirty-one fifty-year-old women were approached. Of these, only eighteen agreed to be interviewed. There was, in other words, a refusal rate of 42 per cent, showing a reluctance to discuss menstruation, which is itself in need of explanation. Subsequently, it was decided that women of all age groups should be interviewed and this work is still in progress.

Interviews were structured, in the sense that they aimed to establish the salient features of the life-history of each woman, how long she had been married, how many children she had had and so on. They also aimed to establish a brief medical history of the woman, with special emphasis on present and past menstrual and menopausal complaints. The medical cards of each of the women were later examined in order to see how the patient's self-image differed from that of her own doctor.[1] However, the most important part of the interview, that which sought to determine the woman's attitudes to her husband and to 'men' generally, to menstruation and the cessation of menstruation, was conducted less formally. Women were asked, for example, whether they thought men treated women fairly or whether they thought men understood women. The quantity and quality of answers to such questions obviously varied enormously. Interviews lasted between thirty minutes and two hours, depending very much upon individual volubility.

After a few weeks of research it became apparent that one of the most crucial items of information related to attitudes concerning the loss of blood in menstruation and the permanent or temporary cessation of bleeding. It was found that women could be divided into one of two clear-cut categories. The first category contains women wishing to lose as much blood as possible and to menstruate for as long as possible, believing this to contribute to the good of their overall health. The second category contains women fearful of 'losing their life's blood', and wishing to cease menstruating as early as possible, believing menstruation to be damaging to their general health. This latter category expressed itself in quasi-scientific terms, saying that they did not, for example, make a fuss about menstruation, 'I just carry on as usual'. By contrast, the former category regard menstruation as a time at which woman is particularly vulnerable and exposed to dangers, especially through the possibilitiy of an obstruction of the menstrual flow.

It is, of course, known that menstrual blood is not the only kind of fluid around which such ideas have collected. Spitting, for example, is a custom illustrating a similar belief which stresses cleanliness and the importance of ridding oneself of saliva. However, it is of significance that the fluid be menstrual blood, which is clearly distinguished from inter-menstrual discharges and bleeding from piles. It was found that the mere discharge of a fluid, irrespective of its source, did not produce a feeling of being cleansed and restored to a former state of efficiency and vigour. Having separated out these two distinct categories of women, an attempt was made to discover what other features were unique to each category. The only correlation which could be found was one between the need for purging through menstruation and a relatively undisturbed conjugal relationship. Conversely, the absence of this need and the viewing of periods as a nuisance seemed to be associated with an irregular or disturbed conjugal relationship.

Tolstoy has said that all happy families resemble one another but each unhappy family is unhappy in its own way. It was decided, however, that the criteria for assessing 'happiness' in marriage were so many as to yield a final category which was unmanageable. Instead an attempt was made to isolate obvious cases of conjugal deficiency under the heading 'irregularity of sexual and reproductive lives'. Under this term are included such conditions as permanent or temporary separations from the husband including widowhood, as are such conditions as childlessness, spinsterhood, as well as extremes of marital conflict. This kind of definition enables us to distinguish a norm for satisfactory marriages which entails the absence of certain negative features. In fact, this division between women having a regular and those having an irregular conjugal relationship is very fruitful, for it emphasises the importance which women not having an irregular sexual or reproductive life attach to the uterus and menstruation. It also highlights the considerable number of gynaecological complaints to which such preoccupations give rise.

These findings, therefore, lead to a conclusion apparently opposed to much of that currently expressed in the medical literature on the subject. Recent literature has pursued a strand of thought which refers pelvic and menstrual complaints to personality difficulties. Estimates of the percentage of emotionally-based pelvic complaints range from 31 per cent. (Miller 1946) to as high as 65 per cent. (Johnson 1939). Incidentally, these figures are almost identical to the estimates for neurosis in general practice (Dr J. B. Loudon, personal communication). Johnson (1939: 374) has claimed that: 'Bodily processes are the common ways in which unconscious attitudes find expression.' Sixty-five per cent of all pelvic complaints are, he claims, of functional origin, revealing upon examination a healthy uterus and being instead the expression of social or sexual maladaptation.

This examination of the kind of role to which menstrual and gynaecological complaints are assigned in medical literature, requires a restatement of the main theme of this article, namely that gynaecological symptoms, rather than being the expression of social or sexual maladaptation are, on the contrary, the expression of social conformity and sexual adaptation. However, we must, of course, allow for the fact that some, if not many, gynaecological symptoms are related to physical conditions such as, for example, fibroids.

The significance attached to menstruation finds expression in a system of related beliefs concerning menstrual bleeding, including the notion of menstrual blood itself, considered as a separate category. The most easily recognisable theme in these beliefs is that focusing on 'bad blood' and the process of menstruation whereby the system is purged of 'badness' and 'excess'. This 'badness' and 'excess' is subjectively experienced as acting as a kind of cog in the wheel, slowing down one's activity, making women feel huge, bloated and poisoned. Surrounding these ideas of female 'badness' and the consequent need for purging are a number of prohibitions to ensure that the body does, in fact, succeed in ridding itself of the 'badness'. Women stated that they would not have a bath for fear the period might 'go away', although they hastened to add that they would, of course, wash. Many would not wash their hair for fear they might go 'funny'. One woman was more explicit, saying that she had once tried to wash her hair whilst menstruating, but had afterwards 'fancied I was not losing as much'. The emphasis here is on losing as much menstrual blood as possible because this is thought to be 'natural' and is a means whereby 'the system rights itself'. The symbolic content of these beliefs appears to be so high as to warrant their description as 'magical'.

In replies to questions about the significance of menstruation, certain key words emerged. These are 'to lose', 'to see' and 'natural'. The analysis of these words which follows is, I am aware, a bit of a linguistic struggle but I shall give it nevertheless. First, the term 'lose'. When women refer to the process of menstruating, they most frequently do so by the intransitive use of the verb 'to lose'. Thus, for example, 'I think it is good to lose'. Alternatively, women say 'I think it is good to see them'. Finally, one of the ways in which all such statements are sanctioned is by reference to their being 'natural'. I do not think it is stretching meanings beyond their natural sphere of reference to say that these words by their very lack of precision and by their ambiguity, are particularly well-suited to convey certain features of the female social situation. The verb 'to lose', for example, can be used transitively, as in 'to lose blood', and, intransitively, in the sense of losing a game. I would maintain that it is this double sense which contributes to the recurrent appearance of the word. Thus in referring directly to the importance of losing large quantities of menstrual blood, they are referring indirectly to the importance of coming to terms with their role as 'losers' in a much wider sense. This sense of loss is expressed most acutely when talking about 'men' generally as a distinct category from women. 'Men' are thought to lack understanding about and consideration for women, especially as regards the constraints which childbearing and housekeeping impose upon a woman. As a class they are thought to be selfish and lacking in responsibility and sensitivity towards their female partners. A similar type of analysis can be given for the word 'see'. For one cannot only be said to 'see' one's periods, but one can also be said to 'see', in the sense of understanding a situation. Finally, the necessity of 'losing' or 'seeing' one's periods is justified on the grounds that 'it's natural' or, alternatively, 'it's got to be'. The felt element of constraint inherent in an external, non-subjective reality would lead me to substitute the word 'social' for 'natural', thus completing the chain of interdependent meanings.

My interpretation of these recurrent words, in terms of which menstruation is talked about, gains added plausibility from the explanatory clauses which qualify the initial statement about the necessity of losing menstrual blood. For example, women say they feel huge, bloated, slow and sluggish if they do not have a period or if they do not lose much. One woman said she felt, 'really great' after a heavy period, whilst most insist on the value and importance of having a 'good clearance'. In more practical terms the side effects of not having a 'good clearance' express themselves in activity, especially in the inability to get on with the housework. One woman in particular, who had already arrived at the menopause, said that she used to find it much easier to do the cleaning whilst she was still menstruating regularly, than she did now in her post-menopausal state.

What has just been said requires an amendment of the previous quotation which claimed that bodily processes were the expression of unconscious emotional attitudes. They may indeed be the expression of such attitudes, but in the case of menstruation, these attitudes will be determined, not by individual conflicts, but by a shared common role, which women themselves see as generating a particular type of conflict in women.

Perhaps what has been said about attitudes to the loss of menstrual blood and cessation of such a loss can best be illustrated by giving the case histories of two women. Their names are, of course, fictitious.

> Mrs Olwen Jones has lived in the village all her life, and was born two doors from the house where she now lives. Her father, now dead, was employed as an undermanager in a pit and her husband, Fred, is a coal merchant. Mrs Jones has just turned fifty, having been married for twenty-five years. She has two children, a son aged twenty-one and a daughter of eighteen. Mrs Jones leaves the impression of being quick-witted and an energetic woman. She takes an obvious delight in saying the unexpected or, to her mind, shocking and then slowly savouring the effect this produces on her audience. She considers herself a happily married woman who is devoted to her husband, Fred. Her worries have been of the common variety, centering on money and anxieties over the children's education. Nevertheless, her speech is permeated with an aura of dissatisfaction which is never quite fully identified. She says she is always depressed, more especially since the children have grown up and her husband has taken to going out in the evenings and leaving her at home by herself. She feels 'sorry for herself'. Her experience of life, and, hence her view of the world, is such that she sees it bisected by an insurmountable communication barrier. Men can 'never in this world of God' understand women. Men she thinks are like animals, although she would exclude Fred from this characterisation. Amplifying on this verdict she said: 'I'm not very fond of my sex life'. She considered it ridiculous at her age. Asked why, she said it was just ridiculous. However, this did not prevent her from acceding to her husband's demands in bed, ridiculous and frustrating though she finds these episodes. Contrasting with this background of ill-defined dissatisfaction about her feminine role, Mrs Jones has very emphatic and definite views about the importance and value of menstruation in her life. She says she would feel very old and 'frustrated' without her periods. 'Frustrated' because she would not be able to get rid of blood, because she would feel unclean. Frustrated also because she would not feel like doing anything about the house and the washing and cleaning would be left undone. Almost as though the energy for housework was generated as a by-product of the process of losing menstrual blood. For the same reasons, Mrs. Jones would dread any gynaecological operations in case they disturbed the menstrual flow.

A very different and contrasting life-history and attitudes to female physiological processes are presented by Mrs Leah Thomas.

> Like Mrs Jones, Mrs Thomas was born in the village in the same year and brought up there. In contrast to Mrs Jones who had only one sister, she comes from a large family of seven children. Her father's occupation was that of blacksmith, whilst her husband has had a succession of occupations, more recently being employed as an ambulance driver and then a bus driver. Mrs Thomas has had a total of five children, four of whom are still living. The youngest girl is still at home, the others all being married. In comparison with Mrs Jones's married life, Mrs Thomas's conjugal relationship has been highly unstable. Although she is still legally married and has been for over thirty years, her conjugal relationship has been punctuated by the intermittent and regular disappearance of her husband. She has now been separated from her husband for four years. At present he is living with another woman on the out-

skirts of a northern city. This woman he met some twenty years ago whilst he was working as an ambulance driver. Their liason started then and has been pursued ever since. Mrs Thomas, however, claims she was totally ignorant of the fact that Frank had 'another woman'. She claims that she considered herself a happily married woman during the years of her marriage, despite the fact that her husband was very little at home. She describes him, somewhat euphemistically, as being 'not a very domestic sort of man'. From her reminiscenses and descriptions of her husband it emerges that she regards herself as still very much in love with him. His sexual prowess, his powerful and melodious voice are still very much sources of admiration and wonder to her. After he had left her to 'live tally' with his friend, Mrs Thomas had made it clear to him that she was willing to forgive him and have him back. Frank, however, had said that he did not deserve such gentle treatment. He had, he said, 'made his bed and must lie in it'.

However, not only is there a difference in the patterns of married life as between Mrs Jones and Mrs Thomas, there is also a striking difference in attitudes about menstruation. Mrs Thomas possesses no theories whatsoever about the value of menstruation or the need to lose menstrual blood. She says she cannot wait to stop menstruating because she is losing such a lot. She said: 'I'm sure I'm no better in health by seeing them'. Menstruation to Mrs Thomas is an unmitigated source of annoyance and discomfort. Prior to and during menstruation, Mrs Thomas feels extremely weak, suffers from sick headaches, dizziness and vaginal irritation. A hysterectomy would not worry her in the least, in fact, she thinks it would provide a welcome relief.

Contrasting with this lack of emphasis on menstruation, merely wishing for its absence, Mrs Thomas expresses marked concern about and attaches great significance to, other bodily ailments. Her complaints are numerous and of such a nature that they lend themselves to lengthy, detailed descriptions. According to her own account and her doctor she suffers from high blood pressure, headaches, dizzy spells, palpitations, backache, indigestion, nervous rashes, sleeplessness and, lastly, depression. In comparison the list of Olwen Jones's ailments is very meagre. Her ailments centre on headaches which she attributes to high blood pressure and depression.

These two case histories, although obviously each unique, illustrate one of the main themes of this article. Namely, that it is the women with relatively undisturbed, though by no means necessarily problem-free married lives who emphasise the loss of large quantities of menstrual blood, who are more sensitive to bodily changes or menstruation and who regard such processes as essential to producing and maintaining a healthy equilibrium. Relationships with other features of the woman's social situation, for example, family size, religion and education, were found to be incidental. In other words, no constant relationship could be established within a larger number of women.

Before concluding this preliminary discussion of menstruation, it may be useful to contrast my approach with that of the psycho-analysts. Freud, not surprisingly in view of his male-centred approach, has very little to say on the subject. In his essay on female sexuality (1931) the subject is significant by its complete absence. In *Civilisation and its discontents* (1930), Freud refers to menstruation in a footnote. In the context of a discussion about the foundations of the monogamous family which results from the transformation of the need for genital satisfaction from the status of 'an intermittent and sudden guest' to that of a 'permanent lodger', Freud draws attention to the changed importance of menstruation. He says: 'the taboo on menstruation is derived from an "organic repression", as a defence against a phase of development that has been surmounted' (1930: 36). By the term 'organic repression' Freud is referring to 'the diminution of the olfactory stimuli' as a significant element in sexual attraction. In other words, Freud is saying that woman is at her most attractive during menstruation. That for some unknown reason the natural process of this attraction has been stemmed, with the result that rigid barriers have been erected against the possibility of experiencing consciously this original attraction. Hence, the prevalence of taboos surrounding menstruating women. Freud's final comment on the significance of menstruation is perhaps most telling. At the menopause, the absence of menstruation is re-experienced by woman as the psychological loss she once felt in early childhood, when she compared her body to a boy's for the first time and concluded that she had been castrated.

Other psycho-analytic writers, among them Horney (1967) in her chapter on 'Premenstrual tension', links menstrual disorders with ambivalent or contradictory attitudes towards motherhood. (For example, where the fear of childbirth or the fear of coitus is coupled with a simultaneous, strong desire for children.)

However, the interpretation which is sociologically of the greatest value is that offered by Deutsch (1965). Deutsch singles out menstruation as being the most interesting gynaecological occurrence. 'And this par excellence "biological event" is to a high degree influenced by psychological factors' (1965: 311). One of the chief aspects of menstruation Deutsch concerns herself with is 'dysmenorrhea', this being the term used to refer to cases of excessively painful menstruation. Of this she states: 'Women suffering from dysmenorrhea assume a priori the attitude toward menstruation that all occurrences in the female genital region are an orgy of painful suffering. The physical discomfort of menstruation mobilizes and substantiates this feeling. Often a feeling of death accompanies the pain.' A concomitant of dysmenorrhea is the belief in the 'poison theory of menstruation'. According to Deutsch this is generally held to consist in the belief that: 'The sexual processes produce poison which is eliminated from the woman's body through menstruation.' The psycho-analytic interpretation of these ideas and symptoms is one which links the poison theory with antecedent guilt feelings surrounding sexuality and a resultant personal need for purification of the body and thus the expiation of sins. In other words, the claimed pain of menstruation serves as a punishment and an outlet for guilty feelings. She concludes: 'Here can be seen the apparent paradox: that women who suffer from dysmenorrhea are hypersensitive to pain, but at the same time, have strongly masochistic tendencies.' Briefly, Deutsch considers all such struggles for purification as an expression of guilt feelings and as attempts to escape the feminine destiny, that is, as an incomplete adaptation to the female identity.

Whilst allowing that, of the psycho-analytic interpretations of menstruation so far considered, Deutsch's comes nearest to grasping its symbolic weight, I should nevertheless like to suggest a rearrangement of the elements in her explanation. It may be true that there exists a category of women who regard all occurrences in the female genital region as a 'painful orgy', but my sample did not in any way corroborate the connexion of this attitude with guilt feelings. Neither did the occurrence of painful menstrual symptoms entail the experience of more directly and obviously sexual experience as painful. Indeed it seems more likely that emphasis on pain at menstruation is among other things a way of safe-guarding the smooth functioning of sexual activity at other times. One is reminded of Harris's (1959) article on possession hysteria among the Taita. It is as though the symbolic destruction of one's inferior status (the insistence on 'a good clearance') left one better prepared to accept the vicissitudes and constraints of being a married woman.

Having considered the part menstruation plays in the symbolic or emotional world of women, it becomes necessary to ask what happens to this when menstruation ceases.

Bearing in mind the importance which menstruation had as a means of conveying a feminine social role, this second part of the article will go on to consider whether the climacteric, in terms of the standardised modes of experiencing it and in terms of the conglomeration of beliefs associated with it, can be better understood when viewed as a *rite de passage*. However, this approach will be exercised with caution. The climacteric may not conform completely to the pattern of a *rite de passage* in the sense of, for example, puberty rituals among primitive peoples, but it may nevertheless share sufficient of the features of transition rituals to make an examination of their basic elements worthwhile.

First, however, a description of the surface features of the 'change' which immediately bring to mind a *rite de passage*. For a start there is the expectation of unknown dangers to be endured, with the emphasis on the uncertainty as to what these dangers actually consist of. Furthermore, these dangers are given a value in themselves. Many women expressed the belief that it was good to experience 'hot flushes' as frequently as possible, otherwise there was a chance of dangerous complications developing. Hence, the popular saying: 'A flush is worth a guinea a box'. And I am told that to anyone who was literate before the second world war, the association with an advertisement for Beechams laxative pills will be immediate. Flushes are thought to 'carry you through the change more quickly and safely'. Again the reference here is to a 'passage' through which one is carried. Some women who were on the change even voiced a regret that they did not flush enough. Asked whether they suffered from hot flushes, they admitted their failure by saying: 'No I'm not very good'. Hot flushes were thought to be the result of menstrual blood rushing to the head so that an absence of flushes implies a deficiency of menstrual blood. Prohibitions surrounding the climacteric incorporate a mixture of medical and magical information. Women are advised not to touch red meat for fear it should 'go off'. They should not attempt to make bread because the dough would not rise. They should not touch salt. Finally, women envisage 'the change' as a period of time when certain ill-defined anatomical or structural changes are taking place within their bodies. This is the reason most often cited to me in answer to the question as to why 'the change' was called the 'change'. One seventy-year-old lady told me that at the menopause, women turned into men inside. She herself had, she said, been aware of this process taking place, and had experienced it as a 'turning and tightening' of the thigh muscles.

The description of menopause attitudes and beliefs will, I hope, justify the analysis of the structure and function of transition rituals which follows. However, it was realised that women who have attached little importance to menstruation, having already had disturbed sexual lives are unlikely to feel that they are moving from one role to another. They have already mentally forsaken their sexual role. Thus of the eighteen fifty-year-old women interviewed, it was the eight women whose sexual lives were described as irregular who adopted a quasi-scientific attitude both to menstruation and to the menopause. These women experienced fewer menopausal symptoms, as well as feeling that the cessation of menstrual bleeding would not be disturbing to their mental or physical equilibrium.

Van Gennep (1909) in his study of rites of passage elaborates one basic theme: namely, that all rites exhibit the same underlying pattern and that this pattern serves a primary function wherever it is found. The bare bones of his argument can be summarised as follows: change exercises a disturbing influence both upon the individual and upon the society; the solution provided by society to deal with these disruptive effects is to ritualise the processes of change, thus minimising the danger inherent in all transitions. 'An individual is placed in various sections of society synchronically and in succession; in order to pass from one category to another and to join individuals in other sections, he must submit from the day of his birth to that of his death, to ceremonies whose forms often vary but whose function is similar' (Van Gennep 1909:189).

The pattern which Van Gennep claims to perceive underlying all ritual activity is divided into three major phases: rites of separation from the original environment, rites of transition, and rites of incorporation into the new environment. This does not, however, mean that each phase is equally accentuated in all rites, as Van Gennep himself stresses. (In fact, it is one of the factors which lends stress to the menopausal situation that rites of incorporation or ritualised ideas expressing incorporation into a new group are remarkably lacking from a time when attitudes and beliefs are otherwise highly ritualised.)

Gluckman (1962: 14) criticises Van Gennep for lacking 'a clearly formulated theory of society' and himself wishes to make rites of passage a class of the more general category of rituals effecting role specialisation. However, it is difficult to see how, for example, rites of pregnancy and childbirth could in the first instance be said to differentiate roles, which are not already secularly defined. The analysis might apply to the case of a man changing his activities, but it hardly seems necessary to use mystical means to identify a pregnant woman, or for that matter a pre-menopausal or a post-menopausal woman.

Gluckman's criticism is centred around the notion to a 'role'. Had Van Gennep realised the importance of this concept for his analysis, he would have been in a far better position to work out the implications of his theory. However, this does not mean that the analysis of ritual has to take an entirely new direction and concern itself with ritual as role differentiation. The notion of a role can be introduced in such a way that Van Gennep's thesis is merely expanded and not rendered otiose.

Parsons (1951: 34) defines role in the following way so that it becomes the Archimedian point for the whole theory of society; 'It is a distinctive feature of the structure of social action, however, that in most relationships the actor does not participate as a total entity but only by virtue of a given differentiated "sector" of his total personality. Such a sector which is the unit of a system of social relationships has come predominantly to be called a "role".' And a page later he says: 'Role is the concept which links the subsystem of the actor as a "psychological" behaving entity to the distinctively social structure.' The notion of a role, therefore, being distinct from the individual, is defined by reference to a norm which is built into the very concept and by means of which it is identified. The rites of passage can thus be seen as not merely marking the transition from one status to another in the passage through society, but as expressing the demands of the new role and the expectations of society on the incumbent of the new role.

Van Gennep's analysis of ritual, therefore, as movement from one status in society to another, or as movement from one group of individuals to another can be left intact. However, we can supply a fuller answer as to why such rites decrease the danger of change. Change is dangerous precisely because one can recognise that the individual, *qua* individual, and not merely as a member of society, is not exhaustively defined by the sum of his roles in society, even though in practice it may be difficult to refer to him other than via one of his roles. The point being that the aspect of individual identity which has been neglected by or has eluded role definition increases ambiguity.

If we use Van Gennep's analysis of rites of passage together with my amendment, we find that it is a peculiarly well-suited theoretical tool with which to approach the climacteric. The very term 'change' is an unambiguous reference to the nature of the climacteric.

The transition in this particular instance is from woman in her reproductive role to woman in her non-reproductive role. In view of the central position which female fertility occupies in the public image of the adult female, the disappearance of this reproductive capacity is bound, at the very least, to present the women with problems. A little girl is taught to expect that she will fall in love, get married and have children, preferably in that order. However, the story tails off rather inconclusively and unsatisfactorily by saying that she will live happily ever after. Again no provision is made for alternatives to this pattern. This theme, of the intrinsic connexion between fertility and 'female adulthood' in our society is extensively dealt with by Kirk (1964) in his study of childless marriages and adoption.

It is also very fruitfully explored by Becker (1963). Becker's article deals with menopausal depression. The question he asks is: 'Why does a woman who to all appearances, has led a satisfying life, suddenly break down at the menopause and decide that her life is not worth living?' (1963: 355). The answer he gives is as follows: 'Women become depressed at the menopause because . . . they do not have enough reasons for satisfying action, and when they lose the one apparent reason upon which they predicated their lives—their femininity—their whole active world caves in. Let us be brutally direct: Menopausal depression is the consequence of confining woman to a too narrow range of life choices or opportunities. It is a social and cultural phenomenon, for which the "designers" of social roles are to blame' (1963: 358). In that quotation, Becker is referring to psychiatrists and psycho-analysts when he uses the term ' "designers" of social roles'. 'We create menopausal depression by not seeing to it that women in their forties are armed with more than one justification for their lives' (1963: 359). Becker illustrates his analysis of menopausal depression by a re-examination of Freud's case-study of a fifty-one-year-old female patient. This woman came to see Freud because she had found that her life was suddenly 'flooded' by an insane jealousy of a young career girl with whom she imagined her husband to be having an affair. Freud's interpretation of the situation was that, through the use of this jealousy language, the woman was trying to conceal her own libidinal urges felt towards her handsome young son-in-law. Becker's view of the situation is very different. From his point of view the significant elements in the situation are, firstly, that 'this woman senses the decline of her only value to men—her physical charm', and, secondly, the difference as between the patient's status as compared with the young girl whom she imagined involved in the affair with her husband. The jealous wife had played the social game according to all the conventional rules, but something had gone wrong. She now found herself alone, without usable skills, no longer with children, without her accustomed beauty. However, the situation is rendered doubly poignant by the fact that the woman is 'without words in which to frame her protest'. The protest against 'helplessness and potential meaninglessness takes the form of jealousy accusations'. This jealousy language is an indirect reference to the woman's exclusion from the man's world. Indirect, of necessity, because the exclusion is so complete as to deprive the woman of the language in which a direct protest could be voiced.

NOTE

1. Permission to look at medical cards was obtained both from the doctor and in writing from each woman concerned.

REFERENCES

BECKER, ERNEST 1963. Social science and psychiatry. *Antioch Rev.* 23, 353–65.

DEUTSCH, HELENE 1965. The psychiatric component in gynaecology. In *Neuroses and character types.* London: Hogarth Press.

DOYLE, JAMES C. 1952. Unnecessary hysterectomies. *J. Am. med. Ass.* 151, 360–5.

FREUD, SIGMUND 1930. *Civilization and its discontents.* London: Hogarth Press.

——— 1931. *Female sexuality* (Collected Papers 5). London: Hogarth Press.

GENNEP, A. VAN 1909. *Les rites de passage.* Paris: Emile Nourry.

GLUCKMAN, MAX (ed.) 1962. *Essays on the ritual of social relations.* Manchester: Univ. Press.

HARRIS, GRACE 1959. Possession 'hysteria' in a Kenya tribe. *Am. Anthrop.* 61, 1046–66.

HORNEY, KAREN 1967. *Feminine psychology.* London: Routledge & Kegan Paul.

JOHNSON, W. O. 1939. Emotional disturbances with pelvic symptoms. *Sth. Surg.* 8, 373–83.

KIRK, DAVID 1964. *Shared fate*. Glencoe, Ill.: The Free Press.
MILLER, NORMAN F. 1946. Hysterectomies: therapeutic necessity or surgical racket? *Am. J. Obstet. Gynec.* 51, 804–10.
PARSONS, TALCOTT 1951. *The social system*. Glencoe, Ill.: The Free Press.

PART 4

Sex Differences

The question of whether or not there are behavioral differences between females and males and, if so, what are they, has long attracted the efforts of psychologists. Beliefs about such differences abound in the popular culture. That both scientists and nonscientists are interested in the matter suggests an asumption that unequivocal data would settle an old human issue. A second question follows upon the first: if it should be shown that behavioral sex differences do in fact exist, is there a biological substratum which makes them inevitable, or do they appear because of massive doses of cultural conditioning?

Based on the research currently available, the answer to the first question is yes, there are behavioral differences between males and females, a few of which appear during childhood. The answer to the second question is by no means certain, but we do know from studies such as those by Margaret Mead that human behavior is enormously malleable, and that learning accounts for much more of our behavior than it does for the behavior of individuals in any other species.

The question of sex differences has become political in recent years, with adherents of the women's movement and promoters of equality for women insisting that there is no basis for discrimination against women on the grounds that women are systematically different from men. Still, there persists in the minds of many the idea that women and men can never be behaviorally similar, that behavioral sex differences are real and natural, and that socialization practices which treat the sexes differently are reflections of biological givens.

The long history of research on sex differences has resulted in a large body of literature on the subject. Only recently have the assumptions and implications of such research been critically examined. The papers in this section are examples of contemporary theoretical and empirical work which demonstrate an awareness of the meaning of sex as a variable in psychological research and as a categorical assignment whose consequences for the person would be difficult to exaggerate.

Since humans are sexually dimorphic, and can be readily categorized, with rare exceptions, as male or female, perhaps it is not surprising that statements about psychological characteristics often seem to imply that these, too, are sexually dimorphic. Such statements as "boys are aggressive" or "girls are emotional" imply that these characteristics are categorically descriptive of the members of one sex and not the other. Therefore, in any discussion of sex differences it is necessary to keep certain important points in mind. The first is that the two sexes overlap greatly on all psychological characteristics. Differences among the members of one sex are much greater than is the difference between the sexes. If a sex difference is shown to exist, it merely means that the average score on the characteristic is somewhat higher for one sex than for the other. Some persons in the lower group will score higher on a measure of the characteristic than will some persons in the higher group. This makes generalizing about the probable strength of a psychological characteristic on the basis of a persons's sex category very risky. For example, the mean perfomance of girls on tests of verbal ability is higher than is the mean performance of boys. But obviously there are some boys who score higher in verbal ability than most girls do. Knowing the sex category of a person does not help one to predict reliably what the person's verbal ability may be.

Another problem in interpreting reports of sex differences is that girls and boys are widely observed to differ in maturity at given ages. Newborn girls are four to six weeks "older" developmentally than are newborn boys, a difference which increases to about one year by age six. Some of the differences are in physical indices, such as skeletal and dental development, and others, which may be more important for behavior, involve brain lateralization and cerebral dominance, both of which occur earlier in girls. Girls also reach puberty a year or so before boys do. Given these developmental differences in maturity, then, the problem of making meaningful observations about sex differences at a given age becomes more complicated.

The question of psychological sex differences among very young infants has not been finally resolved as yet, though the evidence strongly suggests that such differences have not been dmonstrated. An observer of diaper-clad occupants of a nursery for newborns could not do much better than chance if he or she attempted to identify the sex of the infants by either their appearance or their behavior. Yet the baby's sex has very strong stimulus value for others, especially for its parents. That parents perceive boys and girls differently from birth, in accordance with sex role stereotypes, is demonstrated in "The Eye of The Beholder: Parents' Views on Sex of Newborns," by Jeffery Z. Rubin and others. The parents of thirty first-born boys and girls were asked to describe their infants and to rate them on questionnaire within twenty-four hours after birth. The male and female babies did not differ in weight, height, or condition at birth. In describing their infants, parents were more likely to use "big" for their sons and "little" for their daughters. They rated boys as more firm, better coordinated, stronger, and hardier, and girls as softer, weaker, and more delicate. Fathers were more likely to stereotype their babies, seeing greater diferences between boys and girls than mothers did. Since the babies did not in fact differ by sex, the study demonstrates the attribution to them of characteristics which were based entirely on parental beliefs, as they affected their perceptions. If we assume that perception affects behavior, it is reasonable to predict that parents' behavior toward their infants will be influenced by their stereotypic perceptions. If parents respond differentially to their infants from birth on the basis of sex, thus exposing them to different contingencies and expectations, then the problem of evaluating the relative contributions of socialization and biology to later observed sex differences become difficult indeed.

Michael Lewis, in his paper on "Early Sex Differences in The Human," dismisses as fruitless any attempt at this time to untangle the biological-experiential contributions to the development of sex differences. He proposes that the major issue is not whether behavior is more influenced by biology or experience, but rather if and to what extent behavior can be modified. Although certain sex differenes are innately based, they may be modifiable by experience. Instead of looking for etiology, Lewis argues, we should look at process variables—those which affect the development of behavior. Lewis, too, is interested in the differential behavior of parents toward boys and girls. He reports research which shows that parents reward those behaviors which are deemed appropriate to the child's gender. Such processes also mediate the child's development of the concept of gender, its cognitive recognition of its identification with one sex and not the other. Finally, Lewis suggests that the study of sex differences may have little importance as a scientific issue, and that it may indeed be more motivated by social and political interests. A justification for such study is to gain understanding of the processes which affect development. This paper, which was presented at a conference on sex research, concludes with a valuable discussion of infant research and its methodological problems which can result in contradictory findings since procedures for studying infants are not yet sufficiently standardized for researchers to have confidence in the validity of replicated studies.

Reesa Vaughter's paper, "Psychology," is a review essay which looks at the status of several research areas in the psychology of women. In addition to observing the recent literature on sex differences, Vaughter also looks at psychosexual development, achievement motivation, and psychotherapy—areas in which the differential experiences, adaptations, and treatment of girls and women are reflected in currently topical research.

The study of sex differences, Vaughter suggests, may no longer be important for the psychology of women. Even when a difference is found, the determinants of the behavior may not be known nor meet the criteria for biologically based behavior, such as crosscultural observation and species continuity. Vaughter makes a valuable distinction between sex and gender as sources of variance in research on both same and cross sex groups. Sex is a biological characteristic, but gender and gender role are learned from parents and peers in a sociocultural context. Many of the studies reviewed in this paper are concerned not so much with differences between males and females as with differences in the kinds of experiences they have, which then may have affects on later differences between them. For example, a study of sex-typed toys found that boys' toys had a higher potential for eliciting competency than girls' toys had. Another study of the behavior of nursery school teachers found that boys received more instruction and more reward for working on academic tasks.

Current research on female psychosexual behavior, achievement motivation, and psychotherapy, while concerned with disparate behaviors, all illuminate the importance of the situational context within which they occur. Again, the biological variable of sex may turn out to be much less important in producing the adaptations which we call masculine and feminine than are the innumerable noncontradictory messages which the child receives from parents and peers in the formative years. Finally, Vaughter reports on the movement within psychology to bring into the discipline a feminist perspective which will balance both research and practice, thereby facilitating the development of a psychology of human behavior. One aspect of this perspective would place research within its social and political context. Instead of looking for motives inherent in the feminine psyche, such research would have to take into account the environmental context within which these motives occur. In academia, the valuing of cooperative research (instead of competitive) teaching, and a concern with self-growth in the context of research are all examples of shifts in style and priorities which a feminist perspective can affect.

In the last paper in this section, "Androgyny Reconsidered," Kathleen Grady considers psychology's relation to what she calls "the social question of sex." Three questions are posed: What kind of fact is sex? Where do sex differences exist? Why and how should we study sex differences?

Grady echoes Vaughter's concern with the distinction between sex and gender, and argues that the importance attached to discriminations based on sex indicate that sex is primarily a social rather than a biological fact. Discriminations always have a function and, in the case of sex, the function is a social one. That is, its aims and meanings are of social importance. In regard to the loci of sex differences, Grady makes an important distinction between subject and stimulus variables. The view of sex differences as subject variables has characterized traditional research in the area, cataloguing differences between males and females in personality traits, abilities, and similar abstractions. The more recent trend toward examining the affect of sex as a stimulus variable has led to research on sex stereotyping, as well as on beliefs and attitudes which guide behavior. For instance, the attribution of identical works to male and female writers or artists resulted in significantly different evaluations of the work. Here, the sex difference is in the stimulus which because of its sex label calls forth stereotypic attitudes. To the question why and how should we study sex differences, Grady suggests that both androgyny and sexism do exist, and since androgyny is a personality construct and sexism has had the most damaging effects in the area of personality research, attention should focus on these variables.

The papers in this section, then, are less concerned with the documentation and nature of sex differences than they are with the different environmental contexts in which boys and girls grow up, and with the nature of the research itself. As long as the two sexes live in different experiential and existential worlds, it is those worlds which need research attention.

The research itself has been largely a male enterprise, affected by masculine interests and modes of inquiry. It is the correction of social assumptions underlying the research that a feminist perspective can address, with fruitful consequences for a psychology of human behavior.

The Eye of the Beholder
Parents' Views on Sex of Newborns

Jeffrey Z. Rubin, Frank J. Provenzano, and Zella Luria

Thirty pairs of primiparous parents, fifteen with sons and fifteen with daughters, were interviewed within the first 24 hours postpartum. Although male and female infants did not differ in birth length, weight, or Apgar scores, daughters were significantly more likely than sons to be described as little, beautiful, pretty, and cute, and as resembling their mothers. Fathers made more extreme and stereotyped rating judgments of their newborns than did mothers. Findings suggest that sex-typing and sex-role socialization *have already begun at birth.*

As Schaffer[10] has observed, the infant at birth is essentially an asocial, largely undifferentiated creature. It appears to be little more than a tiny ball of hair, fingers, toes, cries, gasps, and gurgles. However, while it may seem that "if you've seen one, you've seen them all," babies are *not* all alike—a fact that is of special importance to their parents, who want, and appear to need, to view their newborn child as a creature that is special. Hence, much of early parental interaction with the infant may be focused on a search for distinctive features. Once the fact that the baby is normal has been established, questions such as, "Who does the baby look like?" and "How much does it weigh?" are asked.

Of all the questions parents ask themselves and each other about their infant, one seems to have priority: "Is it a boy or a girl?" The reasons for and consequences of posing this simple question are by no means trivial. The answer, "boy" or "girl," may result in the parents' organizing their perception of the infant with respect to a wide variety of attributes—ranging from its size to its activity, attractiveness, even its future potential. It is the purpose of the present study to examine the kind of verbal picture parents form of the newborn infant, as a function both of their own and their infant's gender.

As Asch[2] observed years ago, in forming our impressions of others, we each tend to develop a *Gestalt*—a global picture of what others are like, which permits us to organize our perceptions of the often discrepant, contradictory aspects of their behavior and manner into a unified whole. The awareness of another's status,[13] the belief that he is "warm" or "cold,"[2,5] "extroverted" or "introverted,"[6] even the apparently trivial knowledge of another's name[4]—each of these cues predisposes us to develop a stereotypic view of that other, his underlying nature, and how he is likely to behave. How much more profound, then, may be the consequences of a cue as prominent in parents' minds as the gender of their own precious, newborn infant.

The study reported here is addressed to parental perceptions of their infants at the point when these infants first emerge into the world. If it can be demonstrated that parental sex-typing has already begun its course at this earliest of moments in the life of the child, it may be possible to understand better one of the important antecedents of the complex process by which the growing child comes to view itself as boy-ish or girl-ish.

Based on our review of the literature, two forms of parental sex-typing may be expected to occur at the time of the infant's birth. First, it appears likely that parents will view and label their newborn child differentially, as a simple function of the infant's gender. Aberle and Naegele[1] and Tasch,[12] using only fathers as subjects, found that they had different expectations for sons and daughters: sons were expected to be aggressive and athletic, daughters were expected to be pretty, sweet, fragile, and delicate. Rebelsky and Hanks[9] found that fathers spent more time talking to their daughters than their sons during the first three months of life. While the sample size was too small for the finding to be significant, they suggest that the role of father-of-daughter may be perceived as requiring greater nurturance. Similarly, Pedersen and Robson[8] reported that the fathers of infant daughters exhibited more behavior labeled (by the authors) as "apprehension over well being" than did the fathers of sons.

A comparable pattern emerges in research using mothers as subjects. Sears, Maccoby and Levin,[11] for example, found that the mothers of kindergartners reported tolerating more aggression from sons than daughters, when it was directed toward parents and peers. In addition, maternal nurturance was seen as more important for the daughter's than the son's development. Taken together, the findings in this body of research lead us to expect parents (regardless of their gender) to view their newborn infants differentially—labeling daughters as weaker, softer, and therefore in greater need of nurturance, than sons.

The second form of parental sextyping we expect to occur at birth is a function both of the infant's gender *and* the parent's own gender. Goodenough[3] interviewed the parents of nursery school children, and found that mothers were less concerned with sex-typing their child's behavior than were fathers. More recently, Meyer and Sobieszek[7] presented adults with videotapes of two seventeen-month-old children (each of whom was sometimes described as a boy and sometimes as a girl), and asked their subjects to describe and interpret the children's behavior. They found that male subjects as well as those having little contact with small children, were more likely (although not always significantly so) to rate the children in sex-stereotypic fashion—attributing "male qualities" such as independence, aggressiveness, activity, and alertness to the child presented as a boy, and qualities such as cuddliness, passivity, and delicacy of the "girl." We expect, therefore, that sex of infant and sex of parent will interact, such that it is fathers, rather than mothers, who emerge as the greater sex-typers of their newborn.

In order to investigate parental sextyping of their newborn infants, and in order, more specifically, to test the predictions that sex-typing is a function of the infant's gender, as well as the gender of both infant and parent, parents of newborn boys and girls were studied in the maternity ward of a hospital, within the first 24 hours postpartum, to uncover their perceptions of the characteristics of their newborn infants.

Method

Subjects

The subjects consisted of 30 pairs of primiparous parents, fifteen of whom had sons, and fifteen of whom had daughters. The subjects were drawn from the available population of expecting parents at a suburban Boston hospital serving local, predominantly lower-middle-class families. Using a list of primiparous expectant mothers obtained from the hospital, the experimenter made contact with families by mail several months prior to delivery, and requested the subjects' assistance in "a study of social relations among parents and their first child." Approximately one week after the initial contact by mail, the experimenter telephoned each family, in order to answer any questions the prospective parents might have about the study, and to obtain their consent. Of the 43 families reached by phone, eleven refused to take part in the study. In addition, one consenting mother subsequently gave birth to a low birth weight infant (a 74-ounce girl), while another delivered an unusually large son (166 ounces). Because these two infants were at the two ends of the distribution of birth weights, and because they might have biased the data in support of our hypotheses, the responses of their parents were eliminated from the sample.

All subjects participated in the study within the first 24 hours postpartum—the fathers almost immediately after delivery, and the mothers (who were often under sedation at the time of delivery) up to but not later than 24 hours later. The mothers typically had spoken with their husbands at least once during this 24 hour period.

There were no reports of medical problems during any of the pregnancies or deliveries, and all infants in the sample were full-term at time of birth. Deliveries were made under general anesthesia, and the fathers were not allowed in the delivery room. The fathers were not permitted to handle their babies during the first 24 hours, but could view them through display windows in the hospital nursery. The mothers, on the other hand, were allowed to hold and feed their infants. The subject participated individually in the study. The fathers were met in a small, quiet waiting room used exclusively by the maternity ward, while the mothers were met in their hospital rooms. Every precaution was taken not to upset the parents or interfere with hospital procedure.

Procedure

After introducing himself to the subjects, and after congratulatory amenities, the experimenter (FJP) asked the parents: "Describe your baby as you would to a close friend or relative." The responses were tape-recorded and subsequently coded.

The experimenter then asked the subjects to take a few minutes to complete a short questionnaire. The instructions for completion of the questionnaire were as follows:

> On the following page there are 18 pairs of opposite words. You are asked to rate your baby in relation to these words, placing an "x" or a checkmark in the space that best describes your baby. The more a word describes your baby, the closer your "x" should be to that word.
>
> Example: Imagine you were asked to rate Trees.
>
> Good :___:___:___:___:___:___:___:___:___:___:___:___:___:___:___:___:___:___:___: Bad
> Strong :___:___:___:___:___:___:___:___:___:___:___:___:___:___:___:___:___:___:___: Weak
>
> If you cannot decide or your feelings are mixed, place your "x" in the center space. Remember, the more you think a word is a good description of your baby, the closer you should place you "x" to that word. If there are no questions, please begin. Remember, you are rating your baby. Don't spend too much time thinking about your answers. First impressions are usually the best.

Having been presented with these instructions, the subjects then proceeded to rate their baby on each of the eighteen following, eleven-point, bipolar adjective scales: firm-soft; large featured-fine featured; big-little; relaxed-nervous; cuddly-not cuddly; easy going-fussy; cheerful-cranky; good eater-poor eater; excitable-calm; active-inactive; beautiful-plain; sociable-unsociable; well coordinated-awkward; noisy-quiet; alert-inattentive; strong-weak; friendly-unfriendly; hardy-delicate.

Upon completion of the questionnaire, the subjects were thanked individually, and when both parents of an infant had completed their participation, the underlying purposes of the study were fully explained.

Hospital Data

In order to acquire a more objective picture of the infants whose characteristics were being judged by the subjects, data were obtained from hospital records concerning each infant's birth weight, birth length, and Apgar scores. Apgar scores are typically assigned at five and ten minutes postpartum, and represent the physician's ratings of the infant's color, muscle tonicity, reflex irritability, and heart and respiratory rates. No significant differences between the male and female infants were found for birth weight, birth length, or Apgar scores at five and ten minutes postpartum.*

* Birth weight ($\overline{X}_{Sons}$ = 114.43 ounces, $\overline{X}_{Daughters}$ = 110.00, t (28) = 1.04); Birth length ($\overline{X}_{Sons}$ = 19.80 inches, $\overline{X}_{Daughters}$ = 19.96, t (28) = 0.52); 5 minute Apgar score ($\overline{X}_{Sons}$ = 9.07, $\overline{X}_{Daughters}$ = 9.33, t (28) = 0.69); and 10 minute Apgar score ($\overline{X}_{Sons}$ = 10.00, $\overline{X}_{Daughters}$ = 10.00).

Results

In Table 1, the subjects' mean ratings of their infant, by condition, for each of the eighteen bipolar adjective scales, are presented. The right-extreme column of Table 1 shows means for each scale, which have been averaged across conditions. Infant stimuli, overall, were characterized closer to the scale anchors of soft, fine featured, little, relaxed, cuddly, easy going, cheerful, good eater, calm, active, beautiful, sociable, well coordinated, quiet, alert, strong, friendly, and hardy. Our parent-subjects, in other words, appear to have felt on Day 1 of their babies' lives that their newborn infants represented delightful, competent new additions to the world!

Analysis of variance of the subjects' questionnaire responses (1 and 56 degrees of freedom) yielded a number of interesting findings. There were *no* rating differences on the eighteen scales as a simple function of Sex of Parent: parents appear to agree with one another, on the average. As a function of Sex of Infant, however, several significant effects emerged: Daughters, in contrast to sons, were rated as significantly softer ($F = 10.67$, $p < .005$), finer featured ($F = 9.27, p < .005$), littler ($F = 28.83, p < .001$), and more inattentive ($F = 4.44$, $p < .05$). In addition, significant interaction effects emerged for seven of the eighteen scales: firm-soft ($F = 11.22$, $p < .005$), large featured-fine featured ($F = 6.78$, $p < .025$), cuddly-not cuddly ($F = 4.18$, $p < .05$), well coordinated-awkward ($F = 12.52$, $p < .001$), alert-inattentive ($F = 5.10$, $p < .05$), strong-weak ($F = 10.67$, $p < .005$), and hardy-delicate ($F = 5.32, p < .025$).

The meaning of these interactions becomes clear in Table 1, in which it

Table 1 Mean rating on the 18 adjective scales, as a function of sex of parent (*Mother vs. Father*) and sex of infant (*Son vs. Daughter*)[a]

Scale	*Experimental condition*				
(I) – (II)	M–S	M–D	F–S	F–D	$\overline{X}$
Firm–Soft	7.47	7.40	3.60	8.93	6.85
Large featured–Fine featured	7.20	7.53	4.93	9.20	7.22
Big–Little	4.73	8.40	4.13	8.53	6.45
Relaxed–Nervous	3.20	4.07	3.80	4.47	3.88
Cuddly–Not cuddly	1.40	2.20	2.20	1.47	1.82
Easy going–Fussy	3.20	4.13	3.73	4.60	3.92
Cheerful–Cranky	3.93	3.73	4.27	3.60	3.88
Good eater–Poor eater	3.73	3.80	4.60	4.53	4.16
Excitable–Calm	6.20	6.53	5.47	6.40	6.15
Active–Inactive	2.80	2.73	3.33	4.60	3.36
Beautiful–Plain	2.13	2.93	1.87	2.87	2.45
Sociable–Unsociable	4.80	3.80	3.73	4.07	4.10
Well coordinated–Awkward	3.27	2.27	2.07	4.27	2.97
Noisy–Quiet	6.87	7.00	5.67	7.73	6.82
Alert–Inattentive	2.47	2.40	1.47	3.40	2.44
Strong–Weak	3.13	2.20	1.73	4.20	2.82
Friendly–Unfriendly	3.33	3.40	3.67	3.73	3.53
Hardy–Delicate	5.20	4.67	3.27	6.93	5.02

[a] The larger the mean, the greater the rated presence of the attribute denoted by the second (right-hand) adjective in each pair.

can be seen that six of these significant interactions display a comparable pattern: fathers were more extreme in their ratings of *both* sons and daughters than were mothers. Thus, sons were rated as firmer, larger featured, better coordinated, more alert, stronger, and hardier—and daughters as softer, fine featured, more awkward, more inattentive, weaker, and more delicate—by their fathers than by their mothers. Finally, with respect to the other significant interaction effect (cuddly-not cuddly), a rather different pattern was found. In this case, mothers rated sons as cuddlier than daughters, while fathers rated daughters as cuddlier than sons—a finding we have dubbed the "oedipal" effect.

Responses to the interview question were coded in terms of adjectives used and references to resemblance. Given the open-ended nature of the question, many adjectives were used—healthy, for example, being a high frequency response cutting across sex of babies and parents. Parental responses were pooled, and recurrent adjectives were analyzed by X^2 analysis for sex of child. Sons were described as big more frequently than were daughters (X^2 (1) = 4.26, $p < .05$); daughters were called little more often than were sons (X^2 (1) = 4.28, $p < .05$). The "feminine" cluster—beautiful, pretty, and cute—was used significantly more often to describe daughters than sons (X^2 (1) = 5.40, $p < .05$). Finally, daughters were said to resemble mothers more frequently than were sons (X^2 (1) = 3.87, $p < .05$).

Discussion

The data indicate that parents—especially fathers—differentially label their infants, as a function of the infant's gender. These results are particularly striking in light of the fact that our sample of male and female infants did *not* differ in birth length, weight, or Apgar scores. Thus, the results appear to be a pure case of parental labeling—what a colleague has described as "nature's first projective test" (personal communication, Leon Eisenberg). Given the importance parents attach to the birth of their first child, it is not surprising that such ascriptions are made.

But why should posing the simple question, "Is it a boy or a girl?", be so salient in parents' minds, and have such important consequences? For one thing, an infant's gender represents a truly *distinctive* characteristic. The baby is either a boy or a girl—there are no ifs, ands, or buts about it. A baby may be active sometimes, and quiet at others, for example, but it can always be assigned to one of two distinct classes: boy or girl. Secondly, an infant's gender tends to assume the properties of a *definitive* characteristic. It permits parents to organize their questions and answers about the infant's appearance and behavior into an integrated *Gestalt*. Finally, an infant's gender is often a *normative* characteristic. It is a property that seems to be of special importance not only to the infant's parents, but to relatives, friends, neighbors, and even casual passersby in the street. For each of these reasons, an infant's gender is a property of considerable importance to its parents, and is therefore one that is likely to lead to labeling and the investment of surplus meaning.

The results of the present study are, of course, not unequivocal. Although it was found, as expected, that the sex-typing of infants varied as a function of the infant's gender, as well as the gender of both infant and parent, significant differences did not emerge for all eighteen of the adjective scales employed. Two explanations for this suggest themselves. First, it may simply be that we have overestimated the importance of sex-typing at birth. A second possibility, however, is that sex-typing is more likely to emerge with respect to certain classes of attributes—namely, those which denote physical or constitutional, rather than "internal," dispositional, factors. Of the eight different adjective pairs for which significant main or interaction effects emerged, six (75%) clearly refer to external attributes of the infant. Conversely, of the ten adjective pairs for which no significant differences were found, only three (30%) clearly denote external attributes. This suggests that it is physical and constitutional factors that specially lend themselves to sex-typing at birth, at least in our culture.

Another finding of interest is the lack of significant effects, as a simple function of sex of parent. Although we predicted no such effects, and were therefore not particularly surprised by the emergence of "non-findings," the implication of these results is by no means trivial. If we had omitted the sex of the infant as a factor in the present study, we might have been led to conclude (on the basis of simply varying the sex of the parent) that *no* differences exist in parental descriptions of newborn infants—a patently erroneous conclusion! It is only when the infant's and the parent's gender are considered together, in interaction, that the lack of differences between overall parental mean ratings can be seen to reflect the true differences between the parents. Mothers rate both sexes closer together on the adjective pairs than do fathers (who are the stronger sex-typers), but *both* parents agree on the direction of sex differences.

An issue of considerable concern, in interpreting the findings of the present study appropriately, stems from the fact that fathers were not permitted to handle their babies, while mothers were. The question then becomes: is it possible that the greater sex-typing by fathers is simply attributable to their lesser exposure to their infants? This, indeed, may have been the case. However it seems worthwhile to consider some of the alternative possibilities. Might not the lesser exposure of fathers to their infants have led not to greater sex-typing, but to a data "wash out"—with no differences emerging in paternal ratings? After all, given no opportunity to handle their babies, and therefore deprived of the opportunity to obtain certain first-hand information about them, the fathers might have been expected to make a series of neutral ratings—hovering around the middle of each adjective scale. The fact that they did not do this suggests that they brought with them a variety of sex stereotypes that they then imposed upon their infant. Moreover, the fact that mothers, who were allowed to hold and feed their babies, made distinctions between males and females that were in keeping with cultural sex-stereotypes (see Table 1), suggests that even if fathers had had the opportunity of holding their infants, similar results might have been obtained. We should also not lose sight of the fact that father-mother differences in exposure to infants continue well into later years. Finally, one must question the very importance of the subjects' differential exposure on the grounds that none of the typical "exposure" effects reported in the social psychological literature[14] were observed. In particular, one might have expected mothers to have come to rate their infants more favorably than fathers, simply as a result of greater exposure. Yet such was not the case.

The central implication of the study, then, is that sex-typing and sex-role socialization appear to have already begun their course at the time of the infant's birth, when information about the infant is minimal. The *Gestalt* parents develop, and the labels they ascribe to their newborn infant, may well affect subsequent expectations about the manner in which their infant ought to behave, as well as parental behavior itself. This parental behavior, moreover, when considered in conjunction with the rapid unfolding of the infant's own behavioral repertoire, may well lead to a modification of the very labeling that affected parental behavior in the first place. What began as a one-way street now bears traffic in two directions. In order to understand the full importance and implications of our findings, therefore, research clearly needs to be conducted in which delivery room stereotypes are traced in the family during the first several months after birth, and their impact upon parental behavior is considered. In addition, further research is clearly in order if we are to understand fully the importance of early paternal sex-typing in the socialization of sex-roles.

REFERENCES

1. ABERLE, D. AND NAEGELE, K. 1952. Middleclass fathers' occupational role and attitudes toward children. Amer. J. Orthopsychiat. 22(2):366–378.
2. ASCH, S. 1946. Forming impressions of personality. J. Abnorm. Soc. Psychol. 41:258–290.
3. GOODENOUGH, E. 1957. Interest in persons as an aspect of sex differences in the early years. Genet. Psychol. Monogr. 55:287–323.
4. HARARI, H. AND MC DAVID, J. Name stereotypes and teachers' expectations. J. Educ. Psychol. (in press)
5. KELLEY, H. 1950. The warm-cold variable in first impressions of persons. J. Pers. 18:431–439.
6. LUCHINS, A. 1957. Experimental attempts to minimize the impact of first impressions. *In* The Order of Presentation in Persuasion, C. Hovland, ed. Yale University Press, New Haven, Conn.
7. MEYER, J. AND SOBIESZEK, B. 1972. Effect of a child's sex on adult interpretations of its bheavior. Develpm. Psychol. 6:42–48.
8. PEDERSEN, F. AND ROBSON, K. 1969. Father participation in infancy. Amer. J. Orthopsychiat. 39(3):466–472.
9. REBELSKY, F. AND HANKS, C. 1971. Fathers' verbal interaction with infants in the first three months of life. Child Develpm. 42:63–68.
10. SCHAFFER, H. 1971. The Growth of Sociability. Penguin Books, Baltimore.
11. SEARS, R., MACCOBY, E. AND LEVIN, H. 1957. Patterns of Child Rearing. Row, Peterson, Evanston, Ill.
12. TASCH, R. 1952. The role of the father in the family. J. Exper. Ed. 20:319–361.
13. WILSON, P. 1968. The perceptual distortion of height as a function of ascribed academic status. J. Soc. Psychol. 74:97–102.
14. ZAJONC, R. 1968. Attitudinal effects of mere exposure. J. Pers. Soc. Psychol. Monogr. Supplement 9:1–27.

Early Sex Differences in the Human

Studies of Socioemotional Development

Michael Lewis

In any discussion of sex differences one is bound to be confronted with the issue of the etiology of these differences. An implicit belief in the study of a particular individual characteristic such as sex role or gender identity is that the study of how early these differences might be observed would support one theoretical position or another. That is, if sex differences could be demonstrated in the very young, these differences would be due to biological or genetic determinants. It is not uncommon to find writers using early differences in sex role or gender identity as proof for the biological basis of their origin. Thus one of the first issues we must confront in looking at early differences is the issue of learning/experience vs. genetics.

Like many other issues in psychology, this dichotomy is rather useless since we are biological creatures, having sexual dimorphism, and we are also subject to wide and varying early learning experiences. From the outset it is therefore important to state that early sex differences in behavior do not necessarily reflect *either* experiential or genetic roots. Moreover, such questions usually do not add to our understanding of the phenomena.

Our research experience indicates that as early as we can find individual differences as a function of the sexual dimorphism in the infant so we can find a society expressing differential behavior toward the two sexes (Lewis, 1972a). For example, we (as well as others) have reported that girl infants at 12 weeks of age seem to be more attentive to auditory stimulation than boy infants (Lewis *et al.,* 1973). Thus from this early individual difference one might conclude that girls are biologically precocious, *vis à vis*

"Early Sex Differences in the Human: Studies of Socio-Emotional Development" by Michael Lewis, *Archives of Sexual Behavior,* 4, 4 (1975), 329–335. Reprinted by permission of Plenum Publishing Corporation.

boys, in auditory perception—which might account for their precocious language development throughout most of life. At the same time that one can demonstrate early sex differences in auditory perception, however, one can also find that mothers are responding differentially to their girl and boy children. Mothers of 12-week-old infants tend to speak more to those who are girls and, moreover, tend to respond more often to a girl child's vocalization behavior with their own vocalization (Lewis, 1972b; Lewis and Freedle, 1973). From the data it is not possible to determine whether the individual differences on the part of the infants are based on their differential experience via the mother or whether the mother's experience is determined by the child's differential response (biologically determined) to her auditory stimulation.

To repeat, we do not feel that the kind of question that asks us to differentiate the biological from the social will serve us in our exploration of early sex differences in socioemotional development. That is not to say that at some point in the future it may not be possible to untangle the biological-experience effects; however, at this time the expression of genotype in phenotypic behavior can be talked about only in terms of the interaction with the world, that is, with experience. Any attempt to separate them is probably fictional.

Neither in this paper nor in our research efforts do we attempt to discuss the variance accounted for by biology or experience. We recommend, therefore, that in general research not be undertaken with this distinction in mind. Thus the kind of research we are engaged in will not answer the question about the percent of variance accounted for by experience or biology, but rather seeks to explore the dynamics of the relationship and through an understanding of that relationship come to see whether behavior can be modified by experience (Lewis and Lee-Painter, 1974; Lewis and Rosenblum, 1974). The major issue is not the etiology of behavior—that is, whether it is due to biology or experience—but rather whether behavior is modifiable. Indeed, one could well argue that initial differences between the sexes may in fact be biologically determined, yet may be open to alteration by a wide variety of social experiences. It does not seem unreasonable, rather than to address ourselves to the basis of these early individual differences, to look toward the manner in which behavior might be altered.

In order to study the effects of experience, it is probably necessary to investigate an intervention paradigm wherein one tries to alter behavior via altering the environment. (Obviously, intervention of this sort has serious ethical consequences and needs to be approached carefully.)

If the study of early individual differences is not related to trying to separate out the variances accounted for by experience or biology, what use might that study of early differences have? The answer to this question really needs to be posed in terms of a more general question as to why study sex differences at all. In this context, a negative answer—that there is no reason to study sex differences—perhaps is more of the point. What I mean is that the study of socio-emotional development can best be understood through the study of individual differences. Any individual variable which allows for variance in behavior will allow us to study process (Lewis, 1972c; Lewis and Wilson, 1972). Thus the study of individual differences is important inasmuch as it allows us to understand the process variables. In this particular case, by "process variables" we refer to the process of socioemotional development. In a conference on sex differences one point that I have chosen to make is that the study of sex differences needs to be secondary to the study of process. The reasons for this are both scientific and political. It raises the general reason for studying individual differences, and in this case sex differences *per se*. Why should anyone study individual differences as such? It seems to me that the study of individual differences without the study of process must be viewed in the context of an implicit set of assumptions about individual differences and the social consequences of these differences. Thus, rather than a truly scientific endeavor, it is a sociopolitical issue.

In this regard, the study of early differences in socioemotional development must proceed from the study of the socioemotional experience of children, their environment, and their interaction. Moreover, prior to experimentation an ethological approach must be undertaken. To fully appreciate the ethological knowledge, it may be necessary to initiate a series of experiments. The nature of these experiments is, of course, limited by important ethical consideration. What I have in mind, for example, is the observable fact that girl infants cry less than boys (Lewis, 1972b; Moss, 1967). Now this might have to do with the holding position of girl vs. boy infants. Thus it may be possible to show that the holding position, rather than any sex difference, is instrumental in producing the crying behavior and thus separate out the process from individual differences.

While a particular difference between male infant and female infant behavior may be *statistically* significant, this does not mean that the difference has any practical significance in the real world. Research concern should be concentrated on sex differences of practical significance rather than on those which are merely significant in the statistical sense of not being due to chance alone.

Our concern with male-female differences should not blind us to the fact that there are also wide differences among male infants and among female infants. Indeed, within-sex variability probably is as great as the between-sex variability.

Research Examples in the Study of Early Sex Differences

Experiential factors affect male-female differentiation almost from the moment of birth. Thus two studies, one in the United States and one in Britain, have reported differences in mothers' initial reactions during their first encounters with their babies, depending on the sex of the baby (Lewis and Als, 1975). For example mothers feed boy babies more on the first day.

The study of behavioral dimorphism in infants can begin with simple ethological observations:

> Baby cries. Mother comforts baby. Baby stops crying but begins again. This time mother feels diaper, notes it is wet, carries baby to changing table—whereupon baby again stops crying.

We can then ask whether that observed chain of events varies with sex of the baby.

One useful probe for differences in parental and infant response is the study of parent-child interactions in families with opposite-sex twins. Studies of 18 such sets of twins have revealed a wide range of ways in which mothers treat male and female twins differently. Even if a mother does not dress a boy twin in pants and a girl twin in skirts, she is likely to select pants of appropriate color for each sex (Brooks and Lewis, 1974).

Still other experimental situations are possible which tap the young child's other social relationships as a function of sexual dimorphism: for example,

> Four mothers are seated in the corners of a square laboratory room, two holding male babies and two holding female babies. The mothers are instructed to place the babies on the floor facing the middle of the room. Under these conditions, the male babies are significantly more likely to crawl toward and play with each other rather than with a female baby, and female babies are also significantly more likely to crawl toward and play with each other than with a male baby. This is true for babies at twelve months of age as well as at eighteen months. It is true despite the fact that each male baby in this experimental setting faces two female babies but only one male baby (and *vice versa*); hence if the behavior were random one would expect crawling toward a baby of the *opposite* gender to be more frequent than crawling toward a baby of the same gender. The experiment also indicates that babies even at twelve months can distinguish the gender of other babies—though adults often find the distinction difficult to make. (Michalson *et al.,* 1974).

Observations to date indicate that a simple pattern of reward and reinforcement governs much behavioral dimorphism. Both parents and peers reward and thus reinforce those aspects of a child's behavior which are deemed appropriate to his or her gender; they reward negatively and thus inhibit gender-in-appropriate behavior. Touching behavior, for example, is negatively reinforced for boys; this starts extremely early. Touching behavior is neither positively nor negatively reinforced for girls; essentially it is subjected to "benign neglect." Hence girls end up relatively freer to touch (Goldberg and Lewis, 1969; Messer and Lewis, 1972).

It is the mother rather than the father who controls the reward-reinforcement structure during the first year of life, at least in middle-class white American families. In one study, for example, parent-child interactions were recorded for 24-hr periods for babies at the age of 3 months. The fathers interacted with the babies for approximately 37 sec per day (Rebelsky and Hanks, 1971). In another study where families of several social classes were included, fathers were found to interact with their babies for an average of 15 min per day. The range was 0–2 hr. This study probably overstated the amount of interaction, since father-child interaction is socially approved behavior in this context, and fathers were aware that their interactions were being recorded. During the first year of a baby's life, in short, the pattern of nurture is matriarchal. During the second year of life, the father enters the situation. But he enters with male-appropriate behavior; that is, he *plays with* the child rather than tending it (Lewis and Weinraub, 1974).

In addition to biological and socioemotional factors, *cognitive* factors come into play only a little later, further modulating the process by which human behavior becomes dimorphic. Thus children by the age of 4 or 5 know perfectly well—in an explicit cognitive sense—whether they are male or female:

> I am female. There are females and males out there. They behave differently. I will behave in the way appropriate to my femaleness.

The roots of this cognitive recognition of their own dimorphism go back at least to the twentieth to twenty-fourth month of life, when a child first begins to exploit the dimorphism of human language and to apply dimorphic labels—*mummy* vs. *daddy, him* vs. *her* (Michalson and Brooks, 1975). Precocious children may begin making the gender distinction even before the twentieth month; indeed, such gender labels may be the very first labels applied by the child. The ultimate adult human behavioral dimorphism thus has cognitive as well as biological and socioemotional roots (Lewis and Brooks, in press).

It seems to me that research in sex differences in socioemotional development must be based on the understanding of why we are interested in these by implicit variables having more to do with sociopolitical than scientific issues. Remember that for any important psychological variable there is greater within-group than across-group variance. The fact that we seek to concentrate on the across-group variance must reflect certain assumptions we make about the human condition. The study of sex differences in infancy is justified only inasmuch as it allows us to better understand the process at work in producing and affecting development.

Group Discussion

Dr. Rose questioned Dr. Lewis's belief that parental and infant factors in parent-infant reactions cannot be isolated. He pointed out that in ethological studies of monkeys it has been possible to distinguish clearly between sequences of mother-child interaction initiated by the child and sequences initiated by the mother. Dr. Green cited as an example studies showing that at a certain age male monkeys range farther away from their mothers than females—despite the more vigorous efforts of the mothers to retrieve the male infants. Hence it is not, in this case, greater maternal permissiveness which triggers the series of events, it is the male monkey infant who is unilaterally responsible. Dr. Lewis replied that this depends on where the series of observations begins. In the sequence of events described, the infant is clearly the initiator, but this does not mean that there were not maternal influences—perhaps the way in which the mother held the male child during previous weeks—which determined the wider ranging of the male offspring. At this stage in our understanding, it is better to describe the process than to seek to partial out responsibility. It is possible to give differing weights to the maternal and infant contributions during a given sequence of events even though it is not possible to separate them altogether (Lewis and Lee-Painter, 1974).

Dr. Lewis was asked about conflicting reports in the literature—reports of gender differences noted in some studies which could not be replicated. He replied that infant study procedures have not yet been sufficiently standardized to facilitate replication. To take an extreme case, the size and shape of a room may affect infant behavior; infants may respond in one way in a square room, differently in a corridor where their mobility is restricted. In one experiment with divergent-sex twins, one twin is tested with his or her mother while the other twin was kept waiting outside the test room. The usual female-male differences were noted with the twins first tested; that is, the girl twins showed more "proximal behavior" toward their mothers and more touching their mothers, which the mothers accepted. When the second twins were tested, however, they had just suffered 15 minutes of separation—a stressing experience. The stressing did not alter the behavior of the girl twins, but the boy twins tested after the period of separation displayed more than the usual proximal behavior toward and touching of the mothers (Brooks and Lewis, 1974). Thus to replicate an earlier experiment one must not only replicate the actual test situation in full detail but also antecedent conditions and a wide variety of other, as yet not fully explored, variables.

Dr. Lewis was asked why, if intragroup variations among boys and among girls cover a broader range than intergroup differences between boys and girls, his work is in such large part concerned with intergroup differences. He replied that studying the differences between boys and girls is a useful probe in developing hypotheses concerning individual variations in general. By observing boys and girls separately, for example, he was able to note that girls spend more time in proximal relations with their mothers; this in turn may generate a hypothesis concerning the effects of proximal relationships on the developmental process in general. Male-female variations are interesting not only in themselves but also as clues to the determining factors in the developmental process.

Dr. Green pointed out that Dr. Lewis's data could be useful in another way. The data show that male infant behavior is scattered along a bell-shaped curve, and so is female infant behavior. A small percentage of females at one extreme of the bell-shaped curve are more malelike than the typical male, and a small percentage of males at the other end are more femalelike than the typical female. Longitudinal studies might then follow these atypical male and female infants through the years to determine the ultimate outcome of this early atypical behavior. Such longitudinal studies, Dr. Green pointed out, are his own field of interest. He threfore asked what particular behavior variables found in infantological and preschool studies might prove useful in identifying the particular atypical children whose subsequent development should be followed.

Dr. Lewis replied that while there were many differences between boy and girl infants he felt that they were less impressive than might be necessary to serve as the foundation of a logitudinal study. Further, it is not at all clear that a particular difference remains stable through time. For example, numerous studies show that male newborn infants cry more than female newborns (Moss, 1967). But studies also show that the boys who are crying most at 3 months of age are not the same boys who are crying most at 1 year. Indeed, there is a weak *negative* correlation between boys who cry a lot at 1 month and those who cry a lot at 1 year (Lewis, 1967). The reason appears to be that crying at 1 month is a response of vigor, instrumental in getting what an infant wants, while crying at one year is a passive response.

Asked about the next step in infantological studies, Dr. Lewis suggested that what was most needed in considering the relations between infants and their caretakers was to study just what "caretaking" means. To learn this, one must leave the laboratory, adopt ethological techniques, and actually observe how caretaking evolves in the home setting. How much in the course of an ordinary day do an infant and caretaker actually look at each other? How much is a child held? And so on. What are needed now are just data—excluding gender differences or anything else, simply determining what is in fact going on. What does the mother do on the first day she takes over care of the child—and what does the child do? What is happening on day 4?

Such studies are just beginning. Until the results are in, laboratory studies may be premature. For example, the laboratory can be used to study an infant's response to auditory stimulation. But what constitutes auditory stimulation for an infant? We must first observe the sounds to which he responds in a natural setting.

Psychology

Reesa M. Vaughter

The psychology of women[1] is concerned with the construction of a psychology that is relevant to women as well as to men; that studies women as well as men; that employs methodology appropriate, meaningful, and congruent with the lives of women as well as men; that develops theories that predict female as well as male behavior; and that studies questions of interest to women as well as to men. In brief, the goal of the psychology of women is the development of a nonsexist science—a psychology of human behavior.

One significant task of a review is to assemble the questions that psychologists have selected for investigation. Given that scientific research reflects the value system within which it takes place, the questions selected for investigation give us insight into that value system.[2] Within the confines of space, a brief description of methodology and interpretation is presented as it was presumed that these aspects of research are no less reflective of the same value system. Giving thought to the representative questions, methods, and theoretical leanings will hopefully indicate our inheritances from the past, our current status, and how we might proceed to develop feminist perspectives in psychological research to refurbish the "impoverished" psychology of human behavior.[3]

A Selected Guide to the Literature

Sex Differences, Stereotypes, and Gender Roles

Historically, the study of sex differences sought explanations for female "inferiority" and women's subordinate position in society.[4] Sub-

"Psychology" by Reesa M. Vaughter from *Signs: Journal of Women in Culture and Society,* 2, 1 (1976). Reprinted by permission of the University of Chicago Press.

sequently, sex-difference research has evolved as one vehicle to legitimize and to provide a "scientific" reason for including women in psychological research and theory. Demonstrating that females' behavior differed from males' provided an "objective" reason for including both female and male participants. In the face of ample evidence of sex differences,[5] conclusions based upon single-sex methodology came increasingly under attack.[6] Shields has thoughtfully outlined how the research of sex differences has also played handmaiden to social myth and ideologies concerning supposed and suspected real differences. But sex-difference research may also be conducted to test for supposed and suspected unreal differences. Berman et al.[7] found that men were just as attracted as women to pictures of infants and infant behaviors (Harlow's fascination with the sighs of women over baby monkey pictures notwithstanding).

Regardless of the goals, it seems clear that research into the sex differences of characteristics and behaviors has not been an impelling impetus for modifying sexism either in science or in practical affairs. Sexist and sex-biased explanations and recommendations are offered for sex differences obtained, regardless of the direction of the difference, as noted by Maccoby and Jacklin.[8] These two authors have assembled such a massive amount of data and have offered such provocative interpretations of the data regarding sex differences in intellectual skills and social behaviors that their classic work will be the subject of analyses for some time.[9] Meanwhile, the study of sex differences continues. Two reports[10] confirmed previous evidences of increased sex differences with age in skills of reading, social studies, science, writing, literature, and math. Sex differences were also noted regarding the incidence of depression,[11] marriage patterns,[12] and language usage (i.e., sex differences in word choice, syntactic usage, phonology, as well as differences in language acquisition and verbal abilities).[13]

There are several reasons why the study of sex differences may no longer play a dominant role in the development of the psychology of women. As Maccoby and Jacklin's review suggests, sex has not been a consistently powerful predictor.

Even when sex differences are obtained, the determinants of the behavior are likely not to have been identified. Because gender role performance is so homogeneous within the sexes in the case of what is being measured, a significant sex difference may be obtained; but gender, not biological sex, may be the major determinant of the observed difference.[14] The disadvantage of employing sex as the single independent variable becomes evident in cases in which a significant main effect of sex is obtained, such as sex differences in skills and self-esteem,[15] but the sex difference does not meet the criteria employed to deduce biologically based determination. That is, the sex difference does not occur cross culturally, does not show species continuity, cannot be manipulated biochemically, and does not appear early in development.[16]

The problem is that sex differences are confounded with gender differences both within and across sex groups. What is required, then, is a separation of the sources of variances of sex and gender. Progress in making this sophistication in designs has been retarded by psychology's psychometric insistence that that which is male is masculine and that which is female is feminine. Gender and gender role are assigned by the culture on the basis of assigned sex.[17] But sex does not determine gender identity or gender role performance. Gender is a system that emerges out of assigned sex and sex identity; it is related to both but dependent upon neither, with unique properties of its own. The evidence for conceptualizing the development of the related but nondependent sex and gender systems as suggested here comes from many investigations of: (*a*) cross-species and cross-cultural comparisons of sex differences,[18] (*b*) studies of developmental changes in female and male behavior,[19] (*c*) comparisons of sex differences in different ethnic and socioeconomic groups[20] and (*d*) studies of hermaphrodic and cross-gendered persons.[21] Using sex and gender as independent variables[22] will permit us to pull out the amount of variability attributable to sex and the amount attributable to gender (as well as their possible interaction) and begin to make more reasonable inferences of attribution. Recent studies indicate that, for children, sex/sex role[23] and gender/gender role are not synonymous conceptual and behavioral systems. Apparently, both the concepts of sex/sex role and gender/gender role have a developmental sequence, and the child's understanding of sex/sex role and the child's sex role identity develop prior to, develop faster than, and are more complete earlier than the child's understanding of gender/gender roles and the child's gender role identity.[24] Prerequisites for gender role development seem to be: (*a*) learning sex and sex role definitions, and (*b*) learning to use sex as the salient cue for making distinctions and discriminations about all kinds of things that have nothing to do with who has the baby—that is, learning to use sex as a basis for dichotomizing within a gender system that is biologically neuter.

Although Maccoby and Jacklin, questioning the value of parental reports of child-rearing practices, conclude that the principle mechanism by which gender role identity and performance develop lies within the self-socialization process, recent studies indicate that the sexes are indeed treated differently and that knowledge of gender role definitions or stereotypes is evident in children of kindergarten age.[25] Parental descriptions of daughters and sons obtained within the first twenty-four hours after birth demonstrated that parents hold stereotypic views of their newborn infant's physical attributes and personality characteristics.[26] Observational studies found that parents introduced to an infant behaved differently to the child on the basis of the sex that the adult believed the child to be (even if the child was actually of the opposite sex).[27] Margolin and Patterson[28] made home observations of parent-child interactions and classified parental responses, the consequences of the child's "prosocial" and "deviant" responses. A main effect of parental consequences for sex was obtained. Boys received more positive responses from the parents than did girls. Fathers gave twice as many positive responses to sons as to daughters; mothers gave the same amount of positive responses to both sexes. No significant differences were obtained in amount of negative consequences elicited.

Serbin and O'Leary[29] made classroom observations in the nursery school. Teachers were found to act and react in different ways to girls and boys. The teachers' behaviors tended to encourage differential behavioral patterns of aggression, passivity, and assertiveness in girls and boys, and they encouraged the development of sex-typed tactics for getting adult attention. Further, boys received more instruction, more individual instruction, and more reward for working on academic tasks. Overall, the little girls' behaviors had considerably less effect upon their environment in terms of eliciting adult response and attention.

In an imaginative study, Rheingold and Cook[30] counted and classified the contents of children's rooms in the home as an index of differences in behaviors of parents to girls and boys (ages one month to six years). Compared to the girls' rooms, the boys' rooms contained toys of more classes (depots, educational art, machines, military equipment, spatial-temporal objects, sports, animal toys, and vehicles). Boys were provided objects that encouraged activities away from home, whereas girls were provided classes of toys (dolls, houses, and domestic objects) which encouraged housekeeping and child-care activities.

Recent studies have also investigated the consequences of gender role stereotyping upon the individual's development of competence and behavioral adaptability, positive attributes, and positive affect.[31] Having derived a non-sex-biased scale to measure a person's gender role identity, Bem tested the proposition that persons of either sex with different gender role identities (sex × gender design) would behave differently in masculine-defined and feminine-defined situations. Bem found that the problem-solving behaviors of masculine and feminine persons were situation specific, while androgynous persons[32] showed a range of behaviors which cut across masculine-feminine boundaries and were adaptive across problem tasks.

In a paper of theoretical import, Rosenfeld[33] explores the relationship between sex-typed toys, the development of competence, and gender role identification. Rosenfeld assessed sex-typed toys (the same kinds of toys that Rheingold and Cook had found in the rooms of boys and girls) for their competency-eliciting potential, that is, their potential to elicit from the child responses which were measured in terms of fluency (frequency of responses for improving each toy) and flexibility (number of different principles or approaches used to improve the toy). Both girls and boys produced more responses to boys' toys than to girls' toys. Rosenfeld argued that her findings explain why little girls consistently show more "ambivalent sex role identity": toy preferences are typically used as an index of sex role identity, yet boys' toys have a higher competency-eliciting value. In accordance with the theories of Piaget and other developmentalists, Rosenfeld argues that the toys children have available, are encouraged to play with, and learn to prefer may significantly affect the child's developing sense of effectance, competence, and mastery. Apparently, there are more gains to be derived from toys defined for boys than from toys defined for girls. Nash, studying sixth and ninth graders, found no sex differences in visual-spatial aptitude; but among both females and males, participants preferring to be boys showed higher aptitudes in spatial visualization.[34]

Spence, Helmreich, and Stapp[35] found that college students with androgynous gender role identities (scoring high in both feminine and masculine attributes) had significantly higher self-esteem scores than students who were highly feminine or highly masculine or who scored low on both scales of feminine and masculine attributes. Livson[36] reported evidence that both sexes become more androgynous by the age of 50 with an "upsurge of psychological health." And Wetter[37] compared high school and college students' self-esteem scores as a function of gender role identity. Self-esteem scores indicated positive evaluation of self in regard to interpersonal, intellectual, ethical-moral behavior, and overall self-regard. In both samples, the self-esteem of males was significantly higher than that of females, and self-esteem was correlated with masculine, but not feminine, scores. Androgynous persons had the highest self-esteem scores, but their scores did not differ significantly from the masculine-typed person. Significantly lower in self-esteem were feminine-typed persons and persons scoring low on both the masculine and feminine scales. Consistent with previous studies, the findings were interpreted to indicate that successful socialization into the feminine role is accompanied by low levels of self-regard.

As pointed out by Bem and by Berzins,[38] traditional psychology has presumed that the masculine male and the feminine female are the models of "healthy" development. But the current research findings would indicate that the negative consequences of the dichotomized, sex-based gender roles far outweigh the positive.

Gender role definitions for the self and others may continue to be modified and refined throughout development.[39] Since both age and sex are critical features of differentiation in most societies,[40] it seems probable that there are age-related components in both the acquisition and performance of opposite- and same-sex gender role proscriptions and prescriptions.[41] For example, tomboyism may be ignored at age six but punished at age twenty. Gender role definitions may also vary as a function of ethnic group membership. O'Leary and Harrison found that black females and males were less prone to characterize males and females along traditional (white) stereotypic lines and were less likely than whites to devalue females on traditional stereotypic grounds.

At the adult level, studies indicate that adults conceive of masculinity and femininity existing independently of sex of person, but that the evaluations of masculinity and femininity are made, in part, on the basis of the sex of the person displaying those characteristics. How both conceptual systems interact in evaluative decisions received initial attention from researchers in regards to the likability of females who display or "embody" congruities or incongruities with the feminine role definition. Kristal et al.[42] found that college students rated most favorable and likable the masculine-feminine female who adopted certain male-typed characteristics (success oriented and determined) but who "retained" her femininity, that is, was "essentially" feminine and had feminine interests; however, she also "received the lowest ratings on achievement and competency measures." Costrich, Feinstein, and Kidder[43] presented college students with character sketches of women and men who behaved either in line with gender role definitions or counter to them along the behavioral dimensions of assertive-dominant and passive-dependent. Both the assertive (but rated "aggressive") woman and the passive man were less liked and seen as more in need of psychotherapy than their stereotypic counterparts. The authors reported that their results concur with another study[44] in which it was found that the feminine woman was preferred over the masculine woman by all subjects "except profeminist women." The theme that the masculinity of men is more highly valued than the femininity of women is one of the most consistent themes to be found in current research data. In O'Leary and Harrison's study of college students (black, white, female, and male), all subjects agreed that males and masculinity were more valued and valuable than females and femininity. White adult females were rated more negatively by whites than adult black females were rated by blacks. Whites rated the white male more positively than blacks rated the black male, and white females rated the white male even more positively than did white males. Black males, but not black females, adhered to the notion that the masculine stereotype was more positive than the feminine one. The white females' self-ratings corresponded to their ratings of the male stereotype, and their self-ratings were more positive than their ratings of adult women in general. The authors concluded that "even white college women no longer feel compelled to present themselves in light of the 'negative' female stereotype which they recognize but devalue, even more strongly than men."[45]

The evaluation of masculine and feminine is not only dependent upon the sex of the person displaying the characteristics but is apparently based also upon such attributes as her/his political attitudes. In a study with no surprises (and finding no way to report this gracefully), Goldberg, Gottesdiener, and Abramson found that college students think that feminists are ugly.[46] Nielsen and Doyle[47] compared the gender role stereotypes held by women who did and women who did not endorse the women's liberation movement. Liberationists held more positive views of women and depicted men as cooler, more boastful, awkward, and insensitive than did nonliberationists. Nonliberationists rated liberationists as more boastful, excitable, and unattractive than did liberationists. In a study in which liberationist and nonliberationist groups failed to show significant differential rating patterns, Peterson[48] found that college women rated career women, fathers, and closest male peers as aggressive, independent, and dominant. Women were generally perceived as passive, dependent, and submissive. Ditmar, Mueller, and Mitchell[49] found that females with positive feminist attitudes showed less conformity behavior (than females with nonfeminist attitudes) to false evaluations of ambiguous and nonambiguous stimuli by peers.

Given the findings, it may be appropriate to consider gender role development to be a political, rather than an apolitical, aspect of personality development. Concepts of liberationism seem to be defined in part in terms of changes in gender role definitions, but changes primarily in the female gender role definition. Yorburg and Arafat[50] tapped the attitudes of a large sample of college students and housewives about women and careers and house and child care. Both men and women advocated more role sharing. However, only half the sample advocated the total equality of women and men; that more women than men held this belief suggested that the women and men had different expectations and definitions of "role sharing." Luetgert et al.[51] sampled another 500 adults who also expressed a desire for changes in the roles; but again, more changes were advocated for the woman's role, that is, career involvement as well as domestic responsibilities. Participants did not see changes in the home as essential for the equality of women. Attitudes may be predictive of behavior after all: in their study of professional and domestic activities of professional pairs of married psychologists, Bryson et al.[52] found that men with professional wives assumed no more responsibilities in domestic affairs than did husbands with nonprofessional wives.

Thus, within the samples studied, the "changing climate" is primarily defined in terms of the advocacy of women's pursuing occupational involvement. Attitudes about women's participation in the labor force have systematically fluctuated; Rosaldo[53] has maintained, and feminist philosophers concur, that equality for women in any society is not attainable as long as the domestic sphere remains female.

Psychosexuality

The dearth of knowledge concerning the development of human psychosexuality in general, and female psychosexuality in particular, is the most conspicuous anomaly of the entire domain of psychological research. The importance of female psychosexuality to the status of women in society probably cannot be overstated.[54] If social equality for women requires psychosexual freedom for women, then prerequisites for equality are freedom to control our own bodies,[55] freedom in autoeroticism, lesbianism, multiple relations, monogamy, and celibacy; freedom from the energy-draining anxiety about becoming pregnant; and freedom from the "imperfections" of available contraceptives.[56]

For some time, psychologists have been interested in the influence of hormones upon behavior, but we know practically nothing about the effects that gender role and psychosexual behaviors have upon hormonal functioning in the female. Nearly thirty years ago, Taylor (reported in Serhman)[57] found evidence that vasocongestion was an important causal factor of cystic changes in the breast, ovary, and uterus. Vasocongestion is produced by psychosexual arousal unrelieved by orgasm. Most girls begin heavy petting during the teenage years,[58] but the peak of orgasmic frequency in women occurs some fifteen to twenty years later, and only one-fourth of Kinsey's females had masturbated before marriage. This kind of discrepancy between the female's sexual capacities and her typical level of sexual functioning may have critical significance for the general state of her physical and psychological health and raises even more questions as to the relationship between the female's gender role definitions and her psychosexual development. What differences does it make that women are trained in affectionality and not in sexuality and are trained to be sexy but not sexual?[59] What difference does it make that women learn that ladies do not masturbate, ladies do not enjoy sex, and ladies do not make love with other ladies?

Whatever the "differences," it is clear that female psychosexuality is a complex experience of the biological, the social, the emotional/affectional, and the political.[60] Psychosexuality is, apparently, a system that emerges out of sex and gender identities, is related to both but dependent upon neither, with unique properties which are determined neither by sex nor gender.[61] Bell[62] summarized the point succinctly by recommending that it is more appropriate and accurate to speak of *homosexualities* and, presumably, *heterosexualities,* in recognition of the fact that there are multiple routes to and expressions of "homosexuality" and "heterosexuality."

Morin has assessed psychological research of homosexualities during the period from 1967 through 1974 to "clarify the value orientation" of the research. Gay men were studied three times more often than lesbians, most studies were comparative (i.e., comparing homosexualities and heterosexualities), and more than half of all studies were searching for the causes of "homosexuality" or measuring the "adjustment" of "homosexuals." Attitudes toward and assessments of homosexualities were the other major topics of interest to psychologists. As Morin pointed out, research questions provide insight into the value system within which research takes place.[63] The questions in psychological research reflect strong heterosexual biases: "What causes homosexuality?" "Can homosexuals be detected with psychological measures?" "How might homosexuality be prevented?" "Does homosexuality *per se* imply an impairment in judgment, stability, reliability, or general social or vocational capabilities?"[64] Studies of lesbians investigating similar questions and reflecting similar value statements have been reviewed by Morin; Riess, Safer, and Yotive; Brown; and Rosen.[65]

The study of attitudes of mental health practitioners and the public about gays has been of interest and value to the gay community. MacDonald[66] had constructed a scale to measure attitudes toward homosexualities and related homophobia to a number of other attitudes. Significant are MacDonald's findings that homophobia was significantly and consistently related to a lack of support for the equality between the sexes, to authoritarianism, to intolerance of ambiguity, and to cognitive rigidity. MacDonald concluded that the "need" to preserve the double standard between the sexes is the major determinant of homophobia. The connections between psychosexuality, gender roles, and feminism were further explored in several symposia presentations by Love, Trilling, and Sang and Lowenherz at the American Psychological Association's meetings in Chicago.[67] Significant differences have been noted in the study of homosexualities and heterosexualities.[68] It is clear that as we develop models of female psychosexuality, a unidimensional, genitally defined sexuality will not be efficacious; multiple-variable models will be more appropriate. Further, in our investigations and models of female psychosexuality, we have been well advised to understand that both heterosexual and homosexual behaviors require explanation.[69] Neither sex nor gender role identity are singularly predictive of female psychosexuality; neither heterosexuality nor homosexuality is indicative of mental health or healthy development. The position paper on psychosexuality by the Association of Women in Psychology indicates the direction that feminist research is likely to take in this area.[70]

Achievement Motivation and Achievement-related Behaviors

In the psychology of women, achievement research seems to have gained a position of significance similar to the study of sex differences. The event of the year in achievement research was the new anthology edited by Mednick, Tangri, and Hoffman.[71] Offering cross-cultural perspectives, the anthology complements the collection assembled by Knudsin,[72] which also contains discussions of women's career development in relation to family background, educational experiences, economic factors, and childbearing and marriage management. Both collections reflect the two current focuses of research and theory in the area: (*a*) analyses of the social and institutional characteristics which function as barriers and obstacles to women's participation and advancement in occupational, educational, and academic achievement; and (*b*) analyses of the psychological factors and characteristics which function as barriers and obstacles to women's participation and advancement in occupational, educational, and academic achievement.

In achievement research, preoccupation with occupational and educational referrents of achievement is not new. Innovative is the investigation and analysis of situational, social, and institutional characteristics which interact with psychological factors to impede women's participation and advancement in these achievement areas.[73] Psychology has always had a predilection for internal constructs, and the formalized representations of the achievement ideology of the culture have, until recently, dictated the direction of the study of female achievement in spite of the precarious predictive value of such models.[74] The tendency then in research design and interpretation of data has been to imply that achievement and contraachievement motives and behavior are in no way determined by the situational contexts within which women's achievement and achievement-related behaviors occur and develop.

Kanter, Laws, and Liss[75] have explicated yet another aspect in the development of ourselves as psychologists which may act to influence that initial stage of research in which our intuitions dicate the direction the research should take and specify the variables to be examined. Women academicians, no less than men academicians tend to insist that women's educational and occupational achievements are determined solely by abilities and motivations.[76]

Meanwhile, the evidence contrary to these notions continues to accumulate. Available now to psychologists are reviews of job segregation, sex labeling of jobs, sex discrimination in education and academe, and of areas of career conflict.[77] These sources provide points of origin for the construction of models of the environment in which women's achievement behaviors take place[78] and provide directions for ethological research.

From a cursory review of research reports of the past year, one gets the impression that the study of motivational processes and the study of fear of success are synonymous in the psychology of women. A number of investigations attempted to test specific predictions, derived from Horner's formulation of the motive to avoid success, concerning the influence of gender role identity and competition. Caballero, Giles, and Shaver[79] found that adult women with nontraditional attitudes of the role of women in society produced more fear of success (FOS) imagery to achievement cues than did women with traditional attitudes. O'Leary and Hammack,[80] measuring FOS imagery in high school students, found that girls with nontraditional attitudes of women's role had less success-avoidant themes. Further, the imagery in the stories of the nontraditional, but not the traditional, student varied as a function of the gender role prescriptions of the competitive success situations. Apparently, it is not clear how one's attitudes of women's role in society would influence FOS imagery.[81] However, Horner's formulation does explicitly predict that competition in masculine-defined domains of achievement would have deleterious effects upon the performance of the woman high in FOS. Romer[82] measured the motive to avoid success (Ms!) of fifth-, seventh-, eighth-, ninth-, and eleventh-grade girls and boys. Also measured were the participants' performances in scrambled-words tasks under competitive and noncompetitive instructional sets. No significant sex differences or age differences in Ms imagery were obtained. All participants performed better on the word task in the noncompetitive situation. Patty[83] engaged college women in a digit span task, and participants were given the instructions that the task measured either intellectual (masculine defined), interpersonal (feminine defined), or unknown skills (neutral-defined task). Ms-present participants performed more poorly on the digit span tasks under both the intellectual and interpersonal instructional sets than did Ms-absent participants.

Other recent investigations and analyses have been concerned with questions related to the validity of the constructs of fear of success. Are the negative reactions to achievement cues to be conceptualized as reactions to success per se, or do the negative reactions simply indicate the respondent's knowledge that achievement behavior is considered inappropriate or incongruent with the female's gender role definition? If negative imagery (and avoidant behavior) does signal a fear of success because of concern with deviation from gender role prescriptions, is the nature of the fear a fear of being deviant, a fear of visibility, or a fear of recognition?[84] Do negative imagery and success-avoidant behaviors signal fear of success or fear of failure? Does avoidance of potential success experiences derive from established achievement-negative attribution cycles? Should we conceptualize the fear of success as a sex-linked, motivational disposition or as a behavioral pattern of success avoidance and self-sabotage which is not sex linked[85] but is situation specific and controlled by immediate reinforcement contingencies?[86]

Reasoning that women of different career patterns would differ in motivational patterns, Burns[87] compared the scores of married women with no careers, married women in pioneer careers, and married women with traditional careers on Pappo's measure of fear of success (which specifically avoids reference to mixed-sex competitive situations) and on measures of fear of failure, social and monetary risk-taking propensity, and behavioral deviance from gender role prescriptions. Fear of success and fear of failure scores were not significantly different among the three career groups. However, the groups were distinctly different in regard to gender role deviance and risk-taking propensity. Pioneer women reported the highest willingness to take social and monetary risks, and they reported the highest number of behaviors deviant for the feminine gender role definition (e.g., taking trips alone, managing finances, opening doors for oneself, whistling, etc.). The author argued that because of sex labeling of occupations and gender role prescriptions, the pioneer woman is required to maintain a high degree of autonomy to manage emotionally being reacted to as deviant. Burns explores the social and monetary risks for women in regard to the management of child care, family responsibilities, and professional commitment.[88] As Van Dusen and Sheldon point out, the burden of such risks lies with the individual woman in our society since no institutional adjustments have been made for women's increased participation in the labor force.

Jellison et al. vigorously argue that behaviors which have been taken to imply the stable, motivational disposition of fear of success are situationally determined responses controlled by immediate reinforcement contingencies. In a series of studies in which sex of subject and sex of psychologist were varied, it was demonstrated that subjects' performances improved or declined from the first to the second administration of a task as a function of the reward contingency (favorable or unfavorable "impression" from a psychologist) associated with displays of intellectual competence. It was also demonstrated that students would describe themselves as higher or lower in intellectual abilities as a function of the social consequences of their self-descriptions—high self-evaluations were given when a favorable impression from a psychologist for doing so was indicated and low self-evaluations of ability were offered when a favorable impression for doing so was indicated. The researchers maintain that Horner has "incorrectly" equated high performance on intellectual tasks as synonymous with "success" without considering the "desirability" of the consequences of the behavior. To the extent that women avoid the negative consequences associated with being successful on intellectual skills (and, the authors note, women may receive punishment for "outstanding achievement"), women are "successful." Therefore, women do not fear success; by avoiding feared punishments, women are acting in a "reasonable manner."[89]

Alternatively, theories which emphasize the role of cognitive factors in achievement behavior offer the proposition that avoidance of success/achievement experiences may result from established achievement-negative attribution cycles, that is, attributional patterns which are incompatible with continuing achievement-related behavior.[90] Studies of attribution have found that persons tend to attribute their successes and failures to "external" factors (such as task ease or difficulty and good or bad luck) and to "internal" factors (such as ability or lack of it and effort or lack of it). The questions of (*a*) do women, more than men, tend to attribute success to external factors and failure to internal factors; and (*b*) do women tend to attribute both success and failure to external factors more often than men have received considerable attention from researchers in this area. Internality, rather than externality, has been linked with continued achievement involvement and with the experiencing of satisfaction and pride in one's achievement. Noting that consistent sex differences in internality and externality have not been found, Fisher[91] suggests that researchers pay more attention to situational factors and individual differences for a better understanding of the attributional pattern of participants in any particular study. Fisher proposes that extreme modesty, low self-esteem, external locus of control, and high fear of success would result in high externality. She also suggests that situational factors, rather than a stable, dispositional attributional set, may be responsible for an attributional pattern observed. Attributional patterns have been shown to vary as a function of the type of task and the presence of competitive cues.

Called for, then, are careful analyses of the situational influences and pressures that bear upon any specific decision of attribution[92] and of the variables that are typically associated with the consequences of women's achievement-related behaviors. Generalizable patterns of attributions may develop based upon past experiences in similar situations in which positive (or negative) consequences have indeed been capriciously related to effort or ability. As noted previously, little girls' behaviors in the nursery school classroom produced fewer consequences in terms of adult attention. When attention was given, was it related to the child's behavior exemplifying effort or skill or ability? Women's salaries in academe, in contrast to men's, are not invariably associated with number of years' experience, education attained, number of publications, and so forth.[93]

The question of the validity of Horner's construct of the fear of success has not, as yet, been answered. Fear of success, fear of deviancy, fear of recognition, fear of visibility, achievement-negative attribution patterns, or responses to explicitly stated reinforcement contingencies—one need not choose a single determinant from such an array to explain achievement-related behaviors in all women in all situations. Horner's proposition that there is an intrinsic interplay between achievement-related behaviors and the female's feminine gender role definition seems most tenable. For both women and men, being like members of the opposite sex raises implications of deviance in sexual behavior and of general adjustment in our society. Nonetheless, most of the conflicts and fears which researchers indicate as achievement negative are related to the female experience, which can be clarified with ethological approaches.[94]

It would be most advantageous for researchers to define achievement behaviors in many groups (e.g., female minority, male minority, female majority) apart from the value assigned to the behavior by any single group (e.g., white male culture). Achievement motivation in women may be indicated in ways other than task persistence. Achievement motivation in women may be directed toward goals other than, or in conjunction with, "accomplishing the task" and may be directed toward solving problems other than those which define achievement in the male culture.[95] With some exceptions,[96] our achievement research indicates considerable concern with the woman's completing the task and completing it "well"; we have shown little concern about the woman's objectives and about the quality of the woman's experience of achievement.

Psychotherapy

According to one research report,[97] psychoanalytic thought is no longer the most influential theoretical basis for therapeutic practice in psychology. Surely the feminists' efforts in the analyses of Freudian and neo-Freudian theories and the feminists' calls for revision of psychoanalytic thought and practice have played a critical role in this turn of events. Significant advances are being made in psychotherapy for women and, in sum, are directed toward continuing critical analyses of traditional conceptualizations of the "female personality," researching of clinical issues, and developing training materials and programs for the development of feminist therapy.[98]

The report of the APA Task Force, which summarized the findings of a research survey of over 300 women in divisions of the APA, identified two central problems of sexism in the practice of psychotherapy: (*a*) the question of values in psychotherapy, and (*b*) the therapist's knowledge of the psychological processes of women. Based upon its findings, the task force charges therapists with fostering traditional gender role stereotyping in women, biased expectations and devaluation of women, sexist use of theoretical constructs, and responding to women as sex objects, including seduction.

Feminist therapists are addressing themselves to the concerns and needs of women, for example, to issues of competence, interpersonal relationships, and self-actualization. Programs in assertive training for women are presented by Phelps and Austin and by Osborn and Harris—the former more of a self-help guide, the latter a guide for therapists' training.[99] Pendergrass et al. gives therapists and counselors specific information for counseling women filing job discrimination complaints and law suits.[100] Eisenstein and Sacks provide a model for action research and set forth guidelines in developing a therapeutic environment conducive for women to resolve conflicts that may be aroused in the process of seeking autonomy and self-actualization.[101]

Of critical concern for the advancement of feminist therapy is the training of therapists, which requires the definition of feminist therapy[102] and the refinement of methods congruent with the theory. Indicative of these concerns, the first national conference of feminist therapists and two women's institutes of psychotherapy were founded this year.[103] Descriptions of the feminist process in psychotherapy are now available.[104] To examine the identifiable elements is instructive not only from the therapist's perspective but also from the perspective of the development of feminist research.

First, the process of feminist therapy attempts to promote an understanding of women's economic, political, and historical position in the society to promote an understanding of the individual's past and current psychological situation. The working theoretical base appreciates that there are many influences—biological, social, political, and psychological—determining behavior in any situational context. Second, the process attempts to break down the inequality between therapist and client and to promote a model of human interaction that characterizes equality, sharing, and trust. It is proposed that the authoritarian, hierarchical, therapist-client relationship model does not facilitate women's freeing themselves from authority figures. Feminist therapy acknowledges the value of exploring the therapist's own values and encourages negative as well as positive feedback from clients concerning the process, goals, and values of therapy.[105] Third, feminist therapy advocates the use of small groups (instead of, or in conjunction with, individual therapy) as settings for personal change. The therapeutic value of reality-based, problem-solving groups is seen in their getting women away from personal isolation and from singular authority figures.[106]

Feminist Perspectives in Psychology

From conventions to books, from paper sessions to publications, the recurring theme in 1975 was the theme of sexism in the science of psychology. Sex discrimination and sex biases within the profession are widespread in education, therapy, professional opportunities, training, and research.[107]

Thus, when one examines the science from a feminist perspective, with an awareness of sexism or racism, the foundations shake.[108] The response called for is the restructuring of the methods, subjects, apparatus, materials, procedures, discussions, and references.[109] A question frequently raised is, Will the psychology of women contribute to the psychology of human behavior, or is it a passing fad? Will the study of women, by women, for women, enhance our "well-developed" theories in established areas of psychology? To the extent that the psychology of women does not restrict itself to the well-developed theories, methods, and visions of psychology past, the psychology of women may well be the most significant process in the evolution of psychology for the development of a psychology of human behavior. As Carlson notes, psychology's "inability" to deal with the psychological issues of women and femininity "is best construed as a symptom of a far more general impoverishment of current personology"[110] (p. 21). The psychology of women with a feminist perspective, which does not exclude the study of men and the masculine perspective,[111] is discovering new phenomena, redefining concepts, and developing approaches suitable to the study of persons.[112] This feminist perspective in psychology, though early in the process of evolving, has some identifiable elements and may serve as a model for the development of a psychology of human behavior.

One aspect of the feminist perspective involves placing the research enterprise, the methodological and theoretical models of science, within their social and political contexts. As the research findings indicated, there is something political about gender roles, and there is something about the models of inquiry in science which have to do with gender role definitions. Research has been limited because of its reliance upon "masculine" models of inquiry in the pursuit of scientific knowledge.[113]

Analyses of theoretical models from a social-political perspective indicate that we need to get the woman out of the little black box, out of the deep, dark motives of the "feminine psyche," and into the social-political, situational contexts within which her behavior takes place. Though the inadequacies of naive behaviorism are apparent,[114] behavioristic models do encourage us to assume that woman is sane, not crazy; that she is bright and reasonable, not hysterical; and that ill-advised behavioral patterns do not develop endogenously. In fact, the behavioral patterns may not be ill advised at all, given the nature of the environment in which her behaviors take place.[115] Thus, within the context of any single experiment, it would seem advantageous to consider that constructing a psychological analysis requires not only the measurement of some pattern of behavior (e.g., academic achievement) and of cognitions (e.g., expectancies of achievement) but also descriptions and analyses of the situational context and the environment (e.g., a college science class in which the male to female student ratio is four to one and the instructor is male).[116] In brief, ethological approaches can enhance our understanding of the development of behavioral patterns of women. Ethological as well as antecedent-consequence analyses of cognitive and behavioral development encourage us to ask questions of "why." Without investigating "why" questions, we have only traditional theoretical models to call upon, which often lead us back to the mysterious, feminine psyche.

Social-political analyses, in conjunction with psychological analyses, may be facilitated by collaborative, interdisciplinary research. Advances through interdisciplinary research are possible as we change the current policy of isolating psychologists from other scientists. The isolation of men and women in departments of psychology may keep our territories of status clearly intact, but it may also be a significant impediment toward an understanding of human behavior, which is influenced by many factors.

Another aspect of feminist perspectives in research is the development of formats and forums which attempt to engage the constituents of science (the public) and the participants in research (the subjects) in the scientific enterprise, that is, in the establishment of research priorities, data collection, and data interpretation. Women researchers have questioned what women's research priorities should be[117] and are concerned with discovering what kinds of research women consider will advance the status of women and will add to the quality of their lives. The project is critical because of our awareness that what is studied reflects the interests, values, and concerns of the researcher. As predominately well-educated women with high needs to achieve, female psychologists have pioneered in the study of fear of success; but we have not led the way, for example, in the study and analysis of rape and its victims.[118]

That psychologists are investigating research questions that reflect personal interests, values, and concerns is by no means inherently pernicious.[119] The research may well benefit the lives of others as well as one's own. Furthermore, what quality of research would come from dispassionate inquiry? It would seem unreasonable to require that only heterosexual persons study homosexual behavior and that only homosexual persons study heterosexual behavior for the sake of "objectivity." Whatever advantages might be gained in objectivity would surely be offset by narrow perspectives, less persistence, poorly conceived questions, and so forth. But a participatory model which engages the constituents of science in the enterprise would insure that the interests, values, and concerns of nonwhite, less traditionally educated women do influence what is studied and would insure that their passion is brought into the process of research. Furthermore, it is not evident that an authoritarian, hierarchical researcher-subject model is necessary for the acquisition of scientific knowledge. It would seem possible to construct paradigms of the research environment, be it naturalistic or experimental, in which human interaction is characterized by a reasonable degree of equality, sharing, and trust.[120]

A final aspect of the feminist perspective in research can be characterized as the process of integration: integrating the interests and concerns of and for one's research and research productivity with one's concerns for the quality of one's life and the life experiences of others with self-growth and with the methods of research training and practice. The integration necessarily involves a reordering of priorities[121] lowering of the priorities of self-growth, of the competence-enhancing quality of the experiences for the self and others engaged in the practice and teaching of research. Cooperative rather than competitive research with our colleagues may slow down production or speed up production by eliminating duplication and by stimulating new ideas. But the quality of the experience as well as the quality of the research product would be enhanced along with significant gains in our competence to understand human behavior. Likewise, the value of teaching and instruction would be elevated. The integration of valued teaching and research activities in our graduate programs (which at present appear to have more in common with the initiation rites of a male fraternity than with systematic feedback systems to develop skills in research) would benefit students and the profession alike.

To work cooperatively rather than competitively, to value teaching as well as research, and to concern ourselves with self-growth and self-awareness in the context of our research goes against our training as scientists and the atmosphere of most departments and laboratories.[122] Self-examination goes against the masculine model of the scientist. But feminist perspectives are placing not only research but the researcher in her/his social and political perspectives. Self-examination from such a perspective illuminates the degree of integration of the masculine and feminine models in our training, in our teaching, in our interactional patterns with women and men colleagues, and in our preferred methodological and theoretical paradigms.

There is nothing new about women being psychologists. What is revolutionary is the force of women in psychology and in the psychology of women to change the structure of the belief system of science to construct a psychology of human behavior.

NOTES

1. See M. B. Parlee, "Review Essay: Psychology," *Signs* 1 (Autumn 1975): 119–38.
2. Ibid., p. 124; S. F. Morin, "The Past, Present, and Future of Heterosexual Bias in Psychological Research on Homosexuality" (paper presented at the meeting of the American Psychological Association, Chicago, August 1975); and S. A. Shields, "Functionalism, Darwinism, and the Psychology of Women," *American Psychologist* 30 (1975): 739–54.
3. R. Carlson, "Understanding Women: Implications for Personality Theory and Research," in *Women and Achievement: Social and Motivational Analyses,* ed. M. T. S. Mednick, S. S. Tangri, and L. W. Hoffman (Washington, D.C.: Hemisphere Press, 1975).
4. Shields, p. 740.
5. E. E. Maccoby, ed., *The Development of Sex Differences* (Stanford, Calif.: Stanford University Press, 1966).
6. Perhaps some progress has been made in psychology's understanding that "child" and "adult" are meant to include both female and male. W. McKenna and S. J. Kessler, in "Differential Treatment of Males and Females as a Source of Bias in Social Psychology" (paper presented at the meeting of the American Psychological Association, New Orleans, August 1974), had found an overwhelming use of male subjects in research and the development of theory in psychology. From a cursory look at one 1975 volume of the *Journal of Experimental Child Psychology,* 66 percent of the studies utilized about an equal number of female and male participants; however, in 33 percent the sex of subjects was unspecified. Apparently, the possible refinement in methodology has not been complemented in data interpretation and theory construction. A typical case of amateurish data analysis that violates principles of theory construction (sexism aside) is exemplified in the study where both female and male subjects were included, a significant sex × condition was obtained, but only the males' data were used to draw inferences and to construct subsequent hypotheses. In one such case, the authors explained that the interactions with sex were not discussed "for reasons of space." One could hardly be convinced that "space" had a significant bearing upon the decision: the article covered eleven pages of the journal's issue!
7. P. W. Berman, P. Cooper, P. Mansfield, S. Shields, and J. Abplanalp, "Sex Differences in Attraction to Infants: When Do They Occur?" *Sex Roles* 1 (1975): 311–18.
8. E. E. Maccoby and C. N. Jacklin, *The Psychology of Sex Differences* (Stanford, Calif.: Stanford University Press, 1974).

9. J. A. Sherman, "Book Review," *Sex Roles* 1 (1975): 297–301.
10. *Consumer Math: Selected Results from the First National Assessment of Mathematics* (Washington, D.C.: Government Printing Office, 1975); and M. Herman, "A Look at National Assessment Results in Eight Learning Areas in the Light of Female-Male Differences," mimeographed (Denver, Colo.: National Assessment of Educational Progress, Department of Utilization/Applications, 1975).
11. L. Radloff, "Sex Differences in Depression," *Sex Roles* 1 (1975): 249–65.
12. J. Cuca, "Women Psychologists and Marriage: A Bad Match?" *APA Monitor* (January 1976), p. 13; and R. A. Van Dusen and E. B. Sheldon, "The Changing Status of American Women: A Life Cycle Perspective," *American Psychologist* 31 (1976): 106–16.
13. M. R. Key, *Male/Female Language with a Comprehensive Bibliography* (Metuchen, N.J.: Scarecrow Press, 1975); R. Lakoff, *Language and Woman's Place* (New York: Harper & Row, 1975); and N. Henley and B. Thorne, *She Said, He Said: An Annotated Bibliography of Sex Differences in Language, Speech and Non-Verbal Communication* (Pittsburgh: Know, Inc., 1975).
14. Recognizing that angels walk in, I would like to propose the following working definitions: sex is the biological status of a person as congruently female or male or as hermaphroditic. Sex status is defined by the characteristic reproductive system and capacities. The sex role consists of all "irreducible" and nonoptional attributes and behaviors typically characteristic of congruent female or male or of hermaphroditic persons. Sex role behaviors are defined biologically by the structure and function of the reproductive system and include menstruation, gestation, lactation, ovulation, spermatogenesis, and ejaculation. Sex role performance may or may not indicate the biological capacity of the person. Sex role identity is the experiencing of oneself, with concomitant cognitive organization, as female, male, or hermaphroditic. Gender is the perceived or measured status of a female or male in regard to the degree of femininity and the degree of masculinity as pertaining to some attribute or behavior. Prescription of gender is based upon assigned sex. Gender status (feminine, masculine, androgynous) is defined by the female's or male's enactment of gender roles. Gender role consists of all optional and prescribed attributes, attitudes, and behaviors defined appropriate for and expected of females and males within the culture. The gender role definition exists independently of the person's experiencing of, or performing, the role. Gender roles are defined by the culture. Gender role performance may or may not reflect the person's role capacities in any given situation. Gender role identity is the experiencing of oneself, with concomitant cognitive organization, as feminine, masculine, and androgynous to some degree or another in regards to some attribute, attitude, and/or behavior.
15. M. M. Schratz, "A Developmental Investigation of Sex Differences in Perceptual Differentiation and Mathematical Reasoning in Two Ethnic Groups" (Ph.D. diss., Fordham University, 1976); and V. E. O'Leary and A. O. Harrison, "Sex Role Sterotypes as a Function of Race and Sex" (paper presented at the meeting of the American Psychological Association, Chicago, 1975).
16. R. K. Unger and F. L. Denmark, eds., *Woman: Dependent or Independent Variable?* (New York: Psychological Dimensions, Inc., 1975).
17. J. Money and A. A. Ehrhardt, *Man and Woman: Boy and Girl* (Baltimore: Johns Hopkins University Press, 1972).
18. C. S. Ford and F. A. Beach, *Patterns of Sexual Behavior* (New York: Harper & Row, 1951); M. Z. Rosaldo and L. Lamphere, eds., *Woman, Culture, and Society* (Stanford, Calif.: Stanford University Press, 1974); P. L. van den Berghe, *Age and Sex in Human Societies: A Biosocial Perspective* (Belmont, Calif.: Wadsworth Publishing Co., 1973); N. N. Wagner, ed., *Perspectives on Human Sexuality: Psychological, Social, and Cultural Research Findings* (New York: Behavioral Publications, 1974); B. Yorburg, *Sexual Identity: Sex Roles and Social Change* (New York: John Wiley & Sons, 1974); and J. Zubin and J. Money, eds., *Contemporary Sexual Behavior: Critical Issues in the 1970s* (Baltimore: Johns Hopkins University Press, 1973).
19. R. C. Barnett, "Sex Differences and Age Trends in Occupational Preference and Prestige," *Journal of Counseling Psychology* 22 (1975): 35–38; J. S. Hyde, B. G. Rosenberg, and J. A. Behrman, "Tomboyism: Implications for Theories of Female Development" (paper presented at the meeting of the Western Psychological Association, Denver, April 1974); and Maccoby and Jacklin (n. 8 above).
20. N. D. Reppucci, "Parental Education, Sex Differences, and Performance on Cognitive Tasks among Two-Year-Old Children," *Developmental Psychology* 4 (1971): 248–53; and Schratz.

21. R. Green, *Sexual Identity Conflict in Children and Adults* (New York: Basic Books, 1974); and Money and Ehrhardt.
22. S. L. Bem, "Sex-Role Adaptability: One Consequence of Psychological Androgyny," *Journal of Personality and Social Psychology* 31 (1975): 634–43.
23. A. C. Berstein and P. A. Cowan, "Children's Concepts of How People Get Babies," *Child Development* 46 (March 1975): 77–91.
24. R. G. Slaby and K. S. Frey, "Development of Gender Constancy and Selective Attention to Same-Sex Models," *Child Development* 46 (December 1975): 849–56; and S. K. Thompson, "Gender Labels and Early Sex-Role Development," *Child Development* 46 (June 1975): 339–47.
25. J. E. Williams, S. M. Bennett, and D. L. Best, "Awareness and Expression of Sex Stereotypes in Young Children," *Developmental Psychology* 11 (1975): 635–42.
26. J. Z. Rubin, F. J. Provenzano, and Z. Luria, "The Eye of the Beholder: Parents' View on Sex of Newborns," *American Journal of Orthopsychiatry* 44 (1974): 512–19.
27. C. A. Seavey, P. A. Katz, and S. R. Zalk, "Baby X: The Effect of Gender Labels on Adult Responses to Infants," *Sex Roles* 1 (1975):s103–10; and J. A. Will, P. Self, and N. Datan, "Maternal Behavior and Sex of Infant" (unpublished paper available from the authors, West Virginia University, 1975).
28. G. Margolin and G. R. Patterson, "Differential Consequences Provided by Mothers and Fathers for Their Sons and Daughters," *Developmental Psychology* 11 (1975): 537–38.
29. L. A. Serbin and K. D. O'Leary, "How Nursery Schools Teach Girls to Shut Up," *Psychology Today* 9, no. 7 (1975): 56–57, 102–3.
30. H. L. Rheingold and K. V. Cook, "The Contents of Boys' and Girls' Rooms as an Index of Parents' Behavior," *Child Development* 46 (June 1975): 459–63.
31. J. H. Block, J. Block, and D. Harrington, "Sex-Role Typing and Instrumental Behavior: A Developmental Study" (paper presented at the meeting of the Society for Research in Child Development, Denver, April 1975).
32. Bem has measured androgyny in terms of an absence of significant difference between the femininity and masculinity scores regardless of whether the two scores are high or low. However, Spence, Helmreich, and Stapp (see n. 35 below) reserve the term androgynous for persons who have a high degree of both feminine and masculine attributes; persons scoring low on both scales are defined as "indeterminants."
33. E. F. Rosenfeld, "The Relationship of Sex-typed Toys to the Development of Competency and Sex-Role Identification in Children" (paper presented at the meeting of the Society for Research in Child Development, Denver 1975).
34. S. C. Nash, "The Relationship among Sex-Role Stereotyping, Sex-Role Preferences, and the Sex Difference in Spatial Visualization," *Sex Roles* 1 (1975): 15–32.
35. J. T. Spence, R. Helmreich, and J. Stapp, "Ratings of Self and Peers on Sex Role Attributes and Their Relation to Self-Esteem and Conceptions of Masculinity and Femininity," *Journal of Personality and Social Psychology* 32 (1975): 29–39.
36. F. Livson, "Sex Differences in Personality Development in the Middle Adult Years: A Longitudinal Study" (paper presented at the Gerontological Society, Louisville, Kentucky, October 1975).
37. R. E. Wetter, "Levels of Self-Esteem Associated with Four Sex Role Categories" (paper presented at the meeting of the American Psychological Association, Chicago, August 1975).
38. S. L. Bem, "Psychology Looks at Sex Roles: Where Have All the Androgynous People Gone?" (paper presented at the UCLA Symposia on Women, May 1972); J. I. Berzins, "New Perspectives on Sex Joles and Personality Dimensions" (paper presented at the meeting of the American Psychological Association, Chicago, 1975).
39. K. A. Urberg and G. Labouvie-Vief, "Conceptualizations of Sex Roles: A Life Span Developmental Study," *Developmental Psychology* 12 (1975): 15–23.
40. Van den Berghe (n. 18 above), p. 1.
41. See Livson.
42. J. Kristal, D. Sanders, J. T. Spence, and R. Helmreich, "Inferences about the Femininity of Competent Women and Their Implications for Likeability," *Sex Roles* 1 (1975): 33–40.
43. N. Costrich, J. Feinstein, and L. Kidder, "When Stereotypes Hurt: Three Studies of Penalties for Sex-Role Reversals," *Journal of Experimental Social Psychology* 11 (1975): 520–30.
44. J. T. Spence, R. Helmreich, and J. Stapp, "Likability, Sex-Role Congruence of Interest and Competence: It All Depends on How You Ask," *Journal of Applied Social Psychology*, in press.

45. O'Leary and Harrison, p. 11.
46. P. A. Goldberg, M. Gottesdiener, and P. R. Abramson, "Another Put Down of Women? Perceived Attractiveness as a Function of Support for the Feminist Movement," *Journal of Personality and Social Psychology* 32 (1975): 113–15. As a note on the forces which act against women becoming involved in feminism, the study tends to reflect many statements behind the experimental question, e.g., "the most important characteristics of any woman are her physical attributes"; "women are 'libbers' because they are ugly and cannot 'get' a man," etc.
47. J. M. Nielsen and P. T. Doyle, "Sex Role Stereotypes of Feminists and Nonfeminists," *Sex Roles* 1 (1975): 83–96.
48. M. J. Peterson, "The Asymmetry of Sex-Role Perceptions," *Sex Roles* 1 (1975): 267–82.
49. F. Ditmar, N. Mueller, and J. Mitchell, "Females' Attitudes toward Feminism and Their Conformity in Heterosexual Groups" (paper presented at the meeting of the American Psychological Association, Chicago, 1975).
50. B. Yorburg and I. Arafat, "Current Sex Role Conceptions and Conflict," *Sex Roles* 1 (1975): 135–46.
51. M. J. Luetgert, A. H. Armstrong, J. M. Curry, J. W. Creaser, J. A. Ashbaugh, and M. J. LaPlante, "Today's Feminist: Her Place Is in the Home!" (paper presented at the meeting of the American Psychological Association, Chicago, 1975).
52. R. B. Bryson, J. B. Bryson, M. H. Licht, and B. G. Licht, "The Professional Pair: Husband and Wife," *American Psychologist* 31 (1976): 10–16.
53. M. Z. Rosaldo, "Woman, Culture, and Society: A Theoretical Overview," in *Woman, Culture, and Society,* ed. M. Z. Rosaldo and L. Lamphere (Stanford, Calif.: Stanford University Press, 1974).
54. "The emphasis on marriage as the single channel for female sexuality is totally congruent with all other aspects of the feminine character. . . . female sexuality is in our culture constrained by a straight if not narrow path leading to marriage. Marriage, bolstered by a surviving double standard, defines female sexuality in terms of male proprietorship. Not only is a wife her husband's sexual property, but the mores reinforce her dependence on him. . . . The mores also forbid sexual practices which counteract the wife's erotic dependence: autoeroticism, lesbianism, and extramarital affairs. . . . The connection between 'passivity' enforced in sexual and social roles continues to be with us, the one justified in terms of the other" (J. L. Laws, "Towards a Model of Female Sexual Identity," *Midway* 11 [1970]: 39–76).
55. B. Culliton, "Abortion: Liberal Laws Do Make Abbrtion Safer for Women," *Science* 188 (1975): 1091; and S. Stier and N. Russo, "Abortion: Fight Shifts to Congress," *APA Monitor* (June 1975), pp. 1, 5.
56. K. Grimstad and S. Rennie, *The New Woman's Survival Sourcebook* (New York: Alfred A. Knopf, Inc., 1975).
57. J. A. Sherman, *On the Psychology of Sex Differences: A Survey of Empirical Studies* (Springfield, Ill.: Charles C. Thomas, 1971).
58. A. C. Kinsey, W. B. Pomeroy, C. E. Martin, and D. H. Gebhard, *Sexual Behavior in the Human Female* (Philadelphia: W. B. Saunders & Co., 1951); and Wagner (n. 18 above).
59. W. Simon, "The Social, the Erotic, and the Sensual: The Complexities of Sexual Scripts," in *Nebraska Symposium on Motivation,* ed. J. K. Cole and R. Dienstbier (Lincoln: University of Nebraska Press, 1973).
60. P. W. Blumstein and P. Schwartz, "Lesbianism and Bisexuality" (paper available from the authors, University of Washington, Seattle, 1974).
61. J. H. Gagnon, "Scripts and the Coordination of Sexual Conduct," in *Nebraska Symposium on Motivation,* ed. J. K. Cole and R. Dienstbier (Lincoln: University of Nebraska Press, 1973); Green (n. 21 above); and Money and Ehrhardt (n. 17 above).
62. A. P. Bell, "Homosexualities: Their Range and Character," in *Nebraska Symposium on Motivation,* ed. J. K. Cole and R. Dienstbier (Lincoln: University of Nebraska Press, 1973).
63. For an "interesting" statement of values, consult the *Journal of Comparative and Physiological Psychology,* vol. 88 (1975), for studies of "differential rates of exhaustion and recovery of male rat ejaculation," "ultrasonic postejaculatory vocalizations," etc.
64. It is instructive to read the last question substituting the word "female" for "homosexuality" and to review the article by Shields (n. 2 above).
65. S. F. Morin, "An Annotated Bibliography of Research on Lesbianism and Male Homosexuality (1967–1974)" (paper presented at the American Psychological Association, Chicago, 1975); B. F. Riess, J. Safer, and W. Yotive, "Psychological Test Data on Female Homosexuality: A Review of the Literature," *Journal of Homosexuality* 1 (1974): 71–86;

L. S. Brown, "Investigating the Stereotypic Picture of Lesbians in the Clinical Literature" (paper presented at the Second Annual National Conference on Feminist Psychology, Carbondale, Illinois, January 1975); D. H. Rosen, *Lesbianism: A Study of Female Homosexuality* (Springfield, Ill.: Charles C. Thomas, 1974).

66. A. P. MacDonald, "Homophobia: Its Roots and Meanings" (paper presented at the meeting of the American Psychological Association, Chicago, 1975), and "Identification and Measurement of Multidimensional Attitudes toward Equality between the Sexes," *Journal of Homosexuality* 1 (1975): 149–64.
67. B. Love, "A Case for Lesbians as Role Models for Healthy Adult Women"; B. Trilling, "Lesbianism and Its Relation to the Changing Social and Psychological Role of Women"; and B. Sang and L. Lowenherz, "Personism: Towards the Elimination of Personal Oppression" (all papers presented at the meeting of the American Psychological Association, Chicago, 1975).
68. E. Hooker, "The Homosexual Community," in *Sexual Deviance,* ed. J. H. Gagnon and W. Simon (New York: Harper & Row, 1967); see also Kinsey et al.; Rosen; and Wagner.
69. Kinsey et al.
70. E. K. Childs, E. A. Sachnoff, and E. S. Stocker, "AWP Position Paper on Women's Sexuality: A Feminist View," *AWP Newsletter* (March–April 1975), pp. 1–2.
71. M. T. S. Mednick, S. S. Tangri, and L. W. Hoffman, eds., *Women and Achievement: Social and Motivational Analyses* (Washington, D.C.: Hemisphere Press, 1975).
72. R. B. Knudsin, ed., *Women and Success: The Anatomy of Achievement* (New York: William Morrow & Co., 1974).
73. M. T. S. Mednick and H. J. Weissman, "The Psychology of Women—Selected Topics," in *Annual Review of Psychology,* ed. M. R. Rosenzweig and B. W. Porter (Palo Alto, Calif.: Annual Reviews, Inc., 1975).
74. R. M. Vaughter, A. B. Ginorio, and B. A. Trilling, "The Failure of Trait Theories to Predict Success," *Signs,* vol. 2, no. 2.
75. R. M. Kanter, "Women and the Structure of Organizations: Explorations in Theory and Behavior," in *Another Voice: Feminist Perspectives on Social Life and Social Science,* ed. M. Millman and R. M. Kanter (New York: Anchor Books, 1975); J. L. Laws, "The Psychology of Tokenism: An Analysis," *Sex Roles* 1 (1975): 57–68; and L. Liss, "Why Academic Women Do Not Revolt," *Sex Roles* 1 (1975): 209–23.
76. P. J. Bickel, E. A. Hammel, and J. W. O'Connell, "Sex Bias in Graduate Admissions: Data from Berkeley," *Science* 187 (1975): 398–404.
77. G. Rubin-Rabson, "How High Are the Odds against Women?" *American Psychologist* 29 (1974): 916–17; E. M. Westervelt, *Barriers to Women's Participation in Post-Secondary Education: A Review and Commentary* (Washington, D.C.: Government Printing Office, 1975); J. L. McCarthy and D. Wolfe, "Doctorates Granted to Women and Minority Group Members," *Science* 189 (1975): 856–59; J. M. Cuca, "Women PhD's on Rise, But Pay Is Less," *APA Monitor* (January 1975), p. 5; S. R. Sacks and R. M. Vaughter, "APA Workshop Report: Women Doing Research," *APA Division 35 Newsletter* (February 1976), pp. 2–5; J. I. Roberts, *Creating a Facade of Change: Informal Mechanisms Used to Impede the Changing Status of Women in Academe* (Pittsburgh: Know, Inc., 1975); D. Longeward and D. Scott, eds., *Affirmative Action for Women: A Practical Guide for Women and Management* (Reading, Mass.: Addison-Wesley Publishing Co., 1975); E. Spreitzer and E. E. Snyder, "Age, Marital Status, and Labor Force Participation as Related to Life Satisfaction," *Sex Roles* 1 (1975): 235–48; and P. A. Schmuck, "Deterrents to Women's Careers in School Management," *Sex Roles* 1 (1975): 339–54.
78. J. E. Newman, "Sex Differences in the Organizational Assimilation of Beginning Graduate Students in Psychology," *Journal of Educational Psychology* 66 (1974): 129–38; "Guidelines for Nonsexist Use of Language: APA Task Force on Issues of Sexual Bias in Graduate Education," *American Psychologist* 30 (1975): 682–84; N. Russo and S. Stier, "A Rose Is a Rose . . . Is a Four-Letter Word," *APA Monitor* (September 1975), p. 15; "Help Stamp Out Sexism: Change in Language!" *APA Monitor* (November 1975), p. 16; and M. W. Farnsworth, *The Young Woman's Guide to an Academic Career* (New York: Richards Rosen Press, 1974).
79. C. M. Caballero, P. Giles, and P. Shaver, "Sex-Role Traditionalism and Fear of Success," *Sex Roles* 1 (1975): 319–26.
80. V. O'Leary and B. Hammack, "Sex-Role Orientation and Achievement Context as Determinants of the Motive to Avoid Success," *Sex Roles* 1 (1975): 225–34.
81. B. M. Powell, "Role Conflict and Symptoms of Psychological Distress in College Educated Women," *Journal of Consulting and Clinical Psychology,* in press.

82. N. Romer, "The Motive to Avoid Success and Its Effects on the Performance in School-Age Males and Females," *Developmental Psychology* 11 (1975): 689–99.
83. R. M. Patty, "Motive to Avoid Success: Intellectual, Interpersonal, or Neutral Task-Instructions" (paper presented at the meeting of the American Psychological Association, Chicago, 1975).
84. M. E. Lockheed, "Female Motive to Avoid Success: A Psychological Barrier or a Response to Deviancy?" *Sex Roles*1 (1975): 41–50; J. V. Anderson, "Psychological Determinants," in *Women and Success: The Anatomy of Achievement,* ed. R. B. Knudsin (New York: William Morrow & Co., 1974); Kanter (n. 75 above); and S. S. Tangri, "Implied Demand Character of the Wife's Future and Role Innovation: Patterns of Achievement Orientation among College Women," in *Woman and Achievement: Social and Motivational Analyses,* ed. M. S. T. Mednick, S. S. Tangri, and L. W. Hoffman (Washington, D.C.: Hemisphere Press, 1975).
85. M. Pappo, "Fear of Success: A Theoretical Analysis in the Construction and Validation of a Measuring Instrument" (Ph.D diss., Columbia University, 1972).
86. J. M. Jellison, R. Jackson-White, R. A. Bruder, and W. Martyna, "Achievement Behavior: A Situational Interpretation," *Sex Roles* 1 (1975): 369–84.
87. P. Burns, "Profiles of Achievement-related Behaviors in Career and Non-Career Women" (Ph.D. diss., Fordham University, 1976).
88. L. Gray-Shellberg, S. Villareal, and S. Stone, "Resolution of Career Conflicts: The Double Standard in Action" (paper presented at the meeting of the American Psychological Association, Honolulu, August 1972).
89. To the extent that the study's paradigm demonstrates that patterns of underachievement and low self-esteem can be established in response to transmitted messages that negative consequences will follow achievement and confidence, that the same rules of learning apply to both men and women, and that women's fears about the consequences of achieving are not likely to have an unrealistic basis in some malfunctioning perceptual system, the study is instructive. Also valuable is the implication that the goals of the person be considered in evaluating and labeling behavior. However, its theoretical significance is diluted by naive behaviorism. Without exploring the possibility that the study tells us more about the power of the reward contingency manipulated (see n. 92 below), than about the complexities of achievement behavior in men and women, it should have been considered that in the naturalistic world, it is the woman's, not the man's, achievement-related behaviors that are likely to be followed by negative consequences (see studies, for example, of institutionalized sexism cited in the text). Further, in the naturalistic world, the consequences of women's intellectual-related performances are not so typically clearly defined. Thus, generalized expectancies would apparently operate unless there were cues to contradict them. Empirical data would lead us to conclude that gender role definitions are a significant source of information for the construction of generalizable expectancies. The cluster of characteristics which define the masculine gender role, in contrast to those which define the feminine, are congruent with high intellectual performance and positive self-regard. And, finally, the statements of values that can be implied from the interpretation of the data are questionable. I concur with the authors' suggestion that the pattern of negative consequences that typically follow women's achievement-related behaviors must be changed. But until such changes have occurred, the recommendation that success be defined as the avoidance of disapproval from men and that success is avoiding punishment in a sexist society is unacceptable to me.
90. J. Marecek, "Sex Differences in Causal Attributions: Some Thoughts on Methods and Directions for Future Research" (paper presented at the meeting of the Eastern Psychological Association, April 1975); and M. C. McHugh, "Sex Differences in Causal Attribution: A Critical Review" (paper presented at the meeting of the Eastern Psychological Association, April 1975).
91. J. Fisher, "Effects of a Competitive Atmosphere on Causal Attributions: Theoretical Implications" (paper presented at the meeting of the Eastern Psychological Association, April 1975).
92. L. Ross, G. Bierbrauer, and S. Hoffman, "The Role of Attribution Processes in Conformity and Dissent: Revisiting the Asch Situation," *American Psychologist* 31 (1976): 148–57.
93. A. E. Bayer and H. S. Astin, "Sex Differentials in the Academic Reward System," *Science* 188 (1975): 796–802.
94. D. E. Papalia and S. S. Tennent, "Vocational Aspirations in Preschoolers: A Manifestation of Early Sex Role Stereotyping," *Sex Roles* 1 (1975): 197–98; and K. R. Thornburg

and M. Weeks, "Vocational Role Expectations of Five-Year-Old Children and Their Parents," *Sex Roles* 1 (1975): 395–96.

95. See R. M. Vaughter et al. (n. 74 above).
96. E. Spreitzer and E. E. Snyder (n. 77 above), pp. 339–54; and P. S. Sears and A. H. Barbee, "Career and Life Satisfaction among Terman's Gifted Women" (paper available from the authors, Stanford University, 1975).
97. V. E. Garfield and R. Kuntz, "Clinical Psychologists in the 1970s," *American Psychologist* 31 (1976): 1–9.
98. "Report of the Task Force on Sex Bias and Sex-Role Stereotyping in Psychotherapeutic Practice," *American Psychologist* 30 (1975): 1169–75.
99. S. Phelps and N. Austin, *The Assertive Woman* (Fredericksburg, Va.: IMPACT, 1975); and S. M. Osborn and G. G. Harris, *Assertive Training for Women* (Springfield, Ill.: Charles C. Thomas, 1975).
100. V. E. Pendergrass, E. Kimmel, J. Joesting, J. Petersen, and E. Bush, "Sex Discrimination Counseling," *American Psychologist* 31 (1976): 36–46.
101. H. Eisenstein and S. R. Sacks, "Women in Search of Autonomy: An Action Design," *Social Change* 5 (1975): 4–6.
102. D. Tennov, *Psychotherapy: The Hazardous Cure* (New York: Abelard-Schuman, Ltd., 1975); and C. Steiner, H. Wyckoff, D. Goldstine, P. Lariviere, R. Schwebel, and J. Marcus, *Readings in Radical Psychiatry* (New York: Grove Press, 1975).
103. The First National Conference of Feminist Therapists, cosponsored by the Women's Institute of Alternative Psychotherapy and the Women's Studies Program at the University of Colorado, Boulder, Colorado, January 1976; The Women's Institute of Alternative Psychotherapy, Director Anne Schaef, Ph.D., Box 356, Boulder, Colorado; The Women's Institute for Psychotherapy, Directors Jean Mundy, Ph.D.; Rita Sherr, C.W.S.; and Barbara Trilling, Ph.D.; 105 West 13th Street, New York, New York.
104. A. V. Mander and A. K. Rush, *Feminism as Therapy* (New York: Random House, 1974); Osborn and Harris (n. 99 above); E. Sachnoff, "Toward a Definition of Feminist Therapy," *AWP Newsletter* (Fall 1975), pp. 4–5; and E. F. Williams, *Notes of a Feminist Therapist* (New York: Praeger Publishers, 1976).
105. The feminist therapist is likely to value the richness of women's talents and perspectives and to value many of the feminine-labeled aspects of personhood; to value self-definition, autonomy, courage, expert, legitimate, nurturient, and integrative power, as opposed to exploitative, manipulative, and competitive power; to conceive of mental health as competence for change and as acquisition of skills and competency for self-actualization rather than adjustment; to value flexibility in roles (androgyny) and sexual lifestyles; to believe that reciprocal, equalitarian relationships are better than non-equalitarian power-based relationships and to disaffirm social pressure which insists that a woman must surround herself with family life; to value the person's respect of self as well as respect for others; to be sensitive to the human rights of children and to believe that single parenting (regardless of sex or sexual orientation of parent) does not necessarily affect children adversely; to believe that not all women's problems and concerns are related to women's minority-group status and female socialization; to deplore sexual exploitation; and to believe that all women are agents of change in their lives and in the lives of others and that to integrate the personal and the political ("one's relationship to power") is therapeutic.
106. The goals and purposes of the group experience are congruent with those of individual therapy: to learn to differentiate what one can change personally and what requires political organization; to increase political awareness; to learn personal problem-solving skills and interpersonal communication skills which foster self-esteem and confidence; to deal with the psychological effects of true victimization, such as low self-esteem and feelings of helplessness; to increase taking responsibility for one's own actions and to learn to place responsibility where it belongs when it belongs with others; to provide support and feedback, both positive and negative, and to learn to manage self-esteem, social approval, anger, and compassion; to increase one's ability to differentiate unrealistic from realistic criticisms and to learn to manage both; and to learn skills in becoming aware of one's own power and to learn not to exaggerate the power of others.
107. C. Ehrlich, *The Conditions of Feminist Research* (Baltimore: Vacant Lots Press, 1976); M. B. Parlee (n. 1 above); *Report of the Task Force on the Status of Women in Psychology* (Washington, D.C.: American Psychological Association, 1972); and M. J. Mahoney, "Psychology

in Action: The Sensitive Scientist in Empirical Humanism," *American Psychologist* 30 (1975): 864–71.

108. I. S. Reid, "Science, Politics, and Race," *Signs* 1 (Autumn 1975): 397–422.
109. "Guidelines for Correcting Sex-Role Stereotypes in Research," *APA Division 35 Newsletter* (May 1975), pp. 10–11.
110. Carlson (n. 3 above), p. 21.
111. D. S. David and R. Brannon, *The Forty-nine Percent Majority: The Male Sex Role* (Reading, Mass.: Addison-Wesley Publishing Co., 1976).
112. S. Cox, ed., *Female Psychology: The Emerging Self* (Chicago: Science Research Associates, 1976); J. Freeman, ed., *Women: A Feminist Perspective* (Palo Alto, Calif.: Mayfield Publishing Co., 1975), J. S. Hyde and B. G. Rosenberg, *Half the Human Experience: The Psychology of Women* (Lexington, Mass.: D. C. Heath & Co., 1976); and E. Lasky, ed., *Humanness: An Exploration into the Mythologies about Women and Men* (New York: MSS Information Corp, 1975).
113. "Agency operates by way of mastery and control; communion with naturalistic observation, sensitive to qualitative patterning, and greater personal participation by the investigator. . . . I have watched one or another version of it in sociology for almost 50 years. . . . What is new and illuminating, however, is the recognition of a machismo element in research. The specific processes involved in agentic research are typically male preoccupations; agency is identified with a masculine principle, the Protestant ethic, a Faustian pursuit of knowledge—as with all forces toward mastery, separation, and ego enhancement. . . . The scientist using this approach creates his own controlled reality. He can manipulate it. He is master. He has power. He can add or subtract or combine variables. He can play with a simulated reality like an Olympian god. He can remain at a distance, safely behind his shield, uninvolved. The communal approach is much humbler. It disavows control, for control spoils the results" (Jessie Bernard, as cited in M. Millman and R. M. Kanter, eds., *Another Voice: Feminist Perspectives on Social Life and Social Science* [New York: Anchor Books, 1975], p. x).
114. J. W. Sutherland, "Beyond Behaviorism and Determinism," *Fields within Fields* (Winter 1974), pp. 32–46.
115. See Rosaldo (n. 53 above).
116. R. M. Vaughter and W. S. Sullivan, "Achievement-related Behaviors as a Function of Sex of Instructor" (paper presented at the meeting of the American Psychological Association, Washington, D.C., August 1976).
117. P. Crull, "Report from Workshop III: Setting Priorities in Research for Women," *APA Division 35 Newsletter* (February 1976), p. 5.
118. S. Brownmiller, *Against Our Will: Men, Women and Rape* (New York: Simon & Schuster, 1975); N. Connell and C. Williams, eds., *Rape: The First Sourcebook for Women* (New York: New American Library, 1974); and D. E. H. Russell, *The Politics of Rape: The Victim's Perspective* (New York: Stein & Day, 1975).
119. From the perspective of tokenism (J. L. Laws [n. 75 above]), our research of achievement motivation and behavior may reflect the concerns and conflicts of pioneering women in science. The findings of the research reviewed would indicate that in terms of likability and acceptability in our token positions, we can be different and achieve as long as we affirm masculine values, confine competition to competing with other women, do not change established priorities for research, do not change the criteria for evaluating "good" research, and do not modify the well-established and developed areas of psychology. A student related to me that she asked a professor in class one day about the relevance of Erikson's theory to female development. The professor told her to talk to me, that I "take care of females, women, and all that stuff," and proceeded to get back to the "other stuff."
120. "Proposed Revisions of APA Standards on the Conduct of Research with Humans," *APA Division 35 Newsletter* (May 1975), pp. 9–10, 12.
121. H. Holter, "Sex Roles and Social Change," in *Women and Achievement; Social and Motivational Analyses,* ed. M. T. S. Mednick, S. S. Tangri, and L. W. Hoffman (Washington, D.C.: Hemisphere Publishing Co., 1975).
122. J. Walsh, "Science for the People," *Science* 191 (1976): 1033–35; and V. P. White, *Grants: How to Find Out about Them and What to Do Next* (New York: Plenum Press, 1975).

Androgyny Reconsidered

Kathleen E. Grady

There is an enormous literature in psychology and related fields on "sex differences." Technically, sex is an easy and obvious independent variable, and some secondary hypothesis is usually constructed about it and tacked on to any major investigation of some other variable. It is interesting to note that researchers do not usually have the interest or confidence to use sex as a major (or as the only) hypothesis. The result of this approach is a body of "empirical findings" that relates sex tangentially to every conceivable phenomenon from aggressiveness to judging the movement of a dot of light in a dark room. Of course there are also numerous studies in which the sex sub-hypothesis does not work out, but there has not been constructed a matching literature on "sex similarities."

Sifting through this literature is a tedious job warranted only by the great social importance of the task. Shields (1975) and other historians have suggested that psychology and science in general have replaced religion as the justifier for women's inferior position in society. And it is the oppression of women that is at the heart of sex difference research. There is both a social impetus and a social consequence to this research. Sheer intellectual curiosity does not prompt it or there would be matching literatures on other salient personal characteristics such as height, handedness, or eye color, and matching numbers of phenomena to which these characteristics are slightly related. Instead, sex and race are the variables of choice.

If psychological sex differences is the answer, what is the question? What are the phenomena to be explained? It is almost too obvious to men-

"Androgyny Reconsidered" by Kathleen Grady. Paper presented at the Eastern Psychological Association Meeting, New York, April, 1975. Reprinted by permission of the author.

tion that men and women and boys and girls in general lead very different lives in this society in almost any area one could name: employment, education, recreation, in their relations to children and to each other, in their dress and how they spend their time, to name a few. Girls get better grades; boys are class presidents; women care for children; men run corporations. Clearly sex bears an important relationship to these lifestyle differences. They represent social facts around which legal and moral arguments rage now as they have at various other historical points of social change. What has been psychology's contribution to the debate? In this paper, several questions will be addressed to assess psychology's relationship to the social question of sex:

(1) What kind of fact is sex?
(2) Where *do* sex differences exist?
(3) Why and how should we study sex differences?

There is more than one possible answer to the question "What kind of fact is sex?" Garfinkle (1971) calls sex a "moral fact," that is, it is a matter of objective, institutionalized fact that there is a real world of sex persons. There are, from the standpoint of an adult member of our society, two and only two sexes, "natural males, natural females, and persons who stand in moral contrast with them, i.e. [the] incompetent, criminal, sick and sinful (p. 200)." From his work with Agnes, who underwent a sex change, Garfinkle has proposed an anthropological description of our society's members' beliefs about sex. These include the existence of a morally dichotomized population decided on the basis of motivated compliance with the legitimate social order and not on the basis of biological, medical, urological, sociological, psychiatric, or psychological fact. Bem (1970) calls these kinds of beliefs primitive or zero-order in that they represent the non-conscious axioms upon which other beliefs are built.

It would seem, though, that most people have some vague sense that biology supports this position. In fact, it is a trivial statistical point that there are not *two* sexes by any biological measure. If one wanted to differentiate the sexes by using chromosomes, for example, at least four categories emerge: those with XY chromosomes, those with XX, those with extra chromosomes, and those with missing chromosomes. It is a minor point that there are few in these latter categories. Similarly, distributions of hormones may be more or less bimodal, but they are never dichotomous indicators of sex. At any rate the relative bimodality or the number of categories generated by chromosomal or hormonal factors is misleading since these indicators are almost never used as a basis for a decision of gender. Instead a judgment is made at birth by the obstetrician on the basis of genitalia, a categorization that has many more anamolous cases. However, as Money and Ehrhardt (1972) say, "The penis is the final arbiter (p. 14)." If the newborn has anything resembling a penis, a male sex assignment is made; if not, a female sex assignment.

For all practical purposes, this assignment then becomes the crucial factor in determining what social role the individual will play. This social role then proceeds to wash out all the various genetic factors. Many researchers (e.g., Money & Ehrhardt, 1972; Hampson & Hampson, 1961) on the basis of work with ambiguous or contradictory sex assignment cases have advanced the hypothesis that gender role is entirely the result of a learning process which is quite independent of chromosomal, gonadal, or hormonal sex. Nevertheless, from the assignment point on, almost everyone, psychologists included, relies on self-reports for sex, and these self-reports are never anything but the two categories, male or female. No one ever says, "I'm not sure," "I'm waiting to see," or "Chromosomally, I'm male, hormonally, I'm female, and genitally, I'm not sure." From this viewpoint the everyday determination of one's sex and especially the sex of others can be viewed as a Goffmanesque problem to be solved.

Thus, although it is clear that, depending on your measure, there are one or many sexes, it is equally clear that socially there are two and only two sexes. Although there are cases of changes in sex assignment, there are no cases of lack of sex assignment. The reasons for this strict adherence to a dichotomous view of sex must be social. Discriminations, whether they be seventeen different names for snow, or five names for the races, or the rules for determining Jewishness always have a function. The social function of the conception of a male/female dichotomy is in itself a possible object of psychological study. Thus, in answer to our question "What kind of fact is sex?", the response is that it is primarily and most interestingly a social fact not a biological fact.

"Where do sex differences exist?" There are, as I see it, two loci of possible sex differences. Scientific researchers have in no way been immune for the prevailing cultural dichotomy. Thus, the first and most popular locus is within the individual, or, in research terms, *subject sex differences.* Whether researchers have sought the causes of these differences in "nature" or "nurture," biology or socialization, the underlying assumption has been the same: there are two types of people, "females" and "males" who differ in terms of specific capacities, abilities, or traits. As long ago as 1909 Franz Boas pointed out that distributions by sex of virtually any characteristic greatly overlap and warned that "types" such as the male type or the female type could be misleading abstractions (cited in Stocking, 1968, pp. 168–69). Nonetheless, these abstractions have been used, and the research task has been to find the causes for the differences that are presumed to exist between these two groups of individuals.

In the Darwinian beginning, differences were sought in brain weight, brain contours, relative variability, perceptual-motor abilities, emotionality, and intelligence. A recent history dissertation by Rosenberg at Stanford (Rosenberg, 1974) traces the struggle of 19th century and early 20th century feminist psychologists to empirically validate these widespread beliefs that formed the assumptive base for much of the contemporaneous research. They came up with few or no differences. Even periodicity, women's monthly cycle, was found not to affect performance except, as it co-occurred with low blood pressure, a factor that influenced males equally (Mosher, 1911; Hollingworth, 1914).

Much of the later psychological research discarded the biological underpinnings, inserting in their stead the simple labels male and female, which have some amorphous number of biological assumptions underlying them. Hypotheses were advanced that females are more "social" than males, that females are more "suggestible" than males, that females have lower self-esteem, that females are better at rote learning and simple repetitive tasks and males at tasks that require higher-level cognitive functioning and the inhibition of previously learned responses, that males are more "analytic," that females are more affected by heredity and males by environment, that females lack achievement motivation, and that females are auditory and males visual. Maccoby and Jacklin (1974) in their recent review of the developmental literature related to these hypotheses, exploded them all as myths. However, they did find four subject sex differences that they conclude are fairly reliable. Three of them do not show up until adolescence: they are verbal ability for females and mathematical ability and spatial relation for males. The fourth, physical aggressiveness in males, is found only in childhood, disappears by adolescence, and permits a far narrower interpretation than is generally given: it is unrelated to field independence, activity level, or achievement motivation. What little evidence there is then for subject sex differences cannot begin to explain the social facts.

Another locus of sex differences is in the eye of the beholder, or in research terms, sex may be viewed as a stimulus variable. In this category fall all the research on sex-role stereotyping, beliefs, attitudes, and attributions, and here we find large and reliable sex differences. But it is the sex of the stimulus that determines the differences, not the sex of the subject. For example, Horner's (1971) widely quoted "fear of success" study was at first taken to indicate something about females subjects' approach to achievement. Those females who gave bizarre or negative responses to a cue involving female success were presumed to be demonstrating this fear of success. However, subsequent research by Monahan, Kuhn, and Shaver (1974) showed that *both* males and females gave bizarre responses to the female achievement cue and reasonable responses to the male cue. Therefore, the sex difference was located in the stimulus, not in the subjects.

Some work exists which explores the possible consequences of these stereotyped beliefs. When the sex labels attached to the same stimulus materials are varied, subjects hire "applicants" at different levels (Fidell, 1970), grade "students" differently (Goldberg, 1968), and in other ways reward differentially (Pheterson et al., 1971; Deaux & Taynor, 1973; Taynor & Deaux, 1973). Taynor and Deaux call this phenomenon "perceived sex differences." Broverman et al. (1970) using no stimulus materials other than the label "male" or "female" found that clinicians cited different indicators for mental health. Thus, given identical information about a hypothetical stimulus person but different sex labels, subjects stereotyped beliefs appear to control their responses.

There appears to be a wide-ranging psychological phenomenon evident in the findings from the subject and stimulus sex difference literature, namely, the belief in sex differences, or what I call the "illusion of sex differences." Subject sex differences are like what Unger and Siiter (1974) have called the "grain of truth" that supports a huge superstructure of beliefs, most of which are illusory. These beliefs are held identically by males and females and to that extent are independent of the sex of the individual. Sandra Bem's (1972; 1974) work on androgyny makes just that point: it is the extent to which individuals *believe* in sex differences that will predict to their behavior, not their own assigned sex. And Andrea Allen and Daryl Bem's (1975) work would indicate that it is the centrality of that belief that will determine the reliability of the prediction.

Androgyny does not lie in some far-off feminist future. Androgyny is here. The research findings tell us so. It is no longer reasonable to hypothesize subject sex differences in fundamental psychological processes. It seems clear that given the same social situation, the same reinforcement contingencies, the same expectancies, both sexes will react similarly. Men and women are basically alike. They are even alike in terms of their beliefs in their own differences (Unger & Siiter, 1974).

So, why should we study sex differences at all? It could be dangerous, given the way sex differences have been used against us. It could be futile. For example, it is very disheartening to read the work of early feminist psychologists who spent their professional lives rigorously and carefully gathering data to refute a hypothesis we never heard of, engaged in debates that never made official psychological history. Leta Hollingworth spent three years measuring the heads of newborns to refute Havelock Ellis' last ditch effort to salvage the variability hypothesis. Hollingworth not only didn't believe in superior male variability, she didn't believe it could matter or account for the phenomena she was witnessing. Too many lives, too much energy and money has been spent answering other people's questions. Much of the time the hypothesizer was no longer around waiting for the answer.

And yet it is always satisfying to strike down another sex difference. It is a very tempting endeavor. If that is to be the direction of feminist research, probably the most damaging assertions are in the area of personality. Women are no longer held in place by biological arguments in their pure form, although many of us remember a certain Dr. Berman, who advanced some anachronistic and outrageous theories about female biological inferiority and "raging hormonal cycles" in the '60's. Nor do women suffer from slurs on their intelligence as Blacks do, although every one in a while this crops up (for example Donald Broverman in 1968). Rather, it is in the field of personality that women are labelled "field dependent" or having an "external locus of control," and the inferior position of women is subtly supported. Now, we could expend a lot of energy with female superiority arguments, changing the pejorative names from "field dependent" to "field sensitive" for example, and then argue that *everyone* should be more field sensitive, but this strategy basically supports the notion of sex differences and merely shifts the value from one sex to the other. It is equality that the literature most strongly supports, not equivalency.

In addition to the conclusion that androgyny already exists, the other main conclusion to be drawn from the psychological literature is that sexism also exists. The oppression of women is not a paranoid delusion of a few dissidents. The research varying the sex of the stimulus strongly supports the idea that men and women are perceived and treated not only differently but in a direction that is harmful to women.

Given these data, research needs to be done relating the well-documented fact of androgyny to the equally well-documented fact of sexism (and I think we should call it just that, not merely sex-role stereotyping, or perceived sex differences, or the illusion of sex differences). The social facts are still clearly before us. It is time for psychology to address them directly.

BIBLIOGRAPHY

BEM, D. *Beliefs, Attitudes, and Human Affairs.* Brooks/Cole Publishing Co., Belmont, California: 1970.

BEM, D. and A. ALLEN. On predicting some of the people some of the time: the search for cross-situational consistencies in behavior. *Psychological Review,* 1974, *81* (6), 506–520.

BEM, S. Psychology looks at sex roles: Where have all the androgynous people gone? Paper presented at UCLA Symposium on Women, May, 1972.

The measurement of psychological androgyny. *Journal of Consulting and Clinical Psychology,* 1974, *42,* 155–162.

Sex-role adaptability: One consequence of psychological androgyny, *Journal of Personality and Social Psychology,* 1975, *31* (4), 634–643.

BROVERMAN, D. M., KLAIBER, E. L., KOBAYASHI, Y. & VOGEL, W. Roles of activation and inhibition in sex differences in cognitive abilities. *Psychological Review,* 1968, *75* (1), 23–50.

BROEVERMAN, I. K., D. M. BROVERMAN, F. E. CLARKSON, P. S. ROSENKRANTZ, S. R. VOGEL, Sex-role stereotypes and clinical judgments of mental health. *Journal of Consulting and Clinical Psychology,* 1970, *34* (1), 1–7.

DEAUX, K. and TAYNOR, J. Evaluation of male and female ability: Bias works both ways. *Psychological Reports,* 1973, *32,* 261–2.

FIDELL, L. S. Empirical verification of sex discrimination in hiring practices in psychology. *American Psychologist,* 1970, *25,* 1094–98.

GARFINKLE, H. Passing as a woman: A study of sex change. In *Family in Transition,* A. S. Skolnick and J. H. Skolnick (eds.) Little, Brown & Co., Boston: 1971.

GOLDBERG, P. A. Are women prejudiced against women? *Transaction,* 1968,¯¿ 28–30.

HAMPSON, J. L. and J. G. HAMPSON. The ontogenesis of sexual behavior in man. In *Sex and Internal Secretions,* Vol. II, W. C. Young (ed.), Williams & Wilkins, Baltimore: 1961.

HOLLINGWORTH, L. S. *Functional Periodicity,* New York: Columbia University, 1914.

HORNER, M. A. Femininity and successful achievement: Basic inconsistency. In *Roles Women Play,* M. H. Garskoff (ed.), Brooks/Cole, Belmont, Calif.: 1971

MACCOBY, E. E. and C. N. JACKLIN. *The Psychology of Sex Differences,* Stanford University Press, Stanford, Calif.: 1974.

MONAHAN, L., D. KUHN, and P. SHAVER. Intra-psychic versus cultural explanations of the "fear of success" motive. *Journal of Personality and Social Psychology,* 1974, *29,* 60–64.

MONEY, J. and A. A. EHRHARDT. *Man & Woman, Boy & Girl.* The Johns Hopkins University Press, Baltimore, Md.: 1972.

MOSHER, C. D. Functional periodicity in women and some of the modifying factors. *California Journal of Medicine,* Jan.–Feb., 1911.

PHETERSON, G. I., S. B. KIESSLER, and P. A. GOLDBERG. Evaluation of the performance of women as a function of their sex, achievement, and personal history. *Journal of Personality and Social Psychology,* 1971, *19,* 114–118.

ROSENBERG, R. The dissent from Darwin, 1890–1930: The new view of women among American social scientists. (Unpublished doctoral dissertation, Stanford University, 1974). Xerox University Microfilms, Ann Arbor, Michigan 48106 (#75-6915).

SHIELDS, S. Functionalism, Darwinism, and the psychology of women: A study in social myth. American Psychologist, 1975, *30* (7), 739–754.

STOCKING, G. *Race, Culture, & Evolution,* Chicago: University of Chicago Press, 1968.

TAYNOR, J. and K. DEAUX. When women are more deserving than men: Equity, attribution, and perceived sex differences. *Journal of Personality and Social Psychology,* 1973, *28* (3), 360–7.

UNGER, R. and R. SITTER. Sex-role stereotypes: The weight of a "grain of truth." Paper presented at the Eastern Psychological Association Meetings, Philadelphia, Pa., April, 1974.

PART 5

Growing Up Female

Traditionally in our society, girls and boys have been differentially treated from birth and have had different kinds of life experiences. These were generally arranged by family and school along lines which would prepare them for the separate roles they would assume as adults: for the girl, the primary roles of wife and mother; for the boy, the role of worker and economic provider.

In recent years the effects of the socialization of girls on their education, their aspirations, their achievements, and their self-concepts, as well as their evaluation and status in the society, have come under close scrutiny by researchers and feminist theorists. Styles and practices of childrearing and the availability of options to young women have been identified as having profound effects on their subsequent lives, their mental health, and their happiness.

The sex stereotyping of social and work roles, and the prescription for almost all females of domestic, expressive, and nurturant roles have resulted in a waste of female potential. For example, psychologist Lewis Terman's classic study of gifted children showed that the girls in his sample were in general more gifted artistically, and that the seven most talented writers were girls. But when these gifted children became adults, all the eminent artists and writers among them were men. Only eleven percent of the women were in professions, mostly teaching, whereas nearly half the men were professionals in high level occupations. The channeling of capable women into domesticity at the expense of the development of intellectual potential confines them to roles which have built into them a subordinate status for women as well as a devaluing of their characteristics and their productions.

Lisa Serbin and Daniel O'Leary, in "How Nursery Schools Teach Girls to Shut Up," analyze teacher behavior in the classroom and present evidence that teachers unconsciously reward boys for "masculine" and girls for "feminine" behavior. Aggressive or disruptive behavior was far more likely to get attention for a boy than for a girl. By contrast, clinging, or dependency behavior, was more often rewarded for girls. Boys also got more praise, more direction, and more individual instruction on academic tasks than girls received, promoting competence and effectance more for boys than for girls. Such differential treatment actually limits the development of both sexes because they are learning specialized ways of getting their needs met: the boys by aggression and problem solving, the girls by dependency and passivity. While the boys' adaptations may lead to a stronger achievement orientation and to a greater sense of mastery later on, they as well as the girls are learning narrower modes of expression and of coping with life's problems.

Both the typical feminine pattern of personality and behavior, and less typical patterns displayed by some women, can lead to conflict and anxiety. Grace K. Baruch and Rosalind C. Barnett look at these patterns and the conflicts they can engender in vulnerable females in "Implications and Applications of Recent Research on Feminine Development." Since masculine and feminine sex roles are unequal in status in our society, it is not surprising that girls and women socialized in the traditional model tend to overvalue males, their personalities and productions, and to devalue those of their own sex. A high degree of socialization for the feminine role is related to lower levels of self-esteem, autonomy, and adjustment. A girl who identifies with a traditional mother whom she sees as lacking in strength and prestige may develop a self-image which is vulnerable to feelings of inadequacy and self-doubt.

Women who reject the traditional role, however, may experience anxiety and ambivalence about becoming achievers in the world outside the home. Baruch and Barnett describe a double bind situation which affects females more than males: as girls and women become more competent, they may feel less feminine, less secure, and more anxious. As boys and men become more competent, they feel more masculine, more confident, and more secure. The way out of this double bind for females, the authors feel, is to help female children develop independence and competence while letting them feel comfortable with their own individuality as well. Parents, teachers, and therapists need to be sensitive to the effects of child-rearing practices on children's self-concepts; for example, the tendency of mothers to be more protective toward daughters may develop in girls the idea that they are fragile and not competent to take care of themselves.

Because of recent social changes in attitudes toward women, both traditional and "liberated" women may experience conflict. The traditional woman may rely on the long years of investment in her role, on her children's and husband's needs of her, and on the difficulties which change would mean, as a rationalization for not developing an independent, assertive self. The anger generated by this denial of growth in the personal sense can spill over into her relations with her family and her attitudes toward the pattern of her life. The woman who decides to liberate herself from the old constraints, by contrast, may deny her dependency needs in her determination to become self-sufficient, and may have difficulty in expressing legitimate needs in a mutually interdependent relationship with important others. The authors suggest a variety of practical ways to help women with these kinds of conflicts, ways which take into account both the needs of the individual woman and the social context which has contributed to her dilemma.

The next paper, "Social Values, Femininity, and the Development of Female Competence," by Julia Sherman, argues that social change in the sexual caste system involves all aspects of social and personal experience. Sherman makes the points that the goals of femininity and competence may be antithetic to each other, and that not much is known about rearing girls to be competent, since the goal of developing their femininity has typically been prepotent. A model for promoting those social changes which research indicates are constructive for women and for the society as a whole is presented. For example, Sherman shows how making available opportunities in atypical fields for girls and women is not enough by itself to promote significant entry into those fields. Attitudes of the girls and women themselves, as well as their parents, spouses, teachers, and employers, must change too. The whole matter is an interlocking complex of old patterns and resistances, and new opportunities amd motivations for change. Sherman also discusses some specific strategies for social change, for breaking down the sexual caste system which women themselves can implement.

"Growing Up Black" is from Joyce Ladner's study of Black female teenagers living in a low-income area of St. Louis in the 1960s. Ladner's thesis is that the Black community has its own autonomous social system which regulates much of its own characteristic behavior. The Black child's socialization is different from that of the white middle-class child because of differences in sociocultural traditions, values, and beliefs. For the young Black girl growing up in such a community, the agents of socialization, as for the white child, are her family and her peer group. But her family is more likely to be an extended one where she is cared for by a variety of female relatives. For her, the ordinary perquisites of being a child may be unobserved or absent because parents cannot afford them. Harsh social forces of poverty and exposure to violence may engender a precocious emotional development in the young girl which is beyond her ability to manage adequately. At the same time it is impressive, Ladner notes, to see such children handle stress with some competence, to defend themselves against threatening events more capably than could a child brought up in a safer, more protected environment.

The peer goup assumes special salience for the young Black girl when parents who are overburdened or absent cannot provide emotional support, advice, and other services which the white community takes for granted for its children. As she develops, she is helped by the peer group to define her roles, to understand life on a day to day basis, and to survive. Ladner sees in the coping skills that such children develop a healthy adaptation to conditions that are not devised to foster psychological well-being. This paper describes the experience of growing up female for girls who must not only learn the roles prescribed for them in their own society, but who must also learn to function in the dominant culture which views their own as deviant.

The last decade has been the stage for a tremendous emergence of awareness and interest of researchers in the range and processes of the development of girls in our society. No longer are the different tracks which promote one kind of outcome for girls and another for boys taken for granted. While the limitations of those tracks are now widely recognized, they are still the subject of examination, in as much as it is necessary to understand the problem before the problem itself can be addressed and strategies developed to mitigate its effects. Awareness of the limitations and degradations which have characterized scenarios for the lives of girls and women in our society may give rise to feelings of anger and regret for potential and promise unfulfilled. But this awareness also awakens us to the possibility of new ways of being and of a better set of life chances with broader horizons for ourselves and our daughters.

How Nursery Schools Teach Girls to Shut Up

Lisa A. Serbin and K. Daniel O'Leary

Nursery-school teachers are much more likely to react to a boy's behavior, bad or good, than to a girl's. By rewarding boys for aggression and girls for passivity, they mold behavior that will cause both sexes pain later.

As nursery-school children busily mold clay, their teachers are molding behavior. Unwittingly, teachers foster an environment where children learn that boys are aggressive and able to solve problems, while girls are submissive and passive. The clay impressions are transient, but the behavioral ones last into adulthood and present us with people of both sexes who have developed only parts of the psychological and intellectual capabilities.

There has been constant conjecture about when and how sex-role stereotypes develop. We looked into 15 preschool classrooms and found that teachers act and react in quite different ways to boys and to girls. They subtly encourage the very behavioral patterns that will later become painful for children of both sexes.

John was a five-year-old bully. When someone didn't follow his directions or give him the toy he wanted, John lost his temper. He pushed, shoved, shouted, and threw things. When we first watched John in his classroom, he was playing peacefully with another boy at building a Tinker-Toy tower.

Then John asked the other child for a piece of material the boy was using. When he was refused, John began to tear the tower apart. The other boy protested, and John raised his hand threateningly. The other children across the room instantly sang out in chorus: "Teacher, John's hitting!" Mrs. Jones looked over and ordered John to stop. She strode across the room, pulled John away, and spent the next two minutes telling him why he shouldn't hit people. Five minutes later, John was hitting another classmate.

This brief scene shows how a teacher can reinforce exactly the behavior that's causing a problem. For John, as for many children, being disruptive is an effective means of getting a far larger dose of attention than good behavior can bring. Children get attention for good behavior about as often as Congressmen get mail in praise of their activities, so it's not surprising that most children (and some Congressmen) become adept at attracting attention by bad-boy tactics.

Our classroom observations showed that disruption is far more likely to get attention for a John than it is for a Jane. Teachers responded over three times as often to males as to females who hit or broke things, and the boys usually got a loud public reprimand. When teachers did respond to girls, they most often delivered a brief, soft rebuke that others couldn't hear.

How to Cure a Bully

Bullies like John are made, not born. We taught his teacher how to get rid of the problem very simply: we explained that she was to ignore his aggressive acts, except to prevent the victim from being harmed. We suggested that instead she concentrate on the child John was attacking, by saying something warm like, "I am very sorry you got hurt. Let me get a nice game for you to play with." When children learn that they will be ignored for their misbehavior, they stop it almost immediately. John ceased bullying.

Teachers were not usually aware that they reacted differently to aggression from boys and girls. One teacher suggested that the behavior of boys is harder to ignore because "boys hit harder." If teachers really do perceive hitting by boys as potentially more dangerous to other children, it's easy to understand why they're reluctant to ignore the act, but it's ironic that their attention aggravates the problem.

In contrast to the aggression and disruptive behavior typical of boys, girls usually rely on dependency or withdrawal to get adult attention. Feminists have strongly criticized television, educational media and the schools for training girls to be passive and dependent. Television usually depicts women in subservient roles, and the very books from which a child learns to read show girls as unaggressive and dependent. Our observations confirm that these same stereotypes are being encouraged in the classroom. So children of either sex simply use the sex-typed tactic that fits adult prejudice.

We found that teachers were more likely to react to girls when they were within arm's reach, either literally or figuratively clinging to the teachers' skirts (all the teachers we observed were women). Sheila, for example, was so frequently underfoot that Mrs. Cox constantly stumbled over her. Sheila was a bright, attractive child who asked many interesting questions, but she refused to play with the other children. Except for her extreme dependency, Sheila's development was normal for her age.

In an attempt to deal with the problem and give her more self-confidence, Mrs. Cox talked with Sheila frequently, and often touched her affectionately. When she saw Sheila playing alone, Mrs. Cox would go over and encourage her to join the other youngsters. Despite considerable effort, this attention produced no change in Sheila's behavior.

The school director then asked Mrs. Cox to look at or speak to Sheila only when she was with other children. For several days, Sheila clung even more tenaciously to her teacher's skirt, but after a week she ventured out to join the other children. Two weeks later, her extreme dependency had vanished.

Girls Learn to Cling

The pattern of teachers giving attention to nearby, dependent girls repeated itself time and time again. When boys were near, the teacher would praise them and then give them directions to do things on their own. By contrast, she would praise and assist the girls but *not* send them off to work by themselves.

In our study, we sent trained observers into 15 classrooms to record behavior by using a well-defined set of criteria. We identified 13 specific types of teacher response to seven categories of the children's behavior. An observer watched for any of the 91 possible interactions during a 20-second period, then recorded results for 10 seconds. We did the classroom studies in half-hour units. Where we report differences in the teachers' reactions to boys and girls, statistical tests have shown that the differences we observed were far greater than what would be expected by chance alone.

Teachers, we found, actually teach boys more than they teach girls. Many studies show that there are sex differences in important cognitive skills. Boys, on the average, tend to have better analytic problem-solving abilities, to be better at spatial reasoning and to have higher mathematical abilities than girls. Girls, on the other hand, have better reading and other verbal skills [see "What We Know and Don't Know About Sex Differences," *pt,* December *1974*.

These academic abilities may be nurtured, or nullified, by the classroom guardians. Parents make a major contribution to the shaping of social behavior, and there's evidence that they act differently toward boys and girls as early as the first few months of life. Fathers and mothers both turn boy infants out toward the world and push them; little girls more often get hugged up close, face to face. Children learn their academic skills, however, largely in the classroom, where boys learn to do one thing and girls learn to do another.

All 15 of the teachers gave more attention to boys who kept their noses to the academic grindstone. They got both physical and verbal rewards. Boys also received, and were twice as likely as the girls to get individual instructions on how to do things. Whether the directions were delivered by word or by demonstration, they made the boys much more capable of fending for themselves.

Boys Learn to Do

In one classroom, the children were making party baskets. When the time came to staple the paper handles in place, the teacher worked with each child individually. She showed the boys how to use the stapler by holding the handle in place while the child stapled it. On the girls' turns, however, if the child didn't spontaneously staple the handle herself, the teacher took the basket, stapled it, and handed it back.

On another occasion, a teacher was showing a small group of three-year-olds how the same quantity of water can be poured to fill several different containers of varying heights and widths. Three children, Michael, Patty and Daniel, sat nearby, obviously fascinated by the activity, which demonstrates the "conversation" concept that marks a major milestone in a child's development.

The teacher let Michael try to pour the water himself, explaining how water can change shape without changing amount. Patty asked if she could try and was told to wait her turn. The teacher gave Daniel a chance to pour the water, and then put the materials away! Despite another request, Patty never got her turn. She never received the individual instruction the boys got in manipulating the materials.

There is ample evidence, from other studies of the clear relationship between problem-solving ability and the amount of instruction and direction a child receives. So the superiority of boys over girls in spatial and analytic reasoning is at least partially a result of the way each sex learns to manipulate the environment—learning that begins in nursery school with boys who staple and pour, and girls who must sit passively by and watch.

It could be argued, of course, that boys require more instruction than girls, either because girls are more likely to acquire skills by watching others and therefore do not need as much individual instruction. Even if this is the case, however, boys and girls are still receiving a strikingly different amount of a type of adult attention that is important in the development of problem-solving ability. Boys are shown how lawn mowers and erector sets work, and they wind up with better spatial and analytic skills. Girls are encouraged to stay by their mothers and teachers, where they talk and read. It's the girls who rate higher in verbal and reading ability.

We found one exception to the general pattern. When the class engaged in an explicitly feminine, sex-typed activity such as cooking, the teachers did tend to pay more attention to the girls. Even so, they still offered brief conversation, praise and assistance, while the boys got detailed instructions.

Malignant Neglect

With this sole exception, then, we found that in nursery-school classrooms teachers are much less likely to react to a girl's behavior, whether appropriate or not, than to a boy's. The girls' actions have considerably less effect on their environment, at least in terms of adult reaction, than do the actions of boys. Coupled with portrayals of the ineffectual female on television and in books, benign neglect in the classroom rapidly becomes malignant.

The cure, of course, does not lie in reversing the situation so that boys become dependent and girls disruptive, nor does it lie entirely with teachers, who are only one link in an important chain of events, Children of both sexes should learn to be neither too disruptive nor too dependent, and teachers need to be aware of how they can either perpetuate or prevent these qualities, depending on their actions.

We feel that the differential treatment of boys and girls limits the freedom of both sexes to develop psychologically and intellectually. Later psychological problems, as well as differences in academic and on-the-job achievements, may be the price we all pay for preschool inequities. We agree with Sandra Bem [see "Androgyny Vs. the Tight Little Lives of Fluffy Women and Chesty Men," *pt* September] that people need access to the entire spectrum of human behavior in order to cope with the complexity of our current world. That access can be guaranteed to the molders of clay only by the molders of children.

Implications and Applications of Recent Research on Feminine Development

Grace K. Baruch and Rosalind C. Barnett

The traditional feminine role pattern is no longer adaptive and functional for many women, because of pressures for change associated with such components of the social climate as the lengthening life span and concern about the population explosion. It is no longer physically possible nor considered socially valuable to spend a lifetime bearing and rearing children, even for those women who desire to do so. Thus the prospect or actuality of defining one's life by the wife-and-mother role creates anxiety and anger, which is increased by the awareness that society pays only lip service to so-called "feminine" qualities and behaviors, reserving power and prestige for those who achieve high status in the world of work.
Clearly women need alternate bases of gratification and identity. However, these involve interconnected changes that are often painful and that require understanding and support from others which has been slow in coming. The general purpose of this paper is to provide evidence that changes in the feminine role pattern are a matter of urgency and will be beneficial to both sexes.

The paper is organized into two sections. First we will describe relevant research findings in two general areas: difficulties and conflicts associated with typical patterns of femininity, and difficulties and conflicts associated with atypical patterns. Second, since too often research findings that do not fit with existing theory and practice go unnoticed, we will specify ways in which these findings can be implemented by therapists.

Difficulties and Conflicts Associated with Femininity

In general, feminine self-esteem is low. At all ages, girls and women tend to perceive males as having the more desirable personality traits (McKee and

Sheriffs, 1957; Smith, 1939). Many females also make unrealistically low-evaluations, compared with both their own actual abilities and with males' self-evaluations, in such areas as academic ability (Baird, 1973; Crandall et al., 1962; Wylie, 1963) and athletic performance (Clifton and Smith, 1963). At least until recently, many women have tended to devalue other women's professional competence compared to men's (Bernard, 1966; Goldberg, 1967), even where no true differences exist.

With respect to cognition, a recent follow-up study (Kangas and Bradway, 1971) of men and women given IQ tests as preschoolers in the 1930s indicated that the brighter a man was as a youngster, the more he gained in IQ with age; the brighter a woman was as a youngster, the less she gained. The fact that many women—the less intelligent—had patterns of IQ increments similar to males suggests that social rather than biological influences are at work. Further support for this interpretation lies in the fact that the tendency of IQ to increase with age is most negatively associated with femininity scores (Kagan and Moss, 1962) and most positively correlated with emotional independence, a trait rarely encouraged in girls. Moreover, IQs of girls who reject traditional feminine behavior tend to be higher than those of girls who accept it (Kagan and Freeman, 1963).

Similarly, social factors rather than individual psychopathology most likely account for the low self-esteem just discussed. Many women have tended to be socialized according to a sex-role standard of which the component traits—dependence, nurturance, passivity (Kagan, 1964)—are not those most socially valued in our culture. Such highly valued traits as ambition, independence, and assertiveness have been excluded from the feminine sex-role standard.

Challenges have recently been made to the assumption of major personality theories (and of much research and therapy with children) that identification with one's sex-role and with the parent of the same sex both indicates and insures healthy psychological development (Block, 1973; Broverman et al., 1972). Empirical evidence suggests that this assumption is warranted only for males. Examination of research on females shows that, measured by such indices as personality tests of femininity, or identification with the mother, a high degree of sex-role socialization in girls is *negatively* related to such desirable qualities as autonomy (Lozoff, 1972), self-esteem (Connell and Johnson, 1970; Flammer, 1971), and adjustment (Heilbrun, 1968). Perceiving oneself as having traditionally feminine traits has been found to be unrelated to self-esteem, while perceiving oneself as having traditionally masculine traits—i.e., competence, assertiveness, ambition—is associated with high self-esteem (Baruch, 1974a). Thus, the greater the degree of a girl's sex-role socialization, the more vulnerable she is to the problem just described.

Our interpretation of the findings described is not that cross-sex identification is inherently beneficial. All things being equal, identification with one's own sex-role and with the parent of the same sex should be a positive force in development. The problem is that, at present, things are not usually equal; the sex roles are unequal in status. A study of very young children indicated that both girls and boys perceived the father as stronger and smarter than the mother and as "the boss" (Kagan and Lemkin, 1960). Thus, the self-image of girls who identify with their mothers may be impaired, for "the role model that the girls have chosen is not the one they view as the most competent" (Kagan and Lemkin, p. 446). Mothers who occupy the traditional role pattern often lack prestige, power, and satisfaction, attributes that usually characterize an attractive identification model. For example, among comparable groups of able middle-aged women, those who were family-oriented and had not worked since the birth of their first child felt less competent and less attractive, and experienced lower levels of self-esteem and satisfaction than did those who were committed to professional careers (Birnbaum, 1971). Their solely domestic role is perhaps the most common one among women, and girls with such mothers may in turn reflect these associated problems.

Difficulties and Conflicts Associated with Atypical Feminine Patterns

Research described in this section, combined with that described previously, points to a double-bind, no-win situation for women, for despite their dissatisfactions with the traditional role, few women enjoy the stigma of being labeled as masculine or deviant. The desire of most humans to match their own sex-role standard explains much of the willingness, conscious or unconscious, among women to perceive themselves unfavorably when such perceptions constitute "femininity." Typically, women perceive themselves as not only gentle, kind, and tactful, but as illogical, poor leaders, and incompetent, associating the positive side of the latter qualities—i.e., logical, good leaders, competence—with males (Rosenkrantz et. al., 1968).

The motive to avoid success—the fear that success in male-dominated areas will bring social rejection—also revolves around the need to feel and to appear feminine (Horner, 1972). Anxiety and ambivalence about success are found even in girls too young to be concerned about male opinion (Baruch, 1973). The following stories were written by fifth-grade girls (white, middle-class, from suburban Boston homes) who were asked to complete a story beginning with the sentence, "Anne won first prize in the Science Fair for her exhibit on car engines."[1]

> She was so happy, her friends were really mad. They also had a good exhibit, but Anne won. On the way home from the Science Fair she was going to walk with someone, but she had left, so she went to walk with someone else but she ran away. Anne couldn't understand why.
>
> Sue and Mary Ellen got very jealous and started being very mean to Ann. They thought they should win because they took the courses for it and Anne didn't. The Fair manager called and said that they had made a mistake and Anne won second prize. They made friends again even though Ann was disappointed.

Such themes of social isolation and jealousy appeared in about 25% of the stories written by the 10-year-old girls. Tenth-grade girls who were participants in the same study were somewhat more likely to show evidence of anxiety about success (about 33%); their stories reflect more explicit concern about their femininity and about boys reactions:

> Poor Anne, she won first prize for car engines. Now the boy next to her won't stop teasing. All her friends laughed and said, "Car engines, that's for boys." Now the boy she likes is even teasing her. Her parents are proud, but Anne couldn't have done it without her older brother. He actually built the exhibit and that's against the rules. If she tells everyone she didn't make it maybe everyone will leave her alone. She does so and feels better. Now everyone calls her a cheater.

> She is standing in front of her exhibit smiling and feeling proud, yet she also feels sort of funny because she is a girl and girls don't usually think about car engines. Her girlfriends all look at her because they think she is weird and all the boys are laughing at her because they don't think she's feminine. Now she feels hurt and alone and wishes she had gotten the prize for almost anything else. She even feels that she doen't even want the prize at all.

It is probably quite realistic to expect others, perhaps especially friends, to envy one's success. The difficulty is that girls react by withdrawal from competition. Males, in contrast, are more likely to cope with, ignore, or even welcome such envy.

The attitudes toward success and achievement reflected in these findings are paralleled by the actual work-related behavior of women, as is indicated by the literature on feminine career aspirations and actual attainments. The low percentage of women in high-prestige professions is well-documented, as is their concentration in clerical, teaching, and nursing jobs (Barnett and Baruch, 1974). From preschool years on, girls' career aspirations are heavily focused on these few fields. In a study of occupational preferences and aversions, a disturbingly systematic pattern emerged. The higher the prestige of an occupation, the more likely boys were to aspire to it and the more likely girls were to have an aversion to it (Barnett, 1975). These trends increased with age over the range studied, 9 through 17 years.

Obviously, some women do attain high professional status. More may do so in the near future; for example, in the last two years, 30–40% of students entering Harvard Medical School have been women. Social barriers are overcome in some cases, perhaps where inner concerns do not bar a struggle with such barriers. Data available about what facilitates such attainments are only suggestive since successful women are usually studied retrospectively to identify such factors. For example, evidence from studies of black women (Epstein, 1973; Turner, 1972) suggests that expecting to be an economic provider influences girls to aspire to and pursue work-related achievements. Typical qualities among successful white women include being an only child or being the eldest with no male siblings; being close to their fathers; and being encouraged by both parents to achieve and to ignore sexual stereotypes (Helson, 1971; Henning, 1974). But birth order, sex of sibling(s), and closeness to the father are examples of factors that are not inherently necessary for success. The absence of male siblings probably makes it more likely that parental ambitions will be communicated to the oldest daughter, but obviously encouragement of a girl's achievement can take place in the presence of brothers. Similarly, closeness to the mother can facilitate career success, if the mother values or embodies achievement.

Interestingly, women achievers usually have attended a women's college rather than a coeducational college (Tidball, 1973). Women attending a women's college may well feel less threatened by male reactions and therefore be relatively free of conflict about competing intellectually to the best of their ability. The same study also found that the later achievements of an institution's female students are most strongly related to its proportion of women faculty. Thus, having a sufficiently large group of successful female role models seems to have a positive effect on women's achievement. Another intriguing finding is that high-school girls who attended all-female elementary schools were less likely to show fear of success than were girls who had attended coeducational elementary schools (Winchel et al., 1974). Apparently the early learning climate gave some immunity to later social pressures.

Studies of women achievers in turn suggest the importance of considering the sources of inhibition of achievements among women in order to generate strategies for change. Major issues are illuminated by studies of parental—especially maternal—child-rearing behavior and sex-role attitudes. The fact that during the first two years of life mothers differentially encourage and discourage physical closeness, depending on the sex of their child, may contribute to differential male-female achievement (Lewis, 1972). Boys receive earlier and more severe socialization pressure to move from proximal behaviors (such as touching, holding, rocking) to distal behaviors (such as looking, smiling, vocalizing). In other words, mothers encourage independence in sons more than in daughters from the first months of life (Hoffman, 1972). In a recent review of the literature on sex differences, Maccoby and Jacklin (1974) pointed out that such findings are often not replicated, calling into question many of the conclusions of the studies cited by Hoffman. Because of this new debate, one can expect more rigorous studies on these points to be carried out.

Literature on sex differences is not the only fruitful source of insight into women's achievement problems. For children of both sexes, for example, it is now known that parental encouragement of independence and achievement and avoidance of overprotection facilitate the development of competence (Baumrind, 1971). In a study of girls, mothers who valued traits in their daughters that are related to independence and to assertiveness and who did not value traits related to social acceptability and to conformity were more likely to have daughters who perceive themselves as competent, assertive, and independent (Baruch, 1974b). These daughters also had higher self-esteem. The evidence so far is that such maternal patterns enhance self-esteem and competence even though they involve deviations from traditional sex-role socialization.

Finally, two new topics are now producing relevant findings. Most theoretical discussions of socialization and the bulk of the empirical literature, first, have centered on the mother-child interaction, and second, have assumed that it is always the parent who shapes the child's behavior and not vice versa. On the first point, several recent studies suggest the importance of fathers in the socialization process (Fein, 1973; Rubin et al., 1974) and investigators are now beginning to include fathers in their research designs (Osofsky and O'Connell, 1972).

On the second point, it is important to conceptualize the parents' child-rearing behavior as determined at least in part by particular characteristics of the child. In other words, parents may socialize their daughters differently depending on such innate characteristics as their size, intelligence, attractiveness and overall resemblance to the "Dresden doll" female stereotype. It has been speculated (Bell, 1968) that children who more closely "fit" the sex standard of parents and other significant socializers are more likely to evoke stereotypic child-rearing behavior.

Implications and Practical Applications

The double-bind situation described above can be restated as follows: For males, the relationships between a sense of masculinity, self-esteem, and competence are all positive. When a male acts so as to increase one of these—e.g., competence—he reaps additional bonuses by heightened feelings of masculinity and self-esteem. The difference for women lies in the negative relationship between a sense of femininity on the one hand, and self-esteem and competence on the other. For example, when a woman acts so as to increase her competence, she decreases her sense of femininity. Any departure from the traditional sex-role standard may increase her sense of competence, but is also accompanied by anxiety, guilt, and uncertainty.

The way out of this double bind is to make positive the relationships between femininity and competence and between femininity and self-esteem. This is a complex psychosocial problem, but specific steps can be taken to modify the negative relationships and the inherent distress. These depend in part on the age of the females involved. Conflicts are expressed in different ways at various stages in the life cycle, requiring different responses from therapists, parents, teachers, and other concerned people.

Preschool and School-age Girls

Parents of a young girl need to examine their own behavior for its effect, implicit or explicit, on their daughter's competence, independence, and assertiveness behaviors. For a small girl who has fallen and hurt her knee, for example, there are differences in the messages communicated to her depending on whether her mother exhorts her to go back to playing with her friends or commiserates with her and accompanies her into the house. The latter behavior is more frequent where the child is female. Children who are treated as if they were fragile and in need of protection may grow up seeing themselves as vulnerable, insecure, and unsafe unless in the company of some stronger, more competent person. The tendency on the part of parents to overprotect girls seems to have become institutionalized at least to some extent and is often seen as appropriate by child-care professionals. In observing a mother-son interaction, few professionals would find it remarkable if a mother urged her son to climb a previously untried jungle gym or warned her daughter of risks involved and drew her attention to more sedentary activities. If the mother's behaviors were reversed, however, unfavorable evaluations of her maternal efforts might be more likely.

Another common area concerning pre-schoolers is their early interest in what they want to be when they grow up. Often a girl who has said she wants to be a doctor begins to say, perhaps after several months of nursery school, that boys are doctors and girls are nurses. She no longer wants to be the doctor when playing; she wants to be the nurse. If she is encouraged to retain her enthusiasm for becoming a doctor, she might alienate herself from her peers and be forced therefore to deal with such issues as nonconformity and social isolation. Parents, teachers, and therapists are becoming aware of such issues but cannot deal with them effectively until they have thought through their own feelings about them.

Early learning about sex roles is too important to go unmonitored, especially since schools and media still tend to have a traditional stereotyped impact (Saario et al., 1973). Young chldren constructing notions of sex roles, as in searching out rules of language, tend to overgeneralize and to be rigid. Token exceptions to rules—e.g., a few women doctors—are simply not noticed. In one elementary school that proudly acquired a male teacher, the children called him Mrs. X. One writer (Nilsen, 1971) reports that when her sister was accepted at medical school, the sister's young children at first did not believe it since they thought only men could be doctors. When she convinced the children that she was indeed going to be a doctor, they cried bitterly because they knew she would have to turn into a man; they would no longer have a mother.

Adolescence

All of the issues outlined above are especially pronounced when dealing with adolescent girls. Effects of peers become increasingly strong, as do concerns about male opinion, multiplying the perceived risks involved in maintaining nonconformist behavior.

The female teen-ager who is receiving support at home for achievement strivings and is comfortable with her own individuality will probably never present herself as a patient. The girl who is confused about who she is and who is having trouble reconciling parental, peer, and personal aspirations may well seek professional help. Such a patient would be especially sensitive to the therapist's overt and covert reactions to her developing self-concept.

Consider the impact on such a girl if the therapist believes that women really are and should be submissive, subjective, illogical, passive, dependent, and noncompetitive. It has been shown empirically that many therapists of both sexes and of various persuasions hold a double standard of mental health (Broverman et al., 1970). Clinicians asked to describe characteristics of healthy adults (sex unspecified) and healthy adult males include for both groups independence, objectivity, activity, logicality, self-confidence, and so forth. In contrast, therapists perceive mental health in adult women as including such strikingly different characteristics as dependence, passivity, noncompetitiveness, illogicality.

A therapist, parent, or teacher with these disparate views can effectively sabotage the efforts of a girl who is grappling with issues of role definition, with concerns over wanting simultaneously to be feminine and to be competent, and with the difficult task of carving out a new role rather than passively accepting socially-approved traditional roles.

When such a girl seeks help from a male therapist, the interpersonal issues described earlier will undoubtedly affect her self-presentation in therapy and will make her highly sensitive to the therapist's attitudes about femininity, whether they are chauvinistic, liberated, or mixed. A question often raised today is whether a male therapist can do justice to his women patients. Although nonsexist therapy need not be the province of one sex, certain considerations are often overlooked. These are given some perspective by analogy to the relationship of the white therapist and the black patient. First, while today most therapists would have some reservations about accepting at face value the statement "I'm happy I'm black," too few would question the statement, "I only want to be a good wife and mother." Second, therapists need to recognize an obligation to address the issue of male bias, whether it applies to them directly or not, just as they would discuss the difference in race between themselves and their black patients. The racial analogy also illuminates a more subtle problem. Just as blacks, from necessity, know more about whites and white culture than whites know about blacks, women are more knowledgeable about men and masculinity. Therefore, male therapists need to consider whether they are sufficiently aware and informed about the special sociocultural, economic, and psychological forces that exert important influences on today's women. These considerations are of course not limited to work with adolescent patients. In fact, neither are they limited to male therapists, since many professional women have been trained to view the sexes in traditional ways.

Adult Women

Because of rapidly changing attitudes and pressures, both the woman who occupies the traditional role and the liberated career woman, married or unmarried, are likely to experience difficulties that bring them into therapy. For the traditional woman, her role can provide a socially approved excuse for not actualizing her potential. Often such a woman will say, I really want to do something outside the home but women don't have a chance in the real world, it's just too hard to overcome all the prejudice against women, my husband won't let me work. Such a posture often masks the patient's fears about being independent, about asserting herself, about her feelings of femininity, about possible rejection. Women who have adopted this stance have struck a deal in which, at the expense of developing an independent base of self-esteem, they play the part of the dependent "good" wife, while reserving the right to project their anger over this bad bargain onto their husbands, children, parents, society, and perhaps their therapists.

A second adaptation, one seen among career women, has different consequences for marital and familial adjustment. In an effort to deal with internal conflicts and doubts about appropriate sex-role behavior, as well as the guilt attendant on desiring to be self-actualizing, some women adopt a counterdependent posture.

In a typical unfolding of this pattern, such an attitude finds expression in the determination to be completely self-reliant. The defensive nature of this self-view becomes obvious if the woman finds herself in a situation in which there is the possibility of establishing a meaningful relationship with a man. She often continues to avoid dealing with her dependency needs by resolving to be the completely self-sufficient, "perfect" companion and career person. If she decides to get married, she has difficulty in accepting without guilt any willingness on her husband's part to negotiate a co-equal marriage. If she has a child—a necessary part of her definition of being a perfect wife—additional complications arise. The enforced dependency that characterizes the last phase of pregnancy and the period immediately following the birth of the baby is likely to be a blow to her well-maintained façade of super independence and sometimes proves too difficult emotionally for her to handle. In such cases, rejection of the baby and of her husband, and self-punitive depressive reactions can follow. How does a therapist deal with such a woman? First, how does one understand the nature of the problem?

Is it maximally useful to conceptualize sex-role problems as entirely internal? If one did, then in the case of the career woman one might focus treatment on her need to be the perfect wife-mother-career person, on her guilt over departing from traditional sex-role expectations, and on her counterdependence. Assuming that all went well, she would then be ready to return, with more self-understanding, to the situation from which she came. Clearly this approach is incomplete; the social problems that gave rise to the need for her to develop such defenses are still there.

One might say that the problem is largely in the social system—in the rigid sex-role stereotypes that leave no room for a woman like the one we are describing, and in the clearly positive and negative evaluations assigned to these stereotypes and to conformity with them. In a recent study (Maracek, 1974), subjects were presented with statements described as having been made by patients in psychotherapy, and were asked to evaluate how "sick" the patients were. The statements were expressions of either dependency or aggression and were ascribed to either male or female patients. When an aggression statement was ascribed to a female, she was rated as much more disturbed than a male making the same statement. A male making a dependency statement was rated as significantly more ill than a female.

This is an instance in which behavior norms—i.e., descriptive statements about typical behaviors—have become endowed with evaluative connotations. Many other less controversial examples of the same process exist. To illustrate, two cultural norms—bathing regularly and eating with a fork—have attained strong right-wrong, good-bad, aspects. We can appreciate the power of these evaluative attitudes when we are surprised, annoyed, or disgusted while visiting in cultures that do not share these norms. Efforts to change stereotypic attitudes toward men and women are in process, but significant change will not be rapid. Thus, this social attitudinal climate must be kept in mind since it affects all women, even the psychologically healthiest, who try to operate as deviants within it.

Another way to think about the problem is to conceive of it as arising out of the woman's internalization of the social system's stereotypes. Much of her difficulty stems from the fact that she has accepted society's evaluative connotations. The presence in her life space of a sufficient number of women who have successfully combined femininity and competence would go a long way toward loosening these stereotypes.

Perhaps for this reason, a woman who is trying to come to terms with these two aspects of her personality can often benefit greatly from some form of self-help group in which she can find both support from other women for her achievement strivings, and recognition that accepting her legitimate dependent needs does not necessarily threaten her competence or her feelings of self-esteem. Too often a woman trying to define her life's goals is advised by therapists and others to ignore both the opinions of the those around her and such social attitudes as devaluation of motherhood or disapproval of career ambitions in women. But concern about the opinion of others is not a flaw or weakness. It is in fact adaptive, reflecting long years of childhood dependency and perhaps a biologically supported need to be part of group life. Attitudes of significant other people will always have a profound effect; indeed, much of the effectiveness of psychotherapy rests on this insight.

Therefore, many women who have been caught in a double bind and have not developed their potentialities can with the help of other women make remarkable and rapid progress in establishing independent and productive lives. This help is also valuable in offsetting the real opposition and rejection that women who are making transitions do in fact face from those around them. Older women can also benefit from such help, and by developing multiple sources of gratification and status can be enabled to weather more successfully such problems of later years as the empty nest syndrome and widowhood.

In concluding this section on adult women, it is important to mention certain socioeconomic attitudes and norms that interact with the stereotypes and compound the limitations felt by both men and women. The injunction that upon marriage, especially among white middle-class Americans, males should assume the role of sole economic provider acts as a major if unnoticed barrier to women who have been socialized to comply with this injunction. This pattern denies an economic function and hence legitimacy to women's work. If undertaken only for reasons of personal fulfillment, work assumes a hobbylike quality which in our culture is not clearly distinguished from self-indulgence. If their work is not a recognized and valued source of economic support, women will still be expected to have sole or primary responsibility for child care and household maintenance and to relocate willingly if their husbands find better jobs elsewhere. Given such a view of the man's economic function, justice might logically require that a male should be hired over an equally or even a better qualified woman. However, if men and women share the parental functions of nurturance and economic support, each will have more diversified bases for self-esteem and couples will be better able to share each other's lives.

General Considerations

It would be a mistake to conclude that all women should have lifelong high-powered careers. Instead, the goal should be to enlarge women's options and to increase the freedom with which they choose among them. Today, restrictions on women are usually in the area of achievement and the world of work; however, equally rigid prescriptions could conceivably someday make other choices difficult. In any case, the social structure and context must be considered by therapists, health care professionals, and others in a position of influence. Sometimes women, and other minority groups, are told they should not succumb to society's stress on work-related achievement and competence and should somehow be above pursuit of the tainted rewards of status in this sphere. Rather, women are advised to ignore society's devaluation of homemaking and child-rearing activities. Such advice is often unrealistic and presumptuous. It is meaningless to renounce something one could not have had, or to withdraw from a rat-race one is not permitted to enter. All individuals need to feel able and welcome to pursue success as valued by their culture in order to have a sense of efficacy, influence, and importance. When women do have this option, they may then find it easier to value their activities in other spheres. Raising the status of women will raise the status of women's work in whatever arena it is performed.

NOTE

1. This cue was designed to create a situation for young girls parallel to that used in the original fear-of-success research with college women by Matina Horner (1972): "After first term finals, Anne found that she was first in her class at medical school."

REFERENCES

BAIRD, L. *The Graduates;* Princeton, N.J.: Educ. Testing Service, 1973.

BARNETT, R. C. "Sex Differences and Age Trends in Occupational Preference and Prestige," *J. Counsel. Psychol.* (1975) 22:35–38.

BARNETT, R. C., AND BARUCH, G. *Occupational and Educational Aspirations and Expectations: A Review of Empirical Literature;* Natl. Inst. of Educ., 1974.

BARUCH, G. "The Motive to Avoid Success and Career Apirations of 5th- and 10th-Grade Girls," presented at Amer. Psychol. Assn., Montreal, August 1973.

BARUCH, G.: "Correlates of Girls' Evaluation of Their Competence," unpublished, 1974 (a)

BARUCH, G. "Maternal Influences upon Girls' Evaluation of Their Competence," unpublished, 1974 (b).

BAUMRIND, D. "Current Patterns of Parental Authority" *Develop. Psychol. Monogr.* (1971) 4: No. 1.

BELL, R. Q. "Reinterpretation of the Direction of Effects in Studies of Socialization," *Psychol. Rev.* (1968) 75:81–95.

BERNARD, J. *Academic Women;* Cleveland: Meridian, 1966.

BIRNBAUM, J. "Life Patterns, Personality Style and Self-Esteem in Gifted Family-Oriented and Career-Committed Women," doctoral dissertation, Univ. of Mich., 1971.

BLOCK, J. H. "Conceptions of Sex-Role: Some Cross-Cultural and Longitudinal Perspectives," *Amer. Psychol.* (1973) 28:512–527.

BROVERMAN, I. K., et al. "Sex-Role Stereotypes and Clinical Judgments of Mental Health," *J. Consult. and Clin. Psychol.* (1970) 34:1–7.

BROVERMAN, I. K., et al. "Sex-Role Stereotypes: A Current Appraisal," *J. Soc. Issues* (1972) 28:59–78.

CLIFTON, M. A., AND SMITH, H. M. "Comparison of Expressed Self-Concepts of Highly Skilled Males and Females Concerning Motor Performance," *Percept. and Motor Skills* (1963) 16:199–201.

CONNELL, D. M., AND JOHNSON, J. E. "Relationship Between Sex-Role Identification and Self-Esteem in Early Adolescents," *Develop. Psychol.* (1970) 3:268.

CRANDALL, V. J., et al. "Motivational and Ability Determinants of Young Children's Intellectual Achievement Behaviors," *Child Develop.* (1962) 33:643–661.

EPSTEIN, C. G. "Positive Effects of the Multiple Negative: Explaining the Success of Black Professional Women," *Amer. J. Sociol.* (1973) 78:912–935.

FEIN, R. "Men's Experiences Before and After the Birth of a First Child: Dependence, Marital Sharing, and Anxiety," doctoral dissertation, Harvard Univ., 1973.

FLAMMER, D. P. "Self-Esteem Parent Identification, and Sex-Role Development in Preschool Age Boys and Girls," *Child Study J.* (1971) 2:39–45.

GOLDBERG, P. "Misogyny and the College Girl," presented at Eastern Psychol. Assn., Boston, 1967.

HEILBRUN, A. "Sex-Role Identity in Adolescent Females: A Theoretical Paradox," *Adolescence* (1968) 8:79–88.

HELSON, R. "Women Mathematicians and the Creative Personality." *J. Consult. and Clin. Psychol.* (1971) 36:210–220.

HENNIG, M. "Family Dynamics for Developing Positive Achievement Motivation in Women: The Successful Woman Excutive," in R. B. Kundsin (Ed.), *Women and Success;* William Morrow, 1974.

HOFFMAN, L. "Early Childhood Experiences and Women's Achievement Motives," *J. Soc. Issues* (1972) 28:129–155.

HORNER, M. "Toward an Understanding of Achievement-Related Conflicts in Women," *J. Soc. Issues* (1972) 28:157–176.

KAGAN, J. "Acquisition and Significance of Sex Typing and Sex-Role Identification," in M. L. Hoffman and L. W. Hoffman (Eds.), *Review of Child Development Research,* Vol. 1; New York: Russell Sage Foundation, 1964.

KAGAN, J., AND FREEMAN, M. "Relation of Childhood Intelligence, Maternal Behaviors, and Social Class to Behavior During Adolescence," *Child Develop.* (1963) 34:899–911.

KAGAN, J., AND LEMKIN, J. "The Child's Differential Perception of Parental Attributes," *J. Abnormal and Soc. Psychol.* (1960) 61:440–447.

KAGAN, J., AND MOSS, H. A. *Birth to Maturity;* Wiley, 1962.

KANGAS, J., AND BRADWAY, K. "Intelligence at Middle Age: A Thirty-Eight Year Follow-Up," *Develop. Psychol.* (1971) 5:333–337.

LEWIS, M. "Parents and Children: Sex-Role Development," *School Rev.* (1972) 80:440–447.

LOZOFF, M. "Changing Life Style and Role Perceptions of Men and Women Students," presented at Radcliffe Inst. Conference, *Women: Resource for a Changing World,* Cambridge, Mass., April 1972.

MACCOBY, E. E., AND JACKLIN, C. N. *The Psychology of Sex Differences;* Stanford Univ. Press, 1974.

MARACEK, J. "When Stereotypes Hurt: Response to Dependent and Aggressive Communications," presented at Eastern Psychol. Assn., Philadelphia, April 1974.

MCKEE, J. P., AND SHERRIFFS, A. C. "The Differential Evaluation of Males and Females," *J. Personality* (1957) 25:356–371.

NILSEN, A. P. "Women in Children's Literature," *College English* (1971) 32:908–921.

OSOFSKY, J. D., AND O'CONNELL, E. "Parent-Child Interaction: Daughters' Effects upon Mothers' and Fathers' Behaviors," *Develop. Psychol.* (1972) 7:157–168.

ROSENKRANTZ, P., et al. "Sex-Role Stereotypes and Self-Concepts in College Students," *J. Consult. and Clin. Psychol.* (1968) 32:287–295.

RUBIN, J. Z., et al. "The Eye of the Beholder: Parents' Views on Sex of Newborns," *Amer. J. Orthopsychiatry* (1974) 44:512–519.

SAARIO, T. N., et al. "Sex-Role Stereotyping in the Public Schools," *Harvard Educ. Rev.* (1973) 43:386–416.

SMITH, S. "Age and Sex Differences in Children's Opinions Concerning Sex Differences," *J. Genetic Psychol.* (1939) 54:17–25.

TIDBALL, M. E. "Perspective on Academic Women and Affirmative Action," *Educ. Record* (1973) 54:130–135.

TURNER, B. F. "Socialization and Career Orientation Among Black and White College Women," presented at Amer. Psychol. Assn., Hawaii, 1972.

WINCHEL, R., et al. "Impact of Coeducation on 'Fear of Success' Imagery Expressed by Male and Female High School Students," *J. Educ. Psychol.* (1974) 66:726–730.

WYLIE, R. C. "Children's Estimates of Their Schoolwork Ability as a Function of Sex, Race, and Socioeconomic Level," *J. Personality* (1963) 31:203–224.

Social Values, Femininity, and the Development of Female Competence

Julia A. Sherman

An important current question is whether to socialize females to be competent or to be feminine. A second and related problem concerns socialization to promote maximal intellectual development in women. Major points of this paper are: (a) that the goals of femininity and competence are not necessarily the same, and (b) that little is known about how to rear females to be competent, partly because competence, especially intellectual competence, has never been considered an important goal for females. Approaches to social change are discussed.

A key issue in the socialization of females is the question, "Shall we socialize females to be competent or to be feminine?" A second and related problem concerns socialization to promote maximal intellectual development in women. The goals of femininity and competence are not necessarily the same; furthermore, little is known about how to rear females to be competent—partly because competence, especially intellectual competence, has never been considered an important goal for females. This is not to deny that a woman can be a competent cake baker and be stereotypically feminine, but it is to deny that she need necessarily be competent to be stereotypically feminine. It is also to deny that competence is as salient in the stereotypic expectations of females as males.

First let us look at some standard descriptions of the female sex role. Kagan (1964) summarized the female sex role in our culture in this way: Females are supposed to inhibit aggression and to inhibit the open display of sexual urges. They are to be passive with men, to be nurturant, to cultivate attractiveness, and to maintain an emotionally responsive, socially poised, friendly posture with others. In contrast, males are to be aggressive in the face of attack, independent in problem situations, sexually aggressive, in control of regressive urges, and suppressive of strong emotions, especially anxiety.

The Parsonian (Parsons & Bales, 1955) generalization that males specialize in the instrumental role and females in the expressive role, as ampli-

"Social Values, Femininity, and the Development of Female Competence" by Julia Sherman, *Journal of Social Issues* 32, 3 (1976), 181–195. Reprinted by permission.

fied by Johnson (1963), states that the feminine expressive role is characterized by giving rewarding responses in order to receive rewarding responses. The instrumental (masculine) role is defined by a behavioral orientation toward goals which transcend the immediate interactional situation. The instrumental role player is not primarily oriented to the immediate emotional responses of others to him. Rather than soliciting positive responses, instrumental role playing requires ability to tolerate the hostility which it will very likely elicit.

A cross-cultural study of sex differences in socialization (Barry, Bacon, & Child, 1957) found that among 110 cultures surveyed, 82% expected girls to become more nurturant than boys, 87% expected boys to achieve more, and 85% expected boys to be more self-reliant.

Block (1973) reports similar findings for the United States and Western Europe. She found that parents, perhaps especially fathers, emphasize different values in rearing their sons and daughters. For their sons, assertion, achievement, and self-agrandizement are encouraged while their daughters are taught to control aggression, assertion, and self-extension. For girls the emphasis in the parent-child relationship is on relatedness, protection, and support. Her data on cross-national comparisons suggest that sex typing in the United States is more intense than in five European countries. Block notes that "the present American cultural emphasis on masculine machismo and feminine docility appears to impede the development of mature ego functioning" (p. 522).

The key characteristics for purposes of this discussion are passive-dependency, independence in problem solving, and incentive or perhaps even permission to achieve. These sex-role descriptions indicate that passive-dependency is to be expected of the female role and that achievement and independence in problem solving is to be expected of the male role. It is necessary to note that the terms passive-dependency and femininity are vague and stereotypic and different investigators have measured them in different ways (Mischel, 1971). The terms "passive" and "dependent" have multiple meanings: furthermore, dependency is not clearly either a unitary or a bipolar trait (Hartup, 1963)—in other words, independence is not clearly the opposite of dependence. Discussion will be more precise if it is in terms of avoiding extreme passive-dependence rather than in terms of becoming independent. Extreme independence has its own problems and could be difficult to defend as a desirable personality trait. Perhaps it is fair to say that no negative value is attached to traits attributed to the female role per se, that is, when they are appropriate in degree and circumstance; nor is it supposed that females in fact are not competent. The point is that in many ways they are not expected to be competent.

Psychologists and mental health experts have generally assumed that it is good for women to be feminine and good to bring up girls to be well-adjusted to the female sex role. Surprisingly, however, there is considerable evidence to indicate that it is not mentally healthy to be feminine, at least not in the stereotypic sense. The stereotyped characteristics of femininity, including passive-dependent characteristics, were rated by clinicians of both sexes as less mature, less healthy, and less socially competent than the stereotyped description of masculinity (Broverman, Broverman, Clarkson, Rosenkrantz, & Vogel, 1970). In other words, to rear a girl to conform to the stereotype of femininity is to rear her to be less mature, less healthy, and less socially competent according to the judgment of a group of experts. Here is the classic double bind presented to women: Graphically stated, one can be feminine but incompetent or one can be competent but masculine.

Heilbrun (1965, 1968) found from his own studies and from a review of the literature that although masculinity is associated with positive mental health in males, femininity is not necessarily associated with positive mental health in females. For example, one study found that well-adjusted women tended to be identified with low-feminine mothers, while maladjusted women tended to be identified with highly feminine mothers (Heilbrun & Fromme, 1965). Furthermore, when "masculine" women were maladjusted, there was evidence that it was because they were inconsistently masculine. Compared to adjusted masculine women, the maladjusted masculine women were more succorant, abasing, and socially alienated, less need-achieving, dominant, enduring, and instrumental (Heilbrun, 1968). In other words, it was largely their femininity, not their masculinity which was associated with maladjustment.

Though psychoanalytic literature insists that women need to be passive and dependent to function sexually and maternally (Deutsch, 1944–1945), the evidence suggests the contrary. So far as sexuality is concerned, Masters and Johnson (1966), after the most thorough study of female sexuality yet made, decisively rejected passivity as an accurate characterization of sexual response in women.

If the psychoanalytic view were valid, the virtues of the passive-dependent character should be apparent in the intrinsically female task of carrying a fetus to full-term delivery. The evidence, however, does not support this view. One of the most common types among women who have spontaneously aborted three or more times for no known physical reason is the excessively dependent woman (Sherman, 1971). Cohen (1966) reported that the women who best fit the traditional ideal feminine personality of being passive and dependent were simply inadequate—as people, as sexual partners, as wives, as mothers. Locke (1951) found that "directorial" ability in the wife was significantly associated with happy as opposed to divorced marriages. The hysterical, passive, culturally feminine woman was the most frequent type among mothers of children brought to a child-guidance center (Marks, 1961). The evidence therefore indicates that extreme passive-dependency is not mentally healthy and far from being conducive to the performance of female traditional and biological functions, passive-dependency is associated with poor performance. In fact, one investigator was dismayed to find that the more "masculine" women in his sample had been independently rated as more maternal, more attractive, and more competent in their sex role (Peskin, 1968). Peskin found that the so-called masculine women were more effective, directing their energy more to action, while the feminine women were more self-absorbed and concerned with their own bodily functioning.

In addition to being unhealthy, passive-dependency may impede full intellectual development. A longitudinal study of intellectual development (Sontag, Baker, & Nelson, 1953) found that children whose IQs improved with age were competitive, self-assertive, independent, and dominant in interaction with other children; children with declining IQs were passive, shy, and dependent. The hypothesis that sex-related differences in intellectual functioning may be mediated by sex-related differences in independence training has been under consideration for some time, but it is losing empirical support (Maccoby, 1966; Maccoby & Jacklin, 1974; Sherman, 1974).

Another striking instance of an adverse effect related to stereotypic feminine role prescriptions is that identified by Horner (1970), what she has termed the "motive to avoid success." Since this concept is examined at length in Condry and Dyer's article (1976), I will make only these points here about it:

1. Fear of success is probably limited to fear of success in a male domain.
2. It is probably more like a need to avoid turning off men than simply either a fear of success or a fear of sex-inappropriate behavior.
3. The ready acceptance of the fear of success findings stemmed not only from the research findings, but also from the immediate recognition (among women) of a familiar experience.
4. The actual extent to which the sexes understand each other's attitudes is not all clear, i.e., will Jill's success turn John off? (Steinmann & Fox, 1974).
5. Given changing social attitudes, regional differences, the inherent difficulties of consistent scoring of TAT-type stories by researchers across the country, and the varied measures in use (Pappo, 1972; Spence, 1974), the fear of success literature promises to remain a controversial area for some time.

Politics of the Femininity Ideal

Taken together, research from these varied areas indicates that meeting the ideal of stereotypic femininity is not good for mental health, motherhood, marriage, or intellectual development. So what is it good for? Some explanation would seem to be required for the fact that so many maladaptive characteristics should become part of an expected ideal personality.

Freeman (1971) argues that the model most appropriate to explain the relative position of men and women in our society is caste, not role or class. It is possible to adopt a different role, to move to a different class; such mobility is not possible within a caste system. The existence and continuation of a caste system require that those in the lower caste believe it is just and right for them to have lower status. It seems likely that, despite its maladaptive qualities, stereotypic femininity is espoused as a positive cultural value for women because it helps to justify the lower status of women. Inferior intellectual ability and childlike qualities have been ascribed to blacks and to women alike (Hacker, 1951). Female sexual-caste prescriptions encourage women to become inferior, incompetent human beings and that, in turn, is used to justify their inferior status. The term "sexual-caste" socialization appears more appropriate than "sex-role" socialization.

The effects of this pernicious sexual stereotyping do not end with the immediate effects on the individuals but operate also by influencing the kinds of questions scientists ask, what findings are reported, and how interpreted. This problem is clearly illustrated in the literature on sex-related differences in field dependence. The term itself has been recognized as pejorative and "field articulation" has gradually replaced it. The results from these studies have been interpreted in an exaggerated and overgeneralized manner, and the conclusions lend themselves to negative expectations about female intellectual potential. Nonetheless, such conclusions have been comfortably accepted with little critical commentary or concern. The main aspects of the field articulation research negative to women involve first the implication that females are not so analytical as males and second that this characteristic is unmodifiable.

Field articulation is usually measured by one of two devices, the Rod and Frame Test or the Embedded Figures Test. More males score well and more females score poorly on these tasks, so that a small average difference between the sexes is often but not always found (Maccoby & Jacklin, 1974). Accurate performance on these tasks has been interpreted as indicating analytical cognitive style and even analytical ability, despite the fact that there is no evidence that they are general measures of analytical ability and despite the fact that both tests are highly correlated with tests of spatial perception (Maccoby & Jacklin, 1974; Sherman, 1967, 1974). The cause of the sex-related difference in field articulation may well lie in the spatial character of the tasks and not in their "analytical" nature.

Regarding the question of the unmodifiability of field articulation, there is considerable reason to think that this assumption is false. Goldstein and Chance (1965) demonstrated a significant practice effect on the Embedded Figures Test. Kato (1965) demonstrated a significant practice effect and typical learning curves with the Rod and Frame Test. My own findings (Sherman, 1974) also showed a significant practice effect for both sexes on the Rod and Frame Test ($p < .01$); most but not all subjects improved their performance with practice. Further research would be needed to develop more effective methods than mere practice in order to modify field articulation behavior. Introduction of feedback, for example, would be expected to result in even greater improvement. The inherent, unchangeable nature of field articulation behavior no longer appears to be a viable assumption.[1]

Social Change

Social science has not distinguished itself by its constructive role in promoting social change (Caplan & Nelson, 1974). Prescribing for social change involves a wisdom and knowledge that no one can presume to possess, but it may be useful to outline some possible directions within the context of a model suggested by Parsons, Frieze, & Ruble (1976). (See Figure 1.) In terms of the proposed model, all components need to be attacked. Efforts to change the personal attitudes of women (Box C) are not going to be very effective without changes in Boxes A, B, and D. For example, attempting to encourage girls to become engineers will not be so effective if (a) they can see that there are hardly any female engineers (Box A); (b) they have already been socialized away from taking the necessary math courses (Box

B); and (c) not only is engineering school biased against admitting them, but their family and friends think they're pretty peculiar (Box D)!

The model, however, is not complete in that it omits references to biological sex differences. In the case of a model to schematize males and female personality development and caste prescriptions this would seem to be a serious omission (D'Andrade, 1966). To complete the model, a Box AA is needed above Box A with arrows going both directions, and a label, "Sex differences with a direct and indirect biological link." The point of the two-way arrow is to indicate that biologically based sex differences influence cultural norms and also that cultural development can affect the actual biological sex differences—certainly their influence and importance. For example, the impact of women's reproductive capacity has been lessened by birth control, abortion, bottle feeding, better health care. Further changes could be effected by improved understanding, public health provisions, education and research in regard to menstrual cycle changes, pregnancy, childbirth, and menopause and by better childcare provision. Although numerous other possibilities and examples could be cited, I will mention just one more. Attack aggression and/or dominance in males, which is one of the few sex-related differences seriously considered as possibly biologically based (Maccoby & Jacklin, 1974; Money & Ehrhardt, 1972; Sherman, 1971), can also be either augmented and developed by cultural influence—as in our culture—or it can be diminished as in other cultures, e.g., the Arapesh.

Box A, "Cultural norms and economic-political realities," is affected by feedback from the changing behavior in society but is difficult to attack directly. One such effort that would seem worthwhile, however, would be for social scientists to promulgate a new standard for the healthy personality which avoids the constricting, iatrogenic effects of stereotypic masculinity and femininity. Androgyny would appear to be such a standard (Block, 1973; Bem, 1974). Broverman, Vogel, Broverman, Clarkson, & Rosenkrantz (1972) have found that the most highly valued characteristics of the stereotypic male role are competence, rationality, and assertion, while the most

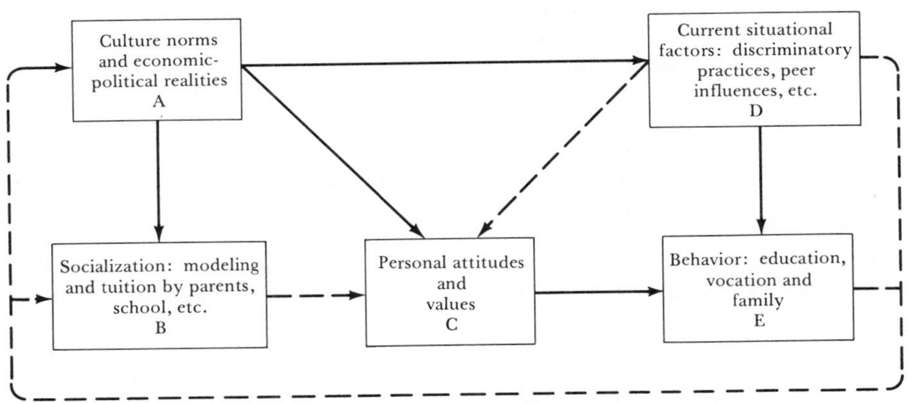

Figure 1 Development and expression of sex-role related behavior in college women.

highly valued characteristics of the stereotypic female role are warmth and expressiveness. It seems highly likely that persons flexible enough to behave in both ways will be more competent in a broad range of situations. Sandra Bem is currently engaged in a program of research testing this hypothesis. Curiously enough the androgynous personality, though advanced now as a new ideal, is much more closely allied to the ideal Christian personality of Western tradition than are stereotyped sex-caste expectations, especially those for masculinity.

Box B, "Socialization," requires adults of a sufficient level of consciousness to socialize their children in a different manner. While Maccoby and Jacklin (1974) imply that there are few important differences in the way boys and girls are reared, this conclusion is disputed (Sherman, 1975). The term "socialize," however, suggests a passive recipient being molded by outside influences. While not denying the influence of modeling, tuition, and imitation, humans defy the mechanistic approach of science. To an important extent in transactional analysis terms they write their own scripts (Berne, 1972), or in terms of cognitive psychology they figure out for themselves what are sex-appropriate behaviors (Kohlberg, 1966). One can, however, alter what is presented on TV and in textbooks, provide models, change attitudes of socializing agents, and thus directly and indirectly effect change.

Common sense and clinical experience suggest that people who have some place they want to go and know how to get there are much more likely to cope with life's problems without undue personal discomfort. As females we are experiencing unsettled values, multiple and conflicting demands, unspoken double binds, lack of information (e.g., likelihood of working as an adult, information about our bodies as females), and the incorporation of a devalued and distorted image of ourselves from advertising, textbooks, psychological theories, the church, and indeed from our whole culture. These realities mean that self-knowledge is very important for females. Without such self-knowledge the continual identity crises of the shifting demands of being the "other" rob us of our personhood.

Specifically in regard to developing female intellectual competence, much needs to be done in regard to the educational institutions. At the level of higher education, one sees refusal of entrenched academic structures to permit courses on women, the near exclusion of women from "track" positions in the major research universities, and many other discriminatory practices. This intellectual castration of women has serious ramifications in terms of producing research which is biased and irrelevant to women, in terms of deprivation of female intellectual models, and in terms of quashing female leadership.

In regard to increasing female competency and/or participation in areas involving mathematics and spatial skill, it is not entirely clear at this point that anything is needed beyond facilitation and encouragement to enter these fields. Although there are genetic and other theories that suggest that fewer females than males inherit a high potential for quantitative reasoning and spatial visualization, sexual disparities in intellectual functioning could not even then account for the scarcity of women in these fields. For example, Kogan[2] has pointed out that the difference between the sexes in their distribution in science-math careers is about two standard deviations while the difference between the sexes in space perception is only about half a standard deviation. Lack of spatial ability could not possibly account for the disparity between the sexes in these fields.

It is important to recognize that education has always meant the education of males. The collective cultural experience has evolved to develop males maximally, and its effect is particularly to develop them in ways in which they might otherwise not function well, i.e., in the verbal area. I think that, therefore, males gain more from schooling than do females, though for the same reason males in their younger years find schooling more demanding than females (Sherman, 1971). Not only are females not immersed in a curriculum featuring their less typically sex-preferred intellectual areas, but the continual verbal emphasis in the education system which is helpful for developing male intellect may even be harmful to females by oververbalizing them.

While it would be helpful to prescribe how the education system should be set up to develop female intellect more fully, well-researched answers are not yet forthcoming. Indeed there is trouble even getting the importance of the question recognized. One suspects, however, that in addition to obvious changes in sexual stereotyping of occupations, textbooks, tests, counseling, the sex ratio of math and science teachers, it may also be important to introduce more nonverbal material in the formal curriculum. Coates, Lord, & Jababovics (1974) found that preschool girls who played more with blocks had greater spatial skill than those who did not. The effect was not found for boys. Although Coates et al. offer another interpretation, the results suggest that fewer of the boys needed this practice, either because their potential skill was greater or because their informal activities already gave them as much practice as they could use in developing spatial skill. This sort of hypothesis (Sherman, 1967, 1971) will have to be further tested and developed before it can be recommended as a policy direction for educational systems; however, it is not premature to suggest this as an important area of research.

Much has already been written about changes needed in "Current situational factors" (Box D). Important areas that seem least developed are: (a) popularization of living complexes with communal cooking and child-care arrangements, and (b) gaining a greater understanding of male attitudes toward women, and of the psychology of the relations between the sexes. Much progress has been made in altering situational factors and of course more needs to be made; this is the focus of numerous feminist organizations.

Box C, "Personal attitudes and values," is an important point of intervention since it is more directly under the control of each woman. What each woman might want to change about herself is of course highly individual. In terms of the ideal, healthy, androgynous personality she will want the characteristics of warmth and expressiveness. Some women (e.g., "queen bees") may want further development in these areas, especially in relation to other women. Of more typical concern, however, are likely to be the valued characteristics of the stereotypic male role: competence, rationality, and assertion. Specialized techniques to develop these characteristics are being increasingly used by women in the classroom, in workshops, in group or individual therapy.

One important technique is explicit instruction in problem solution. The individual attempts to identify her problems and then select a specific problem to work on. The first problem attacked should not be too difficult and hopefully should be important. The individual then generates possible solutions and these are then weighed with the help of the facilitator(s) and other group members. One approach is selected for action and the individual, with the group's support, attempts to put it into effect. Outcomes are then discussed and evaluated. This approach teaches a problem solving method that can be applied to many different situations. It demonstrates techniques to gain mastery over one's own life and often leads to increases in self-esteem and self-confidence.

The second technique, which often plays a role in problem solution as well, is that of assertiveness training (Alberti & Emmons, 1970; Jakubowski-Spector, 1973). Basically, individuals are taught to discriminate between nonassertion (letting others violate your rights), assertion, and aggression (infringing on the rights or dignity of another). Preliminary work also often includes an individual's increased awareness of what her rights are—some persons do not feel that they have a right to assert themselves. Individuals then gain practice in self-assertion through role-play and then in real-life circumstances. Again, it is important to start with something easy and work up to more difficult assertion situations.

In terms of broader aspects of changes in personal attitudes, relevant to the women's movement, the consciousness raising group has of course been a unique vehicle for change (Brodsky, 1973). The focus here has been on recognition of problems, i.e., increased consciousness, more accurate delineation of the sources of problems (i.e., not all from within the self), mutual support and often action.

A more general approach to change in personal attitudes that can combine all of the foregoing is transactional analysis (TA). TA theory describes individuals as living by a script and women as living by a women's script (Wyckoff, 1971; Berne, 1972). In order to change a script that seems maladaptive, its characteristics must be recognized so that the individual can choose whether or not she likes the script. If she should choose to change her script, she must have power and permission to do so. This power and permission comes from the leaders and other group members. The script was originally written to please important others and is now internalized in her own "Parent" (note the implication that sex-role expectations can have superego-like qualities). If she violates the script without support, she is likely to feel uneasy, anxious, and/or depressed. In TA individuals are warned that they may feel depressed when in the process of changing their scripts; forewarned is forearmed. They are also cautioned that the script can be changed only one line at a time, again a precaution against total disarticulation and/or premature discouragement.

Part of changing one's script is also no longer playing the same games, indulging in rackets, and changing one's life position to that of "I'm O.K.—You're O.K." (Harris, 1967). A typical life position for a woman's script is "You (man) are O.K., but I (female) am not O.K." Typical games to accompany such a script are "Kick Me," "Playing Stupid," and "If it Weren't for You" (Berne, 1964). Typical rackets, use of one emotion to avoid facing another, are "Depression" and "Feeling Hurt" which primarily avoid self-assertion and anger expressions. In TA, women learn to discover where they get their strokes and how to rearrange their stroke economies to avoid the stroke deficits so common to women. They learn how to recognize male games—many of which have yet to be described—and they learn counters for them. Changes in male attitudes are of course necessary and to some extent occur as a result of women's changing their scripts and refusing to play the same old games.

Women need to recognize that as they change their scripts, they may be attacked as masculine, selfish, crazy, Lesbian, bitchy, etc., in any case negatively deviant. This is particularly true of female leaders. Actually, in fact, the attacks are usually not so obvious, whispered rather than spoken, implied rather than stated. The so-called paranoia of minority groups arises from this generic, undeserved hostility, provoked merely by being a person, not a black or a female. These external and internal resistances to change are important reasons why women need power and permission in order to change and why they need to change their scripts one line at a time. Realizing that others may not accept script changes, however, helps prevent an attack from hooking one's "Not O.K. Child." It also warns one to be selective about who and what to tackle, when, with what support, and with what likelihood of success. Although it might be nice to tell young women today that they have it made, I think it is unrealistic and a disservice. I would rather they be prepared for the worst, as the best will be easy to cope with.

Social change is a complex of events each acting and reacting on the other, and in the case of breaking down the sexual caste system, social change involves every aspect of personal and social life. The feminist movement is a major social revolution which has not yet reached the full extent of its influence and which has potential for enriching the lives of us all.

NOTES

1. Witkin, H. A. *The effect of training and of structural aids on performance in three tests of space orientation* (Report No. 80). Washington, D.C.: Division of Research, Civil Aeronautics Association, 1948.
2. Kogan, N. *Sex differences in creativity and cognitive styles.* Paper presented at the Conference on Cognitive Styles and Creativity in Higher Education, Montreal, November 1972.

REFERENCES

ALBERTI, R. E., & EMMONS, M. L. *Your perfect right.* San Luis Obispo, CA: Impact, 1970.

BARRY, H., BACON, M. K. & CHILD, I. L. A cross-cultural survey of some sex differences in socialization. *Journal of Abnormal and Social Psychology,* 1957, *55,* 327–332.

BEM, S. L. The measurement of psychological androgyny. *Journal of Consulting and Clinical Psychology,* 1974, *42,* 155–162.

BERNE, E. *Games people play.* New York: Grove, 1964.

BERNE, E. *What do you say after you say hello?* New York: Grove, 1972.

BLOCK, J. H. Conceptions of sex role: Some cross-cultural and longitudinal perspectives. *American Psychologist,* 1973, *28,* 512–526.

BRODSKY, A. The consciousness-raising group as a model for therapy with women. *Psychotherapy: Theory, Research, and Practice,* 1973, *10,* 24–29.

BROVERMAN, I. K., BROVERMAN, D. M., CLARKSON, F. E., ROSENKRANTZ, P., & VOGEL, S. R. Sex-role stereotypes and clinical judgments of mental health. *Journal of Consulting Psychology,* 1970, *34,* 1–7.

BROVERMAN, I. K., VOGEL, S. R., BROVERMAN, D. M., CLARKSON, F. E., & ROSENKRANTZ, P. Sex-role stereotypes: A current appraisal. *Journal of Social Issues,* 1972 *28* (2), 59–78.

CAPLAN, N., & NELSON, S. D. Who's to blame. *Psychology Today,* November 1974, pp. 99–104.

COATES, S., LORD, M., & JABABOVICS, E. Field dependence-independence, social-nonsocial play, and sex differences in preschool children. *Perceptual and Motor Skills,* 1974, *39,* 1307–1313.

COHEN, M. B. Personal identity and sexual identity. *Psychiatry,* 1966, *29,* 1–14.

CONDRY, J., & DYER, S. Fear of success: Attribution of cause to the victim. *Journal of Social Issues,* 1976, *32* (3).

D'ANDRADE, R. Sex differences in cultural institutions. In E. E. Maccoby, *The development of sex differences.* Palo Alto, CA: Stanford University Press, 1966.

DEUTSCH, H. *Psychology of women* (2 vols.). New York: Grune & Stratton, 1944–1945.

FREEMAN, J. The legal basis of the sexual caste system. *Valpariso University Law Review,* 1971, *5,* 203–236.

GOLDSTEIN, A. G., & CHANCE, J. E. Effects of practice on sex-related differences in performance on embedded figures. *Psychonomic Science,* 1965, *3,* 361–362.

HACKER, H. M. Women as a minority group. *Social Forces,* 1951, *30,* 60–69.

HARRIS, T. A. *I'm O.K.—You're O.K.* New York: Avon, 1967.

HARTUP, W. W. Dependence and independence. In H. W. Stevenson (Ed.), *Child psychology.* Chicago: University of Chicago Press, 1963.

HEILBRUN, A. B., JR. Sex differences in identification learning. *Journal of Genetic Psychology,* 1965, *106,* 185–193.

HEILBRUN, A. B., JR. Sex-role identity in adolescent females: A theoretical paradox. *Adolescence,* 1968, *3,* 79–88.

HEILBRUN, A. B., JR., & FROMME, D. K. Parental identification of late adolescents and level of adjustment: The importance of parent-model attributes, ordinal position, and sex of the child. *Journal of Genetic Psychology,* 1965, *107,* 49–59.

HORNER, M. S. Femininity and successful achievement: A basic inconsistency. In J. Bardwick (Ed.), *Feminine personality and conflict.* Belmont, CA: Brooks/Cole, 1970.

JAKUBOWSKI-SPECTOR, P. Facilitating the growth of women through assertiveness training. *The Counseling Psychologist,* 1973, *4,* 75–86.

JOHNSON, M. M. Sex role learning in the nuclear family. *Child Development,* 1963, *34,* 319–334.

KAGAN, J. Acquisition and significance of sex typing and sex role identity. In M. L. Hoffman & L. W. hoffman (Eds.), *Review of child development research.* New York: Russell Sage, 1964.

KATO, N. A fundamental study of the rod and frame test. *Japanese Psychological Research,* 1965, *7,* 61–68.

KOHLBERG, L. A cognitive-development analysis of children's sex-role concepts and attitudes. In E. E. Maccoby (Ed.), *The development of sex differences.* Palo Alto, CA: Stanford University Press, 1966.

LOCKE, H. J. *Predicting adjustment in marriage: A comparison of a divorced and a happily married group.* New York: Holt, 1951.

MACCOBY, E. E. Sex differences in intellectual functioning. In E. E. Maccoby The development of sex differences. Palo Alto, CA: Stanford University Press, 1966.

MACCOBY, E. E., & JACKLIN, C. N. *Psychology of sex differences.* Palo Alto, CA: Stanford University Press, 1974.

MARKS, P. An assessment of the diagnostic process in a child guidance setting. *Psychological Monographs,* 1961, 75 (Whole No. 507).

MASTERS, W. H., & JOHNSON, V. E. *Human sexual response.* Boston: Little, Brown, 1966.

MISCHEL, W. Sex typing and socialization. In P. H. Mussen (Ed.), *Carmichael's manual of child psychology* (Vol. 2). New York: Wiley, 1971.

MONEY, J., & EHRHARDT, A. A. *Man and woman: Boy and girl.* Baltimore: Johns Hopkins, 1972.

PAPPO, M. Fear of success: A theoretical analysis and the construction and validation of a measuring instrument. (Doctoral dissertation, Columbia University, 1972). *Dissertation Abstracts International,* 1973, *34,* 421B. (University Microfilms No. 73–16235)

PARSONS, J. E., FRIEZE, I. H., & RUBLE, D. N. Introduction. *Journal of Social Issues,* 1976, *32* (3).

PARSONS, T., & BALES, R. *Family socialization and interaction process.* Glencoe, Ill.: Free Press, 1955.

PESKIN, H. The duration of normal menses as a psychosomatic phenomenon. *Psychosomatic Medicine,* 1968, *30,* 167–169.

SHERMAN, J. A. Problem of sex differences in space perception and aspects of intellectual functioning. *Psychological Review,* 1967, *74,* 290–299.

SHERMAN, J. A. *On the psychology of women: A survey of empirical studies.* Springfield, Ill.: Charles C Thomas, 1971.

SHERMAN, J. A. Field articulation, sex, spatial visualization, dependency, practice, laterality of the brain, and birth order. *Perceptual and Motor Skills,* 1974, *38,* 1223–1235.

SHERMAN, J. A. Review of *Psychology of sex differences* by E. E. Maccoby & C. N. Jacklin. *Sex Roles,* 1975, *1,* 297–301.

SONTAG, I. W., BAKER, C. T., & NELSON, V. A. Mental growth and personality development: A longitudinal study. *Monographs of the Society for Research in Child Development,* 1953, *23,* No. 68.

SPENCE, J. T. The Thematic Apperception Test and attitudes toward achievement in women: A new look at the motive to avoid success and a new method of measurement. *Journal of Consulting and Clinical Psychology,* 1974, *42,* 427–437.

STEINMANN, A., & FOX, D. *The male dilemma.* New York: Jason Aronson, 1974.

WYCKOFF, H. The stroke economy in women's scripts. *Transactional Analysis Journal,* 1971, *1,* 16–20.

Growing Up Black

Joyce A. Ladner

The life of the young girl in the Black lower class is conditioned by the community's traditions, values, beliefs and, in sum, its culture. Thus, Black child socialization must necessarily be different from that of children reared in the white middle-class tradition, because of the sociohistorical differences that exist between the two groups. It is also vastly different for the life of a girl growing up in the white lower class. For race is a much more powerful variable in this society than social class. It also differs to a great extent from the Black middle class, whose child-rearing practices are often similar to those of the white middle class, but yet dissimilar in the sense that Black parents can never give their children the *ultimate* protection from racism which white parents exercise. Perhaps the most decisive factor that influences the child-rearing patterns of the Black lower class relates to the oppression that even its children must endure and learn to deal with. Unlike the white middle-class child, Black children must also be subjected to the second-class citizenship of their elders. The consequences are manifested in a variety of ways. When one speaks of childhood in the lower-class Black community, it relates to a different phenomenon than what is typically held to be the standard norm in American society. Childhood must be influenced by one's social class and racial background as well as by other factors such as nationality and religion. The type of childhood that is held to be the American norm is peculiar to this society. Philippe Aries observes that the childhood that is characteristic of a great many Western societies was unheard of from the Middle Ages to the seventeenth century. It was only in the seventeenth century that parents became concerned with providing a certain kind of educative resource to children in the preparation for their future roles as adults. Childhood was sharply demarcated from adulthood and a long period of socialization and preparation for the adult world came into being. This had a greater influence on the middle classes, who began providing formal education for their children, than on the lower classes, whose children had to work for the maintenance of the family.[1] This was also the situation with children who worked in sweatshops in the same manner as adults in eighteenth- and nineteenth-century Europe before child-labor laws were enacted. The same, of course, was true for the United States from 1870 to about 1910, when children did not have the protection of child-labor laws.

Lower-class Black children have received less of the protection from these laws, and have been the least likely group of children in the United States to benefit from the general concern with child protection. The socioeconomic status of the Black family has always been such that the income of its children often served a vital need. One only needs to take a cursory view of the biographies of many prominent Black people, who describe their impoverished childhood and the economic contributions they had to make to their family's subsistence, to understand how economic instability, produced by racism, influenced their development as children. Booker T. Washington, the noted Black educator who was born a slave, recalls the time when he was forced to move from the world of childhood to that of adulthood:

> Though I was a mere child, my stepfather put me and my brother at work in one of the [salt] furnaces. Often I began work as early as four o'clock in the morning.[2]

Frederick Douglass also speaks of his childhood as a slave, and the harsh, cruel and inhuman existence he was forced to experience.

> I suffered much from hunger, but much more from cold. In hottest summer and coldest winter, I was kept almost naked—no shoes, no stockings, no jacket, no trousers, nothing on but a coarse tow linen shirt, reaching only to my knees. I had no bed. . . . I must have perished with cold, but that, the coldest nights, I used to steal a bag which was used for carrying corn to the mill. I would crawl into this bag, and there sleep on the cold, damp, clay floor.[3]

Understandably the lives of Washington, Frederick Douglass and other great statesmen of this period would be greatly influenced by slavery. However, the pattern of Black child development in subsequent periods of history was equally influenced by the societal oppression against Black people. Thus, Richard Wright's *Black Boy* and Claude Brown's *Manchild in the Promised Land* address the same problems of child development that is explicit in the lives of Douglass and Washington.

The standard conception of the "protected, carefree, and non-responsible" child has never been possible for the majority of Black children. Parents are unable to offer this protection and comfort to their children because of their own vulnerability to the discriminative practices of the larger society. The consequences of the powerlessness of Black parents and their inability to adhere to the standard child-rearing norm necessitated that they devise their own patterns of child socialization. These patterns were primarily predicated upon the principle that children in the Black community must be taught to survive in a hostile society. Various mechanisms were created for dealing with the strategy of survival. Robert Coles writes:

> If the Negro child's life is one of having to learn how to confront a future of unrelenting harassment, his intimidated parents must prepare him for it. They must teach their child a variety of maneuvers and postures to cope with his baffling lot. By seven or eight most Negro children know the score, and I have seen them draw only faintly disguised pictures of the harsh future awaiting them.[4]

The fact that a parent has to deal openly with this question with his young child probably raises the level of the relationship between parent and child to a more mature one. It also forces an openness and honesty between parent and child on the subject of the external hostile forces that are absolutely necessary. Moreover, the self-defensive mechanisms that are an integral part of the child-rearing process act to protect the child against external as well as internal forces. When a parent berates his child for not defending himself on the playground when attacked by his peers, he is likely to use the same defensive tactics in this situation that he would use against white racists who would launch a similar attack. Black children are, therefore, more totally responsible for their own protection than their middle-class counterparts, especially white. The responsibility they are forced to exercise also lends itself to a deeper involvement with shaping their futures, and ultimately to rendering more control over their destinies. Almost by default, these children are forced to become a vital part of the creative process that determines what kind of individuals they are to become. It is the contention of some behavioral scientists that chronological age probably has little to do with one's maturity when other factors operate in such a forceful way as to be the major determinants of the course an individual's life is to take. Robert Coles provides a perceptive analysis of this aspect of Black childhood in *Children of Crisis:*

> Is a sixteen-year-old [Negro] boy who has lived in stark, unremitting poverty, worked since eight, earned a living since fourteen, married at fifteen, and is soon to be a father, a "child"?[5]

The "adult" responsibility that Coles describes, although less the situation with Black adolescents today than in previous historical periods, is still a very prevalent occurrence. In traditional analysis, the lot of Black children, being "denied" a comforting and protected childhood, is viewed as a negative experience. It falls within the realm of behavior that produces "social problems" and "disorganization" for its participants and the society. However, if the same phenomenon is viewed within the context of its strengths and positive symbols, we can observe the development of maturity and other creative resources that enhance one's ability to be an active agent in the society, instead of a passive recipient. This is the role that poor Black children play in this society.

There is a great need for a new perspective and definition on what childhood means in America and what consequences for particular types of behavior should be viewed as healthy and which ones as pathological. Such a reinterpretation should enable social and behavioral analysts to view the Black child, whose life has often been an unrelenting series of harsh experiences, as a more emotionally stable and well-integrated personality than his white middle-class counterparts, whose protected, sheltered lives are representations of the most fragile personality the society could produce. More simply, a new interpretation of emotional strength and productivity is needed in analyzing socialization patterns and consequences of Black children.

It is within this perspective that the early patterns of learning of preadolescent lower-class girls, growing up in the inner city, will be analyzed.

The young Black girl growing up in this environment becomes consciously socialized into the role of womanhood when she is about seven or eight years old. Human socialization is the period when the individual learns specific forms of behavior through interacting with others in her environment in order to facilitate effective functioning within the social group. It assumes different forms and follows different patterns from one culture or society to another. Different patterns of child rearing, for example, can be observed among various social classes and ethnic groups within a society.[6]

In the Black community the primary agents of socialization for the preadolescent girl are her immediate and extended family. Although she spends more time with her nuclear family, it is often members of the extended family, including aunts and uncles, grandparents, cousins and others, who serve this vital function as well. Frequently, girls spend all of their growing-up years in the care of extended kin. Grandmothers act as permanent baby sitters while the actual parents are away working, and when the absence of parents is more permanent. Often children are "given" to their grandparents, who rear them to adulthood. The influence of the extended family upon the socialization of the young Black girl is often very strong. Many children normally grow up in a three-generation household and they absorb the influences of grandmother and grandfather as well as mother and father.

Another important agent of socialization for the young Black girl is the peer group. During preadolescence girls become strong participants in peer group activities. When the child goes to school her reference group expands from being primarily that of the parents and the extended kin to include her peers. Frequently this process of expansion occurs before school age because the child is often exposed to other children in her age category in a meaningful way. It becomes very important for her to judge and be judged by other children her age. The family begins to slowly lose its position of primary importance. It is also during the preadolescent developmental phase that the Black child begins to engage in conflicts with her family. Her self-assertiveness becomes more pronounced because of the decrease in dependency on the family. What was once taken for granted because of its authoritativeness becomes questioned because one's peers might not agree as to its appropriateness.

As they (ages five to twelve) enter into this psychosocial developmental phase, their lives become attuned to how they should begin to relate to each other and to those around them as aspirant women. Although preadolescent Black girls are very much involved in play activities, sibling rivalry, school and a host of other preoccupations that characterize children in other social, ethnic and racial groups, there is a strong cultural phenomenon directed toward sharpening roles. It is not very easy to articulate what womanhood means to eight-, nine- and ten-year-old girls. Part of the problem is that they do not yet know how to articulate it, but their behaviors are dramatic representations of it. At the age when girls outside this community are playing with dolls and engaging in all of those activities which reflect childhood, girls within its borders are often unable to experience this complete cycle. The societal canon of "childhood" is often unobserved to varying degrees because it is a luxury which many parents cannot afford. Parents in the Black community are often unable to protect their young children from harsh social forces, which protection would ensure that they grow up in this "safe period" emerging relatively unscarred.

In the community in which this study took place, the adult population often envisioned their community as one which had its share of "troubles"—troubles which hindered them from exercising the necessary parental controls over their children's behavior. There is a noticeable absence of formal and informal regulations in the community which would help to counter the socially unapproved behavior. For example, an eight-year-old girl has a good chance of being exposed to rape and violence (such a case will be discussed below) and neither parents nor community leaders have the power to eliminate this antisocial behavior. The community power base still lies outside its borders. In a similar manner, many children are forced to go hungry, without shoes and clothing and an adequate home to live in because of the powerlessness of their parents.

One of the consequences of these pervasive community influences upon the child is that they superimpose emotional precocity on the girl that often exceeds her chronological years. This precocity often enables her to enter networks of individuals and situations wherein traditionally unaccepted behavior for her age group takes place. For example, the thirteen-year-old who can pass for sixteen or seventeen in certain circles not only becomes exposed to but often takes part in behavior that would normally be beyond her range of experience and therefore beyond her capability to manage herself adequately. Among the preadolescents in this study, many of them exhibited behavior patterns and knowledge of "worldly" events that exceeded their years. It was often remarkable to observe these children handle stressful situations with a fair amount of capability.

One of the common themes they relate to is violence, to which they are often exposed. When these children are either witnesses or victims of aggressive activity (or potential victims), they react in a manner of intense fright and displeasure as children elsewhere. However, a difference which is of importance with these children is that they have been educated by older children and adults as to the nature and possible consequences of such aggressive activity. This enables them to, in some ways, defend themselves against antisocial behavior more vigorously than would the child who has not had either vicarious or personal experience with these overt acts.

Rose, an eight-year-old, tearfully described how she had "escaped" the advances of the "rape man" (a middle-aged man who had the reputation for being a child molester) by running through an alley near her home. In this situation Rose expressed both fright and joy about the encounter: She stated that she was frightened when it happened because she knew what he intended to do to her, but was exhilarated that she had been able to maneuver her way out of the situation. A similar occurrence was that of Kim, a ten-year-old, who describes her distress in the following manner:

> INTERVIEWER: Are you afraid of men?
>
> KIM: Yes ma'am. They hang out on the streets drinking and the police come by shooting at them and running. One Sunday I went to a girl friend of my sister's house. Her name was Mary. A man came in this store. His name was Johnny and he had been stabbed . . . in the stomach. It was New Year's Eve. . . . I got scared and started crying. Then the police came by . . . his wife ran out of the store crying and she took her baby with her. The next evening their house caught on fire. . . . [It was set] by the same man who had stabbed Johnny because they didn't like him.

Most of these children could relate directly to some form of violence. They all knew someone who had been involved in it and at least one had experienced rape.

One could say that the mature knowledge they have about antisocial behavior and their abilities to cope with it are symbols of strength that the "protected" child does not share. On the other hand, one of the greatest tragedies is that some parents are often unable to exercise more than minimal control over this rapid developmental process.

Girls growing up in the inner cities in many ways are like their counterparts in other social class, racial and ethnic groups. They share the same concerns, fears, joys and questing ventures as other children. Their preoccupation with youthfulnes is present although situations and events often occur which force them to think and act more grown-up than they are. They share the concerns with boys, peers, games and other play activities as do children in other communities. However, there are other concerns that are thrust upon the young girl through environmental circumstances. Often, a purely childhood experience in the impoverished Black community is considered a luxury. Childhood implies that one grows up in a relatively insulated environment, a protectiveness that keeps her from being exposed to certain facets of grown-up life and the responsibilities that are considered adult. Many parents grew up without the luxuries of the childhood that they are trying to give their children. One mother, who had a sixteen-year-old daughter and a fourteen-year-old son, explained to me why she was so strict on her children, and why she *nurtured* them through a prolonged period of childhood, when compared with most of their peers.

> I had such a short childhood that I wanted my children to have a childhood; not to rush them into being grown people before their time. . . . I had my first boy when I was fifteen years old, nine days before I was sixteen. So that is one thing I wanted to get my daughter through.

The Black child is often forced into "grown-up" activities before he becomes legally an adult. This is the theme of the explosive autobiography of Claude Brown, who described the social, political and economic conditions in Harlem that prevented him and his peers from ever knowing what it meant to be a child in the *traditional* sense. An excerpt taken from this work provides an illustration of this point. Reno, a friend of Claude's, is speaking to Claude:

> Man, Sonny, they ain't got no kids in Harlem. I ain't never seen any. I've seen some really small people actin' like kids. They were too small to be grown, and they might've looked like kids, but they don't have any kids in Harlem, because nobody has time for a childhood. Man, do you ever remember bein' a kid, Sonny? Damn, you lucky. I ain't never been a kid, man. I don't ever remember bein' happy and not scared. I don't know what happened, Man, but I think I missed out on that childhood thing, because I don't ever recall bein' a kid.[7]

The absence of childhood that Reno speaks of is present, to varying degrees, with many preadolescents in the Black community. Some children grow up without the traditional childhood, as described by Reno, and others are given some of the "happiness and protection from fear" that Reno never experienced. Although the experiences are harsh and oftentimes *cruel,* children do develop a great amount of strength and adaptability that enables them to adjust to and cope with the world. The strong personality which emerges is to be viewed as positive because it enhances the child's chances for survival. The childhoods of Kim, whose life has been very similar to Reno's, and Beth, whose parents insulated her from the outside world, are two polar examples.

The Case of Kim

When I first met Kim she was ten years old. She lived in a two-bedroom apartment in the housing project with her mother, two sisters (eleven and sixteen), younger brother (one) and niece (one). Her father had, according to Mrs. Marshal, "gotten tired and just walked away" several years earlier. The family was now supported by Aid to Dependent Children welfare. As a fifth grader, Kim's activities were geared toward her peer group, of which she was the undisputed leader. Most of her time was spent outside the home. As soon as she returned from school each day, she immediately went outside to play until late at night. In the summer she was gone from sunup to sundown. Her mother rarely attempted to prevent her from spending long hours away from home. She and her friends played in other buildings in the housing project, on the project grounds, and often wandered long distances from her home. On occasion she pointed out to me that she had no particular time to be home and was sometimes chased in the building by the housing project security police near midnight. Although Kim was a charming and well-mannered child, she often engaged in "grown-up" activities with her peers. She "played house," played the "dirty dozens," cursed and occasionally imitated sex play with her twelve-year-old boyfriend. Frequently, she also had to baby-sit with the two one-year-olds while their parents were away, help her mother prepare meals, clean house and face the bill collectors when her mother was in hiding because she didn't have the money.

Kim's behavior was similar to that of her mother and sixteen-year-old sister. She laughed about the same things they considered funny and despaired when they did. Her vocabulary was that of her mother. At age ten, she had decided that "men are no good," a sentiment often expressed by her mother, whose husband had deserted her "when things got too rough." Kim had the same attitude toward her mother's boyfriend because he could never stay with them beyond a certain point. He had to go home to his wife.

Earlier in Kim's life, her mother had probably exercised a great amount of control over her activities, but one got the impression now that Mrs. Marshall had grown tired and was unable to express the same amount of concern over Kim's whereabouts as she had when Kim was much younger. Consequently, Mrs. Marshall's discipline over Kim was erratic. Sometimes when she was not in by 11 P. M. she would whip her when she came home, and at other times, she seemed far removed from it. The burden of trying to "make ends meet" with an inadequate welfare allowance took precedent over a preoccupation with her ten-year-old's whereabouts at all times. Mrs. Marshall's sixteen-year-old daughter had given birth to a child at fourteen, and was to become pregnant again at sixteen. She had held high hopes for Elizabeth, but had also reconciled herself to the fact that her resources for rearing her daughters in the desired fashion were too sparse. She could, therefore, only hope for the best. Her second oldest child, Judy, often played hooky from school, talked back to her mother and had taken to smoking. Mrs. Marshall's problems were many. Exercising discipline over Kim was to be counted among the others. The case of Beth, however, is very different.

Beth

Beth, at age nine, lived in the housing project with her mother and father and four sisters and brothers. They lived in a neat apartment that was decorated in lively colors and with fairly good furniture. Her father worked as a skilled laborer in a factory and her mother, on a part-time basis, worked as a cook in a restaurnat. Beth was the second oldest child, and was a close companion of her fourteen-year-old sister. The two of them, in spite of the age difference, shared secrets, went places together (although their parents rarely allowed them to associate with other children except in their own home or under the close supervision of an adult of whom they approved) and viewed each other as close peers. The entire family was a close one and they engaged in frequent outings together, family discussions on issues which the kids raised, etc. Mrs. Robinson was always anxious to involve herself in the lives of her children, particularly her two older daughters, and at age thirty-five (approximately) she was able to understand their day-to-day concerns and problems almost as though they were her very own. Mr. Robinson also played a strong role in the lives of his children, and was as concerned about the problems of his daughters as he was with providing the proper image for his sons (the other three children in the family were boys). However, because of his heavy work schedule which kept him away from home for long hours, he was unable to spend the amount of time with his family that he preferred. Thus, much of the day-to-day guidance and socialization was imparted by Mrs. Robinson. Perhaps for this reason, she was prone to be very strict on her children, especially the two girls. She often described the "troubles" she was afraid they would encounter if she became too lenient and allowed them to "hang out" with the other children in the neighborhood. At one point she told me that she did not feel that Beth was better than her friends, but she could not trust them and their influences upon her because they might unintentionally lead her astray.

Beth was a bright and articulate girl who was always exuberant and easily met challenges from her peers. Whenever I observed her among her peers, she was very creative and the undisputed leader of the group. Her young girl friends looked up to her and sought her childish advice on their problems. She was very mature for her age. Yet the overprotectiveness her mother provided from the outside world seemed to have curbed much of her initiative and creativity. In her mother's presence she rarely spoke to me about any topic without alluding to the fact that "But Mother doesn't feel this way about it," or "Mother said we should do this. . . ." Although she is very close to her mother and father, there are still tensions, which seem to mount from day to day, that border on her insulated home environment and the more mundane involvement with her peers. In Beth we see a young girl coming of age in the Black community whose life is so insulated that she is in the process of developing a reticence and naïveté about life that might prevent her from effectively coping with the harsh realities of her community, should it ever become necessary to do so.

In Kim and Beth, we see two prototypes in the Black community. Kim represents one of the many children whose parents despaired and long since stopped trying to offer the protectiveness afforded other children because they knew they were fighting an uphill battle they would probably lose. They learned not to fight for the unattainable, but they always reserve a gleam of hope that fate will eventually act in their behalf. On the contrary, Beth is one of the many girls whose parents have consciously decided to insulate them because that is the only possible hope, they feel, for coming through the childhood experience relatively unscarred. Beth's mother reasoned that there were too many "bad" people in the streets to allow Beth out there. She could not trust Beth or the "bad" people, so her alternative was always to keep her within specified limits. Mrs. Robinson's recognition of her powerlessness to cope with the environmental conditions is perhaps the only effective strategy of which she is aware. She confided that her experience in the streets as a growing youngster had led her to believe that her children could not adequately handle themselves when confronted by what is out there. On the other hand, this alternative has probably stifled Beth somewhat and rendered her ineffective in dealing with traumatic events. Both girls' childhoods can be considered different from those experienced by middle-class children. Whether little protection (as in Kim's case) or an abundance of protection (as in Beth's case) can be offered is one of the key factors in determining the extent to which Black girls in this kind of environment can expect a relatively restricted, secure life.

These two separate case studies do not cover the entire range of *models,* but represent what I found to be two polarities. Many parents, of course, combine some of the significant elements of both childhood experiences, while others devise even more creative ways of socializing their children for adult roles.

Peer Group and Extended Family

The Black child in this environment is almost born into a strong society of peers who, throughout preadolescence, exert strong influence over their lives. As the child approaches kindergarten age she is exposed to other children on a regular basis. Sometimes the interaction occurs earlier because some parents allow their three- and four-year-olds to spend an almost unrestricted amount of time playing in the buildings and outside with other children in their age group. Frequently, in this community older siblings supervised the play activities of younger sisters and brothers, and sometimes parents conducted the supervision. The early exposure and intimate contact (extended) with other children one's own age allowed for the facilitation of the learning process of certain types of behaviors. The child was no longer under the constant care and influence of parents and extended kin, but of other children his own age. The influence peers exert over each other is remarkable. The formation of attitudes, ideas, behaviors and values can be recognized in the preadolescent as having been a direct result of peer group influence.

One of the reasons peers influence each other so strongly is because they spend so much time together. Mothers and fathers in the Black community are often forced to leave the child in the hands of older sisters and brothers, neighborhood children or alone because they are unable to afford regular baby sitters or nursery school. Grandparents and other elderly women often baby-sit with preschool-age children for a nominal fee from the child's parents, and sometimes no payment is involved. In the housing project a number of elderly women earned much of their income from baby-sitting with several children while their parents worked. In such situations, the children are kept indoors a large portion of the time but usually spend some time outside with the baby sitter. Usually the baby sitter sits with a group of her friends on a bench on the project grounds and talks with them while the children play within a reasonable distance. The children usually do not stray very far from her, and when they do, they are promptly brought back to the area to which they have been restricted. The supervision of these children is usually quite good. They are fed regularly, they take naps and are often taught games and other play activities by the elderly person, depending upon the degree to which she is able to engage in such things. Grandmothers often live in the homes of their children and grandchildren. Here they probably exercise more influence over the behavior of the child than do the parents because of the continuous involvement with them. They not only take care of them in the absence of the parents but the process continues even when the parents return home. Occasionally the child becomes confused about whom he should relate to and be supervised by as the authority figure. If there is some disagreement between the parent and grandparent over the child's behavior, he is prone to take sides with the one he favors.

> There were five children, the parents and grandmother in the Smith home. Grandmother Smith had her own bedroom and worked the night shift as an aide at a nursing home. She slept while the four older children were in school

> and her son and daughter-in-law were at work. However, her sleep was little more than cat naps on some days because she had to take care of four-year-old Freddie. He usually watched television all morning but soon wearied from that and resorted to waking his grandmother for her to take him outside to play. (He was not allowed to go outside by himself.) Usually Grandmother Smith wearily got up and took him outside. Getting up meant that she was not usually able to get back to sleep because the other children were home from school at three and it was impossible to sleep when five children and their friends were running in and out of the house. Although Grandmother Smith was near seventy, she was still very strong and able to make it sometimes on five hours of sleep. All of the kids favored her over their parents because she wasn't strict. She kept cookies and candy in her room and often intervened when their parents were about to discipline them. She usually had her way around the home because her son and daughter-in-law rarely stopped her from interfering with their regulations regarding the children. Whenever young Freddie was about to be spanked by his parents, he ran to Grandmother Smith, who immediately petted him and told her daughter-in-law (who did most of the disciplining) that Freddie was too young to be spanked because he didn't always know right from wrong.

All grandparents are not as permissive as Grandmother Smith. Some are more strict than the parents. Also, some parents feel that the grandparents' ideas about child rearing are somewhat old-fashioned and should not always be adhered to. However, usually this intergenerational conflict is not as strong as it is in the middle class, where parents seem to want to assume far more responsibility for the emotional development of their children. In the low-income Black community a stronger amount of respect is given to the knowledge and experience of the elderly. Very few parents were willing to dismiss their advice as simply being old-fashioned.

The development of the peer society continues from around three years old throughout preadolescence. The process is intensified as the child becomes older because of his increased contact with other children. The peer group seems to serve a somewhat different and broader function with these children than with their middle-class counterparts. There is more unsupervised contact with peers and peers also provide some of the nontangible resources that parents are usually expected to provide. At a very early age many children begin to rely on their peers for company, emotional support, advice, comfort and a variety of other services that parents ideally are expected to offer. In the absence of parents, and in many situations where parents are present but so overburdened with other important matters and do not have the necessary time to give the child, the peer becomes the person to whom the child turns. If an older person is around he is sought out, but many older people have the same concerns and problems his parents have and therefore cannot provide the necessary services. In the most extreme cases, young children rarely communicate with their parents about anything. Five-year-old Ellen Baker is such an example.

> Ellen is one of seven children. Her father is no longer in the home and the family income is received from the welfare allotments. Ellen's first year in school (kindergarten) proved to be a valuable experience because she was able to develop meaningful friendships with three little girls her age. Ellen's

> mother has two children younger than she and must also take care of her four older ones. Although none of the children receive any more attention than Ellen (except perhaps for the baby, two-year-old Buzzy), she is an extremely sensitive child and would, in an ideal situation, depend very heavily upon her parents for guidance. Her four older siblings are also young, the oldest being twelve, and therefore are really unable to relate to her in the manner in which she needs. Her teacher is very nice but largely unavailable. Ellen only spends half a day with the teacher. So she has turned to her three girl friends and looks to them for constant support and approval. Although Mrs. Baker is aware of this, she is unable to do anything about it because there are six other children to care for. Ellen wants to become a nurse but already she wonders whether or not she can. She told me one day, "I want to be a nurse, but that costs money. Can you be a nurse without money?" Ellen's peers had already told her that it costs money and she wanted reassurance from me that it didn't.

Although Ellen is probably an exceptional child, she still represents, in many ways, the typical Black child who ponders these questions with peers because parents are not always able to be available to deal with them.

As the child grows older peers increasingly serve the same function, only the questions they ponder with each other change in terms of the content. The peer group can best be understood as a type of solidarity unit. It is the primary group in which the young girl can share her joys, fears, surprises and disappointments. It is her peers who can always be counted on to understand what it is that she is concerned with. Therefore, the peer group can be viewed for the preadolescent girl as having many integrative functions that help her to survive and understand life from day to day. It is in this context that the process of redefinition of one's roles and the discovery of the many exciting facets of one's young life take place.

Although there is much similarity between a preadolescent girl growing up in the Black community and one growing up in suburbia, because of the impact of the larger society, there are as demonstrated distinct differences between the way the child perceives the world in these two environments. All parents in American society attempt to control the lives of their children as much as possible. Unlike children in many other parts of the world, the American child is expected to be provided a "childhood" and kept from the exposure that is granted adults. This strong protectiveness shapes the child's perspective of his world. He basically views his immediate world as a friendly and protective one, or with suspicion and hostility, or a combination of both. For the Black child, whose parents are unable to provide the constant "surveillance" that is expected by the larger society, the world takes on a strong form of realism. So much of one's survival depends, to some extent, on how independent he can be and how much he can fend for himself when necessary. Children in the community are taught to be strong and not to allow others to take them for granted. Inherent in this attitude, although a very necessary one, is the assumption that if one allows his guards to fall too often, he can be taken advantage of. Suspicion and distrust frequently emanate from such a fear. This is not always the case, however, for many young children accept life in a more realistic manner but nevertheless are not particularly suspicious of every stranger who approaches them.

There is ample reason for even more hostility and suspicion of the unknown to abound than is present. If one considers the fact that children at ages four and five and older are expected to assume sometimes a major responsibility for their own care, such as finding food when there is none in the home, caring for younger siblings, doing major household chores, etc., it is startling that so little of the child's world is perceived as a hostile entity.

The negative experiences which Blacks in this kind of environment have encountered with society have fostered and perpetuated within them suspicion and hostility. This reaction to those individuals who reside outside their environment is often generalized and takes the form of prejudice and stereotyping. Thus, a sentiment which is conveyed is that all Caucasians are not to be trusted, for they are only capable of treating Blacks in an inhuman manner. As a result of such attitudes, self-defense mechanisms are deeply ingrained in children at very early ages. These young children are taught early in the home that they must learn to protect themselves against other children on the playground. For example, a mother can be observed berating her eight-year-old daughter for not "fighting back" on the playground. For them, the only reality which they know is that which they experience.

This is the area in which parents of these children, although often considered children themselves by racist whites, are able to attempt to reconcile the two worlds the child must learn to live in. Children are not only taught to be defensive but also to be positive and hopeful for bright futures. It is to the credit of these parents that they are able to make some projections that their children's lives will be better than theirs were. Thus, the child does not always exercise a "reflexive" defensive response to his encounters, but deals with them in a non-defensive manner. It is perhaps the hope that these parents hold in the future that allows the child to take a dual approach to his existence: (1) understand his role in the society as a *Black* person; and (2) be able to function in the dominant society.

NOTES

1. Philippe Aries, *Centuries of Childhood: A Social History of Family Life* (New York: Random House, 1962).
2. Booker T. Washington, *Up from Slavery* (New York: Bantam Books, Inc., 1963 edition), p. 18.
3. Taken from *Growing Up Black,* Jay David (ed.) (New York: Pocket Books edition, 1969), p. 95.
4. Robert Coles, *Children of Crisis* (New York: Little Brown, 1964), p. 322.
5. P. 319.
6. Allison Davis, *Social Class Influences upon Learning* (Cambridge: Harvard University Press, 1962).
7. Claude Brown, *Manchild in the Promised Land* (New American Library, Inc., 1966), p. 295.

PART 6
Sexuality

The sexuality of women has been the subject of evaluative appraisal, passionate rhetoric, and punitive attempts at control during most of the history of Western civilization. The expression of her sexuality was often viewed as the evidence of her goodness or badness as a person, her designation as asexual and virtuous or lustful and wicked. The dual functions of her body, reproductive and sexual, have caused her to be venerated as mother, on the one hand, and reviled as the seductress, agent of man's downfall, on the other. The true nature of female sexuality has historically eluded philosophers, priests, and scientists alike. The great majority of these commentators have been male, speaking from personal experience, rationalized bias, or staunch fanaticism, mostly quite unembarrassed either by the lack of empirical data or by validation from women themselves.

Beliefs about female sexuality have generally been of two kinds: that woman's lust is insatiable and dangerous to man; or, that she has little or no sex drive at all, being mostly the passive recipient of man's ardor, to which she submits in the service of her potential motherhood. The first of these was exemplified by the witch phobia which swept over Europe during the Middle Ages, causing millions of women to be tortured and put to death because of their suspected sexual liaison with the devil. The second was a modal belief during the Victorian era with its rigid codes of morality and decency which held physical passion to be immoral and unladylike. These two beliefs about female sexuality have coexisted quite comfortably in the minds of men, being incarnated respectively in the prostitute and the virtuous wife.

Scientific attention to sexual behavior is only a few decades old. The works of Alfred Kinsey, William Masters and Virginia Johnson, and others have greatly illuminated the area and have given impetus to its increasing acceptance as a legitimate target of scientific inquiry. The goal of science is knowledge, and the first step toward that goal is observation. Thus recent investigations have included such methods as interviews, questionnaires, and direct observation of sexual responses under controlled conditions. From all these have emerged a beginning of understanding of the impressive diversity and variability of female sexuality. Simple dichotomies and categorizations will not do. Explanations based solely on woman's biology or socialization are equally impoverished. New theories are appearing, out of increasing research attention. Much more is needed before we can begin to feel that we have sampled the range and the variety of female sexuality, its development, its course, and its many experiential qualities.

The first paper, "Women's Liberation and Human Sexual Relations," is concerned with issues of human sexuality which have been raised and examined by scholars whose perspective is illuminated by feminism. Patricia Spencer Faunce and Susan Phipps-Yonas begin with the observation that differences in the ways males and females are socialized in Western society have consequences for sexual behavior and for our experience of ourselves as sexual beings: males learn to be sexually active and nonromantic; and females learn to be nonsexual and romantic.

Feminist issues include male control of sexual relations, the double standard, myths and beliefs about female sexuality, recent research findings, and the "sexual revolution." The authors examine each of these for their meaning for women today. Their concept of the self-affirmed woman—one who functions in a partnership of equals—offers a model for both freedom and responsibility for oneself in the fully human relationship.

Etta Breit and Marilyn Ferrandino are counselors and educators in the areas of sexuality and women's health. Their article, "Social Dimensions of the Menstrual Taboo and the Effects on Female Sexuality," is concerned with the menstrual taboo, reflected in ancient myths as well as in contemporary research and education, and its affects on women's sexuality, attitudes, and behavior. Menstruation research has typically looked for correlatives between the menstrual cycle and behavioral events, for effects of the hormonal changes on mood states and behavior. Such effects are almost always hypothesized as negative, a reflection of old and deeply rooted beliefs that menstruation was bad, dirty, and defiling, and that the menstruating woman had the power to contaminate and to pollute. The authors explore common contemporary attitudes toward menstruation and show how they derogate and mystify this universal female function.

The relationship between attitudes toward menstruation and female sexuality is an intimate one. If menstruation is shameful and unclean, so are the genitals; if menstrual blood has evil power, so do the organs through which woman expresses her sexuality. Girls are admonished not to touch or look at their genitals. Thus are developed inhibitions, psychological barriers to the unfolding of sexuality.

Breit and Ferrandino present an educational model for the restructuring of attitudes and feelings of women students about menstruation and sexuality. With the theoretical background to encourage awareness of how we perceive our bodies and why, the techniques can be used by any woman or group of women to "demystify" our feminine functions, to bring us into psychical contact with our bodies, and to inspire us to celebrate who and how we are.

The last paper in this section is "The Realities of Lesbianism" by Del Martin and Phyllis Lyon. Defining a Lesbian simply as a woman who prefers another woman as a sexual partner, the authors procede to dispel the most common myths and misconceptions about Lesbianism: the Lesbians can be identified by their attempts to dress, look, and act like males (Lesbians in general are indistinguishable from other women); that Lesbians are psychologically disturbed because they are frustrating their "nature" by not having children (there are many ways in which women can work creatively; some Lesbians do have children, just as some heterosexual women do not); Lesbians frequently try to seduce heterosexual women (since the average Lesbian needs to conceal her sexual orientation, she does not typically approach a woman of whose sexuality she is unsure).

The authors describe in particular the problems faced by the woman who is trying to accept her Lesbianism, but has to deal with her own old attitudes, guilts, and values, as well as those of her family and of society. The young woman, especially, faces self-doubt and feelings of isolation as she strives to reconcile her sexuality with her still developing personal identity. Some come close to suicide, as did the 20-year-old who could not resolve the conflict between her Lesbianism and her Christian faith. The only difference between the sexuality of Lesbians and other women is in their choice of partner. This paper promotes understanding and acceptance of women who have suffered dual discrimination as women and as Lesbians.

The papers in this section are unified by their respect for female sexuality, its meanings, diversity, and importance within the contexts of women's lives. Variously regarded as unimportant, dangerous, uncontrollable, or nonexistent, the sexual life of women can now be viewed as a significant part of human behavior and as a legitimate area of inquiry and study. While this interest and openness which we see emerging at the present time is part of the general climate of greater freedom and permissiveness which grew out of the counterculture movement of the 1960s, the research itself, its content and style, partake of the women's movement as it gave women permission to be sexual persons and to investigate with respect and pleasure the phenomena of their own bodies.

Women's Liberation and Human Sexual Relations

Patricia Spencer Faunce
and Susan Phipps-Yonas

A number of issues in relation to human sexual relations are being pursued in the Women's Movement. Some of these issues and their background are explored: the definition of sex, male control of sexual relationships, sexual double standards, historical perspective and current research on female sexuality, and the Sexual Revolution.

What Is Sex?

Any consideration of sexual liberation must begin with the recognition that our Western culture has separated sex from other functions of our lives. As a result, some women and men repress and deny their sexual functioning throughout their lives. (1)

Interestingly, within our society, which misrepresents and derogates sex (as within all societies, even those which are more open and positive in this regard), sexuality has meaning far beyond physical activity. Transcending its biological origins, it is woven into many facets of our existence. While one's gender is typically (although not always) unequivocal at birth—"It's a beautiful girl!" or "It's a husky boy!"—and rarely subject to modification, this is not true cross-culturally for the roles ascribed to individuals on the basis of that physical female- or male-ness. Indeed, rather than being innate, most of the behavioral and psychological characteristics which are designated by a given social matrix as "feminine" and "masculine" are clearly learned. We are molded into "appropriate" female or male roles by our socialization as to what women and men "should" and "should not" do. The expectations that we face are overwhelmingly powerful. Despite the fact that there are few, if any, psychological sex differences, (2) the social definitions of femininity and masculinity have widespread acceptance; the stereotypes are actualized with little realization of the conditioning behind them. Social psychologists Sandra and Daryl Bem (3) have presented an in-

"Women's Liberation and Human Sexual Relations" by Patricia Faunce and Susan Phipps-Yonas from *International Journal of Women's Studies,* published by Eden Press Women's Publications, Montreal.

teresting discussion of this matter in an essay entitled "Case Study of a Non-Conscious Ideology: Training the Woman to Know Her Place."

The significant point here is that these differences in female and male socialization have major consequences for the sexual behaviors of both women and men. Not only are the interpersonal relationships between and within members of each sex affected (4) but their senses of themselves as sexual beings are influenced too. (5) In many ways the lessons taught each sex regarding sexuality and love are opposite and even contradictory. (6) Men, on the one hand, are taught to consider sexual activity as an important part of their masculinity. (7) Adolescent males often learn about sexuality in an atmosphere that encourages masturbation (and thus sexual self-sufficiency) and that fosters detachment in their relationships with female sexual partners (whom they are likely to view as sex objects). They are trained, in this way, to be sexually active but nonromantic; for them, love and sex are separable phenomena. (8)

Females, on the other hand, are socialized to be romantic and nonsexual. Typically, for them, love and sex are intimately related. Thus while they learn to display their sexuality, and to be seductive, they are not yet trained as to how to use their bodies for direct gratification. (9) This is demonstrated, in part, by the fact that masturbatory activity is less common among young (indeed among all age) females, (10) a point to be considered in greater detail momentarily.

Western culture has provided females with very mixed messages about their sexuality. They are, on the one hand "sexually passive, uninterested (the Virgin Mary Image)" and on the other "seductive, flirtatious (the wicked Eve tempting poor innocent Adam)." (11) Whether more or less sexual than men, the lesson either way is that women's sexuality is defined only in relation to that of men; and, parenthetically, either way biology is destiny. Each extreme of this dualistic view results in a comfortable position for men: if women are unmoved by sex they need not be satisfied; if they are unsatiable, they cannot be. Either way, the male is, sexually speaking, off the hook. (12)

Despite major differences in the views held by different social classes and ethnic groups about sexual morality, misconceptions of female and male sexuality remain surprisingly constant across the various segments of society. (13) Such misconceptions may be seen as evidence of the pervasiveness and rigidity of the stereotypes and ideals regarding femininity and masculinity. Furthermore, these misconceptions support one of the primary arguments to be made here, namely that sexual liberation and women's liberation are not one in the same. Indeed, although the two overlap, some of the most sexually liberated segments of society are the most sexist, and conversely some of the most sexually conservative groups are the most "liberated" in their attitudes about women. It should be remembered too that the influences of the women's movement and sexual revolution have not been experienced uniformly across social and ethnic classes.

Returning to the question "what is sex?", the fact that masturbatory activity is less common and frequent for females than for males should be considered. In an intriguing book entitled *Liberating Masturbation,* (14) Betty Dodson argues that the sexual oppression of women begins at the level of masturbation. She contends that in our society female genitals have economic rather than sexual value for women; masturbation is discouraged along with all other activities which seek to make females self-sufficient and independent. Sexual satisfaction which can be secured by a woman alone is clearly undesirable and counter productive in a world where her sexuality is supposed to be directed toward enticing men, serving their sexual needs, and reproducing children. Consequently, many women fail to appreciate the wonder of their own bodies.

In our culture, and especially for women, sexual meanings typically emerge from interaction between persons. To be most meaningful such sexuality requires a fusion of the physical and interpersonal. Such fusion can make sex a humanizing force in life, one that helps to create within individuals a sense of their wholeness.

A humanized view of sexuality recognizes that most human sexual activity does not have reproduction as its purpose, and that pleasure is not the only nor necessarily the major goal in interpersonal sex. In this way of thinking, sex is far more than performance; it is a means of communication and self-expression. Masters and Johnson (15) emphasize this point in their argument that sexual dysfunction often reflects an inability to experience one's sexuality as an expressive part of oneself.

Male Control of Sexual Relationships

As we have seen, however, the ways in which sex is used to express oneself are largely determined by social definitions of sex roles. And because males have held the power over the centuries, they have defined sexual roles and controlled sexual relationships. Today, in theory, sexual expression is determined by the desires of two consenting adults; in practice, men define sexual standards (in and out of the bedroom) and women conform. The male definition dictates that in sexual relationships men are active and dominant while women are passive and submissive, that men "do" while women are "done to." The traditional man-on-top position for intercourse standard found only in Western culture reflects this male definition. Feminists recognize that it is with this male definition of sexuality that women's oppression begins. That definition not only denies the possibility—and thus the validity—of female masturbation and homosexual activity (how can a passive being *do* anything?) but it is also the basic justification for sexual inequality in the distribution of political and economical power. Feminists have maintained (see Firestone (16) for an interesting discussion of this point), that no sexual equality can exist in the bedroom until there is sexual equality on the outside. (17) (Turning out the lights at night cannot hide the psychological consequences of daytime case differences; i.e. it is impossible for two persons who have unequal statuses in all other aspects of their lives to be "equals" in bed.)

The Sexual Double Standard

Male definition and control of female sexuality are clearly illustrated in the pervasiveness of the double standard which has been dominant throughout much of recorded human history. This pattern has included extreme measures to control female sexual behavior. (18) It begins, as Dodson suggests, (19) with attitudes about masturbation but extends to all kinds of sexual activity and relationships. Despite some recent weakening of the double standard as women have moved toward new sexual freedom it is clearly reflected by the American dating pattern (20) which still embodies the sexual ritual whereby the male tries to get all he can and the female teases him with her attempts to preserve her virtue. Most of the population still adheres to the double standard, and even those who have broken from the pattern have usually begun dating according to the standard and only later rejected it.

Feminine Virtue

The double standard implies that the world is divided into two classes of women: good women and bad women, virgins and nonvirgins, procreative women and pleasure-seeking women. Paradoxically, either aspects of the dualistic view of women as both more or less sexual than men can be used to explain (or justify) the standard. Both classes need the "protection" provided by the standard. If women are the virtuous sex and men are lacking in this regard, it can be argued that the ideal of feminine virtue lies at the heart of the double standard. In this case, responsibility for sexual restraint is placed on the female. The male is expected to be concerned with his needs and desires while the female is supposed to overcome her own, as she decides "How far shall I let him go?" One psychiatrist has analyzed the implications of feminine purity as reflecting the following male attitudes 'You, the woman, shall have no pleasure at all,' or 'I alone shall give you pleasure,' or 'I don't care whether you have pleasure or not,' or 'You shall give me pleasure and me alone.' (21) The measure is always male.

Also plausible is the idea that men created the double standard as a defense against their fears of female sexuality. If women are insatiable creatures, their sexuality would, of course, require external constraints, (or sexual chaos would reign), while more reasonable males could function more openly and freely. Such a view could explain the need to keep women ignorant about their sexuality as well.

Premarital and Extramarital Sex

Going far beyond constraints on masturbation, the double standard affects all sexual interaction. One aspect condones both premarital and extramarital sex for men while proscribing it for women. Indeed, premarital sex is thought to establish a man's masculinity and virility. A woman, on the other hand, must refrain from premarital sex to preserve her virtue. Similarly, a man is often allowed discreet extramarital sex if he carries on as usual within the family. The wife, however, is expected to be sexually faithful. (22) It has been noted that while a wife will look the other way when her husband cheats on her, a husband will bring his cheating wife in for counseling, expecting the counselor to persuade his wife to stop her infidelity. (23) Furthermore, during counseling a husband will often even be jealous and suspicious of a faithful wife, and, although he may deny it, he often resents her premarital affairs. Interestingly, it is the case that while men in counseling come from troubled and perhaps atypical marriages, the apprehensions they express about their spouses' fidelity seem no different from those voiced by men everywhere for many centuries. (24)

Initiative in Sexual Behavior

The double standard further dictates that men initiate sexual encounters. (25) A group of husbands interviewed about sexual relationships expressed almost unanimous distaste at the idea of their wives taking the sexual initiative. (26) Female initiative would seem to threaten male sexual control and supremacy and to lift the woman out of her role of sexual servant. After all, the woman's duty is to serve and satisfy the man. The man, however, has no obligation to bring his partner to orgasm; according to the male viewpoint, the woman's satisfaction should result from male ejaculation.

Perspective on Female Sexuality

Many of the early cultures about which we have information (e.g. Hebrew, Arab and Roman) viewed women as sexually insatiable. Her powerful sexuality had to be suppressed in order to provide for order and peacefulness. A passage from Ecclesiastes expresses this attitude: "Women are overcome by the spirit of fornication more than men and in their heart they plot against men." (27)

Thoughts (and rationalizations) change and by the 19th century the Victorians had exchanged this view of female sexuality for its converse. Believing that a woman's sex drive is far weaker than a man's, they felt no "decent" woman could ever enjoy sex. (28)

Freud challenged the Victorian view and in a sense rediscovered (as far as science and medicine were concerned, although women never "lost" their knowledge) women's capacity to enjoy sex and experience orgasm. Unfortunately, Freud found many women "frigid" and declared that they had emotional and psychological problems and were "sexually immature." He was vexed by the fact that those who could reach orgasm freely and quickly through masturbation did so less frequently during standard intercourse. Consequently, Freud postulated two kinds of female orgasm: clitoral and vaginal. The clitoral orgasm, attained by most women, but difficult to achieve in the standard male-gratifying positions, was defined as "adolescent." The vaginal orgasm was declared to be the only true, mature, womanly orgasm. It could occur only during intercourse through vaginal penetration by the penis. Since overwhelming numbers of women were not experiencing the "mature" orgasm, Freud concluded that most women, recognizing their inferiority to men, were loath to accept their femininity. For this dreadful condition he prescribed psychiatric assistance. (29)

Over the decades psychiatrists have treated scores of women with little success at having them "surrender to their destinies" by transferring their orgasms from clitoris to vagina. Generations of women, including the present one, grew up masturbating in secret and faking orgasms during intercourse.

Research on Female Sexuality

In the more recent decades, numerous studies of female sexuality have been conducted by such researchers as Kaplan, Kinsey, et al., Masters and Johnson, Sherfey and Fisher. (30) None of these studies has produced evidence in defense of the double-orgasm theory or any of the other myths regarding female sexuality. Some of the findings from the research on female sexuality are briefly described below:

1. The clitoris is the female analogue to the penis. It, rather than the vagina, is the chief female erogenous zone. Physiologically, there is no difference between so-called clitoral and vaginal orgasm. (31) Anatomically, all orgasms are centered in the clitoris, whether they result from direct manual pressure applied to the clitoris, from indirect pressure resulting from the thrusting of the penis during intercourse, or from generalized sexual stimulation of other erogenous zones such as the breasts.
2. The female sexual response, in terms of its physiological manifestations, is much like that of the male. (32) The female orgasm is as real and identifiable a physiological entity as the male's. It follows the same pattern of erection and detumescence.
3. Females have at least as strong a sex drive as males do if not stronger. (33) In the few cultures where women are allowed full sexual freedom they are as likely to be interested in and to initiate sex as men.
4. Women are multiorgasmic. The female is more capable of multiple orgasms within a defined time period than is the male. (34) That is, if a woman is immediately stimulated following orgasm, she is capable of experiencing several orgasms in rapid succession. This is not an exceptional occurrence, but one of which most women are capable.
5. While women's orgasms do not vary in kind, they vary in intensity. The most intense orgasms experienced by Masters and Johnson's research subjects were by masturbatory manual stimulation, followed in intensity by manual stimulation by the partner. The least intense orgasms were experienced during intercourse. Women are more likely to enjoy and desire an orgasm achieved through clitoral rather than vaginal stimulation.
6. No psychological or physiological differences have been found between readily orgasmic females and those who have less "orgasmic consistency." (35)
7. Masters and Johnson found no woman among all of their subjects who was totally or clinically frigid. (36) Although some females tend to have difficulties in reaching orgasm in heterosexual relationships, apparently most are readily orgasmic when (and if) they engage in masturbation or lesbian relationships. (37)
8. Contrary to much psychiatric theory, females who masturbate are *not* likely to have neurotic problems. In fact they may be more healthy than those who do not. The importance of masturbation for discovering one's own sexuality has been noted by Dodson. (38) Masters and Johnson (39)

observed that female masturbation tends to promote orgasmic response in intercourse. Fisher (40) found that married females who masturbate often do so because they are open to their own sexuality and the pleasure to be derived from it. While they find gratification in the sexual aspects of their marriages, they also enjoy self-stimulation.

The Sexual Revolution

The findings of Masters and Johnson and other researchers would seem to offer hope that women could acknowledge their capacity for sexual enjoyment and thus free themselves from Freudian distortions of their sexual nature. Similarly, the so-called Sexual Revolution should have freed women from the double standard, that other set of psychological bonds which kept them sexually intimidated. The harsh reality of the Sexual Revolution, however, has made it simply a variation on the old theme of exploitation. Instead of freeing women to enjoy their sexuality in a meaningful interpersonal context, it has meant that men continue to control female sexual behavior for male benefit. (41)

The Sexual Revolution has changed standards for a significant majority of our society so that women are no longer expected to remain virgins until they are married. It has freed women from Victorian morality which had dictated that no *nice* woman would ever "go all the way" with a man until marriage.

But, contrary to what many men (and more unfortunately some women) believe, the Sexual Revolution and Women's Liberation are not synonymous. The Sexual Revolution has simply made sex "cheaper" and more readily available to men, with little benefit, indeed perhaps some loss, to women. It has destroyed the sanctuary of maidenhood, pressuring women to give their bodies without respite from late adolescence to sold age, or until their desirability as sex objects has waned. For the first time, women have been shorn of all protection (patronizing as it may have been, and selective in terms of class privilege) and openly exhorted to prostitute themselves in the name of the New Morality.

Some women have come to see that the Sexual Revolution is merely a link in the chain of abuse laid on women throughout history. While purporting to restructure the unequal basis of sexual relationships between women and men, the male "liberators" were in fact continuing their control of female sexuality.

With the advent of the new feminism, women finally began to ask, "What's in it for us?" And the answer was simple. Women had been sold out. The Sexual Revolution was a battle fought by men for the great good of mankind. Womankind was left holding the double standard. Women are supposed to give, but what do they receive in return?

Kinsey's et al. *Sexual Behavior in the Human Female* (42) offered a priceless handbook for the Sexual Revolution in its findings that most women could and did enjoy sex after all; that there were very few frigid women, but many inept men; and that female virginity was no longer considered important or particularly desirable by most men.

What the popularizers of Kinsey's findings neglected to emphasize would have provided the seeds for a *real* revolution in the bedroom. Although the findings are there, the public still remains ignorant about the differences between orgasm and ejaculation, about the speed-of-response differential between female and male orgasm, about the fallacy of the vaginal-clitoral orgasm dichotomy, about women's multi-orgasmic nature, and so on.

The freedom of the Sexual Revolution has been at best a failure, at worst a hoax, because it has caused no significant changes in male attitudes and behavior to correspond with this new Morality forced upon so many women. No real revolution has occurred in the bedroom.

Now, if there was anything the Sexual Revolution should have been able to accomplish, especially with the data made available by Kinsey as early as 1953, it should have been more pleasure for women during intercourse. Yet twenty-four years later, many women have relatively infrequent satisfactory sexual relationships. Not many women are sleeping around for the sheer pleasure of it. (43)

As well as not having secured more pleasure or satisfaction for women, neither has the Sexual Revolution made it more acceptable for women to appear as initiators in sexual encounters. Where they do, they are either declassed as a group (prostitutes) or, like the "groupies" who offer themselves to popular singing stars, they are acting out an inferiority to the men they seek.

The proscriptions against female assertiveness extend not only to initiating a sexual encounter but also to directing activity once it has begun. One experienced sex therapist, Helen Singer Kaplan, (44) has remarked that not reaching orgasm with intercourse alone may be the most normal variant of female sexuality. Women must educate their partners as to what they need (if they are to secure satisfaction) but such directiveness is often frowned upon if not punished.

An even less obvious, but perhaps more important consequence of the Sexual Revolution, is the loss of a female's right to refuse the man's request on general grounds of morality or propriety. In the past, acceptance was seen as a personal sign of affection and favor, but refusal carried no stigma of personal rejection. This now has changed. Because it is now known that women enjoy sex as much as men, men may expect them to agree automatically to a request for sexual relations. The assumption that sex is enjoyable per se thus functions as a pressure on a woman to accept the advance of any date who approaches her, since a refusal will tend to be seen as a personal rejection. She will not be understood as making some general statement ("I don't much like having sex with a stranger") or simply heeding her own physical desires or lack of them. Rather, a refusal will be interpreted as meaning "I don't like *you,*" or "I don't find you sexually attractive." Thus, where it is perfectly possible for a woman to refuse an invitation, on the grounds that she would rather do something else, her refusal to take part in sexual activity is more likely to be misinterpreted. The woman's awareness of this situation means that the man's invitation now seems to contain an element of compulsion. The result is that while a man retains full choice in a sexual encounter since he can approach the woman or not as he chooses, the woman has not gained full freedom. In addition, her decision to take the disapproved choice (that is, to say "No") implicates her in an apparent disparagement of the man which is unpleasant at the time and may negatively influence the future of the relationship. (45)

It is important for us (and for interpreters of the psychology of women) to be aware of complications of this sort. The idea is widespread that current acceptance of female pleasure in sex frees women fully from this disabilities that haunted them in the past, but this is not so. One might say that the content of the female sexual role has changed, but the format has not. A study of recent publications addressed to the mass market indicates that, at this level of class and culture, initiative and dominance in sexual matters are still male prerogatives while the role of the female remains submissive and pleasing. She is structured to be seductive, sexually provocative, alert to her partner's desires rather than to her own, and always ready to accept his advances. This is as true in periodicals addressed to women (*The Cosmopolitan Love Guide*) as it is in those directed to men (*Playboy* and *Penthouse*). (46)

So the emphasis on the pleasing of men has continued. At one time women were chaste, because men wanted wives to be chaste. The Victorian concept of two kinds of women—whores and wives—was well integrated into American mores. To live up to the Victorian standard, women did not go to bed before marriage because *men wanted it that way.* (47)

Clearly, a basic divergence, indeed, a conflict, exists between the ideals of increased independence for women upheld by the Women's Movement and the realities of the Sexual Revolution as it has occurred. Until sexual freedom allows women the rights to initiate and to refuse sexual encounters as they choose (with the same rights allowed to men), and to demand satisfaction in those encounters, it cannot be equated with liberation. It is a mistake to imagine that the forces working for these two different ends are operating in tandem. The end of inhibition and the release of sexual energies thought to be the innovation of a revolutionary humanistic culture are now beginning to be seen as just another fraud for women.

After such events in the early 1970's as the gang-rapes at Altamont and Seattle, after such demands as those raised at People's Park for "Free Land, Free Dope, and Free Women," after the analyses of (male) rock-culture, women are beginning to realize that nothing new has happened at all. (48)

What we have is simply a new, more sophisticated (and thus more insidious) version of male sexual culture. Sexual freedom had meant more opportunity for men for easy sex, but this has not created a new kind of experience for women. Many people have fallen into the trap of equating going to bed with sexual freedom. (49)

Real sexual freedom for women would mean, of course, that one could chose to be celibate, to be monogamous, or to sleep with many men or women—because *she wanted it that way.* Women will be free sexually only when they can choose, when they have the right to respond (or not respond), and when they have the right to initiate. Sexual freedom also means the right-to-sexual-pleasure. (50)

The issue here is not the familiar one of chastity versus promiscuity but the impossibility of forming meaningful equal relationships with continued male domination and definition of roles for both sexes. Despite contradictory research, the myths regarding female sexuality remain and the

Sexual Revolution simply has confused matters by promising freedom that brings women little satisfaction.

The very divergent attitudes created and reinforced by these factors cheapen sex and make it an exploitative tool both in dating and marriage. The competitiveness and manipulativeness with which sex is often imbued present the worst possible condition for real sexual enjoyment.

We do have visions, however, of what life could be like in a truly liberated society, governed by androgynous ideals and populated with people who had real options. (51) New life styles are emerging, and one day perhaps alternatives will abound for both sexes. Feminist therapists, following leads from the consciousness raising/support group movement, already are, along with that movement, providing adaptive, positive, means of change. (52) The number of healthy role models is growing. Some women (and men) are beginning to define themselves in ways unconstrained by sex role stereotypes. Institutions are changing too, with an increasing acceptance, among at least a small minority of the population, of communal living arrangements, of non-monogamous relationships, of open marriages, of celibacy and so on. Finally, the relatively new field of sex counseling (53) is helping to redefine sexuality and to provide means for women to actualize the unfulfilled promise of sexual liberation. Working together with feminism, a real Sexual Revolution could liberate relationships in a previously unknowable manner. Both sexes have very much to gain and very little to lose.

> The self-affirmed woman is a woman who functions as an active member in a partnership of equals—a *total* interaction. That is, an interaction in which the intimacy of the relationship decrees that the woman is free to disagree; that implies that she is free to be active and passive, nurturing and receptive, playful and serious, productive and appreciative. It also implies the woman is free to be judging and loving. The self-affirmed woman is aggressive and constructive; she has survived her own experience.
>
> In a few words, a self-affirmed woman is a woman who:
>
> 1. Can enjoy her own body apart from others. "I have a primary sexual relationship to myself."
> 2. Can have sexual experiences for her own reasons.
> 3. Can experiment and experience.
> 4. Has her own standards and uses herself as the measure of her own experience.
>
> The self-affirmed woman understands the interpersonal issues found frequently in relationships that are sexual. She knows ways to negotiate, to fight, to settle, and to forgive. She knows when to leave relationships that are too costly. These decisions . . . are based on an energy conservation priority. Such a woman relates to other women on an affective and appreciative level. She is able to fully experience both women and men on intellectual and emotional levels as peers. (54)

Summary

In summary, some of the issues which are being pursued in the Women's Movement in relation to human sexual relations are the following:

1. *Pursuing a definition of sex* which emphasizes a humanized view of sexuality, that sex is one of many functions in our lives, that sex is something humans do alone or together to communicate and/or to express themselves. Sex must be lived, not performed.
2. *Doing away with sexual double-standards*-such as those which relate to: feminine virtue; who has the responsibility for preventing sexual intimacies and premarital and extramarital sexual experiences; who should take the initiative in sexual behavior; and service and satisfaction in sexual relations.
3. *Doing away with the myths surrounding female sexuality*—such as those which relate to the female sex drive, the female orgasm and female frigidity. Information available regarding female sexuality should be disseminated and incorporated into human sexual relationships.
4. *Understanding that the Sexual Revolution has often been in conflict with Women's Liberation,* and that the Sexual Revolution has done very little that is positive and much that is negative for women.
5. *Understanding that a true sexual revolution or real sexual freedom for women* would bring them such rights as the right of choice (the right to say no or yes), the right to initiate sexual encounters, and the right to sexual pleasure.

Masters and Johnson (55) have said Women's Liberation is the best thing that has happened to men in a thousand years. If and when we achieve equality of the sexes, that equality will be the very best thing that has happened to men; for when that occurs we will have a basis for *partnership* in all aspects of life including equal sexual expression of androgynous individuals.

NOTES

1. Boston Women's Health Book Collective, *Our Bodies, Our Selves* (New York: Simon and Schuster, 1976); William Masters and Virginia Johnson, Presentation at Symposium on Human Sexuality. Sponsored by Muskegon Health Department, Muskegon, Michigan, U.S.A., November 8–9, 1974.
2. Janet Saltzman Chafetz, *Masculine/Feminine or Human?* (Itasca: F.E. Peacock Publishers, 1974); Eleanor Emmors Maccoby and Carol Nagy Jacklin, *The Psychology of Sex Differences* (Stanford: Stanford University Press, 1974); Shirley Weitz, *Sex Roles* (New York: Oxford University Press, 1977); Juanita H. Williams, *Psychology of Women* (New York: W. W. Norton & Co., 1977).
3. Sandra Lipsitz Bem and Daryl J. Bem, in *Beliefs, Attitudes, and Human Affairs,* ed. Daryl J. Bem (Belmont: Brooks/Cole, 1970).
4. Boston Women's Health Book Collective, *Our Bodies, Our Selves,* 1976; Chafetz, *Masculine/Feminine or Human?* 1974; Lucile Duberman, *Gender and Sex in Society* (New York: Praeger, 1975); Clarice Stasz Stoll, "Female and Male," in *Socialization, Social Roles, and Social Structure* (Dubuque: William C. Brown Co., 1974).
5. Boston Women's Health Book Collective, *Our Bodies, Our Selves,* 1976; Carol Tavris and Carole Offir, *The Longest War* (New York: Harcourt Brace Jovanovich, 1977); Constantina Safilios-Rothschild, *Love, Sex, and Sex Roles* (Englewood Cliffs: Prentice-Hall, 1977).

6. Boston Women's Health Book Collective, *Our Bodies, Our Selves,* 1976; Duberman, *Gender and Sex in Society,* 1975.
7. Warren Farrell, *The Liberated Man/Beyond Masculinity: Freeing Men and Their Relationships with Women* (New York: Random House, 1974); Gene Marine, *A Male Guide to Women's Liberation* (New York: Holt, Rinehart, and Winston, 1972); Joseph H. Pleck and Jack J. Sawyer, ed. *Men and Masculinity* (Englewood Cliffs: Prentice-Hall, 1974).
8. Duberman *Gender and Sex in Society,* 1975.
9. Boston Women's Health Book Collective, *Our Bodies, Our Selves,* 1976; Duberman, *Gender and Sex in Society,* 1975.
10. Masters and Johnson, Presentation at Symposium on Human Sexuality, 1974.
11. Chafetz, *Masculine/Feminine or Human?* 1974.
12. Farrell, *The Liberated Man/Beyond Masculinity,* 1974; Marine, *A Male Guide to Women's Liberation,* 1972; Pleck and Sawyer, *Men and Masculinity,* 1974; Myron Brenton, *The American Male* (Greenwich, Fawcett Publication, 1966).
13. Boston Women's Health Book Collective, *Our Bodies, Our Selves,* 1976; Duberman, *Gender and Sex in Society,* 1975.
14. Betty Dodson, *Liberating Masturbation* (Available from Betty Dodson, Box 1933, New York, N.Y. 10001, 1972).
15. Masters and Johnson, Presentation at Symposium on Human Sexuality, 1974.
16. Shulamith Firestone, *The Dialectic of Sex* (New York: Bantam Books, 1970).
17. Safilios-Rothschild, *Love, Sex, and Sex Roles,* 1977.
18. Tavris and Offir, *The Longest War,* 1977; Farrell, *The Liberated Man/Beyond Masculinity,* 1974; Marine, *A Male Guide to Women's Liberation,* 1972; Pleck and Sawyer, *Men and Masculinity,* 1974; Brenton, *The American Male,* 1966.
19. Dodson, *Liberating Masturbation,* 1972.
20. Chafetz, *Masculine/Feminine or Human?* 1974; Safilios-Rothschild, *Love, Sex, and Sex Roles,* 1977.
21. Abram Kardiner, *Sex and Morality* (New York: The Bobbs-Merrill Co., 1954).
22. Helen Block Lewis, *Psychic War in Men and Women* (New York: New York University Press, 1977)
23. Brenton, *The American Male,* 1966; Lewis, *Psychic War in Men and Women,* 1977.
24. Brenton, *The American Male,* 1966; Lewis, *Psychic War in Men and Women,* 1977.
25. Lewis, *Psychic War in Men and Women,* 1977.
26. Brenton, *The American Male,* 1966.
27. G. Rattray Taylor, *Sex in History* (New York: Ballantine Books, 1954).
28. Williams, *Psychology of Women,* 1977; Tavris and Offir, *The Longest War,* 1977.
29. Anselma Dell-Olio, "The Sexual Revolution Wasn't Our War," in *The First Ms. Reader,* ed. Francine Kagsburn (New York: Warner Books, 1973), pp. 124–132.
30. Helen Singer Kaplan, *The New Sex Therapy* (New York: Brunner-Mazel, 1974); Alfred C. Kinsey, Wardell B. Pomeroy, Clyde E. Martin, and Paul H. Gebhard, *Sexual Behavior in the Human Female* (Philadelphia: W.B. Saunders, 1953); William Masters and Virginia Johnson, *Human Sexual Response* (Boston: Little, Brown, and Co., 1966); William Masters and Virginia Johnson, *Human Sexual Inadequacy* (Boston: Little, Brown, and Co., 1970); Mary Jane Sherfey, "The Evolution and Nature of Female Sexuality in Relation to Psychoanalytic Theory," *Journal of the American Psychoanalytic Association,* 14, 1 (1966), 28–128; Seymour Fisher, *The Female Orgasm* (New York: Basic Books, 1971).
31. Masters and Johnson, *Human Sexual Response,* 1966.
32. Masters and Johnson, *Human Sexual Response,* 1966; and *Human Sexual Inadequacy,* 1970.
33. Masters and Johnson, *Human Sexual Response,* 1966; and *Human Sexual Inadequacy, 1970;* Sherfey, "The Nature and Evolution of Female Sexuality," 1966.
34. Masters and Johnson, *Human Sexual Response,* 1966.
35. Williams, *Psychology of Women,* 1977; Safilios-Rothschild, *Love, Sex, and Sex Roles, 1977;* Fisher, *The Female Orgasm,* 1971.
36. Dell-Olio, "The Sexual Revolution Wasn't Our War"; Catherine S. Chilman, "Some Psychosocial Aspects of Female Sexuality," *The Family Coordinator,* 2, 23 (1974), 123–131.
37. Masters and Johnson, *Human Sexual Response,* 1966; and *Human Sexual Inadequacy,* 1977; Fisher, *The Female Orgasm,* 1971.
38. Dodson, *Liberating Masturbation,* 1972.
39. Masters and Johnson, *Human Sexual Inadequacy,* 1970.
40. Fisher, *The Female Orgasm,* 1971.

41. Karen De Crow, *The Young Woman's Guide to Liberation* (New York: Bobbs-Merrill Co., 1971).
42. Kinsey et al, *Sexual Behavior in the Human Female,* 1953.
43. De Crow, *The Young Woman's Guide to Liberation,* 1971.
44. Kaplan, *The New Sex Therapy,* 1974.
45. Safilios-Rothschild, *Love, Sex, and Sex Roles,* 1977.
46. Elizabeth Janeway, *Between Myth and Morning: Women Awakening* (New York: William Morrow & Co., 1974).
47. De Crow, *The Young Women's Guide to Liberation,* 1971.
48. Linda Phelps, "Death in the Spectacle: Female Sexual Alienation," *Liberation,* 16, 3 (1971), 23–27.
49. Safilios-Rothschild, *Love, Sex, and Sex Roles,* 1977; Lewis, *Psychic War in Men and Women,* 1977; De Crow, *The Young Women's Guide to Liberation,* 1971.
50. Safilios-Rothschild, *Love, Sex, and Sex Roles,* 1977.
51. Chafetz, *Masculine/Feminine or Human?* 1974; Constantina Safilios-Rothschild, *Women and Social Policy* (Englewood Cliffs: Prentice-Hall, 1974); Gayle Graham Yates, *What Women Want: The Ideas of the Movement* (Cambridge: Harvard University Press, 1975).
52. Anica Vesel Mander and Anne Kent Rush, *Feminism as Therapy* (New York: Random House, 1974); Jeanne Maracek, "Dimensions of Feminist Therapy," Unpublished paper, Swarthmore College, Swarthmore, Pennsylvania, n.d,; Dorothy Tennov, *Psychotherapy: The Hazardous Cure* (New York: Abelard-Schuman, 1975).
53. Lewis, *Psychic War in Men and Women,* 1977.
54. E.K. Childs, E.A. Sachnoff, and E.S. Stocker, "Women's Sexuality: A Feminist View," in *Female Psychology: The Emerging Self,* ed. Sue Cox (Chicago: Science Research Associates, 1976), pp. 309–310.
55. Masters and Johnson, Presentation at Symposium on Human Sexuality, 1974.

Social Dimensions of the Menstrual Taboo and the Effects on Female Sexuality

Etta Bender Breit
and Marilyn Myerson Ferrandino

As human beings, we are importantly sexual. That is to say, our sexuality has a metaphysical dimension, existing on a par with rationality and volition. Our sexuality is relatively emancipated from hormonal influences, and our high level of cortical activity leads to the varibility of sexual expression found through history.

As we examine the dynamic of human sexuality, we find that a curious ambiguity exists in the case of half the human species. In both our intellectual traditions and in the majority of our social institutions, women are synomymous with sex: they are defined through their genital organs, with the concomitant philosophy that, for females, "anatomy is destiny." Yet, female sexuality itself has been beyond the control of most women, in terms of practice (sexual repression; involuntary reproduction) and of theory. A provocative feature of human sexuality is the fact that, until quite recently, male specialists (psychologists, sexologists, gynecologists) have consistently analyzed female sexuality in terms of male sexuality. This process has included definition of organs (clitoris = miniature penis) definition of the sex act (vaginal intercourse), and definition of pleasure (pleasing the male partner). Although living in a male body, these specialists have constituted themselves as the authorities on the experience of those who live in a female body. Unsurprisingly, women have started questioning the presumed experts' corpus of knowledge, and have begun to look to women themselves for a re-evaluation and reconsideration of female sexuality.

From this search have emerged new perspectives on women's experiences with fantasy, masturbation, orgasm, and so on.[1] Our focus of attention in this essay is on that quintessential female experience, menstruation, and the effects of our contemporary menstrual taboo on female self-image and sexuality.

The phenomenon of menstruation has itself recently been the subject of new investigation.[2] The menstrual taboo can be used to explain the fact that traditional research focuses on negative aspects of the menstrual cycle (e.g., pre-menstrual tension, dysmenorrhea), and often takes recourse to the categories of hormonal determination and/or psychic disorder to explain these negative features. Two important concerns emerge—the lack of attention given to the cycle in its totality and its positive aspects (e.g., possible surge of well-being and self-esteem at ovulation), and the extent to which socially-derived stereotypic attitudes influence both experimenters and their subjects.

A partial review of the relevant literature on menstruation uncovers the unquestioned assumptions built into research design, and also, and very significantly, shows the emergence of a new research trend which seeks to question previous data and conclusions, and which seeks to establish a new conceptualization from which to investigate menstruation.[3]

Menstruation Research

One typical study on menstruation and personality presents the conclusion that there is a demonstrable relationship between psychological maladjustment and menstrual irregularity, and between psychological maladjustment and specific pre-menstrual and menstrual symptoms.[4] Another reported feature of menstrual irregularity is its association with neuroticism,[5] while women with menstrual flow of six days or longer are considered to be at the extreme feminine position in a model of masculinity-femininity. That is, they are basically submissive, anxious, self-pitying, shallow and unreflective thinkers, or, in the words of the researcher himself, ". . . the personality integration of the long-menstruation subjects relies on immature mechanisms in a variety of areas."[6] This association of femininity with socially undesirable characteristics, or as a deviance model, has been amply commented on elsewhere.[7] Although there may indeed be the occasional case of association between specific menstrual circumstances and psychological problems, the extrapolation and presentation of this as the main model to explain the variations of menstrual experience sets an unfortunate tone for research and speaks ill for a comprehensive psychology of women.

Work on the menstrual cycle by Dr. Katherine Dalton, a frequently cited expert,[8] provides tentative links between pre-menstruation and menstruation and higher incidence of poor examination performances, disciplinary offenses, crime, accidents, psychiatric hospital admissions. These combine to provide an all too familiar picture of women as unfit for responsible positions, and, further, presents the idea that woman's biology is, in and of itself, a liability. In a recent article, Barbara Sommer provides a comprehensive critique of Dalton's methodology and conclusions.[9] Sommer points our that studies which utilize objective performance measures generally fail to demonstrate the suggested menstrual cycle related changes and she offers the view that socially-mediated expectations are to be considered as a possible basis for previous findings. Again, a critical review uncovers implicit assumptions and biases built into research.

The magnitude of emphasis on occurrence of premenstrual symptoms has also recently come under scrutiny. Golub reports that, while anxiety and depression are higher during the premenstrum than during the intermenstrual phase, these changes are, on the average, small, and to be sharply differentiated from psychiatric illness or reactions to unusual stress.[10] Persky's findings substantiate this idea, by indicating that there is little change in such negative moods as anxiety, depression, hostility across the menstrual cycle. Further, the average values for the psychological variables obtained from Persky's subjects closely resembled those obtained from male classmates.[11] In a study comparing men, women taking oral contraceptives, and women non-pill-users, Schrader found that stressful events accounted for more of the variance for the negative mood factors than did menstrual cycle phase.[12] Sommer, in turn, on the basis of a recent study, presents the perspective that self-reported negative affect remained at a low level throughout the subjects' menstrual cycles, while positive affect showed a cyclic variation with a peak at midcycle. As Sommer states, "It is not necessary to conceptualize the menstrual cycle fluctuation as expressing a nadir in mood around the time of menstruation. These data suggest a conceptualization of a menstrual-cycle zenith achieved midcycle—an extra boost in positive mood."[13]

It appears important that the social expectations in regard to menstrual disabilities must be scrutinized for their effect on both women's self-perceptions and experience and on researchers' postulates. One finding that is of significant concern in this regard is the report of Levitt and Lubin that menstrual attitude is related to menstrual complaints.[14] These researchers indicate that subjects with the most unfavorable attitudes toward menstruation from the mental hygiene point of view also tend to have more frequent and more intense menstrual complaints. Certainly, one crucial factor in the etiology of menstrual symptoms is the woman's own system of beliefs about her "condition." As we shall elaborate below, the internalization of the menstrual taboo facilitates the assumption of negative attitudes.[15] At this juncture, we will cite two examples of the effect of negative assumptions.

The Moos' Menstrual Distress Questionnaire (MDQ) is, at the moment, probably the best developed instrument available for measuring menstrual distress. However, the MDQ has recently been criticized for methodological problems and from the consideration of the prevalence of stereotypic responses to the questionnaire.[16] Interestingly, while the MDQ includes feelings of well-being in one of its categories, the predominant focus is on negative factors, while there are no questions about sexual feelings, fantasy, or activity. The conspicuous absence of a Menstrual Satisfaction Questionnaire is to be noted.

Further evidence of the effects of the prevalence of negative attitudes toward menstruation is demonstrated in an article by Rani and Gary Koeske.[17] Following the supposition that social conditioning factors play a large role in menstrual cycle mood swings, these researchers conducted a study, the results of which supported their hypothesis that subjects would judge biology as an important factor in explaining negative (but not positive) moods occurring premenstrually but unimportant for postmenstrual moods. From these data, they draw two important conclusions. First, that the same "hypothesis" about biology and negative moods is accepted by both subjects and experimenters thus resulting in a confound in the design of scores of traditional research studies. Secondly, the role played by this attribution pattern in causing premenstrual tension is to be considered. They present the idea that acceptance of this attribution pattern may adversely affect women's self-esteem, and that women's belief in the biological explanation of premenstrual tension might make action to seek relief more unlikely. They continue, "As part of a complex attributional chain involving biology, behavior, and self-concept, this belief may represent one of the more significant aspects of socialization on female personality and deserves explicit consideration in future research."[18]

The focus on the negative in traditional research tends to obscure emphasis on remedial measures. Premenstrual tension has been shown to be affected or even regulated by dietary changes, e.g., increase in calcium consumption, reduction of salt intake.[19] Given the inadequacies of the typical American diet, there is a need to explore further the relationship between nutrition, nutritional therapy, and premenstrual tension and dysmenorrhea. It has also been shown that orgasm (e.g., by masturbation) can provide relief from menstrual cramps.[20] Other important avenues of research would be more investigation of men's hormonal cycles and mood swings for cross-sex comparison, in addition to much more extensive intrasex research to establish the actual variations of menstrual cycle regularity, duration of flow, cyclicity of emotions and sexual feelings, synchronicity, etc.

A different sort of problem in regard to research on menstruation is described by Sommer. She points out that there exists a publication bias which tends to exclude studies with negative results (e.g., no effect of menstrual cycle phase on performance), with the corollaries of a biased description of the phenomena as well as the discouragement of continued research in this area with its extensive social implications.[21]

As we have seen in the work of Sommer and the Koeskes,[22] e.g., it is high time to explore the reconceptualization of the menstruation process. While we are not rejecting an association between hormonal influences and mood, what we are calling into question is the total identification of the two, with the attendant dismissal of sociocultural factors.

Theories of biological determinism applied to human beings, that is, the reduction of human behavior to purely biological conditions, eventuates in a one-dimensional world which bears little resemblance to the human enterprise as we know it. With respect to the menstrual cycle, we posit that it is not the case that hormones *determine* emotions and/or behavior, nor is it true that hormones are totally irrelevant. Rather, we see emotions, behavior, patterns of sexual sensation and arousal as affected and influenced by hormonal levels as only *one* factor in a coalescence. The error comes in thinking of human behavior as being wholly actuated and determined by physiological states. As humans, we are biocultural things. While the two factors of biology and culture can be seen as formally distinct, their interaction and the resulting holistic process must be analyzed in terms of concepts that cut across the organic and the social.[23] Human behavior is plastic, flexible, educable, and modifiable. Hormones do influence us, set possible tendencies and directions; what is crucial is how we *choose* to deal with these effects. This choice presupposes awareness and knowledge. Hence we can see the importance of knowledge and positive attitudes about menstruation.

It is now time to look at the important determinant of menstrual attitudes—the menstrual taboo.

Menstrual Taboo

George is visiting.
My friend is here.
Falling off the roof.
On the rag.
Sick time
The curse.
Period.

These expressions are our society's ways of referring to menstruation. These phrases reflect some common attitudes toward this bodily process—that is—negativity, avoidance, and denial. As women, we have been socialized to, at best, tolerate menstruation and, at worst, to resent it. In past ages various cultures and societies have treated menstruating women as unhealthy or unclean outcasts. Although we no longer visibly practice similar rituals, there still exists in our current American culture a taboo on menstruation.

Not only are euphemisms used to disguise the fact that women menstruate, but it is also the case that menstruation-related products help to conceal and misrepresent this process. For example, flower symbols are a common theme in the packaging of tampons and napkins; a theme which is far removed from the reality of bleeding. This theme represents implied menstrual/genital shame as opposed to the Dodsonian flower theme used in celebration of women's genitals. Furthermore, the imagery in advertisements for these products reinforces the belief that menstruation is something secretive. For example, pictures of women in white, confirmation-like dresses, and ads which proclaim "no smells, no bulges" add to our fears that someone will know when we are menstruating. This masquerade exemplifies another way in which we as women are taught to reject an integral part of ourselves and our functioning.

Don't go swimming.
Don't wash your hair.
Don't go barefoot.
Don't get a permanent.
Don't get a tooth filled.
Don't have sex.
Don't play sports.

These beliefs, which are in common circulation, tend to inhibit our behavior and prevent us from experiencing menstruation as a normal bodily function. In addition to these beliefs, some usual attitudes are:

Menstruation is God's punishment.
Menstruation is dirty.
Menstruation is a disease.
A menstruating woman is messy, smelly, and crabby.

Taken together, the effects of this cultural thinking about menstruation breed negativity toward ourselves as women.

Another manifestation of the menstrual taboo is the inadequacy of our preparation of menstruation, which results in the menarche (the onset of menses) being cloaked in superstition and ignorance. The main subject of the films we are shown in school centers around cartoon characters or a depersonalized uterus—in either case, it is difficult for the young woman to identify with the on-screen presentation or to be realistically informed about her experience. And certainly there is no basis from which she can view menarche as a positive or joyful event.

Menstruation Education

A sampling of the sex and health education literature reveals a multifaceted impact on the developing girl's body/sexual self-concept. The following implicit dimensions are illustrated by quotes from currently available materials used to present the organization of puberty to a variety of ages.

The first dimension is the insipid negative attitude concerning the menarche itself. While most authors attest to the extreme biological significance of this secondary sex characteristic, menstruation is viewed as non-positive:

> But you'll get used to those few inconvenient days each month, even though they may sometimes make you a little depressed and grouchy. There's no getting away from the fact that periods are more of a chore than a pleasure.[24]

and something to be hidden:

> Don't worry that someone will know that you are having your period, and hesitate to make dates. The only clue an outsider has is your own attitude. . . . If you accept your period as a perfectly normal part of your existence, no one is going to notice at all.[25]

The second dimension involves the differential treatment of girls and boys when authors describe pubescent body changes and awakening sexuality. For boys, major emphasis is placed on the penis becoming thicker and longer, an increase in muscle hardening and strength, and broadening of the shoulders. The cocksman machismo image begins without solace of intrasex variabilities. For girls, emphasis on breast and nipple enlargement and hip broadening begin the objectification of woman as sex symbol. Although it is a fact that estrogen also causes accelerated growth of the external genitals at puberty, including enlargement of the labia and associated structures, and that the clitoris enlarges under the stimulation of androgen from the adrenal glands,[26] these changes are negated behind the descriptions of the facade of pubic hair growth and menstruation, which popularly and inadequately characterizes secondary genital growth in girls.

Concerning the adolescent's new found sexuality, boys are acknowledged and given more permission to be genitally sexual than are girls. When girl's sexuality is recognized, it is with inequality, reservation, or in male defined terms:

> Many boys enjoy rubbing or stimulating their penis because it is pleasurable. This is called masturbation. This sometimes causes the release of semen (the ejaculation) which is also pleasurable. Some girls stimulate themselves sexually, (also called masturbation) but unlike boys, no fluid is released from the genitals.[27]

Also girls may be relegated to parenthetical phrases after a full page description of a boy's wet dream:

> (Girls, *incidentally* have fewer wet dreams and many have none at all. . . .)[28]

The clitoris may be omitted completely from the text or diagram,[29] may be relegated to a parenthetical phrase,[30] or may be discriminatorily described. (It is unheard of for a modern author to treat the penis in any of these ways.)

> When a man is sexually aroused, the spongy tissue of his penis fills with blood. Instead of being limp as in its usual state, it grows firm and erect, increasing both in length and circumference. The erect penis stands up and out from the body. . . .
>
> Where the inner labia meet at the top is the sensitive clitoris, a small projection of normally soft tissue that enlarges and becomes erect when the woman is sexually excited.[31]

The third dimension is the "anatomy is destiny" attitude concerning gender role socialization and the menarche as portrayed by most authors. The preadolescent social scripting for motherhood now dawns a potential reality due to the onset of menstruation. The capacity for motherhood is glorified and the innate desire to be a mother is assumed:

> Motherhood is a natural desire of girls. Since menstruation makes motherhood possible you should think of it as a good and healthy bodily function—just as growth itself is good, just as loving and marrying are good.[32]
>
> You're a girl, and you are getting ready for the special role of childbearing. Like every other woman in the world, this is what your body was planned for.[33]

The beauty of the sexual system and menstruation is irrelevant until the script is fulfilled as in this passage:

> The female reproductive system is a complex and intricate system. When the time comes for it to perform its ultimate roles—the prenatal protection and nourishment of the child, and childbirth—you will have a greater appreciation of its functions.[34]

The final dimension reflects the diverging psychosexual development for girls and boys, a component of which is the formation of the asexual female. The menarche has made the pubescent girl vulnerable to impregnation. The existence of the out-of-wedlock intercourse and pregnancy taboos necessitates that the girl disavow or fear her emerging sexual feelings and guard herself from the faceless enemy of passion. The girl must deny her sexuality as a power within and for herself, and instead, use her externally defined sexuality to fulfill her gender role training. The ambiguity of the controlled chase is illustrated by these two passages:

> The teen years are the perfect time for learing to be a woman . . . for turning from dolls and sandlot ball games to the feminine skills of cooking and sewing and prettying yourself (for this too is a feminine art). It's the time to practice the feminine role of the woman pursued by a man—by your first dating experiences, by practicing your newly discovered womanliness on boys your own age.[35]

however,

> it is important to acknowledge that you, as a young woman, have a very special responsibility to the young men in your life. Male sexual feelings are aroused, in general, much more quickly and easily than your own. A sweater that seems merely fashionable to you may appear sexually provocative to your date. The necking that you consider as little more than friendly communication may stimulate him to physical passion. Obviously, the best way to cope with this unwanted state of affairs is to avoid setting the stage for it or irresponsibly provoking it. Turn off the heat long, long before your date reaches the boiling point.[36]

In summation, one can see patterns emerge from a sampling of popular education materials. The menstrual taboo breeds insidious negativity into the pubescent girl's genital self-image. The menarche may be the girl's first awareness of her genitals. However, no recognition or glorification of the growth of the labia and clitoris is evident. Instead the hallmark of genital puberty for the girl is only to grow hair and bleed. Her genitals are now called cursed, and what flows from them causes inconvenience and is to be endured. A girl is warned to harness her sexual feelings instead of giving free reign to the acknowledgment of her sexuality, a sexuality made positive and powerful by her being adequately informed and having a working knowledge and appreciation of her body. She needs the power of knowledge[37] in order to be in control and make mature, responsible decisions concerning her sexuality. Ignorance is not bliss, but only engenders fear and mystery. This secrecy of the unknown combined with an externally defined value system concerning the acceptability of the girl's body (i.e., when she's attractive and not bleeding) leads to alienation from "the body sexual." How ironic that a woman must be diagnosed as sexually dysfunctional before she is ever given permission to tactually and visually explore her genitals in order to become the authority on her sexual functioning. An adolescent girl should be given the same privilege.

Menstruation and Sexuality

We have noted above the emergence of new perspectives and new directions in research on menstruation. A crucial dimension which is still in the pioneering stages is an exploration of the effects of the menstrual taboo on women's self-image and sexuality, which are important both in and of themselves and as social factors which control women.

As long as menstruation is considered unclean and to be hidden, so are women's genitals unclean; if menstruation is feared or considered unattractive, so are women's sexual organs. This prejudice by association is further enhanced by the cultural taboo on sex during menstruation.[38] A comment about contraceptive methods is relevant at this point. The popularity of birth control pills and I.U.D.'s stems mainly from their relative effectiveness and convenience. However, it is also important to note that these methods are disassociated from the heterosexual experience itself. Use of a diaphragm[39] means that a woman must be familiar with her body, must touch her genitals, and take responsibility—activities that women are socialized away from.[40]

The menstrual taboo reinforces our lack of knowledge; this ignorance leads to fear and shame. It is also the case that we lack systematic knowledge about connections between menstruation and sexuality, and the relationship between the menstrual cycle and a possible sexual cycle, e.g., increased sexual feelings at ovulation and/or premenstrually.

Relearning

Given our socialization process, how then can girls and women learn to perceive and reclaim menstruation as a positive event? In our experience as counselors and educators, we have become acutely aware of the destructive effects of the menstrual taboo. We have utilized our women's health classes as a forum to explore these issues, and, as a result of this work, we have devised teaching models to reframe learning. What follows is a discussion of what and how we teach.

We have found that not only the specific material presented, but also the manner in which we present it, both significantly affect what the woman student learns. Combining a feminist political consciousness with a working knowledge of our bodies, part of our teaching involves modeling of behavior that we would like our students to consider adopting for themselves. Given this situation, even though the age range of the students has varied from seventeen through fifty, there is a common bond of identification as women. Thus our own attitudes toward menstruation become an important factor in the teaching situation. Because we have developed a comfort level with our own bodies, we are able to be self-disclosing and to set a permission-giving tone for the students. The idea and the reality of a group of women seriously and nonjudgmentally discussing menstruation, both theoretical issues and from their own experience, is in itself quite innovative. This protective structure is necessary as a foundation on which all subsequent learning takes place.

The specific material we cover begins with a presentation of historical and crosscultural perspectives on menstruation, and an analysis of the contemporary menstrual taboo. Once the women have gained an understanding of the culture-bound negativity toward menstruation, it is highly appropriate to introduce material and methods intended to increase awareness of how we have internalized harmful attitudes, how these have affected us, and how to then relearn and restructure our experience.

With the aim in mind of creating positive attitudes, we have devised several tools and techniques which we describe and demonstrate in class for the students to utilize for themselves. The following exemplify such learning experiences.

"Puberty Revisited"—In this exercise, the students draw themselves at puberty, in whatever art form they choose, labelling parts and feelings they associate with that time, and with special emphasis on the menarche.

"Celebration Menstruation"—The students bring to class their favorite products relating to menstruation (e.g., tampons, napkins, medications, vibrators) and discuss how and why they use these products and their feelings about them. In addition, each woman who is menstruating that day receives a small red star to paste on her forehead, thereby acknowledging the fact that she is a woman and that she feels good about menstruating.

"Menstrual Chart"—The students are instructed to keep a daily record of observations of the following items: 1) basal body temperature; 2) complexion; 3) weight; 4) feeling of bloatedness; 5) energy level; 6) emotional state (e.g., moodiness, feelings of well-being); 7) appetite; 8) sex drive; 9) characteristics of vaginal environment (e.g., pH, sugar, amount and type of secretions).

"Sex History/Herstory"—The students are asked to write a sexual autobiography discussing any or all aspects of their sexual upbringing and sexual attitudes/beliefs/values formation.

"Sexuality-Raising Group"—Members of the class form themselves into small groups, meeting in weekly sessions outside of class, choosing subjects that pertain to sexuality, e.g., menstruation, masturbation. Each woman relates her feelings about and/or experiences around the topic, in a nonjudgmental, supportive atmosphere. The women are encouraged to draw generalizations when and as appropriate, to further develop their understanding of the socially-conditioned dimensions of our sexuality.

This range of techniques serves to facilitate the process of the woman reowning her body, which consequently overcomes the alienating effects of the menstrual taboo. Thus, through providing basic educational information and structuring an atmosphere in which to share personal information, the women gain self-awareness and potency.

At this point, it is instructive to present the results of a pilot study which utilized the students in this course as subjects. Pre- and post-questionnaires were administered during the first and last classes. The instrument was designed to test for attitudes and experiences about menstruation; body self-image; and attitudes about sexuality. The results of the first (pre-) questionnaire showed that, in general, our sample (n = 66) had high ratings on the body-awareness scale. Most of these students had previously taken the Human Sexual Behavior class and/or other courses offered in our women's studies program, thus this was an expected result. The women's scores on the menstruation scale, however, told a different story—over 80% of the subjects had low ratings, i.e., had answered negatively for over half the items. This finding fits in with previous research, for example, Paula Weideger found that 69% of her respondents, all readers or friends of readers of *Ms.* magazine, would prefer to not menstruate, if they could still retain fertility.[41]

Our pilot study also uncovered a significantly high correlation between attitudes about menstruation and attitudes toward sexuality. Those women with the highest (lowest) scores on the sexuality scale also had the highest (lowest) scores on the menstrual scale. This would seem to be empirical evidence to support the major points raised in the above discussion about menstruation and sexuality, and offers fruitful direction for more extensive research.

The most exciting study result, from a personal perspective, was the change in menstruation scores from pre- to post-questionnaire. We interpret these results to mean that attitudes about menstruation can be changed through the process of education. Positive attitudes about menstruation were reinforced through class discussion and the ceremony of the red star, which was performed at the beginning of every class, so that each woman had the opportunity to participate at least once. We believe that the role-modeling of the teachers, who each spoke of her own experiences and also wore a red star when appropriate, was a further reinforcement factor.

We would like to add some reflections, at this point, on the potential epistemological functions of women's biology and sexuality. It can be hypothesized that a woman's body provides her with various built-in modes of expression for a range of emotions. The argument has even been advanced that women's biological cyclicity can facilitate various cognitive experiences. That is, if a woman is in touch with her processes, her awareness and self-knowledge can provide a base for integration and creativity. The events in a women's life-cycle-menarche, menstrual cycle, pregnancy, childbirth, postpartum, lactation, menopause—can serve as formative learning experiences, as occasions for growth. A fruitful model from which to perceive these processes is that of the maturation crisis, an "intrinsically psychosomatic developmental step,"[42] in which biological changes are accompanied by psychological disequilibrium, which, when resolved, results in emotional growth. The bodily and emotional changes are interdependent, and equally responsible for the successful resolution of the developmental step.[43]

This successful resolution and potential for growth also depends on the cultural context in which the woman learns about these vital experiences. Hence the menstrual taboo, all the more powerful in its nonovert articulation, can have pernicious effects on the women's ability to integrate the menarche and menses. Elimination of the taboo and its replacement with celebratory puberty rites and positive perception of menstruation are thus important as preventative mental health measures.

One of our ultimate goals is to facilitate the process of full acceptance, understanding, and appreciation of one's body and sexuality in all its modes of functioning and expression. And, further, to integrate sexuality—an essential dimension of human existence-into the total life process. The proper education about menstruation plays an essential role in reaching this end.

Political Implications

Contemporary analyses of the mechanisms which perpetuate women's oppression usually revolve around economic structures and the institution of the nuclear family. To these explanations must be added the category of sexuality. Ti-Grace Atkinson speaks of "the institution of sexual intercourse,"[44] but we must not stop here. The whole panoply of myths and distortions which alienate women from positive sexuality, and which thus enhance our powerlessness, must be overturned. Our estrangement from ourselves limits our sexual relationships with ourselves and with others, and consigns us to dependence on others for our orgasms and for our sexual fulfillment (as receptacles).

This dependence renders us vulnerable to all sorts of manipulation and deteriorates our ability to be self-actualizing. This gestalt can be viewed in the light of Reich's analysis of sexuality: repression and alienation prepare the groundwork for our submission to (external) authority.[45] An important link in this process is women's weakened sense of identity and concomitant powerlessness, the corollary features of "depressed" female sexuality. Thus, women's sexual alienation can be seen as one of the main underpinnings of patriarchal social relations.

While we cannot totally recast the current concept of sexuality within the framework of our present social structure, neither can we effect change in our society until we transform our alienation into self-knowledge and potency. The educational methods presented within the theoretical framework of this article thus function as correctives to sociocultural programming, to be ultimately integrated with institutional change.

NOTES

1. See, for example, Nancy Friday, *My Secret Garden: Women's Sexual Fantasies* (New York: Simon & Schuster, 1973); Betty Dodson, *Liberating Masturbation.* (New York: Bodysex Designs, 1974); Lonnie Garfield Barbach, *For Yourself: The Fulfillment of Female Sexuality* (Garden City, New York: Anchor, 1976); Shere Hite, *The Hite Report* (New York: Dell, 1976).
2. See Paula Weideger, *Menstruation and Menopause: The Physiology & Psychology, The Myth and the Reality* (New York: Knopf, 1976).
3. See, for example, Karen E. Paige, "Women Learn to Sing the Menstrual Blues" in James Leslie McCary and Donna R. Copeland, eds., *Modern Views of Human Sexual Behavior* (Chicago; Science Research Associates, 1976); Paula Weideger, *op. cit.;* Barbara Sommer, "The Effect of Menstruation on Cognitive and Perceptual-Motor Behavior: A Review" in *Psychosomatic Medicien* (vol. 35, no. 6, 1973); Barbara Sommer, "Mood and the Menstrual Cycle," presented at the Eighty-Third Annual Convention of the American Psychological Association, Chicago, Illinois, August, 1975; Randi K. and Gary F. Koeske, "An Attributional Approach to Moods and the Menstrual Cycle" in *Journal of Personality and Social Psychology* (vol. 31, no. 3; 1975).
4. Jack D. Hain, Patrick H. Linton, Herbert W. Eber, and Melinda Musgrove Chapman, "Menstrual Irregularity, Symptoms and Personality in *Journal of Psychosomatic Research* (vol. 14; 1970).
5. N. Kessel and A. Coppen, "The Prevalence of Common Menstrual Symptoms" in *Lancet* (ii, 61; 1963), as cited in Hain, *et al, op. cit.*
6. Harvey Peskin, "The Duration of Normal Menses as a Psychosomatic Phenomenon" in *Psychosomatic Medicine* (vol. xxx, no. 4; 1968).
7. See Juanita H. Williams, "Femininity: A Deviancy Modeal of Normal Personality" in Juanita H. Williams, ed., *Interpretations of Woman: Readings in Psychology* (Lexington, Mass: Xerox, 1974) and Broverman, I.K., Broverman, D.M., Clarkson, F.E., Rosenkranz, P. S., and Vogel, S., "Sex-role Stereotypes and Clinical Judgment of Mental Health" in *Journal of Consulting and Clinical Psychology* (vol. 34; 1970).
8. Katherina Dalton's book, *The Menstrual Cycle* (New York: Pantheon, 1969), is considered

to be an excellent source by the Boston Women's Health Book Collective, authors of *Our Bodies, Our Selves* (New York: Simon and Schuster, 1976), p. 35.

9. Sommer (1973), *op. cit.*
10. Sharon Golub, "The Magnitude of Premenstrual Anxiety and Depression" in *Psychosomatic Medicine* (vol. 38, no. 1; 1976).
11. Harold Persky, "Reproductive Hormones, Moods, and the Menstrual cycle" in Richard C. Friedman, M.D., Ralph M. Richart, M.D., Raymond L. Vande Wiele, M.D., eds., *Sex Differences in Behavior* (New York: Wiley Interscience Division, 1969), p. 464.
12. Susan L. Schrader, Linda A. Wilcoxon and Carolyn W. Sherif, "Daily Self Reports on Activities, Life Events, Moods, and Somatic Changes during the Menstrual Cycle," presented at the Eighty-Third Annual Convention of the American Psychological Association, Chicago, Illinois, August, 1975.
13. Sommer (1975), *op. cit.*
14. Eugene E. Levitt and Bernard Lubin, "Some Personality Factors Associated with Menstrual Complaints and Menstrual Attitude" in *Journal of Psychosomatic Research* (vol. 11, 1967).
15. *Cf.* Paige, *op. cit.*
16. See Parlee,.M.B., "Stereotypic Beliefs about Menstruation: A Methodological Note on the Moos Menstrual Distress Questionnaire and Some New Data" in *Psychosomatic Medicine* (vol. 36; 1974), as cited in Golub *op. cit.*, and Glen H. Gruba and Michael Rohrbaugh, "MMPI Correlates of Menstrual Distress" in *Psychosomatic Medicine* (vol. 37, no. 3; 1975).
17. Koeske and Koeske, *op. cit.*
18. *Ibid.*, p. 478.
19. See, for example, Adelle Davis, *Let's Eat Right to Keep Fit* (New York: New American Library, 1970).
20. See The Boston Women's Health Book Collective, *op. cit.*, p. 36.
21. Sommer (1973), *op. cit.*, pp. 531–532.
22. *Cf.* Paige, *op. cit.;* Weideger, op. cit.
23. See Marilyn Myerson Ferrandino, *Patriarchy and Biological Necessity: A Feminist Critique* (unpublished doctoral dissertation, State University of New York at Buffalo, 1977), especially chapter IV.
24. Peter Mayle, "What's Happening to Me?" (Secaucus, New Jersey: Lyle Stuart, 1975), n.p.
25. Mary McGee Williams and Irene Kane. *On Becoming A Woman* (New York: Dell, 1969), p. 25.
26. Herant A. Katchadourian and Donald T. Lunde, *Fundamentals of Human Sexuality* (New York: Holt, Reinhart, and Winston, 1972), p. 85.
27. Sol Gordon, *Facts About Sex for Exceptional Youth* (Plainview, New York: Printing House of Charles Brown, 1969), pp. 16, 25. Note that explicit instructions on what and how to stimulate are missing for the girl. Also, in the author's comparison of girls' process to boys', girls are once again found to be lacking.
28. Mayle, *op. cit;* emphasis added.
29. Evelyn Millis Duvall, *Love and the Facts of Life* (New York: Associated press, 1969), p. 96
30. Mayle, *op. cit.*
31. Benjamin F. Miller, Edward B. Rosenberg, and Benjamin L. Stackowski, *Masculinity and Femininity* (Boston: Houghton Mifflin, 1971), pp. 34, 39.
    It is to be noted that the clitoris consists of two corpora cavernosa and becomes engorged with blood during sexual excitement (Katchadourian and Lunde, *op. cit.*, pp. 35–36). Just prior to orgasm, the clitoris turns 180° and retracts in a flat position behind the symphysis pubis. (Helen Singer Kaplan, *The New Sex Therapy* [New York: Brunner/Mazel, 1974], p. 11). This description is strong and positive as compared to the classical adjectives used, such as small, soft, protected, sheltered.
32. "The Miracle of You" booklet, produced by the Life Cycle Center, Kimberly-Clark corporation, 1968.
33. Williams and Kane, *op. cit.*, p. 18.
34. Cloyd J. Julian and Elizabeth Noland Jackson, *Modern Sex Education* (New York: Holt, Rinehart and Winston, 1972), p. 13.
35. Williams and Kane, op. cit., p. 22.
36. "Your Years of Self-Discovery" booklet, produced by the Life Cycle Center, Kimberly-Clark Corporation, 1968.
    There is no evidence that differing androgen levels in the two sexes will account for differing rates of overt sexual behavior either within or between genders and no evidence

that these same biological events produce variations in meanings attributed to these behaviors. See John H. Gagnon, "The Creation of the Sexual in Early Adolescence" in Jerome Kagan and Robert Coles, eds., *Twelve to Sixteen: Early Adolescence* (New York: W. W. Norton, 1972), p. 235.

37. The power of knowledge, rather than the protection of knowledge (see Williams and Kane, *op. cit.*, p. 33)—having to be protected implies being weak and unable to care for oneself.
38. Studies cited by Weideger, *op. cit.*, suggest that it is more often the male partner's attitude that enforces this taboo. It is also the case that many women report that they do not want their partners to perform cunnilingus because these women believe that their genitals are ugly, unattractive, or have a bad odor, beliefs reinforced by a continuous commercial barrage of "pleasant-smelling" douche preparations and the paradoxically named "feminine hygiene" products. See Thomas Szasz, *Ceremonial Chemistry* (Garden City, New York: Anchor, 1974), p. 106, for a discussion of the extensive history and variations of the notion of "feminine pollution."
39. Contraceptive effectiveness of the diaphragm, when properly used, has recently been reaffirmed. See Robert A. Hatcher, M.D., Gary K. Stewart, M.D., Felicia Guest, Richard Finkelstein, Charles Godwin, eds., *Contraceptive Technology 1976–1977* (New York: Halsted Press, 1976), p. 33, "When the diaphragm is used properly, a failure rate of 3 pregnancies per hundred woman years of use will be observed."
40. Similarly, the newest and most effective therapeutic techniques for nonarousable and preorgasmic women involve the notion that women take responsibility for their own sexuality, an unfamiliar state of affairs and a new behavior to be learned. See, for example, Barbach, *op. cit.*
41. Weideger, *op. cit.*
42. Grete L Bibring, "Recognition of Psychological Stresses Often Neglected in OB Care" in *Hospital Topics*, 44 (September, 1966), pp. 100–103, as cited in the Boston Women's Health Book Collective, *op. cit.*, p. 304.
43. Grete L. Bibring, *et al.*, "A Study of the Psychological Processes in Pregnancy" in *The Psychoanalytic Study of the Child*, vol. XVI (1961), pp. 9–72, as cited in The Boston Women's Health Book Collective, *op. cit.*, p. 305.
44. Ti-Grace Atkinson, "The Institution of Sexual Intercourse" in *Amazon Odyssey* (New York: Link Books, 1974).
45. See Wilhelm Reich, *The Function of the Orgasm*, transl. Vincent R. Carfagno (New York: Farrar, Straus and Giroux, 1973), and Wilhelm Reich, *The Mass Psychology of Fascism*, transl. Vincent R. Carfagno (New York: Farrar, Straus and Giroux, 1970).

The Realities of Lesbianism

Del Martin and Phyllis Lyon

The Lesbian minority in America, which may run as high as ten million women, is probably the least understood of all minorities and the most downtrodden. The Lesbian has two strikes on her from the start; she is a woman and she is a homosexual, a minority scorned by the vast majority of people in our country. If, in addition, she is a member of a racial minority, it is hard sometimes to understand how she survives.

A Lesbian is a woman who prefers another woman as a sexual partner; a woman who is drawn erotically to women rather than to men. This definition includes women who have never experienced overt sexual relations with a woman—the key word is "prefers." There is really no other valid way to define the Lesbian, for outside of the sexual area she is as different in her actions, dress, status and behavior as anyone else. Just as there is no typical heterosexual woman, neither is there any typical Lesbian.

However, there is a popular misconception, or stereotype, of the Lesbian. She is believed to embody all the worst masculine attributes of toughness, aggressiveness, lack of emotion, lack of sentiment, overemphasis on sex, lack of stability—the need and desire to dress as a man or, at least, as much like a man as possible.

At some time in her life the Lesbian may fit this stereotype—usually when she is very young and just finding out about herself. After all, the Lesbian is a product of her heterosexual environment, and all she has to go on, at her first awareness of Lesbian feeling in herself, is society's image. Part of the reason for her over-masculinization is the sexual identity of being attracted to women. At this point the Lesbian feels that in order to be attractive to another woman she must appear masculine. Another reason is for identification purposes. How will she meet other Lesbians? How will they know her to be one of them unless she indicates herself in her outward appearance? A third reason is one of releasing her hostility against society, of defying the mores which she finds stifling to what she considers her very being. A fourth reason is comfort. Any woman who says that girdles and high heels are comfortable is simply lying.

While it is true that occasionally a Lesbian gets trapped in this way of life (emulation of the male) and never finds her way to being a person rather than a symbol, the vast majority pass through this phase and learn to accept their femininity. As a Lesbian she comes to realize she is a human being first, a woman second, and a Lesbian only third. Unfortunately, however, society places the emphasis on the third—sexual identification—and does not acknowledge the Lesbian as a woman or a person.

But the average Lesbian (if there can be anything approaching "average" in our very complex world) is indistinguishable from other women in dress, in manner, in goals and desires, in actions and in interests. The difference lies only in that she looks to women for her emotional and sexual fulfillment. She is a member of the family—a distant cousin, or perhaps a maiden aunt. But more than likely she's closer to home—maybe a daughter, a wife and mother, a grandmother or a sister. She may work in an office, in a factory production line, in the public school system, at the corner grocery. She is not bound by lines of class distinction or educational level, race or religion.

What causes a woman to become a Lesbian? How can it be that two sisters, raised by the same parents in the same home, can turn in two different directions—one toward heterosexuality, the other toward homosexuality? Very simply, the answer is that no one knows. A great deal of research and study has been done in this country on the male homosexual, but very little has been done on the Lesbian. The reason for this, we suspect, lies in the status of women in our country. Because the male—masculinity—is so highly valued, it has been deemed to be imperative to search out the reasons for any deviation from this American norm. Also, the majority of persons working in research are men. Research on the Lesbian has, for the most part, been confined to women who were either psychiatric patients or in prison—which hasn't made for a very full or accurate picture.

Nevertheless, if you begin reading about the "causes" of homosexuality you will find that, as in the Bible, the answer you want to find will be somewhere. Each "expert" on the subject presents a different "cause." Our feeling, which is supported by a growing number of professional persons, is that homosexuality (in both men and women) is merely one dimension of the vastly complicated and varied spectrum of human sexuality. There has always been homosexuality; it has appeared in almost every culture in recorded history; it occurs in every species of animal.

Perhaps the most logical and least hysterical of all statements about homosexuality is the following made by Dr. Joel Fort, psychiatrist and public health specialist; Dr. Evelyn G. Hooker, research psychologist at the University of California at Los Angeles; Dr. Joe K. Adams, psychologist and former mental health officer in California. The statement, made in August of 1966, is as follows:

> Homosexuals, like heterosexuals, should be treated as individual human beings, not as a special group, either by law or social agencies or employers.
>
> Laws governing sexual behavior should be reformed to deal only with clearly antisocial behavior, such as behavior involving violence or youth. The sexual behavior of individual adults by mutual consent in private should not be a matter of public concern.
>
> Some homosexuals, like some heterosexuals, are ill; some homosexuals, like some heterosexuals, are preoccupied with sex as a way of life. But probably for a majority of adults their sexual orientation constitutes only one component of a much more complicated life style.

Why then, if the Lesbian is by and large indistinguishable from other women and if her sexuality is not abnormal, does she face such genuine problems in her search for self-fulfillment? For struggle she does against myriad obstacles presented to her by a hostile society. Through our work with the Daughters of Bilitis, Inc., a Lesbian organization started in San Francisco in 1955, we have talked to literally thousands of Lesbians (and almost as many male homosexuals). And, although each case is different, each person individual, through all is a searching for self-identity and self-fulfillment to the utmost of the person's ability.

Consider the stereotyped "box" most women in this country are placed in from birth: that of becoming wife and mother, nothing else. Consider then, the girl brought up in this box who finds her sexual identification to be Lesbian. How then express the "wife-and-mother" role? This conflict often starts the process of self-searching which goes on for years and which, for some, is never resolved.

Toward a Quaker View of Sex, which came out of England and is more enlightened than most religious treatises on male homosexuality, fails utterly in its chapter on the female homosexual. The only statement with which we can agree is the first sentence: "Homosexuality is probably as common in women as it is in men." The Quaker view of the Lesbian is apparently that of the wishy-washy, namby-pamby old maid who holds hands with another old maid (or preferably an adoring younger girl, if available) because she never was able to catch a man and fulfill her deep yearning for the rewards of the pangs of childbirth. At least the American stereotype of the predatory, aggressive masculine woman has a little more color!

The Quaker view indicates that woman's prime requisite is her "maternal tenderness," that her only reason for being is to have babies, and that the Lesbian is warped and frustrated because she isn't doing her fair share toward the population explosion. To this question of maternity we must point out that the mere possession of biological machinery to produce babies has no correlation whatever with the attributes of motherhood. Let's face it—many women can have babies but make lousy mothers.

The art of motherhood in the human species is not instinctual. It is learned. We have courses in the care of the baby, and there are countless books on the market to help the young mother with the problems she may encounter during the course of her child's growth and development. In some cultures, babies are taken from the mothers and raised by the community without any apparent psychically traumatic results for the biological mothers or their offspring. In other cultures it is the male who tends the young.

It simply does not follow, then, that every Lesbian is suffering untold qualms because she is frustrating her "natural" birthright for giving birth. There are many other ways for women to contribute creatively to society, and at this particular point in the history of the population of our globe, they may also be highly desirable. The Lesbian who does feel frustrated because she doesn't have any children of her own may work in the teaching profession, she may be a playground director or a social worker who comes in contact with families and children. But the majority of Lesbians we have known have not expressed in any way the "void" they feel because they have no children. To the contrary, the expression "I would prefer to lead a heterosexual life if I could," is much more apt to come from the male homosexual than from the female.

It must be said, however, that there are many Lesbians who are raising children—some successfully, some not so successfully. The rate of success is, of course, determined by the degree of self-acceptance and self-assurance of the mother, and the permanence and stability of her relationship to her Lesbian partner. It takes guts, grit and determination. For if a mother is determined to be a Lesbian the courts will assume she is an "unfit mother" on the face of it and take her children away from her. It seems children must have the protection of heterosexuals, regardless. The fact that *all homosexuals are products of heterosexuality* seems to escape those who would judge the homosexual relationship.

The teenage Lesbian has a particular problem which has not been met. Homophile organizations, like the Daughters of Bilitis, have had to refuse membership to those under 21 for fear that they will be charged with "contributing to the delinquency of a minor." The teenager has no one to turn to. Society thinks only in terms of counseling the variety that would tend toward reestablishing the sexual identity in a heterosexual vein, and the teenage Lesbian is whisked off by her parents to the family doctor or clergyman to put a stop to this nonsense. However, in the cases that have come to our attention, the teenager has no doubt about her sexual orientation. What she wants to know is what to do about it. She wants to meet others like herself; she wants to socialize and to discuss the problem she faces. She is looking for Lesbian models, those who have worked out their problems and have established long-term relationships.

When she is denied this social outlet, she very often winds up in unsavory areas of a city like the Tenderloin in San Francisco. There she may find other youth, but she also finds herself in the company of prostitutes, pimps, drug addicts and dope peddlers. There have been several attempts in various cities to set up coffee houses where there is dancing for the teenage homosexual. But they have lacked the influential backing of, say, the church, to provide protection against police harassment while creating a wholesome social fabric for the teenage homosexual.

Because of the absence of role models in working out her way of life, and because the only marriage she has known is that of Mom and Dad, the young Lesbian usually gets hung up in the "butch-femme" syndrome in her early relationships. It is only with painful experience that she learns the Lesbian is attracted to a woman—not a cheap imitation of a man. The lasting Lesbian liaison (and there are many) is one based on mutuality of concern, love, companionship, responsibility, household chores, outside interests and sex.

The successful Lesbian relationship cannot be based on society's exaggerated male-female, dominant-passive roles, as depicted in the flood of Lesbian novels on the newsstands which are, for the most part, written by men for heterosexual male consumption. It is the realization that, contrary to cultural myths, all human beings have both feminine and masculine traits and that a person has to find her own identity as a woman and as a partner in this love relationship that makes for success. The fact that Lesbian relationships are generally long-lasting without benefit of religious ceremony or legal sanction is indicative of a strong bond of love and respect which sees the couple through all the obstacles society places in their way.

Fortunately for all women, there is a growing awareness in this country that woman needs and is more openly demanding an identify for herself as a human being, an identity over and beyond the societal role of housewife and mother. This awareness, coupled with more openness about sexuality and homosexuality, is making it easier now for the young girl, newly aware of her Lesbianism, to cope with the negative sanctions of society. But it is still true that in most areas of our country she has no place to turn for counsel, no one with whom she can talk about her feelings without running the very real risk that the counselor will turn away from her with horror and revulsion.

The Quakers state: "Female homosexuality is free from the legal and, to a large extent, the social sanctions which are so important in the problems of male homosexuals." This is a myth that even the male homosexual has come to believe. It is true that in England there were never any laws pertaining to female homosexuality. But this is not true in the U.S.A. The Lesbian is just as subject to the sanctions of certain laws as the male homosexual; she is just as subject to arrest when she sets foot in a "gay bar"; she is just as subject to blackmail and police harassment. The stigma attached to homosexuality has just as much effect on the Lesbian as she tries to deal with fear and society-imposed guilt in the problem areas of employment, family relationships and religion. Just because the record of arrests is so much smaller is no indication that the Lesbian is relatively free from legal or social sanction. It only means that she is less obvious and less promiscuous. She has done a better job of covering up.

Lesbian problems we have dealt with over the years include the 20-year-old driven to thoughts of suicide because she could not resolve the conflict between her identity as a Lesbian and as a Christian. Or the 40-year-old mother who telephones Daughters of Bilitis 3,000 miles across the country to break "18 years of silence" after reading a book called *The Grapevine* by Jess Stearn. Then there was the nurse with a "perfect work record" in a federal hospital who was interrogated by a government investigator, flown from Washington, D.C., at the taxpayers' expense, because someone wrote to a Congressman accusing her of being a Lesbian.

There was the 19-year-old who was trying to find out what homosexuality was all about because she was drummed out of the armed services on a charge she didn't understand. The daughter who receives a monthly allowance from her wealthy family in the Midwest to stay on the coast lest her district attorney father be threatened with a "family skeleton" by his political foes. And the 25-year-old who, after five years of psychiatric therapy, decides she must make the best of herself as herself—a Lesbian.

The most serious problem a Lesbian faces in life is that of self-acceptance. Like everyone else, she has been taught the cultural folklore that a Lesbian is something less than human—a sick, perverted, illegal, immoral animal to be shunned and despised. Needless to say, with the first glimmering of self-knowledge, of awareness that she has Lesbian tendencies, she becomes bogged down in doubt, fear, guilt and hostility.

Some Lesbians claim they have been aware of their Lesbianism since early childhood. Others first become aware during adolescence. Yet there are some women who make this discovery about themselves much later in life—after they have been married and have had children. Still others, either by choice or lack of opportunity, never admit or act out their Lesbianism.

It isn't easy for a woman to say to herself, let alone anyone else, "I am a Lesbian." But once the words are said, has she really changed? Isn't she still the same person she was—the dear friend, the competent employee, the loving sister? And yet the words become a barrier in her personal and working relationships. To protect her family and her job, she is forced to live a lie, to take on a dual life. No wonder many Lesbians seek out some type of psychiatric or therapeutic help. The miracle is that so many are able to function so well and to contribute so much to society.

The Lesbian is thus a secretive, chameleon creature. She is not easily recognized. The old adage, "It takes one to know one," is not true. Not being distinguishable from other women, she has difficulty meeting others like herself. The "gay bar" is still a meeting place, but there are few such bars which cater to women exclusively because they do not constitute a steady clientele. Besides, a Lesbian, as a woman, has no doubt heard many times the old saw "nice girls don't go into bars," or "no lady would ever go into a bar alone." The Lesbian goes out on the town only occasionally and is more apt to settle down with a partner, to build a home and a lasting relationship, and to develop a small circle of friends—usually both homosexual and heterosexual. Another social outlet for the Lesbian can be homophile organizations throughout the country (if she knows about them), such as Daughters of Bilitis, which has chapters in New York and San Francisco.

The Lesbian, being a woman, comes out of the same cultural pool as do heterosexual women. Therefore, on top of everything else, she may have the same hang-ups and inhibitions about sex, dress, work, actions, etc., as do her heterosexual sisters. Since women have been taught to be passive, to shun the role of the aggressor, the Lesbian finds herself without the slightest idea of how to approach another woman for a date, for a conversation, for sex. It is a rarity for a heterosexual woman to be approached by a Lesbian unless she has given much indication that such advances are welcome.

Even when the Lesbian accepts her sexual identity and herself as a person, she still faces very real discrimination from society. If she has educated herself to a profession (a role doubly difficult for any woman), she can lose her professional status merely because s someone points a finger. This is especially true of teachers, attorneys, doctors, social workers and other professions licensed by the state. But it can also be true for file clerks and secretaries. Very few employers are aware enough to realize that in the Lesbian he has an employee who must work, who will not get married or pregnant, who will devote her energies and capabilities to her job because she will always have to support herself.

As Rabbi Elliot Grafman has stated, "People fear that which they do not understand, and what they fear they despise." It is only through more knowledge and more personal confrontation that the stereotype of the Lesbian can be dispelled. However, to accomplish this feat is to overcome the vicious circle that now envelops the Lesbian who tries to be honest.

If she divulges her identity, she automatically becomes vulnerable. She faces loss of job, family, and friends. Yet, until she opens herself to such possibilities, no one will have the opportunity to come to know and to understand her as the whole person she is.

Through The Council on Religion and the Homosexual, which was formed in San Francisco in 1964 after a three-day retreat attended by clergymen and male and female representatives of the homophile community, such a dialogue began in earnest. Avenues of communication have been opened up not only with the religious community (seminaries and other church groups), but with governmental agencies, the police, business and professional groups, college and high school students. But the task of demythologizing, of education and redefinition of the homosexual is a long and arduous one.

PART 7
Birth Control

Although women have always sought control over their reproductive capability and a choice in the number of children they would have, reliable means for achieving these are only recently available. Even so, the initial enthusiasm for the Pill in its many forms and for the IUD has waned as undesirable or dangerous side effects and consequences have been identified. While the research goes on, many women are turning or returning to such benign methods as the diaphragm, or they are having tubal sterilizations. Whatever the method, should it fail, some women seek abortion as an alternative to continuing the pregnancy. By and large, birth control continues to be women's concern and responsibility.

Freedom from fear of pregnancy can plainly have a liberating affect on the sexuality of women. Even more important, freedom from the specter of many successive pregnancies with their consequent demands for prolonged child nurturing can give women choices about how they want to spend their lives, and can open up new channels for the investment of time, energy, and other resources. As pressures for social change are causing doors to open and more opportunities become available for women to explore, concomitantly they are freer than before from the old exigencies of their bodies. These two factors, freedom from unwanted pregnancy and access to opportunities in the larger world outside the home, together make the liberation of women possible. Without them, or with only one of them, the concept is empty rhetoric.

Obviously birth control is of critical importance to the psychology of women. Without it, woman would continue to be relegated to the traditional roles of wife and mother, her place, functions, and status thereby defined. With control of her fertility, her behavior over both the short and the long range potentially becomes more various and acquires more dimensions as latent possibilities have the chance to grow and mature.

Although contraception is mostly woman's work, research is under way to increase the repertoire of male contraceptive techniques beyond the traditional condom, coitus interruptus, and vasectomy. "Contraceptives for Males" by William Bremner and David de Kretser includes both an informative account of male reproductive physiology and explanations of where and how in the system male contraception might work. Hormonal inhibition of sperm production, prevention of maturation of sperm, a combination of vasectomy and sperm banking, and immunization of a man against his own sperm are all discussed in terms of their feasibility and the status of relevant research.

Estimating that new techniques for male contraception will not be generally available until the 1980s, the authors raise the question of why research on male contraception has lagged so far behind the research on female techniques. They discuss several possible answers, including the important one of the efforts of feminists and birth control advocates such as Margaret Sanger whose interest was in promoting fertility control for women.

Physicians and behavioral scientists have shared with men in general the notion that woman's mental and emotional state was intimately connected with her uterus and its functions. Therefore it was natural to assume that any interference with these would have sinister and fateful sequelae. Abortion, especially, was held to be followed inevitably by guilt, depression, feelings of worthlessness, and loss of femininity. No doubt such consequences did indeed occur, but they could have readily been explained by social stigma, the illegality of abortion, and the conditions under which it often occurred. Since abortion has become more readily available, research on its psychological consequences has forced revisions of old assumptions about it. Lisa Shusterman's essay "The Psychosocial Factors of the Abortion Experience: A Critical Review," looks at the research on both illegal and legal abortions for insight on what the abortion experience means to women.

Data on abortions performed before 1970, when an abortion was illegal in all states except to save the mother's life, are not reliable, but in 1972 when legal abortion was available in some states, more than half a million legal abortions were performed in the United States. Shusterman provides some demographic data from recent studies, revealing the characteristics of women who seek abortions. She also surveys the data on such questions as public opinion about abortion, motivations for unwanted pregnancies and for abortions, and the medical and psychological sequelae of abortion. This is one area of professional concern where informed opinion has made a complete turnabout in the past few years. Shusterman concludes that the more recent research on abortion by request clearly indicates that, for most women, the psychological effects of having an abortion are negligible, if not actually favorable.

The !Kung people of the Kalahari Desert of South Africa are of great interest to behavioral scientists because they have recently forsaken their hunting and gathering life and settled into agrarian villages, thus offering clues to our neolithic past when our ancestors abandoned their nomadic life and settled down to farm and domesticate animals. In "!Kung Hunter-Gatherers: Feminism, Diet, and Birth Control," Gina Kolata reviews some fascinating observations on the !Kung women and how they have been affected by this change in life style. Whereas formerly they had shared equally with men the task of finding food, they now remain in the villages while the men raise food and deal with neighboring tribes. This role segregation along sex lines is reflected in childrearing practices, and has resulted in loss of status and autonomy for women, and greater competitiveness and aggression among children. Of equal interest is the effect of dietary changes on the fertility of !Kung women. The nomadic women had late menarche and low fertility, suspected to be the result of diet and nursing habits. The sedentary women, consuming more calories and lactating for a shorter period owing to use of cow's milk supplements, have experienced a thirty percent decline in birth intervals, resulting in a surge in the population. Such studies of women in other cultures are invaluable for clarifying issues about which our own thinking may be culture-bound. In addition, this study of the !Kung women is a vivid reminder of the interrelatedness of all human experience.

In addition to birth control, it appears that we shall soon have a refinement of technology which will allow parents to select the sex of their children. In "Sex Preferences, Sex Control, and the Status of Women," Nancy Williamson presents a provocative analysis of what this will mean for the status of women. Most parents still want their first-born to be a boy, and numerically boys are preferred over girls. Methods of sex control are now being developed, and research indicates a strong current of approval for its use when it becomes widely available. Sex control has both its positive and negative aspects where women are concerned. On the positive side, it will give women more control with respect to the use of their bodies to have what they want. On the negative side are some interesting personal and demographic considerations. For example, the research indicates that first-borns tend to be favored by higher intelligence and greater achievement. If most first-borns were boys, male dominance of society and culture would be reinforced, and women would be even more securely trapped in a second-class position. Williamson argues for the importance of understanding the impact of sex control technology before its use becomes widespread. And, as she points out, the future is not far off.

Male contraception, effects of abortion, fertility and lifestyle, and sex control—these topics are only a small sample of a growing literature on the complex and far reaching subject of birth control. Woman's ability to bring forth life has been variously valued in human history, honored and encouraged in some times, disparaged in others. At the global level, there is hardly a more important problem facing humanity today than the control of reproduction. As the numbers of people on earth threaten to outstrip the planet's ability to support them, societies try to change people's attitudes about having children and seek to develop ever more refined techniques for avoiding pregnancy. But as important as birth control is to the macrocosm of the world and its cultures, it is just as important, on another level, to the microcosm of the individual. No other issue so intimately affects the lives of so many women.

Contraceptives for Males

William J. Bremner
and David M. de Kretser

In the last twenty years, new contraceptive techniques for females have received wide publicity and use. Over 20 percent of American women in the reproductive age group used oral contraceptives in 1973.[1] Other measures, particularly the intrauterine device, are also very popular. With increasing use of these techniques has come increasing awareness of their hazards. Although the risks for an individual woman using either oral contraceptives or an intrauterine device are extremely small,[2] they are certainly present and have contributed to heightened pressure for alternative means of contraception. An increasingly voiced feeling has been that, if there are to be definite health risks associated with adequate contraception, these risks should be shared between the male and female partners.

Research concerning sexual reproduction in general and possible methods of controlling it has been spurred by awareness of the worldwide threat posed by unchecked population growth. Contraceptive techniques that have been effective on a wide scale in the United States and other developed countries have often not been successful when introduced into different cultural and political climates. The desirability of having a wider range of contraceptive techniques available has become apparent and has led to funding for research along these lines from such organizations as the Population Council, the World Health Organization, the Ford Foundation, the International Planned Parenthood Federation, and the American National Institutes of Health, among others. A significant part of the work that has resulted has been concerned with developing techniques for contraception in the male.[3]

"Contraceptives for Males" by William J. Bremner and David M. de Kretser from *Signs: Journal of Women in Culture and Society,* 1, 2 (1975), 387–96. Reprinted by permission of the University of Chicago Press.

The main methods of contraception that have been available to the male have been coitus interruptus, condoms, and vasectomy. Each has obvious disadvantages in terms of reliability in preventing pregnancy and of acceptability. Vasectomy, while generally quite reliable and increasingly acceptable, has the very significant disadvantage of being irreversible with present techniques in the majority of subjects. The present article will review areas of recent work directed at extending our capabilities for male contraception and consider which methods may become available for general use. We will begin with a description of some of the major relevant aspects of male reproductive physiology.

Normal Male Reproductive Physiology

The pituitary (fig. 1) is a gland about the size of a large pea and is attached to the base of the brain. It secretes many hormones, among which two are directly concerned with testicular function. These are follicle-stimulating hormone (FSH) and luteinizing hormone (LH), the names deriving from their biologic functions in females. The secretion of LH and FSH by the pituitary is stimulated by at least one substance normally formed in the hypothalamus, an area of the brain immediately above the pituitary. This substance, called LH-releasing hormone (LHRH), is necessary for normal secretion of LH and FSH and, if deficient owing to hypothalamic disease or chemical inhibition, will result in inadequate LH and FSH production.

The blood stream carries LH and FSH to the testes, where LH is

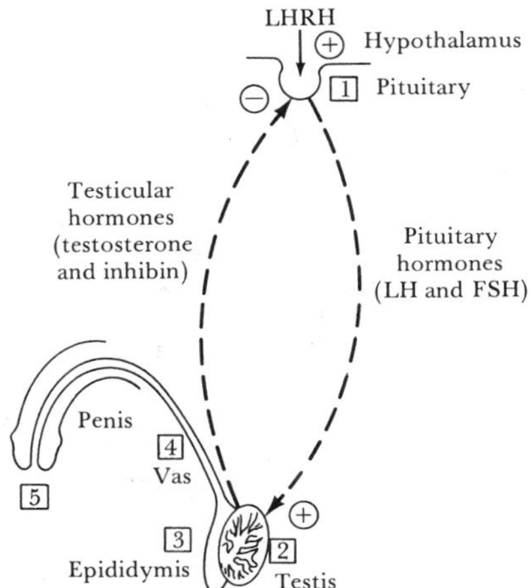

Figure 1. A highly schematic diagram of some of the important anatomic and hormonal factors in human male reproduction. Numbers in squares denote various sites where normal processes theoretically could be blocked, leading to infertility. Symbols: + implies that the hormone(s) exert(s) a stimulatory effect on the organ to which the arrow is directed; − implies an inhibitory effect.

chiefly responsible for stimulating the production of testosterone, the main male sex hormone, and FSH is responsible for the production of sperm.[4] Adequate amounts of both LH and FSH are necessary for normal spermatogenesis; if they are low, sperm production will be decreased or absent. Normal secretion of LH is necessary to maintain normal testosterone production by the testes. If testosterone levels are low, male libido and sexual potency decrease, and many other metabolic functions are adversely affected.

Sperm are produced in the testes from precursor cells by processes of cell division and maturation requiring about seventy days. They are transported through a series of channels into the epididymis, a sacklike structure on the outside of the testis. The epididymis forms the beginning of the vas deferens, which carries sperm to the penis to be expelled during ejaculation. Maturation of sperm, which is necessary for their fertility, occurs during their transit through the epididymis and vas. Abnormalities of any of these structures can lead to deficient or absent production of normal sperm.

Possible Male Contraceptives

The main sites at which a male contraceptive might work are numbered in Figure 1.

1. Potential male contraceptives may be effective through inhibition of FSH and LH production by the pituitary, either by a direct action on the pituitary itself or indirectly through suppression of LHRH secretion. Many steroid hormones,[5] including the male sex hormone testosterone, the female hormones estrogen and progesterone, and numberous similar substances, are known to inhibit the production of both LH and FSH from the pituitary in males and females. Indeed, probably the major mechanism through which most of the oral contraceptives (which are various combinations of female sex hormones) are effective in females is their inhibition of the pituitary hormone secretion necessary to produce eggs from the ovary. Many steroids are available that could be taken orally by the male and would be expected to cause infertility through inhibition of pituitary hormone secretion. A major potential difficulty with this form of therapy is that, if LH secretion is inadequate, the amount of testosterone produced by the testes would be low, causing decreased libido and impotence. A possible solution to this problem is to use testosterone itself as the agent to suppress LH and FSH. High dosages of testosterone taken orally or in shots will suppress LH and FSH, causing infertility, and also will replace the testosterone not produced by the testes. Dosages of testosterone in this range, however, have been found to cause an increase in the red cells of the blood in some men. They may have other harmful metabolic effects. A compromise solution being evaluated in several laboratories, including our own and that of Dr. C. A. Paulsen in Seattle, is that lower dosages of testosterone in combination with one of the progesterone-like hormones or some other derivative of one of the sex steroids would simultaneously induce infertility through suppression of LH and FSH, replace the deficit in endogenous testosterone production, and avoid the undesirable side effects

of excessive testosterone. Preliminary results suggest that this type of therapy does indeed work without, to date, any unacceptable side effects.[6] One disadvantage already recognized is that, because of the length of time (two to three months) between beginning to ingest the drugs and achieving infertility. A similar period intervenes between discontinuing the medication and regaining fertility. Even if such a form of contraception is found to be effective, it will probably be at least five years before it is available for general use, owing to governmental requirements for rigorous demonstration of efficacy and lack of toxicity.

Another class of contraceptive agents under intensive investigation in many laboratories relates to the recent discovery, in the laboratory of Andrew Schally in New Orleans, of the structure and method of synthesis of LHRH, the hypothalamic hormone that causes the release of LH and FSH from the pituitary.[7] Many attempts are under way to develop a chemical analogue of LHRH or an antibody directed against LHRH that would inhibit its action on the pituitary. This would cause decreased production of LH and FSH and infertility in either the male or the female. These lines of investigation have so far met with only partial success, and, if such an agent is effective as a contraceptive, it will be limited by the necessity to replace the testosterone not produced because of decreased secretion of LH.

Perhaps an ideal male contraceptive would be one that blocked pituitary FSH secretion without affecting LH. This would presumably cause deficient spermatogenesis, to the point of infertility, without impairment of testosterone secretion. Work in our laboratories[8] and in those of Dr. Paul Franchimont in Belgium and Dr. Brian Setchell in England has shown that such a substance (a protein, not a steroid) is present in extracts of testicular tissue and seminal fluid of animals. If this protein can be purified in sufficient amounts and is not harmful when given to humans, it will have considerable importance in future contraceptive techniques. It is clear, however, that at least several years' work remains before this substance, named inhibin, reaches the stage of trial in humans.

2. The testis itself is the second major site that could be affected by male contraceptives. Many drugs, such as those used to treat some human tumors, are known to inhibit sperm formation by a direct effect on the testis but are accompanied by unacceptable side effects on other parts of the body, such as the bone marrow and the gastrointestinal tract. Several different classes of drugs have similarly been shown to cause infertility but also other toxicity.[9] Perhaps the most promising was the bis (dichloroacetyl) diamine class, which was developed to the stage of clinical trials in humans in the early 1960s before it was noted that ingestion of alcohol while taking the contraceptive drug caused severe flushing and irregular heartbeats. Therefore, further trials were abandoned.[10] It remains possible that an analogue of one of these drugs or a new chemical may be found which is capable of causing reversible infertility in men without unacceptable toxicity to some other tissue, but no such compound is available to testing at the present time.

3. The epididymis functions as the site for storage and maturation of sperm as well as a channel through which they pass to the vas. If this function is impaired, sperm may be produced in normal numbers but not be able to fertilize eggs. Two drugs have been used, with limited success, in at-

tempts to block normal function of the epididymis. Studies in rats have suggested that cyproterone acetate will impair epididymal function, causing nonfertile sperm without affecting the function of the testis. Some investigators have reported similar results in humans,[11] but others have found that the infertility is associated with decreased libido and potency,[12] which may be related to the drug's known property of antagonizing the effectiveness of testosterone and, at least in high dosage, of inhibiting the secretion of LH. More trials of this compound in humans are under way at the present time.

Another drug thought to affect the epididymis is *a*-chlorohydrin. It has been shown to produce sterility in laboratory animals, but also (at a dosage two to three times that necessary to cause sterility) to cause permanent anatomic changes in the epididymis and at higher dosages to cause death from bone marrow toxicity.

Although satisfactory agents for affecting epididymal function are not available at present, this form of contraception has several theoretic advantages and will be pursued actively in further studies. Among these advantages is the fact that, if epididymal function alone were affected, libido and potency would be normal. Second, the onset and termination of the effect on fertility would be much more prompt (about two weeks) than in the case of agents affecting the pituitary and testis (two to three months).

4. The vasa deferentia are small tubes passing from each testis to meet just prior to entering the penis. Because all sperm have to travel through them to get to the penis and because they are easily accessible to the surgeon as they pass through the scrotum, the vasa have been a common site of surgical intervention to impair fertility. The familiar procedure of "vasectomy" involves taking out a small section of each vas and tying off or cauterizing the blind ends in an attempt to induce permanent sterility without affecting the function of the testis.[13] This has been a remarkably successful procedure, both in preventing pregnancy (over 99 percent effective in most series of operated subjects) and in absence of side effects.[14] Its outstanding disadvantage continues to be that it is essentially irreversible with present surgical techniques and so is not practicable for a man who wants to father children at some time in the future. It is quite commonly possible (50–80 percent of cases) to reattach the two ends of the vas so that sperm can actually get through from the testis to the penis, but these sperm are usually incapable of fertilizing eggs. Only about 20–40 percent of men who have had vasectomies can be made fertile again.

Many variations in surgical technique have been introduced in an attempt to improve the reversibility of vasectomy.[15] In recent years, various devices have been placed in the vas that operate essentially like a faucet that can be opened and closed by a minor surgical procedure. Unfortunately, the rate of ability to induce pregnancy when the devices are open has so far not been significantly greater than that when a vasectomy is repaired.

A technique that theoretically could be used in conjunction with vasectomy in order to guarantee future fertility is freezing sperm, or "sperm banking." Seminal fluid, collected by masturbation, could be frozen prior to a man's undergoing a vasectomy, then thawed and artificially inseminated into a woman at the time pregnancy is desired. The use of sperm banking in animals, particularly cattle, has met with enormous success. In humans, however, the technology of freezing and thawing sperm without killing them has so far not progressed far enough to make this a reliable method of guaranteeing future fertility. The most optimistic recent reports suggest that approximately 70 percent of samples so treated will be capable of inducing fertility.[16] Some men's sperm are able to survive freezing much better than others, but there is no way as yet of predicting which sperm have this characteristic. Although the procedure of sperm banking has severe limitations at present, it is quite possible that improvements in the methods of freezing and thawing may lead to a reliable way of guaranteeing future fertility. If these improvements are forthcoming, sperm banking in combination with vasectomy would be an effective contraceptive technique for many men. Obviously, if sperm banking becomes a practical reality, it will also introduce many sociological and moral problems, for example, the possibility of using frozen sperm from outstanding men for eugenic purposes in women of succeeding generations.

5. Interference with sperm progression from the penis into the vagina by a device such as a condom or by a sexual practice such as coitus interruptus is a well-known contraceptive technique. Coitus interruptus has limitations in terms of acceptability and, even if performed optimally, suffers from the fact that the first few drops of semen ejaculated contain a very high concentration of sperm, which may be produced in some cases before the subjective feeling of an orgasm occurs. Condoms, if used correctly, have a good rate of preventing unwanted pregnancies and are associated with no known health hazard. The necessity of having to employ a condom in each act of intercourse, however, is enough of a burden to cause many men to use them only intermittently, with a subsequent increase in the induction of pregnancy.

A class of techniques for contraception that theoretically might be adapted to act at several of the above sites is that of immunizing a man against some component of his own reproductive system, such as his sperm or his FSH. An effective antibody to one of these components might induce absence of spermatogenesis (FSH antibodies) or production of infertile sperm (sperm antibodies).[17] Efforts have been under way for at least fifty years to develop contraceptives of this type for both males and females but have so far not produced a satisfactory technique.

Antibodies can, in general, be produced in one of two ways. Most commonly they are produced by injecting a person with a substance (the "antigen") that is not normally produced in the body, thereby stimulating the body's immune system to produce its own antibodies. This is the technique employed in vaccination against infectious diseases and is called "active immunization." Alternatively, antibodies can be produced by injecting the antigen into another person or animal and then collecting the antibodies made by that organism and injecting these antibodies into the person whom one desires to make immune. This is called "passive immunization" and has been employed to make antitoxins against diseases such as tetanus.

Either mechanism of antibody production could theoretically be used to produce sterility in humans, but each has serious problems. If FSH or LHRH is employed in active immunization, the man's immune system will produce antibodies to these materials, thereby probably causing infertility.[18] However, the immune system may well continue to produce antibodies for months to years after the injection, since it may be continually restimulated by the hormones produced in the body. This would produce prolonged and possibly permanent sterility and therefore offer no advantage over other methods.

If a sufficiently specific antigen can be prepared from sperm, antibodies to this antigen might be produced in men. Since the antigens associated with sperm normally produced in the body do not enter the blood stream, they would presumably not constitute a continuing source of antigenic stimulation, and the infertility induced by sperm antibodies may be reversible. This series of deductions, however, involves several steps that have not yet been experimentally verified. The technique, although promising, cannot be considered an imminent possibility for effective male contraception.

Passive immunization entails even more difficulties. It involves injecting an extract of blood from another organism, usually an animal, which contains many substances that are foreign to the man being injected. This often induces a disease called serum sickness and may, over a long period of time, cause kidney damage and other serious ill effects. It seems unlikely that passive immunization, at least as presently practiced, will ever be an acceptable contraceptive technique.

To summarize the prospects for male contraception, it is unlikely that new techniques will be available on a wide scale for at least five years. The method that seems likely to be available first is the use of some combination of sex steroids to inhibit the production of LH and FSH. Depending upon the rate of technological improvements, sperm banking in combination with vasectomy may also become a useful procedure. The possibilities of a specific inhibitor of FSH production, of drugs causing infertility through a direct testicular or epididymal mechanism, and of antibody therapy all seem very worthy of further investigation but are not likely to be available for general use in the near future.

As a general comment on the history of research in fertility control, it is of interest that contraceptive techniques for men seem to have lagged somewhat behind those available for women, particularly in the area of oral preparations. Questions about the reason for this discrepancy are often asked of workers in the area of male contraception. The questions are occasionally asked with a certain degree of hostility, with the implication that scientists in the area of reproduction research have been responsive to male opinion, which is held to regard the female as the sex responsible for contraception, and therefore have concentrated on developing techniques for female contraception.

There are undoubtedly many answers to these questions. Certainly one answer relates to the fact that biologists have felt that it is technically easier to disrupt the mechanisms responsible for ovulation in the female than it is to disrupt spermatogenesis in the male. It was pointed out in many early papers on the topic that it was necessary to prevent the production of only one egg each month in a female, while in a male it was necessary to prevent the production of billions of sperm, and that an 80 or 90 percent reduction in sperm production was not sufficient to cause infertility in many cases. In addition, the process of sperm migration from the vagina to the egg, fertilization of the egg, and implantation of the fertilized egg in the uterus all occur in the female only. Therefore, measures such as intrauterine devices can be used in females but not in males.

Another answer may be that there has, in fact, been some degree of prejudice among workers in the area, or in agencies awarding money for research, as to which sex should bear the responsibility for contraception. If so, this has not been mentioned in the scientific literature on the subject, nor has it been part of the personal experience of the authors.

One interesting, and perhaps less widely appreciated answer, is to be found in the writings of two pioneers in the development of oral contraceptives for females, Gregory Pincus and Joseph Goldzieher.[19] Both have stressed the crucial roles played by the feminist and birth control advocate Margaret Sanger and her friend Mrs. Stanley McCormack in enlisting the aid of the scientist Pincus at the Worcester Foundation in Massachusetts and the gynecologist John Rock at Harvard in early studies directed toward an effective contraceptive for women. Both women supplied considerable moral support and social pressure, and Mrs. McCormack furnished large amounts of personal money to finance contraceptive development. Dr. Pincus's book *The Control of Fertility* was dedicated to Mrs. McCormack. As exemplified by the work of those women, a significant factor in the rapid early development of the female oral contraceptive was feminist pressure and support for a method by which a woman could control her own fertility. It is only at the present time that techniques for male contraception may be starting to approach those already available for the female.

As this review has indicated, the traditional male contraceptive techniques of coitus interruptus, condoms, and vasectomy have many limitations in terms of reliability, acceptability, and reversibility. Many of the possibilities for improvement in the technology of male contraception offer promise of significant advancement toward these objectives. We have tried to make some assessment of the potential value of each new technique and the time it may take before the innovations, if successful, are generally available. While it is apparent that it will be at least several years before any of the new techniques has a significant impact on human reproductive practices, it seems quite possible that some of them may eventually have a profound impact. It is, of course, very probable that techniques not considered here will appear. Such new techniques may well surpass those presently envisaged and, with luck, may help give future generations less cause for worry about the related problems of overpopulation and the health hazards of adequate contraception.

NOTES

1. George Washington University Medical Center, Department of Medical and Public Affairs, "Oral Contraceptives," in *Population Report,* ser. A, no. 1 (Washington, D.C., April 1974). The figure quoted is a minimum, since it includes only contraceptives sold in pharmacies and omits those obtained from hospitals, family planning clinics, subsidized programs, and samples. In Australia, Canada, and northern Europe, this figure is approximately 30 percent.
2. The most serious risk of the oral contraceptives for females relates to excessive blood clotting. For healthy women in the reproductive age group not taking the pill, the risk of dying from abnormal blood clotting is approximately 1 in 500,000 per year. For similar

women taking oral contraceptives, the risk is approximately 1 in 60,000 and can probably be decreased by using pills with low estrogen content. The risk of acquiring a clot serious enough to require hospitalization while ingesting the pill is approximately 1 in 2,000.

3. D. M. de Kretser, "The Regulation of Male Fertility: The State of the Art and Future Possibilities," *Contraception* 9 (June 1974): 561–600.
4. Sperm are the cells with mobile tails that, following intercourse, ascend the female reproductive tract and fertilize the ovum. "Seminal fluid" is composed of sperm plus seminal plasma, the fluid secreted by the testes and glands along the male reproductive tract, including the prostate.
5. "Steroid" denotes compounds of a certain chemical structure. Many human hormones, particularly those produced by the adrenal glands, testes, and ovaries, are of this structure. Relatively minor chemical variations superimposed on the basic steroid structure cause the markedly different biological effects of the various steroid hormones. Chemists have added additional variations to produce compounds that in many cases have biological effects different from those of steroids produced in the body.
6. R. Skoglund and C. A. Paulsen, "Danazol-Testosterone Combination, a Potentially Effective Means for Reversible Male Contraception: A Preliminary Report," *Contraception* 7 (May 1973): 357–65.
7. A. Schally, A. Arimura, and A. Kastin, "Hypothalamic Regulatory Hormones," *Science* 179 (January 1973): 341–49.
8. V. W. K. Lee, E. J. Keogh, H. G. Burger, B. Hudson, and D. M. de Kretser, "Studies on the Relationship between FSH and Germ Cells: Evidence for Selective Suppression of FSH by Testicular Extracts," *Journal of Reproduction and Fertility* (1975), in press.
9. H. Jackson, "Antispermatogenic Agents," *British Medical Bulletin* 26 (January 1970): 79–86.
10. C. G. Heller, D. J. Moore, and C. A. Paulsen, "Suppression of Spermatogenesis and Chronic Toxicity in Men by a New Series of Bis (Dichloroacetyl) Diamines," *Toxicology and Applied Pharmacology* 3 (January 1961): 1–11.
11. J. Hammerstein, personal communication.
12. N. Laschet and L. Laschet, "Adrenocortical Function, Corticotrophic Responsiveness and Fertility of Men during Longterm Treatment with Cyproterone Acetate," in *Third International Congress on Hormonal Steroids,* ed. V. H. T. James (Amsterdam: Excerpta Medica, 1970).
13. R. Hackett and K. Waterhouse, "Vasectomy Reviewed," *American Journal of Obstetrics and Gynecology* 116 (June 1973): 438–55.
14. Several studies have found no evidence of hormonal abnormalities in subjects up to two years after vasectomy. Most studies have found a very high proportion of positive psychological adjustments to the procedure. Development of antibodies to sperm occurs in the blood of about 50 percent of men who have undergone vasectomy. This is not known to cause any adverse reaction in men so affected.
15. J. Sciarra, C. Markland, and J. Speidel, eds., *Control of Male Fertility* (New York: Harper & Row, 1975).
16. E. Steinberger and K. Smith, "Artificial Insemination with Fresh or Frozen Semen: A Comparative Study," *Journal of the American Medical Association* 223 (February 1973): 778–83.
17. T. S. Li, "Sperm Immunology, Infertility and Fertility Control," *Obstetrics and Gynecology* 44 (October 1974): 607–23.
18. The hormones would have to be chemically attached to a large protein prior to injection, thereby making a complex that the body's immune system would regard as foreign.
19. G. Pincus, *The Control of Fertility* (New York: Academic Press, 1965); and J. Goldzieher and H. Rudel, "How the Oral Contraceptives Came to Be Developed," *Journal of the American Medical Association* 230 (October 1974): 421–25.

The Psychosocial Factors of the Abortion Experience
A Critical Review

Lisa Roseman Shusterman

The literature on the psychosocial factors of abortion is critically reviewed. It is concluded that due to faulty methodology no general statements can be made about these factors for women receiving illegal abortions. It appears that the data showing that women receiving therapeutic abortions experienced favorable psychological consequences are stronger than the data indicating negative consequences. Studies of abortion on request, which, for the most part, have been methodologically sound, indicate that the new abortion patients are mostly young, unmarried women who are not in a social position to bear and care for a child. They tend to end their pregnancies for social and economic reasons. Further, they are either not aware of or not concerned about the possibility of getting pregnant at the time of intercourse, or they have a contraceptive failure. Finally, the psychological consequences of abortion on request appear to be mostly benign.

Abortion is the termination of pregnancy before the developing embryo or fetus can exist independently. Abortion may be either spontaneous or induced. Spontaneous abortion is the natural death of the embryo or fetus, while induced abortion is the intentional removal of the embryo or fetus. The present review deals mainly with the psychosocial factors of the induced abortion experience.

The role of women in society is in great flux and many of the greatest changes concern women's fertility. In order to understand the nature of these changes and their implications, the psychosocial aspects of abortion must be explored and charted. The woman who interrupts her pregnancy is the central figure in the abortion, and her attitudes, feelings, and behavior in regard to abortion are not well understood. Not only should the psychology of abortion be understood for the sake of knowledge itself, but also so that informed social decisions about abortion can be made.

"The Psychosocial Factors of the Abortion Experience: A Critical Review" by Lisa R. Shusterman in *The Psychology of Women Quareterly,* 1, 1 (1976), 79–106. Reprinted by permission of the Human Sciences Press.

The present paper is a comprehensive review of what has been written about the psychosocial aspects of abortion. There are several recent reviews which deal with one or two aspects of the abortion experience (Simon & Senturia, 1966; Peck & Marcus, 1966; Walter, 1970; Whitman, 1971; Osofsky, Osofsky, & Rajan, 1971), but this paper considers many abortion issues: (a) demographic characteristics of those obtaining abortion, (b) the public's opinion about abortion, (c) the reasons why aborting women have unwanted pregnancies, (d) the motivations of women seeking abortion, and (e) the medical and psychological sequelae of abortion. Since issues (b), (c), and (d) are relevant before the abortion, they can be considered antecedent variables, while (e) constitutes a consequent variable.

This review evaluates the quality of the research on the psychosocial factors of abortion. As would be expected, the more recent studies are better methodologically than the earlier studies. Much of the literature is so poor it can be dismissed on the basis of gross methodological problems, e.g., biased samples and unreliable measurements. The critical analysis here varies with the quality of the studies. More sophisticated critiques can be made of the newer research. The better studies allow for more detailed analyses and demand closer attention because their conclusions can be taken more seriously.

Demographic Characteristics of Those Obtaining Abortion

In this section a summary is presented of the demographic characteristics of the women in each of three groups (a) those who received illegal abortions, (b) those who received therapeutic abortions under restrictive laws, and (c) those who received abortions on request.

Estimates of the number of illegal abortions that occurred in the United States and descriptions of the characteristics of the women who obtained illegal abortions have been difficult to make. Estimates of the number of illegal abortions ranged from 20,000 to 1,500,000 per year prior to 1970 (Calderone, 1958; Lader, 1966; Pipel & Norwick, 1969; Chisolm, 1970). According to Steinhoff, Diamond, Palmore, and Smith (1973), most of the women getting illegal abortions were single, young, middle class, and primaparous.

Before 1970, abortion was illegal in all states except to preserve the life of the pregnant woman. Estimates of the number of therapeutic abortions performed in the United States ranged from 10,000 per year (Lee, 1969; Newman, 1973) to 18,000 per year (Hefferman, 1953; Moore-Čavar, 1974). Women who received therapeutic abortions have been said to be mostly middle-aged, wealthy, and highly educated white women with completed families (Calderone, 1958; Gebhard, Pomeroy & Martin, 1958; Gold, Erhard, & Jacobziner, 1965; Lader, 1966; Peck & Marcus, 1966; Newman, Beck, & Lewit, 1971). However, statements about the characteristics of therapeutic abortion patients are not very reliable for a number of reasons. First, since there were different indications for legal abortions in different states, composite statistics made up of women obtaining therapeutic abortions for extremely diverse reasons are difficult to interpret. Second, the records may have been falsified or distorted (Lader, 1966) so that women with less than technically legal indications could have their pregnancies ended.

Unlike data on the two previous groups of aborting women, data on the women receiving abortion on request are highly reliable. According to Moore-Čavar (1974), in 1972, with legal abortions available in several states, 586,000 abortions were legally induced in the United States. It has been concluded that, in contrast to past legal abortion patients, the recent ones are more likely to be young, single, and primaparous (Duffy, 1971; Pakter & Nelson, 1971; Rovinsky, 1971; Tietze & Lewit, 1972; Steinhoff, *et al.,* 1973). However, Steinhoff, (1973) deduced from Hawaii figures that "when both the age distribution and the probability of pregnancy are taken into consideration, it becomes apparent that women at the two ends of the fertile age range are more likely to terminate a pregnancy by abortion than those in the 25–35 age group" (p. 17). The Hawaii researchers conclude that "the women who utilize legal abortion now, but would not have sought illegal abortion, are primarily older, married women, who already have children. The rest [are] women who would have utilized illegal abortion, plus a substantial number of young women who would have married and begun their families earlier" (Steinhoff *et al.,* 1973, p. 10).

Data on the ethno-racial make-up of the population of women obtaining abortions are available by state; national statistics are unavailable. Statistics indicate that the number of legal abortions per 1000 live births was higher for blacks than for whites in California, Colorado, Delaware, Kansas, Maryland, and New York, although this was not true for Alaska, Arkansas, Georgia, North Carolina, and South Carolina (Pakter & Nelson, 1971; Tietze, 1973; Steinhoff, 1973; Moore-Čavar, 1974).

In Hawaii it has been reported that the recent patients tend to be more highly educated than women in the population at large (Steinhoff, 1973). In that state, for example, over 80 percent of the abortion patients had completed high school and more than 50 percent had been educated beyond high school (Smith, Diamond, & Palmore, 1973). Researchers in Hawaii also concluded that the upper income groups are not overrepresented in the abortion population as they were reported to be in abortion populations prior to abortion on request (Smith, *et al.,* 1973; Steinhoff, 1971). Such a conclusion, of course, needs to be verified in other states and samples.

The Abortion Situation in Foreign Countries

Since many of the abortion studies have been conducted in countries other than the United States, the facts of the abortion situation in several foreign countries are presented.

In Sweden, where most of the foreign studies on the psychology of abortion have been conducted, the abortion law has been fairly liberal since 1938. Abortion during the first twenty weeks of pregnancy is legal on sociomedical, humanitarian, and eugenic grounds (Shaw, 1968), including possible strain on the pregnant woman in rearing her child (Pohlman, 1969). However, in Sweden a substantial number of women seeking legal abortions are refused, and it has been suggested that there are as many or more illegal abortions in that country than legal ones (Ekbald, 1954). Many of the women getting illegal abortions in Sweden have been said to be young, single women (Gebhard *et al.* 1958), the same type of women who, according to Steinhoff *et al.* (1973), had been getting most of the illegal abortions in the United States.

The legality of abortion and the rate of illegal abortion in Denmark is similar to that in Sweden (Genhard *et al.,* 1958). In the Soviet Union, Hungary, Czechoslovakia, and Japan, abortion for any indication has been legal since the mid 1950's.

Antecedents of Abortion

Public Opinion

National opinion surveys of the last decade indicate that the American public generally has approved of abortion under certain circumstances (threat to the woman's life or health, incest, rape or possible fetal deformity), but has disapproved of abortion available on request (Shaw, 1968; Moore-Čavar, 1974). Moore-Čavar (1974) concluded from statistics compiled from 27 studies that in the United States more liberal attitudes are associated with higher education and single marital status. Jews and Protestants are more favorable toward abortion than are Catholics, and males more than females. Further, she states that the findings on the relationship between occupation, income, socio-economic status, race, and age are inconsistent. In a study of currently married women, Miller (1973) found that attitudes toward abortion are not related to a woman's age, the size of her family, the experience of unwanted children, or intentions to have additional children.

It is quite likely that public attitudes toward abortion affect the attitudes and behavior of women who terminate their pregnancies. For instance, it is probably more difficult for a woman to commit an act that is condemned by most of society than an act that is condoned by society. The dynamics of how and to what extent publicly held views influence the decisions and experiences of women needs to be investigated.

Why Aborting Women Have Unwanted Pregnancies

There are many possible reasons why aborting women have unwanted pregnancies. Miller (1973) assessed these reasons directly. A sample of women who were obtaining abortions on request were asked to complete Miller's Contraceptive Sexual Attitude Questionnaire (CSAQ), a list of 53 possible reasons for unwanted pregnancy derived from interviews with physicians and social workers who worked with women applying for abortion or seeking contraceptive advice. On the CSAQ each respondent was asked to check any item which may have played a role in her pregnancy. The sample were mostly young, never married, white, middle- and upper-middle class, private patients.

Miller concluded that several factors were responsible for the unwanted pregnancies of a large proportion of these women. The first factor he referred to as "retrospective rhythm," where the woman "rationalizes the safety of a particular act of sexual intercourse" after it is over. In fact, only a few of the women who reported that they thought they were in a safe period actually knew anything about ovulation and fertility cycles. At the time of conception, 54 percent of the women reported using no form of contraception, 14 percent reported using rhythm, and the rest reported using various kinds of contraceptive devices. Diamond, Steinhoff, Palmore, and Smith (1973) also reported that many of the married women seeking abortions in Hawaii said they did not use birth control because they thought they were in a safe period. Many of the young, single women in the Hawaii population expected intercourse but did not use birth control because they did not want to seem prepared for sex. In that same population, single, unattached women used birth control the least, followed by single women going steady, and then by women living with a man or married.

Another reason for unwanted pregnancy defined by Miller was contraceptive failure, which was indicated as the reason for pregnancy by one-third of the respondents. The accuracy of the women's testimony with regard to contraceptive failure was found to be quite high, as verified by interviewing a subset of 328 respondents and judging whether contraceptive failure or contraceptive misuse had actually occurred. Approximately 19 percent of the aborting women in Hawaii also attributed their pregnancy to birth control failures (Diamond *et al.,* 1973). A third factor was misuse or fear of certain contraceptives, and a fourth factor was denial or refusal to recognize the possibility of getting pregnant.

Miller also found that demographic variables were related to reasons for unwanted pregnancy. Married women, women with higher education, and women with previous induced abortions reported more contraceptive failures than other women, and women with higher education were more likely to be afraid of the side effects of certain contraceptives. In Miller's sample, Catholic women living with their parents were the most likely to get pregnant because they felt such matters as contraception were unimportant in view of their overwhelming love for their partners. High income non-Catholics, living at home, were the most accepting of abortion as a way of coping with an unwanted pregnancy. In a related study, McCormick (1973) concluded that in a group of women seeking abortion, black women are less accepting than white women of abortion as either a primary or a secondary way to control fertility.

The bulk of Miller's data came from the CSAQ responses. Miller reported that the validity of the CSAQ was substantiated by several results: the logical and easily interpretable response patterns in the regression analysis, the accuracy of the reports on contraceptive failure, and the lack of relationship between contraceptive failure and denial, rationalization, or impulsiveness. The CSAQ appears to be a fairly useful method of assessing the way in which women account for their own unwanted pregnancies and is representative of the focus on conscious reasons for unwanted pregnancy.

In much of the older literature, unconscious, psychopathological motivations have been assumed to play a significant role in unwanted pregnancy, although such reasons were endorsed infrequently in Miller's study. Traditionally, women with unwanted pregnancies were said to be manipulative, sado-masochistic, compulsive conceivers, and afraid of disapproval (Deutsch, 1945; Romm, 1954; Bolter, 1962). These conclusions were based solely on the writers' uncorroborated clinical opinion and should not be seen as scientifically founded deductions.

In more recent investigations of unconscious motives for unwanted pregnancy, Simon, Rothman, Goff, and Senturia (1969) and Ford, Castelnuevo-Tedesco, and Long (1972) concluded that women obtaining therapeutic abortions have marked emotional conflict about their female identity and reproductive role and end the pregnancy to satisfy sado-masochistic impulses. Simon *et al.* compared 46 women who obtained therapeutic abortions with 32 women who had spontaneous abortions. Ford *et al.* compared 40 women seeking therapeutic abortion with 52 pregnant women not seeking abortion. Both studies relied on pre-abortion MMPI scores. Since these conclusions were based on pre-abortion data in which women were trying to convince an abortion committee that their mental health was endangered by the pregnancy, the picture presented of women seeking abortions is probably misleading. Since these women were aware that they had to demonstrate their psychopathology as a result of the pregnancy, it appears likely that the pre-abortion assessments of the women reflect the women's attempt to appear as unstable as possible. In fact, Ford *et al.* (1972) reported that women seeking therapeutic abortions had elevated F scale scores on the MMPI which might indicate "intentional exaggeration of symptoms."

Abernathy (1973) also was interested in unconscious motives. She tested the hypothesis that a woman who aborts had assumed elements of her mother's role in the family during adolescence because her mother was alienated from her daughter. Women (N = 65, average age = 28 years) who had an abortion were compared with matched controls who were judged to be effective users of contraception. Two independent judges rated the extent of "role redefinition in the family of origin," assigning each woman a score from 1 to 6 where 1 is high role-redefinition, including an overt incestuous relationship with the father and dating the father, and 6 is normal assignment of roles within the family.

Abernathy reported several differences between the two groups. Women who had obtained induced abortions were more likely to be rated high on role redefinition. They were more likely to have assumed household and child-caring responsibilities in their teens, were more likely to be intimate with men than women, were more sexually precocious, and were more likely to recall that their parents were often hostile to one another than the controls. Abernathy concludes

> that a daughter both fosters and can be the victim of a weak parental coalition, and that because of attraction to the father and alienation from the mother she may be willing to substitute for the maternal figure in domestic spheres and in providing companionship for the father. However, her feelings may then become disturbing because of the excessive intimacy of the ensuing relationship with the father and anxiety may be augmented to the extent that the mother is not warm and supportive. This pressure together with low-self-esteem appear to be major factors in predisposing a woman to risk unwanted pregnancy. (p. 350)

There are a number of problems with Abernathy's methodology that make the conclusions of little value. First, the 1-to-6 scale assumes unidimensionality. However, there are actually two dimensions to the scale which are confounded in the measurement. The two dimensions are the sexual attraction to the father and the assumption of the instrumental mother role. The scale as it was used implies that the two components covary such that if a woman is high on one then she will be high on the other. The scale does not allow for the likely possibility of a woman who was forced by external circumstances to adopt a mother role in the family but who has a very traditional daughter relationship with the father. Second, it may be that the woman's role redefinition score was actually a measure of how disclosing she was about her early history and her feelings about her parents. It seems reasonable that women who admit to abortion are generally more open about themselves and thus revealed certain thoughts or feelings that might have led to a high role-redefinition score. On the other hand, the low role-redefinition scores of the controls may have just indicated a tendency to not reveal intimate feelings. If the controls were more likely to receive high scores, then many may have scored "5," which is "lack of information contrary to normalcy, so it is assumed." Thus an absence of overt role redefinition is classified as normal role development but may really represent nondisclosure of early history.

An additional problem with the Abernathy study is that it assumes that women have some control over unwanted pregnancy. However, given the high percentage of women who have contraceptive failure, the conclusion that adolescent experiences predict unwanted pregnancy would seem to be quite limited.

Why women have unwanted pregnancies should be studied in relation to the woman's decision to have an abortion and the consequences of the abortion procedure. It may be, for example, that women who have unwanted pregnancies because of contraceptive failure have less severe reactions to abortion than women who failed to contracept because they were afraid of how it would appear to their partner. The former may feel less responsible for the pregnancy. Further research might also explore personality correlates of unwanted pregnancy.

Why Women Have Abortions

A review of the literature indicates that the reasons for inducing abortion are different for women who obtained therapeutic abortions under restrictive laws, women who obtained illegal abortions, and women who obtain abortions on request.

Before liberalization of the abortion laws, legal "therapeutic" abortions could be performed for (a) medical indications and (b) psychiatric indications. Since 1950's, the major philosophy regarding medical indications has been that abortion is unnecessary unless pregnancy intensifies the illness (Spivak, 1967). Most sources conclude that the strictly biological reasons for abortion have been declining (Schur, 1955; Routledge, Sparling, & McFarlan 1953; Rosen, 1967; Peel & Potts, 1969). Opinion varies as to what constitutes a medical indication for termination of pregnancy. Frequently cited indications are heart disease, lung disease, kidney disease, malignancy, chorea, ostosclerosis, syphilis, abdominal emergencies, and obstetric and gynecological conditions (Peel & Potts, 1969).

Although the frequency of abortions for medical indications has been decreasing, the frequency of abortions for psychiatric indications had been increasing until psychiatric requirements were dropped with legalization of abortion on request (Schur, 1955; Christakos, 1970). Prior to the broadening of the laws, the only legal psychiatric reason for granting abortion was to prevent a pregnant woman from committing suicide. Rosen (1967) commented that although psychiatrists received many suicidal threats from pregnant women "the suicide rate among pregnant women is less than what would statistically be expected for the population as a whole" (p. 83). However, he also pointed out that "eight percent of all women who committed suicide in Sweden during the twenty-year period from 1925 through 1945 . . . were found on autopsy to be pregnant, and in each case, on investigation, their pregnancy was felt to be the precipitating factor in the suicide" (p. 83). Because of such ambiguity about the real threat of suicide in pregnant women, it had been difficult for American psychiatrists and hospital abortion committees to decide what constituted legitimate psychiatric indications for abortion (Lader, 1966; Rosen, 1967). And since there were no standarized abortion screening practices (Whitman, 1971), a woman could be refused abortion by one hospital and granted abortion by another.

Many authors have asserted that any woman who wants an abortion is necessarily, by reason of her want, emotionally ill (Galdston, 1958; Dunbar, 1954; Bolter, 1962). The only empirical support for such notions comes from an unpublished study cited by Whitman (1971) in which therapeutic abortion applicants scored higher on several MMPI scales than maternity patients. However, the differences were not statistically significant in most cases. In addition, the MMPI scores may have been affected by the abortion applicants' stressful state rather than their general psychopathology. In fact, Ford *et al.* (1972) and Brody, Meikle, and Gerritse (1971) offer evidence that pre-abortion psychological distress can be attributed to the woman's situation and not to any lasting emotional problems. Kane, Lacherbruch, and Lipton (1973) also found that abortion patients are no more neurotic than a comparable group of nonpregnant women, as measured by the Neuroticism Scale Qestionnaire. However, the women who were ending pregnancies were reported to be more anxious than those in the comparison group. Kane *et al.* suggest that high anxiety is due to waiting for the procedure. In light of these writings, it appears unreasonable to conclude that women seeking abortion are emotionally unstable.

In contrast to what has been written about women seeking therapeutic abortions, women who obtained illegal abortions have been said to be concerned mostly about how a baby would affect their lives and the lives of people they cared about, and about the social stigma of being an unwed mother (Lee, 1969). Lee (1969) found that single women who had an illegal abortion terminated their pregnancies because they did not want to be forced into marriage, or because they did not want the responsibility of caring for a child. Engaged or cohabitating women aborted because they did not want to begin a marriage with pregnancy, and married women because they thought a new child would cause or add to family and marital problems, or because they felt too old to raise a baby. Finally, Lee found that divorced or separated women aborted because they felt they could not afford to raise a child. Lee's sample may have been biased since she located her respondents through personal contacts.

Recent research indicates the women receiving abortion on request are aborting for reasons similar to those reasons reported for women seeking illegal abortions before liberalization of the laws. According to the Hawaii studies, women decide to terminate their pregnancies "based on evaluation of objective factors related to the woman's perceived capacity to care for the child" (Steinhoff *et al.,* 1972; Smith *et al.,* 1973). In addition, situational and demographic variables, such as financial status, education, career plans, marital status, and age, were found to be extremely important in determining whether or not a particular pregnancy will be aborted (Steinhoff *et al.,* 1972; Smith *et al.,* 1973).

For example, according to Steinhoff *et al.* (1972), young, single women abort to delay marriage and family, while older, married women abort to prevent their existing family from getting any bigger. In comparison with maternity patients, "women who abort their first pregnancy tend to have become pregnant at an earlier age than those who carry their first pregnancy to term" (Steinhoff *et al.,* 1972). Also, since a large proportion of the Hawaii abortion population is students, while a large proportion of the maternity population is housewives, Steinhoff *et al.* (1972) concluded that "a much higher proportion of maternity patients are already in the occupational position most easily adapted to childbirth and infant care, while a higher proportion of abortion patients are committed to activities outside the home" (p. 5). Also, although over half of the aborting women in Hawaii were reportedly involved in a continuing relationship with a man, it was felt that "women who carry their pregnancy to term seem to have relatively stable family situations into which to bring children, while abortion tends to be chosen by women who do not have those family conditions." In general, the researchers of the Hawaii abortion population concluded that "at the individual level as well as in the overall group comparisons, the reason women give for choosing abortion appear to reflect a fair appraisal of their capacity to provide a satisfactory home for a child" (Steinhoff, *et al.,* 1972).

A variety of methods were used by the Hawaii Pregnancy, Birth Control, and Abortion Study group, including extensive interviews, self-administered questionnaires, and medical charts. The Hawaii studies are all methodologically sophisticated and might well be used as examples for other large scale studies of the psychology of abortion.

Consequences of Abortion

Medical Sequelae

Medical complications of abortion vary with the length of gestation of the pregnancy, the physical condition of the pregnant women, and the method of inducing abortion. The earlier the pregnancy, the better the physical condition of the woman, and the more medically appropriate the abortion procedure, the less likely there will be physical complications (Tietze, 1969; Cushner, 1971; Smith *et al.,* 1973). Also, there is a greater risk of complications for women who have had a previous abortion (Pohlman, 1969). Some of the possible complications of abortion are infection, hemorrhage, perforation, sterility, or risk to subsequent pregnancies (Peel & Potts, 1969).

Before liberalization of the laws, estimates of the mortality rates of women receiving illegal abortions were difficult to make. According to many reports, however, mortality and morbidity rates have been declining and generally there is less risk associated with abortion than with childbirth (Tietze & Lehfeldt, 1961; Lader, 1966; Peel & Potts, 1969; Pipel & Norwick, 1969; Cushner, 1971; Newman, 1973).

Psychological Sequelae

The literature on the psychological effects of induced abortion is quite contradictory: many studies conclude that there are severe psychological consequences; many conclude that there are mild or no consequences, and some conclude that the consequences vary with other factors. Some people have taken the stand that because there are so many divergent results, the after-effects of abortion remain unknown (Population Study Commission, 1966; Newman *et al.,* 1971).

The contradictory results are attributable to methodological differences, differences in the variables investigated, sample differences, and theoretical differences. Many of the conclusions have been drawn from shoddy or nonexistent data. Investigations of the psychological sequelae must be examined separately for the therapeutic abortion population, the illegal abortion population, and the abortion on request population. Several recent reviews of the effects of abortion can be found in Peck and Marcus (1966), Simon, Senturia, and Rothman (1967), Osofsky *et al.* (1971), and Osofsky and Osofsky (1972).

Several investigations, based on women obtaining legal, therapeutic abortions, concluded that the psychological sequelae of abortion were unfavorable. One of the earliest investigations was conducted by Hesseltine, Adair, and Boynton (1940). Through psychiatric records they assessed the outcome of the therapeutic abortions of 82 women after a time period ranging from one to eight years. For 21 women, the outcome was judged to be "satisfactory" ("improved"), for 22 "unchanged," for 3 "unsatisfactory," and for 35 "undetermined." Although so few women actually were judged to be worse for the abortion, and despite the number of women said to be improved, the authors concluded that abortion was very rarely necessary. Further, the exact manner in which evaluations of psychiatric material were made was not reported, and the large number of "undetermined" outcomes was unexplained (Simon & Senturia, 1966). Also, the possible sample biases and the quite variable time spans between the abortion and the assessment are other problems. Therefore, this study is of little value.

The second major study in which unfavorable emotional sequelae of abortion were reported was the Ebaugh and Heuser (1947) investigation. From evaluations of 29 women, they state that feelings of guilt, self-depreciation, and hostility toward one's male partner were the after-effects of abortion. However, since so little of their methodology was presented, it is difficult to evaluate their conclusions.

Wilson and Cain (1951) set out to investigate the consequences of therapeutic abortion of the 226 women who had received them between 1930 and 1949 at a particular medical facility. However, they were able to interview only nine of these women in the follow-up. Two of the women said they felt a loss and felt guilty about the abortion. Four women complained of minor physical discomfort that they felt was related to the abortion. Wilson and Cain concluded that "abortion, regardless of how early it occurs, or whether it is spontaneous or induced, is not without lasting effects and the emotional response may be deep and lasting" (p. 22). This conclusion seems to have been based on the sequelae of two women out of a self-selected group of nine women and to have been overgeneralized to all aborting women. However, in a following study, Wilson (1952) arrived at a different evaluation of the effects of abortion. He interviewed 25 women who had had either a therapeutic, illegal, or spontaneous abortion and concluded only that the consequences of abortion vary with the period of gestation of the pregnancy and the personality of the woman. In addition, Wilson did not use an appropriate comparison group in either study. As Sherman (1975) points out, the appropriate comparison group for abortion patients is women with unwanted pregnancies who deliver at full term.

Using a different approach, Hefferman and Lynch (1953) evaluated the psychology of abortion from questionnaires received from 152 of 367 hospital administrators. Although they did not assess the psychological sequelae directly, they deduced that guilt, disgust, and negative feelings toward one's male partner are the consequences of abortion. Since the data was not gathered from primary care-takers of abortion patients and since the authors appear to have had a strong anti-abortion bias prior to data collection, the value of the study is doubtful.

In Rosen's (1954) compilation of essays on abortion, which had a major impact on the field, three articles strongly argued that abortion leads to adverse psychological reactions. Romm (1954), Dunbar (1954), and Lidz (1954) wrote that the effects of abortion are severe conscious or unconscious guilt, anger toward the male partner, reactivation of the female castration fear, reactive depression, and, in extreme cases, psychosis. The authors' conclusions were based on their own clinical experiences which are subject to reliability and validity problems and, thus, the conclusions have limited scientific worth. However, clinical opinion has constituted much of the literature on the psychology of abortion (Galdston, 1958; Bolter, 1962).

A number of studies of the psychological consequences of therapeutic abortion were conducted in other countries. Malmfors (1958) determined the effect of abortion on 84 Swedish women two years after the abortion had occurred. He concluded that 39 of the women were pleased about the abortion, 4 were unwilling to discuss it, 9 were repressing guilt about it, 22 were openly expressing guilt, and 10 were psychologically impaired because of it. Of those who were granted abortions for psychiatric indications, 12 percent were said to have deteriorated psychologically. Unfortunately the accuraccy of Malmfors' interpretations is difficult to determine since the methodology is not clearly spelled out.

Arén (1958) investigated a random sample of Swedish women who had legal abortions three years prior to the interview. Twenty-three percent of the women had severe reactions, 25 percent had mild guilt, and 23 percent believed problems subsequent to the experience were punishment for the abortion.

Slightly different results were reported in a subsequent study by Arén and Åmark (1961) of a Swedish sample. Of 234 women, 21 percent were judged to be deteriorated emotionally, 43 percent were unchanged, and 37 percent were improved. Arén and Åmark wrote that "a relatively large number of women afterwards regret the performance of the operation or feel more or less pronounced self-reproach . . . guilt and remorse . . . on account of it" (p. 207).

In each of the above studies indicating unfavorable psychological sequelae of abortion there were methodological problems. First, the methodology often is not described fully and most of the measuring devices are not scientifically rigorous, e.g., one therapist's clinical opinion and uncorroborated interviews. Second, most of the studies relied on recall or retrospective data which is always subject to witting or unwitting distortion. Women asked about their abortion might have tended to overemphasize their feelings of guilt or remorse so as not to appear callous and coldhearted. Also, the majority of the interviews were conducted by males. According to Kummer (1963), data on a topic as sensitive as abortion may be different in nature and different in interpretation when collected by male and female researchers. Also, few of the studies indicated the type, frequence, or severity of the sequelae. Further, no studies compared the psychological effects to those of an appropriate control group—women with unwanted pregnancies who bear the child anyway. In spite of these problems, the studies conclude that since the sequelae of abortion are so much worse than full-term delivery for women with unwanted pregnancies, preservation of the mother's health or prevention of suicide are the only legitimate reasons for inducing abortion. Several authors even concluded that there were unfavorable psychological consequences when their own data are ambiguous or mixed regarding the outcome of abortion. Simon and Senturia (1966) noted that "it is sobering to observe the ease with which reports can be embedded in the literature, quoted, and requoted many times without consideration of the data in the original paper. Deeply held personal convictions frequently seem to outweigh the importance of data, especially when conclusions are drawn" (p. 187).

It also may be that a woman's emotional symptoms after the abortion are more a function of her overall mental health then of the interruption of her pregnancy. And, it has been argued that the development of negative after-effects, such as guilt or depression, is dependent upon the attitude of the medical staff and clinic toward the aborting woman. Negative effects have been said to be more likely to develop when the medical environment is not supportive (White, 1966; Walter, 1970). An additional limitation is that the samples in the studies usually have been self-selected and often included women who were sterilized simultaneously with the abortion so the consequences of both procedures could not be assessed independently (Rosen, 1958; Walter, 1970). Therefore, it appears unwarranted to conclude that therapeutic abortion produces negative psychological reactions in women. In fact, there is no high quality study which supports this conclusion.

In contrast to studies which conclude that the emotional effects of therapeutic abortion are severe, others have concluded that the effects are positive or neutral. As the following review shows, the scientific quality of the studies which have concluded that there are mild, negligible, or favorable psychological sequelae is quite varied. Some of the projects are as methodologically poor as those indicating unfavorable consequences, but many meet the standards of good scientific research.

Hamilton (1940, 1941) studied the importance of the length of time between the abortion and the assessment of its emotional outcome. In these studies, only 30 of 537 women interviewed had obtained therpeutic abortions, the rest had had spontaneous or illegal abortions. Immediately after the abortion, 46 percent felt regret, 39 percent felt relief, and 15 percent felt indifferent about the abortion. Fewer women who had therapeutic or illegal abortions felt regret than those who had had spontaneous abortions. Otherwise, no variables were reported that accounted for such different feelings. From such findings, there were no clear indications of the emotional effects of abortion, only that the effects were variable. However, Hamilton (1941) re-interviewed 100 of the women in the first study who came back for a four-week check-up. From these interviews, Hamilton concluded that with time, feelings of relief and satisfaction become more prominent than feelings of regret and guilt. However, there were problems in the two studies, i.e., a self-selected follow-up sample, no distinction made between women who had therapeutic, spontaneous, and illegal abortions, and no correlation made between pre-abortion and post-abortion psychological condition.

In 1963, Kummer (1963) attempted to validate psychiatrists' opinions of the emotional after-effects of abortion by polling 32 psychiatrists in California. According to Kummer, "75% [of the psychiatrists] had never encountered any moderate to severe psychiatric sequelae of abortion. The remaining 25% encountered such sequelae only rarely, the highest figure reported was six cases in fifteen years of practice" (p. 981). On the other hand, the psychiatrists reported treating many more women for unfavorable post-childbirth psychological problems. Kummer concluded that "apparently pregnancy and parturition exert greater stresses than does induced abortion upon women susceptible to mental illness" (p. 982). Kummer did not report how his sample of psychiatrists was selected, how the emotional condition of the women was evaluated, how standardized were the methods of evaluation, or how many and what types of women constituted the population. Further, he did not prorate the occurrence of psychological problems by the occurrence of abortion and live births.

In the same year that Kummer's study appeared, Mumford (1963) published an article that assessed the after-effects of therapeutic abortion by a totally different method. Mumford conducted an in-depth investigation of four married women with two or more children, who had one or more abortions between the ages of 25 and 35. As Mumford pointed out, the sample was quite unique because these four women had ten induced abortions among them. Throughout the entire abortion procedure and one year afterward, the women were interviewed and tested extensively. Mumford reported "no evidence in any case of significant negative ideational or emotional sequelae to the abortion experience" (p. 868). Clearly, his conclusions are quite limited given the small size and uniqueness of his sample.

An in-depth investigation of a larger sample was conducted by Peck and Marcus (1966). Fifty women were interviewed when they applied for legal abortions, and three to six months following the procedure. Demographic, personal history, obstetric and gynecological, and psychiatric data were collected in the pre-abortion interview. In the follow-up, an examination reportedly was made of the woman's psychological condition, her relationships with others, and her attitudes toward future pregnancies. Most of the women in the sample were between the ages of twenty and forty, married, Jewish, well-educated, and private patients. Half of the sample obtained abortions for psychiatric indications and half for nonpsychiatric indications. Of those in the psychiatric group, 72 were schizophrenic, 24 percent were depressed, and 4 percent were neurotic with severe character disorders.

Peck and Marcus reported no significant demographic differences between the psychiatric and nonpsychiatric groups. Only one woman in the psychiatric group had a negative reaction to the abortion, a short-lived depression. Of the nonpsychiatric, 36 percent felt a mild depression and regretted that the abortion had been necessary, but such reactions reportedly did not interfere with their everyday functioning. No woman was hospitalized for psychiatric care following the abortion. Relationships with men did not change for most of the women in the nonpsychiatric group, and improved for 36 percent and worsened for 20 percent of the women in the psychiatric group.

Peck and Marcus concluded that "there would seem to be little reason to fear that a therapeutic interruption of pregnancy will result in psychiatric illness *de novo* or that it will make pre-existing minor psychiatric illness worse . . . On the contrary, it was found to be truly therapeutic in that it alleviated acute states of depression and anxiety, which had resulted from becoming pregnant" (p. 422). While this study is better methodologically than many previous investigations, the validity of the conclusions is questionable on several grounds. First, although the authors claim that few negative consequences occurred and even though hospitalization was evaluated, the post-abortion condition was not assessed rigorously. Second, given that eligibility for abortion was at issue prior to the procedure, it may be that the diagnostic labels were used liberally. Thus, women may have been categorized as being severely disturbed, i.e., schizophrenic, in order to facilitate granting the abortion. Such a practice would make post-abortion normality look like a positive change in contrast. Third, the sample is quite select because although such a large percentage are labelled schizophrenic, they are Jewish, wealthy, private patients who are nonhospitalized—an unusual group.

Niswander and Patterson (1967) found results similar to those of Peck and Marcus (1966) although they used a questionnaire rather than an interview. From a sample of 116 women, they found that immediately after the abortion most women reported feeling better, and that as time passed more women had favorable rather than unfavorable feelings about the procedure. Women who aborted for nonpsychiatric reasons were reported to have more unfavorable responses. According to Niswander and Patterson, "the abortion is usually therapeutic in the best sense of the word—the patient feels better and therefore functions more effectively" (p. 706).

In studying abortion, Simon, Senturia, and Rothman (1967) analyzed interview, MMPI, and Loevinger Family Problem Scale data, rather than depending on only one measurement of post-abortion effects. The sample consisted of mostly white, middle-class, well-educated women. Simon *et al.* reported that 23 women felt relieved and well, 13 felt mild depression, and six felt marked depression immediately after the abortion. Of three groups—those who aborted for psychiatric (35 percent), medical (26 percent), and eugenic (19 percent) reasons—a larger proportion of the women in the psychiatric group had positive responses and a larger proportion of the women in the medical group had negative responses. Although no statistical analyses are presented, Simon *et al.* concluded that the eugenic group were more likely to become depressed and the medical group to feel guilty after the abortion than the other groups. According to Simon *et al.*, "psychiatric illness does occur after therapeutic abortion, but it is not primarily related to the abortion itself. Our study did not produce support for the frequently expressed belief that therapeutic abortion results in involuntary infertility, difficulty in sexual relations, or is a precipitant in involutional depression" (p. 64).

One major problem with such a statement is that it is extremely difficult to determine the precipitant of any psychiatric illness and to eliminate any particular recent event from consideration as a possible contributor to emotional disturbance. However, even though Simon *et al.* do not present strong evidence that subsequent psychiatric illness is not causally related to abortion, they did find a low rate of psychopathology in women obtaining an abortion.

In the same year, an investigation by Kretzchmar and Norris (1967) also concluded that psychological sequelae of abortion are not negative. The sample consisted of mostly non-Catholic, married women who aborted for medical or eugenic reasons. Only two of the 32 women in the study aborted for psychiatric indications, and of the total, one-third were sterilized at the time of the abortion. The follow-up interviews and questionnaires were administered from one to five years after the abortion. The researchers reported that although most of the patients felt anxious and depressed before the abortion, most felt better following a short period of depression after the abortion. The only flaw with the Kretzchmar and Norris study is that a large proportion of the women were sterilized in addition to having an abortion, and so the outcome of abortion cannot be studied as an independent factor, although one would expect that psychiatric reaction to abortion plus sterilization would be more negative than the psychiatric reaction to abortion alone. Overall, the Kretzchmar and Norris investigation is particularly good.

Support for mild or negligible psychological sequelae also was reported by Patt, Rappaport, and Barglow (1969). In a one- to two-hour semi-structured interview, 35 white, middle-class, young women were asked to discuss their reasons for aborting, their feelings about the abortion, their immediate and long-term reaction to abortion, their life situations prior to and after the abortion, their parental and heterosexual relationships, their childhoods, and whether or not they had tried to present exaggerated psychiatric symptoms.

Twenty of the 35 women felt relieved and relaxed immediately after the pregnancy termination. For half of the remaining 15, whose symptoms included suicidal gestures, promiscuity, depression, and physical complaints, the immediate negative consequences were judged to be due to pre-abortion problems and not to the abortion itself. Twenty-six of the 35 felt that in the long term they had improved, four felt unchanged, and six felt worse. However, of the 15 patients who had short-term unfavorable symptoms, "ten considered their long-term emotional status or life functioning improved" (p. 412). Also, half of the women said that their sexual relations had improved. In sum, Patt *et al.* felt that therapeutic abortion generally had positive effects. However, like Simon *et al.,* Patt *et al.* do not present data to support their conclusion that the immediate negative aftereffects were not attributable to the abortion. Yet, even if there were some short-term negative effects in some women, the majority of women obtaining an abortion felt that there were no long-term sequelae. A further problem might be that the study depended on recall data. Reports of past feelings, attitudes, motivations, and behaviors may be distorted, and no attempt was made to analyze the existence, direction, or strength of the distortion. In spite of any possible distortion, however, the Patt *et al.* data are important in that women report that they generally come to feel positively about the abortion in the long run.

In one of the few prospective studies of the effect of therapeutic abortion, Brody, Meikle, and Gerritse (1971) concluded that the procedure is generally very beneficial and effective in reducing psychopathological symptoms. They administered several tests to 117 abortion applicants and to 58 "control" patients who were were in the same state of pregnancy as the abortion applicants. The 94 women who received abortions were retested six weeks, six months, and one year after the procedure, whereas those applicants who were not granted an abortion and the control patients were retested only six weeks after the initial testing.

The MMPl scores of the abortion applicants indicated a significantly greater degree of psychological disturbance than the controls whose scores were essentially normal. Those who received the abortions had MMPI profiles approaching normalcy by six weeks after the abortion. Women who obtained tubal ligation at the time of termination did not differ in improvement from those who only aborted. The rejected applicants ($N = 23$), on the other hand, remained as disturbed as they were on the initial testing. The Borday *et al.* study is good methodologically.

Ford *et al.* (1971) conducted a study very similar in methodology and results to the Brody *et al.* study. Forty abortion applicants scored high on several MMPI scales. In a six month follow-up of 29 of the applicants, the MMPI scores showed much less psychological distress. The only after-effect reported was a short-lived depression. Only those who were initially diagnosed as psychotic did not show any improvement in emotional stability. The Ford *et al.* study also is methodologically sound.

Several studies conducted in other countries also have concluded that the psychological consequences of therapeutic abortion are negligible or favorable (Ekbald, 1954; Brekke, 1958; Gillis, 1969; Todd, 1972; Moore-Cavar, 1974). The comparability of foreign studies with American research is limited because the samples are different.

It is difficult to comment generally on the large number of studies which have indicated no severe sequelae because the studies vary along every research dimension. Several of the studies suffer because they had to rely on self-selected small samples, and others suffer because the length of time between the abortion and assessment of outcome was too variable. Often methods and criteria for evaluation were not presented, and demographic variables were not considered. Further, many of the studies of therapeutic abortion are open to question because of the unreliable use of psychiatric labels in order to enhance the granting of the abortion. Similarly, those studies which concluded that negative reactions were not connected to the abortion do not support this with data. Like studies concluding that the effects of therapeutic abortion are negative, there are few methodologically sound studies which conclude that the effects of therapeutic abortion are essentially benign. However, there are several very good studies and, overall, the evidence is stronger that therapeutic abortion is basically untraumatic than that therapeutic abortion has negative after-effects.

The illegal abortion experience is so radically different from that of therapeutic abortion that the two can hardly be compared. The illegal experience usually is clandestine, expensive, and the abortion is often performed by less than competent operators. First, a women has to find an abortionist who agrees to terminate her pregnancy. Lee (1969) and Schulder and Kennedy (1971) describe such a search as typically frustrating, dangerous, and humiliating. Lee (1969) and Schulder and Kennedy (1971) reported many cases of women who developed medical complications from illegal abortions but were too afraid to go to a hospital for treatment.

Lee (1969) reported that of those women she interviewed, eight percent had severe emotional problems resulting from the abortion, and less than half were depressed following the abortion. The most common complaint was that the women did not feel that their male partners were sufficiently supportive. Lee concluded that any negative emotional effects disappear in a few weeks. Gebhard *et al.* (1958) reported few unfavorable emotional sequelae of illegal abortion.

There are several problems in collecting data about any individual's experience in an illegal activity, i.e., the quality and conditions of the abortion are not standardized, the validity of the disclosed information is not substantiated, and the sample is subject to bias. Well-founded conclusions about the psychological sequelae of illegal abortions cannot yet be made.

Recent reports on the emotional effects of abortion on request concur that the majority of women do not suffer any measurable psychological trauma. In the Osofsky *et al.* (1971) and Osofsky and Osofsky (1972) studies, unfavorable consequences rarely occurred. The Osofsky sample consisted of 380 women, most of whom were young and white; half were single and the rest were split evenly among married, separated, or divorced women. Immediately and one month after the abortion, follow-up data were collected through individual interviews.

Osofsky *et al.* (1971) reported that 64 percent of the patients felt moderately or very happy about the abortion, 20 percent felt neutral, 10 percent felt moderately unhappy, and 5 percent very unhappy. Also, the majority (76 percent) experienced no guilt, although a minority experienced some (15 percent) or considerable (8 percent) guilt. More than three-fourths were satisfied with their decision to terminate the pregnancy. Consistent with the Hawaii studies, most of the women (77 percent) reported that they wanted children in the future. Osofsky *et al.* concluded that "the predominant reactions would appear to be relief and happiness" (p. 230).

In a subsequent article (Osofsky & Osofsky, 1972), intercorrelations among the psychological variables were reported. The data indicated that patients who had more difficulty in deciding to abort also had greater guilt, greater desire for future children, and would have been less likely to abort if it had been illegal. Demographic variables were also important. For example, Catholic patients had a harder time deciding to abort and experienced more guilt. Both of the Osofsky studies were better than most of the previous research. The sample characteristics and methodological procedures were clearly and thoroughly presented.

Athanasiou, Michaelson, Oppel, Unger, and Yager (1973) compared the sequelae of term birth for women with wanted pregnancies, abortion by dilation and curretage, and abortion by saline injection, matching groups on demographic variables ($N = 373$). The original assessment of the woman's emotional status included the Srole Anomie Scale, Rosenberg's Self-Esteem Scale, and a 90-minute structured interview. The follow-up assessment, 13 to 16 months after the delivery or the abortion, included a symptom check list, a shortened version of the MMPI, the Srole and Rosenberg scales, and another interview.

Athanasiou *et al.* found that women ending their pregnancies were not significantly different on any factors from women continuing their pregnancies. In support of the findings of the Osofsky *et al.* and Osofsky and Osofsky studies, they concluded that there were no serious physical or psychological after-effects of abortion. However, women high on scales 4 and 9 of the MMPI have a longer time to emotional recovery. The authors tentatively suggest that such women need special attention when they present themselves for either abortion or term birth. The Athanasiou *et al.* study was good in that it looked at long-term sequlae, used multiple measures of the woman's psychological condition, and compared the effects of abortion with other groups.

In another recent study, Smith (1973) obtained follow-up assessments on 80 women one to two years after their abortions. Most of the women were young, single, and in school. Medical students using very thorough, structured questionnaires interviewed the women. Follow-up interviews were conducted between one and two years later either by mail, by telephone, or in person. At follow-up, 90 percent reported no negative psychological after-effects, and 94 percent were satisfied with their decision to abort. Forty percent said that the abortion had no effect on their lives, and 40 percent said that it had a positive effect in that it was a maturing experience. Most said that their pre-abortion feelings of desperation ended when the pregnancy was terminated and that relief and satisfaction followed. Two of the 15 women who had a history of psychiatric problems sought psychiatric help after the abortion.

A small minority of the Smith (1973) sample reported having negative consequences. According to Smith, this group of women tended to be single teenagers who were ambilvalent about the abortion, who had been concerned about the abortion's possible adverse effect on their fertility, were especially fond of children, and were not involved in a continuing relationship with their sexual partner. The data collection method and length of the follow-up period are strengths of the Smith study.

Still another study, Monsour and Stewart (1973), reported that in 20 randomly selected college women who had aborted, the predominant reaction was positive, not negative. Only one woman felt guilty about ending her pregnancy and her guilt attenuated after five months. The main flaws in the study are that the sample is small and select and the follow-ups ranged from as little as one month to as much as 25 months later. Other studies indicating no negative psychological after-effects for women obtaining abortion on request are Addelson (1973) and Adler (1973).

The recent studies indicate that abortion on request is a relatively benign procedure; no studies conclude negative sequelae. However, there appears to be a certain percentage of women who experience at least mild negative sequelae. These women tend to be less certain about their decision to abort, to be involved in less stable heterosexual relationships, and to be more concerned about the consequences of abortion. In general, however, negative after-effects seem to be short-lived and rarely intense.

There are several methodological limitations of many of the studies of abortion on request. The studies use small, often unrepresentative samples, and measuring devices whose reliability and validity are unclear, or at least not reported. Despite such problems, the recent studies are significantly better than earlier research. That is, the analyses are less subjective, the measures are more reliable, comparisons are made with other groups of women, and, in some cases, statistical analyses are made.

In future research there is a clear need to identify conclusively the significant interrelationships among psychosocial variables in aborting women, to identify what variables account for differences in reaction to abortion, and to cross-validate the findings in a different sample.

Conclusion

Research on the psychosocial factors of abortion has focused on therapeutic abortion, illegal abortion, and abortion on request. The quality of the studies on the first two types of abortion generally has been poor. The literature has included anecdotes, which are not solid scientific material; surveys, which often have lacked depth, particularity, and precision; and interviews, which often have been uncontrolled and retrospective. Furthermore, samples have been incomplete and insufficiently described, and statistical analyses have been almost nonexistent. Reliable information about even the most basic facts of therapeutic and illegal abortions has not yet been established firmly, and so conclusions cannot be drawn.

Studies of abortion on request, however, have been, over-all, sound methodologically, and so the findings have greater validity. Some conclusions can be made. The abortion population seems to be comprised basically of young, single women who are neither prepared for nor willing to adjust their lives to a child. In general, many of the women report that they are not consciously aware of the possibility of conceiving at the time of intercourse. The emotional stability of women who have abortions is another issue of controversy, although there is evidence that the women are no more psychopathological than women who deliver term pregnancies.

The reasons why women have abortions are significant and often ignored variables in the study of the psychology of abortion. For the new abortion patients, the reported rate of contraceptive failure is surprisingly high and, although the rate needs to be validated further, it suggests that to a large extent abortion is being used as a back-up to other means of controlling pregnancy. The data on the abortion on request samples indicate that social and economic reasons account for most abortions. Finally, it appears warranted to conclude that the effects of abortion on request are negligible, if not favorable.

Many dimensions of the psychology of abortion remain unclear. The attitudes of aborting women toward abortion, the reasons why women have unwanted pregnancies, and the reasons why women have abortions need to be clarified and validated further. In addition, the consequences of abortion should be studied further. The extent to which demographic and personality variables influence the psychology of abortion are other issues that warrant investigation. In the past few years great improvements have been made in research methodology; however, the relationships among important variables remain to be studied. In particular, a major study which investigates the relationships among the antecedent psychological variables and the consequent variables is needed to give a coherent shape to the study of the subjective experience of terminating pregnancy.

REFERENCES

ABERNATHY, V. The abortion constellation. *Archives of General Psychiatry,* 1973, *29,* 346–350.

ADDELSON, F. Induced abortion: Source of guilt or growth? *American Journal of Orthopsychiatry,* 1973, *43,* 815–823.

ADLER, N. *Dimensions underlying emotional responses of women following therapeutic abortion.* Presented at American Psychological Association meeting. Montreal, August 30, 1973.

ARÉN, P. Legal abortion in Sweden. *Acta Obstetrica et Gynecologica Scandanavica,* 1958, *36,* supplement 1.

ARÉN, P., & ÅMARK, C. The prognosis in cases in which legal abortion has been granted but not carried out. *Acta Obstetrica et Gynecologica Scandanavica,* 1961, *36,* 203–278.

ATHANASIOU, R., MICHELSON, L., OPPEL, W., UNGER, T., & YAGER, M. *A longitudinal study of sequelae to term birth and therapeutic abortions.* Paper presented at 21st Annual Clinical Meeting of the American College of Obstetricians and Gynecologists, Bal Harbour, May 23, 1973.

BOLTER, S. The psychiatrist's role in therapeutic abortion: The unwitting accomplice. *American Journal of Psychiatry,* 1962, *119,* 312–314.

BREKKE, B. Other aspects of the abortion problem. In M. Calderone (Ed.), *Abortion in the United States,* New York: Hoeber and Harper, 1958, 133–136.

BRODY, H., MEIKLE, S., & GERRITSE, R. Therapeutic abortion: A prospective study. 1. *American Journal of Obstetrics and Gynecology,* 1971, *109,* 347–352.

CALDERONE, M. (Ed.). *Abortion in the United States.* Proceedings of the conference held under the auspices of Planned Parenthood Federation of America in April & June, 1955. New York: Hoeber & Harper, 1958.

CHISOLM, S. Foreward. In D. Schulder & F. Kennedy, *Abortion rap.* New York: McGraw-Hill Book Co., 1971.

CHRISTAKOS, A. Experience at Duke Medical Center after modern legislation for therapeutic abortion. *Southern Medical Journal,* 1970, *63,* 655–661.

CUSHNER, I. Outcomes of induced abortion: Medical-clinical view. In S. Newman, M. Beck, & S. Lewit (Eds.), *Abortion obtained and denied: Research approaches.* Bridgeport, Connecticut: The Population Council, 1971, 21–36.

DEUTSCH, H. *The psychology of women.* (Vol. 2). New York: Grune & Stratton, Inc., 1945.

DIAMOND, M., STEINHOFF, P., PALMORE, J., & SMITH, R. Sexuality, birth control and abortion: A decision-making sequence. *Journal of Biosocial Science,* 1973, *5,* 347–361.

DUFFY, E. *The effect of changes in the state abortion laws.* Washington: United States Government Printing Office, 1971.

DUNBAR, F. A psychosomatic approach to abortion and the abortion habit. In H. Rosen (Ed.), *Therapeutic abortion.* New York: The Julain Press, Inc., 1954, 22–31.

EBAUGH, F., & HESUER, A. Psychiatric aspects of therapeutic abortion. *Post-graduate Medicine,* 1947, *2,* 325–332.

EKBALD, M. Induced abortion on psychiatric grounds: A follow-up study of 479 women. *Acta Psychiatrica Neurologica Scandanavica,* Supplement 99, 1954.

FORD, C., CASTELNUOVO-TEDESCO, P., & LONG, K. Abortion: Is it a therapeutic procedure in psychiatry? *Journal of the American Medical Association,* 1971, *218,* 1173–1178.

FORD, C., CASTELNUOVO-TEDESCO, P., & LONG, K. Women who seek abortion: A comparison with women who complete their pregnancies. *American Journal of Psychiatry,* 1972, *129,* 546–552.

GALDSTON, I. Other aspects of the abortion problem. In M. Calderone (Ed.), *Abortion in the United States.* New York: Hoeber & Harper, 1958, 117–121.

GEBHARD, P., POMEROY, W., & MARTIN, C. *Pregnancy, birth and abortion.* New York: John Wiley & Sons, Inc., 1958.

GILLIS, A. Follow-up after abortion. *British Medical Journal,* 1969, *1,* 506.

GOLD, E., ERHARD, C., & JACOBZINER, H. Therapeutic abortions in New York City: A twenty-year review. *American Journal of Public Health,* 1965, *55,* 964–972.

HAMILTON, V. Some sociologic and psychologic observations on abortion. *American Journal of Obstetrics and Gynecology,* 1940, *39,* 919–928.

HAMILTON, V. Medical status and psychologic attitudes of patients following abortion. *American Journal of Obstetrics and Gynecology,* 1941, *41,* 285–287.

HAMILTON, V. The clinical and laboratory differentiation of spontaneous and induced abortion. *American Journal of Obstetrics and Gynecology,* 1941, *40,* 61–69.

HEFFERMAN, R., & LYNCH, W. What is the status of therapeutic abortion in modern obstetrics? *American Journal of Obstetrics and Gynecology,* 1953, *66,* 135–145.

HESSELTINE, H., ADAIR, F., & BOYNTON, M. Limitation of human reproduction. Therapeutic abortion. *American Journal of Obstetrics and Gynecology,* 1940, *39,* 549–562.

KANE, F., LACHENBRUCH, P., & LIPTON, M. Motivational factors in abortion patients. *American Journal of Psychiatry,* 1973, *130,* 290–293.

KRETZCHMAR, R., & NORRIS, A. Psychiatric implications of therapeutic abortion. *American Journal of Obstetrics and Gynecology,* 1967, *198,* 365–370.

KUMMER, J. Post-abortion psychiatric illness—a myth? *American Journal of Psychiatry,* 1963, *119,* 980–983.

LADER, L. *Abortion.* Indianapolis: The Bobbs-Merrill Co., Inc., 1966.

LEE, N. *The search for an abortionist.* Chicago: The University of Chicago Press, 1969.

LIDZ, T. Reflections of a psychiatrist. In H. Rosen (Eds.). *Therapeutic abortion.* New York: The Julian Press, Inc., 1954, 276–283.

MCCORMICK, P. *Attitudes toward abortion among women undergoing legally induced abortions.* Paper presented at Abortions Research Workshop. New Orleans, April, 1973.

MALMFORS, K. Other aspects of the abortion problem. In M. Calderone (Ed.), *Abortion in the United States.* New York: Hoeber & Harper, 1958, 133–135.

MILLER, J. *The social determinants of women's attitudes toward abortion: 1970 analysis.* Unpublished manuscript, 1973. Available from Ms. J. Miller, Center for Demography and Ecology, University of Wisconsin, Madison, Wisconsin.

MILLER, W. *Psychological antecedents to conception in pregnancies terminated by therapeutic abortion.* Unpublished manuscript, 1973. Available from Dr. W. Miller, Department of Psychiatry, Stanford University, Stanford, California.

MOORE-ČAVAR, E. *International inventory of information on induced abortion.* Division of Social and Administrative Sciences. International Institute for the Study of Human Reproduction. Columbia University, 1974.

MONSOUR, K., & STEWART, B. Abortion and sexual behavior in college women. *American Journal of Orthopsychiatry,* 1973, *43,* 804–813.

MUMFORD, R. An interdisciplinary study of four wives who had induced abortions. *American Journal of Obstetrics and Gynecology,* 1963, *87,* 865–876.

NEWMAN, S. Personal communication, March, 1973.

NEWMAN, S., BECK, M., & LEWIT, S. (Eds.), *Abortion, obtained and denied: Research approaches.* Bridgeport, Connecticut: The Population Council, 1971.

NISWANDER, K., & PATTERSON, R. Psychologic reaction to therapeutic abortion. *Obstetrics and Gynecology,* 1967, *29,* 702–706.

OSOFSKY, J., OSOFSKY, H., & RAJAN, R. Psychological effects of legal abortion. *Clinical Obstetrics and Gynecology,* 1971, *14,* 215–234.

OSOFSKY, J., & OSOFSKY, H. The psychological reaction of patients to legalized abortion. *American Journal of Orthopsychiatry,* 1972, *42,* 48–60.
PAKTER, J., & NELSON, F. Abortion in New York City: The first nine months. *Family Planning Perspectives,* 1971, *3,* 5–12.
PATT, S., RAPPAPORT, R., & BARGLOW, P. Follow-up of therapeutic abortion. *Archives of General Psychiatry,* 1969, *20,* 408–414.
PECK, A., & MARCUS, H. Psychiatric sequelae of therapeutic interruption of pregnancy. *Journal of Nervous and Mental Disease,* 1966, *143,* 417–425.
PEEL, J., & POTTS, M. *Textbook of contraceptive practice.* London: Cambridge University Press, 1969.
PIPEL, H., & NORWICK, K. When should abortion be legal? *Public Affairs Pamphlet No. 429,* January, 1969.
POHLMAN, E. *Psychology of birth planning.* Cambridge: Schenkman Publ. Co., Inc., 1969.
Population Study Commission. State of California, Report to the Governor, 1966.
ROMM, M. Psychoanalytic considerations. In H. Rosen, (Ed.), *Therapeutic abortion.* New York: The Julian Press, Inc., 1954, 209–212.
ROSEN, H. (Ed.), *Therapeutic abortion.* New York: The Julian Press, Inc., 1954.
ROSEN, H. Other aspects of the abortion problem. In M. Calderone (Ed.), *Abortion in the United States.* New York: Hoeber & Harper, 1958, 129–131.
ROSEN, M. Psychiatric implications of abortion: A case study in social hypocrisy. In D. Smith (Ed.), *Abortion and the law.* Cleveland: The Press of Western Reserve University, 1967, 72–95.
ROUTLEDGE, F., SPARLING, A., & MACFARLAND, S. Present status of therapeutic abortion. *American Journal of Obstetrics and Gynecology,* 1953, *66,* 335–345.
ROVINSKY, J. Abortion in New York City, preliminary experience with a permissive abortion statute. *Obstetrics and Gynecology,* 1971, *38,* 333–342.
SCHULDER, D., & KENNEDY, F. *Abortion rap.* New York: McGraw-Hill Book Col., 1971.
SCHUR, E. Abortion and the social system. *Social Problems,* 1955, *3,* 94–99.
SHAW, R. *Abortion on trial.* London: Robert Hall, 1968.
SHERMAN, J. Personal communication, September, 1975.
SIMON, N., ROTHMAN, D., & GOFF, J. Psychological factors related to spontaneous and therapeutic abortion. *American Journal of Obstetrics and Gynecology,* 1969, *104,* 799–808.
SIMON, N., & SENTURIA, A. Psychiatric sequelae of abortion. *Archives of General Psychiatry,* 1966, *15,* 378–389.
SIMON, N., SENTURIA, A., & ROTHMAN, D. Psychiatric illness following therapeutic abortion. *American Journal of Psychiatry,* 1967, *124,* 97–103.
SMITH, E. A follow-up study of women who request abortion. *American Journal of Orthopsychiatry,* 1973, *43,* 574–585.
SMITH, R., DIAMOND, M., & STEINHOFF, P. Abortion in Hawaii: 1970–1971. *Hawaii Medical Journal,* 1973, *32,* 213–220.
STEINHOFF, P. *Ethnic and social class differences in the use of abortion.* Paper presented at Population Studies Seminar, East-West Center, University of Hawaii, November, 1971.
STEINHOFF, P. Background characteristics of abortion patients. In J. Osofsky & H. Osofsky (Eds.), *Abortion experience in the United States.* New York: Harper and Row, 1973, 206–231.
STEINHOFF, P., DIAMOND, D., PALMORE, J., & SMITH, R. *Who are the new abortion patients?* Paper presented at Abortion Research Workshop, New Orleans, April, 1973.
STEINHOFF, P., SMITH, R., & DIAMOND, M. The Hawaii pregnancy, birth control and abortion study: Social psychological aspects. *Conference Proceedings: Psychological Measurement in the Study of Population Problems.* Institute of Personality Assessment and Research, University of California, Berkeley, 1972, 33–40.
TIETZE, C. Mortality with contraception and induced abortion. *Studies in Family Planning,* 1969, *1,* 6–8.
TIETZE, C. Two years' experience with a liberal abortion law: Its impact on fertility trends in New York City. *Family Planning Perspectives,* 1973, *5,* 36–41.
TIETZE, C., & LEHFELDT, H. Legal abortion in Eastern Europe. *Journal of the American Medical Association,* 1961, *175,* 1149–1154.
TIETZE, C., & LEWIT, S. Joint program for the study of abortion (JPSA): Early medical complications of legal abortions. *Studies in Family Planning,* 1972, *3,* 97–122.
TODD, N. Follow-up of patients recommended for therapeutic abortion. *British Journal of Psychiatry,* 1972, *20,* 645–646.
WALTER, G. Psychologic and emotional consequences of elective abortion. *Obstetrics and Gynecology,* 1970, *36,* 482–487.

WHITE, R. Induced abortions: A survey of their psychiatric implications, complications and indications. *Texas Reports of Biological Medicine,* 1966, *24,* 528–558.

WHITMAN, III, H. *Medical and psychiatric factors in decision-making about abortion.* Unpublished manuscript, 1971. Available from Department of Psychology; Harvard University, Boston, Massachusetts.

WILSON, D., & CAINE, B. The psychiatric implications of therapeutic abortions. *Neuropsychiatry,* 1951, *1,* 22.

WILSON, D. Psychiatric indications of abortion. *Virginia Medical Monthly,* 1952, *79,* 448–451.

!Kung Hunter-Gatherers
Feminism, Diet, and Birth Control

Gina Bari Kolata

If results from recent studies of the !Kung* people apply to other societies, anthropologists may now have some new clues as to the social, dietary, and demographic changes that took place during the Neolithic Revolution when people forsook lives of hunting and gathering and began to farm and to keep herds of domestic animals. The !Kung have lived as hunters and gatherers in the Kalahari Desert of South Africa for at least 11,000 years, but recently they have begun to live in agrarian villages near those of Bantus. Investigators who are documenting this change find that, among other things, the settled !Kung women are losing their egalitarian status, the children are no longer brought up to be nonaggressive, and the size of the !Kung population is rapidly increasing rather than remaining stable.

The !Kung's very existence is anomalous since they have lived by hunting and gathering since the Pleistocene. In his archeological studies, John Yellen of the Smithsonian Institution in Washington, D.C., finds artifacts from Late Stone Age hunter-gatherers, of about 11,000 years ago, at the same water holes where modern !Kung set up camp. According to Yellen, these prehistoric hunter-gatherers even hunted the same animals as the contemporary !Kung, including the nocturnal springhare which must be hunted by a special technique because it spends its days in a long deep burrow.

As recently as 10 years ago, many of the !Kung still lived by hunting and gathering. Now, however, less than 5 percent of the 30,000 !Kung live

*The exclamation point refers to an alveolarpalatal click. The tongue tip is pressed against the roof of the mouth and drawn sharply away, producing a hollow popping sound.

in this way; the remainder live in agricultural villages. This period of rapid social change coincided with extensive study of these people by numerous investigators throughout the world and from many disciplines.

It is difficult to distinguish between changes due to settling down and changes due to acculturation to Bantu society. Investigators have drawn on extensive long-term studies of the nomadic !Kung in their documentation of the effects of the !Kung's adoption of an agrarian life, but cannot conclusively state the causes of these effects.

One aspect of the settled !Kung society that has aroused considerable interest among social scientists is the role of women. Patricia Draper of the University of New Mexico reports that !Kung women who belong to the nomadic bands enjoy high status, more autonomy, and greater ability to directly influence group decisions than do sedentary !Kung women. This loss of equality for the agrarian women, Draper believes, may be explained in terms of the social structure of nomadic, as compared to sedentary, groups.

Draper postulates that one reason for the higher status of !Kung hunter-gatherer women is that the women contribute, by gathering, at least 50 percent of the food consumed by a band. Since food gathered by women is so important to the group, the women, of necessity, are as mobile as the men (who hunt), and women and men leave the camp equally often to obtain food. Both the women and men who do not seek food on a given day remain in the camp and share in taking care of the children.

The women in sedentary !Kung societies have far less mobility than the men and contribute less to the food supply. The men leave the village to clear fields and raise crops and to care for for the cattle of their Bantu neighbors. The women remain in the village where they prepare food and take care of the shelters. Since the men work for the Bantus, they learn the Bantu language. Thus when the Bantus deal with the !Kung, they deal exclusively with the men. This practice, together with the !Kung's emulation of the male dominated Bantu society, contributes to increasingly subservient roles for !Kung women.

Also contributing to a loss of female egalitarianism is the different way that agrarian, as compared to nomadic, !Kung bring up their children. Draper points out that the nomads live in bands consisting of very few people so that a child generally has no companions of the same age. Thus play groups contain children of both sexes and a wide variety of ages. This discourages the development of distinct games and roles for boys and girls.

Unlike the nomadic children, the sedentary children play in groups consisting of children of the same sex and similar ages. The boys are expected to help herd cattle, so they leave the village where they are away from adults and on their own. The girls, according to Draper, have no comparable experience but remain in the village and help the adult women with chores.

In addition to promoting sexual egalitarianism by their child rearing practices, the nomadic !Kung also discourage aggression among their children. This is no longer the case when the !Kung become sedentary. The nomadic children observed by Draper do not play competitive games. She attributes this to the wide range of ages of children in a group which would make competitiveness difficult. Moreover, since these children are constantly watched by adults, the adults can and do quickly stop aggressive behavior among children. The children rarely observe aggressive behavior among adults because the nomadic !Kung have no way to deal with physical aggression and consciously avoid it. For example, according to Richard Lee of the University of Toronto, when conflict within a group of adults begins, families leave for other bands. Lee observed that the sedentary !Kung, who cannot easily pick up and leave, rely on their Bantu neighbors to mediate disputes.

In addition to studying social changes taking place when the !Kung settle down, investigators are studying dietary and demographic changes. The !Kung diet is of interest because the nomadic !Kung are exceedingly healthy and are free from many diseases thought to be associated with the diets of people in more complex societies. The sedentary !Kung have substantially altered their diets, thus providing investigators with a unique opportunity to document the effects of diet on the health of these people. The demographic changes taking place among the !Kung are of interest because the settled !Kung seem to have lost a natural check on their fertility rates.

The diet of the completely nomadic !Kung, which has been analyzed by geneticists, biochemists, and nutritionists, consists of nuts, vegetables, and meat and lacks milk and grains. All the investigators agree that the diet is nutritionally well balanced and provides an adequate number of calories. They found very few people with iron deficiency anemia, even when they included pregnant and lactating women in their sample. They also discovered that the nomadic !Kung have a very low incidence of deficiency of the vitamin folic acid and that the concentrations of vitamin B_{12} are higher in their serums as compared to concentrations considered normal for other populations. These findings led Henry Harpending of the University of New Mexico and his associates to suggest that Stone Age people probably had no deficiencies of these vitamins and that deficiencies first appeared when people settled down into agrarian societies.

In addition to being well nourished, the nomadic !Kung are free from many common diseases of old age. For example, Lee and others have found little degenerative disease among elderly !Kung, although it is commonplace for these people to live for at least 60 years and some live for as long as 80 years. A. Stewart Truswell of the University of London also finds that the nomadic !Kung are one of only about a dozen groups of people in the world whose blood pressure does not increase as they grow older.

The medical effects of the altered diet and way of life of the sedentary !Kung are not yet well established. In contrast to the hunter-gatherers, these people consume a great deal of cow's milk and grain. In his studies of a generation of !Kung brought up on such a diet, Lee finds that they are, on the average, taller, fatter, and heavier than the nomadic !Kung. Nancy Howell of the University of Toronto finds that the agrarian women have their first menstrual periods (menarches) earlier than the nomadic women.

The average age of menarche among nomadic !Kung is late—at least age 15.5 according to Howell. Although these women marry at puberty, they have their first children when they are, on the average, 19.5 years of age. This late start to reproductive life helps limit the growth of the population. However, a more significant curb on the size of nomadic populations is the low fertility of the women. Howell finds that the average length of time between giving birth for a nomadic !Kung woman is 4 years. These women have fewer children than any other women in societies that do not practice contraception or abortion. The low fertility of nomadic !Kung contradicts previously held theories that the sizes of hunter-gatherer populations were limited solely by high mortality rates. The !Kung population size remains stable because there are so few children born. Combining her studies of the fertility and mortality rates of !Kung hunter-gatherers, Howell concludes that the long-term growth rate for such a population is only 0.5 percent per year. This is in sharp contrast to the sedentary !Kung whose population is growing rapidly.

The population growth among the sedentary !Kung results from both a decrease in the age of menarche and a decrease in the average time between births. Lee has found that the birth intervals drop 30 percent when !Kung women become sedentary. The causes of these reproductive changes are unknown, but some investigators suspect that these decreased birth intervals may result from changes in nursing or dietary habits.

Nomadic !Kung women have no soft food to give their babies, and so they nurse them for 3 or 4 years, and during this time the women rarely conceive. Sedentary !Kung women, on the other hand, wean their babies much sooner by giving them grain meal and cow's milk. Irven DeVore of Harvard University believes that a contraceptive effect of the long lactation period is not unexpected, since investigators have observed the same phenomenon in many animals, including monkeys and the great apes. A woman who begins to supplement her infant's diet while the child is very young would not experience this effect because her child would require less and less milk.

Howell and Rose Frisch of the Harvard Center for Population Studies believe that an explanation of the decrease in the age of menarche and in the birth intervals of sedentary !Kung women may involve the diet of the sedentary !Kung. They base this idea on a study by Frisch and Janet McArthur of the Massachusetts General Hospital in Boston. These investigators showed that the amount of body fat must be above a certain minimum for the onset of menstruation and for its maintenance after menarche. Howell points out that the !Kung hunter-gatherers are thin, although well nourished. When women from these bands lactate, they need about 1000 extra calories a day. Thus, during the 3 or 4 years that a woman nurses a baby, she may have too little body fat for ovulation to take place. The shorter birth intervals for sedentary !Kung women would follow from their shorter periods of lactation and larger amounts of body fat. Howell notes that this explanation of the low fertility of nomadic !Kung women cannot be verified until more extensive medical studies are performed with these people.

Although no one claims that the changes taking place in the !Kung society necessarily reflect those that took place when other hunter-gatherer societies became agrarian, studies of the !Kung are providing anthropologists with clues relative to the origins of some features of modern societies. Many findings, such as the social egalitarianism, lack of aggression, and low fertility of nomadic !Kung are leading to new perspectives on the hunting and gathering way of life which was, until 10,000 years ago, the way all humans lived.

ADDITIONAL READING

R. B. LEE and I. DEVORE, Eds., *Kalahari Hunter-Gatherers* (Harvard Univ. Press, Cambridge, Mass., in press).

Sex Preferences, Sex Control, and the Status of Women

Nancy E. Williamson

The possible effects on the lives of women of coming technologies should concern feminists of both sexes. This paper systematically analyzes the potential results of new technologies which will enable parents to preselect the sexes of their children. Sex control would be a significant development because parents around the world now tend to have preferences about the number and sex of their children. The majority still prefer boys. Even when parents in the United States want one child of each sex, they would like the boy first. If they want an odd number of children (for example, one, three, or five), most would rather have more boys than girls. These desires already affect some decisions about family size in the United States even without available means of sex control. But a combination of sex preferences with sex-control capability may bring about significant societal and demographic changes having implications for women. In order to assess the likelihood of these changes, I will review the evidence on sex preferences, the extent to which they affect fertility, some of their bases, the techniques of sex control now being developed, and the possible appeal of sex control. Although sex control may have more dramatic consequences for women in some of the developing countries, I will restrict most of my remarks to the United States.

The topic of sex preference has been investigated in the United States since the early 1930s. Then Winston[1] noted that last-born children in a sample of elite families were more likely to be boys. Finding 117 last-born boys per 100 girls, he speculated that perhaps families were stopping child-

"Sex Preferences, Sex Control, and the Status of Women" by Nancy E. Williamson from *Signs: Journal of Women in Culture and Society,* 1 (1976), 847–62. Reprinted by permission of the University of Chicago Press.

bearing after they had the son they desired. In order to see whether son-preference attitudes still existed, Winston polled a very small sample of male college students. He learned that they wanted 165 boys to 100 girls in their ideal future families.

Since Winston's time, over fifty scholarly studies have tried to assess American sex preferences, their source, and their effect on family size. Over this forty-year period, there is little sign of change in attitudes, especially among college students, whose preferences have been studied the most extensively. The sex ratios preferred in the general population have been found to be lower than those of Winston's sample. They range from 106[2] to 113[3] in favor of boys for nonstudent populations. The ratios are higher for student samples. Studies of couples with children have shown that people often consider the sex ratios of their own families to be ideal. For parent samples, then, the desired sex ratios are close to the normal one of 105 boys to every 100 girls. In seven studies, about half of the respondents wanted an equal number of boys and girls.[4] In eight investigations, the majority of respondents wanted first-born boys.[5] Boys were also preferred as only children.[6] In addition, people who wanted three children were more likely to hope for two boys and one girl rather than two girls and one boy.

Evidence from over a dozen studies extending into the early 1970s points to the effect of such preferences on the actual size of families in the United States.[7] Families that did not have one child of each sex were more likely to continue childbearing than those that did. However, some very recent work in the Midwest found evidence that women were not planning to continue this pattern.[8] Indeed, on a national scale, the birthrate is now very low—about fifteen births per 1,000 population, in contrast to twenty-five per 1,000 at the height of the "baby boom" in the mid-1950s. Perhaps financial considerations are assuming precedence over sex preferences in making a decision about a third child.

By this logic, we might expect the effect of sex preferences on fertility to disappear, whether or not sex control becomes available. Yet we can also argue to the contrary. Given that many Americans do have sex preferences and given that most Americans now apparently want comparatively small families, the appeal of sex control could grow. If a couple wanted to have at least one child of each sex, but only two children, there is, of course, a fifty-fifty chance of having two boys or two girls. After the first child, some parents might be tempted to control the sex of the second. However, we cannot be sure that the birthrate will remain as low as it is now. Improvements in the economy, for example, could well raise the birthrate, which would allow more couples to act on sex preferences without resorting to the technologies of sex control.

On balance, it is hard to say confidently how preferences will affect fertility in the future. We can only say that some American parents have continued childbearing to get children of both sexes in the past. Furthermore, many have preferred boys as first-borns. But since parents could do nothing to satisfy this first-born preference, it had no demographic effect. If there were sex control it might, among other things, allow a surplus of boys as first-borns.

Less work has been done on why people have sex preferences. In one interesting study on the value of children, Arnold and Fawcett[9] found for their sample of Hawaii residents that sons were valued because they carry on the family name; daughters were valued for "girlish" traits such as neatness, cuddliness, cuteness, and obedience. In the cross-cultural phase of the same study, the authors generalized that boys were valued for the adults they would become; girls were enjoyed for their contributions as children, which included companionship to the mother and help with housework and child care.

Another way to look at the bases of sex preferences is to study the kinds of people who have them. Results that relate sex preferences to social class, race, education, and other background factors in the United States are inconclusive. A comprehensive review[10] of the economic, social, cultural, and psychological conditions that are associated with different preferences in the United States and Europe found only two consistent results: (1) men tend to prefer boys more than women do,[11] and (2) Catholics and Jews tend to prefer boys,[12] while Protestants are more likely to proceed with childbearing in order to have one child of each sex.[13] However, the son preferences of Catholics and Jews have not been reflected in actual fertility.

The tendency for men to prefer boys more strongly than women do, though a common finding, is not clearly understood. Perhaps men feel that having sons would provide more opportunity for companionship and for joint activities. Perhaps, as Arnold and Fawcett suggest, men are more concerned with the continuity of the family name. Men may fear being outnumbered by females in the family or they may feel that having sons signifies masculinity. Women, in some studies, also prefer boys to girls, but less strongly than do men. They sometimes explain that they want sons to please their husbands.[14] In general, women are more satisfied with having girls than men are. If they have two girls, they are more likely to report that they had wanted two girls originally. In contrast, husbands with two girls are more likely to say they would have preferred a son and a daughter or even two sons.

Assuming that many Americans do have sex preferences they want to fulfill, what are the available methods of control? Three approaches are now being developed: (1) the rhythm and douche method popularized by Rorvik and Shettles, (2) selective abortion that follows either amniocentesis or another sex-detection technique, and (3) separation of androsperms and gynosperms preceding artificial insemination. Let me discuss them in turn.

In 1970 Rorvik and Shettles[15] publicized success rates of over 85 percent with a technique involving the proper timing of intercourse, douches, and specifix sex positions. Forty-eight couples were in their initial study. As far as we know, they have not replicated this study, although a German physician, O. Hatzold,[16] has reported similar results on small samples. Rorvik and Shettles recommended that parents who wanted a boy should have intercourse as close to the time of ovulation as possible. Guerrero,[17] however, found that couples had the best chance of getting a boy if they had intercourse six to nine days before ovulation. (Of course, having sex so long before ovulation reduces the chance of getting pregnant at all.) In any case, this timing and douching method, still experimental, needs to be tested on larger samples. It should also be noted that the technique requires considerable discipline and cooperation on the part of couples.

For the second approach, selective abortion after detection of the sex of the fetus, there are three sex-detection techniques: (1) examination of cells obtained from the amniotic fluid, (2) a blood test, and (3) a test similar to a Pap smear. The first detection technique is now being used on a small scale. The second and third have only recently been announced.

Amniocentesis is a procedure requiring a surgical insertion of a hollow needle through the abdominal wall and the uterus of a pregnant woman in order to obtain amniotic fluid for the determination of either chromosomal abnormality or the sex of the fetus. A very small amount of amniotic fluid, ten to twenty milliliters, is removed.[18] The test is best done from the thirteenth to the sixteenth week of pregnancy. The lymphocytes, or lymph cells, which make up about a quarter of the white blood cells, are cultured for a period of three to six weeks. They are then examined for the presence of XY chromosomes: if these are found, there is a very good chance[19] that the fetus is a male; if no XY chromosomes are found, it is likely to be a female. In either case, the mother's XX chromosomes will also be present. In 4–12 percent of cases, because the first test will not successfully obtain usable material, a second or third will be necessary.

Amniocentesis can be done under local anesthesia in a doctor's office. Presently, the procedure, available mainly at large medical centers, is used for high-risk women only (i.e., women who are over forty and more likely to have a retarded child, women who have a family history of some sex-linked disease, or women who have other reasons for expecting some serious problem with the fetus). According to one researcher, "The limited data available in the literature . . . presently allows no accurate assessment of the true risk of amniocentesis in early pregnancy. . . . An approximate complication risk of 1 to 2 percent is the current working estimate."[20] The risk of amniocentesis (which include hemorrhage, infection, perforation of viscera, and precipitation of labor) are greater for the fetus than for the mother. Moreover, the long waiting period while the cells are being cultured to determine the sex of the fetus necessitates a relatively late abortion, with the attendant difficulties. Finally, in one study,[21] about 20 percent of the women who had the test reported cramps and discomfort lasting from a few hours to a few days after the operation itself.

However, the same study, which followed up 100 women who had the test, found that 96 percent of the women returning the questionnaire would have the test again if they were pregnant. One hundred percent would recommend it to another woman in their situation. Sixty-two percent of the women reported being anxious during the waiting period, which averaged 25.5 days, before the test results were known.

Two other less drastic sex-detection methods[22] are currently being tested. The first, developed by Grumbach, is a blood test. Though less risky to mother and fetus than amniocentesis, it presently requires complex and time-consuming analysis. If this analysis could be computerized, it might reduce the waiting period and permit an early abortion. The second technique, developed by Rhine and Cleary and discussed by Stattman, begins with a smear much like a Pap smear. It can be done in a doctor's office. A technician stains the cells collected on a cotton swab and views them under a fluorescent microscope. The cell structures indicating maleness, called "y-bodies," glow especially bright. If none of these y-bodies is detected, the fetus is probably female. With this method, the sex of the fetus can be detected as early as the ninth week of pregnancy. Researchers hope that detection may be possible as soon as the seventh week. But so far, the accuracy of this vaginal smear method is not as high as with amniocentesis. On a sample of thirty-six pregnant women, it allowed accurate predictions in thirty-one cases, or 86 percent of the time. It was correct on all male births but wrong on some female births.

Sex predetermination techniques are not yet generally available to a couple who want to control the sex of their next child by selective abortion. Furthermore, one might legitimately question whether this method would have much appeal even if it were easily available. To my knowledge, none of the studies on acceptability of sex control to date have asked about selective abortion. And yet, we might speculate, attitudes toward abortion have become more liberal, as studies for the period from 1960 to 1970 have shown.[23] This tolerance is likely to have increased since the January 1973 Supreme Court decision on women's legal right to abort in the first two trimesters, provided certain safety conditions are met. Sex control through abortion, then, might become a logical extension of the social acceptability of abortion itself.

Sex control may also both support and be supported by the idea "every child, a wanted child," which Planned Parenthood has helped to popularize. A child, though planned for and wanted at conception and during the pregnancy, can be a disappointment at birth because it belongs to the "wrong" sex. A study done in the late 1940s[24] found that some children being treated at a mental health clinic for emotional problems had been originally planned for by their parents but had been later rejected because they were of the "wrong" sex. We have no idea how common this is. But if a child can be unwanted because of its sex, and if many people believe all children should be wanted, then sex control, perhaps even through selective abortion, may become a more plausible act.

A third approach to sex control, now being developed, does not require abortion. Some researchers have attempted to separate the heavier X from the lighter Y sperm by physical means. However, according to Jones,[25] ". . . the high centrifugal fields necessary in standard techniques can damage sperm, perhaps differentially with sex." (Lindahl, among others, has worked with this approach).[26] Gordon[27] reports that the two kinds of sperm have been separated by electrophotests, with some success with rabbit semen. Differential staining of sperm has also been suggested.[28] All of these approaches have one thing in common: they would require artificial insemination after the two types of sperm were separated. Apparently, however, in a study to be discussed below, only from 5 to 16 percent of respondents approved of artificial insemination as a method of sex control.

Less research is being devoted to developing techniques that discriminate between the two types of sperm after vaginal intercourse has taken place. If successful, this approach would probably have much more appeal than the rhythm and douche technique of Rorvik and Shettles, selective abortion, or artificial insemination. A sex-control pill might even be more popular, but this technology is probably remote.

Progress on all of these techniques has been slower than Etzioni in *Science* and Markle and Nam in *Social Biology* had predicted.[29] It is hard to say when they will be easily available. Still, there is no reason to doubt the assertion of Kahn and Weiner[30] that sex control will be with us before the year 2000. By then, of course, we will see many changes in technology, attitudes, and institutions which further complicate predictions. But sex control itself is not an intractable scientific problem. Whether or not it becomes widespread will depend on the type of sex-control technique, the resolution of legal problems, the attitudes of the medical profession, the policies of health insurance companies, and many other considerations. In societies such as Korea, Singapore, and Taiwan, where sex preferences tend to be strong and abortion is widespread and quite socially acceptable, the popularity of sex-control techniques, even those involving abortion, could be considerably greater than in the United States.

There is a small amount of empirical research on the acceptability of sex control. Markle and Nam[31] found that about a quarter (26 percent) of their Florida college student sample approved of sex control for themselves. Forty percent approved of sex control for other people who wanted to use it. When the researchers added the condition that the respondent had children of one sex only, 62 percent approved of sex control. Only 16 percent approved of sex control through artificial insemination, as opposed to 30 percent who approved of a prescription pill. For Markle and Nam's respondents, the conditions are so important that they create differentials of from 16 to 62 percent. In general, Markle and Nam found that those approving of sex control tended to be those who were older, black, and male and who had been married, had no religion, and wanted fewer children. Like Markle and Nam, Largey[32] did not include selective abortion when he considered attitudes toward six different sex-control methods: (1) rhythm and douching, (2) a special type of diaphragm, (3) a special type of prophylactic, (4) sperm treatment and artificial insemination, (5) pill taken by wife, and (6) pill taken by the husband. In Largey's sample, which included 126 married couples (with children) who lived in the Buffalo, New York, area, 31 percent approved of rhythm and douching for purposes of sex control, 31 percent approved of the diaphragm, 26 percent approved of the special type of prophylactic, 5 percent approved of artificial insemination, 35 percent approved of a pill for the wife, and 34 percent approved of a pill for the husband. The individuals who approved of at least one method of sex control were considered to have approved of the idea of sex control and were labeled "acceptors." "Rejectors" disapproved of all six methods. According to Largey's findings, 65 percent of the sample were acceptors, 8 percent were undecided, and 27 percent were rejectors of sex control. The acceptors tended to be younger, non-Catholic, had fewer brothers, approved of analogous birth control methods, generally approved of innovations, and had stronger sex preferences. For our purposes, his most interesting finding was that people with stronger sex preferences were likely to approve of sex control. Since my own cross-cultural study[33] revealed that Americans have relatively weak sex preferences as compared with people in many (but not all) developing countries, we might expect that sex control might be more significant outside the United States.

A final study of attitudes toward sex control did not consider different methods of sex control; it merely posed the question: "Some time soon, couples will be able to choose in advance whether they will have a boy or a girl. How would you feel about being able to choose the sex of a child?"[34] They found that 39 percent of a large national sample of American women approved of sex control. (This percentage falls between the 26 percent of Markle and Nam and the 65 percent of Largey.) Women with all girl children were more likely to approve of sex control (43 percent), as were those with all boy children (40 percent), in contrast to women having equal numbers of boys and girls (33 percent).

On the basis of these three recent studies, we can conclude that some Americans would be interested in sex control, particularly those having children of all one sex. We can also say that artificial insemination would not be a popular approach. The rhythm and douche method would probably be more acceptable. Although we have no data on attitudes toward selective abortion, we can speculate that, as with other innovations, there would probably be low approval at first and then a gradual increase.

We can now deal with the question of whether sex control would affect both the quality of women's lives and the status of women relative to men.[35] Looking first at the positive aspects, sex control would of course give the individual woman more choice and less uncertainty. For women who felt strongly about having a certain sex of child, the result might be more satisfaction with childbearing and rearing and a greater acceptance of the child. There would be fewer children of the "wrong" sex, although we have no idea how many such children there are now, and thus more happy children. Women would no longer be "blamed" for producing too many of one sex (unfair as that is, given the fact that the male sperm determines the sex); some women, therefore, would no longer worry about disappointing their husbands or relatives.

Some families would probably be smaller, since sex preferences could be fulfilled without resorting to fifty-fifty chance, but on the other hand, some families might be larger because the parents were able to have the children they wanted. On balance, however, one suspects that smaller families would be more common; this would give women more time for nonfamilial activities.

For a few women, sex-linked diseases would no longer be a worry. In addition, a single woman might feel freer to have a child if she could influence its sex; for example, she might want a girl because she felt she could be a better role model for that sex of child.

On the positive side, then, sex control would allow a woman more control over her body and her life. The possible negative aspects[36] of this question are more complicated. If the rhythm and douche method were used, the woman would have to keep track of her temperature each day to determine the time of ovulation and would have to do the douching. If sex detection were done by amniocentesis, the woman would be the one to have the test, the possible complications, and, perhaps, the abortion. Should she have an abortion, she would have to go through another pregnancy and another test. And because sex detection through amniocentesis requires a late abortion, the woman would bear the resulting special risks. If her doctor had an ethical objection to performing an abortion for so "trivial" a reason as sex preference, a woman would have to go to one doctor for the amniocentesis and another for the abortion. Since some people certainly would not approve of sex control, especially through selective abortion, the woman (and to a lesser extent, the man) would bear that psychic cost as well. Then there is always the chance of a mistake in identifying the sex of the fetus.

For some women, decisions about the desired sex of a child and about the use of sex control might be difficult to make. After making sure that she was pregnant, she would have to decide whether she wanted a child in the first place. She would also have to decide whether to have the amniocentesis operation with its risks. If she decided to go ahead with the test, she would then have to decide whether to abort on the basis of the outcome of the test. Women would have to search their own values and preferences. For some women (and men) these would be hard decisions. With easier sex-detection techniques being developed, there would of course be less risk and a shorter waiting period. Abortions could be earlier and safer, but the decisions would still have to be made. I predict, furthermore, that those decisions would bear down more heavily on women than men.

If artificial insemination were used, women might have to suspend some of their romantic notions about sex, love, and pregnancy. They might also have to be careful not to make their partners feel insecure about not being the direct agent in the conception. No matter what technique were used, disagreement might arise between the potential mother and father about the sex of the child, since men tend to prefer sons more strongly than women do. Some couples might decide that decisions about children are in the wife's (or husband's) province; others might decide on a boy for him first, then a girl for her; some men might pressure women to produce sons. Conflict might also arise after the sex of the fetus had been ascertained; for example, a father might identify with a male fetus and not want it aborted even if the couple had previously agreed on a girl; the reverse could also be true. Such conflict might have more serious effect on women than men since it deals with women's role of childbearing.

The possible negative demographic effects of sex control need to be considered also. The American preference for first-born boys (189 boys to 100 girls for first-borns in the study by Westoff and Rindfuss cited earlier) might be detrimental to women as a group. Let me explain. Consistently, findings show that first-born children are more likely to succeed academically. First-borns (and only children) are overrepresented in American colleges and even more so in elite undergraduate colleges such as Yale or Reed,[37] and in graduate schools. First-borns (and only children) have also been found to be disproportionately high scorers on the National Merit Scholarship test.[38] They are overrepresented among eminent British men and women, distinguished American scientists, people in *Who's Who in America,* and among the gifted California children studied by Terman.[39] Furthermore, a recent analysis of data from roughly 400,000 nineteen-year-old Dutch men found a consistent relationship between birth order and intelligence (measured by tests of language, arithmetic, mechanical comprehension, perceptual speed, and nonverbal intelligence) when social class was controlled.[40] There are various theories which try to explain why first-borns (and only children) have such advantages, or conversely why second-borns and middle-borns seem to be disadvantaged. One is the physiological theory that the uterine environment might be better for the first-born, but this does not explain why last-borns sometimes do well also, or why there are sometimes differences between first-borns and only children. Besides, first-borns are more likely to have difficult births than later-borns. Aside from the physiological argument, which has not been popular of late, there is the economic theory that first-borns (and only children) get more economic resources to go to college. However, Breland's study controlled for economic status and still found an advantage for first-borns. As a result, he favors the "isolation hypothesis: children isolated from other children during early developmental stages may have an advantage as far as achievement is concerned."[41] Such children get more attention from adults, which particularly increases their verbal skills. If, then, first-borns have a greater chance of achieving eminence, and if women are consistently second-borns, then women might consistently be second class. It is only a small compensation that they might at the same time avoid some of the negative aspects of first-borns, such as higher anxiety and greater susceptibility to social pressure. The validity of these speculations, of course, depends to some extent on external factors such as the state of the economy. In a prosperous economy, there would be more opportunity for all children to go to college and we might not see as much favoritism for first-born boys. But even then, some schools will be of higher quality, and there may still be more first-borns in attendance.

Although this argument on birth order is necessarily speculative, previous authors who have considered the possible first-born (male) and second-born (female) pattern have neglected to spell out the possible negative effects for women.[42] Instead, they have pointed to what they regard as a positive effect. Westoff and Rindfuss suggest that the marriage market would be favorable with this birth-order pattern, given the propensity of American women to marry men two or three years their senior. Such a pattern, however, as opposed to an equal-age-at-marriage pattern, perpetuates the inferior position of a woman in a marriage if she is, as a result, the less experienced, less financially independent, and less established partner (although being younger can sometimes be a source of power in our youth-oriented society). Thus I am less enthusiastic about the marriage-market situation. Indeed, some critics like Jessie Bernard have argued that marriage is not as advantageous for women as for men.[43] An age pattern which encouraged marriage might not benefit women as a group. Overall, then, the first-born male and second-born female pattern would not, I believe, better women's status and might well be detrimental.

There is yet another aspect to this question that needs to be considered. If a surplus of males were produced (mainly in families with one or three children), some men would be left without women near their own age to marry and would probably dip into the younger cohorts of women for brides, thereby further increasing the age difference between husband and wife, with the negative consequences discussed above. In addition, with a shortage of women, there might be more pressure on women to marry and to have children. In our society, the importance of the institution of the family, relative to that of the military, business, education, government, and other institutions, has declined. Thus if women were pressured to function primarily within the family, their status relative to that of men could be expected to decline or at least not to rise.

This is not an orthodox argument. An economic analysis might suggest that if women were relatively scarce, their value would go up as men competed for them. Unfortunately, an economic analysis does not seem to hold when the "commodity" is women, especially if the result is a greater difference in the ages of husband and wife, earlier marriage for women, and possibly larger families for women. A similar argument is made by Ridley.[44]

On the other hand, women might successfully oppose these family pressures and some of the negative consequences would not occur. Furthermore, the next wave of children might contain relatively more girls. Such a view implies an "invisible hand" guiding people to adjust their private interests and behavior to the societal good. In my view, however, there is little reason to suppose that such an adjustment would naturally occur. If families felt that having one more boy than girl or having a first-born boy were in their interest, they might continue doing so even if these actions had negative results for the society or for women as a group. This situation seems to be occurring with fertility (but not sex control) in some developing countries. In India, for example, Malmood Mamdani[45] suggests that it is still in the self-interest of many rural families to have moderate-to-large families in the hope of getting two or three sons who provide labor and support their parents in old age. Yet it is clearly not in the interest of the country to have families of five or six children. Aside from the Indian urban middle classes, little adjustment of individual family behavior to the social good is taking place. The same might be expected with sex control in our society.

These, then, are possible negative consequences of control of the sex of children for women. Whether the positive features outweigh the negative ones depends on an individual woman's values and situation. If she does not have a moral or personal objection to one of the three sex-control methods, if she does have strong sex preferences, and if she is not pressured by others, sex control might increase her choice and her satisfaction with child rearing. If these conditions are not met, she might be worse off.

For women as a group, the outcome is more likely to be negative if the burdens of sex control fell on women, if the proportion of first-borns who were female declined, if the age difference between husbands and wives increased, and if women became more tied to family roles rather than societal roles.

Whatever the balance may be, we must be concerned with the impact of such technological changes on our lives before they become widespread. As I was completing the research for this paper (1975), a sex preselection clinic, using the rhythm and douche method, opened up in a very large maternity hospital in Singapore.[46] Within the first ten months, 432 women had enrolled. The future is not far off.

NOTES

1. Sanford Winston, "Burth Control and Sex Ratio at Birth," *American Journal of Sociology* 38 (July 1932–May 1933): 225–31.
2. Pascal K. Whelpton, Arthur A. Campbell, and John E. Patterson, *Fertility and Family Planning in the United States* (Princeton, N.J.: Princeton University Press, 1966).

3. Gerald E. Markle and Charles B. Nam, "Sex Predetermination: Its Impact on Fertility," *Social Biology* 18 (March 1971): 73–82.
4. See Simon Dinitz, Russell R. Dynes, and Alfred C. Clarke, "Preferences for Male or Female Children: Traditional or Affectional?" *Marriage and Family Living* 16 (May 1954): 128–30; Gale P. Largey, "Sociological Aspects of Sex Preselection: A Study of the Acceptance of a Medical Innovation" (Ph.D. diss., State University of New York at Buffalo, 1972); Nancy E. Williamson, Sandra L. Putnam, and H. Regina Wurthmann, *Future Autobiographies: Expectations of Marriage, Children, and Careers,* East-West Population Institute Paper Series, no. 38 (Honolulu, 1976); Jeanne E. Clare and Clyde V. Kiser, "Preference for Children of Given Sex in Relation to Fertility," *Milbank Memorial Fund Quarterly* 29 (October 1951): 440–92; George S. Rotter and Naomi G. Rotter, "Preferred Family Constellations: A Pilot Study," *Social Biology* 19 (December 1972): 401–4; Charles H. Wood, "Ethnic Status and Sex Composition as Factors Mediating Income Effects on Fertility" (Ph.D. diss., University of Texas, 1975); and Charles F. Westoff and Ronald R. Rindfuss, "Sex Preselection in the United States," *Science* (May 10, 1974), pp. 633–36.
5. See Dinitz et al., p. 129; Largey, p. 12; Markle and Nam, p. 77; Wood, p. 96; and Westoff and Rindfuss, p. 634; see also the following studies: Candida C. Peterson and James L. Peterson, "Preference for Sex of Offspring as a Measure of Change in Sex Attitudes," *Psychology* 10 (May 1973): 3–5; Gerald E. Markle, "Sex Ratio at Birth: Values, Variance, and Some Determinants," *Demography* 11 (February 1974): 131–42; and Fred Arnold and James T. Fawcett, *The Value of Children: A Crossnational Study, Hawaii* (Honolulu: East-West Population Institute, 1975), vol. 3.
6. See Clare and Kiser, p. 429; Dinitz et al., p. 129; Peterson and Peterson, p. 4; Largey, p. 12.
7. See Marian Harper, "Parental Preference with Respect to the Sex of Children" (master's thesis, University of Chicago, 1936); D. Cecil Rife and L. H. Snyder, "The Distribution of Sex Ratios within Families in an Ohio City," *Human Biology*s9 (February 1937): 99–103; Robert J. Myers, "Same-Sex Families," *Journal of Heredity* 40 (October 1949): 268–70; Marianne E. Bernstein, "Studies in the Human Sex Ratio: The Proportion of Unisexual Sibships," *Human Biology* 24 (February 1952): 35–43; U.S. Bureau of the Census, *Current Population Reports,* ser. P-20, no. 67 (Washington, D.C.: Government Printing Office, 1956); Charles F. Westoff et al., *Family Growth in Metropolitan America* (Princeton, N.J.: Princeton University Press, 1961); Charles Westoff, Robert Potter, and Phillip Sagi, *The Third Child: A Study in the Prediction of Fertility* (Princeton, N.J.: Princeton University Press, 1963); Robert C. Loyd and Elmer Gray, "Statistical Study of the Human Sex Ratio," *Journal of Heredity* 60 (November–December 1969): 329–31; Larry L. Bumpass and Charles F. Westoff, *The Later Years of Childbearing* (Princeton, N.J.: Princeton University Press, 1970); Robyn M. Dawes, "Sexual Heterogeneity of Children as a Determinant of American Family Size," *Oregon Research Institute* 10 (October 1970): 1–7; Yoram Ben-Porath and Finis Welch, "Chance, Child Traits, and Choice of Family Size," report no. R-1117, prepared for the National Institutes of Health and the Rockefeller Foundation (RAND Corp., 1972); Elmer Gray, "Influence of Sex of First Two Children on Family Size," *Journal of Heredity* 65 (March–April 1972): 91–92; Elmer Gray and N. Marlene Morrison, "Influence of Combinations of Sexes of Children on Family Size," *Journal of Heredity* 65 (May–June 1974): 169–74; Finis Welch, "Sex of Children: Prior Uncertainty and Subsequent Fertility Behavior," report no. R-1510, prepared under a grant from the Rockefeller Foundation (RAND Corp., 1964); Charles H. Wood and Frank D. Bean, "Sex Composition and Fertility: Implications from a Comparison of Mexican Americans and Anglo Americans" (unpublished paper, available from first author, Centro de desenvolvimento e planejamento, Belo Horizonte, Brazil). Comparable results for other countries are mixed. In Korea, Taiwan, and urban India, sex preferences affect fertility. Families who have sons early in marriage tend to limit family size sooner than those who have daughters early. Other developing countries such as Thailand, Bangladesh, and Morocco do not show this pattern.
8. Phillip Cutright, Stephen Belt, and John Scanzoni, "Gender Preferences, Sex Predetermination, and Family Size in the United States," *Social Biology 21* (Fall 1974): 242–58.
9. Arnold and Fawcett, pp. 55–58.
10. Nancy E. Williamson, *Sons or Daughters? A Cross-cultural Study of Parental Preferences* (Beverly Hills, Calif.: Sage Publications, 1976).
11. See Mildred Strunk, "The Quarter's Poll: Children," *Public Opinion Quarterly* 11 (November 1947–48): 641; Ruth E. Hartley, "Children's Perceptions of Sex Preference in Four Culture Groups," *Journal of Marriage and the Family* 31 (May 1969): 380–87; David

Heer et al., "Child Mortality, Son-Preference, and Fertility: A Report with Particular Attention to the Kentucky Pre-Test" (unpublished paper, Harvard Center for Population Studies, 1969); Clyde H. Coombs, Lolagene C. Coombs, and Gary H. McClelland, "Preference Scales for Number and Sex of Children," *Population Studies* 29 (July 1975): 273–98; and Andras Klinger, "The Longitudinal Study of Marriages Contracted in 1974 in Hungary" (paper presented at the Conference on the Measurement of Preferences for Number and Sex of Children, East-West Population Institute, Honolulu, June 2–5, 1975); see also Clare and Kiser, p. 427; Dinitz et al., p. 129; Peterson and Peterson, p. 4; and Wood, pp. 97–101.

12. Dinitz et al., p. 129; Markle, pp. 136–39; Wood, p. 98.
13. Wood and Bean, pp. 13–14 (assuming Mexican Americans are predominantly Catholic and Anglos are predominantly Protestant); see also P. De Wolff and J. Meerdink, "La Fécondité des mariages à Amsterdam selon l'appartenance sociale et religieuse," *Population* 12 (April–June 1957): 289–318; Deborah Freedman, Ronald Freedman, and Pascal K. Whelpton, "Size of Family and Preference for Children of Each Sex," *American Journal of Sociology* 66 (September 1960): 141–46; Francisco J. Ayala and Catherine T. Falk, "Sex of Children and Family Size," *Journal of Heredity* 62 (January–February 1971): 57–59.
14. Gunnar Dahlberg, "Do Parents Want Boys or Girls?" *Acta genetica et statistica-medica* 1 (1948–49): 163–67; N. Uddenberg, P. E. Almgren, and A. Nilsson, "Preference for Sex of the Child among Pregnant Women," *Journal of Biosocial Science* 3 (July 1971): 267–80; and Lois W. Hoffman, "Working Paper on Measurement of Preference for Number and Sex of Children" (paper presented at the Conference on the Measurement of Preferences for Number and Sex of Children, East-West Population Institute, Honolulu, June 2–5, 1975).
15. David M. Rorvik and Landrum B. Shettles, "You Can Choose Your Baby's Sex," *Look Magazine* (April 21, 1970), and *Your Baby's Sex: Now You Can Choose* (New York: Dodd, Mead & Co., 1970). For another popular account of the work of Shettles (and Sophia J. Kleegman), see the article by Sandie North, "Boy or Girl? Now You Can Choose," *Family Circle* (October 1969), pp. 103–4. For a very recent and most useful review of research findings on sex control, see Ward Rinehart, "Sex Preselection Not Yet Practical," *Population Reports* 1 (May 1975): 21–32.
16. Otfried Hatzold, "X or Y? Sex Selection prior to Conception between Utopia and Reality," *Sexualmedizin* 2 (1973): 430–31.
17. Rodrigo Guerrero, "Association of the Type and Time of Insemination within the Menstrual Cycle with the Human Sex Ratio at Birth," *New England Journal of Medicine* 291 (October–December 1974): 1056; see also the summary of Guerrero's article by the editors of *Family Planning Perspectives,* "Timing Intercourse Can Alter Sex Ratio, But There's a Catch," *Family Planning Perspectives* 7 (March–April 1975): 58.
18. Aubrey Milunsky, *The Prenatal Diagnosis of Hereditary Disorders* (Springfield, Ill.: Charles C. Thomas, 1973), p. 4. For another good reference on amniocentesis, see Amitai Etzioni, *Genetic Fix* (New York: Macmillan Co., 1973).
19. The accuracy of the sex determination was 87 percent, 95 percent, and 100 percent, respectively, in the following three studies: M. M. Nelson and A. E. H. Emery, "Amniotic Fluid Cells: Prenatal Sex Prediction and Culture," *British Medical Journal* 50 (February 1970): 523–26; Aubrey Milunsky (see previous note); and M. S. Golbus et al., "Intrauterine Diagnosis of Genetic Defects: Results, Problems, and Follow-up of One Hundred Cases in a Pre-natal enetic Detection Center," *American Journal of Obstetrics and Gynecology* 118, no. 7 (April 1974): 897–905.
20. Milunsky, p. 7.
21. Golbus et al., p. 904.
22. See Melvin M. Grumbach, "Big Step in Sex Production," *Science News* 96 (July 1969): 76–77, and "Boy or Girl? A New Pre-Birth Test Can Tell," *Good Housekeeping* 170 (January 1970): 139; and Ed Stattman, "Boy or Girl?" *Honolulu Sunday Advertiser* (August 24, 1975).
23. See Judith Blake, "Abortion and Public Opinion: 1960–70 Decade," *Science* 171 (February 1971): 540–49; Larry L. Bumpass and Harriet B. Presser, "The Increasing Acceptance of Sterilization and Abortion," in *Toward the End of Growth: Population in America,* ed. Charles F. Westoff et al. (Englewood Cliffs, N.J.: Prentice-Hall, Inc., 1973); John Hedderson et al., "Determinants of Abortion Attitudes in the United States in 1972," *Cornell Journal of Social Relations* 9, no. 2 (Fall 1974): 261–76; and Elise F. Jones and Charles F. Westoff, "Attitudes toward Abortion in the United States in 1970 and the Trend since 1975," in *Research Reports of the Commission on Population Growth and the American Future,* ed. Charles

F. Westoff and Robert Parke, Jr. (Washington, D.C.: Government Printing Office, 1973), vol. 1.

24. Sophie S. Sloman, "Emotional Problems in 'Planned for' Children," *American Journal of Orthopsychiatry* 18 (July 1948): 523–28.
25. Roger J. Jones, "Sex Predetermination and the Sex Ratio at Birth," *Social Biology* 20 (June 1973): 203–11.
26. Eric Lindahl, "Separation of Bull Spermatozoa Carrying X and Y Chromosomes by Counterstreaming Centrifugation," *Nature* 181 (March 1958): 784.
27. Manuel J. Gordon, "The Control of Sex," *Scientific American* 199 (November 1958): 87–94.
28. Peter Barlow and C. G. Bosa, "The Y Chromosome in Human Spermatozoa," *Nature* 226 (June 1970): 959–62.
29. Amitai Etzioni, "Sex Control, Science, and Society," *Science* (September 13, 1968), pp. 1107–12; Markle and Nam (n. 3 above).
30. Herman Kahn and Anthony J. Weiner, "The Next Thirty-three Years: A Framework for Speculation," *Daedalus* (Summer 1967), p. 713.
31. Markle and Nam, p. 80.
32. Largey (n. 4 above), p. 63.
33. See Williamson (n. 10 above).
34. Westoff and Rindfuss (n. 4 above), pp. 635–36.
35. Previous speculations have been more concerned with the possible effects of sex control on the birthrate or on the sex ratio in the population. Some concern has also been expressed about possible effects on society in general if many families choose to have boys. See especially Etzioni (n. 29 above); Largey; and Markle and Nam.
36. Some of these points have been discussed before by the following three writers: Susan Michelmore, "Sexual Reproduction," in *Population in Perspective,* ed. Louise B. Young (New York: Oxford University Press, 1968), p. 412; Richard L. Meier, "Sex Determination and Other Innovations," in ibid., pp. 406–12; and Edward Pohlman, "Some Effects of Being Able to Control Sex of Offspring," *Eugenics Quarterly* 14 (December 1967): 274–81.
37. See Paul C. Capra and James E. Dittes, "Birth Order as a Selective Factor among Volunteer Subjects," *Journal of Abnormal and Social Psychology* 64, no. 4 (1962): 302 and William D. Altus, "Birth Order and Academic Primogeniture," *Journal of Personality and Social Psychology* 2, no. 6 (1965): 872–76.
38. Hunter M. Breland, "Birth Order, Family Configuration, and Verbal Achievement," *Child Development* 45 (December 1974): 1011–19; and R. C. Nichols, "Birth Order and Intelligence" (unpublished research, National Merit Scholarship Corporation, Evanston, Ill., 1964).
39. See Havelock A. Ellis, *A Study of British Genius,* rev. ed. (Boston: Houghton Mifflin Co., 1926); James Cattell, *Men of Science,* 4th ed. (New York: Science Press, 1927); Anne Roe, *A Psychological Study of Eminent Psychologists and Anthropologists, and a Comparison with Biological and Physical Scientists,* in *Psychological Monographs,* vol. 67, whole no. 352 (1953); W. F. Ogburn, "Our Social Heritage," *Survey Graphic* 49 (1927): 227–79, 341–43; Ellsworth Huntington, *Season of Birth: Its Relation to Human Abilities* (New York: John Wiley & Sons, 1938); Stanley Schacter, "Birth Order, Eminence and Higher Education," *American Sociological Review* 28 (October 1963): 757–67; Lewis M. Terman, Catherine M. Cox, and Barbara S. Burks, *Genetic Studies of Genius,* vol. 1, *The Mental and Physical Traits of a Thousand Gifted Children* (Stanford, Calif.: Stanford University Press, 1925); William D. Altus, "Birth Order and Academic Primogeniture" (n. 37 above), and "Birth Order and Scholastic Aptitude," *Journal of Consulting Psychology* 29 (June 1965): 202–5; and Brian Sutton-Smith and B. G. Rosenberg, *The Sibling* (New York: Holt, Rinehart & Winston, 1970).
40. Lillian Belmont and Francis A. Marolla, "Birth Order, Family Size, and Intelligence," *Science* 182 (December 1973): 1096–1101.
41. Breland, p. 1015.
42. See Westoff and Rindfuss (n. 4 above), p. 636.
43. Jessie Bernard, *The Future of Marriage* (New York: World Publishing Co., 1972).
44. See the following articles by Jeanne C. Ridley: "The Effects of Population Change on the Roles and Status of Women: Perspectives and Speculation," in *Toward a Sociology of Women,* ed. C. Safilios-Rothschild (Lexington, Mass.: Xerox College Publishing, 1972), pp. 372–86, "Introduction: Women's Changing Status," in *The Family in Transition,* ed. Arthur A. Campbell et al. (Washington, D.C.: Government Printing Office, 1970), pp. 189–98, and "On the Consequences of Demographic Change for the Roles and Status of Women,"

in *Demographic and Social Aspects of Population Growth,* ed. Charles F. Westoff and Robert Parke, Jr. (Washington, D.C.: Government Printing Office, 1972), pp. 289–304.

45. Malmood Mandani, *The Myth of Population Control: Family, Caste, and Class in an Indian Village* (New York: Monthly Review Press, 1972).
46. Bailyne Sung, "Boy or Girl? How to Make Your Choice," *Singapore Straits Times* (April 18, 1975).

PART 8

Pregnancy, Childbirth, and Breast-Feeding

Pregnancy, childbirth, and lactation are biological events which are exclusively in the female experience. Because of their unmatched importance to the individual and to the species, and because they are the ultimate distinction between male and female, these ephemeral dramas are of great psychological significance to women who experience them—and to men as well.

The psychological importance of reproductive events lies in their meanings to the woman experiencing them. These meanings have several sources whose confluence determines the psychic significance with which they are invested for a particular woman. It is useful to analyze these meanings in terms of their sources: psychodynamic, situational, and cultural. While these sources are related and overlapping, each has distinguishing features which are important theoretically.

Psychodynamic implications of pregnancy include the woman's feelings and perceptions of herself, as woman and as potential mother. Her psychic history, her relationship with her own mother, her resolution of childhood problems and stages, her self-image, her relation to her body, and her motivation for being pregnant—these can be determinants of her intrapsychic response to her pregnancy and its sequelae. Her psychodynamic reaction to her pregnancy may be partly unconscious, but it can powerfully affect the course of the pregnancy and her later response to her child.

Situational variables are identified in her immediate environmental context. The quality of her relationship with her mate, for example, and his presence and reaction to her pregnancy, can significantly interact with and affect her own feelings and attitudes. Her employment and educational status, the life changes necessitated by a child, and the level and quality of emotional and financial resources available to her are variables which enter into her adaptation to this life-cycle milestone.

Cultural meanings of childbearing are those which are shared by most or all others with whom she identifies. These include beliefs and attitudes around pregnancy, birth, and motherhood, values attached to the reproductive functions of women, expectations for the behavior of a woman who is pregnant or mothering, and the limitations which may be placed on her as a function of any of these.

An example of the substance of such an analysis is "Childbirth in Crosscultural Perspective" by Niles and Michael Newton. Based on medical and anthropological literature on cultural patterns of birth practices, the authors show the many variations in the ways that humans handle birth. The Newtons make the interesting point that, while birth is always treated with importance by nonliterate groups, the study of cultural practices has been hampered by the fact that, in most groups, birth is woman's work from which men are excluded. Since most Western observers are male, childbirth has been out of bounds as a subject for study, even for those who were interested in its observances and rituals. Because of this, information is often sparse in regard to this area of behavior.

Attitudes surrounding birth are analyzed by the Newtons in such areas as the attributed importance of childbirth, requirements for secrecy and privacy, beliefs about the contaminating properties of the parturient and postpartum woman, and tendencies to see birth as supernatural, as painful illness, or as normal physiology. Obstetrical techniques vary along several dimensions, including biochemical management, relaxation and activity, sensory stimulation, emotional support, and delivery position. In conclusion, the Newtons note the resistance of establishment systems to the utilization of new data relevant to the facilitation of the birth process. For example, studies have shown that sitting or squatting positions are more advantageous for labor and delivery than is the supine one generally used in Western hospitals. But the suggestion of improving the birth process by changing the position of the woman conflicted with the cultural belief that birth should be experienced lying down, and the research has been ignored by the obstetric profession.

An important event of the postpartum period is lactation, the production of milk for the newborn. While lactation is a normal function of hormonal activity subsequent to birth, not all women choose to breast-feed their infants. In "Breast Feeding" Niles Newton points out that, long before there were any arguments about woman's duty to breast-feed, or any choice for that matter, breast-feeding, along with coitus, was necessary for the survival of the race. Certain similarities between breast-feeding and coitus, including both the obligatory one of duty and the incidental one of sensual pleasure, probably helped motivate women to nourish their children in this way.

The studies reported by Newton offer evidence that maternal behavior and maternal attitudes are related to breast-feeding behavior. Women who were successful in breast-feeding tended to be more comfortable with nudity, and to maintain closer body contact with their infants. Other influences on success with breast-feeding include the woman's cultural setting, her educational level, her social class, and her work status. Newton also examines such factors as the attitudes of hospital personnel and institutional routines on decisions of new mothers to nurse their babies. These, along with prevalent notions of modesty surrounding body functions, make it surprising, she concludes, that breast-feeding continues to be chosen by many young women.

"Maternal Attachment" by Marshall Klaus and others, is a study of the effects on the mother-infant relationship of the amount of close contact the two have in the first few postpartum days. Animal studies show that in some species separation of the mother and infant immediately after birth, a practice in most hospitals, results in the disruption of normal mothering behavior. Klaus *et al.* hypothesized that in humans as well there is a period shortly after birth that is uniquely important for the development of mother-to-infant attachment. To test this hypothesis, they arranged for an experimental group of mothers to have contact with their newborn infants for sixteen hours more than usual hospital procedure permits. A month later they compared the behavior of these mothers with their infants to that of a control group of mothers who had experienced the usual amount of postpartum contact with their infants in the hospital. The results showed that the extended contact mothers were more likely to pick up a crying baby, less likely to have left it with a sitter, and spent more time spontaneously interacting with the baby during feeding.

These results suggest the possibility of a "critical period" in the early postpartum period during which maternal attachment behavior is facilitated. Whether these extended contact effects would persist into later infancy and beyond is not presently known. The authors discuss the implications of their study for the handling of premature as well as normal babies in hospital settings, and raise interesting questions about the effects of high attachment of mothers on babies' later development.

Although Klaus *et al.* do not discuss it, we might raise the hypothetical question of what it would mean if it should be conclusively shown that a critical period exists right after birth during which mother-to-infant bonding occurs, and that such bonding has positive effects on maternal behavior and on infant development. Would this be seen as further evidence of the biological underpinnings of mothering? Would it support the notion that babies are best cared for by their mothers at the time? Would the critical period apply to fathers too? Or is it a phenomenon unique to women, perhaps induced by postnatal hormonal influences? One can visualize such benign effects as changes in hospital procedure to permit parents more time with their newborn child. And it is not farfetched to predict that the notion of a special mother-infant bond, perhaps innately determined, would set up a storm of ideological dispute with traditionalists welcoming scientific support for their views about woman's role as mother and feminists insisting that such findings be interpreted in a perspective which would accommodate them to present and future realities of women's lives, not in one with regressive and constraining consequences.

The biological events which are the bases for the essays in this section are of great significance in human societies everywhere. Because of this, they have become laden with meaning, integrated into cultural patterns of ritual and belief, and celebrated in diverse ways. Only women who experience them can appreciate them fully, and even that experience has been distorted, attenuated, and mystified by fear and ignorance, and by such practices as total anesthesia for childbirth, isolation of the mother, and the depersonalizing effects of institutional care. Stimulated by research findings and by their own consciousness, women are beginning to question the old ways of dealing with childbirth, and to "take back" what is really theirs. Few areas which affect the psychology of women are more deserving of scientific attention, both theoretical and empirical, than this.

Childbirth in Crosscultural Perspective

Niles Newton and Michael Newton

Introduction

All known human societies pattern the behavior of human beings involved in the process of reproduction.[65] Beliefs concerning appropriate behavior in pregnancy, during labor, and in the puerperium appear to be characteristic of all cultures. This review will concentrate on patterns of behavior during and surrounding birth. Special attention will be paid to the primitive and traditional cultures, but examples from modern industrial cultures will also be used. Major trends and contrasts in patterns will be emphasized, particularly in so far as they may have applicability to current clinical issues.

First, attitudes surrounding birth will be discussed: the importance placed on birth, privacy and sexual implications of birth, birth seen in terms of achievement or atonement, birth as dirty or defiling or close to the supernatural, and birth as a painful illness or a normal physiological process.

Then social variations in the management of labor will be discussed, particularly in regard to practices which differ markedly from one society to another, resulting in different types of birth experience for mother and baby. These variations include differences in biochemical management, rules about activity and relaxation, sensory stimulation, emotional support and companionship, and delivery position.

Finally, the effect of social attitudes and beliefs surrounding birth on birth behavior will be discussed, as well as other questions raised by the review.

"Childbirth in Crosscultural Perspective" by Niles Newton and Michael Newton from *Modern Perspectives in Psycho-Obstetrics,* edited by J. G. Howells. New York: Brunner/Mazel, 1972. Reprinted by permission of the publisher.

Limitations on Available Information

Both medical and anthropological literature were searched for information on the patterns of culture in the area of birth. Particularly helpful were the Human Relations Area Files, which, at the time the search was made, contained 222 cultures coded in such a way that materials on childbirth could be located rapidly. Medical literature through the years has also concerned itself with certain aspects of patterns of childbirth and was therefore also searched.

Although both medical and anthropological literatures contain considerable information about certain patterns of obstetrical behavior, information is frequently lacking in regard to areas of behavior most relevant to this review. For example, Teit's[96] record of birth among the Nahane Indians of northern Canada devotes more than 450 words to describing the handling of the umbilical cord and to the beliefs concerning it and fewer than 150 words to the other behavior of the attendants and mother during labor. It was not until the 1920s, when the impact of psychoanalysis began to be felt, that ethnologists turned their attention to variations in emotion and personality and began to make more detailed records in this area.

One of the greatest handicaps in the recording of birth patterning among preliterate peoples is the fact that most primitive peoples exclude men from witnessing normal delivery. Although husbands are sometimes permitted to witness their children born, and medicine men may be called in in case of abnormality, other men are excluded from witnessing birth in many of the preliterature societies that have been studied.

Physicians contributing to medical literature are also handicapped, since they tend to see only the cases of extremely abnormal childbirth. Often modern medical advice is asked only when the primitive woman is on the verge of death. Normal childbirth as it takes place regularly in the tribal community is usually out of bounds for the physician as well as the anthropologist.

Implicit in most historical and anthropological writing and medical case reports is the assumption that relatively few observations of behavior in a culture can be generalized into statements about the whole. Due to the extreme paucity of studies done on broad samples collected with controls for observer bias, the limited data available have been used of necessity.

Nature of Conclusions

The nature of the data available at the present time makes it impossible to draw any precise conclusions. What the data can do is to suggest the many variations in the ways in which human beings handle birth. They can suggest certain aspects that have been muted in industrialized cultures and that are more fully developed in other cultures, thus opening new areas of understanding. They can also give perspective, by raising for question implicit assumptions held within our culture, and by exploring various ways in which behavioral issues in our culture are dealt with in other cultures.

A final word of caution is in order in regard to data gleaned from records of so-called primitive cultures. *The word "primitive" is used only in the anthropological sense, meaning peoples without written language.* It is likely that the *behavior of most peoples mentioned may often be different from that described in the text, due to rapid changes in culture occurring in most parts of the world.* The older accounts are often especially valuable for a study of this nature, since they may record relatively intact societies not yet overwhelmed by excessive contact with industrial culture. Despite the biased and fragmentary records produced by the early ethnographers and other early records, the scholarly world of today owes these men and women a deep debt of gratitude; for they recorded unique patterns of human behavior before they irretrievably disappeared.

Attitudes Surrounding Birth

Birth is an event that is treated with importance. Much cultural patterning surrounds birth as well as other aspects of reproduction. Despite widespread cultural interest in birth, the nature of attitudes toward birth vary greatly. For some it is an open sociable event, while others surround it with secrecy. The sexual implications of birth are developed in some cultures, and strictly taboo in others. Various peoples see birth in terms of pay or praise, dirt, defilement, and/or supernatural involvement; or as normal physiology, or painful illness.

Importance Placed on Birth

Among primitive groups and traditional village culture groups, as well as in modern industrial cultures, childbirth is an event of consequence that changes the behavior not only of the mother but of other people in the social group. In primitive culture, by far the most usual pattern is for the laboring woman to have two or more attendants for labor and delivery. Often special huts are built for delivery, and elaborate postnatal patterns have developed. Even among some primitive people, whose life depends on following the food supply, the group will stop migration if possible when delivery approaches, or leave a helper with the woman who must stay behind.

The intense interest in childbirth is reflected in the high degree of knowledge acquired. Thus some non-industrialized peoples have developed the use of oxytocic drugs,[7, 73, 99] cesarean sections,[105] and operations enlarging the birth passages.[37] Complex cultures have developed sophisticated systems of obstetrics. The medicine that developed in ancient India,[1, 80] Chinese medicine of the thirteenth century,[59] and Roman medicine of the early second century,[80] in some ways matches or surpasses the obstetrical knowledge of western Europe of only one hundred years ago.

Privacy Surrounding Birth

Although all cultures seem to emphasize in one way or the other the importance of childbirth, there are wide variations in specific aspects. One of these variations is in the area of secrecy with which they surround birth.

The frank open approach of some cultures to childbirth is indicated by the frequency with which they portray childbirth in their art. The Egyptian hieroglyphic for "to give birth to" depicts a squatting woman with the fetal head emerging from the perineum.[49] The ancient Mexican civilizations produced figures of women in the birth position with emerging infants.[99]

Many peoples pattern birth as a social event openly accepted by the community. Thus the Navaho of the south-western United States were reported to show "a great interest in birth. The hogan is open when a baby is being born. . . . Anyone who comes and lends moral support is invited to stay and partake of what food is available."[51]

In some cultures, the games of children reflect the frankness with which birth is regarded. For example, it is reported that a favorite game of Pukapuka preadolescents was to play at childbirth, immature coconuts being used to represent babies. "After a pretended cohabitation, the girl mother stuffed the coconut inside her dress and realistically gave birth to her child, imitating labor pains and letting the nut fall at the proper moment."[6]

In contrast to such open attitudes, other peoples feel extreme secrecy or the need for privacy about birth. Among the Cuna of Panama, children were kept in ignorance of birth as long as possible. They were not permitted to see dogs, cats, or pigs giving birth. Ideally they were not told until the last stage of the marriage ceremony about the existence of the sex act and childbirth.[94] Childbirth was called "to catch the deer": children were told that babies are found in the forest between deer horns or put on the beach by a dolphin.[44] The Chagga likewise surrounded birth with secrecy. Children were told that an animal brings babies or that they came from a beehive in the forest or steppe. In 1926 Gutmann reported: "In former years, the whole country was disgraced when a married man in conversation with minors replied to their questions as to the origin of man: *wandu veketsesau*—man happens to be born."[37]

In contemporary industrial cultures childbirth may also be cloaked with privacy. Seeing birth is often considered appropriate only for medical personnel. An illustration of this was the problem of an American obstetrician who bought a sculpture of a Mexican goddess in the act of giving birth. The fetus was half emerged. He tried putting it in his office, but his nurse and patients objected. He brought it home, but his wife felt it was improper to exhibit it in any part of the house.

Secrecy feelings may be so strong that they tend to persist despite administrative attempts to change them. For example, at St. Mary's Hospital in Evansville, Indiana, fathers are encouraged to participate in the childbearing experience. Fathers attend prenatal classes with their wives and usually sit with them during the first stage of labor. Yet when asked whether fathers should be in the delivery room, 59.4% of 267 fathers said that they did not feel husbands belong there.[25]

However, a protest against the taboo on open childbirth may be developing in the United States. Not only is there a strong minority agitating for permission for husbands to be permitted to witness birth of their babies, but the hippies in communes of northern California are patterning birth as a social home event when it's nice to have one's friends around.[72]

Sexual Implications of Birth

Closely allied to feelings about secrecy are feelings about the sexual implications of birth. Niles Newton[77] has pointed out that there are similarities in the level of physiologically based behavior between undrugged childbirth as observed by Dick Read and the female sexual excitement documented by Kinsey *et al.*[46] The following aspects of behavior are similar: (1) type of breathing; (2) type of sounds made and facial expression during second stage labor and orgasm; (3) rhythmic contractions of the upper segment of the uterus; (4) periodic contractions of the abdominal muscles; (5) inhibitions and psychic blockages frequently relieved; (6) unusual muscular strength; (7) increased insensitivity to pain and restricted sensory perception at height of reaction; (8) sudden return of awareness at completion; (9) forceful emotional reaction of satisfaction at completion.

These physiological similarities between birth and sexual excitement are developed and recognized in some cultures and muted in others. A 1901 account of Laotian labor states that relatives, friends, or more often young men, hold the woman up and try to divert her with extremely licentious remarks. Some of the young men bring musical instruments and others bring phalli, to which they address such witty approaches that the patient, despite her pain, responds with an outburst of laughter.[83] A Lepcha man of the Himalayan States in Asia told of peeking at a woman in labor when he was eight or nine years old: "I only went because I was very interested to see how a baby was born and because I wanted to see what a woman's vulva was like. I could not now watch this sort of thing as it would have too exciting an effect on me."[75]

In contrast, other peoples have reacted to the sexual implications of birth by concern over modesty. The following remarks by Chippewa Indians of Ontario, Canada, illustrate this problem.[40]

> Some of the full-bloods don't want men around, not even doctors. I, myself, think it is a disgrace the way women submit themselves to strangers today when their babies are born, especially to those doctors . . . In the old days not even women looked at anyone more than necessary; a big piece of buckskin was placed over the mother to protect her modesty.

The current patterning of the second stage of labor in the United States is in keeping with the tendency to mute any recognition of the relationship between birth and other inter-personal reproductive acts. When delivery seems imminent, the American woman is transported from her bed, wheeled into a room with brilliant lights and medical instruments. She is then put on a special table that has equipment for tying her hands and her feet, and her buttocks are so adjusted that she pushes her baby out into space with no mattress to break its fall should the doctor fail to catch it. Labor is then quite usually artificially shortened by cutting the woman's perineum.[77]

Achievement and Atonement at Birth

In some cultures birth is patterned as representing achievement or an event to be paid for. However, there are marked variations as to who gets the credit and who does the paying. Atlee[2] has pointed out that modern women may derive very little prestige or satisfaction from childbirth. Instead, the feelings of achievement at birth may center around the actions of the obstetrician.

American parlance reflects this feeling. The obstetrician says, "I delivered Mrs. Jones," using the active voice. Mrs. Jones is likely to say, "Dr. Smith delivered me," using the passive voice. The husband and family are more likely to thank the obstetrician for the delivery of the baby than to thank the wife for giving birth.

In contrast to this, the Ila of Northern Rhodesia consider that birth is an achievement for the mother. "Women attending at birth were observed to shout praises of the woman who had had a baby. They all thanked her, saying, 'I give much thanks to you today that you have given birth to a child.' " After the birth, the Ila mother's husband may come in to see her and congratulate her. "Her male relations may also enter the hut, clasp their hand to hers and give her bracelets or leglets by way of congratulation."[88] This feeling of "personal achievement" about labor is so important to some South African tribes that the husband and father may refuse to get medical assistance for a woman in labor on the grounds that she would be better off dead than unable to bring forth a live child by herself.[56]

Perhaps allied with this feeling that birth is an achievement is the attitude that birth must be "paid for". Among the Goajiro of Colombia the father "pays" the relatives of the mother for the suffering and discomfort she experiences in childbirth.[11] The Araucanians of South America may feel that children should be made to "appreciate' their mothers' suffering. Said one informant, "I have often thought that when children grow up they need to be told how much their mothers suffered giving them birth."[41] However, the Laotians felt that the mother herself should "pay" for the birth. After delivery she underwent sitz baths and hot body effusions which are part of the custom known as "You Kam"—"to submit to penitence:"[21]

Birth as Dirty or Defiling

Ordinary birth was frequently regarded as dirty or defiling. Among the Arapesh of New Guinea, "birth must take place over the edge of the village, which is situated on a hilltop, in the 'bad place' also reserved for excretion, menstrual huts, and foraging pigs."[62] Post-partum purification ceremonies were also reported from such widely scattered peoples as the Hottentots of South Africa,[42] the Jordan village peoples of the Middle East,[32] and the Caucasia region of Russia.[55] Hebrew-Christian tradition has firmly imbedded in it the feeling that birth is unclean. The ancient Hebrews felt so strongly about the defiling nature of birth that the whole of Leviticus Chapter 12 is devoted to the ritual purification of women following childbirth,[49] and even today the Catholic church has a special ritual for women after childbirth, although this is falling into disuse.

The "dirty" view of birth was especially strongly held in some parts of Asia. When labor started, the woman of Kadu Gollas of India was required to move into the jungle hut built for the purpose. She was considered impure for three months after delivery. Anyone touching her during labor "caught" the contamination and was isolated as well. Mother and child could not re-enter the house until they got permission from their deity.[92] Some women in India are reported to be considered unclean and "untouchable" during childbirth and for ten days thereafter.[93] The Vietnamese considered birth so contaminating that, although the village father did all he could during and after birth, he could not enter his wife's room but could speak to her only from the door. In order not to bring bad luck to others, Vietnamese mothers avoided going out for 30 to 100 days after delivery.[17]

Birth as Close to Supernatural

Many peoples see birth as a time of particular vulnerability, when death may be near and supernatural forces are at work. This was expressed very clearly in the Jordan village culture, where the midwife admonished: "The mother is in God's hands and she hovers between life and death. . . . Angels go up and down to record what happens . . . and the mother, after safe delivery of a boy, may be congratulated. 'God be thanked that thou hast risen unhurt'."[33] The seventeenth-century diary of Samuel Sewall suggests this same sense of vulnerability and closeness to God in colonial New England culture. A 1690 entry read: "At last my wife bade me call Mrs. Ellis, then Mother Hull, and the Midwife, and throw the Goddness of God was brought to Bed of a Daughter between three and four o'clock."[87] The Moravian village people of Czechoslovakia of the last century are reported to have had strong feelings about vulnerability immediately after birth, when the lying-in woman was susceptible to demoniacal forces, which were particularly strong between sunset and 6 a.m. and again for three hours at mid-day. To avoid their influences, the lying-in woman was supposed to stay in bed and thus obtained some extra postpartum rest.[4]

Death of the laboring woman is widely looked upon as particularly horrifying. Posthumous removal of the fetus was a common pattern, occurring not only in the Pacific Islands.[61] but also in Africa[13] and Burma.[58] In Samoa the child was cut out of the dead woman, since otherwise, it was believed, it would become an avenging ghost.[61] In some areas of West Africa it was considered a disgrace to die in labor. The body of the woman was "treated with contumely" and was burned, as was everything else belonging to her.[105] The deep fears stirred by death during pregnancy or labor were particularly prominent in the report of what happened among the Bambara of Africa. The entire female population of the village was upset, marking the event with an elaborate ceremony.[38]

Birth as Painful Illness or Normal Physiology

Is normal birth really a normal phenomenon or one to be treated as a painful illness? This basic question is viewed in different ways by different people. Many people in many parts of the world regard childbirth as a normal function. Du Bois,[23] observing the people of Alor, of the Lesser Sundas Islands, states: "One gathers the impression that birth is considered an easy and casual procedure. . . . This does not mean that difficulties never occur, but it does indicate that the society has not emphasized such difficulties." The Jarara woman of South America[36] gave birth in a passageway or shelter "in full view of everyone, even her small children. There was no concern at all over this matter; childbirth was considered a normal phenomenon." From the Pacific Islands it was reported: "Extremely realistic attitudes toward childbirth are held by the Pukapukans. No sense of mystery surrounds the event. It is considered of interest to the whole community as natural as any other fact of life."[5]

Indeed, the sensation of normal labor in some cultures may not be thought of as "pain". For instance, the Navaho have two words for labor—one means pain of labor and the other means labor alone.[60] Thus the vocabulary of the Navaho, which embodies the cultural expectation, encourages the Navaho woman to feel that it is possible to have labor sensations without interpreting them as painful. McCammon, after personally attending more than 400 Indian women who were delivered at the Navaho Medical Center, states: "Many appear to suffer severe pain for many hours. These women do not hesitate to request analgesics and anesthetics. . . . However, I am convinced that not a few go through labor and delivery without pain."[60]

One of the most detailed accounts of primitive labor is of the Aranda, an extremely primitive people of central Australia. The observer, de Vidas, reports that the Aranda recognize the onset of labor by strong contractions which are "painful".[20] However, during labor "little fuss" is made by the woman if the labor is normal.

Nor does excessive pain appear to be part of the usual pattern of the people of Alor of the Lesser Sundas Islands. Du Bois writes: "In the half-dozen births I witnessed, the mothers at no time showed signs of pain beyond acute discomfort. They groaned softly and perspired freely, but seemed on the whole to give birth with little difficulty."[23]

In other cultures pain may be quite definite, even among people who have had little contact with Western Industrial culture. For instance, de Lery[19] writes of the Tupinamba of the Brazilian coastal area he observed in 1557–1558, presumably before there was much contact with European culture. He and another Frenchman were lodging in a village, when about midnight they heard a great outcry from a woman. Thinking she had been surprised by a jaguar, they ran to her. They found her in labor with her husband acting as midwife. He caught the baby in his arms and cut the cord with his teeth. A Kurtatchi woman of the Solomon Islands described labor in her culture with these words: "Now it hurts, its mother cries out, now we cut some leaves, we make her drink. Now the child is about to be born. Now she is afraid because the child hurts her. She cries out because of the child."[9] Labor pain has puzzled the Ila of Northern Rhodesia so much that they have developed an elaborate theory concerning its origin as being the result of *mupuka* reluctant to let go of a woman.[90]

A number of primitive peoples do have cultural patterns of stoicism that prohibit women from showing the pain they may feel. In Samoa "convention dictates that mothers should neither writhe or cry out,"[63] In some cultures, where the expectation of pain is intense the culture uses extreme fear to keep screaming under control. The Chagga are told from childhood that it is man's nature to groan like a goat, but women suffer silently like sheep.[81] Clitoridectomy scars may interfere with delivery and increase pain yet the laboring woman believes she will kill her baby if she screams and that her husband may divorce her if, through lack of self control, "the child is killed".[81] She also knows that screams would shame her mother and make her mother-in-law critical of her. Thus most Chagga women are stoic during labor, suppressing loud cries.[81]

American culture has not developed such strong sanctions against expressing pain, but birth customs are patterned around the expectation of pain in labor. Uterine contractions of labor are called "pains" not "contractions," and instead of having separate birth attendants specializing in normal birth, the differences between normal and abnormal are so muted that it is considered desirable for a specialist in obstetrical disease to deliver every woman. Atlee[2] described the attitudes of his North American colleagues as follows:

"We obstetricians seem to think and act as if pregnancy and labor constitute a pathologic rather than a physiologic process. . . . Our entire basic medical education is so obsessed with pathology that it is practically impossible for us to think of any woman who comes to us as other than *sick*."

When there is belief that labor is extremely painful, there may be a kind of resignation about the pain and willingness to add to the inevitable; whereas, when pain is not considered "normal," extra care may be taken to avoid placing the parturient in extra discomfort. For instance, in U.S.S.R., where psychological methods of pain control are widely practised,[14] there is a belief that labor is not necessarily painful. Enemas, often used in American labor upon admission to the hospital, are avoided in U.S.S.R. as "painful stimuli".[67]

Obstetrical Techniques: A Crosscultural View

Since patterning of behavior may be particularly elaborated or particularly rigid when events have emotional impact, it is not surprising to find a large variety of well developed behavior patterns elicited by birth. Differences in management of labor occur in at least five different dimensions, including biochemical management, relaxation and activity, sensory stimulation, emotional support, and delivery position.

Biochemical Management

The culture largely determines the woman's biochemical status during labor. Not only does each society regulate the availability and type of medication, but also determines the availability and type of nutritional support during labor, which in turn influences the parturient's biochemical status.

Non-industrialized peoples have developed the same variety of patterns in regard to biochemical support in labor as have those o. Western culture. Some years ago, the first act of the Ukranian midwife was to give the mother a generous dose of whisky to ease her pains.[47] The Amhara of Ethiopia[70] gave a drink of mashed linseed to "relax the birth tract" and to "lessen the pain". On the other side of the world, in Muskrat, North America, a Crow Indian midwife,[53] was reported to know of two plants that eased the suffering at birth. The Ojibwa[45] had also developed a pharmacological pattern. They had standard medicines for easing childbirth and others to be taken after normal delivery.

Nutritional regulation was also found frequently in primitive labor. For instance, the African Hottentots[86] fed soups to laboring women to "strengthen them". The Yumans[91] and the Pawnee,[22] both of North

America, on the other hand, had developed a strong prohibition against drinking water in labor; it must cease with the first labor pain. Maternal death was ascribed to the breaking of this taboo. The Bahaya of Africa permitted drinking during labor but prohibited eating.[74]

Currently the nutritional approach to labor is so muted in the United States that the idea that food and beverage may play a role in labor may be startling to Americans. American patterns sometimes emphasize the fear that liquid and food given during labor will predispose to the aspiration of vomitus during anticipated anesthesia. A usual pattern is for all food and beverage, and often even water, intake to be prohibited during labor. If labor continues for many hours, dehydration and low blood sugar are combated with intravenous fluids containing glucose. At the same time, a variety of pharmacological supportive measures are administered. The great interest in the United States in the medicinal rather than the nutritional aspect of biochemical support is indicated by the fact that *Williams' Obstetrics*[24] cites 99 references in the chapter on "Analgesia and anesthesia", but only 27 references in the chapter on the "Conduct of normal labor", none of which deals specifically with the problem of nutritional support.

This is a relatively new American pattern. An early-nineteenth-century obstetrical text[69] urges nutritional supplementation in labor but warns against alcohol, an analgesic drug, as follows: "She should be supplied from time to time with mild bland nourishment in moderate quantities. Tea, coffee, gruel, barley water, milk and water, broths, etc., may safely be allowed. Beer, wine or spirits, undiluted or diluted, should be forbidden. . . ."

Current European medicine does not seem to mute the nutritional aspect of labor to the same extent as modern American. For instance, a recent British text[79] states: "The labouring woman requires a certain amount of nourishment . . . her own appetite should be a certain guide to what she wishes to eat or drink." The text goes on to suggest that a patient in "trial labour" who may later need a cesarean section be encouraged to eat and drink such foods as eggs, milk, and glucose drinks. In the late 1940s two papers appeared in the U.S.S.R. concerning the oxytocic and analgesic effects of Vitamin B1 in a series of labors. Europeans, whose cultural orientation included some interest in nutrition in labor, picked up the idea and papers were published in Germany, Italy, Hungary, Bulgaria, Yugoslavia, Austria, France and Greece.[60] Notably absent in a search of literature were American papers, in keeping with their general tendency to mute the nutritional aspects of birth management in this culture.

Relaxation and Activity Implementation

Many cultures feel the need for regulating activity during labor. Patterns involving restriction or augmentation of activity are common.

Preliterate peoples have tended to pattern types of desirable movement during labor, although from birth descriptions it is difficult to tell how far labor has progressed before regulations on movement are invoked. The inactive approach to labor, in which much movement is scarcely possible, is described by Schultze[86] in his study of the Hottentots: "Once I saw six women squatting around in one hut scarcely 3 meters in width. . . . It was difficult to recognize which woman was the cause of this gathering who lay on the floor in the background covered with skins."

Other peoples, however, felt that vigorous exercise was beneficial. Among the Tuareg, a nomadic tribe of the Sahara, the young mother followed the advice of her aunt or mother. She walked up and down small hills from the first labor pain onward, in order "to allow the infant to get well placed". She returned to the tent for delivery in the kneeling position.[10] In another group in the same cultural area women not only walked up and down but "pound grain in mortar to provoke the final labour pains."[29]

In the United States activity in labor is usually strictly patterned only after the parturient arrives at the hospital, regardless of the stage of labor. Upon admission, she is put in a wheelchair and pushed to the labor floor. There she is placed supine in bed. Frequently bedpans may be substituted for walks to the toilet. Labor-room attendants may tell the laboring woman to "relax", but only in hospitals where there is interest in psychological methods of pain control may actual coaching in methods of relaxation be given. Relaxation instruction may aim to relieve muscular tension, focus attention away from the pain, or put the patient in a more suggestible state, depending on theoretical orientations,[15] but in all cases inactivity of the major muscles is required.

Patterned *inactivity* is a relatively new development in American culture, contrasting with previous beliefs that exercise in labor was desirable. An 1816 obstetric text encourages movement:[69] ". . . During the first and second stages (the second stage was defined as terminating before delivery) . . . the patient may be allowed to sit, stand, kneel or walk out as her inclination may prompt her; if fatigued, she should repose occasionally upon the bed or couch, but it is not expedient during these two stages that she should remain very long at a time in a recumbent posture."

As late as 1894 an obstetrical text[54] warns: "The patient should be encouraged not to take to bed at the outset of labor. In the upright or sitting posture gravity aids in the fixation of the head and promotes passive hyperaemia and dilation of the cervix." However, by this time undressing and lying down are recommended as the end of the first stage approaches.

Sensory Stimulation

In quite a number of primitive cultures, sensory stimulation of many sorts plays a prominent part in the management of labor. Music in labor was used by widely separated groups: the Laotians in Indochina,[83] the Navaho of North America,[3] and the Cuna of Panama.[95] Conversation also involves an element of pure sound stimulation and was used by primitive groups who patterned labor as a social event.

Heat is sometimes applied to women in labor in various ways. The Tübatulabel[101] dug a trench inside or outside of the house, depending on the weather, in which a fire was built. The fire was covered with slabs of stone and layers of earth and tule mats were added. The laboring woman lay on top of all this. The North American Comanche[102] simplified the procedure by putting hot rocks on the back of the laboring woman. Farther south, the Tewa[84] fumigated the laboring woman by wrapping her in a blanket and had her stand over hot coals upon which medication was placed.

A common form of sensory stimulation is abdominal stimulation. A tedious labor among the Kurtatchi was treated by an older woman attendant who chewed special roots and vegetation:[9] "She spat the resulting red saliva on to her hand and rubbed Manev's abdomen with it, with a circular motion, all round the edge of the tumid belly. . . . Once in a while the woman kneeling behind moved her clasping hands from the top of the protuberant abdomen to the bottom and shook it violently."

This pattern of abdominal stimulation appears in other widely separated primitive peoples, suggesting independent invention of the technique. The Yahgan midwife of Tierra del Fuego, at the southern tip of South America, made circular strokes on the abdomen with the flat of her hand to stimulate birth.[35] The Navaho sprinkled pollen over the stomach area to make birth easy.[3] The Punjab midwife rubbed melted butter on the abdomen.[30]

Firm pressure applied to parts other than the abdomen was also used in primitive cultures. Among the Pukapuka, the *tangata wakawanau* (medicine man specializing in obstetrics) helped a woman in delivery by pushing with the heel or palm of the hand on the small of her back.[5] The Kurtatchi[9] and the Kazakhs of Kazakhstan in Asia[34] used knee pressure of the attendant holding the woman from the rear. The Punjab village midwife applied strong steady pressure with her feet on either side of the birth canal in the second stage of labor, a measure which was reported to feel "good".[30]

Many primitive peoples provide for skin stimulation by having the woman held in the labor position by others. The contact of body to body skin to skin, may involve considerably more sensation than the support of an inanimate object. Ford[27] lists twenty-five primitive cultures in which women are supported from behind. Abdominal pressure is often applied as well.

Interest in sensory stimulation is muted in the management of labor in the United States today, except for occasional interest among groups that use psycho-physical methods of pain control. The woman using the Lamaze method of preparation for delivery is often instructed to stimulate her abdomen during labor in the manner similar to that used by various preliterate people. A natural childbirth mother may have a warm water bottle placed on her lower abdomen and have her husband put firm pressure on her sore back. Music may be piped into the delivery room and television viewing may be enouraged during labor. However, this use of sensory stimulation in labor, as a diversionary technique to reduce the sensation of pain, is an atypical rather than a typical pattern.

Companionship and Emotional Support

Birth in most societies is patterned not as an unaided solo act but as a social one in which others help in some way. The emotional impact of the labor attendants is a key variable in the patterning of labor.

Curiously, there is a widespread belief that primitive labors are casual unattended affairs, but records indicate otherwise. Unattended birth does occur in many cultures, but it is a rare event to be gossiped about in the same manner as an American birth taking place in a taxi-cab. Granqvist[33] comments, after giving an account of an unusual unattended delivery: "The peasant women move about outside so carefree although they are already in the last stage of pregnancy . . . their hard life full of heavy work does not allow them to spare themselves. Considering this, it is rather surprising that cases of birth in the open air are not much more numerous." Hilger [41] tells of the resentment felt by the South American Araucanian mother who went into labor when no one except her little boy was at home, so that she could not send for help. In the mountains of Yugoslavia it was reported to be "not unusual" for women to give birth in a field or on the mountain,[98] and in a Bulgarian village [85] an "exceptional" woman was reported to prefer to deliver alone. But in neither case is this the "usual way". A most atypical account is that of the South American Talamanca which states: "When the time of parturition approaches, the father goes into the woods and builds a little shed at a safe distance from the house. To this the woman retires as soon as she feels the labor pain coming on. Here, alone and unassisted, she brings forth her young." [28] However, it is to be noted the father built the shed. This was not a "casual delivery," but one which involved considerable preparatory work by a family member.

Often the birth took place in the home of the mother's or the father's mother. Thus, the care of the heavily pregnant and newly delivered woman fell on the grandmother and her younger daughters. Frequently even when later births took place away from the original home, special efforts were made to return the primipara to her own mother for her first confinement. The Punjab girl left her husband and mother-in-law, with whom she still felt shy, and traveled to the home of her birth to be with her own mother and the village midwife, whom she had known for years.[30] Thousands of miles away, in Africa,[50] North America,[103] South America,[36] the Middle East,[33] and in the Pacific Islands,[9] the same return to mother's home for the first baby took place.

In primitive cultures all over the world, the elderly woman, rather than the skilled man, is the predominant attendant at normal labor. Ford [27] found elderly women assisting at birth in 58 cultures and not assisting in only two. In only four of his cultures was information lacking.

When social role differentiation has developed to such an extent that there is a person designated as a regular midwife, her personality and character are usually taken into account. Thus the Ojibwa felt that the midwife "should be a woman of mature years, preferably not under thirty-five. She should have had a few children of her own and be known to have had easy deliveries. She should be of calm temperament." [48] Among the Yahgan some women had the reputation of being good at delivery. "They get this reputation because of their frequent assistance and personal skill. . . . In general a woman will always be attended by the same midwife, because the latter has learned her physical characteristics from experience." [35]

Knowledge does not always come from personal experience, however. Graybull's wife, a North American Crow Indian, gave a horse as payment to obtain her obstetrical knowledge from a visionary.[52] At Tau, in Samoa, barren women past childbearing age compensated for their barrenness by acting as midwives and were reputed to be very wise.[61]

In modern American culture there may be a tendency to mute the help available from older experienced women. Young couples often living many miles from their parents find the help of relatives at the time of childbearing difficult to obtain. Among some families there is even a feeling that it is somehow better to try to manage alone without feeling "dependent" on the help and experience of the older generation. During labor in America, female relatives of the parturient are often excluded. Other women—practical nurses or registered nurses—do look after women in the hospital in the first stage of labor and post-partum, but these women are strangers, not friends or relatives. There is no requirement that a nurse have experienced childbearing herself. A registered nurse who has never had a baby is usually considered more desirable as a labor attendant in normal labor than the practical nurse who has experienced several labors and deliveries.

Although females all over the world attend women in labor, giving them emotional support by their presence as well as ministering to their simple needs, the role of males in labor is extremely variable.

The tendency to feel that birth is woman's business is so strong that men, other than husbands, are usually excluded from entering the same abode as the laboring woman. Even the male healer is frequently excluded. For example, in Africa, the Tuareg midwife, in case of abnormality, may ask for the help of a marabout (a Mohammedan hermit or saint), but he must stand outside the tent, for he may not go near the parturient woman.[50] The Cuna, who consider all labor a fearful ordeal, do call on the shaman for supervision regularly, but he must stay away from the laboring woman and depend on the female attendant's description.[58]

However, the feeling against males attending labor is by no means universal or absolute. In some industrial countries males command a much higher price for officiating at a delivery than does the midwife, and affluent women prefer to have such prestigious persons assist them even in normal deliveries, although the emotional support during labor is still usually left to women.

In preliterate cultures males may be called in under certain circumstances. Quite frequently, when labor is abnormal, male healers participate actively. When the Aranda woman had delayed labor, the male Mura took a hair girdle, and, violating the usual prohibition against men, went to her and tied the belt around her body.[90] The Sakai of Malaya have made the midwife role a hereditary one which both men and women inherit.[104] The Lepcha of the Himalayan mountain region appeared to have no sex preferences—the parents-in-law or anybody who knew how would help the woman in labor.[31] The pattern of the Araucanians of South America was changing at the time they were studied. In one area they had not yet developed a word for male obstetrician, but several middle-aged men were actually assisting at deliveries.[41] The Araucanian husbands also assisted their wives in dire necessity, such as when everyone else had gone to a fiesta or when they were too poor to hire a midwife.

The father very frequently had a patterned role to play, but not necessarily as an emotional supporter and companion to his wife. The Pacific Ocean Easter Islander father got a real sense of participation in birth by having his wife recline against him during labor and delivery.[71] The Kurtatchi father of the Pacific Islands was excluded from the labor, which took place in another hut, but the importance of his impending fatherhood was emphasized by the fact that he must stop work and remain in seclusion. On no account might he lift anything heavy or touch a sharp instrument.[9]

The custom of couvade occurred in many parts of the world. Essentially it involved a period of activity restriction and "regulation" for the father as well as the mother for a time after birth. Ford's sample[27] of 64 cultures contains records of the customs of 18 tribes in this regard. Seventeen tribes from Asia, North America, Oceania, and South America involved the father in couvade after delivery. In only one group was it definitely recorded that there was no couvade. There may be real survival value in this custom, as it may particularly emphasize the father's role and responsibilities at the crucial time as each child is born. It may help him to identify with mother and baby.

Delivery Position

The most essential aspect of birth is the movement of the baby from the uterus to the outside. Thus the body mechanics of second-stage labor are fundamental to the whole problem of normal, spontaneous birth. One would perhaps expect that biological factors would determine the position and movements of the woman at this time, but even here ideas and cultural patterning or customs may overrule physiological and anatomical cues.

Delivery is possible in a great variety of positions.[26] A recent crosscultural survey of 76 non-European societies in the Human Relations Area Files found that 62 used upright positions.[76] Of these upright positions, the most common was kneeling, with 21 cultures represented. The next most common position was sitting, with 19 cultures using this method. Fifteen cultures used squatting, and 5 used standing positions.

Sometimes the culture patterns delivery in more than one way.[82] The Siriono woman lies in her hammock for the delivery of the baby but kneels for the delivery of the placenta.[43] The Sierra Tarascans[7] use both kneeling and flat deliveries, depending on "circumstances", according to a midwife. It is reported that the mother makes the choice for herself. A 1948 report indicated that the Goajiro woman had four different positions to choose from, for the sitting, kneeling, and squatting positions are all included in the traditional cultural pattern, and the supine position was also used occasionally.[36]

Among primitive peoples, the curved back is typical of most birth positions. In the sitting, squatting, and kneeling positions, the back automatically curves forward unless unusual effort is made. Bearing down in the standing position almost automatically forces some curving of the back. It is probable that many supine deliveries also involve a curve in the back. Thus the hammock deliveries[43,57] may take place with backs curved forward. However, two peoples clearly have an opposite pattern. The Bambara woman[78] kneels with her hands thrown behind her while the midwives support the small of her back. The Jordan city woman sits on the side of her bed leaning backwards.[33]

Unfortunately, since most material dealing with primitive peoples does not indicate how far apart the legs were at the time of delivery, there is no way of knowing how much tension is usually put on the perineum at this time. The Laotians were reported to sit with legs folded and spread wide apart.[83] Blackwood[9] reports a Kurtatchi delivery with knees drawn up and wide apart. However, the birth description of the Hottentots, although not specific suggests that the legs may be together, since a hand is kept constantly between the legs of the woman to ascertain the progress of the child's head.[86]

Many primitive peoples used pushing, pulling, and bracing devices to help the parturient in her expulsive efforts. Ropes, which furnish firm resistance to pulling but are easily adjustable in regard to angle and height, are used by groups in Asia,[31] North Africa,[10] North America,[7] and South America.[41,43] Poles and stakes are also used for grasping during delivery.[96,102] In Manus houses, where labor takes place, an extra post or board will be fastened firmly to the leaf wall so that the laboring woman will have something to push her feet against.[64] The Yahgan woman squats, spreading her legs wide apart, and braces herself with hands and feet flat on the ground.[35]

Today in the United States the position for delivery is similar to that used for surgical operations. The body is flat and neck is straight without a pillow to support it, as is the custom on operating tables. Arms are tied so that they will not stray into the sterile field. The legs are mechanically spread wide apart with leg braces to allow the physician to have an unobstructed view of the operative area.

This rigid surgical structuring of position for normal delivery is quite new in American obstetrics. The 1913 edition of the DeLee textbook illustrates delivery with the woman lying on her side in the lateral Sims position, her back curved and her legs only a few inches apart.[18] Lusk[54] in 1894 expressed a permissive attitude toward the position of the woman for delivery: "During the second stage, the patient's posture should be left in general to her own volition. The physician should accustom himself to conduct labor with equal facility, no matter where the woman lies, upon her side or upon her back."

The problem of the body mechanics of labor is mentioned by earlier American obstetrical textbook writers. Adequate foot support to use for bracing during contractions is considered a matter of concern.[12,54] As late as 1947, some thought was being given to a labor as a muscular event. In that year Beck's[8] obstetrical textbook advocated "pullers" and snug abdominal binders to facilitate the body mechanics of delivery and to "retain the advantages of the squat position."

Recent American texts, however, do not appear to give much consideration or discussion to problems of efficient body position and bracing for effective expulsive effort. In a few hospitals a triangular pillow or backrest is occasionally used to help the women achieve a curved back position, but the need for the parturient to push or pull by bracing and holding is almost entirely muted in American hospital practice today.

Concluding Comments

In seeing the possibility of other ways of feeling and acting, one's own way is more clearly delineated. Basically, the questions raised can only be answered by each individual for himself. Questions similar to the following are pertinent. What are my personal attitudes toward birth? What are the attitudes of the majority of persons working with me? Are the attitudes of childbearing women different in my group from those of males and nonreproducing women?

To be sure obstetrical *behavior* is also noteworthy. In so far as it mutes or develops emotional support, sensory stimulation, body mechanics and biochemical manipulation, it can have a profound influence on the emotions of the parturient and those around her. However, emphasis on the varying patterns possible for birth behavior should not obscure the fact that behavior tends to reflect culturally determined attitudes.

An example of the force of attitudes in determining birth behavior is the fate of research studies which conflict with current obstetrical attitudes. For instance, considerable research on the problem of position in labor in relation to ease of delivery suggests that the flat, supine position for delivery may make spontaneous delivery more difficult. Mengert and Murphy,[68] in an extensive experimental study, recorded actual intra-abdominal pressure at the height of maximum straining effort in more than 1,000 observations with women placed in 7 postures. The researchers used sophisticated statistical techniques to analyse their data. They found that the greatest intra-abdominal pressure was exerted in the sitting position. This was due not only to major visceral weight but also to increased muscular efficiency. Vaughan presented X-rays and measurements which indicate that squatting alters the pelvic shape in a way that makes it advantageous for delivery. Had Mengert and Murphy[68] and Vaughan[100] advocated a new drug to speed labor, it is likely that culturally accepting attitudes would have resulted in adoption of their findings—even with far less scientifically controlled data. However, instead, the proposition of improving labor efficiency through sitting and squatting conflicted with the strongly held cultural attitude that birth is an event experienced lying down. This extensive research, instead of becoming part of the fundamental knowledge required of obstetricians, was ignored.

The importance of cultural attitudes in determining birth patterning can also be seen in the history of the "natural childbirth" program set up at Yale University under the leadership of Dr. Herbert Thoms. While Dr. Thoms continued work at Yale, published statistics indicated that 88% of the mothers had spontaneous deliveries and 29% had no anesthesia at birth.[97] Dr. Thoms retired, and some others working closely with him left. The formal patterns of education for childbirth and support during labor continued, but they no longer appeared to influence patterning of birth. A follow-up study,[16] published just eight years after the previous study, indicated that the once deviant Yale practice had quickly changed in the direction of the norm of the surrounding culture. Now only 47% of the women had normal spontaneous deliveries, and less than 1% of the women received no anesthesia at birth, although all of these still received pre-natal training and support in labor.

Socially determined attitudes may also determine how the mother behaves in labor, even to the point of possibly regulating her uterine contractions. Heyns[39] presents statistics showing that Bantu women of South Africa, although their pelves are so small that Western women would require cesarean sections, deliver babies spontaneously. This seems to be accomplished by a moulding of the fetal head by extraordinarily forceful contractions. In extreme cases the baby may be born dead, but the mother's life may be saved through her ability to get rid of the products of conception.

Heyns[39] believes that psychological differences may account for the differences in uterine contractions. "It is submitted that in the European there is an unfavorable emotional background, which has an inhibitory effect on efficient uterine action. . . . Where in any individual parturient there is emotional stability supported by an unwavering resolution to push through with the task of spontaneous delivery, and where the realization that obstetric aid is readily available is not over-emphasized, the achievement of the Bantu woman may always be equalled. . . . Simple dystocia, due to contracted bony passages, can almost be eliminated by fostering the will in the parturient to deliver herself."

This illustration particularly shows the interaction of birth behavior and birth attitudes. The availability of forceps and cesarean sections depends on cultural attitudes which accept the idea of non-spontaneous birth. In turn, the widespread use of operative procedures may decrease the desire to push the baby out spontaneously.

The close interrelation of attitudes and behavior emphasizes that attempts to change obstetrical patterning may meet with unanticipated ramifications. A broad view is required, which takes both attitudes and procedures into account. Perhaps the chief value of reviewing patterns of behavior surrounding birth is that it widens the perspective in the same way as historical knowledge increases understanding. In learning how others have done it, it is possible to get new insight into current patterns, their possible origin and interactions.

REFERENCES

1. ADALJA, K. V., 1940. Ayurvedic midwifery. *E. Afr. med. J.*, 17, 142.
2. ATLEE, H. B. 1963. Fall of the Queen of Heaven. *Obstet. Gynec.*, 21, 514.
3. BAILEY, F. L. 1950. Some sex beliefs and practices in a Navaho community. *Papers of the Peabody Museum of American Archaeology and Ethnology*, 40, 2. Cambridge: Harvard University Press.
4. BARTOS, F. 1897. Volksleben der Slaven. In *Die Osterreichish-Ungarische Monarchie in Wort und Bild: Mähren und Schlesien.* Vienna: Kaiserlich-Koniglichen Staatsdruckerei.
5. BEAGLEHOLE, E. and BEAGLEHOLE, P. 1938. Ethnology of Pukapuka. *Bernice P. Bishop Museum Bulletin,* 150. Honolulu.
6. BEAGLEHOLE, E. and BEAGLEHOLE, P. 1939. Brief Pukapukan case history. *J. Polynesian Soc.,* 48, 135.
7. BEALS, R. L. 1946. *Cherán: a Sierra Tarascan village.* Pub. No. 2, Smithsonian Institute of Social Anthropology. Washington.
8. BECK, A. C. 1947. *Obstetrical practice,* 4th ed. Baltimore: Williams & Wilkins.
9. BLACKWOOD, B. 1935. *Both sides of Buka Passage.* Oxford: Clarendon Press.
10. BLANGUERON, C. 1955. *Le Hoggar.* Paris: Arthaud.
11. BOLINDER, G. 1957. *Indians on horseback.* London: Dennis Dobson.
12. BURNS, J. (with improvements and notes by JAMES, T. C.) 1831. *The Principles of midwifery: including the diseases of women and children.* New York: Clafton and Van Norden.
13. CANE, L. B. 1945. African birth customs. *St. Bartholomew's Hosp. J.*, 49, 94.
14. CHERTOK, L. 1959. *Psychosomatic methods in painless childbirth.* New York: Pergamon Press.
15. CHERTOK, L. 1961. Relaxation and psychosomatic methods of preparation for childbirth, *Amer. J. Obstet. Gynec.*, 82, 262.
16. DAVIS, C. D. and MORRONE, F. A. 1962. An objective evaluation of a prepared childbirth program. *Amer. J. Obstet. Gynec.*, 84, 1196.
17. DÊ, T. D. 1951. Notes on birth and reproduction in Vietnam. Unpublished manuscript by Margaret Coughlin.
18. DELEE, J. B., 1913. *The Principles and practices of obstetrics.* Philadelphia: Saunders.
19. DE LERY, J. 1906. Extracts out of the Historie of John Lerius, a Frenchman, who lived in

Brasill with Mons., Villagagnon, Ann. 1557 and 1558. In *Hakluvtus Posthumus of Purchas His Pilgrimes,* 16, 518. Glasgow: MacLehose.

20. DE VIDAS, J. 1947. Childbirth among the Aranda, Central Australia. *Oceania,* 18, 117.
21. DEYDIER, H. 1952. *Introduction à la connaisance du Laos.* Saigon: Imprimerie française d'Outre-Mer.
22. DORSEY, G. A. and MURIE, J. R. 1940. Notes on Skidi Pawnee society. *Field Museum of Natural History, Anthropology Series,* 27, 2, 65. Chicago: Field Museum Press.
23. DU BOIS, C. 1944. *The people of Alor.* Minneapolis: University of Minnesota Press.
24. EASTMAN, N. J. and HELLMAN, L. M. 1961. *Williams' Obstetrics,* 12th edn. New York: Appleton-Century-Crofts.
25. ENGEL, E. L. 1963. Family-centred hospital maternity care. *Amer. J. Obstet. Gynec.,* 85, 260.
26. ENGLEMANN, G. J. 1883. *Labor among primitive peoples,* 2nd edn. St. Louis: Chambers.
27. FORD, C. S. 1945. *A comparative study of human reproduction.* Yale University Publications in Anthropology, No. 32; New Haven.
28. GABB, W. M. 1876. On the Indian tribes and languages of Costa Rica. *Proc. Amer. Philosoph. Soc.,* 14, 483.
29. GAMBLE, D. P. 1957. *The Wolof of Senegambia.* London: International African Institute.
30. GIDEON, H. 1962. A baby is born in the Punjab. *Amer. Anthropol.,* 64, 1220.
31. GORER, G. 1938. *Himalayan village: an account of the Lepchas of Sikkim.* London: Michael Joseph.
32. GRANQVIST, H. 1935. Marriage conditions in a Palestinian village. *Commentationes humanarum litterarum,* 6, No. 8.
33. GRANQVIST, H. 1947. *Birth and childhood among the Arabs: Studies in a Muhammadan village in Palestine.* Helsingfors: Söderström.
34. GRODEKOV, N. I. 1889. *Kirgizy i Karakirgizy Syr-Dar'inskoi Oblasti,* Vol. I. Tashkent: The Typolithography of S. I. Lakhtin.
35. GUSINDE, M. 1937. *Die Yamana: vom Leben und Denken der Wassernomaden am Kap Hoorns,* Vol. II. Mudling, near Vienna: Anthropos-Bibliothek.
36. GUTIERREZ DE PINEDA, V. 1948. Organizacion social en la Guajira. *Rev. Inst. Etnolog. Nac. (Bogota),* 3.
37. GURMANN, B. 1926. *Das Recht der Dschagga.* Munich: C. H. Beck.
38. HENRY, J. 1910. L'aime d'un peuple Africain. *Bibliotheque-Anthropos,* 1, No. 2.
39. HEYNS, O. S. 1946. The superiority of the South African negro or Bantu as a parturient. *J. Obstet. Gynaec. Brit. Emp.* 53, 405.
40. HILGER, M. I. 1951. *Chippewa child life and its cultural background.* Washington: Bulletin 146, Bureau of American Ethnology, Smithsonian Institution.
41. HILGER, M. I. 1957. *Araucanian child life and its cultural background.* Washington: Smithsonian Miscellaneous Collection, Vol. 133, Smithsonian Institution.
42. HOERNLÉ, A. W. 1923. The expression of the social value of water among the Naman of South-West Africa. *S. Afr. J. Sci.,* 20, 514.
43. HOLMBERG, A. R. 1950. *Nomads of the Long Bow: the Siriono of Eastern Bolivia.* Washington: Publication No. 10, Smithsonian Institute. Institute of Social Anthropology.
44. JELLIFFE, D. B., JELLIFFE, E. F. P., GARCIA, L. and DE BARRIOS, G. 1961. The children of the San Blas Indians of Panama. *J. Pediat.,* 59, 271.
45. KINIETZ, W. V., 1947. *Chippewa village: The story of Katikitegon.* Bloomfield Hills: Cranbrook Press.
46. KINSEY, A. C., POMEROY, W. B., MARTIN, C. E. and GEBHARD, P. H. 1953. *Sexual behavior in the human female.* Philadelphia: Saunders.
47. KOENIG, S. 1939. Beliefs and practices relating to birth and childhood among the Galician Ukranians, *Folk-lore,* 50, 272.
48. LANDES, R. 1937. *Ojibwa Society.* New York: Columbia University Press.
49. LEVIN, S. 1960. Obstetrics in the Bible, *J. Obstet. Gynaec. Brit. Emp.,* 67, 490.
50. LHOTE, H. 1944. *Les Touaregs du Hoggar.* Paris: Payot.
51. LOCKETT, C. 1939. Midwives and childbirth among the Navajo. *Plateau,* 12, 15.
52. LOWIE, R. H. 1922. The religion of the Crow Indians, *Anthropological Papers of the American Museum of Natural History,* 25, 309.
53. LOWIE, R. H. 1935. *The Crow Indians.* New York: Farrar and Rinehart.
54. LUSK, W. T. 1894. *The science and art of midwifery.* New York: Appleton.
55. LUZBETAK, L. J. 1951. *Marriage and the family in Caucasia: a contribution to the study of North Caucasian ethnology and customary law.* Vienna-Modling: St. Gabriel's Mission Press.
56. MARCHAND, L. 1932. Obstetrics among South African natives, *S. Afr. Med., J.,* 6, 329.

57. MARSHALL, D. S. 1950. Cuna Folk. A Conceptual Scheme Involving the Dynamic Factors of Culture, as Applied to the Cuna Indians of Darien. Unpublished manuscript, Department of Anthropology, Harvard University.
58. MARSHALL, H. I. 1922. The Karen people of Burma: a study in anthropology and ethnology. *Ohio State University Bulletin,* 26, No. 13.
59. MAXWELL, P. 1927. Obstetrics in China in the 13th century. *J. Obstet. Gynaec. Brit. Emp.,* 34, 481.
60. MCCAMMON, C. S. 1937. Study of four hundred seventy-five pregnancies in American Indian women. *Amer. J. Obstet. Gynec.,* 61, 1159.
61. MEAD, M. 1928. *Coming of age in Samoa.* New York: William Morrow.
62. MEAD, M. 1935. *Sex and temperament in three primitive societies.* New York: William Morrow.
63. MEAD, M. 1939. *From the South Seas.* New York: Morrow.
64. MEAD, M. 1956. *New Lives for Old.* New York: Morrow.
65. MEAD, M. and NEWTON, N. 1965. Conception, pregnancy, labor and the Puerperium in cultural perspective. In *First International Congress of Psychosomatic Medicine and Childbirth,* p. 51. Paris: Gauthier-Villars.
66. MEAD, M. and NEWTON, N. 1967. Cultural patterning of perinatal behavior. In *Childbearing—its social and psychological aspects,* edited by S. A. Richardson and A. F. Guttmacher. Baltimore: Williams and Wilkins.
67. Medical Exchange Mission to the U.S.S.R. 1960. Maternal and Child Care. *Public Health Service Publication,* 954. U.S. Government Printing Office.
68. MENGERT, W. F. and MURPHY, D. P. 1933. Intra-abdominal pressures created by voluntary muscular effort. *Surg. Gynec. Obstet.,* 57, 745.
69. MERRIMAN, S. (with notes and additions by JAMES, T. C.). 1816. *A Synopsis of the various kinds of difficult parturition, with practical remarks on the management of labours.* Philadelphia: Stone House.
70. MESSING, S. D. 1957. The Highland-plateau Amhara of Ethiopia. Philadelphia: Doctoral (anthropology) dissertation, University of Pennsylvania.
71. MÉTRAUX, A. 1940. Ethnology of Easter Island. Honolulu: *Bernice P. Bishop Museum Bulletin,* 160.
72. MILLER, J. S. 1970. The role of the physician. Unpublished paper given April 30 at Jefferson Medical College: Continuing Medical Education Symposium on Safety and Satisfaction in Childbearing.
73. MOLLER, M. S. G. 1958. Bahaya customs and beliefs in connection with pregnancy and childbirth. *Tanganyika Notes, Records,* 50, 112.
74. MOLLER, M. S. G. 1961. Custom, pregnancy and child rearing in Tanganyika. *J. Trop. Pediat.,* 7, 66.
75. MORRIS, J. 1938. *Living with Lepchas: a book about the Sikkim Himalayas.* London: Heinemann.
76. NAROLL, F., NAROLL, R. and HOWARD, F. H. 1961. Position of women in childbirth. *Amer. J. Obstet. Gynec.,* 82, 943.
77. NEWTON, N. 1955. *Maternal emotions.* New York: Hoeber.
78. PAQUES, V. 1954. *Les Bambara.* Paris: Presses Universitaires de France.
79. PHILIPP, E. E. 1962. *Obstetrics and gynaecology combined for students.* London: Lewis.
80. RAO, K. 1952. Obstetrics in ancient India. *J. Indian Med. Ass.,* 21, 210.
81. RAUM, O. F. 1940. *Chaga childhood.* London: Oxford University Press.
82. RAYNALDE, T. 1626. *The Byrthe of mankynde.* London: Boler.
83. REINACH, L. DE. 1901. *Le Laos.* Paris: Charles.
84. ROBBINS, W. W., HARRINGTON, J. P. and FREIRE-MARRECO, B. 1916. *Ethnobotany of the Tewa Indians.* Washington: Smithsonian Institution.
85. SANDERS, I. T. 1949. *Balkan village.* Lexington: University of Kentucky Press.
86. SCHULTZE, J. 1907. *Aus Nanaland und Kalahari.* Jena: Fischer.
87. SEWALL, S. 1878. *The diary of Samuel Sewall, 1674–1729.* Boston: Massachusetts Historical Society.
88. SMITH, E. W. and DALE, A. M. 1920. *The Ila-speaking peoples of Northern Rhodesia.* London: Macmillan.
89. SORANUS: *Gynecology,* translated by O. Temkin. 1956. Baltimore: John Hopkins Press.
90. SPENCER, W. B. and GILLEN, F. J. 1927. *The Arunta: a study of a Stone Age people.* London: Macmillan.
91. SPIER, L. 1933. *Yuman tribes of the Gila River.* Chicago: University of Chicago Press.
92. SRINIVAS, M. N. 1942. *Marriage and family in Mysore.* Bombay: New Book.

93. STONE, A. 1953. Fertility problems in India. *Fertil. Steril.,* 4, 210.
94. STOUT, D. B. 1947. *San Blas Cuna acculturation: an introduction.* New York: Viking Fund Publications.
95. STOUT, D. B. 1948. The Cuna. *Handbook of South American Indians,* 4, 257. Bureau of American Ethnology Bulletin 143, edited by Julian H. Steward. Washington: Smithsonian Institution.
96. TEIT, J. A. 1956. *Field notes on the Tahltan and Kaska Indians, 1912–15.* Ottawa: The Research Center for Amerindian Anthropology.
97. THOMS, H. and KARLOVSKY, E. D. 1954. Two thousand deliveries under training for childbirth program: a statistical survey and commentary. *Amer. J. Obstet. Gynec.,* 68, 279.
98. TOMASIC, D. 1948. *Personality and culture in eastern European politics.* New York: Stewart.
99. VAN PATTEN, N. 1932. Obstetrics in Mexico prior to 1600. *Ann. med. History, 2d series,* 4, 203–12.
100. VAUGHAN, K. O. 1937. *Safe childbirth: the three essentials.* London: Baillière, Tindall and Cassell.
101. VOEGELIN, E. W. 1938. *Tübatulabal ethnography.* University of California Anthropological Records. 2, 1–90. Berkeley: University of California.
102. WALLACE, E. and HOEBEL, E. A. 1952. *The Comanches: lords of the South Plains.* Norman: University of Oklahoma Press.
103. WHITMAN, W. 1947. *The Pueblo Indians of San Ildefonso.* New York: Columbia University Press.
104. WILLIAMS-HUNT, P. D. R. 1952. *An introduction to the Malayan aborigines.* Kuala Lumpur: Government Press.
105. WRIGHT, J. 1921. Collective review—the view of primitive peoples concerning the process of labor. *Amer. J. Obstet. Gynec.,* 2, 206.

Breast Feeding

Niles Newton

In the 10 years between 1946 and 1956 the number of American mothers who breast fed their newborn babies dropped by almost half. In 1929 in Bristol, England, 77 percent of three-month-old infants were breast fed; twenty years later, 64 percent of the same age Bristol babies depended upon bottles. It took only five years for the number of breast-fed babies at a French obstetric clinic to drop from nearly 70 percent to less than 50 percent.

What has caused this radical change in human behavior? The decrease is far too rapid to be the result of heredity changes. It is too large to be caused by physiological changes short of starvation or widespread, ravaging disease. Instead, the answer seems to lie in psychological factors.

A mother's ability to produce milk for her baby depends upon her own attitude toward breast feeding and toward sex. And her attitude is related to the attitudes of her society. Emotions affect the production of milk through specific psychosomatic mechanisms, several of which have been identified.

The survival of the human race, long before any concept of duty evolved, depended upon the pleasures of two voluntary acts—coitus and breast feeding. Were these acts not so pleasurable that humans sought their repetition, man would have joined the dinosaurs in extinction ages ago.

A woman's body responds similarly to coitus and to lactation. Her uterus contracts, her skin changes measurably and her nipples lengthen and become erect both during suckling and during sexual excitement. Some breast-feeding mothers drip milk more easily than others, possibly due to weaker nipple sphincter muscles. Such women have reported that at times they eject milk during sexual arousal. Breast stimulation alone causes orgasm in some women and during suckling the breast is stimulated extensively. The nipple-erection reflex, which increases nipple length by a centimeter or more, may lead to more efficient nursing.

An aversion to breast feeding appears to be related to a dislike of nudity and of sexuality. E. J. Salber and her associates in Boston worked with American mothers who had never attempted to nurse their babies. The idea of nursing repelled these women, who were embarrassed at the idea of suckling their infants or were too "modest" to nurse. In another study, A. B. Adams, working at Columbia University, interviewed women who were expecting their first child. Both the interviews and tests disclosed that women who said they wished to bottle feed their babies showed significantly more psychosexual disturbances. In a Harvard University Laboratory of Human Development study, R. R. Sears and his colleagues found that mothers who breast fed their infants showed a greater tolerance of masturbation and social sex play in their own children.

Michael Newton and I studied the relation between a woman's own attitude toward breast feeding and her ability to produce milk successfully for her child. I interviewed 91 patients in the maternity wards of the University of Pennsylvania Hospital. Women who refused to suckle their babies, and those who had had premature babies or Caesarean births were excluded from the study. The women were interviewed as soon as possible after delivery, 63 percent of them within 24 hours and 74 percent before the baby had been at the breast. Their answers were recorded verbatim and evaluated by two independent judges who knew neither the patient nor her breast-feeding history.

The judges sorted the answers into three categories: positive, doubtful and negative. Positive women expressed a desire or determination to breast feed. Doubtful women expressed mixed feelings, indifference or indecision about breast feeding their children. Judges placed women who talked of giving both breast and bottle from the start in this doubtful category. Negative women preferred bottle feeding, stated they did not like to breast feed, or were noncommittal but mentioned only the negative aspects of breast feeding.

Feeding procedures were the same for all mothers. Nurses brought the babies to their mothers six times each day and left them together for 45 minutes to an hour each time. This permitted the mother to relax with her baby, cuddling him and suckling him as much as four or five hours a day if she so desired.

After their hospital stay the women were divided into successful, unsuccessful and abortive breast feeders. Successful breast feeders produced so much milk that their babies needed no supplementary formula after the fourth day. Unsuccessful breast feeders continued to feed by breast but had to give supplementary formulas after the fourth day. Abortive breast feeders switched their babies entirely to bottles before they left the hospital.

Breast feeding proved to be closely related to what the mother said about her own attitudes toward breast feeding [*see illustration 1*]. There was also a marked difference in the overall success of breast feeding and in how the mother's attitude affected her milk production [*see illustration 1*].

Illustration 1 Maternal behavior

Maternal behavior	*Nursing members of pairs*	*Non-nursing members of pairs*
Mother sometimes or often sleeps or rests in bed with baby.	71%	26%
Mother definitely states baby not spanked.	87%	95%
Mother holds baby ½ hour or more when not eating.	57%	62%
Mother in different building from baby less than 3 hours daily.	95%	86%

When behaviors of nursing and non-nursing mothers was compared, they differed significantly only in the willingness to share a bed with their babies.

In interviewing these mothers I noticed that the desire to breast feed seemed to be associated with other attitudes. I decided to explore these attitudes further in a new group of 123 women in the wards of Jefferson Hospital in Philadelphia. Again what the mother said was written down verbatim. A judge who knew neither the mother nor how she had answered the other questions categorized her comments on each item. Mothers who expressed the most positive attitude toward breast feeding were found to be quite different from others. They frequently stated that women rather than men have the more satisfying time in life and that labor was easy. Mothers of first babies who strongly wanted to breast feed actually had shorter recorded labors.

Other evidence suggests that maternal behavior and maternal attitude may be related to breast-feeding behavior in women. H. W. Potter of State University of New York College of Medicine at New York City and H. R. Klein of Columbia University College of Medicine studied 25 nursing mothers and babies in a Brooklyn hospital. They scored each mother's "nursing behavior" by observing the way she handled her baby at feeding time. By means of a lengthy interview that centered on questions about doll play in childhood, interest in other people's babies and number of children desired, Potter and Klein also rated each mother on "maternal interest." There was a high correlation between the two measures. Later visits to the homes of 16 mothers showed that all who were rated low on the maternal interest scale had stopped nursing immediately after leaving the hospital. By contrast, all but one of those ranked high on the maternal interest scale continued to nurse their babies.

Michael Newton and I found a similar relation. We recorded the reactions of mothers to the first sight of their babies. Later a different observer, who did not know the first rating, interviewed the mothers and recorded their attitudes toward breast feeding. Mothers who reacted to their babies with visible joy and delight more frequently expressed the desire to breast feed them.

In another study, which I conducted with Dudley Peeler of the University of Mississippi School of Medicine and Carolyn Rawlins, an obstetrician at St. Margaret's Hospital in Hammond, Indiana, an additional difference

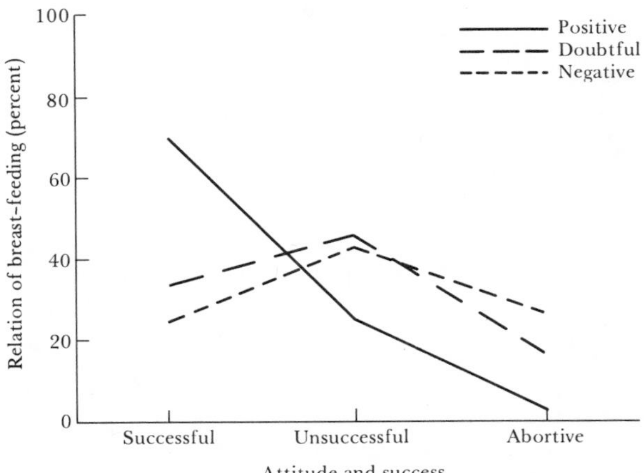

Illustration 2 Attitudes. The desire to breast feed and successful nursing were closely related.

in the behavior of nursing and non-nursing mothers appeared. An anonymous sheet, requiring only checkmarks to answer, was filled out by 177 mothers whose babies were between one and two months old. It was immediately apparent that college-educated mothers and mothers who had other children practiced breast feeding significantly more than mothers with less education or first-time mothers.

We matched breast-feeding mothers who gave neither formula nor solid food to their babies with mothers of the same educational level and the same number of children but who fed their babies by bottle—with or without solid food. Nursing and non-nursing women did not differ significantly on three measures of maternal behavior, but they did differ, markedly, in their willingness to share a bed with their babies [*see illustration 1 below*]. Women who breast feed their children appear willing to disregard current cultural disapproval of bed-sharing. Close body contact, not merely remaining near enough to watch over the baby, may be the determining factor; nursing mothers did not stay in the same building with their babies significantly more than non-nursing mothers.

Strangely enough, Dudley Peeler and I found a somewhat similar tendency in newly delivered mice. Animal research has interested me in the past few years, since controlled experimentation is the best way of demonstrating cause and effect. Most of my work has concerned mice in labor, but it seemed natural to test mice in the nursing situation.

Surgery was performed on some mice so they could not suckle; these were matched with mice who nursed adoptive young. The nursing and non-nursing mice acted in much the same way on tests but the nursing mice seemed to have a much more intense desire for close contact with the mouse pups. They were willing to cross a charged electric grid time after time to get to the young.

The emotions and behavior of the baby—for example, inefficient sucking—also affect the mother's attempts to breast feed. Mothers some-

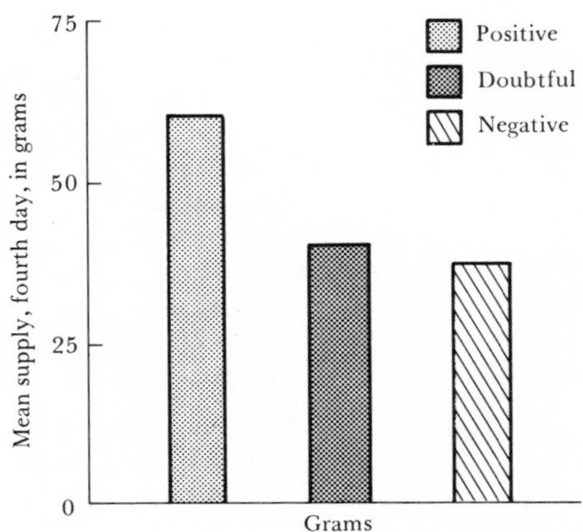

Illustration 3 Milk Supply. A mother's attitude toward breast feeding affects her milk production.

time needlessly feel "rejected" by their babies when the cause of the babies' failure to nurse is not emotional in origin. Drugs given to the mother in labor may have a prolonged effect on the baby's ability to suck after birth. The sucking ability of babies, for as long as four days after birth, has been found to vary with the amount of obstetric sedation given the mother. The baby may also refuse the breast because he has been given a supplementary bottle which is easier to suck, or if the mother schedules feeding far apart, thus presenting the child with an overfull breast that temporarily cuts off his air supply.

The responsiveness of the baby may also influence his enjoyment of breast feeding and his cooperation. This responsiveness can be seen clearly in older babies. Their bodies show eagerness and their hands, feet, fingers and toes may move rhythmically, in time with the sucking. Erection of the penis while nursing is common in male babies. After feeding, the baby often relaxes in a manner characteristic of a satisfactorily concluded sexual response. Sensuous enjoyment of breast feeding probably increases the baby's desire to suckle his mother frequently and fully, thus stimulating the secretion of milk.

The individual attitudes of the mother and the baby are not the only influences on breast feeding. Woman's role in life, as determined by her culture, education, social class and work, has been repeatedly shown to influence her breast-feeding behavior. In what Toynbee has called "times of trouble," breast feeding has been popular. Periods of great wealth and luxury in the western world—Imperial Rome, the Athens of Pericles, the era of Louis XIV, early 18th Century England and Colonial America—were characterized by large numbers of women who use artificial feeding or gave their babies to wet nurses. In these eras, upper-class women may have been objects of amusement rather than contributors to the work of society. Because of this, they may have felt somewhat worthless and insecure. Feelings of security may depend in part on the feeling of being needed and essential.

Industrialization breaks up the wider family as the main economic unit of society and deeply affects the role of woman and the value placed on her contributions. When women and children no longer help produce food or manufacture goods at home, they become economic liabilities. The status of women as bearers of children falls. Women who stay at home under these conditions also contribute less economically to society.

Woman's work role certainly influences breast feeding, but the rate of breast feeding depends on how the work is carried out, not on whether the woman works. In cultures that permit the baby to accompany his mother to work, there is little interference. Some nonwestern cultures—both simple and complex—depend heavily on women in the labor force. Yet breast feeding flourishes for two or more years with each baby because the work does not separate the baby from his mother. On the other hand, even simple cultures can become emotionally indifferent to breast feeding when the mother is the chief source of economic support and when her work requires her to be away from her baby for long periods.

Breast-feeding rates differ with even slight variations in region or culture. The number of babies who receive at least some breast milk on discharge from the hospital differs from region to region in the United States. Some states have more than double the breast-feeding rate of others. Studies have shown that the size of the community or the subcultural grouping affects the breast-feeding rate.

Education and social class influence breast feeding in some cultures. College-educated American mothers are more likely to suckle their children than women whose education ends with high school. In England, America, Switzerland and Sweden high breast-feeding rates have been associated with high social status. But in Belgium and France no hint of class difference has been found. In some cultures the lowest as well as the highest social groups breast feed more than does the middle group.

Many people who work with mothers strongly suspect that the attitude of husband, family and friends has a real bearing on breast-feeding behavior. This is difficult to document. No statistical effort appears to have been made to correlate fathers' attitudes toward nursing with its success.

The effect of medical personnel is clearer. The enthusiastic physician can develop a practice in which his patients breast feed far more than the rest of the society. Carolyn Rawlins began a breast-feeding program with her own patients in 1959. In two years, the hospital breast-feeding rate of her patients jumped from 33 to 65 percent. While previously only 15 percent of her patients had nursed their babies as long as five months, once the program was established, 52 percent were still breast feeding at five months. Enthusiasm about breast feeding frequently is considered improper, however, in cultures with declining lactation rates. A physician may lose status if he shows strong enthusiasm under these conditions.

Lack of interest or rejective feelings in any field tend to hinder the dissemination of knowledge in that field. This makes it hard for those who are interested to obtain facts. Rejective feelings in our own culture have made it necessary to hide breast feeding, thus impeding the flow of knowledge by observation. Just 25 years ago in rural Mississippi, breast feeding in church was acceptable. And 80 years ago in Indiana, upper-class women naturally took their babies to afternoon parties to nurse them as needed. Now there is a strong taboo on public nursing in the United States. Even photographs of babies suckling their mothers are frowned upon, yet bottle feeding in public and photographs of bottle-feeding babies are completely acceptable. As a result, a young girl often starts breast feeding without ever once in her life having seen another woman suckle a child. She is ignorant, even if she is interested.

The attitudes of the mother, the baby, the husband, friends, the physician and the culture work together in several ways to determine the success or failure of breast-feeding attempts. Although some psychosomatic mechanisms are probably unknown, three different factors have been identified: the milk-ejection reflex, suckling stimulation and other sensory contact between mother and baby.

The milk-ejection reflex has long been recognized in cattle, where it is called the let-down reflex. As good dairy farmers know, animals who are frightened, placed in unfamiliar suroundings or treated unkindly will not let down their milk. Impulses to the posterior pituitary gland release oxytocin, the same hormone used to induce labor. When the oxytocin travels through the bloodstream to the breast, it acts on the cells surrounding the alveoli. These cells contract and force the milk into larger ducts where it is available to the nursing animal or the milking machine.

Assuming the let-down reflex worked similarly in cattle and in people, Michael Newton and I inhibited the reflex experimentally by distracting a mother with techniques that did not appear to disturb her baby. The mother was a 25-year-old woman in good health, who had successfully breast fed her first baby for 11 months. The baby in the experiment, her second, was seven months old and had been entirely breast fed on a demand schedule from birth. At the time of the experiment, the baby was taking orange juice and additional solid food.

Each morning the baby was weighed before and after feeding. On control mornings the mother and baby were not disturbed during the 10-minute nursing period. On the other mornings, the mother was distracted four minutes before the baby was brought to her. Two minutes later, she received an injection of either oxytocin or a sterile saline solution. The mother was not told which solution was used.

The distractions took three different forms. In the first, the mother's feet were immersed alternately in ice water for 10 seconds out of every 30.

Illustration 4 Ejection reflex

Maternal disturbance	*Mean amount of milk obtained by baby*
No distractions—no injection	168 grams
Distraction saline injection	99 grams
Distraction oxytocin injection	153 grams

Interrupted milk flow can be restarted with hormone injection.

(This was reported as the worst distraction.) In the second, she was asked a rapid series of mathematical questions. When the mother answered incorrectly or delayed her answer more than 10 seconds, she was given an electric shock of moderate intensity. This shock disturbed the mother emotionally and made her angry, although the effect diminished when the baby was suckling. At these times she tended to have difficulty hearing the question and frequently delayed answering. In the last distraction, surgical gauze was tied around each of the mother's big toes. The bandage was pulled intermittently, causing sharp pain.

On control days, where there was no disturbance, the baby obtained significantly more milk than when the mother was disturbed [*see illustration*]. The amount of milk rose to nearly normal levels, however, when the injection of oxytocin set off the milk-ejection reflex artificially.

Another way to demonstrate the relation of the milk-ejection reflex to the success of breast feeding is to study the clinical signs that accompany milk ejection. The signs are easily recognized and can be reported by the mother: milk dripping from the breasts before the baby starts to nurse; uterine cramps during nursing; cessation of nipple discomfort as the baby obtains milk easing the negative pressures on the nipples.

Michael Newton and I compared 53 successful breast feeders, whose babies received no supplementary formula, with 50 unsuccessful breast feeders, whose babies required supplementary bottle feedings. The total average milk-ejection symptoms were significantly higher among the successful mothers: 72 percent of this group reported symptoms, as compared to 58 percent of the unsuccessful mothers. The milk-ejection reflex appeared to be sensitive to small differences in the mother's oxytocin level, suggesting that minor psychosomatic change may influence the amount of milk the baby receives.

When inhibition of the milk-ejection reflex occurs, much milk already in the breast simply cannot be obtained by the baby. To demonstrate this, Michael Newton had mothers nurse their babies. The babies were weighed before and after feeding to determine the amount of milk obtained. Then the mothers' breasts were pumped by machine. Finally, their breasts were repumped after an injection of oxytocin which set off the milk ejection reflex artificially. After the injection of oxytocin, mothers whose attempts at breast feeding were unsuccessful produced almost as muck milk as both baby and machine had been able to extract. Before the injection, 47 percent of their milk had been unavailable to either the baby or milking machine.

Sucking stimulation may be even more important than the ejection reflex to the success of breast feeding. Cultures where breast feeding meets the disapproval seem to permit far less sucking by the baby, and babies in these cultures are weaned earlier. The regulated, restricted, short breast feeding now common in Western industrial countries developed only recently. In 1906, T. S. Southworth, writing in a standard American pediatric textbook, recommended 10 feedings a day for most of the first month, declining gradually to six feedings each day through the 11th month. Southward approved of night feedings through the fifth month.

There is considerable evidence that the restriction of suckling inhibits milk production. In a study of 1,057 newborn infants, E. J. Salber assigned each baby to one of three groups. Those she placed on a true self-demand schedule gained weight most rapidly. Those on three-hour schedules, although they gained less weight than the babies on self-demand, gained faster than the group on four-hour schedules.

Both the milk-ejection reflex and suckling stimulation depend primarily on sensory stimulation of the nipple, but other sensory contacts—hearing, seeing, smelling and touching the baby—may be important. In cultures where breast feeding is enjoyable enough to continue without restriction, neither the mother nor the baby easily tolerates separation. Mother and baby stay in continuous close sensory contact even when not in the act of nursing.

In contrast to this, Western cultures raise many barriers to sensory contact between mother and baby. Modern Western styles of dress make breast-baby contact difficult. Families no longer sleep together in one room and the baby is expected to sleep alone. Many hospitals practice separation of mother and child at birth, except for brief feeding periods, and at home the baby frequently has his own room where he spends much of his time. These customs are relatively new—in American hospitals, housing the baby away from the mother started only about 65 years ago.

Here again, the cause for the decline of breast feeding may lie in the changes in attitudes toward family life that accompany full industrialization. A common way in which human beings express mixed feelings or ambivalence is to put distance between themselves and the object in question.

In this country, barriers placed between a mother and her child often begin in the delivery room, when the infant, after brief inspection by the groggy mother, is whisked away to be weighed, cleaned and placed in an aseptic nursery and then presented briefly to the mother every four hours along with a bottle of supplementary formula. If the mother insists on breast feeding, she may be greeted by a skeptical nurse and physician and the raised eyebrows of friends, and be expected to sequester herself at feeding time as if she were enacting a somewhat shameful ritual. Thus the mother who breast feeds her child must go to considerable trouble to do so. Perhaps it is less surprising that the breast-feeding rate continues to decline than that it does not decline faster.

Maternal Attachment
Importance of the First Post-Partum Days

Marshall H. Klaus, Richard Jerauld, Nancy C. Kreger, Willie McAlpine, Meredith Steffa, and John H. Kennell

To determine whether present hospital practices may affect later maternal behavior, we placed 28 primiparous women in two study groups shortly after delivery of normal full-term infants. Fourteen mothers (control group) had the usual physical contact with their infants, and 14 mothers (extended contact) had 16 hours of additional contact. Mothers' backgrounds and infants' characteristics were similar in both groups. Maternal behavior was measured 28 to 32 days later during a standardized interview, an examination of the baby and a filmed bottle feeding. Extended-contact mothers were more reluctant to leave their infants with someone else, usually stood and watched during the examination, showed greater soothing behavior, and engaged in significantly more eye-to-eye contact and fondling. These studies suggest that simple modification of care shortly after delivery may alter subsequent maternal behavior.

In certain animals such as the goat, cow and sheep, separation of the mother and infant immediately after birth for a period as short as one to four hours often results in distinctly aberrant mothering behavior, such as failure of the mother to care for the young, butting her own offspring away and feeding her own and other infants indiscriminately.[1,2] In contrast, if they are together for the first four days and are then separated on the fifth day for an equal period, the mother resumes the protective and mothering behavior characteristic for her species when the pair is reunited. Thus, there is a special period immediately after delivery in the adult animal. If the animal mother is separated from her young during this period, deviant behavior may result. An early short period of separation does not produce as severe a distortion of mothering behavior in all species.[3]

In recent years several investigators have studied whether a similar phenomenon occurs in mothers of premature infants.[4,5] Does the prolonged separation experienced by the mother of a premature infant affect

"Maternal Attachment: The Importance of the First Post-Partum Days" by Marshall Klaus and others from *New England Journal of Medicine*, 286 (1972), 460–463. Reprinted by permission.

the formation of her affectional bonds and change her mothering behavior months and years after the delivery? Early results from these studies suggest that the long period of physical separation common in most nurseries may adversely affect maternal performance of some women.

Studies of human mothers of premature infants necessarily differ in design from the classic studies of separation in the animal mother. The gestation of the mothers is severely shortened, the infant is small and appears fragile, the period of separation after birth is greatly extended, and it has not been possible to provide close physical contact immediately after birth similar to the natural human and animal situation.

In most nurseries in the United States, however, even full-term mothers are separated from their infants for a short, but possibly important time. Thus, it seemed essential to determine whether present hospital practices for the mother of a full-term infant influence later maternal behavior. This report tests the hypothesis that there is a period shortly after birth that is uniquely important for mother-to-infant attachment in the human being.

Material and Methods

We placed each of 28 primiparous mothers of normal full-term infants in one of two study groups, depending on the day of delivery. Neither group knew of this study in advance or to our knowledge was aware of the arrangements made for the other. (The mothers, however, were not questioned on this subject.) The 14 mothers in the control group had the traditional contact with their infants: a glimpse of the baby shortly after birth, brief contact and identification at six to 12 hours, and then visits for 20 to 30 minutes every four hours for bottle feedings. In addition to this routine contact, the 14 mothers in the extended-contact group were given their nude babies, with a heat panel overhead, for one hour within the first three hours after birth, and also five extra hours of contact each afternoon of the three days after delivery. (A heat panel was also placed over the control mothers' beds for one hour during the first three hours.)

To eliminate any influence from the enthusiasm or interest of the nurse that might obscure the results, the special nurses who cared for the mothers during the extended-contact period (five hours per day) spent an equal amount of time with the control mothers. After an initial standardized introductory statement they only answered questions, did not instruct any of the women in caretaking unless this was requested, and most the time were available just outside the room.

The mean age, socioeconomic and marital status, color, premedication, sex of the infant and days hospitalized in both groups were nearly identical (see Table 1). Only mothers who intended to keep their infants and to bottle-feed them were admitted to the study. The mean birth weights of the two groups of infants differed by 110 g.

To determine if this short additional time with the infant early in life altered later behavior, we asked the mothers to return to the hospital a month after delivery for three separate observations. These observations were made between the 28th and 32d post-partum days and consisted of a

Table 1 Clinical data for 14 mothers in the extended-contact and 14 in the control group

Group	*Maternal characteristics*				*Mean score**			*Nurses' time*	*Hospital stay*	*Mean birth weight*	*No. of infants*	
	Age	*Married*	*N*†	*W*‡	*A*	*B*	*C*				*M*§	*F*¶
	yr	*no. of mothers*						*min/day*	*days*	*g*		
Extended contact	18.2	4	13	1	6.7	6.7	4.9	13	3.8	3184	6	8
Control	18.6	5	13	1	6.5	6.9	4.9	14	3.7	3074	8	6

*In this (Hollingshead) scoring system, on a scale of 1 to 7, residence (A) of 7.0 = poorest housing, occupation (B) of 7.0 = unskilled workers, & education (C) of 5.0 = reaching 10th to 11th grade in high school.
†Negro ‡White. §Male. ¶Female.

standardized interview, an observation of maternal performance during a physical examination of the infant and a filmed study of the mother feeding her infant.

The first seven questions on the interview concerned the general health of the infant, such as the number of stools and the amount of milk taken. Three separate questions were related to caretaking and were scored 0, 1, 2, 3.

FIRST: "When the baby cries and has been fed, and the diapers are dry, what do you do?" A score of 0 was given for letting the baby cry it out, and 3 for picking up the baby every time. An intermediate score was given for gradations of behavior.

SECOND QUESTION: "Have you been out since the baby was born, and who sat?" A score of 0 was given for "yes," and if the mother felt good and did not think about her infant while she was out. A score of 3 was given if she did not go out or leave the baby with anyone, or if she did go out but thought constantly about the baby.

The third question related to spoiling and could not be scored.

A second measure of maternal behavior was the observation of the mother during a standardized examination of her infant. A score of 3 was allotted if, during the examination of the infant, she was standing by the pediatrician and watching continuously; a score of 0 was given if she remained seated and looked elsewhere. We also noted whether or not the mother attempted to soothe the baby when it cried. If she did not interact with the baby, she was given a score of 0; if she was consistently soothing, she was given a score of 3. The scoring of the interview and observation of maternal performance was then determined by independent raters who did not know to which group the mothers belonged.

To study maternal behavior in another situation, we made time-lapse films of the mothers feeding their infants. They all knew they were being photographed and were told to spend as much time as they wished. Filming was done through a one-way mirror for 15 minutes at a speed of 60 frames per minute. Mothers' and babies' reactions could then be analyzed in detail at one-second intervals. Each frame of the first 600 was scored by analyzers who did not know which group the mothers were in. We analyzed each frame for 25 specific activities, ranging from caretaking skills (such as the position of the bottle) to measurements of maternal interest and affection such as "en face" (defined as when the mother aligned her face in the same vertical plane of rotation was the infant's[6]), whether the mother's body was touching the infant's trunk, and whether she fondled the infant. (We defined fondling as any active spontaneous interaction initiated by the mother not associated with feeding, such as stroking, kissing, bouncing or cuddling.) Inter-observer reliability coefficients were calculated for the individual behaviors. The average of the reliability coefficients was 0.83 for "en face" and 0.99 for fondling.

Results

Analysis of the interview data is shown in Figure 1. The extended-contact group (the solid black bars) had scores of 2 and greater, whereas the control mothers (cross-hatched bars) were at the lower end of the scale. The chance of this occurrence is less than 0.05, with the use of the Mann-Whitney U-test.[7]

The two groups scored differently on the results of the observations during the physical examination (Fig. 2). The extended-contact group did not score below 3, whereas the scores of the control mothers were distributed from 1 to 6 (p less than 0.02). When the scores on the interview questions and the observations made during the examination are combined (Fig. 3), there is a separation of the scores of the two groups of mothers. The controls have scores of 2 to 10 spread out over the entire range, whereas mothers in the extended-contact group have scores ranging from 7 to 12 (p less than 0.002).

Figure 4 indicates the fondling and "en face" scores for both groups of

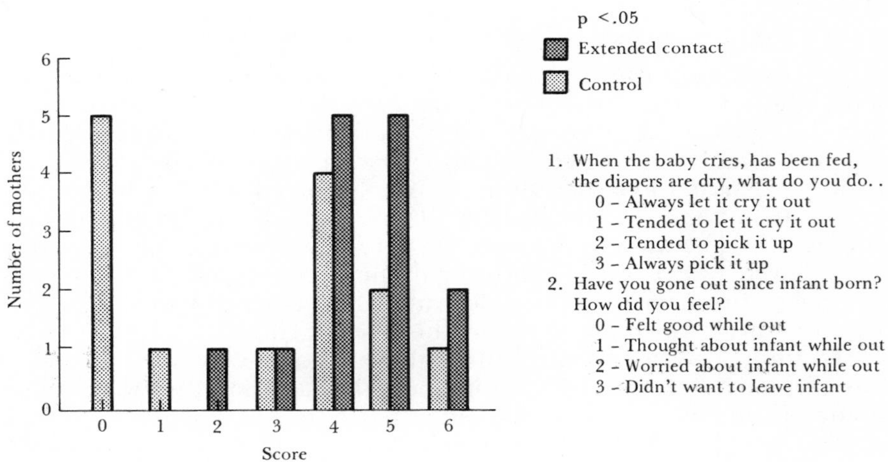

Figure 1 Maternal Scores from a Standardized Interview at One Month.

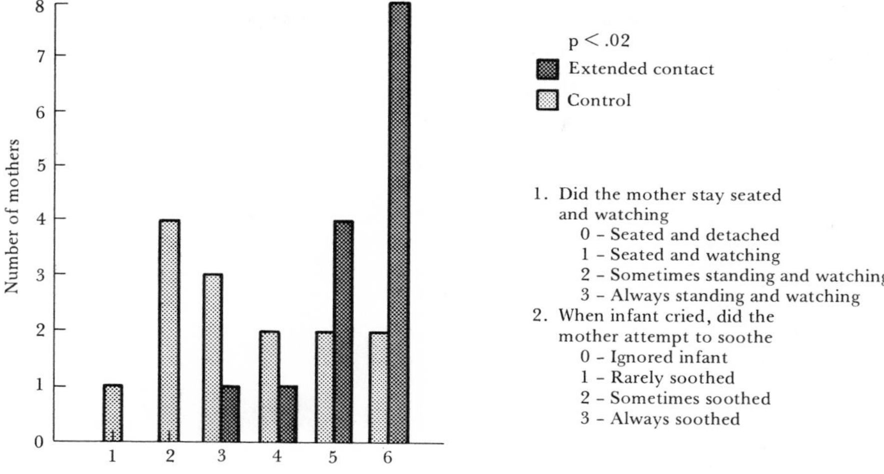

Figure 2 Scored Observations of the Mother Made during a Physical Examination of Her Infant at One Month.

mothers. Although the amount of time the mothers were looking at their babies was not significantly different in the two groups, the extended-contact mothers had significantly greater "en face" and fondling (11.6 per cent and 6.1 per cent of the total scored time, as compared to 3.5 per cent and 1.6 per cent in the control group). There were no significant differences in measures of caretaking, although the bottle was held away from the perpendicular more often in the control group. By all three measurements studied, differences between the two groups of mothers are apparent.

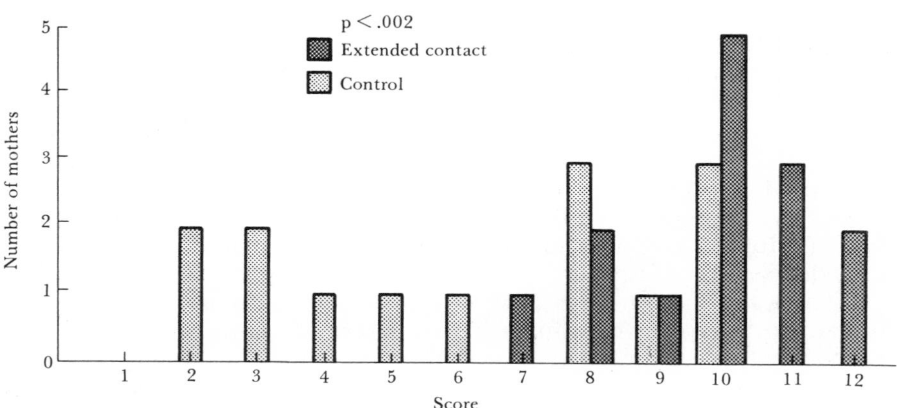

Figure 3 Summation of Scores of Performance from Both the Interview and the Observation of the Mother during an Office Visit at One Month Post Partum.

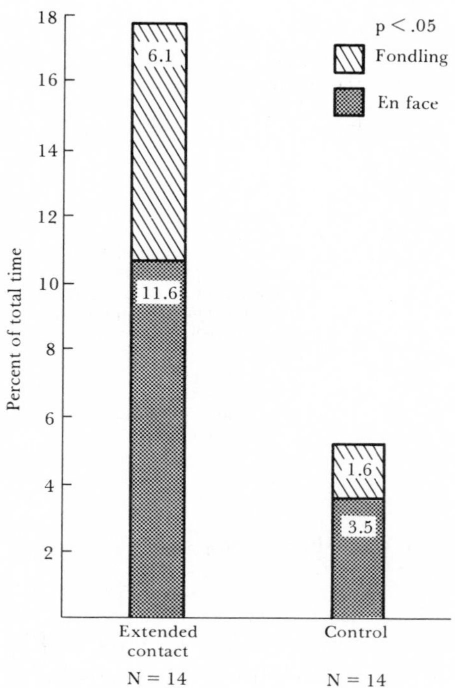

Figure 4 Filmed Feeding Analysis at One Month, Showing Percentage of "en Face" and Fondling Times in Mothers Given Extended Contact with Their Infants and in the Control Group.

Discussion

It is surprising with the multitude of factors that influence maternal behavior[8] (such as the mother's genetic and cultural background, her relations with her husband and family, the planning and course of her pregnancy, her own mothering as an infant, and her experiences in her family) that just 16 extra hours in the first three days had an effect that persisted for 30 days. From our study we are unable to determine if the initial hour, the five hours of additional contact per day or a combination produced the differences. The previously observed intensive interest of mothers[6,9] in their infants' eyes matched with the unusual ability of the newborn infant to attend and follow, especially in the first hour of life, suggest that the period immediately after birth may be uniquely important.

Though these findings suggest a special attachment period in the human mother somewhat similar to that described in animals, it is possible that the early presentation of a baby shortly after birth is taken by a mother as a special privilege or recognition that in itself may have altered her behavior. In either case, it does affect behavior.

Extensive studies have focused on the process by which the infant becomes attached to his mother. Our observations help in describing the process in the opposite direction—the attachment behavior of the mother. It is tempting to consider this a form of imprinting or a critical period for an adult human. However, this process does not fit the precise definition for either imprinting or a critical period.[10] Both processes are defined in terms of the infant animal and refer to events that occur only once in the life of an individual. Our data suggest that this may be a special attachment period for an adult woman—special in the sense that what happens during this time may alter the later behavior of the adult toward a young infant for at least as long as one month after delivery. It would be useful to have a special term for this period, such as "maternal sensitive period."

An understanding of this intricate process may be vital during planning for the mother of the full-term infant as well as for the mother of the high-risk infant, the premature infant and even the adopting mother. Should the adopting mother receive her baby immediately after delivery to optimize maternal attachment? If there is a "sensitive period," this question and many others require study.

The differences between the two groups in eye-to-eye contact and in tactile stimulation that have probably occurred in the first month in over 200 feedings, and in countless other encounters between mother and infant, may have definite effects on the infant. If these differences in attentiveness and in responsiveness to the babies' cries that we observed are to continue, they could assume additional consequence when taken in the light of the observations of Rubenstein,[11] Bell[12] and others, who have shown that increased maternal attentiveness facilitates exploratory behavior and the early development of cognitive behavior in infants. Early and extended contact for the human mother may have a powerful effect on her interaction with her infant and consequently its later development.

We do not know whether these differences in maternal behavior will disappear after two or three months, will be present in other social and economic groups, or will affect the later development of the two groups of infants. Thus, it is premature to make any recommendations regarding which caretaking regimen is preferable. Caution is recommended before any drastic changes are made in hospital policies as a result of this report, particularly in facilities for mother and infant care, where changes have been made in the past without study of the long-term effects on the mother and infant. It has been the custom of health professionals to make major changes affecting behavior and environment to promote what appeared to be a beneficial innovation without a careful study of the side effects.

We are indebted to Harriet Wolfe. Robin White, Susan Davis and the nursing staff for their helpful ideas and criticism.

REFERENCES

1. COLLIAS, N. E. The analysis of socialization in sheep and goats. Ecology 37:228–239, 1956.
2. HERSHER, L., MOORE, A. U., RICHMOND, J. B. Effect of post partum separation of mother and kid on maternal care in the domestic goat. Science 128:1342–1343, 1958.
3. RHEINGOLD, H. Maternal Behavior in Mammals. New York, John Wiley and Sons, 1963.
4. BARNETT, C. R., LEIDERMAN, P. H., GROBSTEIN, R. et al Neonatal separation: the maternal side of interactional deprivation. Pediatrics 45:197–205, 1970.

5. KLAUS, M. H, KENNELL, J. H. Mothers separated from their newborn infants. Pediatr. Clin. North Am. 17:1015–1037, 1970.
6. ROBSON, K. The role of eye-to-eye contact in maternal-infant attachment. J Child Psychol Psychiatry 8:13–25, 1967.
7. SIEGEL, S. Non-parametric Statistics for the Behavioral Sciences. New York, McGraw-Hill Book Company, 1956.
8. BOWLBY, J. attachment and Loss. Vol 1. New York, Basic Books Inc, 1969.
9. KLAUS, M., KENNELL, J. H., PLUMB, N., et al Human maternal behavior at the first contact with her young. Pediatrics 46:187–192, 1970.
10. CALDWELL, B. The usefulness of the critical period hypothesis in the study of filiative behavior. Merrill-Palmer Q 8:229–242, 1962.
11. RUBENSTEIN, J. Maternal attentiveness and subsequent exploratory behavior in the infant. Child Dev 38:1089–1100, 1967.
12. BELL, S. The development of the concept of object as related to infant-mother attachment. Child Dev 41:291, 1970.

PART 9

Lifestyles: Tradition and Change

In many countries throughout the world, woman's place, the roles she plays, and the kind of life she leads are being examined and evaluated with a scope and intensity which are new in human history. This interest began with the new feminism of the 1960s, and since then it has grown to a point where it affects all our important institutions: the family, law and government, religion, industry, education, and the professions. With the advent of the means to limit fertility and the opening of educational and vocational opportunities for women came the motivation for major changes in the lives many women lead.

When part of a social system changes, the rest of it must make an adaptation to that change. The process is attended by strain, tension, and often disruption as old customs and attitudes are challenged by proponents of the new order. Today's woman feels this, too. The middle-aged housewife, having followed all the rules, hears that her life with all its definitions is held in low esteem in the new scheme of things. Even if she works outside the home she is made aware that her job is considered to be of low status and poorly rewarded, compared to her male counterparts, or compared indeed to what she herself could have done had she not dedicated all those years to the care and well-being of others.

The younger woman, in her twenties or thirties, looks at her mother and says, "It won't happen to me." So she tries to develop her skills, to keep in touch by going to school or working part time while the children are young, or by continuing with full-time committment, babies or no babies. But for many the old expectations are still there, and in even the most "progressive" countries we hear that women come home from work and, without missing a beat, pick up where they left off that morning with their other jobs: rearing children and doing housework.

Young women of college age and younger have other kinds of problems. While uncommitted to social, personal, or career roles, they have choices their mothers never had. Hence they feel the burden of having to make decisions. What do I want to do with my life? Should I get married? Should I have children? How can I combine a satisfying personal life with the work I want to do? Where can I find a man who will willingly share the work at home so that both of us can explore other areas as fully as we wish to do?

Women today are experiencing life across a wider spectrum than ever before. But tradition, layered through centuries, yields slowly to change, especially in areas invested with powerful emotions and deep personal meanings. The papers in this section deal with just such areas of women's lives as they attempt to discover new identities for themselves, and at the same time to hold on to the best of the old ones.

"Anger and Tenderness" is the first chapter of Adrienne Rich's *Of Woman Born.* Subtitled *Motherhood as Experience and Institution,* the book combines an intensely personal account of her own experience of being a mother with a historical examination of the social institution of motherhood. In interweaving the personal with the scholarly, Rich's work is part of a new tradition which more and more feminist writers are finding compatible. In this excerpt from her book she begins her own story with segments from her journal at the time she was rearing her three young sons, in the 1950s and 1960s. She captures with great poignancy the assumptions of those days which held mothers and children in the unrelieved bondage of each other's company, and describes her conflicts as she tried to fill the role, to meet her own creative needs, and to hold herself together as a person. Except that it is written by a poet, her story is not unique. It shares feelings with which most of us are, or might become, familiar.

Increasingly, women are attempting to combine the old primary roles of wife and mother with other roles outside the home. The dilemma which may be inherent in the attempt to succeed in both arenas is analyzed by Susan A. Darley in "Big-Time Careers for the Little Woman: A Dual-Role Dilemma." "Women who try to combine the traditional feminine role of wife and mother with a career are caught between two reference groups which have conflicting values and standards for self-appraisal of their members." While the practical obstacles and difficulties confronting such women are obvious, Darley describes a more subtle problem: the contradictory nature of the roles themselves. This leads to the inference that a person who is highly successful in a career can hardly be successful as a mother as well. Whether or not this is true her awareness of such inferences leads to self-doubt and anxiety, and ultimately to the inhibition of achievement. Present trends, however, are more promising for the woman who wants the best of both worlds. As the number of such women increases, a reference group will emerge wherein woman's combined role choice can be evaluated and validated. When her status becomes less deviant and more acceptable, energies now bound up in conflict resolution can be applied to achievement—in both worlds.

A common problem for women trying to succeed in male-dominated professions is the absence of female role models. Elizabeth Douvan explores this situation in "The Role of Models in Women's Professional Development." In the absence of role models young women must develop their own coping strategies as they seek acceptance from their male colleagues. Some of these strategies, such as trying to be "one of the boys" or downplaying one's professional competence, are stressful and require sacrifices which no woman should have to make. In either case, the woman is sacrificing something of herself in her efforts to adapt to a masculine work environment. Douvan's interest is in the integrator, the woman who wants to be her female and feminine self, and to achieve professionally as well. She is in particular need of models, other women who have done just that.

As examples Douvan presents a fascinating group: those women who gathered around Freud to learn and to participate in the development of psychoanalysis in its early days in Vienna. Unusually gifted and unconventional, they used each other, much as women graduate students do today, to validate their self-concepts as intellectuals who were also women. Douvan notes a special dilemma for them: the very discipline within which they worked and taught defined women such as themselves as victims of abnormal feminine development, manifesting an ancient and unresolved envy of the male and a denial of their womanliness. Even so, each saw that she was not alone. It is this critical need that women professionals can meet for each other. As an example it can serve for those who are beginning a long and difficult preparation and who may be wondering if, indeed, achievement can be accomplished without distortion of the self.

The emergence of research attention to the psychology of women and to sex roles has generated a similar interest in male sex roles and their affects on men's lives. In "The Male Sex Role: Definitions, Problems, and Sources of Change," Joseph H. Pleck looks at how male sex roles are defined in our society, in particular at four current perspectives of the strains experienced by men in their roles, identifying sources for change.

Pleck distinguishes between the traditional and the modern versions of the male role. For example, in the traditional role, the kinds of achievement most valued for men were physical; interpersonal and emotional skills, along with such feelings as tenderness and vulnerability, were discouraged. In the modern male role, however, achievement in work settings requires intellectual *and* interpersonal skills, even as romantic psychosexual relationships require the cultivation of emotional intimacy.

Dramatic changes which have occurred in women's definitions of themselves and their place in the society have been an urgent stimulus for men to examine their own lives if they are to accommodate women in interdependent relationships. Less obvious, Pleck believes, is the need for men to change in their relationships with other men, with children, and with their involvement in their work. While external pressure for change is much less intense in these last three areas than in the first, they too are sources for change because of the binding and constraining effects that are presently built into them.

We are living in a period of rapid social change and transition from one era to the next. No longer do we live in a society characterized by rigid sex role segregation, guided by values and expectations handed down from one generation to the next. Nor have we yet built a society which is truly egalitarian and tolerant of pluralistic life styles, where women and men are free from the old constraints which defined behavior along lines laid down by anatomy. The movement, disorderly as it seems at times, is an authentic one, and the consciousness which informs it has emerged and taken shape, as exemplified by the papers in this section.

The essays here focus mainly on the lifestyle dimension which defines work roles for women, either in or out of the home, or a combination of both. That is, it is an activity dimension, relating to what women do with their time. Plainly there are other dimensions as well, defining, for example, living arrangements: living alone, living with another woman, living with a man in a nonmarital relationship, living in a commune. While none of these is new, each seems more viable today as an alternative lifestyle, either on a temporary or permanent basis, for women who are so inclined.

It seems, though, that the work dimension is the most important lifestyle determinant for most women. A woman may marry and spend the rest of her life engaged in domestic activities. Or she may choose to remain single and spend as much time in the work force as a typical man does. Variants of these patterns, modified by such contingencies as divorce and widowhood, account for the ways that most women spend their time. Increased understanding of the options and what they entail as lifestyles may make the transition to the brave new world a little smoother.

Anger and Tenderness

Adrienne Rich

. . . to understand is always an ascending movement; that is why comprehensions ought always to be concrete. (One is never got out of the cave, one comes out of it.)

–Simone Weil, First and Last Notebooks

Entry from my journal, November 1960

My children cause me the most exquisite suffering of which I have any experience. It is the suffering of ambivalence: the murderous alternation between bitter resentment and raw-edged nerves, and blissful gratification and tenderness. Sometimes I seem to myself, in my feelings toward these tiny guiltless beings, a monster of selfishness and intolerance. Their voices wear away at my nerves, their constant needs, above all their need for simplicity and patience, fill me with despair at my own failures, despair too at my fate, which is to serve a function for which I was not fitted. And I am weak sometimes from held-in rage. There are times when I feel only death will free us from one another, when I envy the barren woman who has the luxury of her regrets but lives a life of privacy and freedom.*

And yet at other times I am melted with the sense of their helpless, charming and quite irresistible beauty—their ability to go on loving and trusting—their staunchness and decency and unselfconsciousness. *I love them.* But it's in the enormity and inevitability of this love that the sufferings lie.

April 1961

A blissful love for my children engulfs me from time to time and seems almost to suffice—the aesthetic pleasure I have in these little, changing creatures, the sense of being loved, however dependently, the sense too that I'm not an utterly unnatural and shrewish mother—much though I am!

*The term "barren woman" was easy for me to use, unexamined, fifteen years ago. As should be clear throughout this book, it seems to me now a term both tendentious and meaningless, based on a view of women which sees motherhood as our only positive definition.

May 1965

> To suffer with and for and against a child—maternally, egotistically, neurotically, sometimes with a sense of helplessness, sometimes with the illusion of learning wisdom—but always, everywhere, in body and soul, *with* that child—because that child is a piece of oneself.
>
> To be caught up in waves of love and hate, jealousy even of the child's childhood; hope and fear for its maturity; longing to be free of responsibility, tied by every fibre of one's being.
>
> That curious primitive reaction of protectiveness, the beast defending her cub, when anyone attacks or criticizes him—And yet no one more hard on him than I!

September 1965

> Degradation of anger. Anger at a child. How shall I learn to absorb the violence and make explicit only the caring? Exhaustion of anger. Victory of will, too dearly bought—far too dearly!

March 1966

> Perhaps one is a monster—an anti-woman—something driven and without recourse to the normal and appealing consolations of love, motherhood, joy in others . . .

Unexamined assumptions: First, that a "natural" mother is a person without further identity, one who can find her chief gratification in being all day with small children, living at a pace tuned to theirs; that the isolation of mothers and children together in the home must be taken for granted; that maternal love is, and should be, quite literally selfless; that children and mothers are the "causes" of each others' suffering. I was haunted by the stereotype of the mother whose love is "unconditional"; and by the visual and literary images of motherhood as a single-minded identity. If I knew parts of myself existed that would never cohere to those images, weren't those parts then abnormal, monstrous? And—as my eldest son, now aged twenty-one, remarked on reading the above passages: "You seemed to feel you ought to love us all the time. But there *is* no human relationship where you love the other person at every moment." Yes, I tried to explain to him, but women—above all, mothers—have been supposed to love that way.

From the fifties and early sixties, I remember a cycle. It began when I had picked up a book or began trying to write a letter, or even found myself on the telephone with someone toward whom my voice betrayed eagerness, a rush of sympathetic energy. The child (or children) might be absorbed in busyness, in his own dreamworld; but as soon as he felt me gliding into a world which did not include him, he would come to pull at my hand, ask for help, punch at the typewriter keys. And I would feel his wants at such a moment as fraudulent, as an attempt moreover to defraud me of living even for fifteen minutes as myself. My anger would rise; I would feel the futility of any attempt to salvage myself, and also the inequality between us: my needs always balanced against those of a child, and always losing. I could love so much better, I told myself, after even a quarter-hour of selfishness, of peace, of detachment from my children. A few minutes! But it was as if an invisible thread would pull taut between us and break, to the child's sense of inconsolable abandonment, if I moved—not even physically, but in spirit—into a realm beyond our tightly circumscribed life together. It was as if my placenta had begun to refuse him oxygen. Like so many women, I waited with impatience for the moment when their father would return from work, when for an hour or two at least the circle drawn around mother and children would grow looser, the intensity between us slacken, because there was another adult in the house.

I did not understand that this circle, this magnetic field in which we lived, was not a natural phenomenon.

Intellectually, I must have known it. But the emotion-charged, tradition-heavy form in which I found myself cast as the Mother seemed, then, as ineluctable as the tides. And, because of this form—this microcosm in which my children and I formed a tiny, private emotional cluster, and in which (in bad weather or when someone was ill) we sometimes passed days at a time without seeing another adult except for their father—there *was* authentic need underlying my child's invented claims upon me when I seemed to be wandering away from him. He was reassuring himself that warmth, tenderness, continuity, solidity were still there for him, in my person. My singularity, my uniqueness in the world as *his mother*—perhaps more dimly also as Woman—evoked a need vaster than any single human being could satisfy, except by loving continuously, unconditionally, from dawn to dark, and often in the middle of the night.

2

In a living room in 1975, I spent an evening with a group of women poets, some of whom had children. One had brought hers along, and they slept or played in adjoining rooms. We talked of poetry, and also of infanticide, of the case of a local woman, the mother of eight, who had been in severe depression since the birth of her third child, and who had recently murdered and decapitated her two youngest, on her suburban front lawn. Several women in the group, feeling a direct connection with her desperation, had signed a letter to the local newspaper protesting the way her act was perceived by the press and handled by the community mental health system. Every woman in that room who had children, every poet, could identify with her. We spoke of the wells of anger that her story cleft open in us. We spoke of our own moments of murderous anger at our children, because there was no one and nothing else on which to discharge anger. We spoke in the sometimes tentative, sometimes rising, sometimes bitterly witty, unrhetorical tones and language of women who had met together over our common work, poetry, and who found another common ground in an unacceptable, but undeniable anger. The words are being spoken now, are being written down; the taboos are being broken, the masks of motherhood are cracking through.

For centuries no one talked of these feelings. I became a mother in the family-centered, consumer-oriented, Freudian-American world of the 1950s. My husband spoke eagerly of the children we would have; my parents-in-law awaited the birth of their grandchild. I had no idea of what *I* wanted, what *I* could or could not choose. I only knew that to have a child was to assume adult womanhood to the full, to prove myself, to be "like other women."

To be "like other women" had been a problem for me. From the age of thirteen or fourteen, I had felt I was only acting the part of a feminine creature. At the age of sixteen my fingers were almost constantly ink-stained. The lipstick and high heels of the era were difficult-to-manage disguises. In 1945 I was writing poetry seriously, and had a fantasy of going to postwar Europe as a journalist, sleeping among the ruins in bombed cities, recording the rebirth of civilization after the fall of the Nazis. But also, like every other girl I knew, I spent hours trying to apply lipstick more adroitly, straightening the wandering seams of stockings, talking about "boys." There were two different compartments, already, to my life. But writing poetry, and my fantasies of travel and self-sufficiency, seemed more real to me; I felt that as an incipient "real woman" I was fake. Particularly was I paralyzed when I encountered young children. I think I felt men could be—wished to be—conned into thinking I was truly "feminine"; a child, I suspected, could see through me like a shot. This sense of acting a part created a curious sense of guilt, even though it was a part demanded for survival.

I have a very clear, keen memory of myself the day after I was married: I was sweeping a floor. Probably the floor did not really need to be swept; probably I simply did not know what else to do with myself. But as I swept that floor I thought: "Now I am a woman. This is an age-old action, this is what women have always done." I felt I was bending to some ancient form, too ancient to question. *This is what women have always done.*

As soon as I was visibly and clearly pregnant, I felt, for the first time in my adolescent and adult life, not-guilty. The atmosphere of approval in which I was bathed—even by strangers on the street, it seemed—was like an aura I carried with me, in which doubts, fears, misgivings, met with absolute denial. *This is what women have always done.*

Two days before my first son was born, I broke out in a rash which was tentatively diagnosed as measles, and was admitted to a hospital for contagious diseases to await the onset of labor. I felt for the first time a great deal of conscious fear, and guilt toward my unborn child, for having "failed" him with my body in this way. In rooms near mine were patients with polio; no one was allowed to enter my room except in hospital gown and mask. If during pregnancy I had felt in any vague command of my situation, I felt now totally dependent on my obstetrician, a huge, vigorous, paternal man, abounding with optimism and assurance, and given to pinching my cheek. I had gone through a healthy pregnancy, but as if tranquilized or sleep-walking. I had taken a sewing class in which I produced an unsightly and ill-cut maternity jacket which I never wore; I had made curtains for the baby's room, collected baby clothes, blotted out as much as possible the woman I had been a few months earlier. My second book of poems was in press, but I had stopped writing poetry, and read little except household magazines and books on child-care. I felt myself perceived by the world simply as a pregnant woman, and it seemed easier, less disturbing, to perceive myself so. After my child was born the "measles" were diagnosed as an allergic reaction to pregnancy.

Within two years, I was pregnant again, and writing in a notebook:

November 1956

Whether it's the extreme lassitude of early pregnancy or something more fundamental, I don't know; but of late I've felt, toward poetry,—both reading and writing it—nothing but boredom and indifference. Especially toward my own and that of my immediate contemporaries. When I receive a letter soliciting mss., or someone alludes to my "career", I have a strong sense of wanting to deny all responsibility for and interest in that person who writes—or who wrote.

If there is going to be a real break in my writing life, this is as good a time for it as any. I have been dissatisfied with myself, my work, for a long time.

My husband was a sensitive, affectionate man who wanted children and who—unusual in the professional, academic world of the fifties—was willing to "help." But it was clearly understood that this "help" was an act of generosity; that *his* work, *his* professional life, was the real work in the family; in fact, this was for years not even an issue between us. I understood that my struggles as a writer were a kind of luxury, a peculiarity of mine; my work brought in almost no money: it even cost money, when I hired a household helper to allow me a few hours a week to write. "Whatever I ask he tries to give me," I wrote in March 1958, "but always the initiative has to be mine." I experienced my depressions, bursts of anger, sense of entrapment, as burdens my husband was forced to bear because he loved me; I felt grateful to be loved in spite of bringing him those burdens.

But I was struggling to bring my life into focus. I had never really given up on poetry, nor on gaining some control over my existence. The life of a Cambridge tenement backyard swarming with children, the repetitious cycles of laundry, the nightwakings, the interrupted moments of peace or of engagement with ideas, the ludicrous dinner parties at which young wives, some with advanced degrees, all seriously and intelligently dedicated to their children's welfare and their husbands' careers, attempted to reproduce the amenities of Brahmin Boston, amid French recipes and the pretense of effortlessness—above all, the ultimate lack of seriousness with which women were regarded in that world—all of this defied analysis at that time, but I *knew* I had to remake my own life. I did not then understand that we—the women of that academic community—as in so many middle-class communities of the period—were expected to fill both the part of the Victorian Lady of Leisure, the Angel in the House, and also of the Victorian cook, scullery maid, laundress, governess, and nurse. I only sensed that there were false distractions sucking at me, and I wanted desperately to strip my life down to what was essential.

June 1958

These months I've been all a tangle of irritations deepening to anger: bitterness, disillusion with society and with myself; beating out at the world, rejecting out of hand. What, if anything, has been positive? Perhaps the attempt to remake my life, to save it from mere drift and the passage of time . . .

The work that is before me is serious and difficult and not at all clear even as to plan. Discipline of mind and spirit, uniqueness of expression, ordering of daily existence, the most effective functioning of the human self—these are the

> chief things I wish to achieve. So far the only beginning I've been able to make is to waste less time. That is what some of the rejection has been all about.

By July of 1958 I was again pregnant. The new life of my third—and, as I determined, my last—child, was a kind of turning for me. I had learned that my body was not under my control; I had not intended to bear a third child. I knew now better than I had ever known what another pregnancy, another new infant, meant for my body and spirit. Yet, I did not think of having an abortion. In a sense, my third son was more actively chosen than either of his brothers; by the time I knew I was pregnant with him, I was not sleepwalking any more.

August 1958 (*Vermont*)

> I write this as the early rays of the sun light up our hillside and eastern windows. Rose with [the baby] at 5:30 A.M. and have fed him and breakfasted. This is one of the few mornings on which I haven't felt terrible mental depression and physical exhaustion.
>
> . . . I have to acknowledge to myself that I would not have chosen to have more children, that I was beginning to look to a time, not too far off, when I should again be free, no longer so physically tired, pursuing a more or less intellectual and creative life. . . . The *only* way I can develop now is through much harder, more continuous, connected work than my present life makes possible. Another child means postponing this for some years longer—and years at my age are significant, not to be tossed lightly away.
>
> And yet, somehow, something, call it Nature or that affirming fatalism of the human creature, makes me aware of the inevitable as already part of me, not to be contended against so much as brought to bear as an additional weapon against drift, stagnation and spiritual death. (For it is really death that I have been fearing—the crumbling to death of that scarcely-born physiognomy which my whole life has been a battle to give birth to—a recognizable, autonomous self, a creation in poetry and in life.)
>
> If more effort has to be made then I will make it. If more despair has to be lived through, I think I can anticipate it correctly and live through it.
>
> Meanwhile, in a curious and unanticipated way, we really do welcome the birth of our child.

There was, of course, an economic as well as a spiritual margin which allowed me to think of a third child's birth not as my own death-warrant but as an "additional weapon against death." My body, despite recurrent flares of arthritis, was a healthy one; I had good prenatal care; we were not living on the edge of malnutrition; I knew that all my children would be fed, clothed, breathe fresh air; in fact it did not occur to me that it could be otherwise. But, in another sense, beyond that physical margin, I knew I was fighting for my life through, against, and with the lives of my children, though very little else was clear to me. I had been trying to give birth to myself; and in some grim, dim way I was determined to use even pregnancy and parturition in that process.

Before my third child was born I decided to have no more children, to be sterilized. (Nothing is removed from a woman's body during this operation; ovulation and menstruation continue. Yet the language suggests a cutting- or burning-away of her essential womanhood, just as the old word "barren" suggests a woman eternally empty and lacking.) My husband, although he supported my decision, asked whether I was sure it would not leave me feeling "less feminine." In order to have the operation at all, I had to present a letter, counter-signed by my husband, assuring the committee of physicians who approved such operations that I had already produced three children, and stating my reasons for having no more. Since I had had rheumatoid arthritis for some years, I could give a reason acceptable to the male panel who sat on my case; my own judgment would not have been acceptable. When I awoke from the operation, twenty-four hours after my child's birth, a young nurse looked at my chart and remarked coldly: "Had yourself spayed, did you?"

The first great birth-control crusader, Margaret Sanger, remarks that of the hundreds of women who wrote to her pleading for contraceptive information in the early part of the twentieth century, all spoke of wanting the health and strength to be better mothers to the children they already had; or of wanting to be physically affectionate to their husbands without dread of conceiving. None was refusing motherhood altogether, or asking for an easy life. These women—mostly poor, many still in their teens, all with several children—simply felt they could no longer do "right" by their families, whom they expected to go on serving and rearing. Yet there always has been, and there remains, intense fear of the suggestion that women shall have the final say as to how our bodies are to be used. It is as if the suffering of the mother, the primary identification of woman *as* the mother—were so necessary to the emotional grounding of human society that the mitigation, or removal, of that suffering, that identification, must be fought at every level, including the level of refusing to question it at all.

3

"Vous travaillez pour l'armée, madame?" (You are working for the army?), a Frenchwoman said to me early in the Vietnam war, on hearing I had three sons.

April 1965

> Anger, weariness, demoralization. Sudden bouts of weeping. A sense of insufficiency to the moment and to eternity . . .
>
> Paralyzed by the sense that there exists a mesh of relations, between e.g. my rejection and anger at [my eldest child], my sensual life, pacifism, sex (I mean in its broadest significance, not merely physical desire)—an interconnectedness which, if I could see it, make it valid, would give me back myself, make it possible to function lucidly and passionately—Yet I grope in and out among these dark webs—
>
> I weep, and weep, and the sense of powerlessness spreads like a cancer through my being.

August 1965, 3:30 A.M.

> Necessity for a more unyielding discipline of my life.
>
> Recognize the uselessness of blind anger.

Limit society.
Use children's school hours better, for work & solitude.
Refuse to be distracted from own style of life.
Less waste.
Be harder & harder on poems.

Once in a while someone used to ask me, "Don't you ever write poems about your children?" The male poets of my generation did write poems about their children—especially their daughters. For me, poetry was where I lived as no-one's mother, where I existed as myself.

The bad and the good moments are inseparable for me. I recall the times when, suckling each of my children, I saw his eyes open full to mine, and realized each of us was fastened to the other, not only by mouth and breast, but through our mutual gaze: the depth, calm, passion, of that dark blue, maturely focused look. I recall the physical pleasure of having my full breast suckled at a time when I had no other physical pleasure in the world except the guilt-ridden pleasure of addictive eating. I remember early the sense of conflict, of a battleground none of us had chosen, of being an observer who, like it or not, was also an actor in an endless contest of wills. This was what it meant to me to have three children under the age of seven. But I recall too each child's individual body, his slenderness, wiriness, softness, grace, the beauty of little boys who have not been taught that the male body must be rigid. I remember moments of peace when for some reason it was possible to go to the bathroom alone. I remember being uprooted from already meager sleep to answer a childish nightmare, pull up a blanket, warm a consoling bottle, lead a half-asleep child to the toilet. I remember going back to bed starkly awake, brittle with anger, knowing that my broken sleep would make next day a hell, that there would be more nightmares, more need for consolation, because out of my weariness I would rage at those children for no reason they could understand. I remember thinking I would never dream again (the unconscious of the young mother—where does it entrust its messages, when dream-sleep is denied her for years?)

For many years I shrank from looking back on the first decade of my children's lives. In snapshots of the period I see a smiling young woman, in maternity clothes or bent over a half-naked baby; gradually she stops smiling, wears a distant, half-melancholy look, as if she were listening for something. In time my sons grew older, I began changing my own life, we began to talk to each other as equals. Together we lived through my leaving the marriage, and through their father's suicide. We became survivors, four distinct people with strong bonds connecting us. Because I always tried to tell them the truth, because their every new independence meant new freedom for me, because we trusted each other even when we wanted different things, they became, at a fairly young age, self-reliant and open to the unfamiliar. Something told me that if they had survived my angers, my self-reproaches, and still trusted my love and each others', they were strong. Their lives have not been, will not be, easy; but their very existences seem a gift to me, their vitality, humor, intelligence, gentleness, love of life, their separate life-currents which here and there stream into my own. I don't know how we made it from their embattled childhood and my embattled motherhood into a mutual recognition of ourselves and each other. Probably that mutual recognition, overlaid by social and traditional circumstance, was always there, from the first gaze between the mother and the infant at the breast. But I do know that for years I believed I should never have been anyone's mother, that because I felt my own needs acutely and often expressed them violently, I was Kali, Medea, the sow that devours her farrow, the unwomanly woman in flight from womanhood, a Nietzschean monster. Even today, rereading old journals, remembering, I feel grief and anger; but their objects are no longer myself and my children. I feel grief at the waste of myself in those years, anger at the mutilation and manipulation of the relationship between mother and child, which is the great original source and experience of love.

On an early spring day in the 1970s, I meet a young woman friend on the street. She has a tiny infant against her breast, in a bright cotton sling; its face is pressed against her blouse, its tiny hand clutches a piece of the cloth. "How old is she?" I ask. "Just two weeks old," the mother tells me. I am amazed to feel in myself a passionate longing to have, once again, such a small, new being clasped against my body. The baby belongs there, curled, suspended asleep between her mother's breasts, as she belonged curled in the womb. The young mother—who already has a three-year-old—speaks of how quickly one forgets the pure pleasure of having this new creature, immaculate, perfect. And I walk away from her drenched with memory, with envy. Yet I know other things: that her life is far from simple; she is a mathematician who now has two children under the age of four; she is living even now in the rhythms of other lives—not only the regular cry of the infant but her three-year-old's needs, her husband's problems. In the building where I live, women are still raising children alone, living day in and day out within their individual family units, doing the laundry, herding the tricycles to the park, waiting for the husbands to come home. There is a baby-sitting pool and a children's playroom, young fathers push prams on weekends, but child-care is still the individual responsibility of the individual woman. I envy the sensuality of having an infant of two weeks curled against one's breast; I do not envy the turmoil of the elevator full of small children, babies howling in the laundromat, the apartment in winter where pent-up seven- and eight-year-olds have one adult to look to for their frustrations, reassurances, the grounding of their lives.

4

But, it will be said, this is the human condition, this interpenetration of pain and pleasure, frustration and fulfillment. I might have told myself the same thing, fifteen or eighteen years ago. But the patriarchal institution of motherhood is not the "human condition" any more than rape, prostitution, and slavery are. (Those who speak largely of the human condition are usually those most exempt from its oppressions—whether of sex, race, or servitude.)

Motherhood—unmentioned in the histories of conquest and serfdom, wars and treaties, exploration and imperialism—has a history, it has an ideology, it is more fundamental than tribalism or nationalism. My individual, seemingly private pains as a mother, the individual, seemingly private pains of the mothers around me and before me, whatever our class or color, the regulation of women's reproductive power by men in every totalitarian system and every socialist revolution, the legal and technical control by men of contraception, fertility, abortion, obstetrics, gynecology, and extrauterine reproductive experiments—all are essential to the patriarchal system, as is the negative or suspect status of women who are not mothers.

Throughout patiarchal mythology, dream-symbolism, theology, language, two ideas flow side by side: one, that the female body is impure, corrupt, the site of discharges, bleedings, dangerous to masculinity, a source of moral and physical contamination, "the devil's getaway." On the other hand, as mother the woman is beneficent, sacred, pure, asexual, nourishing; and the physical potential for motherhood—that same body with its bleedings and mysteries—is her single destiny and justification in life. These two ideas have become deeply internalized in women, even in the most independent of us, those who seem to lead the freest lives.

In order to maintain two such notions, each in its contradictory purity, the masculine imagination has had to divide women, to see us, and force us to see ourselves, as polarized into good or evil, fertile or barren, pure or impure. The asexual Victorian angel-wife and the Victorian prostitute were institutions created by this double thinking, which had nothing to do with women's actual sensuality and everything to do with the male's subjective experience of women. The political and economic expediency of this kind of thinking is most unashamedly and dramatically to be found where sexism and racism become one. The social historian A. W. Calhoun describes the encouragment of the rape of black women by the sons of white planters, in a deliberate effort to produce more mulatto slaves, mullattos being considered more valuable. He quotes two mid-nineteenth-century southern writers on the subject of women:

> "The heaviest part of the white racial burden in slavery was the African woman of strong sex instincts and devoid of a sexual conscience, at the white man's door, in the white man's dwelling." . . . "Under the institution of slavery, the attack against the integrity of white civilization was made by the insidious influence of the lascivious hybrid woman at the point of weakest resistance. In the uncompromising purity of the white mother and wife of the upper clases lay the one assurance of the future purity of the race."[1]

The motherhood created by rape is not only degraded; the raped woman is turned into the criminal, the *attacker*. But who brought the black woman to the white man's door, whose absence of a sexual conscience produced the financially profitable mulatto children? Is it asked whether the "pure" white mother and wife was not also raped by the white planter, since she was assumed to be devoid of "strong sexual instinct?" In the American South, as elsewhere, it was economically necessary that children be produced; the mothers, black and white, were a means to this end.

Neither the "pure" nor the "lascivious" woman, neither the so-called mistress nor the slave woman, neither the woman praised for reducing herself to a brood animal nor the woman scorned and penalized as an "old maid" or a "dyke," has had any real autonomy or selfhood to gain from this subversion of the female body (and hence of the female mind). Yet, because short-term advantages are often the only ones visible to the powerless, we, too, have played our parts in continuing this subversion.

5

Most of the literature of infant care and psychology has assumed that the process toward individuation is essentially the *child's* drama, played out against and with a parent or parents who are, for better or worse, givens. Nothing could have prepared me for the realization that I *was* a mother, one of those givens, when I knew I was still in a state of uncreation myself. That calm, sure, unambivalent woman who moved through the pages of the manuals I read seemed as unlike me as an astronaut. Nothing, to be sure, had prepared me for the intensity of relationship already existing between me and a creature I had carried in my body and now held in my arms and fed from my breasts. Throughout pregnancy and nursing, women are urged to relax, to mime the serenity of madonnas. No one mentions the psychic crisis of bearing a first child, the excitation of long-buried feelings about one's own mother, the sense of confused power and powerlessness, of being taken over on the one hand and of touching new physical and psychic potentialities on the other, a heightened sensibility which can be exhilarating, bewildering, and exhausting. No one mentions the strangeness of attraction—which can be as single-minded and overwhelming as the early days of a love affair—to a being so tiny, so dependent, so folded-in to itself—who is, and yet is not part of oneself.

From the beginning the mother caring for her child is involved in a continually changing dialogue, crystallized in such moments as when, hearing her child's cry, she feels milk rush into her breasts; when, as the child first suckles, the uterus begins contracting and returning to its normal size, and when later, the child's mouth, caressing the nipple, creates waves of sensuality in the womb where it once lay; or when, smelling the breast even in sleep, the child starts to root and grope for the nipple.

The child gains her first sense of her own existence from the mother's responsive gestures and expressions. It's as if, in the mother's eyes, her smile, her stroking touch, the child first reads the message: *You are there!* And the mother, too, is discovering her own existence newly. She is connected with this other being, by the most mundane and the most invisible strands, in a way she can be connected with no one else except in the deep past of her infant connection with her own mother. And she, too, needs to stuggle from that one-to-one intensity into new realization, or reaffirmation, of her being-unto-herself.

The act of suckling a child, like a sexual act, may be tense, physically painful, charged with cultural feelings of inadequacy and guilt; or, like a sexual act, it can be a physically delicious, elementally soothing experience, filled with a tender sensuality. But just as lovers have to break apart after sex and become separate individuals again, so the mother has to wean herself from the infant and the infant from herself. In psychologies of child-rearing the emphasis is placed on "letting the child go" for the child's sake. But the mother needs to let it go as much or more for her own.

Motherhood, in the sense of an intense, reciprocal relationship with a particular child, or children, is *one part* of female process; it is not an identity for all time. The housewife in her mid-forties may jokingly say, "I feel like someone out of a job." But in the eyes of society, once having been mothers, what are we, if not always mothers? The process of "letting-go"—though we are charged with blame if we do not—is an act of revolt against the grain of patriarchal culture. But it is not enough to let our children go; we need selves of our own to return to.

To have borne and reared a child is to have done that thing which patriarchy joins with physiology to render into the definition of femaleness. But also, it can mean the experiencing of one's own body and emotions in a powerful way. We experience not only physical, fleshly changes but the feeling of a change in character. We learn, often through painful self-discipline and self-cauterization, those qualities which are supposed to be "innate" in us: patience, self-sacrifice, the willingness to repeat endlessly the small, routine chores of socializing a human being. We are also, often to our amazement, flooded with feelings both of love and violence intenser and fiercer than any we had ever known. (A well-known pacifist, also a mother, said recently on a platform: "If anyone laid a hand on *my* child, I'd murder him.")

These and similar experiences are not easily put aside. Small wonder that women gritting their teeth at the incessant demands of child-care still find it hard to acknowledge their children's growing independence of them; still feel they must be at home, on the *qui vive,* be that ear always tuned for the sound of emergency, of being needed. Children grow up, not in a smooth ascending curve, but jaggedly, their needs inconstant as weather. Cultural "norms" are marvelously powerless to decide, in a child of eight or ten, what gender s/he will assume on a given day, or how s/he will meeet emergency, loneliness, pain, hunger. One is constantly made aware that a human existence is anything but linear, long before the labyrinth of puberty; because a human being of six is still a human being.

In a tribal or even a feudal culture a child of six would have serious obligations; ours have none. But also, the woman at home with children is not believed to be doing serious work; she is just supposed to be acting out of maternal instinct, doing chores a man would never take on, largely uncritical of the meaning of what she does. So child and mother alike are depreciated, because only grown men and women in the paid labor force are supposed to be "productive."

The power-relations between mother and child are often simply a reflection of power-relations in patriarchal society: "You will do this because I know what is good for you" is difficult to distinguish from "You will do this because I can *make* you." Powerless women have always used mothering as a channel—narrow but deep—for their own human will to power, their need to return upon the world what it has visited on them. The child dragged by the arm across the room to be washed, the child cajoled, bullied, and bribed into taking "one more bite" of a detested food, is more than just a child which must be reared according to cultural traditions of "good mothering." S/he is a piece of reality, of the world, which can be acted on, even modified, by a woman restricted from acting on anything else except inert materials like dust and food.

6

When I try to return to the body of the young woman of twenty-six, pregnant for the first time, who fled from the physical knowledge of her pregnancy and at the same time from her intellect and vocation, I realize that I was effectively alienated from my real body and my real spirit by the institution—not the fact—of motherhood. This institution—the foundation of human society as we know it—allowed me only certain views, certain expectations, whether embodied in the booklet in my obstetrician's waiting room, the novels I had read, my mother-in-law's approval, my memories of my own mother, the Sistine Madonna or she of the Michelangelo *Pietà,* the floating notion that a woman pregnant is a woman calm in her fulfillment or, simply, a woman waiting. Women have always been seen as waiting: waiting to be asked, waiting for our menses, in fear lest they do or do not come, waiting for men to come home from wars, or from work, waiting for children to grow up, or for the birth of a new child, or for menopause.

In my own pregnancy I dealt with this waiting, this female fate, by denying every active, powerful aspect of myself. I became dissociated both from my immediate, present, bodily experience and from my reading, thinking, writing life. Like a traveler in an airport where her plane is several hours delayed, who leafs through magazines she would never ordinarily read, surveys shops whose contents do not interest her, I committed myself to an outward serenity and a profound inner boredom. If boredom is simply a mask for anxiety, then I had learned, as a woman, to be supremely bored rather than to examine the anxiety underlying my Sistine tranquility. My body, finally truthful, paid me back in the end: I was allergic to pregnancy.

I have come to believe, as will be clear throughout this book, that female biology—the diffuse, intense sensuality radiating out from clitoris, breasts, uterus, vagina; the lunar cycles of menstruation; the gestation and fruition of life which can take place in the female body—has far more radical implications than we have yet come to appreciate. Patriarchal thought has limited female biology to its own narrow specifications. The feminist vision has recoiled from fremale biology for these reasons; it will, I believe, come to view our physicality as a resource, rather than a destiny. In order to live a fully human life we require not only *control* of our bodies (though control is a prerequisite); we must touch the unity and resonance of our physicality, our bond with the natural order, the corporeal ground of our intelligence.

The ancient, continuing envy, awe, and dread of the male for the female capacity to create life has repeatedly taken the form of hatred for every other female aspect of creativity. Not only have women been told to stick to motherhood, but we have been told that our intellectual or aesthetic creations were inappropriate, inconsequential, or scandalous, an attempt to become "like men," or to escape from the "real" tasks of adult womanhood: marriage and childbearing. To "think like a man" has been both praise and prison for women trying to escape the body-trap. No wonder that many intellectual and creative women have insisted that they were "human beings" first and women only incidentally, have minimized their physicality and their bonds with other women. The body has been made so problematic for women that it has often seemed easier to shrug it off and travel as a disembodied spirit.

But this reaction against the body is now coming into synthesis with new inquiries into the actual—as opposed to the culturally warped—power inherent in female biology, however we choose to use it, and by no means limited to the maternal function.

My own story, which is woven throughout this book, is only one story. What I carried away in the end was a determination to heal—insofar as an individual woman can, and as much as possible with other women—the separation between mind and body; never again to lose myself both psychically and physically in that way. Slowly I came to understand the paradox contained in "my" experience of motherhood; that, although different from many other women's experiences it was not unique; and that only in shedding the illusion of my uniqueness could I hope, as a woman, to have any authentic life at all.

NOTE

1. Arthur W. Calhoun, *A Social History of the American Family from Colonial Times to the Present* (Cleveland: 1971). See also Gerda Lerner, *Black Women in White America: A Documentary History* (New York: Vintage, 1973), pp. 149–50 ff.

Big-Time Careers for the Little Woman
A Dual-Role Dilemma

Susan A. Darley

An explanation is presented for differential career achievement in women and men. The analysis proposed is based on social psychological theories, such as role theory and social comparison and attribution theory, rather than on the genetic or personality theories which have been advanced in the past. The paper focuses on the situational factors which operate on women to shape their domestic and professional choices and behavior. These factors are analyzed from the perspectives of traditional housewives and mothers; career women; and women who attempt to combine the responsibilities of housewife, mother, and professional.

Impressive data support the contention that men and women show differential career achievement (Epstein, 1970). Historically this apparent difference has suggested to some (Freud, 1927) that women are genetically inferior to men; to others (Horner, 1972), that women have deficient personalities as a result of early socialization. (See Condry & Dyer, 1976, for a discussion of this issue.) This paper contends that to understand women's apparent lack of achievement we might do better to analyze social rather than genetic or personality variables. While allowing for genetic contributions to sex differences and for the fact that boys and girls are indeed socialized differently from an early age, the following analysis is based on the belief that the importance and the influence of biological and personality variables have been overstated, and that variables stemming from the more immediate social situations in which adult men and women find themselves have been relatively understated.

Role Behavior

The particular nature of a given social situation, including the expectations of real or imagined other people, can shape the kind of behavior that will be displayed. Some expectations may relate to the individual's sex, so that different kinds of behavior will be expected of men than of women,

"Big-Time Careers for the Little Woman: A Dual-Role Dilemma," from *Journal of Social Issues*, 32, 3 (1976), 85–98. Reprinted by permission of *Journal of Social Issues* and the author.

and for the most part people's behavior conforms to such sex-role expectations. When a person fails to behave role-appropriately, she/he violates role expectations and is likely to meet with disapproval and perhaps outright hostility from others. By such social sanctions one tends to learn to avoid roles that are inappropriate. While Horner (1972) suggests that women develop a motive to avoid success through rewards and punishments received during childhood, the alternative proposed here extends through adulthood the implicit social reinforcement focus of Horner's thinking and avoids the assumption of personality traits. Here it is suggested instead that in a particular situation women will choose to avoid behaviors that might make them appear to be filling a male-appropriate rather than female-appropriate role; and conversely, that men will choose not to display behaviors which would, in a particular situation, be generally expected of women. This hypothesis suggests that men would not competitively or aggressively clean house and that as a rule women would not competitively or aggressively discuss sports. On the other hand, it might explain why men vie avidly for office space and promotions in the office hierarchy, while women compete equally vigorously for cleaner laundry and fluffier rice.

My working hypothesis, then, is that qualities like competitiveness, assertiveness, and competence are not uniquely possessed by men either by virtue of genetics, anatomy, or early socialization. They are characteristic of both men and women but will be displayed by the two sexes in different kinds of situations. Unlike Horner's model, it is not assumed here that women as compared to men have a general disposition to avoid success, but rather that both sexes will avoid success when such success conflicts with social norms relating to sex role, and both will seek success when the norms allow for or require success (Howe & Zanna, Note 1).

Role Clarity and Stability

So far we have been discussing behavior in terms of sex role as though these roles are defined equally clearly for men and women and, in both cases, clearly enough that the behaviors appropriate to each role may be determined with ease and lack of ambiguity. If this were true, one would expect that men and women would have the same general kind of role choices to make and that qualitatively the consequences of these choices would be essentially similar. There are some suggestions in the literature, however, that this may not be the actual state of affairs; and if it is not, perhaps we have uncovered a second factor deriving from a role theory approach that might help explain achievement differences between men and women. That is, it may not be only the kind of behaviors demanded by the different sex roles that lead to differences in achievement, but also differences in the clarity and consistency with which these sex-role demands are defined.

It has been hypothesized by Rose (1951), for example, that "the social changes accompanying the industrial revolution left the middle-class urban woman's roles relatively less specific and less definite than those of comparable men and hence her pre-adult expectations are less adequate" (p. 69). Sarbin and Allen (1968) make a similar observation, using women's role expectations of marriage as an example. The obligations and responsibilities of wifehood are not validly depicted in movies and popular magazines nor are they clear simply from observing the behavior of one's parents, especially when such observations are made from the perspective of a child. As a result, it is difficult for girls to prepare adequately for the role of wife, and often they come into the role with vague and unrealistic ideas about what will be required or expected of them. According to Sarbin and Allen, boys grow up with a relatively clear and accurate picture of a husband's role.

The problem stems not so much from lack of role models—for certainly little girls have more opportunity to observe the daily life and work of their mothers than do little boys that of their fathers—as from the disparity between what our formal system of education is designed to prepare children to do as adults and what, in fact, they will likely be doing as adults. In school, children are taught academic and vocational skills which presumably prepare them for job responsibilities as adults. As former U.S. Education Commissioner S. P. Marland has recently written, "whether we acknowledge it or not, our society expects our schools and colleges to equip young men and women for successful entry into the world of work" (cited in *Newsweek,* 1974). And in our schools, girls follow the same general curricula as boys and are even encouraged to excel. In fact, they often outperform the boys on such measures of academic success as grades (Maccoby, 1966).

Having completed the educational gamut, however, girls are typically encouraged not to use directly the skills they have learned but rather to abandon them for a new set of skills—housekeeping, childcare, and husband tending—skills which are not typically an important part of public education. Boys, on the other hand, are encouraged if not actually pushed into using their marketable skills. To the extent that this is true, the educational preparation is more compatible with the activities involved in the stereotypic adult-male role than it is with the stereotypic adult-female role. Thus, it may be not only the career woman who faces an ambiguous role situation for which much of her experience and training have been inadequate but also the homemaker. Before analyzing the role problems confronting a career woman, then, let's turn briefly to the more traditional but far from simple role situation with which a housewife-mother must cope.

The Role of Homemaker

Before the industrial revolution, the roles of housewife and mother were relatively clearly defined in terms of keeping the hearth and ministering to the needs of children and husband. In earlier days, too, formal education outside the home was neither as widespread nor as intensive for girls as for boys. The activities involved in homemaking were relatively unambiguous, and the role training received by girls in childhood was more consistent with the traditional adult-female role than it is at present.

Today too the criteria for a well-kept hearth are not so clearly related to the personal efforts of the individual homemaker. Many essential services are provided by outside personnel and institutions, and with the development of almost limitless household appliances, the work of running a household has become more mechanical. In this sense, perhaps, the domestic role of homemaker has become less challenging.

On the other hand, most of the evidence (Linder, 1970; Morgan, Sirageldin, & Baerwaldt, 1966) suggests that despite modern conveniences, running a home has not become less time-consuming. Built-in obsolescence makes tracking down repair services a constant chore for homemakers, and the fact that the repairs are often costly and only to be accomplished by the intervention of experts may make the role of homemaker a more frustrating experience than ever.

And what of the role of mother? The explosion of books, articles, and television talk shows on the subject of motherhood suggests that the expectations for this role are almost without limit, stunningly unclear, and highly variable. Is a good mother permissive or firm or both? Is she a friend to her children or an advisor or both? Should she provide a lot of structure for them or allow them to schedule their own patterns of eating, sleeping, and play? "What's a mother to do?" a cliché plaint, aptly reflects the state of affairs in matters of motherhood. Note that what is expected of a good father is also unclear, but the parent role is not generally taken to be as salient for a man as it is for a woman.

In one sense, the activities involved in the role of parent, like that of houseworker, may be diminishing. With the increase in day-care facilities and organized after-school programs, a parent's physical presence is not as necessary as it once was for the proper care of young children. Again, like the homemaker role, however, a parent's job has probably increased in complexity, despite or perhaps because of the fact that more and more aspects of the role have been taken over by outside institutions and personnel.

With their children at school relatively early in life, many women turn to active involvement in community affairs. This aspect of the woman's role, i.e., voluntary involvement in community good works, however, is only partially institutionalized and perhaps as a result is accompanied by what Parsons (1942) has called "marks of strain and insecurity" (p. 612). Also, the possible social rewards to be gained for activity in this area are moderate at best; volunteerism is not a highly regarded pursuit and in fact has come under increasing attack from the feminist movement as exploitative.

A woman's lot, therefore, even if she restricts herself to the traditional and socially acceptable roles of wife, mother, and community volunteer is not an easy one, nor it is rich in extrinsic rewards. The strains and insecurities with which it is marked, however, are probably no greater, and perhaps less, than those facing the woman who seeks to combine the traditional role with that of career person.

The Dual-Role Woman: Homemaker and Career Person

Both Maccoby (1963) and Horner (1972) have emphasized the incompatibility between qualities traditionally associated with the role of wife-mother (e.g., nurturance, emotionality, responsiveness to people rather than ideas) and qualities associated with the role of achiever in the occupational and professional world (e.g., aggressiveness, rationality, and independence). A woman who exhibits such achievement-oriented characteristics in her career, or even simply by virtue of having a career, is usually considered to be fulfilling a socially inappropriate sex role and thus will most likely experience some anxiety and possibly some real social sanctions as well.

As difficult as the satisfactory performance of either the housewife-mother role or the career-woman role may be, the satisfactory performance of the two in conjunction appears almost impossible. Certainly, there are a myriad of practical and logistical problems that make the combination difficult and often exhausting. Furthermore there are as yet no clear-cut norms for such a combination of roles, and one would expect that women who attempt such a combination experience many strains and insecurities indeed.

Perhaps this would not be the case if performance in one role had no implications for performance in a different role, but the correspondent inference theory of attribution processes (Jones & Davis, 1965) suggests that such generalization does occur. The generalization is mediated by inferences made by an observer about an individual's personality. People are likely to infer, for example, that a successful career woman has an aggressive competitive nature, rather than that she is simply capable of behaving in an aggressive, competitive way when her immediate role requires such behavior. People interpret behavior as reflecting stable underlying traits of the behaving individual. This is the same kind of inference that Horner makes in her theory, and it is an inference which often works against women. If the fact that a woman succeeds at a career implies that she has a tough, contentious, hard-driving nature, it also implies, given current stereotypes, that she must not be a good mother—for insofar as anything is clear about what a good mother should be, this set of qualities, taken as personality traits, does not describe the ideal. In fact, these traits are often assumed to be the opposite of the ideal mother and of the ideal wife.

The strains and insecurities associated with the combined role of wife/mother and career woman, then, derive in part from the tendency for people to make inferences about an individual's personality from his/her behavior. Whether or not a woman combining the two roles is aware of the inferences being made about her, she suffers the effects. If she is unaware of them, she is nonetheless likely to be derogated as a mother and thus treated less cordially by her neighbors, and also likely to be taken less seriously at work, in which case her performance on the job may actually be impaired. If though, as is often the case, she is aware of the kinds of inferences, i.e., personality judgments, that are being made about her, the self-doubt and internal tension she must sustain are further increased.

One case in which such inferences are probably not made should be mentioned: the case of the wife/mother who has no choice but to work. These women may not be negatively sanctioned for working, perhaps because the fact that they work does not imply a set of nonfeminine personality characteristics, nor does it suggest that they have rejected the traditional female role. The assumption can easily be made that these women would not freely choose to work if conditions did not force them to it. It is only women who *choose* to work who are violating role expectations and whose personalities are assumed to be warped. If a woman has to work, for example, if she is widowed or living separately from her husband, it is usually the man who is negatively sanctioned and who is assumed to have a defective personality. If, on the other hand, a woman works because she enjoys it, she is usually assumed to be somehow lacking in the womanly qualities that make for good wives and mothers.

In addition to the negative inferences that dual-role women may face, there are also problems that stem from particular nature of the spouse/parent and occupational roles that may work against career success in women. Sarbin and Allen (1968) have provided a theoretical conceptualization of role conflict that may elucidate what some of these problems might be and help explain apparent sex differences in career achievement. They describe two kinds of roles, ascribed and achieved, and differentiate them primarily in terms of the degree of choice one exercises in entering them. Ascribed roles, of which the role of parent is an example, are attained by virtue of one's inherent characteristics or by virtue of one's necessary relationship to another person. One may choose to have children, for instance, but if one has them, one is a parent regardless of how one acts. Achieved roles, on the other hand, are usually attained through processes like training, personal achievement, or election. Sarbin and Allen hypothesize that roles that are predominantly ascribed differ from those that are predominantly achieved in terms of the range of valuations that may be assigned to the respective role enactments or performances. Specifically, they suggest that valuations for poor or nonperformance of achieved roles are at or near the neutral point; whereas proper or good enactments of such roles may be very positively evaluated and marked by real rewards, e.g., Pulitzer prizes, military medals. Possible evaluations for achieved roles, then, are assumed to range from neutral to highly positive. For ascribed roles, like mother or father, however, the range is from negative for poor or nonperformance to neutral for proper role enactment. Mothers, for example, are not generally rewarded for enacting the parent role well, but they are severely judged if they fail. Note that fathers who work to support their families are simultaneously filling two roles, one that is ascribed and one that is achieved. If they are economically unsuccessful or achieve less than their class background demands, they may be evaluated quite negatively. The Sarbin and Allen hypothesis would hold, however, that it is the fact that they are fathers, i.e., failing in their ascribed role, that accounts for the negativity and not the simple fact that they did poorly on the job, i.e., failure in their achieved role. The hypothesis suggests that a man who fails to achieve at work but who is not responsible for supporting a family will be only mildly sanctioned.

Sarbin and Allen hypothesize further that there is a tendency for the standards used in evaluating ascribed roles to be more ambiguous than those used in evaluating achieved roles. It's not nearly as clear what a good parent is, or does, as it is what a successful job holder is or does. So the rewards, even though only moderate for proper fulfillment of ascribed roles, are probably more difficult to come by than are those for proper fulfillment of achieved roles. Even though the clearer standards for achieved roles make failure in these roles relatively unambiguous, the sanctions for such failure are mild compared to the sanctions applied for poor performance of ascribed roles.

Sarbin and Allen also point out, "Perhaps for the male the occupational role is most salient and central, while the mother role seems to have similar saliency for most females" (p. 539). If this is true, and it does seem to be a fairly widespread assumption, then men are clearly more likely to be positively evaluated in the performance of their characteristic role since this role happens to be an achieved one. The situation for women, unfortunately, is just the reverse; not only are the possible rewards available to them for good performance of their salient role less striking, but also the possible punishments are greater than they are for men. The Sarbin and Allen analysis also lends support to the point made earlier about the lack of clarity associated with the traditional female role. Since the salient role for women is the parent role, an ascribed role, the standards they must meet will be more ambiguous than those of men, whose salient role is an achieved one.

It is possible to analyze in these terms the case of women who try to combine both kinds of roles, the ascribed role of parent and the achieved role of job holder. If it is correct that good mothers are assumed to be rather less good as job holders or conversely that a woman who is a success in her occupation is assumed to be necessarily lacking as a mother, then it is clear that working women are in an unresolvable conflict. They cannot reap whatever positive evaluations might accrue to them because of good performance on the job when such performance implies poor performance in their ascribed role as mothers. And failure to fulfill ascribed roles has the potential for being severely punished. The implicit moral to women is don't try such a combination, you simply can't win. On the other hand, a man who is successful at his work not only gains positive evaluation in that role but at the same time is highly evaluated in his ascribed roles of father and husband. One really can't help feeling that the "game," such as it is, is rigged.

Although the ascribed vs. achieved role analysis suggests that women have a more difficult role situation to resolve than do men, note that the reference is to extrinsic rewards and sanctions and almost exclusively to how people other than the individual role occupant evaluate his/her activities. The intense and profoundly personal experience of parenting, however, has intrinsic rewards (and anxieties) that may far exceed whatever external trappings of success or failure the career world has to offer.

Whatever the intrinsic pleasures and pains involved in the parent role, however, men who have careers and for whom the parent role is as salient as it is for women, i.e., dual-role men, find themselves in a role conflict every bit as difficult as that described for dual-role women. In fact, the situational approach suggests that the conflict for men might be even worse than for women. After all, a man who devotes a lot of time and emotional energy to domestic activities will be doubly sanctioned. Not only is he violating sex-role expectations, but also he is pursuing a kind of activity that is not generally highly regarded in our culture. This double-sanction effect may account in part for the apparent fact that more women are currently crossing sex-role boundaries to enter careers than are men to expand and develop activities in the domestic domain.

The issue of choice may play an important part in creating strains for dual-role women and in creating the apparent difference between men and women in terms of professional or occupational achievement. Rose (1951) reports:

> The modern woman has a choice between "career" and marriage, or she can work out some combination of them almost by herself. Since she has a choice, she may later question whether the goals she chose are the ones she "really" wants. A man has no such choice facing him: He must get an occupation. . . . Other people measure his success in terms of achievements in his occupation whereas even if a woman is a success in what she sets out to do, public acclaim will not be at all universal. (p. 70)

Possible Solutions to Dual-Role Conflict in Women

Let us assume, then, that women who seek to combine a career with wifehood and motherhood are confronted with an ambiguous situation. On the face of it, they have a great deal of free choice about the role combination. The standards that must be met, however, are contradictory, i.e., to be good in one role implies relative failure in the other, and the range of evaluations associated with each of the combined roles are different. It is probably safe to assume that this kind of role conflict may well inhibit occupational and professional achievement in women and that to realize fully their achievement potential, women must somehow resolve the conflict. How might such resolution be accomplished?

One useful strategy for dual-role women is to seek to compare their performance in the two roles with relevant others, most often other people who are in the same kind of situation. Festinger (1954) has postulated that all people will seek to compare their opinions and abilities with people who are similar to themselves. This hypothesis has been examined in many investigations (Schachter, 1959; Wrightsman, 1960; Radloff, 1966; Zanna, Geothals, & Hill, 1975), and has received considerable support.

Unfortunately, for the career/wife-and-mother there are still not many other mothers or wives in the office with whom she can compare her performance on the job, and there are still not many women in her neighborhood who leave their homes and children every day to pursue careers. There simply aren't many relevant others with whom these women can compare themselves in either of the two roles, and the self-evaluative information they get therefore will not be very stable. The information must be frequently verified and validated, and it is in the effort to gain such validation, which can only be obtained in social contexts, that women may appear to be more dependent and affiliative than men. Because the role requirements of having a career and being a good husband and father are not contradictory and because most husbands and fathers have careers and many men with careers are also husbands and fathers, men can evaluate their role performances and their attitudes far more easily and reliably than can women. For men, an occasional check is sufficient; for women, it is not.

The drive for evaluation, as postulated by Festinger (1954), "is a force acting on persons to belong to groups, to associate with others. And the subjective feelings of correctness in one's opinions and the subjective evaluations of adequacy of one's performance on important abilities are some of the satisfactions that persons attain in the course of these associations with other people" (pp. 135–136). But the chances are that dual-role women often find less satisfaction in any one social-comparison encounter than do men, mainly because the relevant other for a woman is usually less relevant than is the relevant other for a man. Most of the woman's colleagues are likely to be men, which makes them dissimilar on an important dimension; and of the few colleagues that are women, not all will be married or have children, and so they too may be importantly different and thus not ideal social-comparison referents. On the other hand, many of the woman's evaluators for her enactment of the wife-mother role will not be career women and so will not understand the full range of responsibilities and role demands that she must meet. They too are less than perfect social-comparison referents.

Women who try to combine the traditional feminine role of wife and mother with a career are caught between two reference groups which have conflicting values and standards for self-appraisal of their members. In their discussion of the research reported in *The American Soldier,* Merton and Kitt (1950) consider the patterns of self-evaluation that are often displayed by people who "are subject to multiple reference groups operating at cross-purposes" (p. 63). One pattern involves a compromise self-appraisal, intermediate between the evaluation of the two conflicting reference groups. A second alternative when two membership groups exert opposing pressures for self-evaluation is for the individual to adopt a third group for social-comparison purposes. Additional possibilities suggested by Lazarsfeld, Berelson, and Gaudet (1948) "range all the way from individual neurotic reactions, such as inability to make a decision at all, to intellectual solutions which might lead to new social movements" (p. xxii).

Whatever the solution, however, an individual who tries to maintain membership simultaneously in two groups whose values are contradictory is likely to engender hostility from both groups. As Merton and Kitt (1950) point out: "What the individual experiences as estrangement from a group of which he is a member tends to be experienced by his associates as repudiation of the group, and this ordinarily evokes a hostile response" (p. 93). While the deviant may at first receive considerable attention and communication from other group members (Festinger, 1950; Schachter, 1951), the tendency for the group to reject the individual will increase as the person orients him/herself toward outgroup values, either verbally or in his/her behavior. And of course for an individual who from the outset maintains some affiliation with each of two opposing groups, such orientation is constant. Each group is continuously being threatened by the individual's membership in the other. Women who seek to combine the traditional feminine role with a career are bound to be viewed as deviants within each of their role-reference groups.

What options are open to a woman contemplating both family and career? She can, for instance, give up professional aspirations and decide to stay home where, supposedly, she belongs and to devote herself exclusively to her husband and children; or she can forswear a family and devote herself entirely to a career. Since in the latter case she is failing to fill the role that is considered most appropriate for women in current American society, she is likely to suffer various negative social sanctions. Still, if she adopts the standards of an appropriate career-oriented reference group, she may receive enough social support within her profession or occupation to withstand the general pressures to conform to traditional role expectations.

For women who do not want to give up either the opportunities for self-development and the monetary and other tangible rewards involved in a career or the satisfactions of family life, the situation is more complicated but perhaps not as bleak as it might appear. If the number of women choosing to combine previously contradictory roles increases, a third kind of reference group will emerge and will validate the combined role choice. It will also be a source of stable social-comparison information for group members. And as self-evaluation becomes more stable for these women, their behavior may appear to become more independent since they will no longer have to check with as many and as conflicting social-comparison referents. Their status in the social order will become less deviant, certainly in a statistical sense but also perhaps in a social sense. Finally, as their status becomes more acceptable, women who combine family life and careers may have less energy bound up in internal conflict and more energy available to channel into their work. Thus they may more visibly achieve in areas currently reserved for men. If women, in other words, can free themselves from the kind of role conflict outlined in this paper, their apparent overdependence on others for social support and their seemingly nonachieving "natures" may be revealed as largely or wholly epiphenomenal.

NOTE

1. Howe, K. G., & Zanna, M. P. *Sex-appropriateness of the task and achievement behavior.* Paper presented at the meeting of the Eastern Psychological Association, New York, April 1975.

REFERENCES

CONDRY, J., & DYER, S. Fear of success: Attribution of cause to the victim. *Journal of Social Issues,* 1976, *32*(3).

EPSTEIN, C. F. *Woman's place: Options and limits in professional careers.* Berkeley: University of California Press, 1970.

FESTINGER, L. Informal social communication. *Psychological Review,* 1950, *57,* 271–282.

FESTINGER, L. A theory of social comparison processes. *Human Relations,* 1954, *7,* 117–140.

FREUD, S. Some psychological consequences of the anatomical distinction between the sexes. *International Journal of Psychoanalysis,* 1927, *8,* 133–142.

HORNER, M. Achievement-related conflicts in women. *Journal of Social Issues,* 1972, *28*(2), 157–175.

JONES, E. E., & DAVIS, K. E. From acts to dispositions: The attribution process in person perception. In L. Berkowitz (Ed.). *Advances in experimental social psychology* (Vol. 2). New York: Academic Press, 1965.

LAZARSFELD, P. F., BERELSON, B., & GAUDET, H. *The people's choice.* New York: Columbia University Press, 1948.

LINDER, S. *The harried leisure class.* New York: Columbia University Press, 1970.

MACCOBY, E. Women's intellect. In S. M. Farber & R. H. L. Wilson (Eds.), *The potential of women.* New York: McGraw-Hill, 1963.

MACCOBY, E. Sex differences in intellectual functioning. In E. E. Maccoby, *The development of sex differences.* Stanford, CA: Stanford University Press, 1966.

MERTON, R. K., & KITT, A. S. Contributions to the theory of reference group behavior. In R. K.

Merton & P. F. Lazarsfeld (Eds.), *Continuities in social research: Studies in the scope and method of "The American Soldier."* Glencoe, Ill.: Free Press, 1950.

MORGAN, J. N., SIRAGELDIN, I. A., & BAERWALDT, N. *Productive Americans.* Ann Arbor: University of Michigan Press, 1966.

Newsweek, November 1974, p. 112.

PARSONS, T. Age and sex in U.S. social structure. *American Sociological Review,* 1942, *7,* 604–616.

RADLOFF, R. Social comparison and ability evaluation. In B. Latané (Ed.), *Studies in social comparison.* New York: Academic Press, 1966.

ROSE, A. M. The adequacy of women's expectations for adult roles. *Social Forces,* 1951, *30,* 69–77.

SARBIN, T. R., & ALLEN, V. L. Role theory. In G. Lindzey & E. Aronson (Eds.), *The handbook of social psychology* (Vol. 1). Reading, Mass.: Addison-Wesley, 1968.

SCHACHTER, S. Deviation, rejection, and communication. *Journal of Abnormal and Social Psychology,* 1951, *46,* 190–207.

SCHACHTER, S. *The psychology of affiliation.* Stanford: Stanford University Press, 1959.

WRIGHTSMAN, L. S., JR. Effects of waiting with others on changes in level of felt anxiety. *Journal of Abnormal and Social Psychology,* 1960, *61,* 216–222.

ZANNA, M. P., GOETHALS, G. R., & HILL, J. F. Evaluating a sex-related ability: Social comparison with similar others and standard setters. *Journal of Experimental Social Psychology,* 1975, *11,* 86–93.

The Role of Models in Women's Professional Development

Elizabeth Douvan

If modeling represents a significant process in socializing candidates to professions, the question arises as to how young women have negotiated the acquisition of professional identities in fields where there are no (or virtually no) established women to serve as models. This article explores aspects of the situation of women in male-dominated fields; the techniques of adaptation they use and the effects on the intellectual styles and personal integrations women develop in these circumstances.

We hear a good deal these days about the importance of models for young women in the intellectual world, the professions, the business world—in all those spheres women have traditionally not entered. We take it on faith that knowing a woman academician and being close enough to see something of the reality of her life and action will help the young intellectual woman to concretize her own role conception, invest her aspirations with greater reality, and perhaps offer her some useful clues about ordering her spheres of action. It seems plausible. But we must take it on faith because identification and modeling have not been studied systematically except in preschool children. We know little about the nature of identification and its outcomes in young adults. We have hints: anyone who has spent much time in the company of young psychoanalytic trainees will certainly have noted the high incidence of cigars and trim beards in their ranks—and this before the current hirsute turn of fashion. In graduate school young men of my acquaintance were wont to affect stylish cigarette holders and certain distinctive gestures that were easy to trace to a particular figure in the faculty. We have all probably noted these charming gestures of respect and admiration in the young—at any rate, before current generations became so markedly counter-dependent. Adelson (1962) has catalogued significant features of the teacher as model and has described with great force the confusion that overtook young intellectuals when their faculty, under stress, failed to provide them with a model of integrity.

"The Role of Models in Women's Professional Development" by Elizabeth Douvan from *Psychology of Women Quarterly,* 1 (1976), 5–20. Reprinted by permission of Human Sciences Press.

If we assume that the model does provide a kind of relay for the youngster struggling up the cliff of his aspiration, we are led to ask again where young women have found appropriate models and how they managed to supply the modeling functions in the absence of adult women models. Or is modeling somehow not as critical a function for women as for men with their Oedipal remnants and authority crises?

It seems possible to me that modeling is more important for young men, or at least that its forms are quite different in males and females. In his references to character formation in the girl, Erikson (1950) stresses the girl's use of peers as identification figures and the negative strain to avoid identification with her mother. It may be that the enveloping, preoedipal mother is still sufficiently dangerous to the forming identity of the young women to disqualify older women as models. I am certainly struck—in looking back at my own graduate school experience and in my discussions with women currently in graduate school—at the extent to which young women altercast for each other and reinforce the reality of their self-concepts as working intellectuals.[1] Yet my experience and impressions as well as some shards of data that do exist lead me to conclude that many women also need and use older models, however specially, for their own purposes and growth.

The role of a crucial older women model is prominent in the biographies of women successful in politics (Kirkpatrick, 1974), poetry (Dickinson, 1894), the academic world (Almquist & Angrist, 1975; Mead, 1972), and psychoanalysis (Deutsch, 1973; Erikson, 1965). In her recent autobiography Helene Deutsch (1973) writes of her experiences at a socialist congress. "I was seeking models with whom I could identify; these could only be found among the feminine leaders . . . I found two who corresponded to the ego ideal I needed. These were Rosa Luxemburg and Angelica Balabanoff . . . In this gathering that swarmed with famous men, both of these women were treated with significant respect, and their speeches had a strong, often decisive influence on the proceedings. I heard these speeches with awe."

There are also the data from studies of the effects of working mothers. Studies of adolescents and of college women consistently report that girls and women whose mothers worked outside the home are more likely to aspire to higher-skill innovative and prestigious jobs than are those women whose mothers were full-time housewives (Baruch, 1972; Tangri, 1972; Douvan & Adelson, 1966). Furthermore, in studies where the question is asked, it turns out that the daughters of employed women more often choose their own mothers as models, as the person they would most like to be like (Douvan & Adelson, 1966).

In a focused study of 25 married women Ph.D.'s, Walum (1974) found that her subjects, all of whom were managing to integrate professional activities with traditional family roles, had strong positive identifications with their fathers as well as with some female model. "This female was not necessarily the mother: in some cases it was a grandmother, teacher, or aunt. Nearly all of the women spoke with passion [of] the importance these women had in stimulating them, not only toward professional careers but in alleviating guilts that might have been incurred being working mothers." She also asked respondents about books they remembered from childhood.

They often alluded to books about famous women and spoke of their own identification with the heroines in these books.

In a further study of undergraduate women, Walum (1974) found a significant association between career aspirations and the remembrance of heroines from books read in childhood.

A somewhat more inferential line of evidence for the importance of older women models can also be drawn. For example, the eastern women's colleges produce a disproportionate number of women who achieve prominent positions in the arts, professions, business, and politics. These schools traditionally select students from privileged backgrounds and powerful families. But they were not different in this respect from most universities through the Second World War. Yet they have consistently stimulated outstanding personal achievement in their alumnae—more so than coeducational institutions.

Girls attending these women's colleges experience a serious and intense intellectual climate that has been described by a number of observers (Newcomb, 1943; Sanford, 1962), and they are credited by their teachers with having outstanding and serious minds. They are regarded and respected for their ideas by faculty who value the intellectual life. This is likely to have a powerful impact on young women; for many, it is a first and unique experience. The absence of male peers in the classroom may also allow a freedom from sexual competitiveness and heterosexual concerns—and so facilitate the young woman's consolidation of a self-conception that stresses competence, independence, and academic achievement.

All of this is important and may contribute to the high incidence of real achievement among the alumnae of these schools. But I suspect that modeling is also important in the process that allows these women to integrate achievement strivings and the industry and discipline needed to realize their talents. Familiarity with adult women who have integrated achievement into gratifying lives and who have a stake in encouraging intellectual excellence in younger women must ease some of the anxieties that so commonly accompany and inhibit success in women (Horner, 1970). Being in daily close touch with working intellectual women (who integrate their own work and achievement with feminine fulfillment) must for many students open and facilitate the development of new conceptions of what is possible in their own lives.

Comparing notes with a college classmate and colleague recently, it emerged that while college had been crucial for both of us in offering models of intellectual women, the particular models and styles that had been most compelling and illuminating to us were different. She had never previously known women who combined roles and so was particularly affected by the many women on the Vassar faculty who were committed intellectuals and scholars at the same time that they had husbands and children and led rich, full family lives. Given her traditional background and her unquestioning acceptance of traditional goals, she could never have entertained serious thought of a profession without this real-life demonstration that it was possible to commit oneself to work without yielding feminine goals. (We were the generation raised on ideals of "togetherness" and large families. We were warned in sociology classes about the dreadful implications of the reproductive figures for upper-status, highly-educated women: we were not replacing ourselves! The eugenics movement still held sway in the ideology of some older faculty.)

The model who most impressed me—the one who provided the most startling and fresh view of what was possible in life—was an unmarried woman, a social scientist of international reputation in a specialty within her field so male-dominated that it was my impression at the time that she was the unique woman—an impression the years since have affected only slightly. She was exceptional in other ways: a department chairperson with a staff that included men, a consultant to state and federal agencies, and a frequently-called expert witness at legislative hearings.

My contact with this great woman was primarily social. Her courses were by and large too advanced and too specialized for students not majoring in her department. I had heard her as guest lecturer and in one introductory course and had served on a student-faculty committee with her, but mainly I saw her and knew her because she was a much sought-after dinner guest in the dormitories.

She was sought after because of her great charm. Essentially a shy woman, she had firm convictions and an inner integrity and competence that allowed her both unambivalent self-assertion and a gentle, beautiful personhood. She was my first experience with an unmarried woman who clearly contradicted two stereotypes which I had brought to college as part of my baggage from home: a) that a woman who didn't marry was by definition unhappy and unfulfilled, and b) that unmarried women could not conceivably have chosen their status. A man might choose to be a bachelor, but outside of religious orders a woman who didn't marry had obviously never been asked. (My background was by no means extreme in providing me these assumptions. In 1957, 30 percent of a national sample of adults shared similar views.)

My model stood as the simplest and clearest concrete evidence that these assumptions were wrong. Embryonic empiricist that I was, it was clear to me that the premises must be rejected out of hand in the face of evidence that was both elegant and incontrovertible. I was delighted and enlarged by the discovery. There were plenty of other cases to support my observation, but later evidence is never so exciting as the first encounter with a reality that stimulates insight. In any event, no case could have been clearer than my friend: a more beautifully integrated, warmly feminine, attractive, and fulfilled human being can hardly be imagined. It was obvious that many men must have wanted to marry her.

There were other models available who represented different integrations. One woman described elsewhere by Katz (1962) was a strikingly influential model for many women in my generation at the college. She represented and explicity taught an ideological position about marriage and motherhood that would offend many feminists today. At the same time, she also held historically advanced views about varieties of experience and ways of knowing, about the importance and legitimacy of human feeling as both a source of information and a fascinating area of study. She continually used examples from her family life to concretize concepts she was eager to convey. She was a brilliant thinker and sound scholar. And she was generous with her time and her inclusion of students into her full, busy family life. Even those of us who argued with her most vigorously were objects of her generous concern and warm humanity.

We also had our share of brisk, old-style feminists who were out of step with the then-current dominion of the values of large families and intense togetherness. One delightful economist, wife, and mother took every opportunity to impress on us her version of Parkinson's Law: that a woman who worked outside the home while she maintained a family managed housework in the time she had, while the full-time homemaker moved furniture and dusted full-time. She carried her maiden name in the tradition of the feminists. She was one of several bright-eyed ideologists who swam against the tides and the ethos of the time with verve and determination.

It was not, I think, the style or views of any particular faculty member that had such an important effect on students. It was the number of models available, their diversity, and their obvious pleasure in their active roles—their lively exchange with each other and with women students—that impressed many of us with the gratifications available through the route of involvement-commitment and the life of the mind.

Graduate school in a large coeducational institution was rudely disjunctive with my undergraduate life at Vassar. The virtual absence of women faculty was by no means the only or most striking way in which it was different, though that certainly was the case and registered on my awareness. I had a number of women colleagues in the student group, and we provided each other with support and collateral models. We were concerned about the absence of older models, noting that in a large and distinguished male faculty, only one man was married to a woman who worked at her profession. Later in our graduate careers, a friend and I who were by this time working wives and students were invited several times to speak to a group of young faculty wives in the department about job possibilities and the demands of a work commitment. Our personal relationships with these women were warm and gratifying, and many in the group did commit themselves eventually to jobs of various kinds. There was a subtle unarticulated strain in our initial discussions in that each side obviously represented an alternative that had been rejected by the other. Only the warmth and openness of the women in the group permitted us to transcend the different and be helpful to each other. We have continued to be friends and boosters of each other's accomplishments in various spheres over the years.

But what about professional modeling? What do young women do for professional identifications when there are no older female figures available? Do they use male models and split their identifications between the masculine-professional and feminine-family ones? Do they develop an internal model based on distant, historical, abstract ideals? Do they use close relationships with women in their own age group to support their internal conceptions? All of these and other techniques very likely play some part for the young woman in her developing fantasy of her future self-in-role.

The problem for the young woman entering a male-dominated field can be seen and treated conceptually as a mobility problem exactly the same as the situation of the minority group member, the immigrant, or a member of any underclass moving into a higher-status world. The problem is to become socialized to the higher-status world without losing one's identity and touch with one's own history.

There are three routes available. The first is to become just like the dominant group and abandon one's past. A form of overlearning, we identify this solution clinically as identification with the aggressor; in the particular case at issue here, it signifies a defeminization or abandonment of feminine goals. The second adaptation is deprofessionalization, the abandonment or de-emphasis of competence, and the third is a trenchant, continuing effort to integrate professionalism and feminine goals. Let me comment briefly on the first two routes and then look in greater detail at the mechanisms women use to effect an integration of professional and feminine goals.

De-emphasizing Femininity

The classic example of this style was the woman physician of the nineteenth century who adopted the style—in manner and dress—of a general of the Army. Surrounded on all sides by trenchant antifeminism, certain young women medical students did thbeir utmost to become invisible and nondistinctive in a sea of male colleagues. Determined to be judged on their talents alone, and struggling to ease both their own and their male colleagues' anxieties, these young pioneers lapsed occasionally into a literalness that bordered on caricature.

While we may no longer see this style in pure form (and I would argue that it declined as the incidence of women role models increased), remnants abound in certain fields. I have a friend, a distinguished woman architect, who describes the initial ploy she used as a young woman on entering new firms. Aware of the hush and chill that descended whenever she first walked into a drafting room, she would wait for the first good opportunity to express frustration and let go with a longshoreman's string of curses. She claims that the relaxation of tension was palpable once she had thus established herself as "one of the boys." The natural sciences, which have been especially inhospitable to women, probably still create conditions for this kind of masculine identification in women students. One woman scientist has described the confusion that overtook her when her first child was born. She had modeled her life and her concept of her professional future on the only examples available—her male teachers—and was completely unprepared for the disruption in her life that her baby implied.

Identification of her intellectual self with the male models who surround her is obviously crucial to the young woman in fields dominated by men. The fact of her sex is not crucial to all of her activity—much of the life of the mind and soul is truly androgynous. A young person of either sex can—and should—aspire to the informed naivete of Einstein, the industry and verve of Russell or W. E. B. DuBois, the humanity, creativity, and generosity of Erikson and Margaret Mead. Great human and intellectual traits come in many personalizations which are available to all irrespective of sex or age, class or ethnic background.

But males and females are different in many ways, including styles of conceptualizing and tastes for particular kinds of work. And it can make a difference to the growth and security of a young woman to interact with women scholars as well as with admirable men.

The style of thought women develop will be affected by training within a system dominated by a male point of view. Inevitably those of us who have developed and succeeded through such a system carry its imprint in subtle or blatant form in our intellectual styles.

Fields like medicine and law require to a high degree the objectification and depersonalization of people, and we would expect women to find the training process in these fields wrenching in its demands for intrapsychic changes and for alienation from aspects of the self as well as from feelings developed during normal feminine socialization. In addition, there are the more obvious problems that stem from role expectations in such high-status occupations, from overt discrimination, and from the unavailability of women models and colleagues.

In fields like psychology, anthropology, and literature—where intellectual content is entirely congenial to women and departments have been relatively tolerant of women students—these effects are for the most part subtle, at least in contrast to fields like physics, engineering, medicine, and law.

Lourie (1974) refers to and analyzes the "masculating" effects of academic training on women literary scholars and critics. Through a subtle analysis of the writing of women critics and of changes developing in the work under the influence of the women's movement, she provides a compelling demonstration that even women working in a field entirely consonant with traditional concepts of femininity (i.e., requiring intraceptiveness, concern with interpersonal nuance, interest in character and personality) do not escape the effects of their training in a male-dominated tradition that systematically demotes the creative work of women by labeling them "women novelists."

Finally let my give an example from my own field. Psychologists have always been interested in the question of how one person comes to apprehend and appreciate the experience of another person, and how the child growing up develops this human capacity for understanding mental contents that are not in the last analysis accessible in any direct or absolute sense. Numerous terms have been used to designate the process—empathy and taking the role of the other are two of the most common. I would suggest that empathy is a more feminine term—implying as it does a kind of union of subject and object, a swaying together or melding of the interpreter and the person interpreted. Empathy does not take as its central focus the separateness of the two but implies fluidity of boundaries and joining of consciousness. "Taking the role of the other" is a designation that contrasts with empathy in all these features. It addresses a phenomenon of merging but imposes articulated separateness in the process of conceptualizing it. I suspect that men prefer this label while women are more likely to use the term empathy. It would be instructive to do content analysis of the writings of male and female psychologists, and even more interesting to see whether young women shift from empathy to role-taking as they progress through their graduate training. This kind of analysis would translate some of Carlson's (1972) conceptual interests into specific empirical tests.

De-emphasizing Professional Goals or Styles

In one of its forms, this looks like a feminine version of the "gentleman's C" ideology: the young woman wants to be smart, but not so smart that it will offend anyone (male). It can also be more subtle, focussing on surprise. The goal in this case is to be asked, "How can anyone as cute as you have brains?"

Although in its most stereotyped form this alternative brings seductive sexuality into play as an instrument of professional ambition, it can also take less sexual forms. For example, the brilliant woman graduate student can attach herself as an intellectual daughter to an older male colleague, emphasizing loyalty and dependency rather than seductive sexuality.

Integrating Identifications

The choices and behaviors described in the previous outcomes are, of course, only exaggerations of forms that all professional women try out at one time or another. The difference is one of the degree and consistency with which a particular element is emphasized. Is there a professional woman alive who has not at one time or another enjoyed being treated as one of the boys or as the little princess? The main difference between those who settle solidily on one or the other element in the duality and those who try continuously for integration may be omnipotence—the desire to be all things and have all the rewards. Or it may be the degree to which surprise and a gaming attitude are valued. The integrator wants to use rough language and dirty words (just like her "boyish" colleagues) but enjoys the impact that's added by virtue of her also being a delicate, womanly woman.

The woman who insists on integrating her duality can be compared to the immigrant who came from Eastern Europe in the twenties who neither joined the American Legion nor refused to learn English, who neither sentimentalized nor rejected the Europe of his childhood, who embraced what he valued in the U.S. without either giving up his right to criticize or identifying with the xenophobic, misanthropic elements prominent in American society of the time. Such integration is difficult, for it requires a willingness to remain forever marginal, to live between and partake in two realities without negating or invalidating either of them.

The integrator, then, has particular need of models. To return to our young intellectual or professional woman, she needs to see that the integration is possible. The woman who chooses the route of professional identification and suppresses feminine goals can use her male teachers as models. The woman who suppresses her professional side will probably not stay in the competitive arena after school. But the integrator will remain and cannot use exclusively male models. For her, then, the adult woman who has managed the balance to which she aspires may be of pivotal importance in determining the outcome of her training and development.

Currently I am working on an analysis of the writings of women in the early Vienna circle in an effort to grasp the special roles women played in the group and the special nature of their relationships to Freud, their male colleagues, and each other. The women in psychoanalysis are ideal subjects for such a study—they are preoccupied with individual growth and autonomy; they have verve, intellectual quality, and commitment, and a degree of articulateness rare in any group and certainly extraordinary for women of the time.

In those days, the *only* available model of a psychoanalyst was the inventor of the role. And he was a Victorian patriarch. The theory he propounded included assumptions about feminine development clearly at odds with the experience of the young women students who came to learn to be psychoanalysts. Nonetheless, the reality of Freud's interaction with women and of the women students' reception and experience in Vienna was complex and ambiguous, as most social reality is.

Psychoanalysis developed as an intellectual movement in an era of radical political and intellectual movements. Revolution and socialism, modern anti-Semitism and Zionism, and new ideas of freedom and feminism all had been stirring in European consciousness since 1848.

Mitchell (1974) has recently articulated the impact the rising feminist movement had on psychoanalytic thought. Freud was aware of the movement and responded to it directly and explicitly on numerous occasions. The Vienna circle was a radical group in more ways than the fact that it represented a radical intellectual departure. Many of the women who entered the circle were attracted to the image of modern woman symbolized in Ibsen's Nora and Shaw's Candida. Ferenczi, Helene Deutsch, and other members of the group were also political radicals who contributed theory and/or practical leadership to the growing socialist movement. We have come to think of psychoanalysis principally as a conservative force, countering in essential ways the notion of change through social or political revolution, and I think it is hard for us to imagine the degree to which psychoanalytic ideas entered the confluence of radical ideas roiling European consciousness and intellectual life at the turn of the century.[2]

Life in the psychoanalytic circle was by no means a sexist nightmare. There was first of all a large group of women students who took active and effective roles in the seminars, in the journal, and in the training institute. At the international meeting held in Berlin in 1911, one-sixth of the participants—8 out of 46—were women. That figure compares very favorably with most any profession in the U.S. today.

Though he was a Victorian in personal style, Freud in fact had unusually authentic, respectful relationships with a significant number of brilliant and autonomous women. He worked with them, argued with them, and was, I think, influenced by them in a degree and with less defensiveness than he could ever allow in the case of male students and colleagues. Sexuality and the relationship between men and women was, of course, a central issue in psychoanalysis. It is critical to note that when his women students argued with Freud—and they often did—their point of contention was always feminine development and the essential theory of psychosexual stages. The males might disagree over cosmology, the basic psychic mechanisms and motivation, the relative force of biology and culture, metatheory, or specific psychopathologies and their interrelations. But the women argued about female development. Even when they finally broke over other issues—as, for example, Karen Horney did—the initial differentiation for the women usually arose over the question of female development.

There is a good deal of evidence that Freud's later crucial statements on female psychology were heavily influenced by the work of Jeanne Lampl de Groot. And in those later works Freud uses a peculiar prose convention, which, as far as I have been able to determine, is unique in the body of his work. It consists of inserting into the line of reasoning a critical comment or objection by a woman student and following the comment with a palpable shift in the subsequent direction of his own thought. (Davis, 1974). It may be as one cynical colleague of mine commented, that Freud could be responsive to his women colleagues because, after all, they didn't have penises. Whatever the unconscious sources, it is clear that Freud demonstrated both respect for the intellectual competence of his women students and openness to their intellectual influence. Perhaps the clearest demonstration of his objectivity about intellectual quality is the fact that he chose a woman—Helene Deutsch—for the critical position of head of the Vienna training institute.

In spite of all this, the circle was not without its problems for women. The theory, which began with the assumption of bisexuality, rather quickly took a path, via the notions of penis envy and the notorious triad of passivity, narcissism, masochism, that created conflict for these autonomous, ambitious women and clearly shunted them outside the category of normal feminine development. The problem was compounded by the peculiar nature of psychoanalytic training, which includes personal didactic analysis. To be fully trained a woman had to deal with—and perhaps be converted to—the theory of feminine development and her own "masculine" ambition, her strivings based on penis envy.

How did the women cope with this situation? Who did they use as models in their efforts to integrate professional and personal goals? Let me point at the outset to the fact that they were almost uniformly integrators, abandoning neither professional development nor fulfillment of their sexual identities.

They had no older female models to look to. Lou Andreas-Salome, the only older woman in the group, presented a highly deviant feminine adaptation and, more importantly, was both competitive and exploitive in her relationships with younger women (Binion, 1968). She seems to have had no close relationships with the women in Freud's circle. Though she and Freud both cherished some hope that she might serve as an intellectual mother to Anna, it is clear that Anna Freud's intellectual interests moved in a direction very different from Andreas-Salome's and also that Miss Freud was gifted with a mind and a style of thought that were lucid, analytic, rational, and orderly in contrast to Lou's romantic, vague obscurantism. Deutsch (1973) dismisses Andreas-Salome as a potential intellectual model without mincing or wasting words:

> Acceptance into the Society involved one formality: every prospective member had to read a paper on the basis of which he was either accepted or rejected.

> The topic assigned to me was a critical review of Lou Salome's article *Vaginal and Anal.* This article was unnecessary, speculative, hard to comprehend, and completely alien to my own psychological thinking. Perhaps the antipathy I felt from the beginning for this highly gifted woman stemmed from the labor her article cost me. (pp. 139–140)

The women students used Freud and their male colleagues and each other as mentors and models of integration. They used a variety of mechanisms to deprofessionalize or defeminize their stance at various times and to handle the conflicts and anxieties that confronted them both in psychoanalytic theory and in the very ambitious, avant garde integration they undertook.

In Andreas-Salome we find the clearest examples of deprofessionalization (let me quickly add that none of the examples I use are meant to imply that any of these women ever gave up the effort to integrate). In her relationship with Victor Tausk she acted out the sexual mistress-mentor role that she had created earlier in her relationship with the poet Rilke. Her relationship with Freud was a sublimated version of the same role. The letters they exchanged are rich with sexual imagery applied to intellectual intercourse and progeny (Andreas-Salome, 1972; Binion, 1968).

Helene Deutsch adopted the less obvious and less explicitly sexual form of feminine adaptation. In much of her relationship with Freud she was his favored, exceptional intellectual daughter. Both Freud and she used the father-daughter image in referring to their relationship, and, when Freud chose to interrupt her analysis (in order to resume the analysis of a former male patient), he did so with the assurance that she was in any case so nonneurotic that she had no real need of analysis. Deutsch had demonstrated her filial obedience earlier when she gave up her patient Tausk at Freud's insistence.

Defeminization was not used to any great extent or in any obvious ways by the women analysts, certainly not in comparison to women in other areas of medicine or in other professions at the time. They were not generals, and they did not look like generals.

Yet they did have—at least intellectually—to dissociate themselves from normal feminine development as it was described in the psychoanalytic model. When they did this—and there are clearly exceptions like Melanie Klein, Therese Benedek, and Clara Thompson, who never yielded to the idea that the bisexual dilemma was an exclusively feminine problem or that the unconscious demand to be male was the central motive or key to feminine development—they had to rationalize their personal intellectuality, achievement, and autonomy. They did so by saying, in essence, "But, of course, my development was not normal." Given the norms of the Vienna group, this was not an impossible or even extraordinarily difficult thing to say. Neurosis was accepted as part of the human condition by Freud and his colleagues. They really believed that the normal and abnormal formed a continuum and that we all participate in all that is human, whether normal or abnormal. The norm of candor and the freedom to be both intraceptive and nondefensive were much more a part of this small intimate group than we can easily imagine.

The woman students used Freud and their respective male analysts as intellectual models—and reserved the feminine side of their identities to be worked out separately. And they used each other, much as young women in graduate school do today, as models and legitimizers of the self-concept of woman intellectual they were all working through and anticipating in their fantasies of the future. There were many very close friendships that withstood the years as well as political and geographic dislocations.

The women in the Vienna circle were rare women who would have been in some avant garde movement with or without psychoanalysis. They had unusual intellectual gifts and ambitions, and they also had backgrounds of status and wealth that allowed them choices—an uncommon freedom for women then or now. In their small intimate circle they were able to find at least a few of their contemporaries who had innovative aspirations similar to their own. While the existence of this modeling opportunity may not have been the most crucial element in their professional development, I think that it was a significant element. And for the young woman of less determination and talent, the chance to see her own aspirations *in vivo*—realized and concretized—can be a crucial support at those moments of strain when she might otherwise decide that the integration is too difficult and abandon the effort.

NOTES

1. Alice Rossi (1973) has made a compelling case for the importance of the sibling paradigm in her analysis of friendships among nineteenth-century feminists. The notion of sisterhood in the women's movement calls on the same idea: that women will support each other—like sisters—in the effort to win greater self-realization. I have been impressed with the extent to which one ambitious and assertive woman on a faculty serves to encourage and disinhibit other women in their professional activities.
2. In the second of her autobiographical volumes, *Pentimento,* Lillian Hellman (1974) tells a fascinating, suspenseful story of her childhood friend who continued to see Freud and receive thoughtful personal counsel from him while she was a central figure in the anti-fascist underground network. He could not but have known that she was aligned with the Communists since she was injured in street-fighting and was a target of fascist search and violence. This story reminds us again that on a personal basis Freud had significant ties to the revolutionary political movement.

REFERENCES

ADELSON, J. The teacher as model. In N. Sanford (ED.), *The American college.* New York: Wiley, 1962, 396–417.

ALMQUIST, E. M., and ANGRIST, S. S. *Careers and contingencies.* Amherst: University of Massachusetts, 1975.

ANDRES-SALOME, L. *The Freud journal.* New York: Harper, 1972.

BARUCH, G. Maternal influence upon college women's attitudes toward women and work. *Developmental Psychology,* 1972, *6,* 32–37.

BINION, R. *Frau Lou.* Princton: Princeton University Press, 1968.

CARLSON, R. Understanding women: Implications for personality theory and research. *Journal of Social Issues,* 1972, *28* (2), 17–32.

DAVIS, N. Personal communications, 1974.

DEUTSCH, H. *Confrontations with myself.* New York: Norton, 1973.

DICKINSON, E. *Letters.* M. L. Todd, Ed. Boston: Roberts Bros., 1894.

DOUVAN, E., & ADELSON, J. *The adolescent experience.* New York: Wiley, 1966.

ERIKSON, E. H. *Childhood and society.* New York: W. W. Norton & Co., 1950.

ERIKSON, J. M. Nothing to fear: Notes on the life of Eleanor Roosevelt. In R. J. Lifton, (Ed.), *The woman in America.* Boston: Beacon Press, 1965, 267–287.

HELLMAN, L. *Pentimento.* Boston: Little, Brown, 1973.

HORNER, M. Femininity and successful achievement: A basic inconsistency. In J. Bardwick, et al., *Feminine personality and conflict.* Belmont, Calif.: Brooks/Cole, 1970, 45–76.

KATZ, J. Personality and interpersonal relationships in the college classroom. In N. Sanford (Ed.), *The American college.* New York: Wiley, 1962, 396–417.

KIRKPATRICK, J. *Political woman.* New York: Basic Books, 1974.

LOURIE, M. Literary women and the masculated sensibility. In D. McGuigan, (Ed.), *New research on women.* Ann Arbor: University of Michigan Center for Continuing Education of Women, 1974, 11–15.

MEAD, M. *Blackberry winter; my earlier years.* New York: Morrow, 1972.

MITCHELL, J. *Psychoanalysis and feminism.* New York: Random House, 1974.

NEWCOMB, T. M. *Personality and social change.* New York: Dryden, 1943.

ROSSI, A. Feminist history in perspective: sociological contributions to biographic analysis. In D. McGuigan (Ed.), *A sampler of women's studies.* UMCCEW, 1973, 85–108.

SANFORD, N. (Ed.). *The American college.* New York: Wiley, 1962.

TANGRI, S. S. Determinants of occupational role innovation among college women. *Journal of Social Issues,* 1972, *28* (2), 177–199.

WALUM, L. Personal communication, 1974.

The Male Sex Role
Definitions, Problems, and Sources of Change

Joseph H. Pleck

This article examines some persistent paradoxes in the definition of the male role, and proposes a distinction between traditional and modern male roles. Four current perspectives on the problems of the male role are distinguished: individual-level sex-role identity, cultural-level sex-role identity, contradictory socialization role strain, and inherent role strain. Finally, sources and forms of change in the male role are analyzed in terms of a distinction between the male role in relationship to women and the male role in other areas of life experience.

After a period of intense interest in the female sex role in the social sciences and in the wider culture, the male sex role is now beginning to emerge as an important and legitimate complementary topic. Three recent publications (Fasteau, 1974; Farrell, 1974; Pleck & Sawyer, 1974) herald the beginning of a new body of writing which explicitly takes the perspective that the male role contains many constricting and limiting features from which men need to free themselves. This article aims to put in analytical focus some central issues which need to be taken up as the male role is investigated in more social scientific perspective, specifically, issues in the definition of the male role, current perspectives about the problems of the male role, and sources of change in the male role.

Definitions

There have been a number of persistent paradoxes about what traits, attitudes, and interests men are expected to show or actually do show in contemporary society. Popular imagery about the male role is contradictory and confusing on many points. For example, physical strength and accomplishment are dominant images of masculine achievement, but it is intellectual and interpersonal competencies which are necessary for the kinds of achievement most rewarded in men by society. Males are expected to

"The Male Sex Role: Definitions, Problems, and Sources of Change" by Joseph Pleck from *Journal of Social Issues,* 32, 3 (1976), 155–164. Reprinted by permission of *Journal of Sound Issues* and the author.

show greater emotional control than women, and are often described as being more alienated from their feelings; but at the same time, men appear to become angry or violent more easily than women and are often rewarded for doing so, covertly if not directly. To give a third example, males appear to have stronger social bonds with others of the same sex than do women (a thesis popularized by Tiger, 1969) but they are reputed also to avoid emotional intimacy with same-sex others and have greater fears about homosexuality than do women. These and other apparent contradictions in the definition of the male role and typical male personality style need to be better understood.

The analysis proposed here is based on Sawyer's (1970) suggestion that the two fundamental themes in the male role are stress on achievement and suppression of affect. Employing the familiar Parsonian dichotomy between instrumental (or task) and expressive (or social-emotional) spheres of action (Parsons & Bales, 1955), Sawyer identifies the male orientation to each. I would additionally distinguish *traditional* and *modern* versions of the male role, in which these primary instrumental and expressive themes take on somewhat different meaning.

In the traditional male role—that described in classic community and working-class studies (W. F. Whyte, 1943; Komarovsky, 1964) as well as in Tiger's (1969) statement—the major forms of achievement which validate masculinity are physical. By contrast, in the modern male role—that depicted in W. H. Whyte (1956), Seeley, Sim, and Loosey (1956), and more recent studies by Komarovsky (1973, 1974)—positively sanctioned male achievement takes other forms, requiring more interpersonal and intellectual skills than physical strength.

The characteristic patterns of emotional and interpersonal life also differ in the two roles. In the traditional male role, interpersonal and emotional skills are relatively undeveloped, and feelings of tenderness and vulnerability are especially prohibited. Anger and impulsive behavior are encouraged, especially with other males, and are often experienced as particularly validating of masculinity. By contrast, in the modern male role, interpersonal skills are expected, especially insofar as these promote smooth collaboration with others toward achievement, as in management. Capacity for tenderness and emotional intimacy are also encouraged, but closely restricted to romantic heterosexual relationships and excluded elsewhere. Staying emotionally "cool" is a major value, and anger and impulsive behavior are particularly prohibited.

Traditional and modern male roles entail different patterns of relationships with women and men. Following the classic distinction between institutional and companionship marriage (Burgess & Locke, 1945), the traditional male expects women to acknowledge and defer to his authority. Marital relationships are primarily functional, without the contemporary concept of intimacy, and other relationships with nonkin females are at a minimum. The more modern male expects companionship and intimacy in his relationships with women. He sees heterosexual relationships as the only legitimate source of the emotional support he needs in his daily struggle. Compared to the traditional male's expectation that women defer to his authority in the family, the modern male's expectation that women soothe his wounds and replenish his emotional reserves places different demands on women, but ones at least equally limiting.

The traditional male role prescribes that men have strong emotional bonds to other men. Though these male-male bonds often take ritualized forms which limit their intimacy (Pleck, 1975a), these bonds are nonetheless important and often stronger than men's ties to women. By contrast, in the modern male role, emotional relationships with other men are weak and often absent, though a high level of competence in conducting work relationships is expected. Komarovsky (1974), for example, reports in an elite college sample that men now disclose more to female friends than to male friends. Compared to the traditional role, it is now men's relationships with other men—rather than with women—that seem only pragmatic and functional.

This distinction between traditional and modern male roles can be elaborated further, and a similar dichotomy made in female roles. The distinction parallels some developmental analyses of national character, particularly Reich's (1970) formulation of the character types, Consciousness I and Consciousness II. It also clearly parallels a distinction between working-class and middle-class culture. The argument is not that all males used to have traditional roles and now all have modern ones. Rather, as contemporary culture has evolved, the modern male role has emerged, and its elements increasingly represent the expectations and values by which males evaluate their behavior. Elements of the traditional male role clearly persist, both in culturally conservative groups and in the personalities of modern males, but these elements are increasingly less dominant.

Current Perspectives

In current literature, there are four major views of the difficulties and stresses in the male role. The first two, reflecting *sex-role identity* perspectives, assume that the behaviors and traits of traditional masculinity are desirable and functional for men; they focus on the difficulties men have in attaining them. The second two approaches, reflecting *sex-role strain* perspectives, question the content of traditional and modern male roles, and examine the strains men experience even if they do internalize the traits expected of them.

Individual-Level Sex-Role Identity

The individual-level sex-role identity perspective is currently the dominant analysis in developmental and personality psychology of the difficulties in the male role (Biller, 1974). This approach holds that persons develop their sex-role identities through identification with or imitation of the parent of the same sex and, to a lesser extent, other same-sex adults. However, males' earliest relationship in infancy tends to be exclusively with their mothers, and fathers (and other same-sex adults) are less available to sons than mothers are to daughters. Further, boys are more likely to experience complete absence of the same-sex parent than are girls—Herzog and Suda (1971) report 3 million boys in fatherless families in the United States in 1967. Thus, males are predicted to have greater difficulty attaining their sex-role identity and to show more insecurity in their sex-role identity than do females. This perspective obviously differs from the classical psychoanalytic view that females have greater difficulty in sex-identity development.

According to the individual-level sex-role identity perspective, the special vulnerability of male sex-role identity development leads to certain direct outcomes which are viewed as negative, such as effeminacy and homosexuality. In addition, the insecurity of male sex-role identity generates the less direct negative outcomes of compensatory overconformity to the male role and "hypermasculinity," including a predisposition to violence (Toby, 1966). This theoretical perspective also makes possible a special analysis of males' fears of and negative attitudes toward women. In this view, men fear and try to control women because they fear the feminine part of their own identity generated by their early attachment to the mother (Chodorow, 1971), and more generally because boys are socialized to be masculine by avoiding femininity rather than by directly imitating male models (Hartley, 1959). The solution to the problem of the male role suggested by this perspective is to increase the role of men in childcare to provide developing males with the means to attain more secure sex-role identities.

Cultural-Level Sex-Role Identity

This familiar perspective argues that at some time in the past it was easier for males to validate masculinity than it is today. In the past, men felt like men because they took a dominant role in relationships with women and because they engaged in work that was directly related to physical survival, such as hunting and farming. But today, goes this analysis, men are expected to accept women as equals, and the work males do is increasingly sedentary and increasingly unrelated to physical survival. Comparing themselves against the past, adult males today cannot feel fully masculine because society does not now provide them the means to do so. In short, the shift from the traditional to the modern male role has left men without activities and experiences which validate their masculinity. Though men create and seek compensatory experiences which offer this validation, such as outdoor sports and do-it-yourself crafts, these are not enough.

Sexton's (1969) argument can be interpreted as a variant of the cultural-level sex-role identity perspective, focussing on one particular social institution, the schools. Sexton depicts traditionally masculine working-class boys as discriminated against by contemporary schools which devalue masculine skills and instead reward boys who are compliant and effeminate. Where the cultural-level sex-role identity perspective holds that the economy and the family have changed so that males are not provided with masculinity-validating experiences, Sexton indicts the schools as not giving validation to traditional masculinity. In both analyses, the overall point is that current cultural institutions do not provide experiences in which males can feel traditionally masculine. Though Sexton overlooks the extent to which the schools in fact support traditional masculinity, through their emphasis on sports, she is correct in noting a discrepancy between traditional male styles and the modern male role valued in contemporary social institutions such as the schools. She is also correct in noting that it is working-class males who typically have the fewest resources for meeting modern male role demands. However, other solutions can follow from this analysis besides calling for a re-masculinization of the schools.

The individual-level and cultural-level sex-role identity perspectives are structurally similar in that they both unquestioningly assume the desirability of traditional forms of the male role. Both assume a theory of how males acquire a secure sex-role identity, and both attribute difficulties in its attainment to deficiencies in what the culture provides males—in opportunities for sex-role learning in childhood, in the former, and in masculinity-validating marital and economic roles, in the latter. Clearly, the adequacy of both perspectives depends on the validity of their assumptions about the desirability of traditional male styles and the processes by which they are acquired and supported.

Contradictory-Demands Role Strain

This perspective holds that the problem of the male role is that males are confronted by contradictory demands and expectations in their socialization and in adult life. Such was a major theme in Hacker's pointedly-titled "The New Burdens of Masculinity" (1957), in which she argued that males have traditionally been expected to be instrumental but are now expected to be expressive as well. In Hacker's analysis, these two expectations lead to role strain, because they conflict with each other and cannot be satisfied simultaneously.

Another formulation of this view (Hartley, 1970; Knox & Kupferer, 1971) holds that there is a strain-generating discontinuity between the expectations applied to males in different phases of the life cycle. To use our earlier distinction, males tend to be socialized in childhood for a traditional male role, but in late adolescence and adulthood find themselves measured against the standard of the modern male role. Where childhood socialization valued physical strength and athletic ability and taught boys to shun girls, adulthood confronts males with expectations for intellectual and social skills and for the capacity to relate to females as work peers and emotional intimates. Thus, where Hacker argues that the contradiction is between traits expected simultaneously, Hartley and Knox and Kupferer argue that the contradiction is between expectations applied in early and later parts of the life cycle.

Hartley (1959, 1970) does not take a neutral stance with respect to these early and later expectations; she believes that the traditional role socialization typical of male childhood is tragically inappropriate to the modern world. There is empirical support for this view in Mussen's (1962) finding in a major longitudinal study that while traditionally masculine boys show positive adjustment (compared to less masculine boys) in adolescence, they show poorer adjustment in adulthood, apparently because they lack the social and intellectual skills needed for successful adaptation in the adult world. Bem (1975) provides further evidence that males who have only sex-typed masculine traits are not able to adapt to situations requiring expressive or nurturant skills.

Inherent Role Strain

The inherent role strain perspective on the problems of the male role is just beginning to emerge. Where Hartley's analysis implies that males would have no difficulties if they were consistently socialized for the modern male role, the inherent strain perspective holds that males would still experience role strain. This role strain would not be between different features of the role or between norms internalized at different periods in development, but between modern male role demands and more fundamental personality needs. In this analysis, the obsolescence and dysfunctionality of the traditional male role is becoming increasingly clear, but the inherent limitations and constraints of the modern male role are not yet so obvious, partly because we are so much closer to it. Males need deeper emotional contact with other men and with children, less exclusive channeling of their emotional needs to relationships with women, and less dependence of their self-esteem on work than the modern male role allows.

The goal of this analysis has been to differentiate four perspectives on the male role, not to evaluate them fully. Recent reviews of sex-role identity development (Maccoby & Jacklin, 1975; Pleck, 1975b) find little support for the identification assumption central to the first perspective, or for the view that males are more insecure in their sex-role identities than females. Far less data are available for the evaluation of the other three perspectives. Each needs fuller evaluation, but I am convinced that future work on male roles will depend increasingly less on the sex-role identity perspectives and increasingly more on the sex-role strain perspectives.

Sources of Change

A basic distinction needs to be made in understanding the sources of contemporary change in the male role, a distinction between the new demands and opportunities presented by current changes in women's role, and the constraints and opportunities present in areas of male experience other than relationships with women. It is clear that a major stimulus for men to examine and change their sex role is the dramatic recent change in women's definitions of themselves and their place in society. Many men have been confronted with the need to change because of their relationships with women who have felt the impact of feminism. Insofar as women and men relate to each other and are interdependent, change in one sex's role requires accommodating change in the other's. In this analysis, the major form of change in the male role is in males' relationships to women, and it is stimulated by feminism. This change encompasses men accepting women as peers in work settings, acceptance of female careers, and equal sharing of power and initiative in marital or other heterosexual relationships, including equal division of household work and childcare.

A second source of change in the male role is the restriction and constraint men face in other areas of living. Need for change in men's relationships with men, their relationships with children, and their involvements with work is less obvious than in heterosexual relationships, because these areas depend more on an internal sense of dissatisfaction and limitation than on external demands and confrontation. Nonetheless, men encounter norms for their behavior which are limiting in each of these three areas, and each represents a potential arena of change.

It is important to make the distinction between these two general sources (and forms) of change because the second area is often neglected or not made explicit. It is sometimes asked, for example, what could motivate men to change their role since change means giving up power and privilege relative to women. Such a question assumes that there are no potential gains for men in changing current patterns of male-female relationships. But in addition to this debatable assumption, the question betrays an even deeper assumption that the only area in which men might be motivated or choose to change is in relationship to women. When the full range of life spheres is examined, there is ample reason to believe that men have considerable gains to make in loosening and changing their roles. Needs in relationships with women and needs in the other three life spheres are equally legitimate sources of change for men (Pleck & Sawyer, 1974), and the relationship between role changes in these different domains is an intriguing topic awaiting empirical investigation. These four life spheres (relationships with women, relationships with other men, relationships with children, and involvements with work), along with the more general issue of male sex-role strain, constitute a major set of topics for research on the male role in the time to come.

REFERENCES

BEM, S. Sex role adaptability: One consequence of psychological androgyny. *Journal of Personality and Social Psychology,* 1975, *31,* 634–643.

BILLER, H. B. *Paternal deprivation: Family, school, sexuality, and society.* Lexington, Mass.: Heath, 1974.

BURGESS, E. W., & LOCKE, H.J. *The family, from institution to companionship.* New York: American Book Co., 1945.

CHODOROW, N. Being and doing: A cross-cultural examination of the socialization of males and females. In V. Gornick & B. K. Moran (Eds.), *Woman in sexist society.* New York: Basic Books, 1971.

FARRELL, W. T. *The liberated man: Freeing men and their relationships with women.* New York: Random House, 1974.

FASTEAU, M. F. *The male machine.* New York: McGraw-Hill, 1974.

HACKER, H. The new burdens of masculinity. *Marriage and Family Living,* 1957, *3,* 227–233.

HARTLEY, R. E. Sex role pressures in the socialization of the male child. *Psychological Reports,* 1959, *5,* 457–468.

HARTLEY, R. E. American core culture: Continuity and change. In G. Seward & R. J. Williamson (Eds.), *Sex roles in changing society.* New York: Random House, 1970.

HERZOG, E., & SUDIA, C. E. *Boys in fatherless families* (DHEW No. OCD 72-33). Washington, D.C.: U.S. Government Printing Office, 1971.

KNOX, W., & KUPFERER, H. A discontinuity in the socialization of males in the United States. *Merrill-Palmer Quarterly,* 1971, *17,* 251–261.

KOMAROVSKY, M. *Blue collar marriage.* New York: Vintage, 1964.

KOMAROVSKY, M. Some problems in role analysis. *American Sociological Review,* 1973, *38,* 649–662.

KOMAROVSKY, M. Patterns of self-disclosure in male undergraduates. *Journal of Marriage and the Family,* 1974, *36,* 677–687.

MACCOBY, E. E., & JACKLIN, C. N. *The psychology of sex differences.* Stanford: Stanford University Press, 1975.

MUSSEN, P. H. Long-term consequents of masculinity of interests in adolescence. *Journal of Consulting Psychology,* 1962, *26,* 435–440.

PARSONS, T., & BALES, R. F. *Family socialization and interaction process.* Glencoe, Ill.: Free Press, 1955.

PLECK, J. H. Man to man: Is brotherhood possible? In N. Glazer-Malbin (Ed.), *Old family/new family: Interpersonal relationships.* New York: Van Nostrand Reinhold, 1975. (a)

PLECK, J. H. Masculinity-femininity: Current and alternate paradigms. *Sex Roles,* 1975, *1,* 161–178. (b)

PLECK, J. H., & SAWYER, J. (Eds.). *Men and masculinity.* Englewood Cliffs, N.J.: Prentice-Hall, 1974.

REICH, C. *The greening of America.* New York: Random House, 1970.

SAWYER, J. On male liberation. *Liberation,* 1970, *15,* 32–33.

SEELEY, J., SIM, R. A., & LOOSEY, E. W. *Crestwood Heights.* New York: Simon & Schuster, 1956.

SEXTON, P. C. *The feminized male: Classrooms, white collars, and the decline of manliness.* New York: Random House, 1969.

TIGER, L. *Men in groups.* New York: Random House, 1969.

TOBY, J. Violence and the masculine ideal: Some qualitative data. *The Annals,* 1966, *36*(5), 19–27.

WHYTE, W. F. *Street corner society.* Chicago: University of Chicago Press, 1943.

WHYTE, W. H. *The organization man.* New York: Simon & Schuster, 1956.

PART 10

Psyche and Society: Variations from the Norm

The course of life seems to run smoother for young females compared to their brothers, at least until puberty. Their mortality rate is lower and they have fewer congenital defects. They have a lower incidence of all kinds of problems, both physical and behavioral, than boys have. They display much less of the kind of behavior which is likely to bring them into conflict with authority. The research suggests that several factors interact to produce this effect. These include the extra genetic material on the second *X* chromosome which protects girls from sex-linked disorders which add stress to the life of the effected individual; the advanced developmental maturity of girls which facilitates their early socialization, giving them an advantage in developing interpersonal skills; the "feminine" tone of the early environment in which girls are cared for and later taught by same-sex models with whom they can relate and identify perhaps more easily than boys can; and the lower level for girls of aggressive and resistive behaviors which facilitates their adaptation to adult expectations.

This auspicious (for girls) sex difference gives way to a less bright picture following puberty, however, and adult women are not exempt from the conflicts and problems of adjustment which afflict men as well. The reported crime rate has drastically increased among women in the past few years, and women are overrepresented among the clients of mental health professionals. Many explanations have been advanced for these phenomena. Regarding crime, it is asserted by some that the changed social climate wherein women are freer and more active outside the home has weakened old inhibitions against showing aggressive behavior and increased opportunities to commit crimes. It is also possible that police are more willing to arrest women, and juries to convict them, than they once were. Regarding the high representation of women among those who seek help for psychological problems, interlocking hypotheses have been presented: women's adult roles are frustrating and unsatisfying; women are more likely to express problems and to seek help; women find the role of patient less dissonant since the therapist is usually a male, and the woman client is accustomed to a dependency role with a male authority figure. An old and resilient explanation ties women's emotions to the events of their bodies. The menstrual cycle in particular has been held to affect women such that by nature they are nervous, fearful, and erratic in behavior.

The papers in this section examine the data on problem behavior in women, both antisocial and psychological, and present theories to account for them. In "The Nature of Female Criminality," Dale Hoffman-Bustamante proposes that differences in rates and types of crimes committed by women and men are the result of social factors: differences in role expectations, socialization patterns, opportunity, access to criminal subcultures, and sex differences built into the crime categories themselves. While women account for only about one in six of all arrests, their arrest rate is higher than that for some kinds of crimes and lower for others. Their arrest rate is lower for crimes associated with "masculine" behavior, such as armed robbery, except as auxiliaries to men. By contrast, they are arrested in large numbers for offenses less inconsistent with female sex roles, such as forgery, fraud, prostitution, and runaway. Many of the crimes committed by women center around dependency on men, such as the pimp-prostitute relationship, and are minor in character. Major crimes typically require active independence and at least the threat of violence, both less congruent with the socialization of women than of men in our society.

As men and women differ in the rates and kinds of crimes they commit, so do they differ, in some respects, in the rates and kinds of mental disorders they develop. In "Sex Differences and Psychiatric Disorders," Bruce and Barbara Dohrenwend examine data reported in more than 80 studies of North American and European populations since the turn of the century. They were interested in sex differences in total rates of functional mental disorders, in types of disorders, in variations of sex differences over time, and in the implications of their findings for theory relating sex roles to psychiatric disorder.

According to their analysis, the total rates of functional mental disorders are not higher for women than for men. However, a look at the major subclassifications of mental disorders reveals that the rates of manic-depressive disorder and of the psychoneuroses are higher for women, while the rates of personality disorders are higher for men. The authors suggest that the common denominator for the former is depression, whereas the common denominator for the latter is irresponsible and antisocial behavior. This explanation fits rather well with the observation that the typical client of the mental health professional is an individual woman, while the typical prison inmate is a man. Of course, there is much overlap between male and female populations on these variables, as there is for all behavioral characteristics. But to the extent that systematically different trends appear, it becomes important to understand what there is in the female experience and in the male experience which biases them toward different kinds of maladaptive or deviant behavior.

Contrary to earlier demographic studies, the Dohrenwends did not find a change in the sex differences in rates or kinds of disorders when they looked at pre- and post-1950s data. While the incidence for both sexes had increased greatly, the relative distributions of males and females in the subclassifications stayed about the same. Since World War II is often seen as an event marking the emergence of women into new roles in the society, the separation of studies into those made before and after that period should help to test the hypothesis that adult sex roles are related to incidence of mental disorders. That is, if women's roles did change in the post-war period, one would expect, according to the hypothesis, that this change would be reflected in the statistics. Since the patterns for women and men did not shift from the earlier to the later studies, the Dohrenwends argue, ideas which hold that one sex or the other is under greater stress and therefore more vulnerable to mental disorder in general are not supported. Rather, the issue is posed by the higher rates of females with depressive symptomatology and of males with personality disorders. The question then becomes, what is different in the bodies and lives of men and women that moves them in different deviant directions?

Marlene Boskind-Lodahl's essay, "Cinderella's Stepsisters: A Feminist Perspective on Anorexia Nervosa and Bulimia," is a fine example of a feminist analysis of a pair of peculiarly female disorders which have received considerable attention by earlier generations of traditional theoreticians. Anorexia nervosa is a prolonged self-starvation which sometimes alternates with bulimia, gorging on food. Typical psychoanalytic explanations of these two disorders, mostly manifested by young women, include the elements of hatred of the mother, rejection of the feminine role, and conflicts between fears of oral impregnation and desire for pregnancy. Boskind-Lodahl's theory, however, is that such women, far from rejecting the stereotyped model of femininity, are completely captured by it. Having identified with it since childhood, they have learned a passive and accommodating approach to life which has two opposing tensions: a desperate requirement of self-validation from a man and, at the same time, a fear of men because of their power to reject. Success is defined as the ability to attract and to hold a man and these patients are preoccupied with a fear of failure, of not being good enough to please a man. Thus the problem is basically one of self-worth and self-esteem.

Boskind-Lodahl notes that traditional approaches to therapy with women would recommend a male therapist for such women on the grounds that he could replace her inadequate father with a good father, and would not be identified with her bad mother. The author argues, however, that such women need female therapists, positive role models in contrast to their experiences of their mothers, to help them grow toward a healthier, more independent sense of self.

The rebirth of the feminist movement in the 1960s brought with it a need felt by many women to explore with each other identity issues, feelings, and situational complexities which were widely shared; consciousness-raising (C-R) groups for that purpose became part of the American scene. The last paper in this section, "The Consciousness-Raising Group as a Model for Therapy with Women," by Annette Brodsky, contrasts C-R groups with traditional therapy, and suggests that the values, behaviors, and outcomes of such groups can offer insights to therapists who work with women clients today.

Many women who present themselves to a psychologist or a psychiatrist for help in dealing with their problems are not mentally ill. Very often their distress is the result of a situational or interpersonal problem, such as an unhappy marriage, occupational frustration or boredom, or problems with children and other family members. Such complaints as these, however, may screen a deeper problem: a pervasive disillusionment with their lives, a sense of promise unfulfilled, or as Betty Friedan called it, the problem that has no name.

Many therapists who are practicing today were trained in a model which included for women adaptation to the "feminine role," a model which tends to locate the woman's problems within herself rather than to identify those parameters in society and in her life which impinge upon her and cause stress and unhappiness. Brodsky analyzes the attitudes and assumptions which are present in the traditional therapist-client dyad, and shows how stereotypes of the feminine role can restrict the therapist's perception of the client's problems, as well as of her needs and potential for growth. Her insistence that therapists enlighten themselves with regard to current issues relating to women, and not rely on their personal knowledge and training, is well-taken indeed. Consciousness-raising is not a substitute for all women, but the insights it provides enrich our knowledge about ourselves, other women and the human condition. Likewise, those insights can enrich and facilitate other models used by the helping professions.

In summary, we see that women are different from men in the ways that they manifest behavior that deviates from the important social norms which define and regulate antisocial behavior and define and treat mental disorders. Crime rates in general are much higher for men, whereas women's crimes are clustered in more "feminine" areas such as prostitution and shoplifting. Differences in roles, in socialization, and in society's attitudes toward the sexes, which give men more physical freedom and supervise women more closely, interact to make at least part of the difference.

The data on incidence and types of mental disorders for men and women lend themselves to similar explanation. Men have a higher incidence of personality disorders which include antisocial behavior and substance abuse, "acting-out" kinds of behaviors which are more consistent with male socialization than with female. The data that find women more likely to develop depressive disorders are harder to explain. Depression has been variously interpreted as anger turned against the self and as a resignation to powerlessness. It is not farfetched to hypothesize that both self-recrimination and definition of oneself as powerless are more characteristic of women than of men for reasons that are imbedded in social values and tradition.

More research is needed on disorders that are peculiarly female such as anorexia nervosa. Here again, one sees a connection between the Gestalt of the disorder and the socialization process whereby some young women believe that they must, like Cinderella's stepsisters, alter their bodies to fit a rigid mold which they both desire and fear.

Finally, the motif of women helping women is reflected both in the egalitarian peer format of the consciousness-raising group and in the increasing valuing of women therapists for women clients. This reflects the emergent recognition and appreciation of the commonalities among those who live the female experience in our society.

The Nature of Female Criminality

Dale Harrentsian

The question of whether or not female criminality is uniquely different from male criminality is one that remains largely unanswered. A survey of current literature on women in crime graphically illustrates the gap in data in this area and shows the lack of interest among researchers in the field. Much of what has been written is highly moralistic in tone, based on common sense and has little if any supporting data (Pollak, 1950). According to one sociologist, "Our knowledge of the character and causes of female criminality is at the same stage of development that characterized our knowledge of male criminality some 30 or more years ago" (Ward, *et al.*, 1969:847).

The present paper attempts to strip away the moralistic assumptions of previous research and delve into the nature of female crime patterns from a more sociological perspective. It appears that when such an approach is taken, crimes committed by women are the outcome of five major factors. These include differential role expectations for men and women, sex differences in socialization patterns and application of social control, structurally determined differences in opportunities to commit particular offenses, differential access or pressures toward criminally oriented subcultures and careers and sex differences built into the crime categories themselves.

Each of the above-mentioned factors may be more or less important for a given crime, yet each will operate differently for both men and women. The difficulty lies in determining exactly how each factor operates differentially by sex. For instance, if we took the crime of armed robbery, it

"The Nature of Female Criminality" by Dale Harrentsian from *Issues in Criminology,* (1973), 117–136. Reprinted by permission of the author.

becomes fairly easy to see how each of the above-mentioned factors makes it more likely that a man will commit the crime. Use of weapons is more likely to be learned by males as children, during military service or in the course of an adult occupation, than by females. Structurally determined differences in opportunities to commit the crime, although less important for this than for many other offenses, may be significant in terms of access to weapons or knowledge of places or persons that may be profitably robbed. Differential access to criminal subcultures and pressures toward criminal careers are decidedly more significant for males, both in terms of early socialization and possible prison experiences. Finally, the category itself is really a type of theft, separated from other categories of stealing by the particular way in which the crime is committed, a method that embodies more male than female role expectations.

This framework not only enables us to see why, in an overall sense, men commit more crimes than do women, but also gives us a clue as to why the percentage of women arrestees varies by crime. Although the importance of each factor depends on the nature of the crime, such a framework provides a sound basis of comparison between the sexes and between crimes. It also allows us to use already available statistical data that can be integrated with detailed descriptive studies that focus on individual crimes or particular aspects of crime.

In order to explore the nature of female criminality from this perspective, use will be made of data on female arrest rates from *Crime in the U.S.* (Federal Bureau of Investigation, 1970), which covers thirty crime categories, on the assumption that while arrest is admittedly an imperfect measure of criminality, it is the most comprehensive and systematic of available sources. In addition, data on female arrest rates from *Crime and Delinquency in California* (Bureau of Criminal Statistics, 1968) has been used for comparative purposes where appropriate. Where it is available, data from more specific studies has been used in order to better understand the meaning of arrest rates for particular crimes and the dynamics of women's roles in crime. Finally, consideration has also been given to the question of whether patterns of female criminality are changing, and if so, the direction of change.

Even a cursory examination of the data on arrest rates suggests the different ways in which the problem can be examined. Percentages of arrests of women in comparison to men can be made for each crime, or the pattern of crime, *i.e.*, % of women's crimes that are homicide, theft, arson, etc., can be compared to the pattern exhibited by men. Another possibility is to compare either major or minor types of crime or both to each other. Still another approach is to go beyond the mere figures of arrest and compare the methods of committing the various crimes in order to determine whether women use different techniques, or commit different types of crimes that happen to fall into categories which mask the differences.

Sex Differences in Arrest Rates

When the relative percentages of men and women committing each type of crime are compared, it becomes evident that at least two categories are by definition sex linked. Arrests for forcible rape are exclusively male, while those for prostitution and commercialized vice are nearly all female (79.3% in 1970) (see Appendix B). According to Cooper and Podolsky (1971), prostitution statutes are often phrased as "the practice of a female offering her body to an indiscriminate intercourse with men, usually for hire" (*Ibid.,*:12), making it by definition an exclusively female crime.

For the year 1970 women averaged 14.4% of all arrests (see Appendix B). With the exception of prostitution, the only other categories in which they constituted more than 15% of all arrests were under murder/manslaughter (15.4%), larceny (27.9%), forgery and counterfeiting (23.7%), fraud (27.1%), embezzlement (24.6%), narcotic drug laws (15.6%), vagrancy (19.7%), curfew violation (21.2%) and runaway (51.6%) (see Appendix B).

The most obvious question is why women's arrest rate averages only 14.4% of arrests for all crimes. Since women are about 51% of the total population, we would expect that they would commit at least 50% of the crimes and make up 50% of those arrested. As can be seen from the F.B.I. figures, this is nowhere close to the actual situation.

In the past, some sociologists have tried to account for this apparent discrepancy. One of the more recent attempts to develop a comprehensive theory of female criminality is that of Otto Pollak. In his book, *The Criminality of Women* (1950), Pollak bases his theory on three premises. The first is that those offenses most often committed by women (shoplifting, thefts by prostitutes, domestic thefts, abortion, perjury and disturbance of the peace) are greatly underreported (*Ibid.*:1). The high incidence of disturbing the peace is due to "her irritability at certain times" (*Ibid.*:2), and perjury is usually committed by "young girls still in a state of pubescence, or women suffering from hysteria" (*Ibid.*:25). These contentions seem hardly supported by the references Pollak uses, one of which is Lombroso (*Ibid.*:2). It should be noted that all of these crimes, with the exception of abortion, are petty in nature and are by no means the most underreported (Sutherland, 1949:8–13). Sutherland attempts to support the hypothesis that white collar crime is more prevalent both in terms of frequency and in dollar cost than all forms of so-called lower class crime (*Ibid.*).

The next premise of Pollak's theory is that the male attitude of protectiveness creates a situation in which males perform crimes at the instigation of women (1950:2–3). No data is provided in support of such a conclusion. In fact, Ward's study (1969:867) tends to confirm that, at least for violent crimes where women act with others, theirs is definitely a secondary role. Here Pollak brings in the idea that women are basically deceptive and that this is well expressed by their use of poison to commit murder, a contention not supported by the data (*Ibid.*:871; Wolfgang, 1958:85).

Pollak's final premise is that the law deals more leniently with women than with men (1950:3–4). Women who are convicted are given lighter sentences (Nagel and Weitzman, 1971:176). But even the table used by Pollak to illustrate this point does not fully support his thesis. Pollak shows that of those arrested for homicide, a higher percentage of women than men are convicted (1950:4). Yet, there is no reason to believe that arrest is used equally against both male and female suspects. In fact, it seems plausible that the reason the conviction rate for males is higher in comparison to their arrest rates is that female accomplices may be picked up without sufficient evidence. This is particularly pertinent when we see that the widest differences exist in robbery (13%), grand larceny (12%), receiving stolen property (11%), and forgery (13%).[1]

A more plausible explanation for the vast differences in arrest rates between males and females is accounted for by differential socialization and differential use of social control. Females are more closely supervised and more strictly disciplined in our society. Yet social control in the form of informal sanctions applied by primary and secondary groups is imposed more consistently and for more minor deviations from accepted standards. This results in a situation where females have been taught to conform to more rigid standards and rewarded for such behavior, whereas males are told to conform, yet rewarded for flaunting many conventional standards. Culture heroes, such as cowboys, private eyes, football players, adventurers and two-fisted cops, are evidence of the types of models emulated by many boys. Culture heroes for girls are either non-existent or portrayed as successful suburban housewives and mothers. As Sutherland and Cressey point out, the rates of arrest for women are lowest in those societies in which they are most closely supervised, and highest in those where women have the greatest equality with men (1970:127).

Major Crimes

Women in 1970 made up 15.4% of all those arrested for murder/manslaughter, one of the subcategories of criminal homicide (see Appendix B). If we combine the two subcategories (murder and manslaughter with and without negligence), we find that women account for 14.5%[2] of the arrests or only one-tenth of one percent over their average rate of arrest for all crimes. The classification used by the F.B.I. separates homicides according to whether or not the killing was willful (1970:6), thus excluding deaths resulting from criminal negligence. This separation appears to be closely tied to differences in opportunities available to women to be in positions, such as owners of businesses, supervisors of workers, purchasers of equipment or professional drivers of motor vehicles, where they could, in fact, be blamed for such deaths. This is reflected in the smaller than expected percentage of female arrests in the category of manslaughter by negligence (10.7%) (see Appendix B). The slight increase in the percentage of women arrested for manslaughter by negligence between 1958 and 1970, 1.2% (see Appendix B), may possibly be the result of changing female roles. At the same time, the percentage of women arrested for murder/manslaughter has dropped by 4.5%, and for aggravated assault it has declined by 3.1% (see Appendix B). If we examine the ways in which women are involved in willful homicides, we may be able to begin to account for this decrease.

Both Wolfgang's study of homicide (1958) and the more recent analysis of women and violent crime by Ward, Jackson and Ward (1969) support the hypothesis that the role of women in murders and their choice of victims is closely tied to the female sex role. According to Wolfgang's data, 51.9% of female victims had a family relationship to the offender, whereas for male offenders, the rate was 16.4% (1958:207). An additional 20.9% of women's victims were paramours (*Ibid.*). Wolfgang also brings out some important racial as well as sex differences in the rates of homicide. He points out that racial differences are greater than sex differences (*Ibid.*:32–33). The Black rate as a whole is twelve times greater than the White rate, while the male rate is just under four times the female rate (*Ibid.*:33). It has been proposed that this may be due to differential law enforcement as well as culturally acquired predispositions to violence (Ward, *et al.*, 1969:848; Piliavin and Briar, 1968:153–154; Goode, 1969:948). Despite the wide differences between racial groups, the patterns within each race are substantially similar, with women accounting for disproportionately fewer of the offenders and having a primary group relationship with a far greater percentage of their victims (Wolfgang, 1958:32–34).

Ward's data (1969:847) supports the major findings reported by Wolfgang, using more recent data drawn from two populations of women incarcerated in state prisons for crimes of violence. One area explored in this study was the woman's role in the crime. Women involved in murders were the sole perpetrator in 77% of the cases (*Ibid.*:867). In over half of the cases a family member or lover was the victim (*Ibid.*). Nearly half (47%) of the homicides took place in the common residence of the victim and offender with an additional 13% occurring in the offender's home (*Ibid.*:868). Only 21% of these crimes were premeditated (46% unpremeditated, 33% undetermined) (*Ibid.*:870).

Physical strength was not used in committing the crime in 51% of the cases (*Ibid.*). Over one-third of the weapons were knives or other household implements and another third of the weapons were guns (*Ibid.*:871). Wolfgang's data shows a greater use of knives and household implements (62.4%) and less use of guns (20.4%) (1958:85). In comparing male and female offenders we find a greater incidence of guns used (35.6%) and a significantly greater incidence of beatings (27.9%) as opposed to 2.8% for women (*Ibid.*). These differences in weapons used in committing homicide support the originally proposed hypothesis. Women more often use household objects, a reflection of the fact that they most often commit homicide in their own homes against their own kin or a paramour. The fact that men more often beat their victims to death or use a gun is related to the fact that males more often kill close friends and strangers (*Ibid.*:207) and that the crimes more frequently take place in the residence of the victim (26.7%) or outside either the victim or the offender's home (17.5%) (*Ibid.*:123).

Another important factor is the degree to which the victims were unable to defend themselves. Forty-two percent of the victims in Ward's sample were ill, drunk, off-guard, asleep or infirm, and another 19% were children (1969:871). Wolfgang breaks down his sample in terms of violence and non-violence. In his sample, 67% of the women committed non-violent homicide, whereas for men the rate of nonviolent homicide was 45.5% (1958:160). The standard used for this categorization was the inflicting of two or more stab wounds, gunshot wounds or beating the victim (*Ibid.*:159). Non-violent homicide would involve only a single stab wound, blow or gunshot wound. This difference in the use of violence by men and women is related to both the condition of the victim and differences in sex roles. As has been pointed out, women's victims are largely (61%) incapacitated

(Ward, 1969:871). Women in the course of growing up are also less likely to have the opportunity to learn the skills of fighting to the same degree as boys. This is reflected in the larger percentage of homicides men commit by beating their victims. The fact that women overwhelmingly use knives and household implements further supports the hypothesis that the commission of homicide by women is closely related to the nature of the female sex role, the types of skills women learn as they grow up and the network of social relations in which adult women are involved.

The category of larceny is defined by the F.B.I. as "the unlawful taking of property or articles of value without the use of force or violence or fraud. It includes such crimes as shoplifting, pocket-picking, purse snatching, thefts from autos, thefts of auto parts and accessories, bicycle thefts, etc." (Federal Bureau of Investigation, 1970:21). The stolen property must be worth at least fifty dollars for the F.B.I. to consider it a larceny. In 1970 women constituted 27.9% of the arrests for this crime (see Appendix B). In contrast, a burglary is defined as "the unlawful entry of a structure to commit a felony or theft even though no force was used to gain entrance" (*Ibid.*:18). The main distinctions between these categories are, first, the type of entrance made by the arrestee and, secondly, the value of what was taken. These distinctions are closely linked to sex role differences.

If we use Cameron's estimate that approximately 80% of all arrests of women on larceny charges are for shoplifting (1964:125), we can readily see that in 1970, 23.7% of the larceny arrests involved shoplifting.[3] The concentration of women in the arrest figures in this area is closely tied to her pattern of everyday life. Most department and grocery store shopping is done by women. Changes in marketing patterns that rely on self-service encourage such pilfering. When adult women are caught for shoplifting, the average value of the merchandise they have taken is considerably lower, $16.40, than for men, $28.36 (Cameron, 1964:71–72). Amateurs make up 90% of the arrestees (*Ibid.*:56). This gives us the picture that most women who are arrested for larceny are accused of having taken small items and are decidedly nonprofessional and, as Cameron suggests, do not repeat their crime after arrest (*Ibid.*:151). The pettiness of women's larcenies is again supported by a comparison with data from California. In 1968 the national rate for women was 24.4% (Federal Bureau of Investigation, 1968:118) of the arrests, while in California it was 10.7% of the larceny arrests (Bureau of Criminal Statistics, 1968:74). The difference can be found in the definition of the two categories. California uses the classification grand theft which is defined as including "theft of material amounting to $200 or more, certain fruits and nuts having a value of $50 or more, any horse, cow, pig, sheep or goat, embezzlement, fraudulant conversion of property, obtaining money under false pretenses and the receiving of stolen property" (*Ibid.*:178). The major difference here is the discrepancy in the money value of property taken, since according to Cameron (1964:71–72), women on the average shoplift goods of lesser worth than do men.

In comparing the categories of burglary and larceny, again we find differences closely linked to sex roles. Burglaries usually involve forcible entry, 77% in 1970 (Federal Bureau of Investigation, 1970:21). Half are committed during the day and the other half at night (*Ibid.*). Once more we find that this follows the expected pattern of everyday activities. Men are much more likely to be out at night than are women. Women out at night are likely to be supervised or escorted by men. Burglary is also the type of offense for which boys in the normal process of growing up would be more likely to acquire the necessary skills. If we combine the categories of burglary and larceny, we find that women account for 18.5% of the arrests. Although women still account for a larger than their average percentage of arrests for this offense, the size of the difference is largely reduced.

This brings up a broader issue of the inherent sex related aspect of several of the categories. What seems to be true is that one type of act, such as taking another person's property without his consent (theft), is subdivided by type of technique into, legally speaking, "different" crimes. Thus, we find nearly all women who steal are arrested for larceny, and men for larceny, burglary and robbery.

The categories of homicide and larceny are the only two types of major crimes in which women constitute a higher percentage of arrestees than their average for all crimes. For the other major crimes, their arrest rate is exceedingly low (0% rape, 6.1% robbery, 4.7% burglary, 5.1% auto theft) (see Appendix B). This situation is again related to differential role expectations for and training of women as well as differences in available opportunities to commit such offenses.

Rape is an obviously sex defined category. With the exception of statutory rape it would be difficult for a woman to commit this crime. Another factor is the double standard. In the area of sex there is a culturally conditioned presumption that the male is always the aggressor and that the female is in the submissive role. Thus, even in the case of an underage male having relations with an older woman, there is a reluctance to bring charges. Many statutory rape cases also involve disputes over financial responsibility for birth expenses rather than indignation over sexual exploitation. Such a factor would not operate in the case of an underage male. In any case, statutory rape is specifically excluded from the F.B.I. statistics on rape (Federal Bureau of Investigation, 1970:61).

In the case of robbery, the low female arrest rate is closely tied to the nature of the offense. The crime takes place in the presence of the victim and involves an attempt to take property or some article of value by force or the threat of it (*Ibid.*:15). According to Ward (1969:867), 80% of the female robbers in his sample were either accessories or partners, and in only 14% of the cases were they sole perpetrators. In 40% of the cases the partner was a husband or lover (*Ibid.*). No weapon was used in 53% of the offenses, even though 44% of the victims were adults who were not incapacitated (*Ibid.*:871). This further illustrates the peripheral nature of female participation. Ward comments that the most striking aspect of these crimes are their degree of poor planning, the spur-of-the-moment nature of the offense, the great risk for small possible financial success and the secondary nature of female participation in the crime (*Ibid.*:873).

Other Crimes

In the division of "other crimes," female arrest rates exceeded their average for all crimes for forgery and counterfeiting (23.7%), fraud (27.1%), embezzlement (24.6%), prostitution and commercialized vice

(79.3%), narcotic drug laws (15.6%), disorderly conduct (15.0%), vagrancy (19.7%), curfew (21.2%) and runaway (51.6%) (see Appendix B).

If we examine the category of forgery and counterfeiting, we find a sex related pattern similar to those described for theft. According to one study of forgery (Lemert, 1971:139), the vast proportion of arrestees either had no record or only previous forgeries. Many of those with previous records had been convicted of grand theft or petty theft which actually involved forgery. Lemert estimated that 75% of all persons convicted of forgery were "naive check forgers" (*Ibid.*). The socioeconomic characteristics of forgers also stand out in comparison with other types of criminals. They are usually of higher intelligence, have completed more years of schooling than the average of the population, and follow clerical, professional or skilled occupations (*Ibid.*:140). Forgery, like larceny, is a low visibility crime. Particularly among the middle and upper classes, both males and females are equally likely to acquire the skills of committing such crimes in the normal process of growing up. In support of this contention, Lemert asked a college class how they would go about obtaining and passing a bad check. He found that they proposed to use about the same types of techniques as had been used by the actual forgers in his sample (*Ibid.*:146–147). Although no breakdown by sex is given for the sample, we can again propose that as in the case of larceny, the high proportion of women is due to the fact that the crime fits well into the everyday round of activities in which women engage, especially their role of buying most family necessities and paying the family bills. These patterns are particularly typical of middle-class families. In addition to having the opportunity and skills to commit the crime, the woman who handles family finances is much more likely to feel the type of economic pressure that might cause her to see this as a way out of financial difficulty, especially when she feels she has an unshakable problem and no alternative resources.

Fraud as defined by the F.B.I. includes "fraudulent conversion and obtaining money or property by false pretenses. It includes bad checks except forgeries and counterfeiting" (Federal Bureau of Investigation, 1970:61). This category also contains such offenses as postal fraud, welfare fraud, writing insufficient funds checks, false advertising, con games, investment and land frauds checks and violation of consumer protection statutes, to name a few. According to Sutherland and Cressey, "it is probable, also, that fraud is the most prevalent crime in America" (1970:42). The amount of fraud in business practices is particularly large. Most of the misrepresentation in advertising and concealed defects in products go unreported, and reported offenses go unprosecuted (Sutherland, 1949:8–13). As Sutherland and Cressey indicate many occupations have developed expert techniques of concealment, not only in the production of commodities, but in the area of insurance (by insurers and the insured), in the legal profession, in tax reports, and in charities (1970:43–44). Direct and indirect bribery is also a common feature of much political and business practice (*Ibid.*:44–45). In Sutherland's study of white collar crime (1949:17), he investigates the various legal violations committed by seventy corporations. In this analysis, several typical white collar crimes are discussed. These include restraint of trade, rebates, patents, trademarks, copyrights, misrepresentation in advertising, unfair labor practices, financial manipulations, war crimes, and others (*Ibid.*:xv). Such offenses are nearly all committed by males. Enforcement of laws in these areas is often almost impossible, as it involves the arrest and prosecution of responsible members of the community who have the influence and often the ingenuity to avoid detection and/or prosecution.

There has been little study of women who are arrested for fraud. It is possible that most women arrested in this category are involved in con games, welfare fraud or possibly as accessories in fraudulent business practices. The high arrest rate for women may be due to the fact that the types of fraud for which women are arrested tend to be fairly easily detected and ones which police would be more likely to investigate, *i.e.*, con games, welfare or land schemes. These are crimes in which there is likely to be a victim who is aware of the crime. The bulk of fraud, false advertising, product defects and occupationally oriented frauds, (Sutherland and Cressey, 1970:42–43) are not detected or prosecuted (Sutherland, 1949:8–13). These would be more likely committed by men who are owners or managers of large companies or corporations, well able to protect themselves against detection, arrest or prosecution. If these persons were arrested, it is likely that the arrest rate for women would go down drastically.

Embezzlement, like fraud, is an extremely underrated crime in terms of the numbers of arrests made as compared to known losses. It has been estimated that employees take over $8 million per day in cash and merchandise (Sutherland and Cressey, 1970:21). One of the factors operating here is the reluctance of employers to prosecute, especially when there is the possibility of recovering part or all of the money through restitution. In many cases employers are not able to prove or discover who the offender is. The fact that these losses are passed onto the customer in the form of higher prices (*Ibid.*:22) reduces the incentive for vigorous prosecution. Sutherland and Cressey propose a theory to account for embezzlement in which the individual in a position of financial trust has no intention of violating his trust. It is only when the potential violator defines his financial problems as unshareable and sees that his position offers a possible solution. Even when they begin to take money, many embezzlers see their actions as borrowing rather than stealing (*Ibid.*:253–254). Like forgers, the embezzler is typically well educated, middle-class and respected, as evid denced by the attainment of a position of financial trust. As Sutherland and Cressey point out, being caught usually bars the individual from further positions of financial trust (*Ibid.*:255), so most arrestees are first offenders.

Women constitute 24.6% of those arrested for embezzlement (see Appendix B). One way in which they differ somewhat from male offenders is that female embezzlers frequently steal from charities that are rarely audited, where income is often not watched as closely as in banks or businesses (Elliott, 1952:246–247). Women who embezzle from banks usually "shingle" small amounts from large accounts (*Ibid.*:247). The very high arrest rate of female offenders probably reflects the effects of several factors. One important fact is that women generally hold positions of lesser authority in banks and businesses, which means that their work would be more closely and more frequently checked than that of a bank president or vice president, for example. Another related consideration is that all persons in these lower positions have less education in accounting and financial manipulations than do those in higher status positions. This would probably mean that those in low status positions would use less sophisticated, more easily discovered methods of concealing their crime. This would be especially true of persons who embezzle from charities and often have no training and little experience in financial manipulation. In addition, since persons in low status jobs have fewer economic resources, they would be less able to replace the money before being detected, as Sutherland reports is true of many embezzlers (1970:254). Thus, we see that although the ways in which the crime is committed is the same for both men and women, the lesser training, low status positions and lesser ability to offer restitution that characterizes the jobs open to women, make it more likely that the women offender will get caught. Here we can again see dynamics similar to those described for larceny. The sex role link concerns the differential in both skills and economic opportunities of men and women which result in women being concentrated at the bottom of the economic ladder and in positions that make their crimes more vulnerable to detection.

In looking at these three categories of offenses, forgery and counterfeiting, fraud, and embezzlement in which women constitute over 23% of those arrested for each offense, it is clear that both sex role behavior and the particular way in which the category is defined operate to account for the larger than expected rate of female arrests. Each of these offenses is a type of theft in which force or confrontation is absent. In fact the victim may never know a crime has been committed. Women tend to have low arrest rates in those categories of theft involving use of force, threat of force and real or possible confrontation with the victim, *i.e.,* burglary, robbery, auto theft. If all the arrests in all categories of "taking other people's property" (robbery, burglary, larceny, auto theft, forgery and counterfeiting, fraud and embezzlement) are combined into a single one, then women account for only 18.5% of those arrested.[4] This is still above the 14.4% average for all arrests. Again, in the area of thefts of all types, it is important to keep in mind the large numbers of undetected crimes and the fact that women are often arrested for smaller thefts that are less well planned and more visible to the police. This is especially true in the case of larceny (shoplifting), check forgery, fraud and embezzlement.

As has been previously noted, the offense of prostitution is in many states defined as a female offense (Cooper and Podolsky, 1971:12). With the addition of commercialized vice to the category, we find that in 1970 women accounted for 79.3% of the arrests (see Appendix B). It is ironic that in some states it is also illegal for a person to be a customer of a prostitute, just as it is illegal to either buy or sell other illegitimate goods and services, *i.e.,* buy or sell narcotics, steal or receive stolen property. Yet in the case of prostitution, it is only the female who is arrested (*Ibid.*:2, 16–18). If we included one customer for each prostitution arrest, the proportion of female arrests would be reduced considerably. If male prostitutes and "street walkers" were added to the category, the female arrest rate would again go down some. In addition to these discrepancies, it seems curious that prostitution is separated from "other sex offenses" for which there was nearly an identical number of reported arrests in 1970 (see Appendix B). According to the F.B.I. this category includes "statutory rape, offenses against chastity, common decency, morals and the like" (Federal Bureau of

Investigation, 1970:62). One problem with this category is that the offense tends to be a status crime in which a woman is subject to arrest for "being a prostitute" as well as for specific acts of prostitution (Cooper and Podolsky, 1971:12–14). In some states this has given rise to subsidiary violations based on the prostitute's special status, *i.e.,* walking on the street at night, walking on the street at any time (*Ibid.*: 13–14; Elliott, 1952:231–232). This is a strong indication that prostitution is one crime around which a subculture exists. Subcultures both help individuals cope with outside pressures and perpetuate the behavior around which the subculture is built. Other sex offenses such as rape, statutory rape, sodomy violations and sexual attacks against children are based on specific acts and lack the status characteristic many prostitution statutes embody. A possible exception to this would be laws governing homosexual activity, but arrests for these offenses would not be of the magnitude of prostitution arrests. One reason for the large number of arrests for prostitution (nearly 50,000 in 1970) (see Appendix B) seems to be that arrest and subsequent fines operate as an informal licensing system in which the offender is arrested, posts bail, is freed and later pays a fine, depending on the number of previous arrests (Cooper and Podolsky, 1971:22–23). There appears to be a definite parallel to the way in which white collar crime by corporations is handled. In some areas the accused prostitute must submit to a VD test before the case may be concluded (*Ibid.*:23). Both the ways the laws are written and the ways in which they are enforced make it inevitable that most of those arrested for prostitution and commercialized vice will be women. If all categories of sex offenses (rape, prostitution and commercialized vice, other sex offenses) are combined, the percentage of female arrestees drops to 31%.[5]

In the category of narcotic drug law violations, women accounted for 15.6% of those arrested in 1970 (see Appendix B). According to the F.B.I., this includes "unlawful possession, sale or use" (1970:62). It is of interest to note that since 1958 the percentage of women arrested for these offenses has decreased slightly: 1958, 16.4% to 1970, 15.6% (see Appendix B).

Little study has been done on the female narcotic drug offender. Most available material focuses on males without mentioning women (Becker, 1964; Lindesmith, 1952). A descriptive study by Alan Sutter (1970) sheds some light on the role of the female drug user. He describes one category which he calls "The Dope Fiend Broad as a Hooker and Booster." These are women who, under the supervision of "an old man" support their and his habit by shoplifting or by prostitution (*Ibid.*:673–674). The sex role character of this type of drug user is obvious. Here the woman plays a dependent, secondary role in exchange for the love and protection of a man. In all the other categories Sutter describes, he implicitly assumes that only men are involved. While this may or may not be true, as no statistics are given, the pattern described does coincide with many facets of female crime in other categories. It centers around dependency on a man and tends to be petty in terms of the nature of the offense, thus making the woman vulnerable to arrest. Aside from such speculation, it is difficult to draw any more definite conclusion from the available data.

Women accounted for 19.7% of all vagrancy arrests in 1970 (see Appendix B). This category includes "vagabondage, begging, loitering, etc." (Federal Bureau of Investigation, 1970:62). Vagrancy laws are a means by

Appendix B Major crimes in the U.S.

	1958 [1]			1964 [2]			1970 [3]			Net Chg.
	Total	%♂	%♀	Total	%♂	%♀	Total	%♂	%♀	%♀
TOTAL (all crimes)	2,340,004	89.4	10.6	4,685,080	88.3	11.7	6,570,473	85.6	14.4	+ 3.8
Criminal homicide										
(a) murder/mansl.	2,303	80.1	19.9	6,412	82.2	17.8	12,836	84.6	15.4	– 4.5
(b) mansl. by negl.	1,166	90.5	9.5	2,685	90.1	9.9	3,020	89.3	10.7	+ 1.2
Forcible Rape	3,680	100.0	–	9,415	100.0	–	15,411	100.0	–	0
Robbery	14,968	95.5	4.5	39,134	94.7	5.3	87,687	93.9	6.1	+ 1.6
Aggravated Assault	25,824	84.3	15.7	79,895	86.4	13.6	125,971	87.4	12.6	– 3.1
Burglary (B/E)	61,045	97.6	2.4	187,000	96.3	3.7	285,418	95.3	4.7	+ 2.3
Larceny (theft)	118,325	85.7	14.3	358,569	79.7	20.3	616,099	72.1	27.9	+13.0
Auto Theft	30,240	96.8	3.2	97,356	95.8	4.2	127,341	94.9	5.1	+ 1.9
SUBTOTAL	257,551	90.4	9.6	780,501	87.4	12.6	1,273,783	83.1	16.9	+ 7.3

Major crimes in California

	1958 [4]			1964 [5]			1968 [6]			Net Chg.
	Total	%♂	%♀	Total	%♂	%♀	Total	%♂	%♀	%♀
TOTAL	53,634	91.9	8.1	100,690	89.4	10.6	168,789	87.9	12.1	+ 4.0
Homicide	628	88.1	11.9	1,158	83.9	16.1	1,660	84.3	15.7	+ 3.8
Robbery	4,523	95.1	4.9	9,934	94.0	6.0	13,687	92.1	7.9	+ 3.0
Burglary	12,468	95.8	4.2	24,047	93.0	7.0	30,857	92.6	7.4	+ 3.2
Aggravated Assault	6,010	89.4	10.6	12,992	86.1	13.9	18,591	86.9	13.1	+ 2.5
Grand Theft (ex. auto)	3,349	89.3	10.7	8,150	83.6	16.4	11,114	84.2	15.8	+ 5.1
Forgery & Checks	8,300	84.4	15.6	9,411	80.2	19.8	10,681	72.5	27.5	+11.9
Sex Offenses	3,844	99.2	0.8	6,276	98.9	1.1	2,398	97.1	2.9	+ 2.1
Narcotics	6,029	88.6	11.4	10,919	84.8	15.2	49,274	85.4	14.6	+ 3.2
Rape							2,818	100.0	0	0
All Others	3,835	91.9	8.1	8,108	88.2	11.8	12,437	89.6	10.4	+ 2.3

[1] Federal Bureau of Investigation, *Uniform Crime Reports* (1958:96).
[2] Federal Bureau of Investigation, *Uniform Crime Reports* (1964:112).
[3] Federal Bureau of Investigation, *Crime in the United States* (1970:129).
[4] Bureau of Criminal Statistics, *Crime in California* (1958:36).
[5] Bureau of Criminal Statistics, *Crime in California* (1964:46).
[6] Bureau of Criminal Statistics, *Crime & Delinquency in California* (1968:53).

Other crimes in the U.S.

	1958 [1]			1964 [2]			1970 [3]			Net Chg.
	Total	%♂	%♀	Total	%♂	%♀	Total	%♂	%♀	%♀
Other Assaults	82,454	90.4	9.6	191,455	89.8	10.2	287,027	87.0	13.0	+ 3.4
Arson	–	–	–	5,220	91.3	8.7	9,409	90.8	9.2	+ 0.5
Forgery & Counterfeit.	11,317	84.9	15.1	30,637	81.8	18.2	43,833	76.3	23.7	+ 8.6
Fraud	19,489	85.7	14.3	45,998	81.0	19.0	76,861	72.9	27.1	+ 8.1*
Embezzlement				8,610	82.7	17.3	8,172	75.4	24.6	+ 7.3*
Rec. Stolen Property	5,504	92.3	7.7	18,152	90.2	9.8	61,517	90.7	9.3	+ 1.6
Vandalism	–	–	–	76,814	94.0	6.0	111,671	94.2	7.6	+ 1.6*
Weapons	18,611	95.0	5.0	47,287	93.4	6.6	102,725	93.3	6.7	+ 1.7
Prostitution & Com. Vice	17,482	31.0	69.0	28,190	22.0	78.0	49,344	20.7	79.3	+10.3
Sex Offenses	24,517	79.9	20.1	58,082	84.4	15.6	49,328	87.2	12.8	– 7.3
Narcotic Drug Laws	9,863	83.6	16.4	37,802	86.0	14.0	346,412	84.4	15.6	– 0.8
Gambling	61,546	90.1	9.9	103,814	91.8	8.2	84,804	91.9	8.1	– 1.8
Offenses ag. Family & Children	23,701	91.6	8.6	57,454	90.7	9.3	56,620	91.1	8.9	+ 0.3
Driving Under Infl.	102,219	94.7	5.3	225,672	93.4	6.6	423,522	93.4	6.6	+ 1.3
Liquor Laws	52,707	84.7	15.3	153,829	87.8	12.2	222,464	87.1	12.9	– 2.4
Drunkenness	908,957	92.6	7.4	1,458,821	92.0	8.0	1,512,672	92.9	7.1	– 0.3
Disorderly Conduct	281,997	85.0	15.0	475,756	86.6	13.4	589,642	85.0	15.0	0
Vagrancy	88,351	92.4	7.6	132,955	90.9	9.1	101,093	80.3	19.7	+12.1
All Others	–	–	–	510,624	85.7	14.3	804,780	83.8	16.2	+ 1.9*
Suspicion	96,740	89.7	10.3	102,106	89.3	10.7	70,173	85.9	14.1	+ 3.8
Curfew	–	–	–	64,784	81.0	19.0	105,548	78.8	21.2	+ 2.2*
Runaway	–	–	–	70,517	55.9	44.1	179,073	48.4	51.6	+ 7.5*

*Change from 1964 to 1970 only.

[1] Federal Bureau of Investigation, *Uniform Crime Reports* (1958:96).

[2] Federal Bureau of Investigation, *Uniform Crime Reports* (1964:112).

[3] Federal Bureau of Investigation, *Crime in the United States* (1970:129).

which local officials attempt to control migratory cheap labor and undesirables (Chambliss, 1969:60–61). When applied to women, it appears that such laws are often directed at known or "potential" prostitutes (Cooper and Podolsky, 1971:12–13). Using vagrancy statutes is often an easier and less time-consuming way for police to control prostitution or suspected prostitution. It requires less explicit evidence, does not involve the customer, and yet serves the same end of clearing an area of prostitutes for a time (*Ibid.*:25–27). In addition to vagrancy charges, disorderly conduct arrests are often made with the same objective (*Ibid.*:27).

The only other two categories in which female arrest rates exceed their expected average are for the juvenile offenses of curfew (21.2% in 1970) and runaway (51.6% in 1970). The large percentage of female arrests in both cases are related to sex roles. In the case of curfew, girls are more likely to be stopped if out after dark, unaccompanied by an adult or a male. Such curfew arrests are also a means by which police can control suspected underage prostitutes or girls parking with older males. The large number of female arrests for runaway appear to be related to the following factors. Parents are probably more likely to attempt to find underage girls who have run away, and police are probably more likely to question strange young girls than boys in a similar situation. In addition, girls are probably less able than boys of the same age group to support themselves except by prostitution or shoplifting which makes it more likely that they will be picked up by the police. At any rate, these two categories represent status offenses that are probably often used in place of other charges, *i.e.*, larceny, vagrancy, prostitution, disturbing the peace, drunkenness. They also graphically illustrate the tendency to treat women in a paternalistic manner (Nagel and Weitzman, 1971:197–198) and to express concern for their "state of living" or what "they are becoming," over and beyond specific offenses they commit. Prostitution, curfew and runaway are excellent examples of these attitudes toward women offenders.

Conclusion

When we look at crimes in which female arrest rates are well below their average for all crimes, we again find a close relationship to sex roles. Women tend not be arrested for crimes that require stereotyped male behavior, *i.e.*, robbery, burglary. When they are arrested on such charges, it appears that they have played secondary, supportive roles. Even in crimes where women are more frequently arrested, their involvement in the offense is closely tied to the female sex role. Where women are often sole perpetrators, *i.e.*, homicide, shoplifting, the close ties are still evident. Where the crime requires behavior that is consistent with expected female roles, women appear to make up a large number of the petty criminals (forgery, fraud, embezzlement, prostitution, vagrancy, curfew and runaway). Thus, women seem to commit crimes in roles auxiliary to men, in keeping with their sex roles and for lesser returns, often making them more vulnerable to arrest. In addition, those acts for which women have received adequate training in the normal process of growing up, *i.e.*, forgery, are more likely to have high rates of women arrestees. Those for which more masculine skills and techniques are required, *i.e.*, auto theft, will likely show a lower than expected rate of female participation.

In addition to these characteristics of female arrestees and their techniques of committing the various offenses, the rates are definitely affected by the ways in which the category boundaries are drawn. For example, the general term theft encompasses the offense categories of robbery, burglary, larceny, auto theft, forgery and counterfeiting, fraud and embezzlement. Indeed, when the arrest rates for all these offenses are combined, women's arrest rate is much closer to the female average for all crimes. This also appears true in the area of sex offenses, when we combine rates of arrest for rape, prostitution and other sex offenses. Thus, there seems to be a tendency in the law itself to classify offenses in ways that correspond to sex role differences. This principle operates even more obviously when we compare major and other crimes. Those classified as major, with the exception of theft, are typically ones that require active independence on the part of the offender and the use or threat of violence.

NOTES

1. Calculated from data given in Otto Pollak (1950:4).
2. Percentage calculated from figures in Appendix B.
3. Calculated by using Cameron's 80% figure and rate in Appendix B.
4. Calculated from 1970 figures in Appendix B.
5. Calculated from figures in Federal Bureau of Investigation (1970:129).

REFERENCES

Becker, Howard
1964 Outsiders: Studies in the Sociology of Deviance. New York: The Free Press.

Bureau of Criminal Statistics
1958 Crime in California. Sacramento: State of California, Department of Justice.
1964 Crime in California. Sacramento: State of California, Department of Justice.
1968 Crime in California. Sacramento: State of California, Department of Justice.

Cameron, Mary Owen
1964 The Booster and the Snitch. New York: The Free Press.

Chambliss, William
1969 Crime and the Legal Process. New York: McGraw-Hill.

Cooper, Janice and Raphael Podolsky
1971 "Prostitution." Unpublished manuscript (June 5).

Elliott, Mabel
1952 Crime in Modern Society. New York: Harper and Row.

Federal Bureau of Investigation
1958 Uniform Crime Reports for the United States. Washington: U.S. Department of Justice.
1964 Uniform Crime Reports for the United States. Washington: U.S. Department of Justice.
1968 Crime in the U.S. Washington: U.S. Department of Justice.
1970 Crime in the U.S. Washington: U.S. Department of Justice.

Goode, William
1969 "Violence Among Intimates." Crimes of Violence. Edited by Donald Mulvihill, *et. al.* Washington: U.S. Government Printing Office (December).

Lamert, Edwin
1971 Human Deviance, Social Problems, and Social Control. Second Edition. Englewood Cliffs, New Jersey: Prentice-Hall.

Lindesmith, Alfred
1952 Opiate Addiction. Bloomington, Indiana: Principia.

Nagel, Stuart and Lenore Weitzman
1971 "Women as Litigants." The Hastings Law Journal 23(1)(November):171–198.

Piliavin, Irving and Scott Briar
1968 "Police Encounters With Juveniles." Deviance: The Interactionist Perspective. Edited by Earl Rubington. New York: Macmillan.

Pollak, Otto
1950 The Criminality of Women. Philadelphia: University of Pennsylvania Press.

Sutherland, Edwin
1949 White Collar Crime. New York: Holt, Rinehart and Winston.

Sutherland, Edwin and Donald Cressey
1970 Criminology. Eighth Edition. Philadelphia: J. B. Lippincott Company.

Sutter, Alan
1970 "A Hierarchy of Drug Users." The Sociology of Crime and Delinquency. Edited by Marvin Wolfgang. New York: John Wiley & Sons.

Ward, David, Maurice Jackson and Renée Ward
1969 "Crimes of Violence by Women." Crimes of Violence. Edited by Donald Mulvihill, *et. al.* Washington: U.S. Government Printing Office.

Wolfgang, Marvin
1958 Patterns in Criminal Homicide. Philadelphia: University of Pennsylvania Press.

Sex Differences and Psychiatric Disorders

Bruce P. Dohrenwend
and Barbara Snell Dohrenwend

Since the turn of the century, over 80 studies designed to count both untreated and cases of psychiatric disorder have been carried out in different parts of the world; in the majority of these, data were reported for males and females separately. The procedures and results of these epidemiological studies of "true" prevalence are analyzed with respect to several questions: Are total rates over all types of functional disorder higher among males or among females? Which types of disorder are more prevalent among males and which among females? How do sex differences in overall rates and in different types of disorder vary over time? What are the implications of the findings for theory about sex roles and psychiatric disorder?

In their 1973 study of sex roles and mental illness, Gove and Tudor discovered much in the writings of contemporary social scientists to suggest that "women find their position in society to be more frustrating and less rewarding than do men and that this may be a relatively recent development" (p. 816). Accordingly, they "postulate that, because of the difficulties associated with the feminine role in modern Western societies, more women than men become mentally ill" (p. 816).

To investigate this hypothesis, Gove and Tudor focused on research conducted since World War II, on the grounds that the war marked a high point of change in the role of women, with significant portions of married women entering the work force for the first time. They also restricted their coverage to North America and Europe where, they assumed, economic and technological conditions related to industrialization have promoted the posited change in the role of women. They concluded that the epidemiological evidence demonstrates that women do in fact have higher rates of "mental illness" than do men and that this is, indeed, a relatively recent development.

However, most of the evidence on which they base their conclusion is inadequate for the problem: It does not deal with trends over time; it omits data on the personality disorders; it includes treatment statistics that are

"Sex Differences and Psychiatric Disorders" by Bruce P. Dowrenwend and Barbara Dowrenwend from *American Journal of Sociology,* 81, 6 (1976), 1447–1454. Reprinted by permission of the University of Chicago Press.

limited and can often be misleading (e.g., Dohrenwend and Dohrenwend 1969); and, where it consists of a presentation of results from some community studies that are not restricted to treated rates (Gove and Tudor 1973, p. 819), the findings are refracted through Gove and Tudor's highly idiosyncratic definition of "mental illness" (p. 812). In this definition, such disparate types of diagnosed psychiatric disorder as psychoses and neuroses are lumped together and tallied along with objective measures of milder signs and symptoms of personal distress whose relation to clinical psychiatric disorder is far from evident, especially when, as in some of the studies considered by Gove and Tudor, the test items are not calibrated against psychiatric evaluations or patient criterion groups (e.g., Dohrenwend 1973).

The most important data that Gove and Tudor bring to bear on the issue, and the only data on trends over time, consist of overall rates of functional disorder (not excluding the personality disorders) that we summarized in our 1969 review of epidemiological studies of "true" prevalence conducted since the turn of the century (Dohrenwend and Dohrenwend 1969). All of these studies identify cases of psychiatric disorder in general populations by one of the following procedures or some combination of them: evaluations by psychiatrists of data from key informants and agency records; evaluations by psychiatrists of data from direct interviews with community residents; and, especially in more recent studies, scores on screening test questions that have been calibrated against psychiatric evaluations or against criterion groups of psychiatric patients (Dohrenwend and Dohrenwend 1969, 1974*b*).

Perceptively, Gove and Tudor divided the North American and European studies that we included in our 1969 review into, roughly, pre–World War II and post–World War II groups (because of the gap in publication between 1943 and 1950, the division is actually on the basis of whether they were published before 1950 or in 1950 or later). They found that overall rates were consistently higher for men in the earlier studies and for women in the later ones (Gove and Tudor 1973, p. 828). Other things being equal, it would seem that these results provide the strongest support that Gove and Tudor have for their hypothesis. Other things, however, are not equal.

Analysis of Epidemiological Studies of "True" Prevalence Conducted in the United States and Europe

Since our 1969 review, we have updated our coverage of the epidemiological literature. Altogether, we have found over 80 studies of the "true" prevalence of pschiatric disorder in community populations. The majority of them provide at least some relevant data on sex differences, and 33 of those that do were conducted in North America and Europe.[1]

Table 1 shows that, as Gove and Tudor found on the basis of data from our 1969 review, overall rates in the North American and European studies are consistently higher for men in the pre-1950 investigations and for women in those published in 1950 or later. Accepted at face value, this apparent change provides striking support for Gove and Tudor's hypothesis. Note, however, that by contrast with the overall rates trends on sex dif-

Table 1 Number of European and North American studies reporting higher rates of psychiatric disorders for men or for women according to publication prior to 1950 or in 1950 or later

Date of publication and type of psychopathology	*Studies in which rate is higher for (N)*	
	Males	Females
Before 1950:		
All types	7	2
Psychosis	3	3
Neurosis	1	2
Personality disorder	3	0
1950 or later:		
All types	2	22
Psychosis	5	10
Neurosis	0	15
Personality disorder	11	3

ferences for the major subclassifications of functional psychiatric disorder do not show such reversals between the earlier and the later studies. Rates of personality disorder in particular are consistently higher for men in both the earlier and the later studies, and there is no consistent evidence of higher male rates of either neurosis or psychosis in the pre-1950 studies. These results for the various subtypes of disorder are difficult to explain in terms of Gove and Tudor's theory of changing sex roles.

Table 2 shows that something else has happened to reported rates of psychiatric disorders since 1950. Overall rates and rates for the major subclassifications of psychosis, neurosis, and personality disorder have all increased dramatically from the earlier to the later studies—for men and for women. Accepted at face value, these results not only would be consistent with the hypothesis that the role of women has become more stressful, but also would imply more stress in the male role since World War II. Moreover, the increase in the median of the overall rates from under 2% to over 15% for both sexes appears to be of epidemic proportions.

Amidst a plethora of possible speculations about the reasons for such an extraordinary increase, there is one firm fact. One thing that we know has increased is the breadth of our definitions of what constitutes a psychiatric case. A great impetus to this expansion was provided by the experience of psychiatrists in screening and treatment during World War II. As Raines wrote in his foreword to the 1952 *Diagnostic and Statistical Manual* of the American Psychiatric Association, which reflected that experience: "Only about 10% of the total cases fell into any of the categories ordinarily seen in public mental hospitals. Military psychiatrists, induction station psychiatrists, and Veterans Administration psychiatrists, found themselves operating within the limits of a nomenclature specifically not designed for 90% of the cases handled" (p. vi).

The expansion has been a continuing process. One can see it in the development of such concepts as "pseudoneurotic schizophrenia" (Hoch and Polatin 1949) and, reflecting the efforts of the mental health education

Table 2 Medians and ranges of percentages of psychiatric disorder reported for European and North American studies before 1950 and in 1950 or later

	Before 1950		*1950 or later*	
	Males	Females	Males	Females
Overall:				
Median	1.89	1.91	15.4	23.5
Range	1.1–9.0	1.0–6.0	2.0–51.8	2.7–75.2
Studies (*N*)	9		22*	
Psychosis:				
Median	0.445	0.43	.120	1.69
Range	0.23–0.90	0.247–0.91	0.006–4.6	0.009–56.0
Studies (*N*)	6		14†	
Neurosis:				
Median	0.20	0.26	3.56	8.0
Range	0.14–0.22	0.11–0.42	0.30–44.0	0.31–64.0
Studies (*N*)	3		15	
Personality disorder:				
Median	0.63	0.12	5.85	2.94
Range	0.11–1.08	0.01–0.18	0.046–18.0	0.047–11.0
Studies (*N*)	3		13†	

*Two studies reported only the relative ranking of men and women.
†One study reported only the relative ranking of men and women.

movement, in a dramatic increase between the 1950s and the 1960s in the willingness of the public to broaden its own definition of what it identifies, at least attitudinally, as "mental illness" (e.g., Dohrenwend and Chin-Shong 1967). Consistent with these changes in conceptions of what constitutes a case, there has been an increase, as table 3 shows, in rates of psychiatric disorder reported in the true prevalence studies not only between the pre- and post–World War II periods but also during the latter period.

While the expanding concepts of what constitutes a case appear to provide an economical explanation of the general tendency for reported rates of all types of functional psychiatric disorders to increase over time for both men and women, they do not explain why the rate of increase should be so much greater for women than for men (table 2) that sex differences in overall rates are actually reversed between the earlier and the later studies (table 1). We think that the most plausible and parsimonious explanation is again methodological rather than substantive.

In the studies published prior to 1950, there was a far greater tendency than in later ones for the investigators to rely on key informants and official records to identify potential cases (Dohrenwend and Dohrenwend 1974*b*, p. 425). Such procedures are well suited to identifying the types of personality disorder characterized by chronic antisocial behavior and addiction to alcohol or drugs: persons, disproportionately male, who show such problems tend to leave records with police and other agents of social control or, at the least, to develop unfavorable reputations in their communities (cf. Cawte 1972; Mazer 1974).[2] Correspondingly, such procedures are less likely to identify persons, disproportionately female, whose neurotic problems are more private (cf. Cawte 1972).

By contrast with the earlier epidemiological studies of true prevalence,

Table 3 Medians and ranges of overall percentages of psychiatric disorder reported for European and North American studies, by date of publication

	Before 1950		*1950–59*		*1960 or later*	
	Males	Females	Males	Females	Males	Females
Median	1.89	1.91	12.1	13.6	18.43	26.75
Range	1.1–9.0	1.0–6.0	2.0–22.1	2.7–26.0	4.8–51.8	2.4–75.2
Studies (*N*)	9		6		16	

the investigations published in 1950 or later tended to rely for the most part on direct interviews with all respondents for data collection. Moreover, beginning in the 1960s when, as can be seen in table 3, the strong trend for women to show higher overall rates than men emerged, a growing number of the investigators have adopted screening inventories such as the ones developed by Langer (1962), Macmillan (1957), and several investigators who have used variations on the Cornell Medical Index (e.g., Rawnsley 1966) to identify cases. Typically, these inventories focus on symptoms of anxiety, depression, and physiological disturbances that are more indicative of neurosis and some aspects of manic-depressive psychosis than of personality disorders or schizophrenia. Given their content, it is not surprising that scores on such measures are generally higher for women than for men (cf. Cawte 1972; Mazer, 1974).

These contrasts in method are confounded with date of publication in the studies whose results are sumarized in table 2, so that a direct test of their impact is difficult to make. There are, however, four studies concerning the United States and Europe published after 1950 that relied on key informants and records instead of direct interviews with all subjects to identify potential cases. The median of the ratio of female to male overall rates for these studies is 1.18. By contrast, the corresponding median for the seven post-1950 studies in Western communities that relied on the Langner screening items or a similar measure is 1.92. Moreover, one study reports for the same subjects both sex differences based on key informant reports and sex differences based on self reports to questions adapted from the Cornell Medical Index (CMI) (Cawte 1972). The men are found by the informants to be more disturbed (p. 59); the women report more symptoms on the CMI (pp. 74–75).

It is possible, then, to speculate that the results in tables 2 and 3 indicate that there have been increases in rates of the functional psychiatric disorders in modern Western societies since World War II and that, particularly since 1960, these increases have been greater for women than for men. It seems more plausible, however, to interpret these results as being a function of changes in concepts and methods for defining what constitutes a psychiatric case.

Where Truth Lies in the Epidemiological Studies of True Prevalence

For us, the truth of these epidemiological studies does not lie in the accuracy of their estimates of rates for this or that type of psychiatric disorder, much less for overall rates. Such estimates, as we have shown, vary with contrasts in the concepts and methods used at different times and in different places by the various investigators. Instead, their truth lies in the consistent relationships they report between various social variables and various types of disorder across—even in spite of—such methodological differences. We have found such relationships with social class (Dohrenwend and Dohrenwend 1969, 1974*b*) and with rural versus urban location (Dohrenwend and Dorenwend 1974*a*).

More recently we have been able to reach certain conclusions about sex differences, which we summarize here. With time since the turn of the century specified as pre– and post–World War II, with place specified as rural and urban settings in selected United States and European communities in contrast with selected communities in the rest of the world, and with the functional psychiatric disorders defined as operationalized by the various epidemiological investigators who have worked in these communities: (1) There are no consistent sex differences in rates of functional psychoses in general (34 studies) or one of the two major subtypes, schizophrenia (26 studies), in particular; rates of the other subtype, manic-depressive psychosis, are generally higher among women (18 out of 24 studies). (2) Rates of neurosis are consistently higher for women regardless of time and place (28 out of 32 studies). (3) By contrast, rates of personality disorder are consistently higher for men regardless of time and place (22 out of 26 studies).

These results cannot easily be explained by role theories arguing that at some time and place one or the other sex is under greater stress and, hence, more prone to psychiatric disorder in general. Instead, the findings suggest that we should discard undifferentiated, undimensional concepts of psychiatric disorder and with them false questions about whether women or men are more prone to "mental illness." In their place we would substitute an issue posed by the relatively high female rates of neurosis and manic-depressive psychosis, with their possible common denominator of depressive symptomatology, and the relatively high male rates of personality disorders with their possible common denominator of irresponsible and antisocial behavior. The important question then becomes, What is there in the endowments and experiences of men and women that pushes them in these different deviant directions?

NOTES

1. However, some of these studies present findings based on ratings or screening scores that do not distinguish among diagnostic types and can be tallied with other studies only for total or overall rates of functional psychiatric disorder. Moreover, not all of the studies that give diagnostic breakdowns do so for the same subtypes of disorder; hence, the more detail we seek beyond overall rates, the more studies we are forced to omit from our analysis. Because of space limitations, we present summary tables only. Interested readers can obtain more detailed tables and bibliography by writing to us at the Social Psychiatry Research Unit, Columbia University, 100 Haven Avenue, New York, New York 10032.
2. It can be argued, in fact, that none of the "true" prevalence studies, cross-sectional in nature, use the appropriate methods for identifying the mobile and hazard-prone individuals who show the antisocial types of personality disorder. Far better for this purpose would be prospective studies of cohorts identified from birth records or early childhood records and followed to their destinations, whether residence in the community of birth, another com-

munity, a jail or other institution, or an early grave (cf. Robins 1966). Such studies, unfortunately, are extremely rare in psychiatric epidemiology.

REFERENCES

CAWTE, J. 1972. *Cruel, Poor and Brutal Nations.* Honolulu: University of Hawaii Press.

DOHRENWEND, B. P. 1973. "Some Issues in the Definition and Measurement of Psychiatric Disorders in General Populations." Pp. 480–89 in *Proceedings of the 14th National Meeting of the Public Health Conference on Records and Statistics.* DHEW Publication no. (HRA) 74-1214, National Center for Health Statistics. Washington, D.C.: Government Printing Office.

DOHRENWEND, B. P., and E. Chin-Shong. 1967. "Social Status and Attitudes toward Psychological Disorder: The Problem of Tolerance of Deviance." *American Sociological Review* 32 (June): 417–33.

DOHRENWEND, B. P., and B. S. DOHRENWEND. 1969. *Social Status and Psychological Disorder.* New York: Wiley.

———. 1974*a*. "Psychiatric Disorders in Urban Settings." Pp. 424–47 in *American Handbook of Psychiatry.* 2d ed. Vol. 2. *Child and Adolescent Psychiatry, Sociocultural and Community Psychiatry,* edited by S. Arieti and G. Caplan. New York: Basic.

———. 1974*b*. "Social and Cultural Influences on Psychology." *Annual Review of Psychology* 25:417–52.

GOVE, W. R., and J. F. TUDOR. 1973. "Adult Sex Roles and Mental Illness." *American Journal of Sociology* 78 (January): 812–35.

HOCH, P., and P. POLATIN. 1949. "Pseudoneurotic Forms of Schizophrenia." *Psychiatric Quarterly* 23 (April): 248–76.

LANGNER, T. S. 1962. "A Twenty-two Item Screening Score of Psychiatric Symptoms Indicating Impairment." *Journal of Health and Social Behavior* 3 (Winter): 269–76.

MACMILLAN, A. M. 1957. "The Health Opinion Survey: Technique for Estimating Prevalence of Psychoneurotic and Related Types of Disorder in Communities." *Psychological Reports* 3 (September): 325–39.

MAZER, M. 1974. "People in Predicament: A Study in psychiatric and Psychosocial Epidemiology." *Social Psychiatry* 9 (July): 85–90.

RAINES, G. N. 1952. "Foreword." Pp. v–xi in *Diagnostic and Statistical Manual: Mental Disorders,* Committee on Nomenclature and Statistics of the American Psychiatric Association. Washington, D.C.: American Psychiatric Association.

RAWNSLEY, K. 1966. "Congruence of Independent Measures of Psychiatric Morbidity." *Journal of Psychosomatic Research* 10 (July): 84–93.

ROBINS, L. N. 1966. *Deviant Children Grown Up.* Baltimore: Williams & Wilkins.

Cinderella's Stepsisters: A Feminist Perspective on Anorexia Nervosa and Bulimia

Marlene Boskind-Lodahl

Reading the literature on female socialization reminds one of the familiar image of Cinderella's stepsisters industriously lopping off their toes and heels so as to fit into the glass slipper (key to the somewhat enigmatic heart of the prince)—when of course it was never intended for them anyway. [1]

During my early months of internship in 1974 in the mental health section of a university clinic, I encountered Anne, a lively, attractive, and slim young woman of eighteen. For three years she had been on a cycle of gorging and starving which had continued without relief. She felt desperate and out of control.

Anne was the first in a series of 138 binger-starvers that I was to treat. It became clear that the exaggerated gorging and purging reported by these patients was part of a self-perpetuating syndrome that was primarily a problem of women.[2] The women I interviewed were consumed by constant but self-defeating attempts to change their bodies so that they might each fit into the glass slipper. Anne was well informed about her symptoms. She even recommended books for me to read. I searched the traditional literature for insights into her problem. Bruch, who has written extensively on eating disorders, has most clearly diagnosed the starvation or anorexic aspect of this syndrome. According to her, characteristics of primary anorexia nervosa are: (1) severe weight loss; (2) a disturbance of body image and body concept which Bruch calls "delusional"; (3) a disturbance of cognitive interpretation of body stimuli, combined with the failure to recognize signs of nutritional need; (4) hyperactivity and denial of fatigue; (5) a paralyzing sense of ineffectiveness; (6) a family life in which (*a*) self-expression was neither encouraged nor reinforced. (*b*) the mother was frustrated in career aspirations, subservient to her husband, and generally conscien-

"Cinderella's Stepsisters" by Marlene Boskind-Lodahl, *Signs* 2, 1 (1976), 120–146. Reprinted by permission of the University of Chicago Press and the author.

tious and overprotective, (*c*) the father was preoccupied with outer appearances, admired fitness and beauty, and expected proper behavior and measurable achievements from his children.[3] Little else, however, was helpful. Most writers treated the starvation and the binge-ing (bulimia) as separate and distinct diseases, although several researchers had noted in passing the compulsion of the self-starver to binge.

This paper is intended to provide the nucleus of a new approach. Relating anorexia to bulimia, it may also help to stimulate successful therapies for the young women whom I shall describe as "bulimarexics."

Psychoanalytic Interpretation of Anorexia and Bulimia

The view of anorexia as a rejection of femininity which often manifests itself as a fear of oral impregnation is widely held (see fig. 1). Szyrynski observes:

> They appear to be afraid of growing and maturation and they find it difficult to accept . . . their sexual identity. In the case of girls, fear of pregnancy often dominates the picture; pregnancy being symbolized by food, getting fat means becoming pregnant. Such fantasies are also quite often formulated as oral impregnation. The girl, after kissing a boy for the first time, gets panicky lest pregnancy should follow. She pays particular attention to her gaining weight and not infrequently a casual remark of a visitor, a relative, or a friend, that she is looking well and probably has gained some weight will unleash the disastrous ritual of self-starvation.[4]

Behind such fears is said to be an unconscious hatred of the mother, who is ineffective and discontent but castrating. Wulff, writing in the early 1930s, describes such psychodynamics.

> This neurosis is characterized by the person's fight against her sexuality which, through previous repression, has become greedy and insatiable. . . . This sexuality is pregenitally oriented and sexual satisfaction is perceived as a "dirty meal." Periods of depression in which patients stuff themselves and feel themselves "fat," . . . "dirty," or "pregnant," . . . alternate with "good" periods in which they behave ascetically, feel slim and conduct themselves normally. . . . Psychoanalysis discloses that the unconscious content of the syndrome is a preoedipal mother conflict, which may be covered by an oral-sadistic Oedipus conflict. The patients have an intense unconscious hatred against their mothers and against femininity.[5]

Lindner, describing the case of Laura in *The Fifty-Minute Hour,* is a more modern proponent of traditional theory.[6] His patient, Laura, complained of the same gorging-fasting symptoms as my patient, Anne, but his interpretation of these symptoms diverges sharply from mine. He fits Laura neatly into a stereotyped feminine role, maintaining that her symptoms show a neurotic, unhealthy resistance to that role. His cure involves putting an end to that hatred of femininity by helping the woman learn to accept and to act out the traditional female role, often described as accommodating, receptive, or passive. What Lindner's Laura "really wanted" was to become pregnant. He observes Laura's desperate desire for a man, but

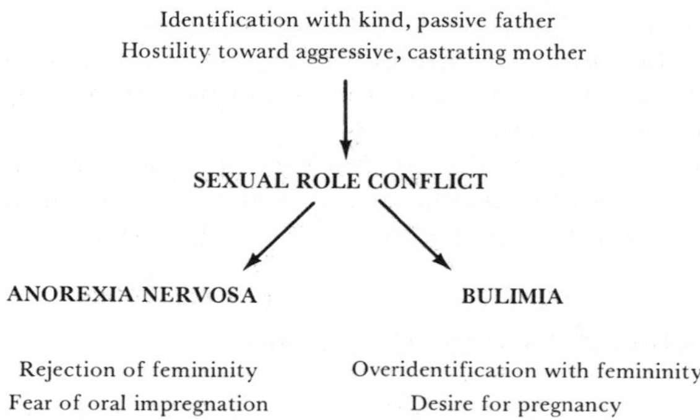

Figure 1 Psychoanalytic model of anorexia nervosa and bulimia

presupposes that it is healthy for a woman to feel desperate without a man and likewise to feel completely fulfilled once she is in a relationship.

Bruch writes more critically on the oral impregnation interpretation. She states that "modern psychoanalytic thinking has turned away from this merely symbolic, often analogistic etiological approach and focuses now on the nature of the parent-child relationship from the beginning." However, she confirms that "even today fear of oral impregnation is the one psychodynamic issue most consistently looked for."[7] The fact that most anorexic women suffer from amenorrhea, interruption of the menstrual cycle, is seen as further evidence that these women are rejecting their "femininity."[8] Medical evidence has shown, however, that amenorrhea is consistently observed in women with abnormally low body weight who do not have symptoms of primary anorexia. This suggests that it is low body weight that is the key factor in initiating hormonal changes associated with amenorrhea.[9]

Women Who Become Bulimarexic

My experience with bulimarexics contradicts standard psychoanalytic theory (see fig. 2). Far from rejecting the stereotype of femininity—that of the accommodating, passive, dependent woman—these young women have never questioned their assumptions that wifehood, motherhood, and intimacy with men are the fundamental components of femininity. I came to understand that their obsessive pursuit of thinness constitutes not only an acceptance of this ideal but an exaggerated striving to achieve it.[10] Their attempts to control their physical appearance demonstrate a disproportionate concern with pleasing others, particularly men—a reliance on others to validate their sense of worth.[11] They have devoted their lives to fulfilling the feminine *role* rather than the individual person. None has developed a basic sense of personal power or of self worth.

Bruch says that these women have a basic *delusion* "of not having an identity of their own, of not even owning their body and its sensations, with the specific inability of recognizing hunger as a sign of nutritional needs." She attributes this to, among other things, "the mother's superimposing on the child her own concept of the child's needs."[12] Thus the child, believing that she is hungry because her mother says so, has little sense of what hunger is about internally. In my experience with these women, the feeling of not having any identity is not a delusion or a misperception but a reality which need not be caused solely by the stereotyped protective mother but by other cultural, social, and psychological pressures as well.

Anne, for example, was a good, generally submissive child. She had lived her life the way "she was supposed to"—precisely her problem. She had been socialized by her parents to believe that society would reward her good looks: "Some day the boys are going to go crazy over you." "What a face! With your good looks you'll never have to worry about getting a job." Clinging and dependent, she could not see herself as a separate person. Our early sessions had an unreal quality. I searched for a glimpse of unique

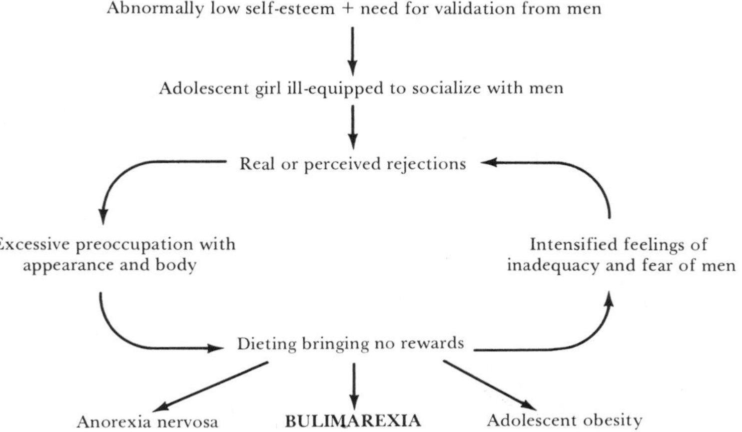

Figure 2 Development of bulimarexic behavior

character, but Anne had no identifiable sense of self from which to project a real person. Her dependency on others prevented any development of self. Most of the women in my study had been rewarded for their physical attractiveness and submissive "goodness," while characteristics such as independence, self-reliance, and assertiveness were generally punished by parents, grandparents, teachers, and peers. Peggy said, "I was always a tomboy. In fact at the age of ten to twelve I was stronger and faster than any of the boys. After I won a race against a boy, I was given the cold shoulder by the rest of the boys in my class. The girls teased me and my parents put pressure on me to 'start acting like a girl should.' I did, and stopped having as much fun."

Wulff refers to an intense, unconscious mother hate in these women. In my experience they were, on the contrary, painfully conscious of despising their mothers, most of whom they described as weak and unhappy, women who had abandoned careers in order to raise children. "My mother wanted to be a lawyer but gave it all up when she married my father." Though the mothers are painted as generally ineffectual, they do exercise power in one limited realm: over their children. There, as if they are compensating for their misery elsewhere, they are often suffocating, dominating, and manipulative. Rather than rejecting the passive aggressive behavior of their mothers and with it the more destructive results of such behavior, the women to whom I listened described their struggle for a social acceptance that would allow them to enact their mother's role. Most of them also strongly identified with their fathers, despite the fact that many fathers spent little time with their families. Instead, they concentrated on interests outside the home. Some of the women reported that the fathers were more persistent in their demands for prettiness and feminine behavior than the mothers. Fathers were objects of hero worship, even though they were preoccupied, distant, or emotionally rejecting.

A distorted concept of body size, a characteristic of the anorexics described by Bruch and of the bulimarexics I have studied, is related to the parental and societal expectations that emphasize physical appearance. At the first session with Anne, I was struck by the utter distortion of her body size. She complained frequently of how fat she was; I saw her as exceedingly thin.

M. B.-L. Why don't you stand up and point out to me where you experience yourself as fat.

ANNE Here . . . here . . . everywhere. [She jabbed and pulled.]

I noted at this session that Anne's "distorted body image" was linked to a complete lack of confidence in her own ability to control her behavior. She reported that she felt inadequate as a woman and that she had never been able to sustain a loving relationship with a man.

As well as striving to perfect and control their physical appearance, the bulimarexics displayed a need for achievement. All the women were high achievers academically and above average in intellect. However, in most cases the drive to achieve had as its goal pleasing parents and marrying "well." Continued success in academe was essential to feelings of self worth, but the pressure to achieve, with its rewards, was expected to be forgotten and tucked away in exchange for the fulfillments that marriage and childbearing could bring. These women saw achievement mainly in terms of what rewards it could provoke from others. For example, a doctor is more likely to meet and desire for a mate a woman who is educated; a woman is most likely to meet this man in a university. Achievement was not seen in terms of intrinsic rewards to the self.

Obviously, women who grew up struggling to perfect the female role expect that perfection to be rewarded by fulfillment. Their expectations are founded on what they perceive to be the expectations and standards of the rest of the world for them. It is expectation that has left the women I interviewed sadly vulnerable to rejection. In adolescence they begin to look eagerly for their reward, for the men who will see them as they have struggled to be seen. But rather than being offered rows of handsome princes waiting to court, many women suffer male rejection about this time. For others the rejection was *perceived* rather than actual (i.e., these adolescent girls felt rejected if they were not pursued by males and socially active). The experience of male rejection often precipitates dieting. The girl somehow believes that the appearance of her body must be related to the reason for her rejection. Bruch describes a young woman who could trace the beginning of her anorexic behavior to an incident she experienced as a rejection.

> Celia (No. 12) had begun her noneating regimen during her second year in college, when her boyfriend commented that she weighed nearly as much as he. He was of slight build weighing only 130 lbs. and was sensitive about this, feeling that his manliness was at stake. He expressed the desire that she lose a few pounds and she went on a diet in an effort to please him. However she resented that he had "fixed" their relationship at a certain weight. When she first talked about this she said, "I completely lost my appetite"; later she added that she had been continuously preoccupied with food but denied it to herself. . . . As she began to lose weight she experienced a great sense of strength and independence.[13]

Some women reported that they were, in fact, chubby at this time, but others described themselves as slim but not slim enough, according to their ideal image of what they believed a beautiful body should look like. Along with these slimming efforts, other attempts were sometimes made to beautify the body; three women reported having their noses straightened. However, these dieting attempts also do not produce anticipated rewards (i.e., male attentiveness).

When the expectations of these women of being desired and pursued by men did not materialize, they believed themselves to be undesirable, unattractive, and unworthy. These beliefs reinforced their already existing pervasive sense of inadequacy. Fear of rejection then became a crucial motivating force in their behavior. A rejection, real or perceived, shatters the self-image of the person who has constructed that image around the expectations of others. The person adopts a behavior that will protect her against future rejection. Lee supports this view: "There was an overwhelming preoccupation with weight and a tendency to view others according to their weight as a way of defending against feelings of inadequacy and fear of rejection by others. The struggle consists of a 'relentless pursuit of thinness.'"[14]

A fear of rejection as a source of Anne's symptoms appeared rather dramatically one day. After three months, she had not been able to recall her first food binge or the circumstances that had led to it. This day she was describing a binge she had had the night before. Using Gestalt techniques, I suggested she try a role-playing fantasy, something with which she was familiar.

M. B.-L. OK—in that chair is your *body*. The chair you are sitting in is *the food*. Now *be the "food"* and tell your body what you are doing and why.

ANNE I'm your food and I'm going into you now . . . stuffing you . . . making you disgusting . . . fat. I'm your shame and I'm making you untouchable. No one will ever touch you now. That's what you want . . . that no one will touch you. [She looked up in surprise.]

M. B.-L. Are you surprised about something you just said?

ANNE About not being touched . . . [silence].

M. B.-L. Is that something you feel you could get into talking about now?

ANNE Yes, I guess it might be important. . . . When I was fifteen [three years ago] I was on a cruise down the Snake River. I impulsively decided I didn't want to be a virgin anymore and since I liked the boat man, I decided to let him make love to me. The only thing is I got drunk, passed out, and that's when he did it to me. I didn't remember anything the next day except feeling miserable and disgusted with myself. And the worst part was this guy didn't want anything to do with me after that. After this happened I lost some weight because I felt maybe I was too fat and that this is what had turned him off. Shortly after I lost weight I had my first binge, and it's gone on ever since.

The first rejection often becomes a pattern. Many women revert to dependent behavior, which assures the repetition of the rejection. Anne would meet a man, "fall in love," and eventually drive him away by growing increasingly possessive and clinging. She then tried to compensate for what she perceived as a failure, attempting to alter herself through fasting in order to accommodate to some mysterious standard of perfection men held. Other women become supercritical of most men they encounter, thereby eliminating the possibility of warm and loving relationships.

Another of my patients, Linda, petite, soft-spoken, and lovely, says of her first binge:

> Well, my mother thinks it all started after I was rejected by a boy in my junior year of high school . . . [silence] . . . he was my first boyfriend, and I was really crazy about him. One day he just dropped me without any explanation. . . . I never did find out what I had done. It was so confusing. . . . I was really depressed. Shortly after I had my nose fixed and began to diet. I wasn't fat, but it was the Twiggy era, and I can't remember exactly, but I started to binge somewhere around that time, but I don't really know if there's any connection.

The Psychodynamics of the Binge and Purge

The cycle the bulimarexic endures can be physically damaging (see fig. 3). The women report fasting, habitual forced vomiting, and amphetamine

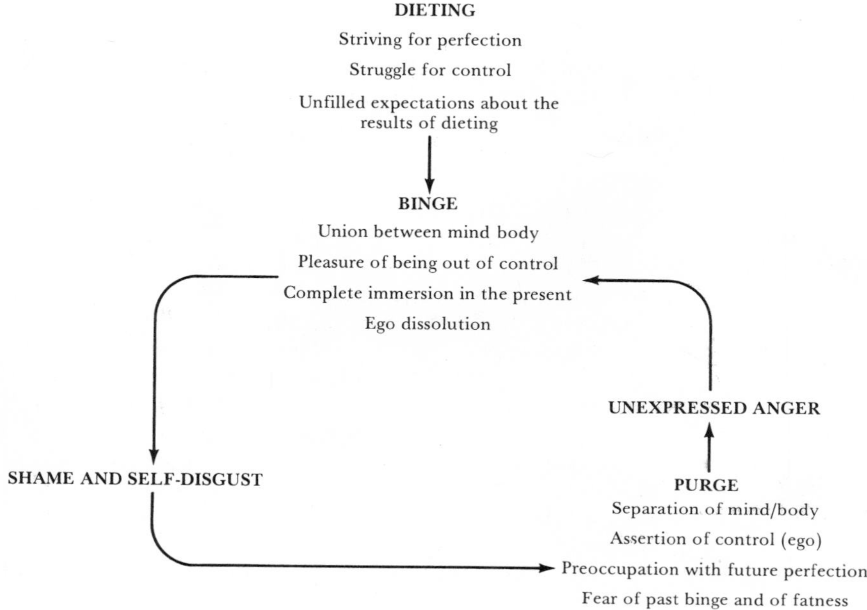

Figure 3. The psychodynamics of bulimarexia

and laxative abuse as means to counteract a binge. However, for these young women who have been "good" girls, and who are afraid of parental disapproval and the rejection that might result from sexual activity, food is one of the few elements in their tightly regulated lives that they can choose to indulge excessively. For the person who is struggling to meet unrealistic goals by imposing severe and ascetic control over herself, the binge is a release.

> ANNE When I am into a binge it doesn't matter if I have just eaten . . . I just go crazy . . . completely out of control. Whatever is around I eat . . . candy . . . four or five bars . . . a whole quart of ice cream. If I am in the cafeteria, I fill my plate with everything. I then go back for seconds, thirds, and even more. I eat until I feel sick. After I binge I feel disgusted with myself and start my fast. I don't eat anything except liquids for a few days. I usually stick to this for as long as a week.

Moreover, the binge brings about a union between the mind and body. One gives one's self to the food, to the moment completely. There is a complete loss of control (ego). It is an absolute here-and-now experience, a kind of ecstasy.

However, the giving over of one's self to this kind of experience leads to shame and guilt. Socialization and cultural pressures intrude to initiate the purification rites, purging or fasting. The purging represents a concentration on past and future. In reliving the past, the self is a helpless child, rewarded for beauty and feminine passivity, punished for being assertive and rebellious. In anticipating the future, the self preoccupies itself with the repercussions of having a fat body in American culture, which will bring about male rejection. For the bulimarexic, ego manifests itself in social symbols (i.e., beautiful body = male approval = self-validation). Because the binge will bring about an ugly body, it carries with it the threat of ego dissolution and social humiliation. In purging, the mind separates itself from the body by focusing on the shame of being out of control.

A feature of fasting that feeds the persistence of the syndrome is the false sense of power that the faster derives from her starvation. The woman feels "good," "in control," and "disciplined" when her life has narrowed to self-denial. Bruch refers to anorexia as a "struggle for control for a sense of identity, competence, and effectiveness." She writes that many of these youngsters "had struggled for years to make themselves over and to be perfect in the eyes of others."[15] What her otherwise reasonable interpretation of the syndrome overlooks is the fact that the fasting behavior in this syndrome also strives for power and control over the bulimic behavior. Thus, the bulimarexic is involved in a struggle against a part of the self rather than a struggle toward a self. In the early stages of the syndrome, the adolescent girl may be asserting ownership rights over her body. She also may be using this behavior as a passive-aggressive reaction to her mother whom she perceives as controlling and suffocating. The refusal of food—along with compulsive masturbation, nailbiting, etc.—are all behaviors that the parents cannot completely control. The child chooses privacy and isolation for her acting out. However, when bulimia first occurs the nature of the syndrome undergoes a transformation. The underlying beliefs about one's self ("I am unlovable, unattractive, and inadequate") are pervasive and make the woman extraordinarily sensitive to the reactions of other people toward her. The most minor or insignificant slight is exaggerated and distorted, creating massive self-loathing, and is used as an *excuse* for binge-ing. The anger the woman feels toward her imagined rejector is not acknowledged, and this unexpressed anger is turned inward, adding to the fury of the binge.

The fast-binge cycle of the bulimarexic is confining. It consumes enough energy to prevent the woman from looking beyond it or outgrowing it. It serves to keep her socially isolated. Binge-ing wards off people with a "wall of [perceived] fat." It is a way of "filling up" without needing others. A fairly typical example from Anne's case supports this hypothesis. Anne was invited to go out to dinner by a boy she really liked; she wanted to go but was on the fasting part of her cycle. She feared the temptation and thus worked herself into a high state of anxiety, fearing a binge and vacillating between going and staying home. On the date, she ate moderately and had an enjoyable time. When the man dropped her off, she proceeded to binge grotesquely.

The fact that the behavior is a secret one, carried out in private, further isolates the bulimarexic. For her food becomes a *fetish,* as Becker uses the term in "Fetishism as Low Self-Esteem."

> "General inactivity," "low self-esteem," and "sense of inadequacy" indicate that the fetishist is a person who has sentenced himself (herself) to live in a certain kind of object world. It will be shallow in terms of the complexity and richness

of its objects; it will represent a narrow commitment instead of a broad and flexible one; yet it will be a segment of the world which has to bear a full load of life meaning. In other words, the fetishist will be a behaviorally poor person, who has the resourceful task of creating a rich world. As we said, the record of that resourceful contriving is the fetish behavior itself.[16]

A Feminist Perspective

None of the women in this study had ever experienced a satisfying love relationship in spite of their attractiveness and high intelligence. All longed for one. Most were virgins. Others froze up when sexual overtures were made or developed severe anxiety or depression during or after sex. The sexual conflicts that are evident in these women do not reflect a rejection of femininity or a bizarre fear of oral impregnation.[17] Rather, these women have already learned a passive and accommodating approach to life from their parents and their culture. This accommodation is combined with two opposing tensions: the desperate desire for self-validation from a man, and an inordinate *fear of men* and their power to reject. Since most of the women have already experienced a real or perceived rejection by a male or males, this perpetuates the already larger than life belief in the power and importance of men. The sexual fears of these women are often associated with intercourse, which is viewed as an act of surrender exposing their vulnerability to rejection. Rather than finding an obsession with bizarre fantasies (oral impregnation), I found a preoccupation with the fear of rejection in sex, of not being good enough to please a man.

If the woman is able to find a male companion who loves her, in spite of the obstacles her behavior presents to the relationship, a remission of symptoms might occur. This relationship, while relieving the surface of the bulimarexic's problem, can be more ultimately destructive. If the woman has not strengthened her sense of self and self-worth, the future of the relationship can be at best uncertain; failure of the relationship can be devastating.

Why is it that the bulimarexic gives men the power to reject her? Why does she give up her own power and make men larger than life? A reasonable answer, one more direct than that found in a theory of the innate psychology of women, lies in our heritage of sexual inequality. As Miller says, "our male dominated society creates a system of values in which men and women tend to believe that the only meaningful relationships are with men. Men attempt to win esteem by achievement and their attention lies in the sphere outside the family. And since the women define themselves in terms of their success in holding the love of men, a system of mutual frustration develops and the children become the repository."[18] Between the ages of thirteen to seventeen, these adolescent girls find that society in general and men in particular do not reward them as they have been socialized by both their parents and their culture to *expect.* Obviously this image of men affects a woman not only as a daughter but as a mother. It is my conviction that the mothers of these women became what they are for the same reasons that their daughters became bulimarexics. Most women are socialized to dependency to some degree. Laws has summarized ways in which this affects women:

> Social dependence, as a habit of responding, has a number of consequences. . . . First, the reliance on rewards coming from others makes the individual very flexible and adaptable, ready to alter her behavior (or herself) in response to words and threats. Second, she is limited to others as a source of rewards, including self-esteem, for two reasons: (1) the necessity of being accommodating and responsive works against the development of a sense of self which might oppose the demands of others, and (2) any evidence of the development of the self as a source of approval or of alternative directions is punished by others. The "responsiveness" and the sole reliance on social support make the woman extraordinarily vulnerable to rejection (meaning failure).[19]

Many traditional approaches to therapy with women see men as solutions to problems of low self-esteem. Szyrynski exaggerates these assumptions when he suggests that "since a great majority of such patients are adolescent girls, a male therapist may be probably more effective than a woman. He can replace for the girl her inadequate father figure; on the other hand, he will not be identified by the patient with her hostile mother."[20] I believe, on the contrary, that female therapists can provide positive female role models for these women which are a marked contrast to the negative experiences they recount in relationships with their mothers. In addition, it is unrealistic to expect that the presence of a man, or any other person, can compensate for a nonexistent sense of self. It is equally unrealistic to expect a man to want to serve this function. I can only offer a pessimistic prognosis for the woman who looks at the accession of an approving man as the solution to her psychological conflicts.[21] Since anorexia nervosa and bulimarexia are appearing with greater frequency,[22] I can only hope that the increasing number of women suffering from these syndromes can avail themselves of a humane therapy to help alleviate the low self-esteem that is at the root of their problems.

NOTES

1. Judith Long Laws, "Woman as Object," *The Second XX* (New York: Elsevier Publishing Co., in press).
2. Four men who reported the binge-ing-starving behavior were also treated. I saw three of these men in individual therapy. Since the writing of this paper I have been engaged in therapeutic interventions and research designed to test some of these theoretical arguments. Taking advantage of a new philosophical and innovative movement within our mental health clinic, I attempted an outreach program designed to break through the isolation and shame experienced by women who are food bingers. In September 1974, an ad was placed in our university newspaper describing the symptom and offering a group experience with a feminist orientation that would utilize Gestalt and behaviorist techniques. Sixty women responded; fifteen were admitted to the group. Some of the before, after, and follow-up measurements administered were: questionnaires specifically dealing with the binge-fast behavior and early childhood training; a body cathexis test (P. Secord and S. Jourard, "The Appraisal of Body-Cathexis: Body-Cathexis and the Self," *Journal of Consulting Psychology* 17 [1953]: 343–47); and the Sixteen Personality Factor questionnaire (R. B. Cattell, *The 16 P-F* [Champaign, Ill.: Institute for Personality and Ability Testing, 1972]). Based on the success of this initial group, two subsequent groups have been run and data collected. Our outreach program, designed as a preventive intervention, re-

vealed a much larger population manifesting this behavior than had been suspected. After seeing 138 women and four men in two years at our clinic and systematically studying eight of these with a variety of tests and other measurements, we are now working on developing an operational definition of the bulimarexic syndrome, analyzing our data for publication, and outlining a new therapeutic approach to this problem.

3. Hilda Bruch, *Eating Disorders* (New York: Basic Books, 1973), pp. 82, 251–54.
4. V. Szyrynski, "Anorexia Nervosa and Psychotherapy," *American Journal of Psychotherapy,* 27, no. 2 (October 1973): 492–505.
5. M. Wulff, "Ueber einen interessanten oralen Symptomenkomplex und seine Beziehung zur sucht," in *The Psychoanalytic Theory of Neuroses,* ed. Otto Fenichel (New York: W. W. Norton & Co., 1945), p. 241.
6. Robert Lindner, "The Case of Laura," *The Fifty-Minute Hour* (New York: Holt, Rinehart & Winston, 1955).
7. Bruch, p. 217.
8. J. V. Waller, R. M. Kaufman, and F. Deutsch, "Anorexia Nervosa: A Psychosomatic Entity," *Psychosomatic Medicine* 2 (September 1940): 3–16.
9. R. M. Boyer et al., "Anorexia Nervosa: Immaturity of the 24-Hour Luteinizing Hormone Secretory Pattern," *New England Journal of Medicine* 291 (October 24, 1974).
10. I am indebted to Dr. Ronald Leifer for his insights into the implications of bulimarexic behavior and to Janet Snoyer and Holly Bailey for their assistance.
11. The four male bingers I interviewed exhibited the following striking commonalities with the women in the study: (1) all complained of feelings of inadequacy and helplessness and exhibited abnormally low self-esteem; (2) all were extremely dependent and passive individuals who worked very hard at pleasing their parents through academic achievement; (3) all expressed feeling inadequate because they had never been able to sustain relationships with women, and, indeed, all had suffered female rejection in adolescence, which left them fearful of women and further encouraged their isolation; (4) all described their parents as excessively repressive. Unlike the women in the study, the men strongly identified with their mothers and expressed hostility toward their fathers whom they experienced as demanding and authoritarian. All had been pushed into athletics at an early age by their fathers. Although none were overweight as children and some were, in fact, slight of build, they became preoccupied with weight because of their desire to maintain slim and athletic bodies.
12. Hilda Bruch, "Children Who Starve Themselves," *The New York Times Magazine* (November 10, 1974), p. 70.
13. Bruch, *Eating Disorders,* p. 268.
14. A. O. Lee, "Disturbance of Body Image in Obesity and Anorexia Nervosa," *Smith College Studies in Social Work* 44 (1973): 33–34.
15. Bruch, *Eating Disorders,* p. 251.
16. Ernest Becker, *Angel in Armor* (New York: Free Press, 1969), pp. 18–19.
17. Normal adolescent girls often express a fear of oral impregnation. These fears occur between the ages of ten and thirteen and usually are connected with inaccurate sexual information and imagined parental disapproval. Since such fears are so often experienced by normal women, I can see no basis for assuming that these fears foster anorexic behavior.
18. Jean B. Miller, "Sexual In-Equality: Men's Dilemma; a Note on the Oedipus Complex, Paranoia, and Other Psychological Concepts," *American Journal of Psychoanalysis* 32, no. 2 (April 1972): 140–55.
19. Laws (n. 1).
20. Szyrynski (n. 4), p. 502. In the cases of the three men I saw in individual therapy, the same Gestalt-behaviorist approach used with women was utilized. It emphasized awareness, responsibility, assertiveness training, and male consciousness raising. In all cases, at a particular stage in the therapy it was decided that a male therapist would be useful to deal with issues of sexuality, and these patients were then referred to a male counselor with a similar therapeutic orientation. All eventually gave up the bulimarexic behavior and reported many positive changes in their attitudes toward themselves, women, and their parents.
21. The extent to which such attitudes prevail in our culture is indicated by the account of a "cured" anorexic. "I fell in love. By no means do I want to suggest that love is the answer to everything. For me, loving someone shifted my attention away from the compulsive, convoluted world of self I had created inside me, toward another person. Finally, I felt some self-esteem because I had been found worthy by someone else" (Kathryn Lynch, "Danger! You Can Overdo Dieting," *Seventeen* 24 [March 1974]: 107).

22. With a few exceptions, most of the literature on these behaviors has not acknowledged this upward trend. One exception is the British study by May Duddle, "An Increase of Anorexia Nervosa in a University Population," *British Journal of Psychiatry* 123 (December 1973): 711–12. Most of the food bingers I have encountered know of other women who binge. I suspect that most cases are seen in a high school guidance office or college mental health service. Many more women probably suffer secretly from this compulsion and do not seek help because of inordinate shame about their behaviors.

The Consciousness-Raising Group as a Model for Therapy with Women

Annette M. Brodsky

By now, almost everyone is familiar with a sense of growing unrest among women with many of their traditional sex role stereotypes. There is no evidence that women are more like each other psychologically than men are like each other. In fact, the bulk of evidence on gender role differences points out that the differences between individuals of each sex are greater than differences between men and women (Mischel, 1966). Yet, for a woman in particular, her sex determines to a large degree her future roles in life, dictating limitations on the options for her development, regardless of intellect, activity level, or physical and emotional capacity (Epstein, 1970; Amundsen, 1971). This role confinement has been psychologically frustrating to many women and is a major basis for identification as feminists of many of the therapists on the Feminist Therapist Roster of the Association for Women in Psychology (Brodsky, 1972). Epidemiological studies (Gurin et al., 1960; Chesler, 1971) reveal that women complain more of nervousness, impending breakdown, and attempts at suicide (and they are beginning to achieve this goal more often). They are more frequently seen in therapy, and more likely to be hospitalized for their mental disorders. As Chesler (1971) points out, women are the most "treated" category in our society. The Task Force on Family Law and Policy (1968) concluded that the married woman, in the traditional feminine role of housewife, has the most difficulty psychologically, and the discrepancy between married women and other groups increases with the years of marriage. Bart (1971) noted that depression in middle-aged women was most likely to occur when

"The Consciousness-Raising Group as a Model of Therapy with Women" by Annette M. Brodsky in *Psychotherapy: Theory, Research, and Practice,* 10 (1973), 24–29. Reprinted by permission.

there was an overly strong commitment to the mother role so that other forms of individual identity were lacking when the children left home.

Directing women into narrowly confined roles is a long socialization process that starts with the toys and books of young children that encourage specific social models that differentiate instrumental and expressive tools of development (Bardwick, 1971). The realization that women are not to make a significant impact upon the world, that their role in life is not only different from that of their brothers, but qualitatively inferior in terms of rewards of the society in which they live, occurs in vivid and demonstrable form by high school years. Horner (1970) demonstrates dramatic evidence of the suppression of self-esteem and self-actualization in adolescent girls. The motive to avoid success becomes a powerful inhibition on the academic achievement of girls. The fears of loss of femininity associated with being competitive, the social disapproval of intellectual females, and the actual denial in bright women that a woman is capable of high levels of achievement, were all themes repeatedly related in projective stories of Horner's subjects. Sixty-five per cent of the sample of females, compared to less than ten per cent of the males, showed this phenomenon of avoiding success.

The identity crisis is perhaps most noted in the married, middle-class women who have been over-educated and under utilized. The gulf separating the life style of the upper-middle class housewife and her mate is perhaps wider than any other strata in our society. By definition these women are happy. They have husbands, families, and household help. Why don't they feel fulfilled? Freidan (1963) refers to the uneasiness and disillusionment of the bored middle-class housewives as the "problem that had no name." These women continued to live out their proscribed roles in spite of vague, undefined needs for more variability and needs for more opportunity to reveal individual talents that were often not consonant with the roles of "kinder, kuche, and kirche" (children, kitchen, and church).

With the re-awakening of the feminist movement in the 60's, women began to investigate the problem with no name. Bird (1968) discovered what women in the working world suspected, but dared not voice aloud. That is, when a woman leaves the stereotyped roles, she fights a battle of subtle and often blatant discrimination and resentment. The battle is a lonely one for those who can overcome the initial fears of loss of femininity, social disapproval and disdain of men and women alike for daring to compete in the male domain.

Consciousness-raising (C-R) groups grew out of both the sense of restless constraint noted by Freidan and the awareness of being different and alone noted by Bird. These feelings were finally exposed as a common occurrence and C-R groups developed a very important aspect of the women's movement, the awareness of women that others shared these same self-doubts.

The small group structure of the women's movement was ideally suited to the exploration of personal identity issues. The technique of heightening self-awareness by comparing personal experiences was as basic to the continuance and solidarity of the movement as any other tactic. Women found themselves eliciting and freely giving support to other group members who often were asserting themselves as individuals for the first time in their lives. They gained strength from members who confronted others, and they learned to ask for their own individual rights to adopt new roles and express new behaviors.

The individual changes that occurred in the context of C-R groups were unique from many therapeutic techniques that women had previously experienced. Many C-R group members had previously been in therapy (Newton & Walton, 1971). Many others had considered the entire mental health profession as implying illness and abnormality and had no contact with individual or group experiences until they joined a C-R group.

By education and training, women had been encouraged to be conformists and passive. In their traditional roles, they had been isolated from each other and from events in the larger political and economic world beyond their narrowly confined psychological space. The C-R group offered a sense of closeness or intimacy with other women as opposed to a media-produced sense of competition and alienation from each other. The development of the concept of sisterhood arose as a shared understanding of the unique problems of being a woman in a man's world.

Movement women (Allen, 1971) and professionals (Newton & Walton, 1971) have begun to study consciousness-raising groups for their perspectives on the social movement, and on exploration of new life styles. The present analysis focuses on the psychological impact, with therapy groups, the C-R group starts with the assumption that the environment, rather than intrapsychic dynamics, plays a major role in the difficulties of the individuals. The medical model of abnormal behavior based on biological, innate causes is not acceptable to these groups. They are struggling to redefine these very concepts that have been seen as assigning women to a helpless patient role, destined as victims of their biological nature to behave in certain ways (Weisstein, 1969; Chesler, 1971).

Women in C-R groups do not react in traditional female interaction patterns that are commonly seen in all-female groups of mothers of patients, institutional groups, etc. The typical response is that women are catty, aggressive, competitive, and much tougher on each other for digressions, than they are toward men.

In C-R groups, women are confronted with acting as individuals. They are encouraged to examine their uniqueness apart from their roles toward others such as wife, mother, or secretary. It appears easier for a woman to reveal taboo subjects and feelings such as not liking the caring of young children, wishing one had never married, feeling more intelligent than one's boss or husband, or being tired of boosting his self-esteem at the expense of her own. Finding that not only are these feelings not abnormal, but common experiences among other women, can have an almost religious conversion reaction in some women (Newton & Walton, 1971).

A sense of trust in other women and a closeness based on common problems that arise from external sources as well as internal deficiencies, serves to bind the groups into continuing, relatively stable units. The attrition rate for the groups I and my colleagues have encountered as well as those studied by Newton & Walton (1971) appear to be lower than those of typical voluntary therapy groups, or sensitivity groups. They appear to move to an intimacy stage rapidly and maintain a strong loyalty. Dropouts occur early, often due to conflict with male relationships that are threatened by changes in dependency behaviors.

The therapeutic processes that occur in these groups are akin to assertive training, personal growth groups, achievement-oriented training or simply self-development groups. In assertive training, the key technique seems to involve the role models provided by other group members. Women as models are more convincing then male authoritarian leaders for whom the assertive role is a cultural expectation. The identification with other women who achieve is more real than transference to a model outside the situation of direct discrimination experiences. In this sense, like Synanon, Recovery, Inc., or Alcoholics Anonymous, in C-R groups some experienced members give strength to the neophyte.

I have seen faculty women return to long forgotten dissertations and take advanced courses, and housewives who have confronted their husbands for more rights or domestic help. Others went through divorces from marriages that had been security traps, and childless women stood up for their right to refuse to have children simply because others thought they should.

One difficulty with the groups comes at a stage when the women try to transfer their new found behaviors outside the group. In a parallel fashion to the sensitivity group member who expects others outside the group to respond as positively as the group, C-R group members often find that the group understands, but the outside world does not change to correspond with the groups' level of awareness. It is at this stage that women tend to become angry with their employers, lovers, and old friends for continuing to act in chauvinistic, stereotyped patterns. A new response from a woman may be either ignored, misunderstood, patronizingly laughed at, or invoke a threatened retaliatory confrontation. Unlike the individual in a more traditional assertive training situation, these women are behaving often in new ways that society usually does not condone. In frustration, women may overreact and as a result, provoke just the response they fear to get. For example, loud demands for better treatment on the job by a previously meek woman may well meet with a backlash response leading to termination of her entire job.

This type of frustration often leads to a period of depression, either of individuals or the group as a whole. They feel that while they can become aware of their situation and make individual changes, they cannot make much of an impact on the outside world. There is little outside reinforcement to carry on their motivation. At this later dropout stage, the faculty women gets pregnant instead of completing her dissertation, the potential divorcée decides that security is more important after all, the frustrated housewife announces that "Joe thinks this group is making me unhappy and he wants me to quit," or the graduate student can not find time because she is up nights typing her boyfriend's thesis.

If these regressive tendencies are weathered by the group, the most crucial, and often the most effective, stage of the group experience develops. The women plan to actively alter the environment in a realistic manner to make it more compatible with the developing growth needs of the members. The direction of the group turns from personal, individual solutions (except for occasional booster-shot sessions as the need arises) to some sort of group action. Actions that groups may take vary according to talents, age and needs. They might consist of organized protests, political lobbying, educational programs, or missionary goals of helping to organize other groups to expand the population of the enlightened. The C-R group works to give a sense of social as well as personal worth to the members, and as a by-product, serves to help modify an environment insensitive to the needs of an increasingly growing population of restless women.

The premise of this paper is that the C-R groups of the women's movement have implications for the treatment of identity problems of women in therapy. The following ways are suggested possibilities for transfering the C-R groups dynamics to use individual therapy. First, in working with women on identity issues, therapists should be aware of the increasingly wider range of valid goals for healthy functioning of women in terms of roles and personality traits (Maccoby, 1971). For example, exuberance should not be interpreted as aggression because the behavior occurs in a female. Second, a good therapist is aware of the reality of the female patient's situation. Many factors are beyond her control. She cannot realistically expect to attain achievement comparable to a man, unless she has greater intellectual and/or motivational abilities. Discrimination does exist (Amundsen, 1971; Bernard, 1971; Astin, 1969; Epstein, 1970; Bird, 1968, etc.). Because of this discrimination, the importance of encouragment through assertive training and independence from others, including the therapist, is paramount to counteract the many years of discouragement through subtle, cultural mores. The therapist can serve as supporter and believer in the patient's competence through the regressive, dropout stages and finally, in the face of individual frustrations he or she can recognize the need for some direct and meaningful activity related to improvement of the societal situations.

Working with women's C-R groups offers a number of insights to a therapist for the particular problems women face in trying to resolve the difficulties of living in a world that revolves around men's work. For example, those women who report patterns of intrusive male behavior often appear to be oversensitive to slights and minor brushoffs. C-R group experiences help women to confirm the reality of such slights, rather than deny their existence or pass them off an projections. For a man, such incidents can be overlooked as exceptional, and not integrated into the broader experience of being taken seriously and accepted as a thinking individual. For a woman, the experience is more a rule, than an exception (unless she is an exceptional woman). Her sensitivity to such slights comes out of an awareness of the situation, and a concomitant frustration in being unable to defend herself in the situation without appearing pompous, uppity, or paranoid.

The accumulation of experiences of being interrupted in conversations, having her opinions ignored or not taken seriously can severely affect a woman's feelings of competence and self-worth. Her desire to be assertive, or to make an impact on the environment is continuously weakened by this lack of affirmation of her self by others.

There are therapists who maintain that women who act insecure or inferior in such situations are doing so in order to get secondary gains from such postures (using feminine wiles) and her verbalizations of a desire for independence or responsibility are not genuine. Such therapists probably do not understand that without role models or encouragement from the environment, these women have no real choice in not accepting the only reality they have been indoctrinated to believe about the capabilities of their sex.

Other major themes that some therapists are apt to misjudge or overlook when dealing with women clients can be briefly mentioned here. Unaware therapists still tend to consider marriage uncritically as a solution for women's problems without realizing that, like with men, divorce or no marriage may often present the best available alternative for the individual. When a woman proposes such a solution, the therapist may become more concerned with her non-traditional life style than with her personal feelings in living out such a style.

Some therapists also automatically assume that a woman's career is secondary to her mate's career. The conflict over "having it both ways," by wanting a career and family is still seen as the wife's burden, not the husband's also. Unusual patterns of division of household tasks, child care, etc. are no longer stigmas that label individuals as deviant. Therapists have been guilty of producing iatrogenic disorders in women who felt comfortable with what they were doing until the therapist suggested that they were selfish, unreasonable, or pointed out how no one expected them to accomplish so much and they would be loved and accepted without this unrealistic drive to compete.

Perhaps related to the foregoing is the frustration women have experienced with therapists who can empathize readily with a man who is stifled by a clinging, nagging wife, but who interprets the same complaint from a woman as her being cold and unfeeling for not responding affectionately to an insecure, demanding husband. The crucial issue surrounding such misunderstandings is an unconscious tendency for many therapists to have a double standard for men and women in mental health and adjustment (Broverman, et al., 1970). This attitude restricts their capacity to allow their clients a free expression of the various available roles. Women, after all, have needs for self-esteem, independence, expression of anger and aggression; and men have needs for security, affection and expression of fear and sorrow. While, at present, men may have more diverse models in our society for the development of an adequate masculine role, women's models have been restricted for the most part to housewives or the more narrow traditional feminine occupations.

Perhaps the strongest message to be seen from the success of these C-R groups is that women are capable of using other women as models. Identification of women with role models of their own sex has been largely limited to the traditional homemaker roles or the feminine occupations such as teaching and nursing. The acceptance of more varied roles and personality traits in women will help to integrate a larger portion of women into the "mentally healthy" categories.

Until this happens to a greater extent, perhaps, as Chesler (1971) suggests only women should be therapists for other women. On the other hand, if therapists must have the same experience as their patients in order to help them, we would be a sorry lot indeed. The important lesson for clinicians, male and female alike, is to make a particular effort to study the facts and reasoning behind the women's movement. We help neurotics, psychotics, children, handicapped, any group of which we are not a member by keeping educated with the current literature written by those in close touch with large numbers of that particular population. In the same vein, any male therapist who has not kept abreast of current theory and issues relating to women, is treating from a position of ignorance. The sample of women in his personal life does not provide sufficient clinical data or theory on which to base therapy. Women have a great need today for allies in their struggles to alter a constricting environment. Legal and political allies are not sufficient. Understanding, enlightened therapists are necessary if we want to avoid psychological casualties of today's transitional cultural changes.

REFERENCES

ALLEN, P. *The small group in women's liberation.* New York: Times Change Press, 1971.

AMUNDSEN, K. *The silenced majority: Women and American democracy.* Englewood Cliffs, New Jersey: Prentice Hall, 1971.

ASTIN, H. *The woman doctorate in America.* Hartford: Russell Sage Foundation, 1969.

BARDWICK- J., & DOUVAN, E. Ambivalence: The socialization of women. In V. Gornick & B. Moran (Eds.), *Woman in sexist society: Studies in power and powerlessness.* New York: Basic Books, 1971, 147–159.

BART, P. Depression in middle-aged women. In V. Gornick & B. Moran (Eds.), *Woman in sexist society: Studies in power and powerlessness.* New York: Basic Books, 1971, 99–117.

BERNARD, J. *Women and the public interest.* New York: Aldine-Atherton, 1971.

BIRD, C. *Born female: The high cost of keeping women down.* New York: McKay, 1968.

BRODSKY, A. (Ed.) *Feminist therapist roster of the Association for Women in Psychology.* Pittsburgh: KNOW, Inc., 1972.

BROVERMAN, I. K., BROVERMAN, D. M., CLARKSON, F., ROSENKRANTS, P. & VOGEL, S. R. Sex-role stereotypes and clinical judgments of mental health. *Journal of Consulting Psychology,* 1970, 34, 1–7.

CHESLER, P. Patient and patriarch: Women in the psychotherapeutic relationship. In V. Gornick & B. Moran (Eds.), *Woman in sexist society: Studies in power and powerlessness.* New York: Basic Books, 1971, 251–275.

EPSTEIN, C. *Woman's place: Options and limits in professional careers.* Berkeley: California Press, 1970.

FRIEDAN, B. *The feminine mystique.* New York: Dell, 1963.

GURIN, G., VEROFF, J., & FELD, S. *Americans view their mental health.* New York: Basic Books, 1960.

HORNER, M. Femininity and successful achievement: A basic inconsistency. In J. Bardwick, *Feminine personality and conflict.* Belmont, Calif.; Brooks/Cole, 1970, 45–76.

MACCOBY, E. Sex differences and their implications for sex roles. Paper presented at American Psychological Association, Sept. 1971, Washington, D. C.

MISCHEL, W. A social-learning view of sex differences in behavior. In E. Maccoby, *The development of sex differences.* Stanford: Stanford University Press, 1966, 56–81.

NEWTON, E., & WALTON, S. The personal is political: Consciousness-raising and personal change in the women's liberation movement. In B. G. Schoepf (Chw), *Anthropologists look at the study of women.* Symposium presented at the American Anthropological Association, November 19, 1971.

REEVES, N. *Womankind: Beyond the stereotypes.* New York: Aldine .Atherton, 1971.

Report of the Task Force on Family Law and Policy to the Citizen's Advisory Council on the Status of Women, Washington, D. C., 1968.

WEISSTEIN, N. Kinder, kuche, kirche as scientific law: Psychology constructs the female. *Motive,* 1969, 29, 6–7.

PART 11

Middle Age and Aging

In a society which adulates youth, its bouyancy, its firm, unlined beauty, and its lifestyle, the perception of oneself as aging, as no longer young, can be a sobering if not unpleasant experience for anyone. Physically, aging brings changes which are associated with a slowing of physical and mental processes, with a loss of flexibility and elasticity, decreased muscle tone, and the appearance of lines and wrinkles. Psychologically, the experience is often associated with a motif of loss—loss of youthful beauty, loss of vigor, loss of children, loss of reproductive capacity, sometimes loss of job or spouse. In our society, cultural attitudes toward aging and toward older people are generally negative, constructing a model for the middle and later years which is quite unattractive to contemplate. On the other hand, many who are in mid-life and older are quite happy, experiencing new found freedom, greater financial security, and personal maturity of values and attitudes, glad to be relieved of the *Sturm und Drang* of their youthful years.

While adaptations to aging vary greatly among both women and men, it is a safe generalization that aging in our society has different meanings for the two sexes. Women have been valued primarily for their sexual and reproductive functions, both expressed in the context of youth. Men are more likely to be valued for successful achievement and economic productivity, characteristically expressed in the context of maturity. A glance at any newsstand will confirm that the favored style of being female is the "girl" model who, above all, is young and sexually attractive. A man, on the other hand, has greater permission to age attractively. An unattached man of 40 or 50 may be quite sought after as a mate or companion, whereas a single woman of that age has been relegated to the category of old maid —she whom no man found desirable enough to marry.

While differential valuing of aging for men and women is a reflection of cultural attitudes and perceptions, there are also realities which discriminate the mid-life experiences of the two. Women who are socialized to build their lives and their identities around the primary roles of wife and mother find these roles attenuated or lost as children leave and husbands die or go elsewhere. Such role shrinkage occurs earlier for women than it does for men who typically occupy their major role of worker until they are well into their seventh decade or older. Thus appears for women the often noted "empty nest" syndrome, whose chief symptom is depression. Depression—loss of enthusiasm for living, apathy, feelings of boredom and fatigue, alienation and loss of purpose—has been called by sociologist Jesse Bernard epidemic among American women. Others, such as Therese Benedek, see this developmental phase with its freedom from pregnancy and childrearing as a challenge for the development of one's own identity, for the reorganization of one's personality, for the identifying of new objectives—time at last for the search for one's self.

The culturally different criteria for the meaning of aging for women and men are examined in depth in "The Double Standard of Aging" by Susan Sontag. Her balanced analysis of the problem shows how men too can feel diminished if they feel they have not been successful as defined by middle-class standards, and how beset they can be with anxieties about health and loss of virility and sexual potency. Women are exempt from the panic of being evaluated as a failure in the outside world since they are not expected to achieve in that arena to the same extent that men are. Women also are healthier and live longer, and need not have the same fears about sexual potency. Young women, though, are not encouraged to develop qualities of intellectual competence and resourcefulness which can be reservoirs for a full and satisfying life as one grows older.

There is always for women the correlation between youthful beauty and desirability. A man may take for his wife a woman young enough to be his daughter, an event which suggests that he is strong, potent, still to be reckoned with. But a woman who marries a man much younger than she is has broken a taboo and is condemned as an exhibitionist clearly in her dotage. In such a case, the man, too, is censured; he is acting out an eternal quest for Mother, victim of an unresolved Oedipal conflict.

By denying our age, Sontag says, we corrupt ourselves. Instead of striving to be "girls" as long as possible, we should become women earlier. We should let ourselves age naturally, she believes, disobey the conventions of the double standard, and—tell the truth.

Researchers do not agree on what years should be included in the phrase "middle age." Most define a range of 20 or 30 years which lies somewhere between the ages of 30 and 70. Perhaps its lack of clarity as a developmental period as well as its generally negative connotations in the popular culture have contributed in the past to a lack of interest by theoreticians and researchers. In "Women in the Middle Years: A Critique of Research and Theory," Rosalind C. Barnett and Grace L. Baruch review some of the literature on middle-aged women and consider the requirements which must be met by an adequate theory of women in mid-life.

The studies reviewed by the authors focus on the areas of mental health, effects of marriage, children, and work, and the relationships among these variables. In general, the findings suggest that it is the relationship between marital status (whether or not children are still at home) and employment status which determines the psychological well-being of women in this age group. At greatest risk is the educated woman who is married, still has children at home, and has not worked since her marriage. Employment is an important variable, perhaps because it provides an alternate source of gratification not available to women whose lives revolve around their families.

Barnett and Baruch propose that an adequate theory for adult women must account for the variation of mental health problems with marital status, work status, and children's age and dependency; and for variations in satisfaction, self-esteem, and other components of well-being in relation to these patterns. Additionally, it must account for the little noted (and perhaps more prevalent than we know) findings on the positive effects of the empty nest as well as for the healthful aspects of the single life and of being an economic provider. The authors discuss some reasons why such a theory has not appeared. These include familiar myths about women, including the belief in the crucial importance of her reproductive life such that the only significant thing which can happen to her in the middle years is the menopause. Welcome indeed is the authors' attention to the need for investigation of positive variables such as personal control, competence, and a sense of the self. And it is even possible that there are women who, instead of sitting and weeping in their empty nests, are savoring it with joy—free at last!

If studies of middle-aged women in our own society are scarce, studies of their counterparts in other cultures are even more rare. A recent study is "Cross-Cultural Investigation of Behavioral Changes at Menopause," by Joyce Griffen. For many women in our society the cessation of the menses during the developmental period of the climacterium is intimately associated with aging. A tangible reminder of the loss of youth and reproductive capacity, it has not only personal but also cultural connotations far beyond its simple biological importance. Using data from the Human Relations Area Files, Griffen looks at the ways that other cultural groups manage the transition of women from their reproductive years to the status of older woman.

One is struck by the diversity of attitudes and reactions. At one extreme are groups wherein it is common for women to renounce sex, take vows as nuns, or retire permanently to bed. Poignantly, some even believe that they have a bewitched pregnancy which will never grow. On the other hand there are groups which allow menopausal women greater freedom than they had when they were young. They may eat and drink what they wish, swear, appear at male gatherings, and speak their minds. Occasionally they may become witches with curative powers. Griffen concludes that the behavior proper to the status of "old lady" is shaped by the culture. For the individual it is a pattern of responses reflecting an interplay between biology and the behavioral alternatives available to women in their cultures.

Since women live longer than men, and since most women tend to marry men who are a few years older than they are, married women in our society have a high probability of becoming widows as they grow older.

Carol J. Barrett reviews the stresses of widowhood and the implications for social policy in "Women in Widowhood," the last paper in this section.

The stresses of widowhood include grief, economic burdens, and social isolation, among others. Studies of grief show that widows vary in the extent to which they are psychologically impaired by their bereavement. Those who take the initiative in activity and in coping attempts and those who have the most interpersonal support seem to fare the best as they begin to adjust to being alone. Most widows face reduced financial resources resulting from their husband's death. Loss of husband's income and large bills from illness are usual consequences. In addition to the bereavement, the widow often must reduce her standard of living, curtail social and recreational activities, and seek employment with few marketable skills. The most frequently reported problem of widows, however, is not money but loneliness. Loneliness comes in several forms: missing the interaction with the particular other, lacking someone to care for, missing an in-depth relationship with another human being, and missing the feeling of being loved. Widows do not remarry as often as divorced women do, and many do not want to. Others may want to but have not the opportunity in that widows outnumber widowers four to one. Barrett points out that considerable variation exists among widowed women as they attempt to handle the stresses associated with their new status. Age, educational level, employment status, and presence of children in the home are all important variables.

An important component of social policy planning to improve the adjustment of widows is education dealing in a realistic way with widowhood as a life-cycle stage for most women. Such education could include preparation for living alone, both emotional and economic, stressing the importance of developing early in life autonomous interests and occupational skills. Public education could correct stereotypes about widows, and help to lift the stigma sometimes associated with the designation.

Running through these essays are two themes which we may identify as the closing of the gates, to use Helene Deutsch's phrase, and the opening of the gates, in happier terms. The conception of middle age for women in terms of loss—loss of youth with its particular beauty, vigor, and grace, loss of the capacity to bring forth new life, loss of the mother role as children leave and perhaps the wife role when husband dies—has been the more prevalent theme in both the research literature and the popular consciousness, conveying the idea that the most important part of life is over. But more recent data emerging in a new social climate call for a reevaluation of that conception. Middle age can be the beginning of a time of life when one is freer than ever before from the old exigencies of role and place, when time and opportunity become available for exploration of oneself, and of one's relation to an expanded world, when one is less bound than in earlier years by the necessity of putting others first and oneself second. Even the popular media are beginning to reflect the view that maturity in women may be an attractive attribute. A recent essay in *Time* (April 24, 1978) is titled "In Praise of Older Women." Remarking on the "slightly amazing" observation that contemporary culture heroines are mostly in their thirties and older, the author comments on the changed perceptions of women and men as to what constitutes attractiveness in women: independence, self-confidence, a sense of identity—those qualities which many women acquire in maturity, "when they seem finally to have taken permanent possession of themselves." To be in possession of ourselves seems indeed a happy consequence of growing older.

The Double Standard of Aging

Susan Sontag

"How old are you?" The person asking the question is anybody. The respondent is a woman, a woman "of a certain age," as the French say discreetly. That age might be anywhere from her early twenties to her late fifties. If the question is impersonal—routine information requested when she applies for a driver's license, a credit card, a passport—she will probably force herself to answer truthfully. Filling out a marriage license application, if her future husband is even slightly her junior, she may long to subtract a few years; probably she won't. Competing for a job, her chances often partly depend on being the "right age," and if hers isn't right, she will lie if she thinks she can get away with it. Making her first visit to a new doctor, perhaps feeling particularly vulnerable at the moment she's asked, she will probably hurry through the correct answer. But if the question is only what people call personal—if she's asked by a new friend, a casual acquaintance, a neighbor's child, a co-worker in an office, store, factory—her response is harder to predict. She may side-step the question with a joke or refuse it with playful indignation. "Don't you know you're not supposed to ask a woman her age?" Or, hesitating a moment, embarrassed but defiant, she may tell the truth. Or she may lie. But neither truth, evasion, nor lie relieves the unpleasantness of that question. For a woman to be obliged to state her age, after "a certain age," is always a miniature ordeal.

If the question comes from a woman, she will feel less threatened than if it comes from a man. Other women are, after all, comrades in sharing the same potential for humiliation. She will be less arch, less coy. But she probably still dislikes answering and may not tell the truth. Bureaucratic formalities excepted, whoever asks a woman this question—after "a certain age"—is ignoring a taboo and possibly being impolite or downright hostile. Almost everyone acknowledges that once she passes an age that is, actually, quite young, a woman's exact age ceases to be a legitimate target of curiosity. After childhood the year of a woman's birth becomes her secret, her private property. It is something of a dirty secret. To answer truthfully is always indiscreet.

The discomfort a woman feels each time she tells her age is quite independent of the anxious awareness of human morality that everyone has, from time to time. There is a normal sense in which nobody, men and women alike, relishes growing older. After thirty-five any mention of one's age carries with it the reminder that one is probably closer to the end of one's life than to the beginning. There is nothing unreasonable in that anxiety. Nor is there any abnormality in the anguish and anger that people who are really old, in their seventies and eighties, feel about the implacable waning of their powers, physical and mental. Advanced age is undeniably a trial, however stoically it may be endured. It is a shipwreck, no matter with what courage elderly people insist on continuing the voyage. But the objective, sacred pain of old age is of another order than the subjective, profane pain of aging. Old age is a genuine ordeal, one that men and women undergo in a similar way. Growing older is mainly an ordeal of the imagination—a moral disease, a social pathology—intrinsic to which is the fact that it afflicts women much more than men. It is particularly women who experience growing older (everything that comes *before* one is actually old) with such distaste and even shame.

The emotional privileges this society confers upon youth stir up some anxiety about getting older in everybody. All modern urbanized societies—unlike tribal, rural societies—condescend to the values of maturity and heap honors on the joys of youth. This revaluation of the life cycle in favor of the young brilliantly serves a secular society whose idols are ever-increasing industrial productivity and the unlimited cannibalization of nature. Such a society must create a new sense of the rhythms of life in order to incite people to buy more, to consume and throw away faster. People let the direct awareness they have of their needs, of what really gives them pleasure, be overruled by commercialized *images* of happiness and personal well-being; and, in this imagery designed to stimulate ever more avid levels of consumption, the most popular metaphor for happiness is "youth." (I would insist that it is a metaphor, not a literal description. Youth is a metaphor for energy, restless mobility, appetite: for the state of "wanting.") This equating of well-being with youth makes everyone naggingly aware of exact age—one's own and that of other people. In primitive and premodern societies people attach much less importance to dates. When lives are divided into long periods with stable responsibilities and steady ideals (and hypocrisies), the exact number of years someone has lived becomes a trivial fact; there is hardly any reason to mention, even to know, the year in which one was born. Most people in nonindustrial societies are not sure exactly how old they are. People in industrial societies are haunted by numbers. They take an almost obsessional interest in keeping the score card of aging, convinced that anything above a low total is some kind of bad news. In an era in which people actually live longer and longer, what now amounts to the latter *two-thirds* of everyone's life is shadowed by a poignant apprehension of unremitting loss.

The prestige of youth afflicts everyone in this society to some degree. Men, too, are prone to periodic bouts of depression about aging—for instance, when feeling insecure or unfulfilled or insufficiently rewarded in their jobs. But men rarely panic about aging in the way women often do. Getting older is less profoundly wounding for a man, for in addition to the propaganda for youth that puts both men and women on the defensive as they age, there is a double standard about aging that denounces women with special severity. Society is much more permissive about aging in men, as it is more tolerant of the sexual infidelities of husbands. Men are "allowed" to age, without penalty, in several ways that women are not.

This society offers even fewer rewards for aging to women than it does to men. Being physically attractive counts much more in a woman's life than in a man's, but beauty, identified, as it is for women, with youthfulness, does not stand up well to age. Exceptional mental powers can increase with age, but women are rarely encouraged to develop their minds above dilettante standards. Because the wisdom considered the special province of women is "eternal," an age-old, intuitive knowledge about the emotions to which a repertoire of facts, worldly experience, and the methods of rational analysis have nothing to contribute, living a long time does not promise women an increase in wisdom either. The private skills expected of women are exercised early and, with the exception of a talent for making love, are not the kind that enlarge with experience. "Masculinity" is identified with competence, autonomy, self-control—qualities which the disappearance of youth does not threaten. Competence in most of the activities expected from men, physical sports excepted, increases with age. "Femininity" is identified with incompetence, helplessness, passivity, noncompetitiveness, being nice. Age does not improve these qualities.

Middle-class men feel diminished by aging, even while still young, if they have not yet shown distinction in their careers or made a lot of money. (And any tendencies they have toward hypochondria will get worse in middle age, focusing with particular nervousness on the specter of heart attacks and the loss of virility.) Their aging crisis is linked to that terrible pressure on men to be "successful" that precisely defines their membership in the middle class. Women rarely feel anxious about their age because they haven't succeeded at something. The work that women do outside the home rarely counts as a form of achievement, only as a way of earning money; most employment available to women mainly exploits the training they have been receiving since early childhood to be servile, to be both supportive and parasitical, to be unadventurous. They can have menial, low-skilled jobs in light industries, which offer as feeble a criterion of success as housekeeping. They can be secretaries, clerks, sales personnel, maids, research assistants, waitresses, social workers, prostitutes, nurses, teachers, telephone operators—public transcriptions of the servicing and nurturing roles that women have in family life. Women fill very few executive posts, are rarely found suitable for large corporate or political responsibilities, and form only a tiny contingent in the liberal professions (apart from teaching). They are virtually barred from jobs that involve an expert, intimate relation with machines or an aggressive use of the body, or that carry any physical risk or sense of adventure. The jobs this society deems appropriate to women are auxiliary, "calm" activities that do not compete with, but aid, what men do. Besides being less well paid, most work women do has a lower ceiling of advancement and gives meager outlet to normal wishes to be powerful. All outstanding work by women in this society is voluntary; most women are too inhibited by the social disapproval attached to their being ambitious and aggressive. Inevitably, women are exempted from the dreary panic of middle-aged men whose "achievements" seem paltry, who feel stuck on the job ladder or fear being pushed off it by someone younger. But they are also denied most of the real satisfactions that men derive from work—satisfactions that often do increase with age.

The double standard about aging shows up most brutally in the conventions of sexual feeling, which presuppose a disparity between men and women that operates permanently to women's disadvantage. In the accepted course of events a woman anywhere from her late teens through her middle twenties can expect to attract a man more or less her own age. (Ideally, he should be at least slightly older.) They marry and raise a family. But if her husband starts an affair after some years of marriage, he customarily does so with a woman much younger than his wife. Suppose, when both husband and wife are already in their late forties or early fifties, they divorce. The husband has an excellent chance of getting married again, probably to a younger woman. His ex-wife finds it difficult to remarry. Attracting a second husband younger than herself is improbable; even to find someone her own age she has to be lucky, and she will probably have to settle for a man considerably older than herself, in his sixties or seventies. Women become sexually ineligible much earlier than men do. A man, even an ugly man, can remain eligible well into old age. He is an acceptable mate for a young, attractive woman. Women, even good-looking women, become ineligible (except as partners of very old men) at a much younger age.

Thus, for most women, aging means a humiliating process of gradual sexual disqualification. Since women are considered maximally eligible in early youth, after which their sexual value drops steadily, even young women feel themselves in a desperate race against the calendar. They are old as soon as they are no longer very young. In late adolescence some girls are already worrying about getting married. Boys and young men have little reason to anticipate trouble because of aging. What makes men desirable to women is by no means tied to yough. On the contrary, getting older tends (for several decades) to operate in men's favor, since their value as lovers and husbands is set more by what they do than how they look. Many men have more success romantically at forty than they did at twenty or twenty-five; fame, money, and, above all, power are sexually enhancing. (A woman who has won power in a competitive profession or business career is considered less, rather than more, desirable. Most men confess themselves intimidated or turned off sexually by such a woman, obviously because she is harder to treat as just a sexual "object.") As they age, men may start feeling anxious about actual sexual performance, worrying about a loss of sexual vigor or even impotence, but their sexual eligibility is not abridged simply by getting older. Men stay sexually possible as long as they can make love. Women are at a disadvantage because their sexual candidacy depends on meeting certain much stricter "conditions" related to looks and age.

Since women are imagined to have much more limited sexual lives than men do, a woman who has never married is pitied. She was not found acceptable, and it is assumed that her life continues to confirm her unacceptability. Her presumed lack of sexual opportunity is embarrassing. A man who remains a bachelor is judged much less crudely. It is assumed that he, at any age, still has a sexual life—or the chance of one. For men there is no destiny equivalent to the humiliating condition of being an old maid, a spinster. "Mr.," a cover from infancy to senility, precisely exempts men from the stigma that attaches to any woman, no longer young, who is still "Miss." (That women are divided into "Miss" and "Mrs.," which calls unrelenting attention to the situation of each woman with respect to marriage, reflects the belief that being single or married is much more decisive for a woman than it is for a man.)

For a woman who is no longer very young, there is certainly some relief when she has finally been able to marry. Marriage soothes the sharpest pain she feels about the passing years. But her anxiety never subsides completely, for she knows that should she re-enter the sexual market at a later date—because of divorce, or the death of her husband, or the need for erotic adventure—she must do so under a handicap far greater than any man of her age (*whatever* her age may be) and regardless of how good-looking she is. Her achievements, if she has a career, are no asset. The calendar is the final arbiter.

To be sure, the calendar is subject to some variations from country to country. In Spain, Portugal, and the Latin American countries, the age at which most women are ruled physically undesirable comes earlier than in the United States. In France it is somewhat later. French conventions of sexual feeling make a quasi-official place for the woman between thirty-five and forty-five. Her role is to initiate an inexperienced or timid young man, after which she is, of course, replaced by a young girl. (Colette's novella *Chéri* is the best-known account in fiction of such a love affair; biographies of Balzac relate a well-documented example from real life.) This sexual myth does make turning forty somewhat easier for French women. But there is no difference in any of these countries in the basic attitudes that disqualify women sexually much earlier than men.

Aging also varies according to social class. Poor people look old much earlier in their lives than do rich people. But anxiety about aging is certainly more common, and more acute, among middle-class and rich women than among working-class women. Economically disadvantaged women in this society are more fatalistic about aging; they can't afford to fight the cosmetic battle as long or as tenaciously. Indeed, nothing so clearly indicates the fictional nature of this crisis than the fact that women who keep their youthful appearance the longest—women who lead unstrenuous, physically sheltered lives, who eat balanced meals, who can afford good medical care, who have few or no children—are those who feel the defeat of age most keenly. Aging is much more a social judgment than a biological eventuality. Far more extensive than the hard sense of loss suffered during menopause (which, with increased longevity, tends to arrive later and later) is the depression about aging, which may not be set off by any real event in a woman's life, but is a recurrent state of "possession" of her imagination, ordained by society—that is, ordained by the way this society limits how women feel free to imagine themselves.

There is a model account of the aging crisis in Richard Strauss's sentimental-ironic opera *Der Rosenkavalier,* whose heroine is a wealthy and glamorous married woman who decides to renounce romance. After a night with her adoring young lover, the Marschallin has a sudden, unexpected confrontation with herself. It is toward the end of Act I; Octavian has just left. Alone in her bedroom she sits at her dressing table, as she does every morning. It is the daily ritual of self-appraisal practiced by every woman. She looks at herself and, appalled, begins to weep. Her youth is over. Note that the Marschallin does not discover, looking in the mirror, that she is ugly. She is as beautiful as ever. The Marschallin's discovery is moral—that is, it is a discovery of her imagination; it is nothing she actually *sees.* Nevertheless, her discovery is no less devastating. Bravely, she makes her painful, gallant decision. She will arrange for her beloved Octavian to fall in love with a girl his own age. She must be realistic. She is no longer eligible. She is now "the old Marschallin."

Strauss wrote the opera in 1910. Contemporary operagoers are rather shocked when they discover that the libretto indicates that the Marschallin is all of thirty-four years old; today the role is generally sung by a soprano well into her forties or in her fifties. Acted by an attractive singer of thirty-four, the Marschallin's sorrow would seem merely neurotic, or even ridiculous. Few women today think of themselves as old, wholly disqualified from romance, at thirty-four. The age of retirement has moved up, in line with the sharp rise in life expectancy for everybody in the last few generations. The *form* in which women experience their lives remains unchanged. A moment approaches inexorably when they must resign themselves to being "too old." And that moment is invariably—objectively—premature.

In earlier generations the renunciation came even sooner. Fifty years ago a woman of forty was not just aging but old, finished. No struggle was even possible. Today, the surrender to aging no longer has a fixed date. The aging crisis (I am speaking only of women in affluent countries) starts earlier but lasts longer; it is diffused over most of a woman's life. A woman hardly has to be anything like what would reasonably be considered old to worry about her age, to start lying (or being tempted to lie). The crises can come at any time. Their schedule depends on a blend of personal ("neurotic") vulnerability and the swing of social mores. Some women don't have their first crisis until thirty. No one escapes a sickening shock upon turning forty. Each birthday, but especially those ushering in a new decade—for round numbers have a special authority—sounds a new defeat. There is almost as much pain in the anticipation as in the reality. Twenty-nine has become a queasy age ever since the official end of youth crept forward, about a generation ago, to thirty. Being thirty-nine is also hard; a whole year in which to meditate in glum astonishment that one stands on the threshold of middle age. The frontiers are arbitrary, but not any less vivid for that. Although a woman on her fortieth birthday is hardly different from what she was when she was still thirty-nine, the day seems like a turning point. But long before actually becoming a woman of forty, she has been steeling herself against the depression she will feel. One of the greatest tragedies of each woman's life is simply getting older; it is certainly the *longest* tragedy.

Aging is a movable doom. It is a crisis that never exhausts itself, because the anxiety is never really used up. Being a crisis of the imagination rather than of "real life," it has the habit of repeating itself again and again. The territory of aging (as opposed to actual old age) has no fixed boundaries. Up to a point it can be defined as one wants. Entering each decade—after the initial shock is absorbed—an endearing, desperate impulse of survival helps many women to stretch the boundaries to the decade following. In late adolescence thirty seems the end of life. At thirty, one pushes the sentence forward to forty. At forty, one still gives oneself ten more years.

I remember my closest friend in college sobbing on the day she turned twenty-one. "The best part of my life is over. I'm not young any more." She was a senior, nearing graduation. I was a precocious freshman, just sixteen. Mystified, I tried lamely to comfort her, saying that I didn't think twenty-one was *so* old. Actually, I didn't understand at all what could be demoralizing about turning twenty-one. To me, it meant only something good: being in charge of oneself, being free. At sixteen, I was too young to have noticed, and become confused by, the peculiarly loose, ambivalent way in which this society demands that one stop thinking of oneself as a girl and start thinking of oneself as a woman. (In America that demand can now be put off to the age of thirty, even beyond.) But even if I thought her distress was absurd, I must have been aware that it would not simply be absurd but quite unthinkable in a *boy* turning twenty-one. Only women worry about age with that degree of inanity and pathos. And, of course, as with all crises that are inauthentic and therefore repeat themselves compulsively (because the danger is largely fictive, a poison in the imagination), this friend of mine went on having the same crisis over and over, each time as if for the first time.

I also came to her thirtieth birthday party. A veteran of many love affairs, she had spent most of her twenties living abroad and had just returned to the United States. She had been good-looking when I first knew her; now she was beautiful. I teased her about the tears she had shed over being twenty-one. She laughed and claimed not to remember. But thirty, she said ruefully, that really is the end. Soon after, she married. My friend is now forty-four. While no longer what people call beautiful, she is striking-looking, charming, and vital. She teaches elementary school; her husband, who is twenty years older than she, is a part-time merchant seaman. They have one child, now nine years old. Sometimes, when her husband is away, she takes a lover. She told me recently that forty was the most upsetting birthday of all (I wasn't at that one), and although she has only a few years left, she means to enjoy them while they last. She has become one of those women who seize every excuse offered in any conversation for mentioning how old they really are, in a spirit of bravado compounded with self-pity that is not too different from the mood of women who regularly lie about their age. But she is actually fretting much less about aging than she was two decades ago. Having a child, and having one rather late, past the age of thirty, has certainly helped to reconcile her to her age. At fifty, I suspect, she will be ever more valiantly postponing the age of resignation.

My friend is one of the more fortunate, sturdier casualties of the aging crisis. Most women are not as spirited, nor as innocently comic in their suffering. But almost all women endure some version of this suffering: A recurrent seizure of the imagination that usually begins quite young, in which they project themselves into a calculation of loss. The rules of this society are cruel to women. Brought up to be never fully adult, women are deemed obsolete earlier than men. In fact, most women don't become relatively free and expressive sexually until their thirties. (Women mature sexually this late, certainly much later than men, not for innate biological reasons but because this culture retards women. Denied most outlets for sexual energy permitted to men, it takes many women *that* long to wear out some of their inhibitions.) The time at which they start being disqualified as sexually attractive persons is just when they have grown up sexually. The double standard about aging cheats women of those years, between thirty-five and fifty, likely to be the best of their sexual life.

That women expect to be flattered often by men, and the extent to which their self-confidence depends on this flattery, reflects how deeply women are psychologically weakened by this double standard. Added on to the pressure felt by everybody in this society to look young as long as possible are the values of "femininity," which specifically identify sexual attractiveness in women with youth. The desire to be the "right age" has a special urgency for a woman it never has for a man. A much greater part of her self-esteem and pleasure in life is threatened when she ceases to be young. Most men experience getting older with regret, apprehension. But most women experience it even more painfully: with shame. Aging is a man's destiny, something that must happen because he is a human being. For a woman, aging is not only her destiny. Because she is that more *narrowly* defined kind of human being, a woman, it is also her vulnerability.

To be a woman is to be an actress. Being feminine is a kind of theater, with its appropriate costumes, *décor,* lighting, and stylized gestures. From early childhood on, girls are trained to care in a pathologically exaggerated way about their appearance and are profoundly mutilated (to the extent of being unfitted for first-class adulthood) by the extent of the stress put on presenting themselves as physically attractive objects. Women look in the mirror more frequently than men do. It is, virtually, their duty to look at themselves—to look often. Indeed, a woman who is not narcissistic is considered unfeminine. And a woman who spends literally *most* of her time caring for, and making purchases to flatter, her physical appearance is not regarded in this society as what she is: a kind of moral idiot. She is thought to be quite normal and is envied by other women whose time is mostly used up at jobs or caring for large families. The display of narcissism goes on all the time. It is expected that women will disappear several times in an evening—at a restaurant, at a party, during a theater intermission, in the course of a social visit—simply to check their appearance, to see that nothing has gone wrong with their make-up and hairstyling, to make sure that their clothes are not spotted or too wrinkled or not hanging properly. It is even acceptable to perform this activity in public. At the table in a restaurant, over coffee, a woman opens a compact mirror and touches up her make-up and hair without embarrassment in front of her husband or her friends.

All this behavior, which is written off as normal "vanity" in women, would seem ludicrous in a man. Women are more vain than men because of the relentless pressure on women to maintain their appearance at a certain high standard. What makes the pressure even more burdensome is that there are actually several standards. Men present themselves as face-and-body, a physical whole. Women are split, as men are not, into a body and a face—each judged by somewhat different standards. What is important for a face is that it be beautiful. What is important for a body is two things, which may even be (depending on fashion and taste) somewhat incompatible: first, that it be desirable and, second, that it be beautiful. Men usually feel sexually attracted to women much more because of their bodies than their faces. The traits that arouse desire—such as fleshiness—don't always match those that fashion decrees as beautiful. (For instance, the ideal woman's body promoted in advertising in recent years is extremely thin: the kind of body that looks more desirable clothed than naked.) But women's concern with their appearance is not simply geared to arousing desire in men. It also aims at fabricating a certain image by which, as a more indirect way of arousing desire, women state their value. A woman's value lies in the way she *represents* herself, which is much more by her face than her body. In defiance of the laws of simple sexual attraction, women do not devote most of their attention to their bodies. The well-known "normal" narcissism that women display—the amount of time they spend before the mirror—is used primarily in caring for the face and hair.

Women do not simply have faces, as men do; they are identified with their faces. Men have a naturalistic relation to their faces. Certainly they care whether they are good-looking or not. They suffer over acne, protruding ears, tiny eyes; they hate getting bald. But there is a much wider latitude in what is esthetically acceptable in a man's face than what is in a woman's. A man's face is defined as something he basically doesn't need to tamper with; all he has to do is keep it clean. He can avail himself of the options for ornament supplied by nature: a beard, a mustache, longer or shorter hair. But he is not supposed to disguise himself. What he is "really" like is supposed to show. A man lives through his face; it records the progressive stages of his life. And since he doesn't tamper with his face, it is not separate from but is completed by his body—which is judged attractive by the impression it gives of virility and energy. By contrast, a woman's face is potentially separate from her body. She does not treat it naturalistically. A woman's face is the canvas upon which she paints a revised, corrected portrait of herself. One of the rules of this creation is that the face *not* show what she doesn't want it to show. Her face is an emblem, an icon, a flag. How she arranges her hair, the type of make-up she uses, the quality of her complexion—all these are signs, not of what she is "really" like, but of how she asks to be treated by others, especially men. They establish her status as an "object."

For the normal changes that age inscribes on every human face, women are much more heavily penalized than men. Even in early adolescence, girls are cautioned to protect their faces against wear and tear. Mothers tell their daughters (but never their sons): You look ugly when you cry. Stop worrying. Don't read too much. Crying, frowning, squinting, even laughing—all these human activities make "lines." The same usage of the face in men is judged quite positively. In a man's face lines are taken to be signs of "character." They indicate emotional strength, maturity—qualities far more esteemed in men than in women. (They show he has "lived.") Even scars are often not felt to be unattractive; they too can add "character" to a man's face. But lines of aging, any scar, even a small birthmark on a woman's face, are always regarded as unfortunate blemishes. In effect, people take character in men to be different from what constitutes character in women. A woman's character is thought to be innate, static—not the product of her experience, her years, her actions. A woman's face is prized so far as it remains unchanged by (or conceals the traces of) her emotions, her physical risk-taking. Ideally, it is supposed to be a mask—immutable, unmarked. The model woman's face is Garbo's. Because women are identified with their faces much more than men are, and the ideal woman's face is one that is "perfect," it seems a calamity when a woman has a disfiguring accident. A broken nose or a scar or a burn mark, no more than regrettable for a man, is a terrible psychological wound to a woman; objectively, it diminishes her value. (As is well known, most clients for plastic surgery are women.)

Both sexes aspire to a physical ideal, but what is expected of boys and what is expected of girls involves a very different moral relation to the self. Boys are encouraged to *develop* their bodies, to regard the body as an instrument to be improved. They invent their masculine selves largely through exercise and sport, which harden the body and strengthen competitive feelings; clothes are of only secondary help in making their bodies attractive. Girls are not particularly encouraged to develop their bodies through any activity, strenuous or not; and physical strength and endurance are hardly valued at all. The invention of the feminine self proceeds mainly through clothes and other signs that testify to the very effort of girls to look attractive, to their commitment to please. When boys become men, they may go on (especially if they have sedentary jobs) practicing a sport or doing exercises for a while. Mostly they leave their appearance alone, having been trained to accept more or less what nature has handed out to them. (Men may start doing exercises again in their forties to lose weight, but for reasons of health—there is an epidemic fear of heart attacks among the middle-aged in rich countries—not for cosmetic reasons.) As one of the norms of "femininity" in this society is being preoccupied with one's physical appearance, so "masculinity" means *not* caring very much about one's looks.

This society allows men to have a much more affirmative relation to their bodies than women have. Men are more "at home" in their bodies, whether they treat them casually or use them aggressively. A man's body is defined as a strong body. It contains no contradiction between what is felt to be attractive and what is practical. A woman's body, so far as it is considered attractive, is defined as a fragile, light body. (Thus, women worry more than men do about being overweight.) When they do exercises, women avoid the ones that develop the muscles, particularly those in the upper arms. Being "feminine" means looking physically weak, frail. Thus, the ideal woman's body is one that is not of much practical use in the hard work of this world, and one that must continually be "defended." Women do not develop their bodies, as men do. After a woman's body has reached its sexually acceptable form by late adolescence, most further development is viewed as negative. And it is thought irresponsible for women to do what is normal for men: simply leave their appearance alone. During early youth they are likely to come as close as they ever will to the ideal image—slim figure, smooth firm skin, light musculature, graceful movements. Their task is to try to maintain that image, unchanged, as long as possible. Improvement as such is not the task. Women care for their bodies—against toughening, coarsening, getting fat. They *conserve* them. (Perhaps the fact that women in modern societies tend to have a more conservative political outlook than men originates in their profoundly conservative relation to their bodies.)

In the life of women in this society the period of pride, of natural honesty, and unself-conscious flourishing is brief. Once past youth women are condemned to inventing (and maintaining) themselves against the inroads of age. Most of the physical qualities regarded as attractive in women deteriorate much earlier in life than those defined as "male." Indeed, they perish fairly soon in the normal sequence of body transformation. The "feminine" is smooth, rounded, hairless, unlined, soft, unmuscled—the look of the very young; characteristics of the weak, of the vulnerable, eunuch traits, as Germaine Greer has pointed out. Actually, there are only a few years—late adolescence, early twenties—in which this look is physiologically natural, in which it can be had without touching-up and covering-up. After that, women enlist in a quixotic enterprise, trying to chose the gap between the imagery put forth by society (concerning what is attractive in a woman) and the evolving facts of nature.

Women have a more intimate relation to aging than men do, simply because one of the accepted "women's" occupations is taking pains to keep one's face and body from showing the signs of growing older. Women's sexual validity depends, up to a certain point, on how well they stand off these natural changes. After late adolescence women become the caretakers of their bodies and faces, pursuing an essentially defensive strategy, a holding operation. A vast array of products in jars and tubes, a branch of surgery, and armies of hairdressers, masseuses, diet counselors, and other professionals exist to stave off, or mask, developments that are entirely normal biologically. Large amounts of women's energies are devoted into this passionate, corrupting effort to defeat nature: to maintain an ideal, static appearance against the progress of age. The collapse of the project is only a matter of time. Inevitably, a woman's physical appearance develops beyond its youthful form. No matter how exotic the creams or how strict the diets, one cannot indefinitely keep the face unlined, the waist slim. Bearing children takes its toll: the torso becomes thicker; the skin is stretched. There is no way to keep certain lines from appearing, in one's mid-twenties, around the eyes and mouth. From about thirty on, the skin gradually loses its tonus. In women this perfectly natural process is regarded as a humiliating defeat, while nobody finds anything remarkably unattractive in the equivalent physical changes in men. Men are "allowed" to look older without sexual penalty.

Thus, the reason that women experience aging with more pain than men is not simply that they care more than men about how they look. Men also care about their looks and want to be attractive, but since the business of men is mainly being and doing, rather than appearing, the standards for appearance are much less exacting. The standards for what is attractive in a man are permissive; they conform to what is possible or "natural" to most men throughout most of their lives. The standards for women's appearance go against nature, and to come anywhere near approximating them takes considerable effort and time. Women must try to be beautiful. At the least, they are under heavy social pressure not to be ugly. A woman's fortunes depend, far more than a man's, on being at least "acceptable" looking. Men are not subject to this pressure. Good looks in a man is a bonus, not a psychological necessity for maintaining normal self-esteem.

Behind the fact that women are more severely penalized than men are for aging is the fact that people, in this culture at least, are simply less tolerant of ugliness in women than in men. An ugly woman is never merely repulsive. Ugliness in a woman is felt by everyone, men as well as women, to be faintly embarrassing. And many features or blemishes that count as ugly in a woman's face would be quite tolerable on the face of a man. This is not, I would insist, just because the esthetic standards for men and women are different. It is rather because the esthetic standards for women are much higher, and narrower, than those proposed for men.

Beauty, women's business in this society, is the theater of their enslavement. Only one standard of female beauty is sanctioned: the *girl*. The great advantage men have is that our culture allows two standards of male beauty: the *boy* and the *man*. The beauty of a boy resembles the beauty of a girl. In both sexes it is a fragile kind of beauty and flourishes naturally only in the early part of the life-cycle. Happily, men are able to accept themselves under another standard of good looks—heavier, rougher, more thickly built. A man does not grieve when he loses the smooth, unlined, hairless skin of a boy. For he has only exchanged one form of attractiveness for another: the darker skin of a man's face, roughened by daily shaving, showing the marks of emotion and the normal lines of age. There is no equivalent of this second standard for women. The single standard of beauty for women dictates that they must go on heaving clear skin. Every wrinkle, every line, every grey hair, is a defeat. No wonder that no boy minds becoming a man, while even the passage from girlhood to early womanhood is experienced by many women as their downfall, for all women are trained to want to continue looking like girls.

This is not to say there are no beautiful older women. But the standard of beauty in a woman of any age is how far she retains, or how she manages to simulate, the appearance of youth. The exceptional woman in her sixties who is beautiful certainly owes a large debt to her genes. Delayed aging, like good looks, tends to run in families. But nature rarely offers enough to meet this culture's standards. Most of the women who successfully delay the appearance of age are rich, with unlimited leisure to devote to nurturing along nature's gifts. Often they are actresses. (That is, highly paid professionals at doing what all women are taught to practice as amateurs.) Such women as Mae West, Dietrich, Stella Adler, Dolores Del Rio, do not challenge the rule about the relation between beauty and age in women.

They are admired precisely because they *are* exceptions, because they have managed (at least so it seems in photographs) to outwit nature. Such miracles, exceptions made by nature (with the help of art and social privilege), only confirm the rule, because what makes these women seem beautiful to us is precisely that they do not look their real age. Society allows no place in our imagination for a beautiful old woman who does look like an old woman—a woman who might be like Picasso at the age of ninety, being photographed outdoors on his estate in the south of France, wearing only shorts and sandals. No one imagines such a woman exists. Even the special exceptions—Mae West & Co.—are always photographed indoors, cleverly lit, from the most flattering angle and fully, artfully clothed. The implication is they would not stand a closer scrutiny. The idea of an old woman in a bathing suit being attractive, or even just acceptable looking, is inconceivable. An older woman is, by definition, sexually repulsive—unless, in fact, she doesn't look old at all. The body of an old woman, unlike that of an old man, is always understood as a body that can no longer be shown, offered, unveiled. At best, it may appear in costume. People still feel uneasy, thinking about what they might see if her mask dropped, if she took off her clothes.

Thus, the point for women of dressing up, applying make-up, dyeing their hair, going on crash diets, and getting face-lifts is not just to be attractive. They are ways of defending themselves against a profound level of disapproval directed toward women, a disapproval that can take the form of aversion. The double standard about aging converts the life of women into an inexorable march toward a condition in which they are not just unattractive, but disgusting. The profoundest terror of a woman's life is the moment represented in a statue by Rodin called *Old Age:* a naked old woman, seated, pathetically contemplates her flat, pendulous, ruined body. Aging in women is a process of becoming obscene sexually, for the flabby bosom, wrinkled neck, spotted hands, thinning white hair, waistless torso, and veined legs of an old woman are felt to be obscene. In our direst moments of the imagination, this transformation can take place with dismaying speed—as in the end of *Lost Horizon,* when the beautiful young girl is carried by her lover out of Shangri-La and, within minutes, turns into a withered, repulsive crone. There is no equivalent nightmare about men. This is why, however much a man may care about his appearance, that caring can never acquire the same desperateness it often does for women. When men dress according to fashion or now even use cosmetics, they do not expect from clothes and make-up what women do. A face-lotion or perfume or deodorant or hairspray, used by a man, is not part of a disguise. Men, as men, do not feel the need to disguise themselves to fend off morally disapproved signs of aging, to outwit premature sexual obsolescence, to cover up aging as obscenity. Men are not subject to the barely concealed revulsion expressed in this culture against the female body—except in its smooth, youthful, firm, odorless, blemish-free form.

One of the attitudes that punish women most severely is the visceral horror felt at aging female flesh. It reveals a radical fear of women installed deep in this culture, a demonology of women that has crystallized in such mythic caricatures as the vixen, the virago, the vamp, and the witch. Several centuries of witch-phobia, during which one of the cruelest extermination programs in Western history was carried out, suggest something of the extremity of this fear. That old women are repulsive is one of the most profound esthetic and erotic feelings in our culture. Women share it as much as men do. (Oppressors, as a rule, deny oppressed people their own "native" standards of beauty. And the oppressed end up being convinced that they *are* ugly.) How women are psychologically damaged by this misogynistic idea of what is beautiful parallels the way in which blacks have been deformed in a society that has up to now defined beautiful as white. Psychological tests made on young black children in the United States some years ago showed how early and how thoroughly they incorporate the white standard of good looks. Virtually all the children expressed fantasies that indicated they considered black people to be ugly, funny looking, dirty, brutish. A similar kind of self-hatred infects most women. Like men, they find old age in women "uglier" than old age in men.

This esthetic taboo functions, in sexual attitudes, as a racial taboo. In this society most people feel an involuntary recoil of the flesh when imagining a middle-aged woman making love with a young man—exactly as many whites flinch viscerally at the thought of a white woman in bed with a black man. The banal drama of a man of fifty who leaves a wife of forty-five for a girlfriend of twenty-eight contains no strictly sexual outrage, whatever sympathy people may have for the abandoned wife. On the contrary. Everyone "understands." Everyone knows that men like girls, that young women often want middle-aged men. But no one "understands" the reverse situation. A woman of forty-five who leaves a husband of fifty for a lover of twenty-eight is the makings of a social and sexual scandal at a deep level of feeling. No one takes exception to a romantic couple in which the man is twenty years or more the woman's senior. The movies pair Joanne Dru and John Wayne, Marilyn Monroe and Joseph Cotten, Audrey Hepburn and Cary Grant, Jane Fonda and Yves Montand, Catherine Deneuve and Marcello Mastroianni; as in actual life, these are perfectly plausible, appealing couples. When the age difference runs the other way, people are puzzled and embarrassed and simply shocked. (Remember Joan Crawford and Cliff Robertson in *Autum Leaves*? But so troubling is this kind of love story that it rarely figures in the movies, and then only as the melancholy history of a failure.) The usual view of why a woman of forty and a boy of twenty, or a women of fifty and a man of thirty, marry is that the man is seeking a mother, not a wife; no one believes the marriage will last. For a woman to respond erotically and romantically to a man who, in terms of his age, could be her father is considered normal. A man who falls in love with a woman who, however attractive she may be, is old enough to be his mother is thought to be extremely neurotic (victim of an "Oedipal fixation" is the fashionable tag), if not mildly contemptible.

The wider the gap in age between partners in a couple, the more obvious is the prejudice against women. When old men, such as Justice Douglas, Picasso, Strom Thurmond, Onassis, Chaplin, and Pablo Casals, take brides thirty, forty, fifty years younger than themselves, it strikes people as remarkable, perhaps an exaggeration—but still plausible. To explain such a match, people enviously attribute some special virility and charm to the man. Though he can't be handsome, he is famous; and his fame is understood as having boosted his attractiveness to women. People imagine that his young wife, respectful of her elderly husband's attainments, is happy to become his helper. For the man a late marriage is always good public relations. It adds to the impression that, despite his advanced age, he is still to be reckoned with; it is the sign of a continuing vitality presumed to be available as well to his art, business activity, or political career. But an elderly woman who married a young man would be greeted quite differently. She would have broken a fierce taboo, and she would get no credit for her courage. Far from being admired for her vitality, she would probably be condemned as predatory, willful, selfish, exhibitionistic. At the same time she would be pitied, since such a marriage would be taken as evidence that she was in her dotage. If she had a conventional career or were in business or held public office, she would quickly suffer from the current of disapproval. Her very credibility as a professional would decline, since people would suspect that her young husband might have an undue influence on her. Her "respectability" would certainly be compromised. Indeed, the well-known old women I can think of who dared such unions, if only at the end of their lives—George Eliot, Colette, Edith Piaf—have all belonged to that category of people, creative artists and entertainers, who have special license from society to behave scandalously. It is thought to be a scandal for a woman to ignore that she is old and therefore too ugly for a young man. Her looks and a certain physical condition determine a woman's desirability, not her talents or her needs. Women are not supposed to be "potent." A marriage between an old woman and a young man subverts the very ground rule of relations between the two sexes, that is: whatever the variety of appearances, men remain dominant. Their claims come first. Women are supposed to be the associates and companions of men, not their full equals—and never their superiors. Women are to remain in the state of a permanent "minority."

The convention that wives should be younger than their husbands powerfully enforces the "minority" status of women, since being senior in age always carries with it, in any relationship, a certain amount of power and authority. There are no laws on the matter, of course. The convention is obeyed because to do otherwise makes one feel as if one is doing something ugly or in bad taste. Everyone feels intuitively the esthetic rightness of a marriage in which the man is older than the woman, which means that any marriage in which the woman is older creates a dubious or less gratifying mental picture. Everyone is addicted to the visual pleasure that women give by meeting certain esthetic requirements from which men are exempted, which keeps women working at staying youthful-looking while men are left free to age. On a deeper level everyone finds the signs of old age in women esthetically offensive, which conditions one to feel automatically repelled by the prospect of an elderly woman marrying a much younger man. The situation in which women are kept minors for life is largely organized by such conformist, unreflective preferences. But taste is not free, and its judgments are never merely "natural." Rules of taste enforce structures of power. The revulsion against aging in women is the cutting edge of a whole set of oppressive structures (often masked as gallantries) that keep women in their place.

The ideal state proposed for women is docility, which means not being fully grown up. Most of what is cherished as typically "feminine" is simply behavior that is childish, immature, weak. To offer so low and demeaning a standard of fulfillment in itself constitutes oppression in an acute form—a sort of moral neo-colonialism. But women are not simply condescended to by the values that secure the dominance of men. They are repudiated. Perhaps because of having been their oppressors for so long, few men really *like* women (though they love individual women), and few men ever feel really comfortable or at ease in women's company. This malaise arises because relations between the two sexes are rife with hypocrisy, as men manage to love those they dominate and therefore don't respect. Oppressors always try to justify their privileges and brutalities by imagining that those they oppress belong to a lower order of civilization or are less than fully "human." Deprived of part of their ordinary human dignity, the oppressed take on certain "demonic" traits. The oppressions of large groups have to be anchored deep in the psyche, continually renewed by partly unconscious fears and taboos, by a sense of the obscene. Thus, women arouse not only desire and affection in men but aversion as well. Women are thoroughly domesticated familiars. But, at certain times and in certain situations, they become alien, untouchable. The aversion men feel, so much of which is covered over, is felt most frankly, with least inhibition, toward the type of woman who is most taboo "esthetically," a woman who has become—with the natural changes brought about by aging—obscene.

Nothing more clearly demonstrates the vulnerability of women than the special pain, confusion, and bad faith with which they experience getting older. And in the struggle that some women are waging on behalf of all women to be treated (and treat themselves) as full human beings—not "only" as women—one of the earliest results to be hoped for is that women become aware, indignantly aware, of the double standard about aging from which they suffer so harshly.

It is understandable that women often succumb to the temptation to lie about their age. Given society's double standard, to question a woman about her age is indeed often an aggressive act, a trap. Lying is an elementary means of self-defense, a way of scrambling out of the trap, at least temporarily. To expect a woman, after "a certain age," to tell exactly how old she is—when she has a chance, either through the generosity of nature or the cleverness of art, to pass for being somewhat younger than she actually is—is like expecting a landowner to admit that the estate he has put up for sale is actually worth less than the buyer is prepared to pay. The doubtle standard about aging sets women up as property, as objects whose value depreciates rapidly with the march of the calendar.

The prejudices that mount against women as they grow older are an important arm of male privilege. It is the present unequal distribution of adult roles between the two sexes that gives men a freedom to age denied to women. Men actively administer the double standard about aging because the "masculine" role awards them the initiative in courtship. Men choose; women are chosen. So men choose younger women. But although this system of inequality is operated by men, it could not work if women themselves did not acquiesce in it. Women reinforce it powerfully with their complacency, with their anguish, with their lies.

Not only do women lie more than men do about their age but men forgive them for it, thereby confirming their own superiority. A man who lies about his age is thought to be weak, "unmanly." A woman who lies about her age is behaving in a quite acceptable, "feminine" way. Petty lying is viewed by men with indulgence, one of a number of patronizing allowances made for women. It has the same moral unimportance as the fact that women are often late for appointments. Women are not expected to be truthful, or punctual, or expert in handling and repairing machines, or frugal, or physically brave. They are expected to be second-class adults, whose natural state is that of a grateful dependence on men. And so they often are, since that is what they are brought up to be. So far as women heed the stereotypes of "feminine" behavior, they *cannot* behave as fully responsible, independent adults.

Most women share the contempt for women expressed in the double standard about aging—to such a degree that they take their lack of self-respect for granted. Women have been accustomed so long to the protection of their masks, their smiles, their endearing lies. Without this protection, they know, they would be more vulnerable. But in protecting themselves as women, they betray themselves as adults. The model corruption in a woman's life is denying her age. She symbolically accedes to all those myths that furnish women with their imprisoning securities and privileges, that create their genuine oppression, that inspire their real discontent. Each time a woman lies about her age she becomes an accomplice in her own underdevelopment as a human being.

Women have another option. They can aspire to be wise, not merely nice; to be competent, not merely helpful; to be strong, not merely graceful; to be ambitious for themselves, not merely for themselves in relation to men and children. They can let themselves age naturally and without embarrassment, actively protesting and disobeying the conventions that stem from this society's double standard about aging. Instead of being girls, girls as long as possible, who then age humiliatingly into middle-aged women and then obscenely into old women, they can become women much earlier—and remain active adults, enjoying the long, erotic career of which women are capable, far longer. Women should allow their faces to show the lives they have lived. Women should tell the truth.

Women in the Middle Years
Conceptions and Misconceptions

Rosalind Barnett and Grace Baruch

Although it is now widely acknowledged that the middle years, for both men and women, are a time of development and change rather than of stability and decline, relatively little is known about these years. In 1968, Bernice Neugarten commented on the state of knowledge about human adulthood: "Not only is there a paucity of data, but more important, we are without a useful theory." Again in 1975, Brim and Abeles described the middle years as a "largely unexplored phase of the human life cycle." Particularly with respect to women, theoretical work is in its infancy and empirical findings tend to be scattered and non-cumulative.

Yet the need for knowledge about the middle years in women is increasingly urgent. A longer life span and overpopulation, combined with women's increasing educational attainments and labor force participation, have made obsolete much of previous research and theory. Moreover, there is evidence, although not completely consistent, that women are especially vulnerable to distress and dissatisfaction.

In this paper we review selected theories and research in order to examine such impediments to understanding as assumptions and biases, limitations and stereotypes. We then briefly point to conceptual areas that promise to be fruitful for the study of adult women.

An illustration of certain weaknesses of current theory and research can be found in the literature concerning the mental health and well-being of women in the middle years.

"Women in the Middle Years: A Critique of Research and Theory" by Rosalind Barnett and Grace Baruch from *Psychology of Women Quarterly*. Reprinted by permission of Human Sciences Press and the authors.

A Case of Conflicting Evidence: The Well-Being of Adult Women

In their study of the perceived quality of life, Campbell, Converse, and Rodgers (1976) find no evidence that women's lives are any less rewarding or satisfying than are men's. Yet findings from a variety of research studies indicate a significantly higher level of distress among women. Lowenthal, Thurnher, and Chiriboga (1975), in their study of four groups of men and women facing life transitions (high school seniors, newlyweds, "empty nest" [middle-aged] and pre-retirement couples) found that the middle-aged women were the most distressed group. They had poorer self-concepts, were the lowest in life satisfaction, most pessimistic, highest in existential despair, and most negative toward their spouses. Other studies, for example, that of Gurin, Veroff, and Feld (1960), indicate that women have poorer self-concepts, feel more inadequate as parents and more dissatisfied with their marriages, and report more problems and psychiatric symptomatology than do men, although they do not differ from men in global ratings of general happiness.

Recent careful re-analyses of mental health data suggest that if one considers all forms of mental illness, including for example such often ignored categories as alcoholic disorders, women are no more disturbed than men. However, compared to men they do suffer more from such specific disabilities as depression, neurotic disorders, and functional psychoses. Several researchers report that this finding is not due to artifacts of reporting nor to women's greater willingness to admit symptoms, nor to biases of mental health professionals (Radloff, 1975; Guttentag, Salasin, Legge, & Bray, Note 1; Weissman & Klerman, Note 2).

We shall now analyze theoretical and empirical approaches that may have impeded efforts to resolve these conflicting findings.

Theoretical Considerations

In two major theories of adult development, those of Erikson (1959) and Levinson (1976), adult development is seen as proceeding linearly through a series of stages, each of which poses certain tasks for resolution. For Erikson, for example, the task of identity formation is associated with late adolescence and early adulthood. However, for women, especially those who have children, issues of personal identity often do not become critical until childrearing responsibilities diminish in the late 30's and 40's. Recognizing problems of fit between his theory and the experiences of many women, Erikson suggests that the resolution of their identity crises occurs after choice of a mate. The implications of Erikson's theoretical position are ominous. Women, but not men, require a spouse before they can complete as crucial a task as identity formation; not marrying implies never establishing one's identity.

Similar problems of fit occur with respect to Levinson's theory, which was developed through intensive interviewing of a small sample of men. He views one's 20's as a time for entering marriage and the world of work;

and one's 30's as a time for establishing oneself in these arenas. Toward 40 there is reconsideration of one's commitments and often attempt to free oneself from a previously central mentor, the famous BOOM phenomenon—becoming one's own man. It is hard to know how to think of women within this theory—a woman may not enter the world of work until her late 30's, she seldom has had a mentor, and even women with life-long career commitments rarely are in a position to reassess their commitment pattern by age 40.

Both Erikson's and Levinson's models reflect male experience. Perhaps for this reason, they focus on chronological age as a key variable and they assume a continuous, uninterrupted series of events such as marriage and occupational commitment. (Loevinger's stage theory of ego development [1966] is not based on chronological age. However, the theory has not yet had a major impact on the mainstream of research and theory on the middle years.)

It is true that men and women share certain universal experiences linked to age. Near 40, both may have a sense of time running out and may have to deal with stresses associated with adolescent children and aging parents. Yet if one begins with a consideration not of the male experience but of the reality and variations of women's lives, it is unlikely that chronological age would be seen as the central variable. Furthermore, the concept of stage, which is also central to these theories, is not used with sufficient rigor: the processes and mechanisms underlying the sequence of stages and accompanying crises remain to be worked out (Brim, 1966).

For women, then, the approach of these theorists seems inappropriate, particularly because they fail to take into account varying role patterns a woman may occupy. Numerous combinations of career, marriage, and children may occur with respect to both the timing and the degree of commitment, and each has different ramifications. Independent of role pattern, the stage of a woman's family life cycle—whether she has no children, young children, or grown children—also has a powerful impact upon her life experience.

Empirical Studies: Limitations and Biases

The link between theoretical and empirical work concerning women in the middle years is weak. For example, in attempting to explain the high level of distress in the middle-aged women they studied, Lowenthal *et al.* (1975) suggest that the findings may be evidence for Freud's view of adult women. He saw women in the menopausal years as frequently suffering from unresolved, recurrent Oedipal conflicts and perceived most women as rigid and worn out developmentally, because of their early, difficult psychosexual development. Such theoretical formulations at best reflect the social realities and mores of earlier times and thus seem out-moded and inadequate explanations. When such formulations guide the design and interpretation of empirical studies, their value is greatly diminished.

Underlying many studies of women in the middle years is a belief in the biological determinism of feminine behavior. Certain subtle assumptions about women are widely shared and reflected in research, although not always stated: that the mind-body relationship is somehow closer for women than for men; that biological influences are thus stronger for women (Parlee, Note 3). Because of this view, a woman's life is too often seen only in terms of her reproductive role; menopause and the "empty nest" become the major events of the middle years. Furthermore, marriage and children are conceptualized as crucial to a woman's well-being. Evidence to the contrary is greeted with surprise (Maas & Kuypers, 1974) or its significance not understood. For example, the middle-aged women studied by Lowenthal *et al.* (1975) reported that they were looking forward to the empty nest. Given the assumption of centrality of the childrearing function to women's well-being, the researchers doubted these self-reports, which have since been supported by follow-up studies (Lowenthal, 1975). The researchers suggested that the women's anxiety and despair about their children leaving home must be too deep to be tapped, even in lengthy interviews.

Indeed, the very use of the term "menopausal" women or "empty nest" women to describe certain groups of subjects reflects fixed assumptions about the centrality of these events. The work of Neugarten, Wood, Kraines, and Loomis (1968) and McKinlay and Jeffries (1974) has shown that menopause is not seen as a central or distressing event by women in or past that stage. And Campbell (1976), reflecting on the results of his recent survey, has stated that "the empty nest has a reputation that is not deserved." Findings from several studies (Campbell *et al.,* 1976; Lowenthal, 1975; Radloff, 1975) confirm that the well-being of women whose children have left home is higher, and the incidence of depression lower, than in women living with young children. Yet, despite contradictory evidence, the assumption persists that certain life styles are necessary for happiness among women.

Perhaps the best illustration of the impact of out-moded assumptions, stereotypes, and biases is the way researchers deal with the variable of work. Although 90% of all women work for pay at some point in their lives, paid employment has not been conceptualized as central to the lives of women, who are not expected to function as economic providers nor to derive self-esteem and identity from this role. Since industrialization separated work and family life, women have been seen as primarily committed to the family and as thus out of place and unreliable at places of employment (Coser & Rokoff, 1970).

This view is reflected even in the selection of subjects for study. In one major study of the impact of menopause, women who worked were simply excluded from the sample, apparently because they were too deviant (Van Keep & Kellerhals, 1975). In a major ongoing longitudinal study of retirement, married women are excluded on the grounds that it is their husband's retirement that has the important impact on their lives (Sherman, 1974). Whatever validity such decisions once had, their function today is to limit the usefulness of the findings.

When women who work *are* included in studies, and even when work is treated as an important variable, as in comparisons of working versus nonworking women, relevant differentiations among workers are rarely made. Physicians and sales clerks, the career-committed and those who would prefer to be at home, are too often treated as one group. In studies based upon probability samples, the numbers of women working in high-prestige professions are too small to be useful in data analysis (Campbell *et al.*, 1976).

Yet aspects of work status such as level of occupation and of commitment appear to have a profound effect upon women's experiences, particularly in the second half of the life span. Judith Birnbaum (1975) studied satisfaction and self-esteem at mid-life in comparable groups of married professionals with children, single professionals, and "home-makers," women who had not worked since the birth of their first child. Both groups of professional women were more satisfied and had higher self-esteem than did the women who had lived out the traditional role pattern. In Sears and Barbee's (1977) analysis of Terman's sample of gifted women, married women were less satisfied with their life patterns than were women who were single, divorced, or widowed. Satisfaction was highest among women who were both single and income producers.

These studies do not address the problem of cohort effects. Furthermore, there may be an interaction of age and work status. In Birnbaum's (1975) study, the women were from about 35 to 50; in Sears and Barbee's they were in their 60's. During the early adult years commitment to work might not have been a more satisfying pattern than a solely domestic pattern. Moreover, working women in these studies were in relatively high-prestige occupations. Most women who work hold routine, low-level jobs. Thus assessment of occupational level is crucial for understanding the impact of work on women's lives.

Kanter's (Note 4) recent analysis of the impact of structural conditions of employment suggests other specific components of the work situation which may affect satisfaction, self-esteem, and well-being, as well as women's work-related behavior and attitudes. She points out that the conditions under which many women work, namely: low level of occupation, the absence of opportunity for advancement, lack of power, and tokenism, are related to low career aspirations and commitment, and to low self-esteem (in men as well as women). Because most studies fail to take into account those qualitative aspects of work, the studies conclude that for women, in contrast to men, work satisfaction has little effect on well-being (Bradburn & Caplovitz, 1965; Campbell *et al.*, 1976).

The failure to deal adequately with the variable of work reflects assumptions about the centrality of marriage and children, menopause and empty nest, over work-related issues. One cannot understand the impact of marriage and children upon women in a vacuum; without careful consideration of work status, the heated debate about whether marriage and children are a "health hazard" for women (Bernard, 1972; Campbell *et al.*, 1976; Glenn, 1975) may not be resolvable.

Another limiting assumption concerning women and work is that for women who are married and have children, the work role has been seen almost exclusively as a source of conflict, ambivalence, and overload (Hall & Gordon, 1973); beneficial, invigorating, health-maintaining aspects of combining roles have been overlooked. Yet Gove and Tudor (1973) have argued that, for men, access to sources of satisfaction in both work and family accounts for their lesser tendency to psychiatric symptomatology. Moreover, in a study of stressful events and mitigators of stress among women living in London, Brown, Bhrolchain, and Harris (1975) found that for women who were both under stress and unable to turn to a confidante, work served to prevent the development of psychiatric symptomatology; only 14% of such women who worked developed symptoms, compared with 79% of those who did not work. Thus the traditional role pattern, as Bailyn (Note 5) points out, although perhaps still adaptive in early adult years, soon begins to "exact a toll." Perhaps it is this toll that has led researchers to focus so much on problems and dysfunctions—on losses such as the menopause and the empty nest—rather than on positive influences on women's mental health.

Future Theory and Research

How can a theory of women in the middle years be developed? We have already suggested the necessity of including certain variables as elements in such a theory—work status and conditions; role pattern; and stage of the family life cycle. At present, no theoretical framework links these variables. Indeed, it is premature to expect to formulate a comprehensive theory. As Lowenthal (1975) points out, given the present state of knowledge, researchers should "systematically explore concepts of a number of disciplines in order to locate potentially useful building blocks toward the eventual development of an interdisciplinary science of adult development and aging."

In the spirit of Lowenthal's suggestion, we suggest two additional "potentially useful" conceptual areas: (a) locus of control and attributions; and (b) support systems and social networks. The task of integrating these into other areas of research remains.

Locus of Control and Attributions

Locus of control (Rotter, 1966) refers to whether one believes that what happens to one is mainly contingent on one's own behavior (internal locus) versus is independent of one's behavior or outside one's own control (external locus). Attribution research deals with how people understand and explain the causes of their successes and failures, e.g., luck, effort. The causes tend to fall on two dimensions—stable/unstable and internal/external (Weiner, Frieze, Kukla, Reed, Rest, & Rosenbaum, 1971).

Although there is conflicting evidence on this point it appears that women are more likely to see what happens to them as independent of their own behavior than are men, and they also more often attribute their successes to external and/or unstable factors. However, one's confidence, self-esteem, and sense of competence are best served by attributing success to internal stable factors and failure to external unstable ones (Frieze, 1975). Furthermore, the sense of being in charge of one's life fosters self-esteem while feelings that one is not in charge are associated with depression and a sense of helplessness (Seligman, 1974). Thus research on locus of control and attributions is highly relevant to understanding women's experiences and attitudes.

Social Networks and Support Systems

Campbell (1976) has stated that progress in understanding well-being requires exploration of social networks and supports. Empirical evidence is consistent with this view. Support systems and social networks can be conceptualized as buffers against stress, as "protective social processes" (Caplan, 1974). Social networks usually refer to the number, frequency, proximity, and quality of social contacts; support systems are most typically studied in relation to patterns of help utilization—what persons or institutions are turned to for help with problems.

Bradburn and Caplowitz (1965) found that positive components of happiness correlated highly with participation in social networks and social interactions. Brown *et al.* (1975) found that, for women under stress, the most powerful mitigator was a confidante, a person who is rated highest on a scale of practical and emotional support.

In a study of the differential use of helping systems by men and women, Warren (Note 6) found that women relied on help from a spouse less than did men; sex differences were more pronounced in blue-collar, compared with white-collar subjects. She also found social class differences in the helping sources available to women. White-collar women had a greater variety of resources than did blue-collar women (co-workers, physicians), who typically experience more stress. Research on patterns of networks and supports thus bear directly upon understanding women's lives.

Conclusion

Our concern that research and theory on women in the middle years go beyond a focus on problems and dysfunctions ought not to be taken to mean that we are complacent or sanguine about women's well-being. Recent studies document the increasing incidence of depression in women, which is occurring at earlier ages, particularly in women with young children. Those who are single parents and who work at low-paying jobs are particularly at risk, and it is fortunate that intervention attempts are not awaiting the final word from academe (Guttentag *et al.*, Note 1).

The situation of older women, particularly those living out the traditional role pattern, also requires thoughtful intervention. In an interview study of a sample of U.S. women, Weiss, and Samuelson (1958) asked, "What are the things you do that make you feel useful or important?" They report, "A rather substantial proportion of women in the older age groups said that nothing made them feel useful and important." Judith Bardwick (Note 7) has commented that only the sense of challenge and commitment and the possibility of new undertakings can make the middle years rewarding. Yet Marjorie Lowenthal (1975) has pointed out the painful situation of middle-aged women whose deepest desire is for a way to grow and develop, but who see no way to do so. We are hopeful that sound theoretical and empirical work on women in the middle years will point to ways of preventing and mitigating such distress and will thus promote well-being.

NOTES

1. Guttentag, M., Salasin, S., Legge, W. W., & Bray, H. *Sex differences in the utilization of publicly supported mental health facilities.* Unpublished manuscript, Harvard University.
2. Weissman, M. M. & Klerman, G. L. *Sex differences and the epidemiology of depression.* Unpublished manuscript, Yale University.
3. Parlee, M. Psychological aspects of menstruation, childbirth and menopause: An overview with suggestions for further research. Paper presented at conference *New Directions for Research on Women,* Madison, Wisconsin, 1975.
4. Kanter, R. N. Women and hierarchies. Paper presented at the meeting of the American Sociological Association, San Francisco, 1975.
5. Bailyn, L. Discussant's comments at symposium, *Will the real middle-aged women please stand up: Toward an understanding of adult development in women.* Presented at the meeting of the Eastern Psychological Association, New York, April 17th.
6. Warren, R. B. *The work role and problem coping: Sex differentials in the use of helping systems in urban communities.* Paper presented at the meeting of the American Sociological Association, San Francisco, 1975.
7. Bardwick, J. M. *Middle age and a sense of the future.* Paper presented at the meeting of the American Sociological Association, San Francisco, 1975.

REFERENCES

BERNARD, J. *The future of marriage.* New York: World-Times, 1972.

BIRNBAUM, J. A. Life patterns and self-esteem in gifted family-oriented and career-committed women. In M. Mednick, S. Tangri, & L. Hoffman (Eds.), *Women and achievement: Social and motivational analysis.* New York: Wiley, 1975.

BRADBURN, N. M., & CAPLOVITZ, D. *Reports on happiness.* Chicago: Aldine, 1965.

BRIM, O. G., JR. Theories of the male mid-life crisis. *The Counseling Psychologist,* 1976, *6,* 2–9.

BRIM, O. G., JR., & ABBELES, R. P. Work and personality in the middle years. *Items,* Social Science Research Council, 1975, *29.*

BROWN, G. W., BHROLCHAIN, M. N., & HARRIS, T. Social class and psychiatric disturbance among women in an urban population. *Sociology,* 1975, *9,* 225–254.

CAMPBELL, A. Subjective measures of well-being. *American Psychologist,* 1976, *31,* 117–124.

CAMPBELL, A., CONVERSE, P. E., & RODGERS, W. L. *The quality of American life.* New York: Russell Sage, 1976.

CAPLAN, G. Support systems. In G. Caplan (Ed.), *Support systems and community mental health.* New York: Behavioral Publications, 1974, 1–40.

COSER, R. L., & ROKOFF, G. Women in the occupational world: Social disruption and conflict. *Social Problems,* 1970, *18,* 534–541.

ERIKSON, E. H. Identity and the life-cycle. *Psychological Issues,* 1959, No. 1.

FRIEZE, I. H. Women's expectations for and casual attributions of success and failure. In M. Mednick, S. Tangri, & L. Hoffman (Eds.), *Women and achievement: Social and motivational analysis.* New York: Wiley, 1975.

GLENN, N. D. The contribution of marriage to the psychological well-being of males and females. *Journal of Marriage and the Family,* 1975, *37,* 594–601.

GOVE, W. R., & TUDOR, J. F. Adult sex roles and mental illness. *American Journal of Sociology,* 1973, *78,* 812–835.

GURIN, G., VEROFF, J., & FELD, S. *Americans view their mental health.* New York: Basic Books, 1960.

HALL, D. T., & GORDON, F. E. Career choices of married women: Effects on conflict, role behavior, and satisfaction. *Journal of Applied Psychology,* 1973, *59,* 47–58.

LEVINSON, D. J., DARROW, C. M., KLEIN, E. B., LEVINSON, M. H., & MCKEE, B. Periods in the adult development of men: Ages 18 to 45. *The Counseling Psychologist,* 1976, *6,* 21–25.

LOEVINGER, J. The meaning and measurement of ego development. *American Psychologist,* 1966, *21,* 195–206.

LOWENTHAL, M. F. Psychosocial variations across the adult life course: Frontiers for research and policy. *The Gerontologist,* 1975, *15,* 6–12.

LOWENTHAL, M. F., THURNHER, M., & CHIRIBOGA, D. *Four stages of life.* San Francisco: Jossey-Bass, 1974.

MCKINLAY, S. M., & JEFFREYS, M. The menopausal syndrome. *British Journal of Preventive and Social Medicine,* 1974, *28,* 108–115.

NEUGARTEN, B. L. Adult personality: Toward a psychology of the life cycle. In B. L. Neugarten (Ed.), *Middle age and aging.* Chicago: University of Chicago Press, 1968.

NEUGARTEN, B. L., WOOD, V., KRAINES, R J., & LOOMIS, B. Women's attitudes toward the menopause. In B. L. Neugarten (Ed.), *Middle age and aging.* Chicago: University of Chicago Press, 1968.

RADLOFF, L. Sex differences in depression: The effects of occupation and marital status. *Sex Roles,* 1975, *1,* 249–265.

ROTTER, J. B. Generalized expectancies for internal versus external control of reinforcement. *Psychological Monographs: General and Applied,* 1966, *80,* 1–28.

SEARS, P. S., & BARBEE, A. H. Career and life satisfaction among Terman's gifted women. In J. Stanley, W. George, & C. Solano (Eds.), *The gifted and the creative: Fifty-year perspective.* Baltimore, Md.: Johns Hopkins University Press, 1977, in press.

SELIGMAN, M. Depression and learned helplessness. In R. J. Friedman & M. Katz (Ed.), *The psychology of depression: Contemporary theory and research.* Washington, D.C.: Winston, 1974.

SHERMAN, S. R. Labor-force status of nonmarried women on the threshold of retirement. *Social Security Bulletin,* September, 1974, DHEW Publication No. (SSA), 75–11700.

VAN KEEP, P. A., & KELLERHALS, J. M. The aging woman. *Acta Obstetricia et Gynecologica, Scandinavica Suppl.,* 1975, *51,* 17–27.

WEINER, B., FRIEZE, I., KUKLA, A., REED, L., REST, S., & ROSENBAUM, R. *Perceiving the causes of success and failure.* New York: General Learning, 1971.

WEISS, R. S., & SAMUELSON, N. M. Social roles of American women: Their contribution to a sense of usefulness and importance. *Journal of Marriage and Family,* 1958, *20,* 358–366.

A Cross-Cultural Investigation of Behavioral Changes at Menopause

Joyce Griffen

Two basic questions are addressed in this article: first, in what cultures are there rites of passage to move women from their reproductive years to their status as "old," and second, in what other ways is this transition eased for women in various cultures? It was hypothesized that the discipline of anthropology, which has detailed rituals performed at menarche, would also have recorded instances of rituals and their content at menopause. Further, it was hypothesized that cultures which do not provide such ceremonies will in some other way or ways indicate acceptable and unacceptable behavior during and after menopause.

Proceeding from these logical hypotheses, there are further questions. Given the presence or absence of ceremonies, what correlations exist with, for example, comparative dominance or submission of females within various cultures, or with types of descent systems, or the different activities of women within and outside the family and the household at different ages or with changed behavior of significant others in the culture vis-à-vis the menopausal woman who may be changing her roles?

Unfortunately, the cross-cultural data on menopause are so limited that the only conclusions that can be drawn are tentative at best. Because of their scarcity, these data are treated descriptively rather than statistically in this presentation. The very paucity of data suggests further explanatory hypotheses, which will be presented at the conclusion of the discussion.

The McKinlay and McKinlay "Selected Studies of the Menopause" appears to be the only recent synopsis of studies of menopause.[1] Their bibli-

"A Cross Cultural Investigation of Behavioral Changes at Menopause" by Joyce Griffen from the *Social Science Journal,* 14, 2 (1977). Reprinted by permission of the *Social Science Journal* and by Greenwood Press, Inc.

ography annotates 84 articles, fifteen of which are concerned solely with clinical trials in the area of menopausal therapy. Only three of the remaining 69 references include data from other than Caucasian women. Of the three, one is a study of 55 women in Israel "of European and Oriental origin"; another includes just over 1,300 Bantu women but reports only on an attempt to discover mean age at menopause in South Africa (Bantu women reportedly cease menstruation nine months earlier than white women in the same area); while a book published in 1897 and long out of print compares the menopausal experience of Eskimos and American Indians with that of French and Irish women.

The McKinlays pose six research questions for future investigation, two of which might profitably be investigated with reference to cross-cultural data, it seemed (special attention is given here to the second question):

(1) How can the intra- and inter-societal differences in the appearance of symptoms be explained? Why is it, for example, that in some societies there is no apparent evidence of "menopausal symptoms"?

(2) If the menopause signals for women the end of such socially important roles as reproducer, mother, and perhaps even wife, could it be that "menopausal" symptomatology is a manifestation of difficulties of role readjustment experienced at about this time of life?[2]

To research these questions cross-culturally, the Human Relations Area Files were used. Category 886, "Senescence," in *Outline of Cultural Materials* deals with "cultural criteria of senescence and the onset of old age, menopause (e.g., cultural interpretation, adaptive changes in behavior) . . . and retirement from active life."[3] However, 191 of the cultures indexed in the Human Relations Area Files-Microfiles collection had no entry whatsoever in the "Senescence" category, and an additional 41 had no material relevant to the hypotheses. Of the remaining approximately 35 cultures, ten noted changed behavior of both males and females in "old age." For example, both Nahane males and females restrict activities with increasing age; Burmese women are expected (as are Burmese men) to be retiring and unobtrusive in their behavior when the third age of life is reached, and in the Soviet Union management is legally obliged to release male employees at age sixty if they have completed 25 years of work or females at age 55 if they have completed 20 years of work.[4]

In eight cultures, it was specifically noted that no behavior changed for post-menopausal women. Elwin notes that "as elsewhere in aboriginal India, the climacteric does not appear to be dreaded or even especially noticed. In India, women are old at forty-five and they greet the cessation of the menstrual period with relief. . . ."[5] For the Marias, " 'As it appears, so it disappears.' If an elderly woman or her husband dreams of a dried-up tank or stream, it means that this crisis is approaching."[6] With the Lepcha, "It is realised that after a certain age women cease to conceive, but there is no break in their sexual activities."[7]

Changed behavior obviously has been recorded in only a small number of the world's cultures. One type of change noted is that of withdrawal from previous social activities. Bohannan and Bohannan noted, for example, an elderly Tiv woman who "had again 'put on the snail shell' (i.e., had declared herself no longer sexually available and had donned the insignia of this situation, usually seen only on very young girls and very old women), and had returned to live in her natal lineage with her brother."[8] The Amhara observe that "women fade more rapidly than men. As a result, the 'mabalat' or 'baltét,' a greying woman past menopause, or widow of serious mind and spirit, often takes vows as a nun. . . ."[9] More traumatically among the Rural Irish "it is commonly believed that the menopause can induce insanity; in order to ward it off, some women have retired from life in their mid-forties and, in at least three contemporary cases, have confined themselves to bed until death years later."[10]

In two other cultures, both African, menopause is reportedly viewed as a disorder, although perhaps not an unfortunate one. "A Yoruba woman is unable to accept the menopause as a natural occurrence; she rather supposes that it is a pregnancy prevented by witchcraft from terminating normally."[11] Among the Twi of Ghana, "most women, quite apart from the depressives, are worried by these social hazards of the menopause [such as the husband taking younger wives, upon whom he lavishes presents] and many of them, when they first become aware of amenorrhea, go from shrine to shrine over several years with the plaint, 'I am pregnant, but the pregnancy doesn't grow.' "[12]

There are several cultures in which behavior for post-menopausal women changes in the direction of much greater freedom. Yet, no data are recorded on women learning to operate in these heady new dimensions, or if exercise of the new privileges was sudden or gradually assumed, or if, indeed, it was not merely exercised increasingly with increasing age with no reference whatever to cessation of menses. For example, the strength of the avoidance relationship between Yap brother and sister 'diminishes markedly once the woman is past menarche and when her brother is of advanced years too, and obtains only primarily during the years when both are sexually mature."[13]

Gustatory adventures await post-menopausal Thonga women. "When women have passed the time of child-bearing, most of the taboos [primarily cattle-associated taboos] cease, and they can eat monkeys and porcupine if they wish!"[14] In Tepoztlán, both old men and old women "may get drunk, insult others, use sexual terms, laugh and cry, and even urinate in public without censure, although younger people may find it embarrassing."[15] In Thailand,

> men and women in this old age group [after sixty] become freer in behavior and manner. In warm weather old women often go about the house compound with their breasts uncovered even when outsiders are present. . . . The old can break many language prohibitions and speak among themselves of things that younger men and women would not mention in a mixed group.[16]

Much the same lessening of bonds is reported for the Taiwan Hokkien, of whom it is reported that "old women smoke in public, appear at public dinners normally attended by men only, and are generally outspoken."[17] These references and others seem entirely secular in tone. The Kanuri, for example, often "use old women for such purposes" as taking kola nuts as a wooing present.[18] Among the Dogon,

> it is only at the moment when the woman, arriving at the threshold of old age, ceases to be a woman that she may finally feel herself truly integrated in the more stable element of the population; to observe henceforth with a critical eye the conduct of the young women whom her sons, in their turn, bring to the village, to give orders in the house, in which she will work less and less. . . .[19]

How much is such secular freedom accomplished as a result of independence from males, and what are the dimensions of acquiring such independence? Among the Kapauku, "senescence has an opposite influence on the status curve of the woman. The older she grows, the more she becomes emancipated from the powers of her husband."[20] In China "The *lao-nien* [aged—past sixty] stage was often an unusual one for women. It was often a stage in which a woman was released from male domination."[21] A final observation in this category relates to a rite among the eastern Timbira where Nimuendajú

> witnessed a ceremony that publicly and formally expressed the principle that old women merit respect as much as old men. Ordinarily there is no feminine counterpart to the men's council in the plaza; but on that day [the close of the pepyé retreat in 1933] the old women were invited by the councilors to take the male elders' places in the plaza, the councilors themselves withdrawing to a spot on the margin. Then two youths and a girl hauled in a huge meat pie on a mat and handed it over to the old women, who forthwith divided it up and ate it precisely in the manner of the councilors, whereupon they went home.[22]

Finally, there are cultures in which menopause signals accession to increased social and perhaps also supernatural power.

All of these cultures, with one exception, are New World, and they are—again with only one exception—North American. The one Old World instance comes from Iran, where it is said that "making the prophet Hrezr appear is only possible for a woman who has passed the menopause."[23] Although not specifically reported to be post-menopausal, it seems obvious that the Gros Ventre women of the following quotation are just that:

> Other women could join the Dance with the chief vower, but under what general conditions and procedures we did not ascertain except that to qualify either as associates or as chief vower, women had to be 'old' or 'very old,' to be 'women who had seen all of life,' and were 'beyond their prime,' not 'young women.' This would probably mean in Gros Ventre age terminology women beyond the age of about forty-five or fifty.[24]

Winnebago women could participate in construction of ceremonial lodges only if they had passed their climacterics, and after this they also could work on the buckskins of a war bundle. Attendance at feasts was possible then as well:

> All the young girls nearing the age of puberty will be absent, but the old women, who have passed their climacteric, sit right next to the men, because they are considered the same as men as they have no menstrual flow any more.[25]

The same equation is made by the Northern Ojibwa, where women may exercise professional services that require supernatural license "after menopause when they are considered to be much more like men."[26]

Although not retrieved from the Human Relations Area File, three further instances belong here. The first of these relates to the Munducuru of South America, where it is reported that

> all these strictures are suspended in the case of postmenopausal women. An old woman will sit where she pleases, and men will actually defer by making room for her. She may talk on whatever subject interests her, and if this requires that she interrupt the men, then so be it. Her opinions are freely given—and listened to—on matters of community concern, and they are shown marked respect. By graduating from sex and child-bearing, she has graduated from a female role and, in a legal sense, has become a man, albeit an old one.[27]

Second, Kessler noted that in Indian villages in Mexico the *curandera* "is often a woman past the menstrual cycle."[28] Finally, the Cree of western Saskatchewan have the knowledge that women cannot exercise shamanistic power until after menopause, "for women and *manito,* the force necessary to healing, are antithetical."[29]

As mentioned earlier, any attempt to draw conclusions in any way definitive from such scanty data is tentative. To begin, however, it is difficult to accept without question Kessler's assertion that "in all probability, not many women in early societies lived long enough to achieve this stage."[30] Second, and apropos of this stage of cessation, when is something "the last" (e.g., the last rainbow or the last snowfall one is to see)? "The first" is easier descriptively, if not also conceptually, and this may well hinder categorization. Clinical papers dealing with menopause, for instance, frequently resort to "no menstrual periods within the last twelve months" as a working definition.

A third possible conclusion is that most ethnographers have been male and hence barred from gathering data about the female life cycle. Fourth, perhaps all ethnographers, female as well as male, have been more oriented to youth than to old age and are thus uninterested in changes in behavior related to cessation of childbearing.

Some combination of culture area and time of investigation seems to be part of a fifth possible explanation. Are cultures which see access of females to increased power (and hence ceremonial associations, as with the making of war bundles) indeed North American almost exclusively? Or is some factor at work which made the male ethnographers working in North America more perceptive and perhaps more painstaking? And is there some correlation between the time in which these men were in the field (Radin in the Twenties and Hallowell in the Thirties) and fashions in emphasis or in training so that they recorded changed behavior in women past the menopause and other ethnographers at other times and places did not?

It would seem that the inadequate reporting may well be a combination of many of the above factors but particularly of the anti-woman, anti-aging biases within U. S. culture, the culture in which so many ethnographers have been trained. These two strikes against the gathering of data on post-menopausal behavior may be augmented by a third if the ethnographer is a female who has internalized a sexless, if not an actual anti-female, bias in order to have progressed far enough in professional training to be doing field work. For example, this author believes that without the influence of these three biases while in the field in the early Sixties, she would have been more sensitive to the behavior of three elderly women who clearly wielded power in the workings of the Southern Ute tribe.[31] Indeed, two of the three were thought to have had supernatural power. And was that power caused by or correlated with their social power? That, too, should have been investigated. Such questions would have been perceived as more legitimate, had the McKinlays only asked ten years earlier if menopausal symptoms are not indeed caused by loss of "such socially important roles as reproducer, mother, and . . . wife."[32]

Clearly the cross-cultural data available, at least as indexed in the Human Relations Area File, are inadequate to correlate physical symptoms associated with a predictable biological phenomenon with the array of sociocultural factors found in the modern United States. Data from aboriginal North American Indian cultures strongly suggest that loss of the role of reproducer-mother-wife signals at least access to the role of curer, and that the two roles are mutually exclusive. Certainly, the hypothesis should be entertained that the magnitude of symptoms associated with menopause is positively correlated with the paucity of roles (or of availability of demeaning roles only) available to the post-menopausal woman. The Rural Irish example would seem important here.

In future research the following questions are among those which should be addressed: Why no rites of passage? Why no instruction in requisite new behavior? What must be learned, and under what conditions, to play adequately the role of "old lady"?[33] In cultures in which post-menopausal women actually gain in power, is it solely because they "have become men, albeit old ones"?

In addition to the professional challenge of seeking answers to these questions and to others which will inevitably be generated by further research, there may well be vitally important physical reasons for answering such questions. For example, without cross-cultural knowledge, women in complex industrialized nations such as the United States almost inevitably will be treated by some physicians on the basis of perceptions such as those of Wilson and Wilson. These authors published a paper entitled "The *Fate of Non-treated* Post-menopausal Women: A *Plea* for the Maintenance of *Adequate* Oestrogen *Therapy* from Puberty to the Grave."[34]

Scanty as are the data presented in this discussion, the author believes they make clear that no female at the approximate age of fifty suddenly faces fate. Rather, they seem to demonstrate that behavior proper to the role of elderly female is shaped by culture, as are all sex- and age-linked roles. From long before puberty the behavior of any female is a product of the interplay between her unique biological heritage, her shared sociocultural environment, and the choices she as an individual makes from among the behavioral alternatives available to her in her culture.

NOTES

1. Sonia M. McKinlay and John B. McKinlay, "Selected Studies of the Menopause," *Journal of Biosocial Science,* vol. 5, no. 4 (1973), pp. 533–55.
2. *Ibid.,* p. 537.

3. George P. Murdock *et al., Outline of Cultural Materials,* vol. 1, Behavior Science Outlines (4th rev. ed.; New Haven, Conn.: Human Relations Area Files, Inc., 1961), p. 143.
4. John Joseph Honigmann, *Culture and Ethos of Kaska Society* (New Haven: Yale University Press, 1949), p. 199; Charles S. Brant and Mi Mi Khaing, "Burmese Kinship and the Life Cycle: An Outline," *Southwestern Journal of Anthropology,* vol. 7 (1951), p. 451; Wladyslaw Wszebòr Kulski, *The Soviet Regime; Communism in Practice* (Syracuse, N. Y.: Syracuse University Press, 1954), p. 358.
5. Verrier Elwin, *The Muria and Their Ghotul* (Bombay: Oxford University Press, 1947), p. 152.
6. Wilfrid Vernon Grigson, *The Maria Gonds of Bastar* (London: Oxford University Press, 1949), p. 364.
7. John Morris, *Living with the Lepchas; A Book About the Sikkim Himalayas* (London, Toronto: W. Heinemann, 1938), p. 237.
8. Paul Bohannan and Laura Bohannan, "Three Source Notebooks in Tiv Ethnography" (manuscript; New Haven, Conn.: Human Relations Area Files, 1958), p. 268.
9. Simon David Messing, "The Highland-Plateau Amhara of Ethiopia" (Ph.D. dissertation, University of Pennsylvania, 1957), p. 481.
10. John C. Messenger, *Inis Beag, Isle of Ireland* (New York: Holt, Rinehart and Winston, 1969), p. 109.
11. P. Morton-Williams, "The Atinga Cult Among the Southwestern Yoruba: A Sociological Analysis of a Witch-Finding Movement," Institut Français d'Afrique Noire, Bulletin, Serie B, *Sciences Humaines,* vol. 18 (1956), p. 329.
12. M. J. Field, *Search for Security; An Ethno-Psychiatric Study of Rural Ghana* (New York: W. W. Norton, 1970), p. 150.
13. Edward E. Hunt, Jr., *et al., The Microesians of Yap and Their Depopulation* (Washington, D.C.: Pacific Science Board, National Research Council, 1949), p. 103.
14. Henri Alexandre Junod, *The Life of a South African Tribe* (2nd ed.; London: Macmillan, 1927), vol. 2, p. 185.
15. Oscar Lewis, *Life in a Mexican Village; Tepoztlán Restudied* (Urbana: University of Illinois Press, 1951), p. 411.
16. John E. De Young, *Village Life in Modern Thailand* (Berkeley and Los Angeles: University of California Press, 1955), p. 35.
17. Bernard Gallin and Hsin Hsing, *Taiwan: A Chinese Village in Change* (Berkeley and Los Angeles: University of California Press, 1966), p. 215.
18. Ronald Cohen, *The Kanuri of Bornu* (New York: Holt, Rinehart and Winston, 1967), p. 41.
19. Denise Paulme, *Organisation sociale des Dogon (Soudan français) [Social Organization of the Dogon (French Sudan)]* (Paris: Editions Domat-Montchrestien, F. Loviton et Cie., 1940), pp. 417–18.
20. Leopold J. Pospisil, *Kapauku Papuans and Their Law* (New Haven, Conn.: Yale University Press, 1958), p. 59.
21. Marion Joseph Levy, *The Family Revolution in Modern China* (Cambridge, Mass.: Harvard University Press, 1949), p. 129.
22. Curt Nimuendajú, *The Eastern Timbira,* trans. and ed. Robert H. Lowie (Berkeley and Los Angeles: University of California Press, 1946), p. 133.
23. Henri Massé, *Croyances et coutumes persanes [Persian Beliefs and Customs*], trans. Human Relations Area Files (2 vols.; Paris: Librairie Orientale et Americaine, 1938), p. 363.
24. John Montgomery Cooper, *The Gros Ventres of Montana: Part 2, Religion and Ritual,* ed. Regina Flannery (Washington, D. C.: Catholic University of America, 1956), p. 243.
25. Paul Radin, *The Winnebago Tribe,* U. S. Bureau of American Ethnology, Annual Report, vol. 37 (1915/1916), p. 106, p. 137, p. 442.
26. A. Irving Hallowell, *The Role of Conjuring in Saulteaux Society* (Philadelphia: University of Pennsylvania Press, 1942), p. 20.
27. Yolanda Murphy and Robert F. Murphy, *Women of the Forest* (New York and London: Columbia University Press, 1974), pp. 105–06.
28. Evelyn S. Kessler, *Women: An Anthropological View* (New York: Holt, Rinehart and Winston, 1976), p. 25.
29. Alice B. Kehoe, "The Metonymic Pole and Social Roles," *Journal of Anthropological Research,* vol. 29, no. 4 (1973), p. 270.
30. Kessler, p. 25.
31. The author completed field research with the Southern Utes from July 1 through August 15, 1962, as a research assistant for the Tri-Ethnic Research Project of the University of

Colorado at Boulder. In addition, from August 15, 1962, through May 30, 1963, the author served as secretary to the director of the Southern Ute Rehabilitation Program.

32. McKinlay and McKinlay, p. 37.
33. The author is indebted to M. Jean Haviland, of the University of Southern Colorado, who suggested at the 1976 Western Social Science Association meeting in Tempe, Ariz., where this presentation was originally made, that no rite of passage and no instruction in behavior may be felt necessary. Her thought was that a woman freed of child-bearing could also now pursue her life freely and hence need not be socialized to approved behavior, a situation very different from that of the pubescent female.
34. R. A. Wilson and T. A. Wilson, "The Fate of Non-Treated Post-Menopausal Women: A Plea for the Maintenance of Adequate Oestrogen Therapy from Puberty to the Grave," *Journal of the American Geriatric Society,* vol. 11 (1963), p. 347. Words considered to be biased have been emphasized.

Women in Widowhood

Carol J. Barrett

There are almost 10 million widowed women in this country, constituting almost 5 percent of the total population.[1] Their median age is sixty-four.[2] As a minority group they suffer from sexism, ageism, and in some cases, racism.[3] All of them suffer because they are perceived to be carriers and transmitters of the reality of death. They may be abused by bureaucracies and insensitive professionals, shunned by relatives and former friends, exploited by racketeers and Don Juans, discriminated against by employers, and berated by others in similar circumstances. They belong to a subculture whose members live in relative oblivion, submerged in the despair of loneliness, chiding each other for self-pity, advising each other to keep busy, individually hoping for an avenue of escape, and collectively succumbing to an attitude of hopelessness.

Most widows hate the word "widow." Many have told me that people respond to them as if they have an infectious disease. The model of a pervasive illness is suggested by their questions. They want to know when—if ever—they will "get over it." They want to know if anyone ever "completely recovers," if anyone is ever "cured."

The Stresses of Widowhood

The death of a spouse is consistently seen as a major source of stress requiring more readjustment than any other event in life. This finding has been replicated with subjects of varying ages and diverse cultural backgrounds

"Women in Widowhood" by Carol J. Barrett from *Signs,* 2 (1977), 856–868. Reprinted by permission of the University of Chicago Press and the author.

by a group of researchers attempting to determine the life changes associated with susceptibility to illness.[4]

Grief

The pain of bereavement itself is the first stress facing the widow. The grief process has been described by a number of writers, most notably Marris, Lindemann, and Parkes.[5] Marris's study of seventy-two British lower-class widows recognized the following frequent phenomena: a sense of futility and the suspicion that nothing in life is worthwhile; an inability to understand the loss; a sense of injustice at one's fate; reliving of shared experiences; and a need to blame. A wide range of physical symptoms which the widow herself or her physician thought were caused or aggravated by the shock of the husband's death were reported, most often an inability to sleep. In the initial struggle to accept death some were bothered by obsessive memories of the circumstances of the death or illusions of the husband's presence. Some widows appeared to cultivate a sense of his presence, for example, by talking to his photograph and imagining him giving advice. For others any reminder of the deceased revived the grief. Marris also found a tendency for the widows to withdraw from others and reject consolation.

In a milestone paper in the study of grief, Parkes reported the experience of twenty-two London widows under age sixty-five studied longitudinally for thirteen months after bereavement. Most had failed to accept warnings of their husbands' impending deaths. The immediate reaction to the death was a phase of numbness, followed by a phase of yearning in which the "pangs" of grief occurred. The loss itself was often avoided or denied. Restlessness and an urge to search for the husband were also observed. Some widows tended to behave or think more like the spouse, developed symptoms closely resembling the husband's last illness, or experienced the husband as inside themselves or one of the children. It is not uncommon for persons in the midst of grief to feel they are "going insane," as many of the lay books on this subject will attest.[6]

An important question is whether differences in grief reactions will predict later adjustment to widowhood. In a retrospective study of aged Americans who cited the death of a loved one as a major stress, Anderson found that those later judged as psychiatrically impaired tended to be unable to act at the time of the stress compared with a more normal group who took initiative in coping with the stress.[7] Maddison and Walker's retrospective study of Boston women widowed for three months confirms that those in best health experienced fewer unmet interpersonal needs during their grief.[8]

Several writers have postulated that bereavement is less distressing in cultures which sanction elaborate public displays of grief. Marris, for example, has pointed to the perfunctory style of mourning in Western cultures, and Gorer has described it as deinstitutionalized.[9] The ambiguity with regard to "proper" mourning in the United States probably contributes to the difficulties in early widowhood.

The Economic Burden

Vitually every study of widows has commented on the reduced financial resources characteristically resulting from the husband's death. Aside from the loss of income from the husband's employment and the possible freeze on bank accounts in some states, there are apt to be large bills from prolonged illness and funeral arrangements. In a major study of widowed families receiving survivors' benefits in 1962, Palmore and her co-workers found that they spent considerably more of their income on food and housing than the average family.[10] Thus, fewer had enough money for other needs, including life or health insurance or cars. Working widows frequently used relatives to care for the children in the widow's own home, but others had to leave their school-age children unattended while they worked. (Fifteen percent of children aged six to eleven years were not supervised.) The average earnings of employed widows were only about three-fourths the average earned by all female workers. One-fourth of these families had incomes below the poverty level established by the Social Security Administration.

In a more recent study, Nuckols described the financial situation of 1,744 women who were widowed "prematurely"; that is, their husbands died before reaching age sixty-five.[11] The subjects, 5 percent of whom had remarried, were obtained through their spouse's death certificate on file in Boston, Houston, Chicago, or San Francisco, and were interviewed approximately two years after the husband's death. The typical widow faced $2,860 worth of final expenses; the average final expense was $3,900. Over half of those receiving life insurance benefits received their first check within two weeks of filing a claim, whereas social security payments typically took more than three months to be processed. Few widows reported having anyone to talk with concerning options for settling life insurance claims, and many were not aware they had any options. Furthermore, the majority of husbands (71 percent) had died without a will. The average per capita monthly income payment received from all sources was only $155. Family incomes were reduced an average of 44 percent from predeath levels. The change varied from a 4 percent increase among families accustomed to less than $3,000 income to a 57 percent decrease among families formerly receiving over $15,000. About one-half of the widows were able to maintain their standard of living, but only one-fourth were living comfortably and reasonably free from financial worries. The most frequent cutbacks were for clothing, social and recreational activities, and food. The highest source of income received by the widows was their own earnings (40 percent). Whereas 47 percent of these women were working prior to the husband's death, two years later 56 percent were working.

Widows are much more likely to work than married women of the same age. They are also more likely to work full time during the week and during the year.[12] (Widowers are *less* likely to be employed than same-age married men, but still more likely than widows to work.) Overall, 26.9 percent of white widows are employed, 35.5 percent of nonwhite widows.[13] The majority of widows in the main working ages are employed. Mothers receiving survivors' benefits are more than twice as likely to work as mothers with husbands, even controlling for age and number of children.

Yet their unemployment rate is about three times as high as that of other *women.*[14] A recent study of employment patterns in a Chicago sample of widows found that the most frequent source of information leading to employment was the widow's own friends. Other sources, including employment agencies, had been helpful less often.[15]

Social Factors

Loneliness is the most consistent and frequently reported problem of widows. Lopata has conceptualized ten forms of loneliness based on her interviews with 300 widows in the Chicago area:[16] (1) missing the particular other, with whom interaction is no longer available; (2) lacking the feeling of being loved; (3) lacking someone to care for; (4) longing for an in-depth relationship with another human being; (5) missing the presence of the other in the dwelling unit; (6) absence of the other to share work with; (7) homesickness for a certain style of life; (8) drop in status of the unescorted female; (9) strain in other relationships; and (10) inability to make new friends.

More recently, Lopata has described widowhood as an event marking reduced social roles.[17] Those apt to be disrupted or eliminated with the husband's death involve his prior roles as sexual partner, father of the children, partner in couple-oriented leisure activities, contributor to home management, and comember in voluntary association groups. His death may remove the wife's link to his relatives, his work associates, mutual friends, and the community at large.

Most evidence shows that widowhood does indeed lead to social isolation. Lay books on the subject abound with the difficulties of finding satisfying social events that widows may enjoy. Relationships with married-couple friends may deteriorate. Interview data indicate that the widow does indeed see far less of her husband's relatives than before his death.[18] Marris's study found that contact with the widow's own relatives was not increased after the death either. Among the explanations he considers are the widow's desire to be independent, her resentment of an attitude of pity, the social apathy characteristic of grief, the family's frustration at trying to console someone who will not be consoled, and the side effects of poverty, such as reduced funds for transportation and entertainment. A more detailed study by Adams comparing 263 middle-aged adults and their widowed or married mothers indicated that the widow's contact with her sons diminished, while visits with her daughters increased. Adams also looked at the interaction between widows and their children: daughters tended to increase in almost all types of interaction.[19] For sons, however, the only increase was in the category of aid to the parent. Similarly, Lopata found that daughters of widows appeared more often in their emotional support networks than sons.[20] One-fourth of all widows over age fifty in a large Chicago sample have no living children,[21] and almost half of the total sample live alone.[22] The children of most widows are no longer dependents.

The major dissenting vote for the hypothesis that widowhood increases social isolation comes from a study by Lowenthal.[23] A large group of mental patients and a stratified random sample of San Francisco residents over age sixty were classified as isolates or interactors on the basis of their reports of the number of contacts with friends or relatives in a two-week period. There were proportionately more widows and widowers among the interactors than among the isolates, both within the hospital and nonhospital groups.

Remarriage may be seen as one solution to the apparent isolation of widowhood. Second marriages in general are as happy as first marriages.[24] Yet the widowed do not remarry as often as the divorced. Only one-fourth of widows remarry within five years. (One-half of widowers and three-fourths of all divorced persons do so.) The likelihood of remarriage decreases more sharply with advancing years for widows than for widowers.

A number of studies have found that the majority of widows do not *want* to remarry.[25] Marris has described the guilt associated with bereavement and the subsequent feeling of loyalty to the deceased as an obstacle to remarriage. Marsden has poignantly pointed out that remarriage may be a financial risk for the widow who would lose her admittedly meager government benefits.[26] The widow's typical denial of interest in remarriage may not accurately reflect her desires. It may reflect the lack of opportunity; men die seven to eight years sooner than women, and grooms are usually older than brides. There are more than four times as many widows living as there are widowers. The problem of unfulfilled sexual needs was readily discussed in my Los Angeles sample of widows participating in small discussion groups when the opportunity to do so was sanctioned,[27] yet we have very little information about this particular stress experienced by widowed women.

Physical and Mental Health

That the physical and mental health of widows is impaired compared with their married sisters' has been repeatedly demonstrated in the past. The reasons for this discrepancy are less clear. Woolsey documented higher rates of disabling illness among unmarried women than among married women.[28] The gap is large by age thirty and continues to be substantial through age sixty. Widowed, divorced, or separated women also had a greater number of days in disability per person and a higher frequency and duration of hospitalization than married women.[29] Confrey and Goldstein concluded that illness among unmarried women, primarily widows, constitutes a large part of the total problem of illness in later life.[30]

Two studies have documented health decrements in *younger* widows relative to a matched group of married women.[31] In both Boston and Australia the widowed women had more physical complaints. However, Heyman and Gianturco did not find health deterioration associated with bereavement in their longitudinal study of forty-one *elderly* persons who became widowed.[32]

Even more striking than the health decrement in young widows is the fact that widows die sooner than married women. The mortality rates of widowed persons from all causes of death, for every age group, for both sexes, and for both whites and nonwhites are higher than those for married persons.[33] (The rates for single persons are slightly lower than widowed rates; rates for the divorced are even higher.) The relative excess mortality in unmarried groups is greater at the *younger* ages. Unmarried persons between the ages of twenty and thirty-four are more than twice as likely to die as married persons of the same age, sex, and race. The death rates attributable to the twenty leading causes of death in the twenty to forty-four age range were calculated by marital status. In every case the rate was higher among the widowed than among the married individuals.

Kraus and Lilienfield describe several factors which may account for the high death rates endured by the widowed.[34] One is that persons with poor health risks may tend to marry each other. Second, a widowed individual may have shared an unfavorable environment with the deceased spouse which contributed to both deaths. Finally, there is the hypothesis that *widowhood itself* has such deleterious consequences that an excessive death rate ensues. The stresses of widowhood outlined here should make that hypothesis seem plausible. In conjunction with the difficulties already described, widowhood may lead to a less nutritious diet and lowered standards of personal hygiene. Frank has documented a phenomenon in other cultures whereby deaths are produced literally by group pressure and individual decision to die.[35] Perhaps there is some semblance between the pressures of widowhood in this society and the circumstances of such "inexplicable" deaths in other cultures.

A relationship between mental illness and widowhood has also been observed.[36] Suicides occur more frequently among the widowed than the married.[37] An increase in psychiatric symptoms such as anxiety, depression, insomnia, and tiredness has been noted in widows under age sixty.[38] Older widows again escaped this phenomenon. The high proportion of widowed in-patients in mental hospitals is known, but further analysis of mental illness by marital status is needed controlling for the influence of variables such as age and income level.

Individual Variation

Every widow will not experience exactly the same stresses nor respond to them in the same way.[39] The age at widowhood may be an important variable. Research suggests that more negative outcomes may engulf younger widows,[40] perhaps because the spouse's death has seldom been anticipated and emotional preparation is minimal. Older widows also have an opportunity to develop a social network among already widowed individuals of the same age. In their initial contact with a therapeutic program I directed, older widows were more self-disclosing.[41] Wyly discerned differing needs among middle-aged and elderly widows interviewed in the state of New York,[42] and Abrahams found differential rates in the reasons why young and old widowed persons called the Widowhood Service Line, a crisis intervention hotline.[43] Despite such differences, widows of diverse ages can participate meaningfully in discussion (Twenty-nine to seventy-four, in my experience), and the majority recommend diverse age groupings in future programs for widows.[44]

The widow's educational level is related to her subsequent participation in a variety of social roles; greatest social isolation occurs among women with the least education.[45] Current employment status and presence or absence of children in the home may also be associated with different life-styles as widows. Those who are employed are more likely to ask how to meet people,[46] and those without children at home are more likely to complain of loneliness.[47] Both Nuckols's study and my own clinical experience suggest that widows are more concerned about the difficulties of being single parents when sons are involved; they often feel more competent in dealing with daughters. The widow's ethnic background and religious affiliation may also be important determinants of her response to widowhood, but relevant empirical data are scarce.

Social Policy Implications

The pervasive negative effects of the death of one's spouse demand extensive changes in our social policies, both with regard to widowhood and with regard to our life-styles prior to widowhood.

Broad-scale public education dealing realistically with widowhood as an inevitable life-cycle stage for most women is needed. A substantial measure of the agony of widowhood might be prevented. Daughters of six as well as wives of sixty must realize that as women they will live alone for a substantial period of their adult years. The average widow who does not remarry and dies a natural death will have spent eighteen and a half years in this final stage of life.[48] For many women, this is longer than the entire period of life from entrance into the first grade until marriage. (The comparable period for widowers is thirteen and a half years.) From this awareness can come effective preparation. The shock of widowhood can be muted with death education. Skills relevant to a single life-style can be cultivated before they are needed. Marriages can accommodate plans for life after a spouse's death.

In my research I have asked widows what advice they have for women whose husbands are still living. Their suggestions are abundant, but two themes are strong. One is concerned with financial preparation for widowhood, the other with emotional preparation. Widows urge other women to learn financial management and become familiar with all documents and financial transactions bearing on their present and future lives. They advise women to develop occupational skills and to keep them alive during marriage. They recommend life insurance and wills and saving money.

In the second category appear suggestions aimed at developing independent interests and resources in marriage. Some urge wives to be employed, others to pursue individual goals or hobbies. Widows have learned the hard way what Lopata has predicted: the more areas of one's life which are dependent on the spouse's participation, the greater the role discontinuity at widowhood.[49] Widows sense that an autonomous stream of interests and/or associates would provide a continuous anchor of identity as the losses of bereavement are experienced.

Finally, public education can correct the stereotypes of widows, teach us how to deal effectively with our own and others' grief, and help destroy a leprosy-like stigma. We can make a dent in the fears and accusations born out of ignorance about the normal reactions to grief. Friends and relatives can learn an explanation for the angry rebuffs that may greet their initial offers of help. With this understanding they may be able to extend their support six months later, when many widowed persons feel abandoned again.

Government Support

Federal policies can ease the transition to widowhood in three ways: through the provision of adequate survivors' benefits, through sponsorship of research, and through direct support to ameliorative service programs.

The recent bills and revisions of Social Security law demonstrate an increasing awareness of the inadequacy of current benefits. But they have not gone far enough. The majority of elderly persons are women, the majority of elderly women are widowed, and the majority of elderly widows are living in poverty. We must provide financial compensation for the years of toil spent as homemakers and insure that new policies are not sex biased.[50]

Widowhood should be a high priority in the funding of research on aging and on women's roles. Our data base has only begun to describe the needs and concerns of widows. We need to know much more about how to predict diverse psychological reactions to widowhood. A variety of demographic, interpersonal, and personality variables require investigation. We need to know how best to facilitate the grief process and how best to prepare widowed persons for its consequences. And we need to study this life-cycle stage intensively from a developmental point of view to increase our understanding of the experience of widowed persons as it evolves over a period of months and years.

Institutional Support

Silverman has surveyed mental health agencies in the United States and concluded they are underutilized by widowed persons.[51] Services have not been oriented to the needs of this particular group. The ignorance of professionals in the field can be appalling. Severe psychopathology may be attributed to the intense depression often experienced in widowhood. The not infrequent illusions of the husband's presence during the early stages of grief may be interpreted as "visual hallucinations" symptomatic of schizophrenia. Psychotropic drugs are used to treat loneliness, the complexities of which may never be untangled.

Religious institutions have rarely fared better than mental health institutions. Widows seldom describe their minister, priest, or rabbi as particularly helpful. Rather, they are more likely to find comfort in their religious beliefs per se. Few religious organizations sponsor special programs for widowed persons. Two exceptions are a Catholic organization called NAIM, and Theos, a nondenominational spiritual organization based in Pittsburgh.[52]

The Widowhood Service Program of Boston inspired a variety of volunteer service programs using widowed persons themselves as helpmates to the recently bereaved.[53] Sponsorship of such programs may include the American Association of Retired Persons,[54] funeral homes,[55] the YWCA, or other community organizations. The New York Widowhood Consultation Center provides diverse counseling services on a fee-for-service basis. Continuing-education programs have begun to implement courses on widowhood, with therapeutic results.[56]

I developed a program of group interventions for widows of all ages and duration of widowhood in the Los Angeles area.[57] Three types of group format were evaluated: self-help groups, women's consciousness-raising groups for widows, and "confidant" groups inspired by Lowenthal and Haven's research on the relationship between intimacy and mental health in old age.[58] The women's consciousness-raising participants consistently gave the program the highest ratings of helpfulness and educational value, although all responses were generally positive. They also reported the most positive life changes during the five- to six-month follow-up period. Rates of contact between members were substantial in all groups but were particularly high in one of the confidant groups. Four out of six groups elected to continue meeting as groups even after the follow-up period.

Clearly, the enormous stresses of widowhood demand a societal commitment that will require the participation of a variety of institutions. The needs are too great for us to discourage prematurely any model of helping that can be developed. Evaluation measures should be instituted as such programs are planned.

Social Change

Many of the stresses of widowhood could be avoided. If we become more flexible in our patterns of intimacy we can provide alternatives to the prolonged desolation of widowhood. If traditionally couple-oriented activities were to become more inclusive, the "fifth-wheel" phenomenon of widowhood could give way to meaningful, socially diverse experience. (Widowhood may be avoided altogether by an older woman married to a younger man or by the lifelong single.) The fact is that there are more adult women than men. As society becomes more tolerant of diverse life-styles at all ages, the widow or potential widow will have more viable options.

Half of Lopata's widowed sample described specific advantages to their status.[59] Among them were enjoying living alone, having less work (such as housework) to do, and being independent. An occasional widow in my research was jubilant in her new-found freedom and sense of personal growth. Widowhood may be the first time in a woman's life that she is living alone. She is a member of a group that could wield substantial political power. She has the potential for self-mastery and discovery at a time of her life when new social roles can be pursued.

NOTES

1. U.S. Bureau of the Census, *U.S. Census of the Population: 1970. Characteristics of the Population* (Washington, D.C.: Government Printing Office, 1970), vol. 1, pt. 1.
2. H. Carter and P. C. Glick, *Marriage and Divorce: A Social and Economic Study* (Cambridge, Mass.: Harvard University Press, 1970).
3. H. Z. Lopata, *Living Arrangements of American Urban Widows* (Washington, D.C.: U.S. Administration on Aging, 1971).

4. T. H. Holmes and M. Masuda, *"Life Change and Illness Susceptibility"* (paper presented at the annual meeting of the American Association for the Advancement of Science, Chicago, 1970).
5. P. Marris, *Widows and Their Families* (London: Routledge & Kegan Paul, 1958); E. Lindemann, "Symptomatology and Management of Acute Grief," *Death and Identity* (New York: John Wiley & Sons, 1965); C. M. Parkes, "The First Year of Bereavement," *Psychiatry* 33 (1970): 444–67.
6. J. Z. Owen, *Widows Can Be Happy* (New York: Greenberg, 1950); E. Richford, *Mothers on Their Own* (New York: Harper & Bros., 1953); M. Langer, *Learning to Live as a Widow* (New York: J. Messner, Inc., 1957); M. M. Champagne, *Facing Life Alone, What Widows and Divorcees Should Know* (Indianapolis: Bobbs-Merrill Co., 1964); L. Caine, *Widow* (New York: William Morrow & Co., 1974).
7. B. G. Anderson, "Bereavement as a Subject of Cross-cultural Inquiry: An American Sample," *Anthropological Quarterly* 38 (October 1965): 181–200.
8. D. Maddison and W. L. Walker, "Factors Affecting the Outcome of Conjugal Bereavement," *British Journal of Psychiatry* 113 (1967): 1057–67.
9. G. Gorer, *Death, Grief, and Mourning* (New York: Doubleday & Co., 1965).
10. E. B. Palmore, G. L. Stanley, and R. H. Cormier, "Widows with Children under Social Security," *The 1963 National Survey of Widows with Children under OASDHI,* Social Security Administration, Research Report no. 16 (Washington, D.C.: Department of Health, Education, and Welfare, 1963).
11. R. C. Nuckols, "Widows Study," abstracted in the Journal Supplement Abstract Service's *Catalog of Selected Documents in Psychologfy* 3 (1973): 9.
12. Carter and Glick.
13. Ibid.
14. Palmore et al.
15. F. Steinhart, "Labor Force Characteristics of Widows" (paper presented at the American Psychological Association Annual Convention, Chicago, 1975).
16. H. Z. Lopata, "Loneliness: Forms and Components," *Social Problems* 17 (1969): 248–61.
17. H. Z. Lopata, "The Social Involvement of American Widows," *American Behavioral Scientist* 14 (1970): 41–58, and *Widowhood in an American City* (Cambridge, Mass.: Schenkman Publishing Co., 1973); H. Z. Lopata, T. Philblad, D. Adams, N. Smolic-Krovic, and A. Kurzynowski, "Widowhood in Selected Areas of the U.S., Poland and Yugoslavia," *Sociological Abstracts* 18, no. 5, suppl. 9 (1970): 889 (abstract no. E4162).
18. Lopata, "The Social Involvement of American Widows"; Marris.
19. B. N. Adams, "The Middle-Class Adult and His Widowed or Still-married Mother," *Social Problems* 16 (1968): 50–59.
20. H. Z. Lopata, "Support Systems Involving Widows" (paper presented at the American Psychological Association Annual Convention, Chicago, 1975).
21. Lopata, n. 18 above.
22. Lopata, n. 3 above.
23. M. F. Lowenthal, "Social Isolation and Mental Illness in Old Age," *American Sociological Review* 29 (1964): 54–70.
24. J. Bernard, *Remarriage: A Study of Marriage* (New York: Dryden Press, 1956).
25. B. J. Cosneck, "A Study of the Social Problems of Aged Widowed Persons in an Urban Area" (Ph.D. thesis, Florida University, 1966); Lopata, *Widowhood in an American City.*
26. D. Marsden, "Mothers Alone: Their Way of Life," *New Society* 13 (1969): 705–7.
27. C. J. Barrett, "A Comparison of Therapeutic Interventions for Widows" (paper presented at the 26th Annual Meeting of the Gerontological Society, Miami Beach, 1973. Abstract published in the *Gerontologist* 13 [1973]: 66).
28. T. D. Woolsey, "Estimates of Disabling Illness Prevalence in the U.S., Based on the Current Population Survey of February 1949, and September 1950," *Public Health Service Publication 181* (Washington, D.C.: Government Printing Office, 1952).
29. L. S. Rosenfeld, F. D. Mott, and M. D. Taylor, "Health Services for the Aging in Saskatchewan," in *Illness and Health Services in an Aging Population,* Public Health Service Publication no. 170 (Washgington, D.C.: Government Printing Office, 1952); L. S. Rosenfeld, S. Donabedian, and J. Katz, *Medical Care Needs and Services in the Boston Metropolitan Area* (Boston: United Community Services of Metropolitan Boston, 1957); California Department of Public Health, *California Health Survey, Health in California* (Sacramento: State Printing Office, 1958).

30. E. A. Confrey and M. S. Goldstein, "The Health Status of Aging People," *Handbook of Social Gerontology* (Chicago: University of Chicago Press, 1959).
31. D. Maddison and A. Viola, "The Health of Widows in the Year Following Bereavement," *Journal of Psychosomatic Research* 12 (1968): 297–306.
32. D. K. Heyman and D. T. Gianturco, "Long Term Adaptation by the Elderly to Bereavement," *Journal of Gerontology* 28 (1973): 359–62.
33. A. A. Kraus and A. M. Lilienfeld, "Some Epidemiologic Aspects of the High Mortality Rate in the Young Widowed Group," *Journal of Chronic Diease* 10 (1959): 207–17.
34. Ibid.
35. J. D. Frank, *Persuasion and Healing: A Comparative Study of Psychotherapy* (New York: Schocken Books, 1963).
36. S. S. Bellin and R. H. Hardt, "Marital Status and Mental Disorders among the Aged," *American Sociological Review* 28 (1958): 155–62.
37. Cosneck; B. E. Segal, "Suicide and Middle Age," *Sociological Symposium* 3 (1969): 131–40.
38. C. M. Parkes, "Effects of Bereavement on Physical and Mental Health: A Study of the Medical Records of Widows," *British Medical Journal* 2 (1964): 274–79.
39. C. J. Barrett, "The Development and Evaluation of Three Therapeutic Group Interventions for Widows" (doctoral diss., University of Southern California, 1974).
40. Heyman and Gianturco.
41. C. J. Barrett and L. Snyder, "Letters of Inquiry: Initial Self-disclosure in a Program for Widows" (paper presented at the American Psychological Association Annual Convention, Chicago, 1975).
42. M. V. Wyly, "Problems and Compensations of Widowhood: A Comparison of Age Groups" (paper presented at the American Psychological Association Annual Convention, Chicago, 1975).
43. R. B. Abrahams, "Mutual Help for the Widowed," *Social Work* 17 (1972): 54–61.
44. Barrett, n. 39 above.
45. Lopata, n. 25 above.
46. Abrahams.
47. Nuckols.
48. Carter and Glick.
49. H. Z. Lopata, "Role Changes in Widowhood: A World Perspective," *Aging and Modernization* (New York: Appleton-Century-Crofts, Inc., 1972).
50. V. P. Reno, "Women under Social Security" (paper presented to the Gerontological Society Annual Meeting, Portland, Ore., 1974); P. Nathanson (address delivered at the Gerontological Society Annual Meeting, Louisville, Ky., in a symposium entitled "Women as They Age: Now and Tomorrow," 1975).
51. P. R. Silverman, "Services to the Widowed during the Period of Bereavement," *Social Work Practice* (New York: Columbia University Press, 1966), and "How You Can Help the Newly-Widowed," *American Funderal Director* 93, no. 5 (1970): 43–44, 72.
52. B. Decker and G. Kooiman, *After The Flowers Have Gone: Coping with the Problems of the Widowed* (Grand Rapids, Mich.: Zondervan Corp., 1973); *Theos Newsletter* (Pittsburgh: Theos Foundation, 1975).
53. See Abrahams; Silverman, "Services to the Widowed . . . ," "Services to the Widowed: first Steps in a Program of Prevention Intervention," *Community Mental Health Journal* 3 (1967): 37–44, "The Widow-to-Widow Program," *Mental Hygiene* 53 (1969): 333–37, and "Widowhood and Preventive Intervention," *Family Coordinator* 21 (1972): 95–102.
54. L. Baldwin (personal communication, 1975).
55. H. Antoniak, "The Widowed to Widowed Prgram" (pamphlet financed by the San Diego County Funeral Directors Association, 1973).
56. V. Van Coevering, "Exploring Group Counseling as a Technique for Ameliorating Morbidity, Mortality, and Lowered Life Satisfaction of Widowhood" (paper presented at the Gerontological Society Annual Meeting, Portland, Ore., 1974).
57. Barrett, nn. 27 and 39 above.
58. M. F. Lowenthal and C. Haven, "Interaction and Adaptation: Intimacy as a Critical Variable," *American Sociological Review* 33 (1968): 20–30.
59. Lopata, n. 25 above.